NEW PERSPECTIVES

Microsoft® Windows® 10

INTERMEDIATE

June Jamrich Parsons
Dan Oja
Lisa Ruffolo

Australia • Brazil • Mexico • Singapore • United Kingdom • United States

New Perspectives Microsoft® Windows® 10 Intermediate
June Jamrich Parsons, Dan Oja, Lisa Ruffolo

SVP, GM Skills & Global Product Management: Dawn Gerrain

Product Director: Kathleen McMahon

Senior Product Team Manager: Lauren Murphy

Product Team Manager: Andrea Topping

Associate Product Managers: Reed Curry, William Guiliani

Senior Director, Development: Marah Bellegarde

Product Development Manager: Leigh Hefferon

Senior Content Developer: Kathy Finnegan

Developmental Editor: Jane Pedicini

Product Assistant: Erica Chapman

Marketing Director: Michele McTighe

Marketing Manager: Stephanie Albracht

Senior Production Director: Wendy Troeger

Production Director: Patty Stephan

Senior Content Project Manager: Jennifer Goguen McGrail

Designer: Diana Graham

Composition: GEX Publishing Services

Cover image(s): schankz/Shutterstock.com

Mac users: If you're working through this product using a Mac, some of the steps may vary. Additional information for Mac users is included with the Data Files for this product.

Library of Congress Control Number: 2015957535
ISBN: 978-1-305-57939-2

Cengage Learning
20 Channel Center Street
Boston, MA 02210
USA

Cengage Learning is a leading provider of customized learning solutions with employees residing in nearly 40 different countries and sales in more than 125 countries around the world. Find your local representative at **www.cengage.com.**

Cengage Learning products are represented in Canada by Nelson Education, Ltd.

To learn more about Cengage Learning, visit **www.cengage.com**

Purchase any of our products at your local college store or at our preferred online store **www.cengagebrain.com**

Printed at CLDPC, USA, 05-20

BRIEF CONTENTS

WINDOWS

TABLE OF CONTENTS

MODULE 1

Exploring the Basics of Microsoft Windows 10

Investigating the Windows 10 Operating System

WINDOWS

OBJECTIVES

Session 1.1

- Start Windows 10
- Explore the Start menu
- Start and close apps
- Run apps, switch between them, and close them
- Identify and use the controls in windows and dialog boxes

Session 1.2

- Navigate your computer using File Explorer
- Change the view of the items in your computer
- Get help when you need it
- Turn off Windows 10

Case | *For Pet's Sake*

For Pet's Sake is a nonprofit pet-adoption agency in Glencoe, Illinois, dedicated to placing adoptable companion animals in suitable homes and educating the public about responsible pet ownership. The agency depends on its volunteers to help with daily operations, pet care, and fundraising. As the volunteer coordinator at For Pet's Sake, Ashley Cramer recruits, trains, and manages volunteers. Some of her training sessions involve teaching volunteers how to perform their daily tasks using the agency's computers.

Ashley recently hired you as her assistant. She has asked you to lead the upcoming training sessions on the fundamentals of the Microsoft Windows 10 operating system. As you prepare for the sessions, she offers to help you identify the topics you should cover and the skills you should demonstrate while focusing on the new features in Windows 10.

In this module, you will start Windows 10 and practice some fundamental computer skills. You'll tour the desktop, start applications, and then navigate a computer using File Explorer. Finally, you'll find and use help topics and turn off Windows 10.

Note: With the release of Windows 10, Microsoft is taking a new approach to software publication called "Windows as a Service." With this approach, Microsoft is constantly providing updates to Windows instead of releasing new versions periodically. This means that Windows features might change over time, including how they look and how you interact with them. The information provided in this text was accurate at the time this book was published.

STARTING DATA FILES

There are no starting Data Files needed for this module.

Session 1.1 Visual Overview:

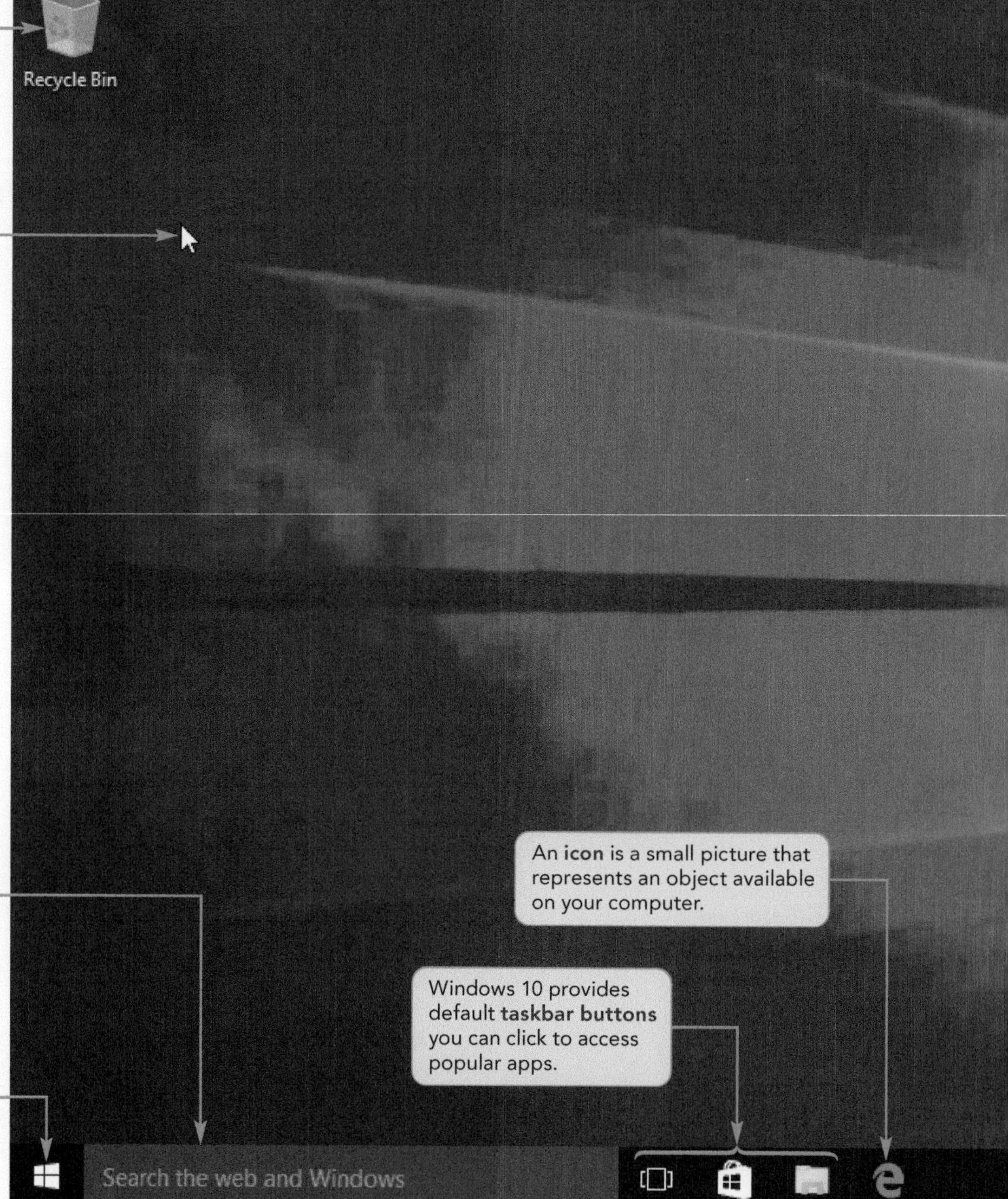

The **Recycle Bin** holds deleted items until you remove them permanently.
Recycle Bin
The **pointer** is a small object, such as an arrow, that moves on the screen when you move the pointing device.
This box provides access to **Cortana**, an electronic personal assistant.
The **Start button** provides access to Windows 10 apps, documents, and settings.
An **icon** is a small picture that represents an object available on your computer.
Windows 10 provides default **taskbar buttons** you can click to access popular apps.
Search the web and Windows

Windows 10 Desktop

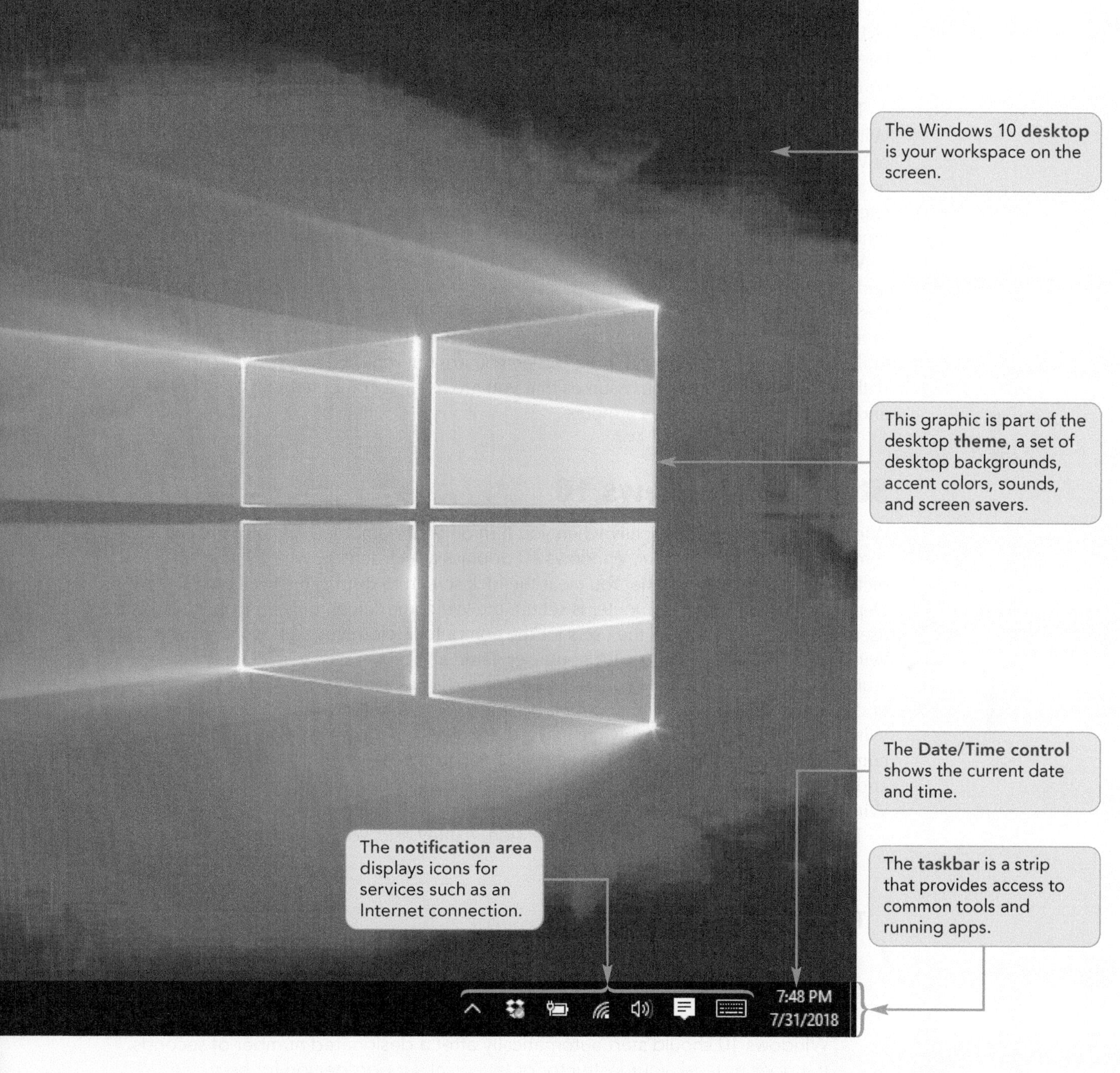

The Windows 10 **desktop** is your workspace on the screen.
This graphic is part of the desktop **theme**, a set of desktop backgrounds, accent colors, sounds, and screen savers.
The **Date/Time control** shows the current date and time.
The **notification area** displays icons for services such as an Internet connection.
The **taskbar** is a strip that provides access to common tools and running apps.
7:48 PM
7/31/2018

Introducing Windows 10

The **operating system** is software that manages and coordinates activities on the computer and helps it perform essential tasks, such as displaying information and saving data. (The term *software* refers to the **programs** a computer uses to complete tasks.) Your computer uses the **Microsoft Windows 10** operating system—**Windows 10** for short. Windows is the name of the operating system, and 10 identifies the version you are using.

The most popular features of Windows 10 include its speed, flexibility, and design. Windows 10 runs software created specifically for Windows 10 and for earlier versions of Windows, such as Windows 7 and 8. This type of software is called an **application**, or **app** for short. You use apps to perform specific tasks, such as writing a document or exchanging messages with another computer user. You can use more than one app at a time and switch seamlessly from one app to another to perform your work efficiently.

Windows 10 is designed to run on computers that use a touchscreen, such as tablets and some laptops, and those that use a keyboard and mouse, such as other laptops and desktop computers. A **touchscreen** is a display that lets you touch areas of the screen to interact with software. To select a button, for example, you touch the button on the tablet display with your fingertip. However, you are not required to use a touchscreen with Windows 10. This book assumes that you are using a computer with a keyboard and pointing device, such as a mouse.

Starting Windows 10

TIP

If you have a Microsoft account, you can use the user name and password for that account to sign in to Windows 10.

Windows 10 starts automatically when you turn on your computer. After completing some necessary start-up tasks, Windows 10 displays a **lock screen**, which includes a picture, the date, and the time. You clear the lock screen to display the Welcome screen. Depending on how your computer is set up, the Welcome screen might list only your user name or it might list all the users for the computer. Before you start working with Windows, you might need to click your user name and type a password. A **user name** is a unique name that identifies you to Windows, and a **password** is a confidential series of characters that you must enter before you can work with Windows. If you installed Windows yourself, you probably created a user name and password as you set up your computer. If not, the person who created your account assigned you at least a user name and possibly a password. After selecting your user name or entering a password, the Windows 10 desktop appears (as shown in the Session 1.1 Visual Overview).

To begin preparing for your training session, Ashley asks you to start Windows 10.

To start Windows 10:

1. Turn on your computer. After a moment, Windows 10 starts and the lock screen appears.

   Trouble? If you are asked to select an operating system, do not take action. Windows 10 should start automatically after a designated number of seconds. If it does not, ask your instructor or technical support person for help.

2. Press any key to clear the lock screen and display the Welcome screen.

   Trouble? If the Welcome screen does not appear, click the lock screen, hold down the mouse button, and then drag the lock screen picture up to display the Welcome screen.

3. If necessary, click your user name, type your password, and then press the **Enter** key.

   The Windows 10 desktop appears, as shown in the Session 1.1 Visual Overview. Your screen might look different.

   Trouble? If your user name does not appear on the Welcome screen, try pressing the Ctrl+Alt+Del keys to enter your name. If necessary, ask your instructor or technical support person for further assistance.

   Trouble? If a blank screen or an animated design replaces the desktop, your computer might be set to use a **screen saver**, a program that causes a display to go blank or to show an animated design after a specified amount of idle time. Press any key or move your mouse to restore the desktop.

   Trouble? If your computer is using a screen resolution other than 1366 × 768, the figures shown in this book might not match exactly what you see in Windows 10 as you work through the steps. Take the screen resolution difference into account as you compare your screen with the figures.

The background area that appears after you sign into Windows 10 is called the desktop because it provides a workspace for projects and the tools you need to manipulate your projects. The desktop displays icons that represent items on your computer, such as apps, files, and folders. A computer **file** is a collection of related information. Typical types of files include text documents, spreadsheets, photos, and songs. A folder is a container that helps you organize the contents of your computer.

Windows gets its name from the rectangular areas called **windows** that appear on your screen as you work, such as those shown in Figure 1-1.

Figure 1-1 **Two windows open on the desktop**

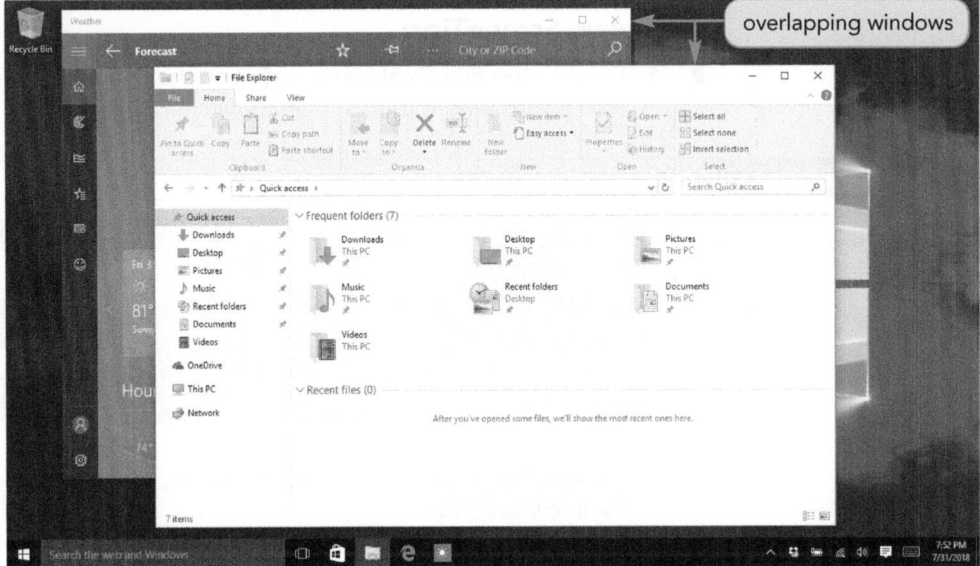

You can open two types of windows in Windows 10: those for Windows apps (also called universal apps), such as the Weather app, and those for traditional desktop applications, such as **File Explorer**, a tool you use to navigate, view, and work with the contents and resources on your computer. You'll explore both types of windows later in the module.

Touring the Desktop

The first time you start a computer after installing Windows 10, the computer uses **default settings**, those preset by the operating system. The default desktop you see after you first install Windows 10, for example, displays a large background image. However, Microsoft designed Windows 10 so that you can easily change the appearance of the desktop. You can, for example, change pictures or add color to the desktop.

Interacting with the Desktop

If you are using a laptop or desktop computer, you use a **pointing device** to interact with the objects on the screen. Pointing devices come in many shapes and sizes. The most common one is called a **mouse**, so this book uses that term. If you are using a different pointing device, such as a trackball or touchpad, substitute that device whenever you see the term mouse. Some pointing devices are designed to ensure that your hand won't suffer fatigue while using them. Most mice work wirelessly and provide access to your computer without being plugged into it. Others are attached directly to your computer by a cable.

You use a pointing device to move the pointer over locations and objects on the screen, or to **point** to them. The pointer is an on-screen object, often shaped like an arrow as shown in the Session 1.1 Visual Overview, though it changes shape depending on its location on the screen and the tasks you are performing. As you move the mouse on a surface, such as a table top, the pointer on the screen moves in a corresponding direction.

When you point to certain objects, such as the objects on the taskbar, a ScreenTip appears near the object. A **ScreenTip** is on-screen text that tells you the purpose or function of the object to which you are pointing.

Ashley suggests that during your class, you introduce For Pet's Sake volunteers to the desktop by viewing ScreenTips for a couple of desktop objects.

To view ScreenTips:

1. Point to the **File Explorer** icon on the taskbar. A ScreenTip identifying the icon appears near the icon, as shown in Figure 1-2.

Figure 1-2 Viewing a ScreenTip

Trouble? If you don't see the ScreenTip, make sure you keep the pointer still for a few seconds.

Clicking refers to pressing a mouse button and immediately releasing it. Clicking sends a signal to your computer that you want to perform an action with the object you click. In Windows 10, you perform most actions with the left mouse button. If you are told to click an object, position the pointer on that object and click the left mouse button, unless instructed otherwise.

Selecting and Opening Objects

> **TIP**
>
> If you are using a device with a touchscreen, a check box appears near an on-screen object when you point to the object. A checkmark appears in the box when you select the object.

You need to select an item, or object, before you can work with it. To **select** an object in Windows 10, you point to or click that object. Windows 10 indicates an object is selected by highlighting it, typically by changing the object's color or displaying a box around it. For example, when you point to the Start button, it changes color. The change shows it is the **active object**. You can interact with active objects by clicking them, for example. When you click the Start button, the Start menu opens. A **menu** is a group or list of commands, and a **menu command** is text that you can click to perform tasks.

The **Start menu** provides access to apps, files, settings, and power options. Ashley suggests you click the Start button to open the Start menu.

To open the Start menu:

1. Click the **Start** button on the taskbar. The Start menu opens, as shown in Figure 1-3; your Start menu might show different commands.

Figure 1-3 Start menu

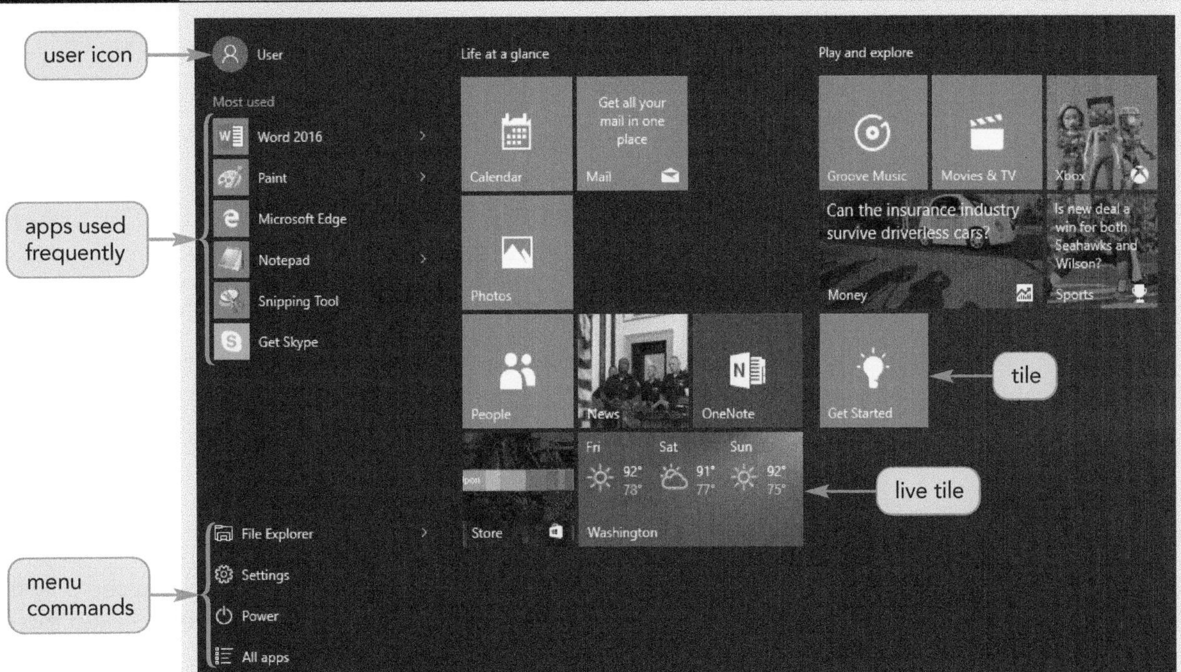

2. Click the **Start** button on the taskbar to close the Start menu.

Besides menu commands, the Start menu includes colored rectangles called **tiles**, which represent apps. Some tiles display icons, such as the Calendar tile. Other tiles display information that previews the contents of the app, such as the Sports tile, which displays photos and headlines for current sports stories. A tile that displays updated content is called a **live tile**. Tiles such as the Weather tile become live tiles after you open their apps for the first time.

If clicking an object doesn't open its app, you probably need to double-click it. **Double-clicking** means clicking the left mouse button twice in quick succession. For example, you can double-click the Recycle Bin icon to open the Recycle Bin and see its contents. The **Recycle Bin** holds deleted items until you remove them permanently.

Ashley suggests that you have volunteers practice double-clicking by opening the Recycle Bin.

To view the contents of the Recycle Bin:

1. Point to the **Recycle Bin** icon, and then click the left mouse button twice quickly to double-click the icon. The Recycle Bin window opens, as shown in Figure 1-4.

Figure 1-4 Contents of the Recycle Bin

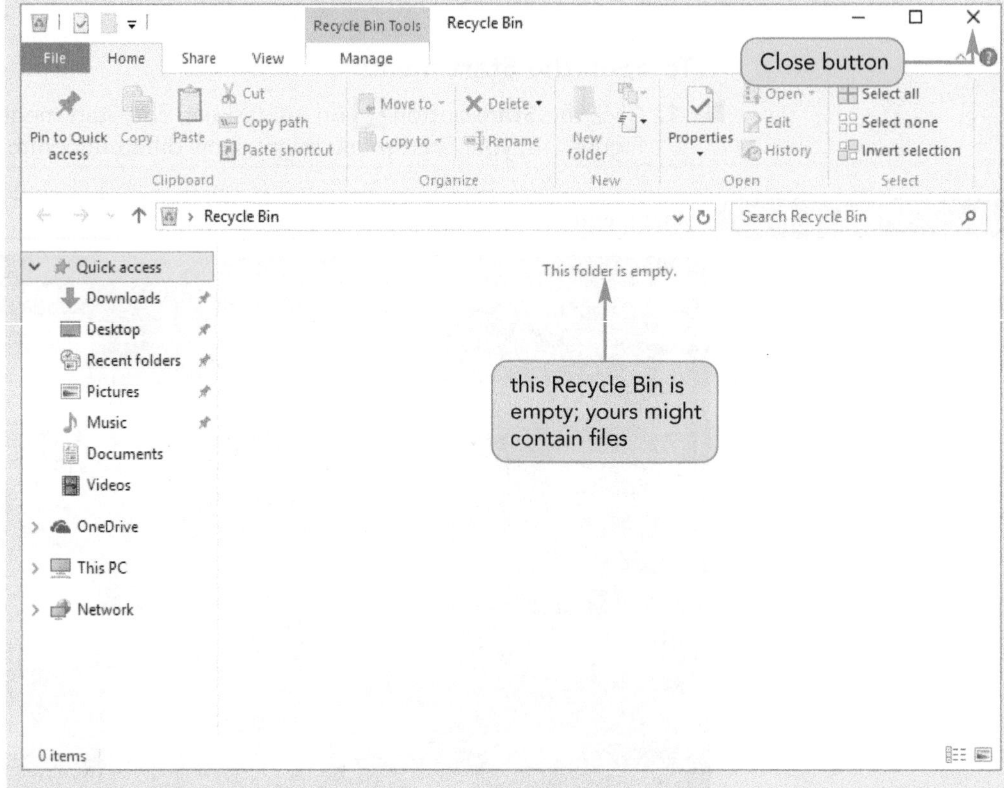

Trouble? If the Recycle Bin window does not open and you see only the Recycle Bin name highlighted below the icon, you double-clicked too slowly. Double-click the icon again more quickly.

Now you can close the Recycle Bin window.

2. Click the **Close** button [X] in the upper-right corner of the Recycle Bin window.

You'll learn more about opening and closing windows later in this session.

Displaying Shortcut Menus

Your mouse most likely has more than one button. In addition to the left button, the mouse has a right button that you can use to perform certain actions in Windows 10. However, the term *clicking* refers to the left button; clicking an object with the right button is called **right-clicking**. (If your mouse has only one button, you right-click by pressing the right side of the button.)

In Windows 10, right-clicking usually selects an object and opens its **shortcut menu**, which lists actions you can take with that object. You can right-click practically any object—a tile on the Start menu, a desktop icon, the taskbar, and even the desktop itself—to view commands associated with that object. Ashley suggests that when you're not sure what to do with an object in Windows 10, you should right-click it and examine its shortcut menu. Now you can right-click the Recycle Bin icon to open its shortcut menu.

To right-click an object on the desktop:

1. Point to the **Recycle Bin** icon on your desktop, and then right-click the icon to open its shortcut menu. This menu offers a list of actions you can take with the Recycle Bin icon. See Figure 1-5.

Figure 1-5 **Recycle Bin shortcut menu**

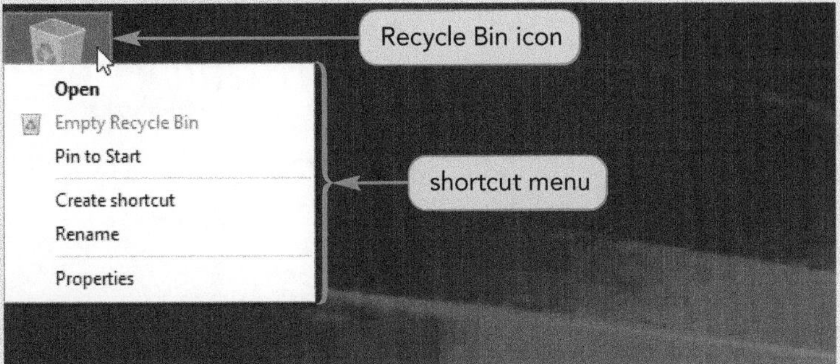

Trouble? If the shortcut menu does not open and you are using a trackball or a mouse with a wheel, make sure you click the button on the far right, not the one in the middle.

2. Click **Open** on the shortcut menu to open the Recycle Bin window again.
3. Click the **Close** button [X] in the upper-right corner of the Recycle Bin window.

Now that you've explored the desktop, you can return to the Start menu and use it to start applications.

Exploring the Start Menu

The Start menu is the central point for accessing apps, documents, and other resources on your computer. The Start menu is organized into two **panes**, which are separate areas of a menu or window. See Figure 1-6.

Figure 1-6 Two panes of the Start menu

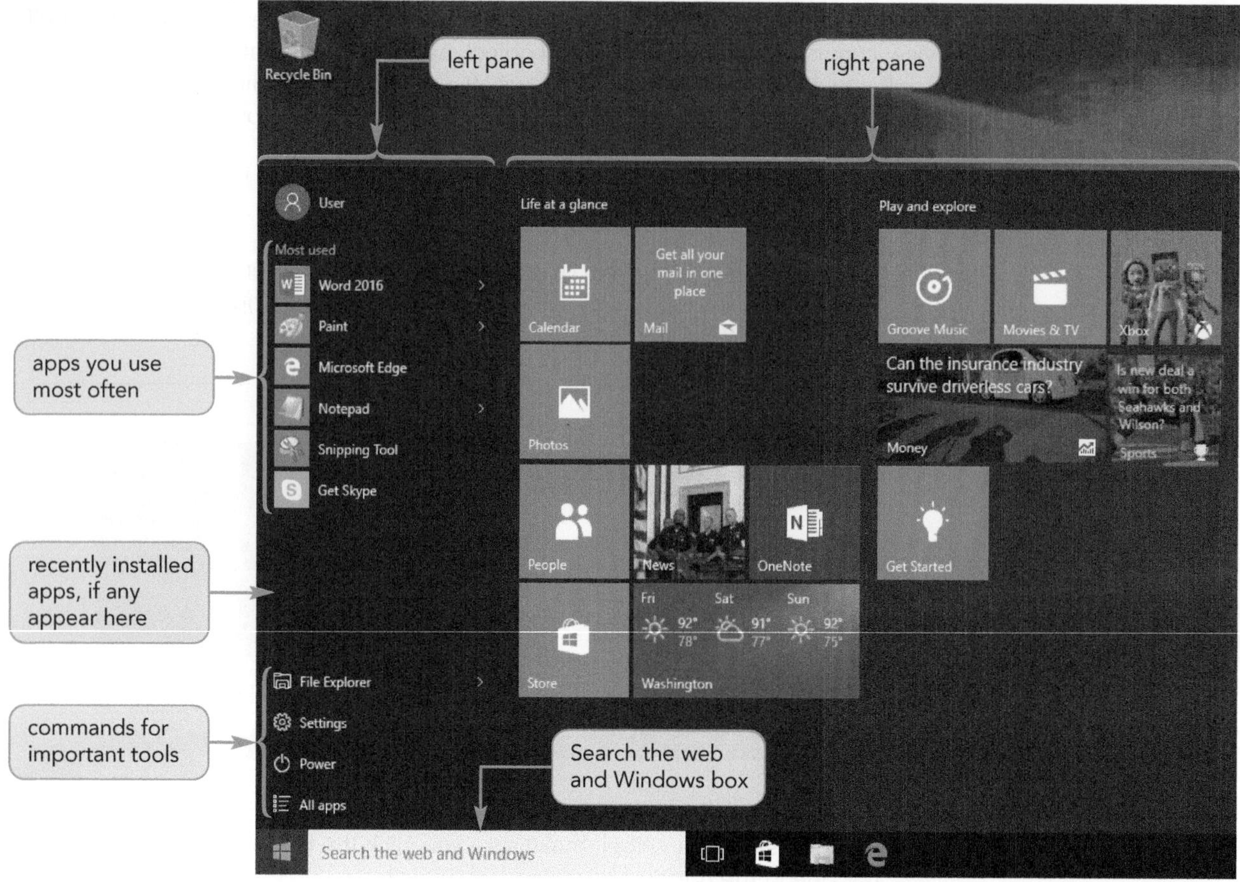

For easy access, the left pane lists the apps you use most often in the Most used list. If you have recently added apps, the left pane also lists those apps in the Recently added list. When you first install Windows 10, the Most used list contains a few apps already installed on your computer. After you use an app, Windows 10 adds it to this list so you can find it quickly the next time you want to use it. The Most used list can contain only a certain number of apps—after that, the apps you have not opened recently are replaced by the apps you used last.

Near the bottom of the left pane are commands for the following important tools:

- File Explorer: Navigate, view, and work with the contents and resources on your computer.
- Settings: Select and change system settings.
- Power: Control the power to the computer by shutting it down, for example.
- All apps: Select from an alphabetic list of all the apps on the computer.

Use the **Search the web and Windows box** to access Cortana, an electronic personal assistant that can search the web, find files, keep track of information, and respond to your questions. You can activate Cortana by typing text or talking. For example, you can ask Cortana to tell a joke, remind you about an appointment, or find a file. See Figure 1-7.

Figure 1-7 Cortana electronic personal assistant

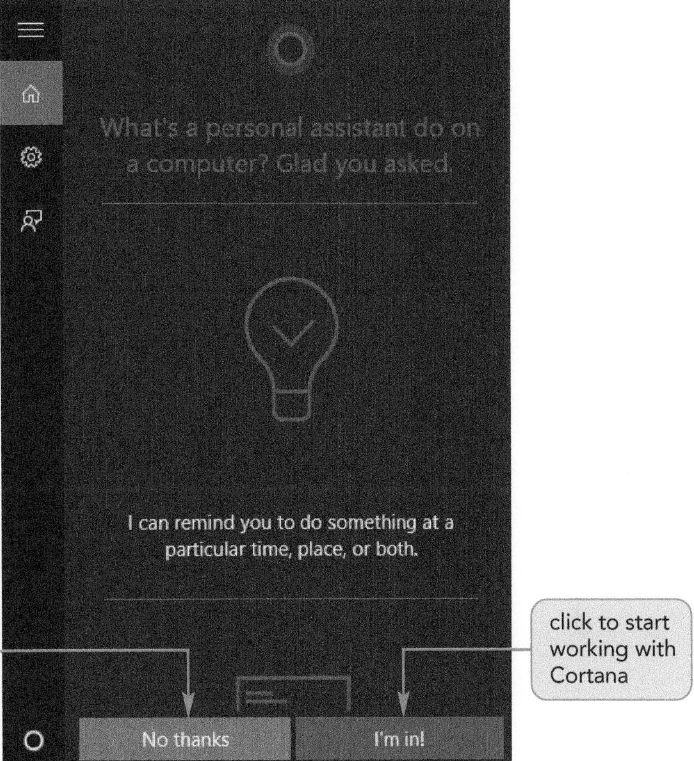
What's a personal assistant do on a computer? Glad you asked.
I can remind you to do something at a particular time, place, or both.
click if you don't want Cortana to track your preferences
click to start working with Cortana
No thanks
I'm in!

INSIGHT

Cortana

Cortana comes from the Halo series of games where she is a smart and powerful character that provides information and helps the master chief complete missions. In Windows 10, Cortana is not a character, but a personalized assistant. The **Notebook** is where Cortana keeps track of what you like, such as your interests and favorite places, and what you want it to do, such as display reminders or information that might interest you. Settings in the People and Maps apps also affect Cortana. For example, if you identify a contact as a friend, Cortana can remind you to call that person. If you identify locations on the map as your home and workplace, Cortana can estimate the time of your commute. As you work, Cortana can take note of your preferences and what you're doing when you ask for information to give personalized answers and recommendations. Because you control the type of information you share with Cortana, the interactions are on your terms and are personalized to your benefit.

From the right pane of the Start menu, you can select tiles for **Windows apps**, or **universal apps**, a type of app that can run on many devices, including laptops, tablets, and mobile phones. You purchase, download, and install Windows apps from the Windows Store, an online resource for games, music, video, and other types of apps, including social and productivity apps. In contrast, many apps in the left pane of the Start menu are **desktop apps**, which run only on personal computers (PCs) such as laptops and desktop computers.

Now that you've explored the Start menu, you're ready to use it to start an app.

Starting Apps

Computers can run two types of software: system software and apps. **System software** is the software that runs a computer, including the operating system. As you know, an app is the software you use to perform tasks, such as writing a screenplay or viewing a webpage. In general, a computer runs system software to perform computer tasks, and you run apps to carry out your work or personal tasks.

REFERENCE

Starting an App

- Click the Start button on the taskbar.
- Click the tile or command for the app you want to start.
- If the app you want does not appear on the Start menu, click All apps, and then click the app you want to start.

or

- In the Search the web and Windows box, type the name of the app until the app appears in the search results on the Start menu; or click the Start button, and then type the name of the app until the app appears in the search results on the Start menu.
- Click the app in the search results.

Ashley suggests that you demonstrate how to start the Calendar app, a Windows app that displays a full-screen calendar where you can schedule appointments and other events.

To start the Calendar app:

1. Click the **Start** button on the taskbar to display the Start menu.
2. Click the **Calendar** tile to start the Calendar app. If this is the first time you are starting the Calendar app, click the **Get started** button to set up the calendar. See Figure 1-8.

   Trouble? If a screen appears asking you to let Mail and Calendar access your location, click the No button.

Figure 1-8 Calendar app

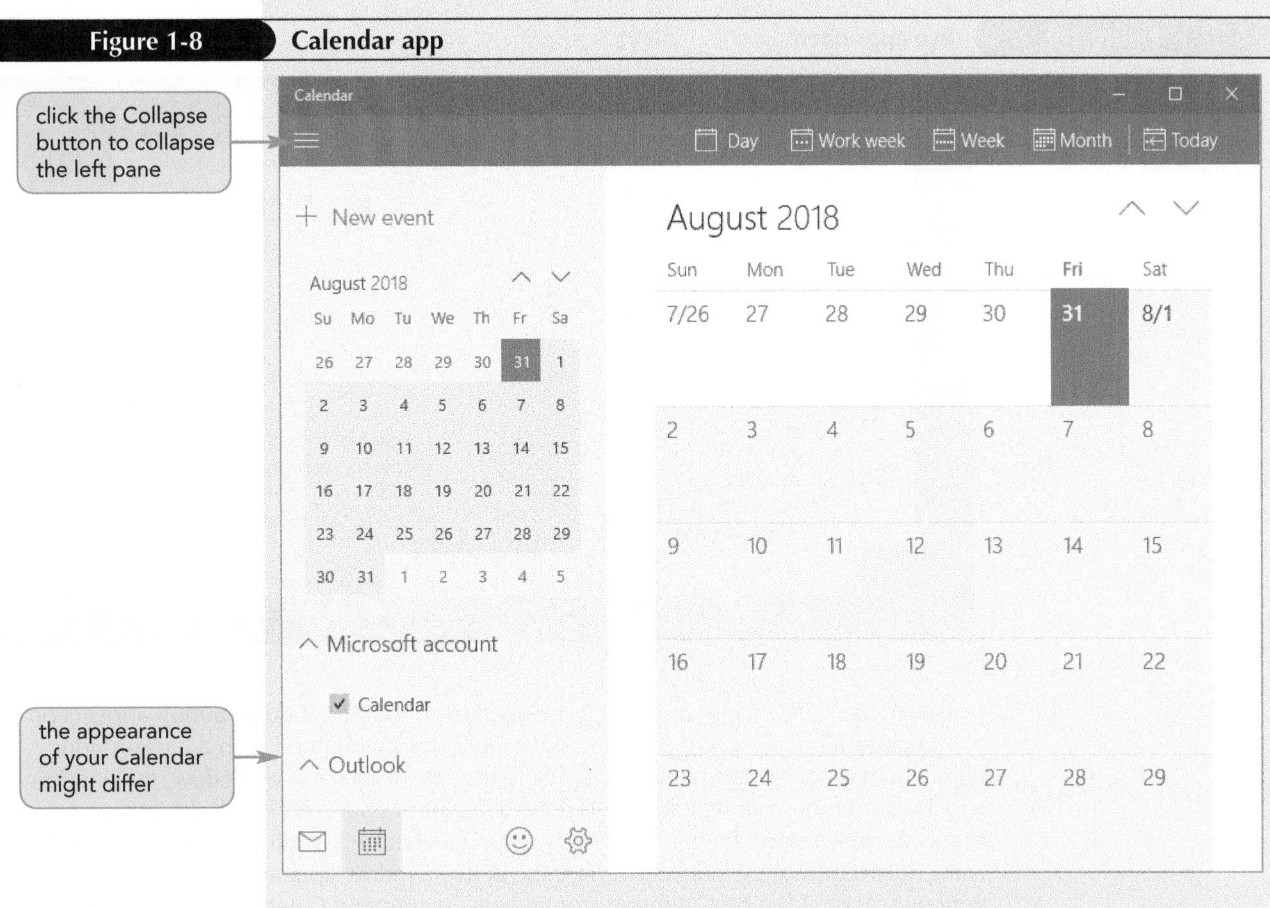

Now that you have started one app, you can start another app and run two at the same time.

Running Multiple Apps

One of the most useful features of Windows 10 is its ability to run multiple programs at the same time. This feature, known as **multitasking**, allows you to work on more than one task at a time and to switch quickly between projects.

To demonstrate multitasking and switching between apps, Ashley suggests that you start Paint, a desktop app you use to draw, color, and edit digital pictures. Paint appears on the Start menu by default.

To run Calendar and Paint at the same time:

1. Click the **Start** button on the taskbar to display the Start menu.
2. In the left pane, click **Paint** to start the app. Now two apps are running at the same time.

   Trouble? If Paint does not appear in the left pane of the Start menu, click All apps, scroll the list of apps, click Windows Accessories, and then click Paint.
3. If the Paint window fills the entire screen, click the **Restore Down** button in the upper-right corner of the Paint window to reduce the size of the window. See Figure 1-9.

Figure 1-9 Two apps open

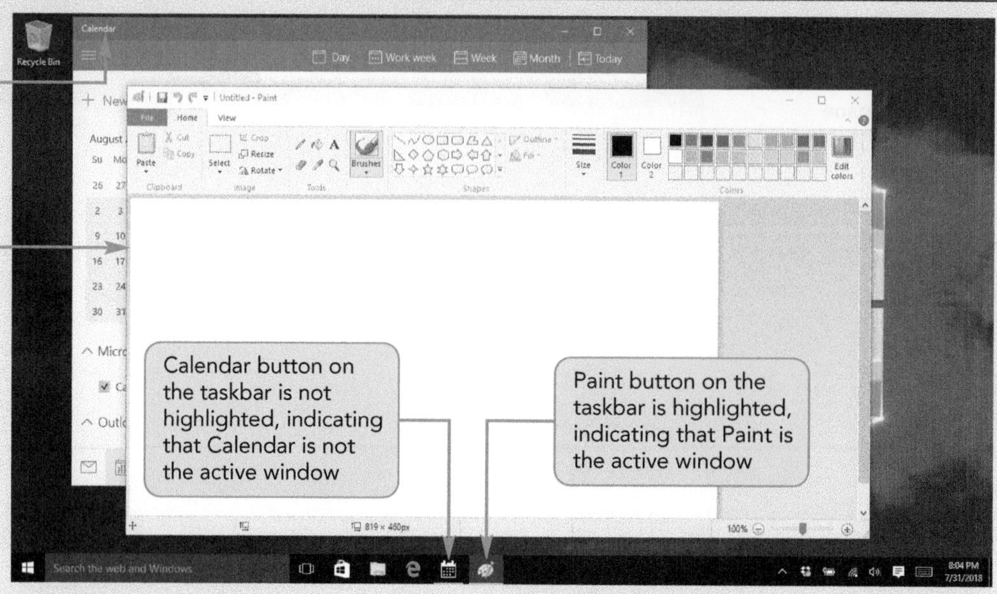
Calendar window; yours might be hidden by the Paint window
Paint window appears in front of the Calendar window
Calendar button on the taskbar is not highlighted, indicating that Calendar is not the active window
Paint button on the taskbar is highlighted, indicating that Paint is the active window

When you start an app, it is said to be open or running. A taskbar button appears on the taskbar for each open app. One taskbar button is highlighted with a background lighter than the other taskbar buttons. This button is for the **active window**, the window you are currently working with—Windows 10 applies your next keystroke or command to the active window. Paint is the active window because it is the one you are currently using. If two or more windows overlap, the active window appears in front of the other windows. Even if the Paint window completely covered the Calendar window, you could still access the Calendar app by using its taskbar button. The taskbar organizes all the open windows so you can quickly make one active by clicking its taskbar button.

Switching Between Applications

Because only one app is active at a time, you need to switch between apps if you want to work in one or the other. The easiest way to switch between running apps is to use the taskbar buttons.

To switch between Calendar and Paint:

1. Click the **Calendar** button on the taskbar. The Calendar window moves to the front, and the Calendar taskbar button appears highlighted, indicating that Calendar is the active window.
2. Click the **Paint** button on the taskbar to switch to the Paint app. The Paint window is again the active window.

TIP

You can also click an inactive window to make it the active window.

Another way to use the taskbar to switch between open apps is to use the Task View button. By default, the Task View button is the first button to the right of the Search the web and Windows box. Click the Task View button to display thumbnails of all running apps. (A **thumbnail** is a miniature version of a larger image, such as a window.) See Figure 1-10.

Figure 1-10 Task view

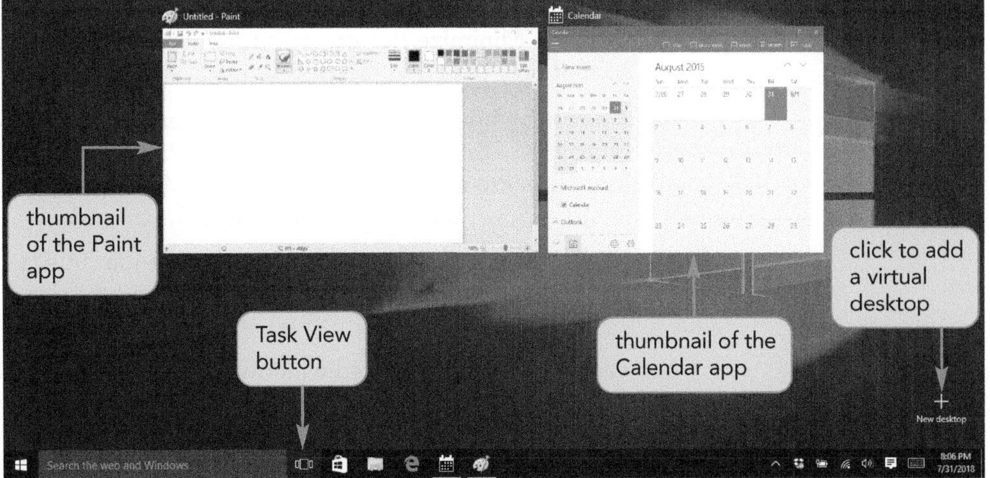

You can switch to one of the running apps by clicking its thumbnail or close it by clicking its Close button. Clicking a thumbnail displays its full window as the active window. To close the Task view, click the Task View button again.

Besides switching apps, you can click the New desktop button in Task view to add a new desktop to the interface, called a **virtual desktop**. For example, you might use the default desktop for school or work projects, and another desktop for entertainment, such as a music player and games.

Another way to switch apps is to bypass the taskbar altogether and use keyboard shortcuts to switch from one open window to another. A **keyboard shortcut** is a key or combination of keys that performs a command. Use the Alt+Tab keyboard shortcut to switch between running apps. To do so, you hold down the Alt key and then press the Tab key to display thumbnails of all running apps, press the Tab key again to select a thumbnail, and then release the Alt key to make that app active. Pressing the Alt+Tab keys displays thumbnails similar to Task view. However, when you release the keys, the thumbnails no longer appear. In Task view, the thumbnails remain on the screen until you select one.

Manipulating Windows

After you open a window, you can manipulate it to display as much or as little information as you need. In most windows, three buttons appear on the right side of the title bar. See Figure 1-11. The first button is the Minimize button, which hides a window so that only its button is visible on the taskbar. Depending on the status of the window, the middle button either maximizes the window or restores it to a predefined size. The last button is the Close button, which closes the window.

Figure 1-11 Window buttons

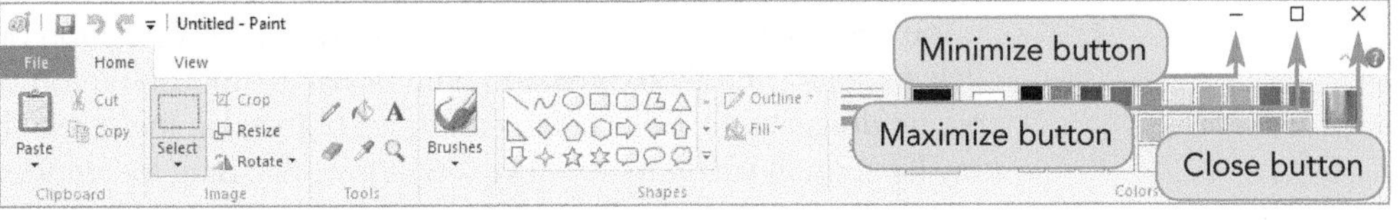

Paint and Calendar are open on the desktop, so Ashley encourages you to show volunteers how to use their window controls. Start with the Minimize button, which you use when you want to temporarily hide a window but keep the app running.

To minimize the Paint and Calendar windows:

1. Click the **Minimize** button on the Paint title bar. The Paint window shrinks so that only the Paint taskbar button is visible.

   Trouble? If the Paint window closed, you accidentally clicked the Close button. Use the Start menu to start Paint again, and then repeat Step 1. If you accidentally clicked the Maximize button or the Restore Down button, repeat Step 1.

2. Click the **Minimize** button on the Calendar title bar. The Calendar window is minimized.

You can redisplay a minimized window by clicking the window's taskbar button. When you redisplay a window, it becomes the active window.

To redisplay the Paint window:

1. Click the **Paint** button on the taskbar to redisplay the Paint window.

   The taskbar button provides another way to switch between a window's minimized and open states.

2. Click the **Paint** button on the taskbar again to minimize the window.
3. Click the **Paint** button once more to redisplay the window.

The Maximize button enlarges a window so that it fills the entire screen. Ashley recommends that you work with maximized windows when you want to concentrate on the work you are performing in a single app.

To maximize the Paint window:

TIP

You can also double-click a window's title bar to maximize the window. Double-click the title bar again to restore the window to its previous size.

1. Click the **Maximize** button on the Paint title bar.

The Restore Down button reduces the window so that it is smaller than the entire computer screen. This feature is useful if you want to see more than one window at a time. Also, because the window is smaller, you can move it to another location on the screen or change its dimensions.

To restore a window:

1. Click the **Restore Down** button on the Paint title bar. After a window is restored, the Restore Down button changes to the Maximize button.

You can use the mouse to move a window to a new position on the desktop. When you click an object and then press and hold down the mouse button while moving the mouse, you are **dragging** the object. You can move objects on the screen by dragging them to a new location. If you want to move a window, you drag the window by its title bar.

To drag the restored Paint window to a new location:

1. Position the pointer on the Paint title bar.
2. Press and hold down the left mouse button, and then move the mouse up or down a little to drag the window. The window moves as you move the mouse.
3. Position the window anywhere on the desktop, and then release the left mouse button. The Paint window stays in the new location.
4. Drag the Paint window near the upper-left corner of the desktop.

You can also use the mouse to change the size of a window. When you point to an edge or a corner of a window, the pointer changes to the resize pointer, which is a double-headed arrow. You can use the resize pointer to drag an edge or a corner of the window and change the size of the window.

To change the size of the Paint window:

1. Position the pointer over the lower-right corner of the Paint window. The pointer changes to ⤡. See Figure 1-12.

Figure 1-12 Preparing to resize a window

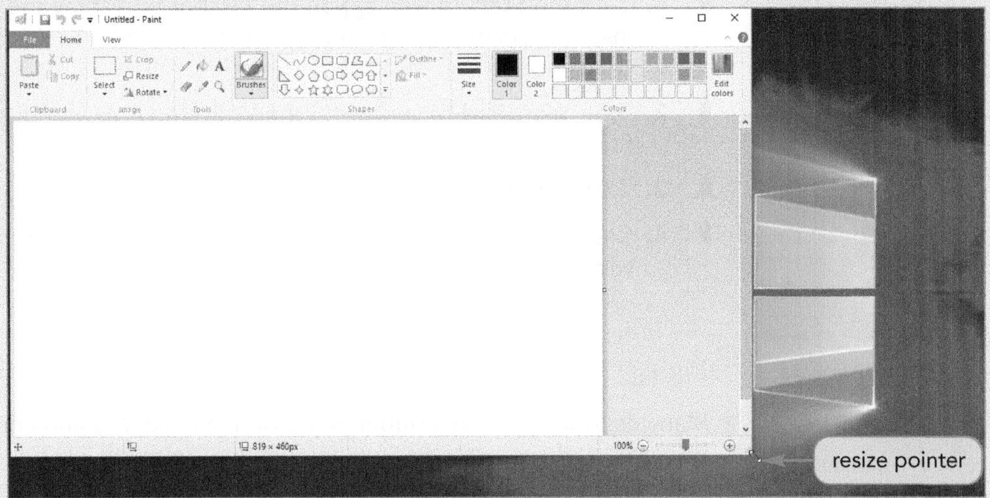

2. Press and hold down the mouse button, and then drag the corner down and to the right.
3. Release the mouse button. Now the window is larger.
4. Practice using the resize pointer to make the Paint window larger or smaller.

You can also use the resize pointer to drag any of the other three corners of the window to change its size. To change a window's size in any one direction only, drag the left, right, top, or bottom window borders left, right, up, or down.

Using App Tools

When you run an app in Windows 10, it appears in a window that contains **controls**, graphical or textual objects used for manipulating a window and for using an app. All apps organize controls in dialog boxes. A desktop application also uses a ribbon to provide controls.

Ashley mentions that Windows 10 comes with a basic word-processing app called WordPad. You use WordPad to create and format basic documents. The WordPad app displays the controls you are likely to see in most windows, including the ribbon, which might be unfamiliar to For Pet's Sake volunteers. Ashley suggests that you start WordPad and identify its window controls during your first training session. You have already started apps using the left and right panes on the Start menu. To start WordPad, you can use the Search the web and Windows box.

As you enter text in the Search the web and Windows box, the Start menu displays search results, including the installed apps, folders, documents, and settings whose names include the text you typed. The search results might also include web search text and Windows Store apps. Two buttons appear at the bottom of the search results: the My stuff button and the Web button. Click the My stuff button to restrict the search to locations on your computer, OneDrive, or network. Click the Web button to start a browser and search the web using the text you entered as the search text.

To start WordPad:

1. Click the **Start** button on the taskbar to display the Start menu. The insertion point appears in the Search the web and Windows box so you can search for an app or other information.
2. Type **WordPad** to search for the WordPad app and display the results in the Start menu.
3. Click **WordPad** on the results list to start the app.
4. Click the **Maximize** button on the WordPad title bar to maximize the window.

Using the Ribbon

TIP

By default, the ribbon displays the Home tab when you start WordPad. To display the contents of the View tab, you click the View tab on the ribbon.

Many desktop apps use a **ribbon** to consolidate features and commands. The ribbon is located at the top of a desktop app window, immediately below the title bar, and is organized into tabs. Each **tab** contains commands that perform a variety of related tasks. For example, the Home tab has commands for tasks you perform frequently, such as changing the appearance of a document. You use the commands on the View tab to change your view of the WordPad window.

To select a command and perform an action, you use a button or other type of control on the ribbon. Controls for related actions are organized on a tab in **groups**. For example, to enter bold text in a WordPad document, you click the Bold button in the Font group on the Home tab. If a button displays only an icon and not the button name, you can point to the button to display a ScreenTip and identify the name or purpose of the button. Figure 1-13 shows examples of the types of controls on the ribbon.

Figure 1-13 Examples of ribbon controls

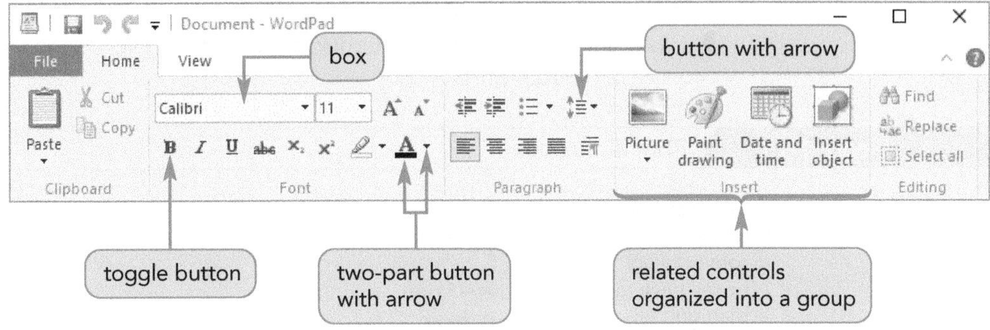

Figure 1-14 describes the types of ribbon controls.

Figure 1-14 Types of controls on the ribbon

Control	How to Use	Example
Button with arrow	Click the button to display a menu of related commands.	
Box	Click the box and type an entry, or click the arrow button to select an item from the list.	Calibri
Toggle button	Click the button to turn on or apply a setting, and then click the button again to turn off the setting. When a toggle button is turned on, it is highlighted.	B
Two-part button with arrow	If an arrow is displayed on a separate part of the button, click the arrow to display a menu of commands. Click the button itself to apply the current selection.	A

Using Dialog Boxes

When you click some buttons on the ribbon, you open a **dialog box**, a special kind of window in which you enter or choose settings for how you want to perform a task. For example, you use the Print dialog box to enter or select settings for printing a document.

You open dialog boxes by selecting a command on a ribbon tab. For example, the File tab lists commands such as Open, Save, and Print in its left pane. If you point to the Print command, a list of three printing options appears in the right pane, including Print, Quick print, and Print preview. Choose Print to open the Print dialog box, where you can change settings such as the number of copies to print. If you want to print the open document without changing any settings, choose Quick print. Choose Print preview to display the document as it will appear when you print it. If you click the Print command in the left pane without displaying the three printing options, the Print dialog box opens.

Dialog box controls include command buttons, tabs, option buttons, check boxes, and boxes to collect information about how you want to perform a task. Ashley says a good way to learn how dialog box controls work is to open a typical WordPad dialog box, such as the Print dialog box.

To work with a typical Windows 10 dialog box:

1. Click the **File** tab on the ribbon, and then click **Print** to open the Print dialog box. See Figure 1-15.

Figure 1-15 Print dialog box

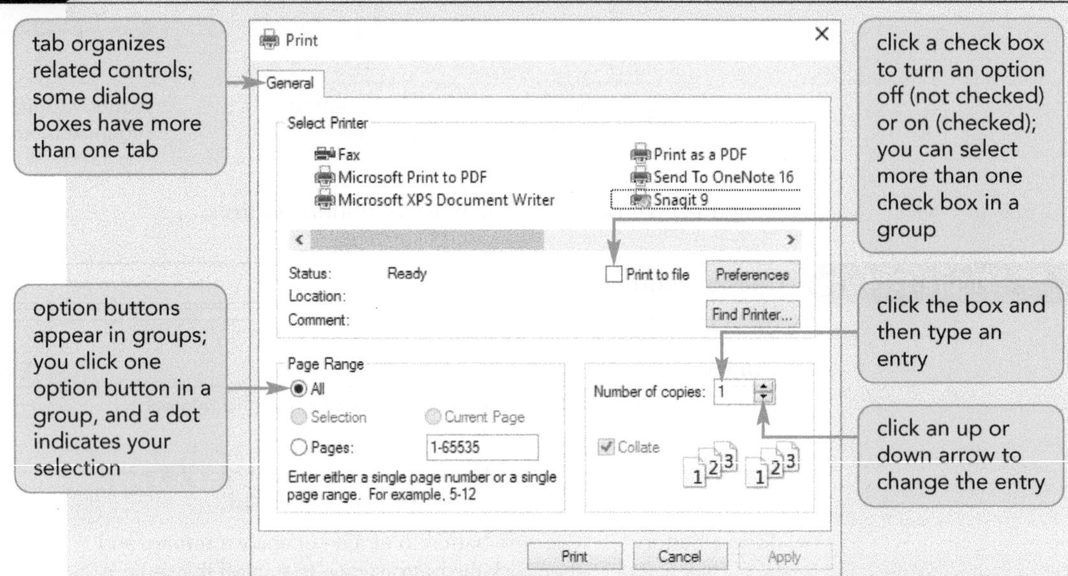
tab organizes related controls; some dialog boxes have more than one tab
option buttons appear in groups; you click one option button in a group, and a dot indicates your selection
click a check box to turn an option off (not checked) or on (checked); you can select more than one check box in a group
click the box and then type an entry
click an up or down arrow to change the entry
Print
General
Select Printer
Fax
Microsoft Print to PDF
Microsoft XPS Document Writer
Print as a PDF
Send To OneNote 16
Snagit 9
Status:
Ready
Location:
Comment:
Print to file
Preferences
Find Printer...
Page Range
All
Selection
Current Page
Pages:
1-65535
Enter either a single page number or a single page range. For example, 5-12
Number of copies:
1
Collate
Print
Cancel
Apply

2. Click the **Pages** option button. You use this control to print only specified pages, not the entire document.
3. Double-click the **Number of copies** box to select the current value, and then type **2**. You use this control to indicate how many copies of the document you want to print.
4. Click the **Cancel** button to close the Print dialog box without printing.

TIP

You can also click an arrow button in the Number of copies box to change the number of copies you want to print.

If you wanted to print a document with the settings you specified, you would click the Print button instead of the Cancel button. To retain your selections while you perform other tasks in a dialog box, such as setting preferences or finding a printer, you can click the Apply button, complete the other tasks, and then click the Print button.

You're finished working with apps for now, so you should close all open apps.

Closing Apps

You should close an application when you are finished using it. Each application uses computer resources, such as memory, so Windows 10 works more efficiently when only the applications you need are open.

REFERENCE

Closing an App

- Click the Close button on the title bar.

or

- Point to the app's taskbar button to display a thumbnail, point to the thumbnail, and then click the Close button on the thumbnail.

or

- Click the File tab on the ribbon, and then click Exit.

You can close an app in at least three ways, and you use all three to close the WordPad, Calendar, and Paint apps.

To close WordPad:

1. Click the **Close** button in the upper-right corner of the WordPad window. WordPad closes while the Paint and Calendar windows remain open. (Recall that the Calendar window is minimized.)

   Trouble? If a dialog box opens with a message asking if you want to save changes, click the Don't Save button.

The Calendar app is still running, though its window is minimized. In this case, the fastest way to close the Calendar app is to use the Close button on the app's thumbnail.

To close Calendar using the thumbnail:

1. Point to the **Calendar** button on the taskbar to display a thumbnail of the Calendar window.
2. Point to the thumbnail, and then click the **Close** button on the thumbnail. The Calendar app closes and its button no longer appears on the taskbar.

TIP

You can also right-click the app's taskbar button and then click Close window on the shortcut menu, or click the Task view button, point to a thumbnail, and then click its Close button.

Only the Paint app is still open and running. You can use the Exit command on the File tab to close the Paint window and exit the app.

To close Paint using the Exit command:

1. Click the **File** tab on the Paint ribbon to display a list of commands for working with Paint files.
2. Click **Exit** to close the Paint app.

   Trouble? If a message appears asking if you want to save changes, click the Don't Save button.

PROSKILLS

Problem Solving: Working with Apps Efficiently

As you work on your computer throughout the day, you may end up with quite a few apps open and running at the same time. This situation can lead to two common problems that affect your productivity: Finding the information you need becomes more difficult as you switch between apps, and the performance of your computer can slow significantly.

To address both these issues, decide which apps need to be running, and then close the ones you don't need. Closing unnecessary apps allows you to focus on the information you need for the tasks at hand. It also frees up system resources, which makes your computer faster and more responsive and can solve performance problems.

REVIEW

Session 1.1 Quick Check

1. What is the difference between system software and apps?
2. The ____________ is the central point for accessing apps, documents, and other resources on your computer.
3. A tile that displays updated content is called a(n) ____________.
4. Describe the appearance of the Start menu.
5. Name two tasks you can perform with Cortana.
6. What is a Windows (or universal) app?
7. How can you display an app if its window is minimized?
8. In a desktop app, the ____________ is located at the top of the window, immediately below the title bar, and is organized into tabs.

Session 1.2 Visual Overview:

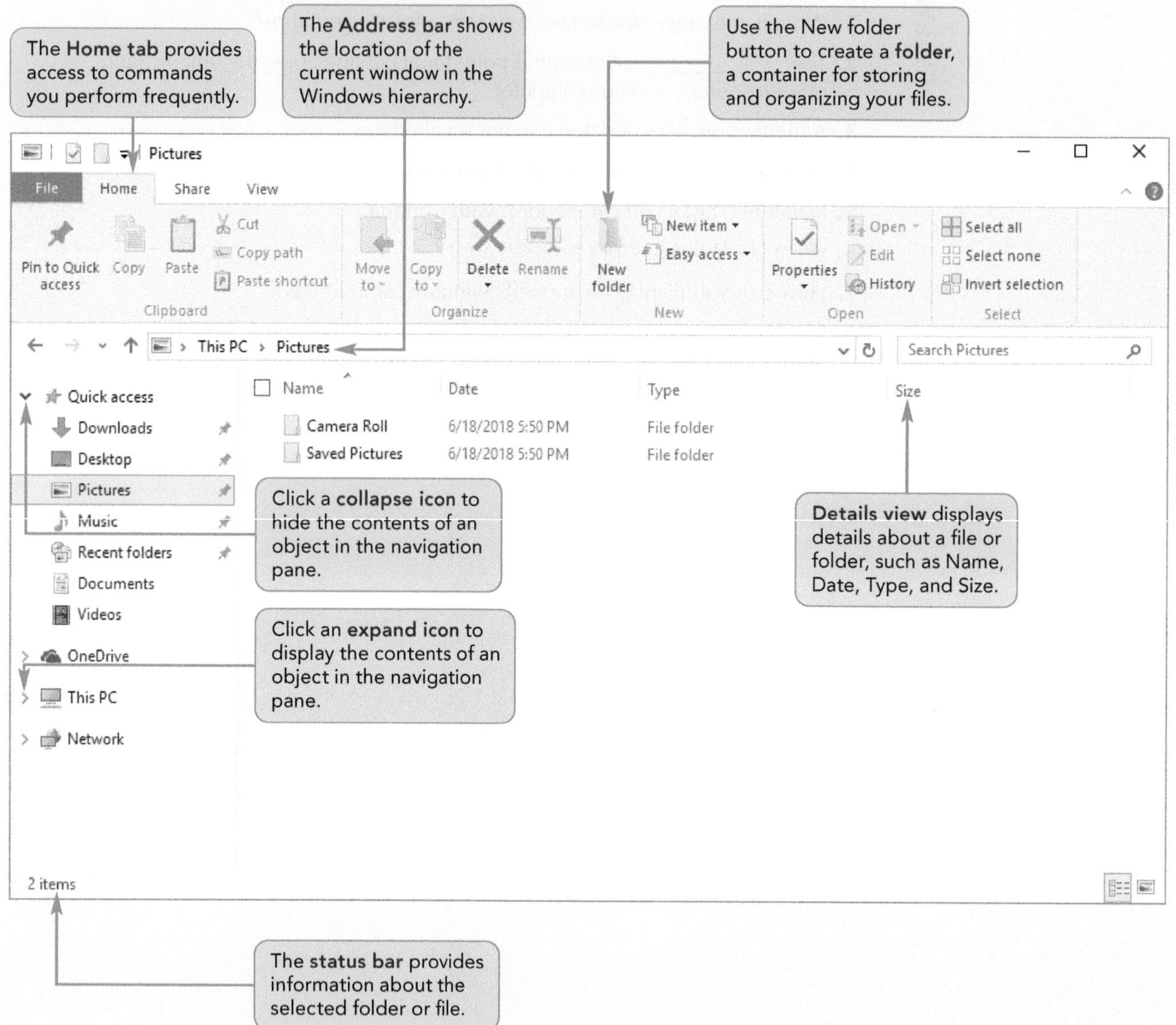
The Home tab provides access to commands you perform frequently.
The Address bar shows the location of the current window in the Windows hierarchy.
Use the New folder button to create a folder, a container for storing and organizing your files.
Pictures
File
Home
Share
View
Pin to Quick access
Copy
Paste
Cut
Copy path
Paste shortcut
Clipboard
Move to
Copy to
Delete
Rename
Organize
New folder
New item
Easy access
New
Properties
Open
Edit
History
Open
Select all
Select none
Invert selection
Select
This PC > Pictures
Search Pictures
Quick access
Downloads
Desktop
Pictures
Music
Recent folders
Documents
Videos
OneDrive
This PC
Network
Name
Date
Type
Size
Camera Roll
6/18/2018 5:50 PM
File folder
Saved Pictures
6/18/2018 5:50 PM
File folder
Click a collapse icon to hide the contents of an object in the navigation pane.
Details view displays details about a file or folder, such as Name, Date, Type, and Size.
Click an expand icon to display the contents of an object in the navigation pane.
2 items
The status bar provides information about the selected folder or file.

Working in File Explorer

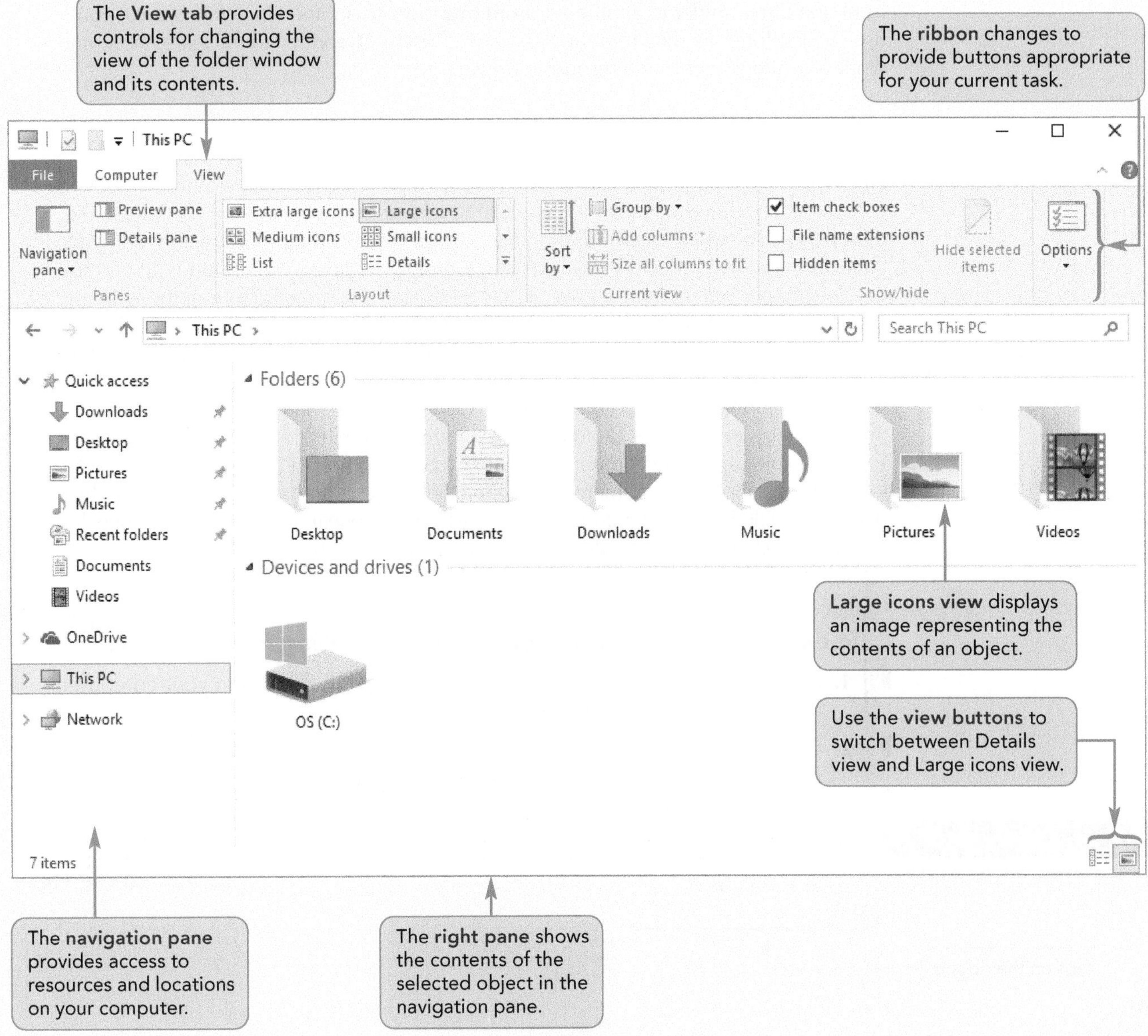
The View tab provides controls for changing the view of the folder window and its contents.
The ribbon changes to provide buttons appropriate for your current task.
This PC
File
Computer
View
Preview pane
Details pane
Navigation pane
Panes
Extra large icons
Large icons
Medium icons
Small icons
List
Details
Layout
Sort by
Group by
Add columns
Size all columns to fit
Current view
Item check boxes
File name extensions
Hidden items
Hide selected items
Show/hide
Options
Search This PC
Quick access
Downloads
Desktop
Pictures
Music
Recent folders
Documents
Videos
OneDrive
Network
Folders (6)
Devices and drives (1)
OS (C:)
7 items
Large icons view displays an image representing the contents of an object.
Use the view buttons to switch between Details view and Large icons view.
The navigation pane provides access to resources and locations on your computer.
The right pane shows the contents of the selected object in the navigation pane.

Exploring Your Computer

To discover the contents and resources on your computer, you explore, or navigate, it. **Navigating** means moving from one location to another on your computer, such as from one file or folder to another, or from one drive to another. In Windows 10, you use File Explorer (as shown in the Session 1.2 Visual Overview) to navigate, view, and work with the contents and resources on your computer.

Navigating with File Explorer

File Explorer is a window that is divided into two panes. The left side of the window is called the navigation pane, which you use to access locations on your computer. The right pane displays the details of the location you navigated to, so you can work with your files, folders, or devices easily. At the top of the window is a ribbon with buttons that let you perform common tasks. A status bar appears at the bottom of the window and displays the characteristics of an object you select in the File Explorer window. You use File Explorer to keep track of where your files are stored and to organize your files.

Ashley Cramer, the volunteer coordinator of For Pet's Sake, is helping you plan a training session for volunteers on the basics of Windows 10. She wants you to start this session by opening File Explorer and exploring the contents of your computer. She suggests exploring the locations in the Quick access list. These locations include standard folders for storing your documents, music, pictures, videos, and other files. In the right pane of the File Explorer window, the standard folders appear in the Frequent folders list. If you have opened files recently, they appear in the Recent files list.

To explore the contents of your computer using File Explorer:

1. If you took a break after the previous session, make sure that your computer is on and Windows 10 is running.
2. Click the **File Explorer** button on the taskbar. A window opens showing folders in the Quick access list. See Figure 1-16.

Figure 1-16 Quick access folders

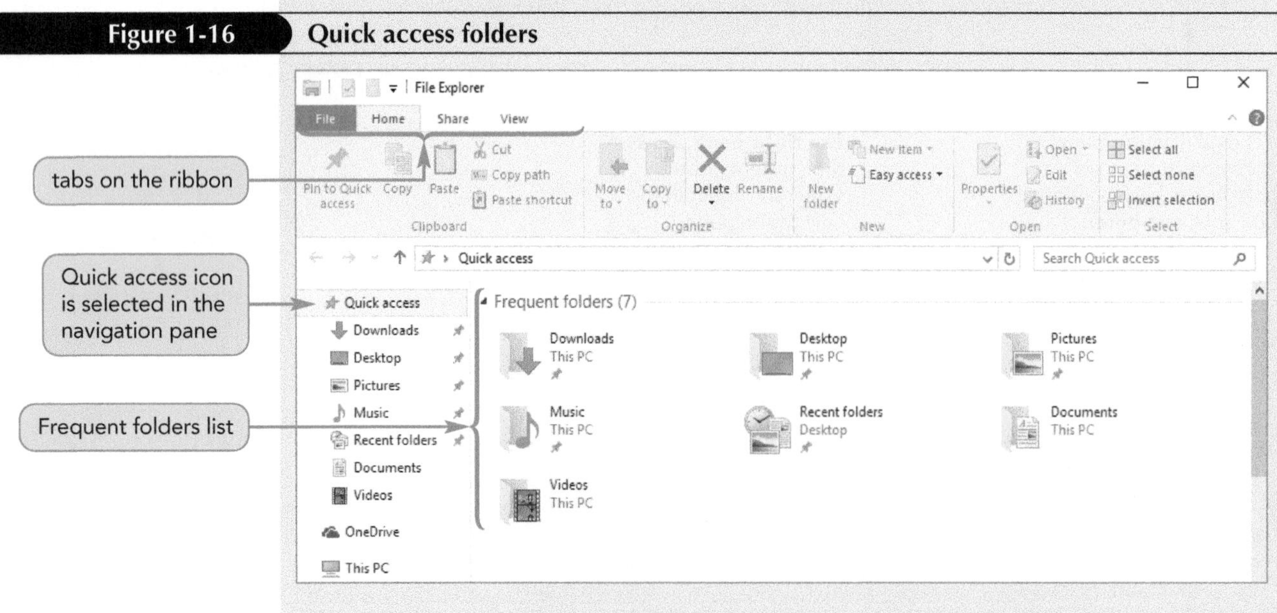

3. In the navigation pane, click **Pictures**. The right pane of the window shows the contents of the Pictures folder, which is designed for storing your photos and other picture files. The Pictures folder might contain two folders by default: Camera Roll, for saving photos taken with the camera on your device, and Saved Pictures, for storing other images.
4. In the right pane, click the **Saved Pictures** folder to select it. See Figure 1-17. Your Pictures folder might contain other files and folders.

Figure 1-17 **Pictures folder in File Explorer**

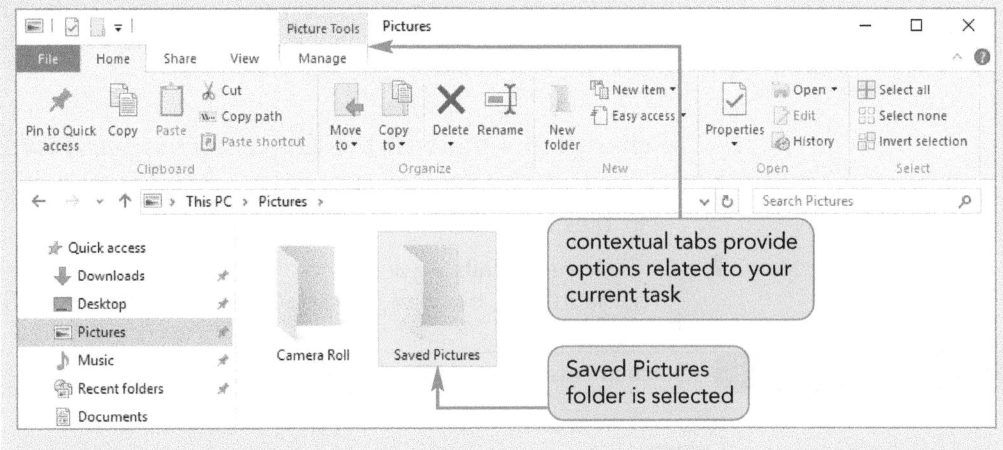

As you open folders and navigate with File Explorer, tabs might appear at the top of the window just above the standard ribbon tabs. For example, the Picture Tools Manage tab appears when you select a file or folder in the Pictures folder. This type of tab is called a **contextual tab**, and it contains options that apply to the object you have selected. For example, the Picture Tools Manage tab contains options for working with pictures.

Ashley mentions that you can change the appearance of most windows to suit your preferences. You'll change the view of the File Explorer window next so you can see more details about folders and files.

Changing the View

Windows 10 provides eight ways to view the contents of a folder: Extra large icons, Large icons, Medium icons, Small icons, List, Details, Tiles, and Content. The default view for the Pictures folder is Large icons view, which provides a thumbnail image of the file contents. (If thumbnails are turned off on your computer, the Large icons view displays a larger version of the file icon.) The default view for other types of folders is Details view, which displays a small icon instead of a thumbnail and lists details about each file. Although only Details view lists all file details, such as the date a photo was taken and its size, you can see some of these details in any other view by pointing to a file to display a ScreenTip.

INSIGHT

Selecting a View

When you display files in Medium icons view or larger, the icon displays a preview of the file's content. The preview images are big and easy to see; however, the window shows fewer files with large icons. When you display files using smaller icons, the window can show more files, but the preview images are not as easy to see. The view you select depends on your preferences and needs.

REFERENCE

Changing the Icon View

- In File Explorer, click a view button on the status bar.

or

- Click the View tab on the ribbon.
- In the Layout group, point to a view option to preview its effect in the folder window, if necessary, and then click a view option.

To demonstrate switching from one view to another, Ashley says you can display folders in Details view. To do so, you'll use the Details view button on the status bar.

To change the view of the Quick access window:

1. In the navigation pane, click **Quick access** to display the Frequent folders list in Tiles view, which is the default for this window.
2. Click the **Details view** button on the status bar. The window shows the same folders, but with more details and smaller icons. See Figure 1-18.

Figure 1-18 **Quick access folders in Details view**

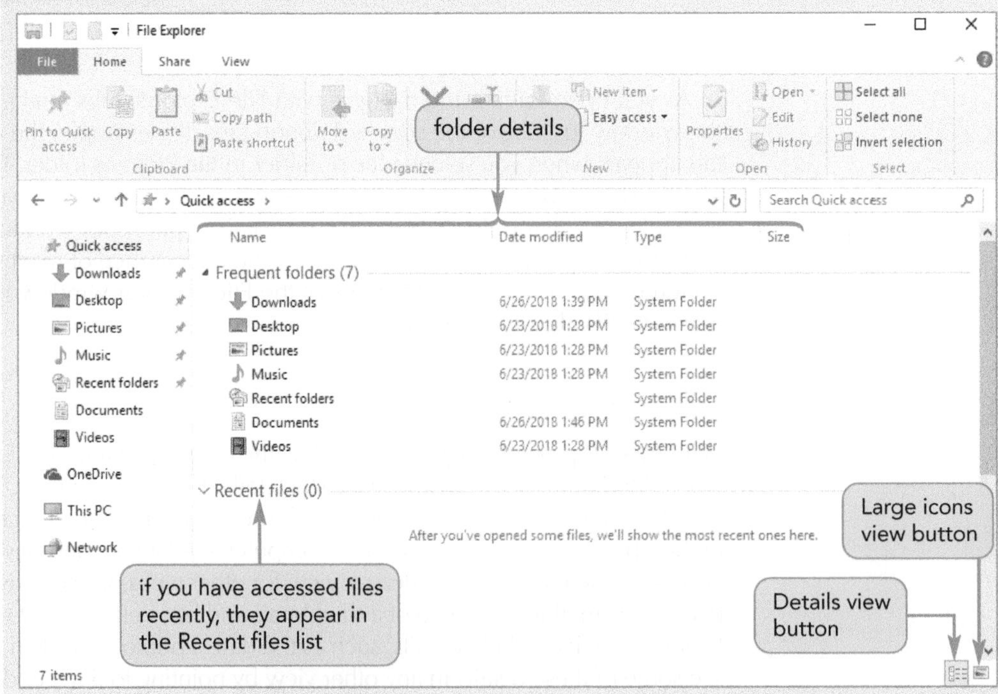

3. Click the **Large icons view** button on the status bar. The window shows the folders with large icons and no details.

Ashley suggests that you now use File Explorer to navigate your computer.

Using the Navigation Pane

To navigate your computer, you use the navigation pane on the left side of the File Explorer window. By default, the navigation pane organizes computer resources into four categories: Quick access (for locations you access frequently), **OneDrive** (for files and folders stored online in your OneDrive folder), This PC (for the folders, drives, and devices on your computer), and Network (for network locations your computer can access).

INSIGHT

OneDrive

File Explorer lists OneDrive as a location in the navigation pane by default. OneDrive is a service from Microsoft that provides 15 GB of free storage space and lets you use software on a **server**, a powerful, high-capacity computer you access using the Internet or other network. You can increase the amount of storage space, if necessary. You use OneDrive to store, synchronize, and share files with people and devices. For example, if you are working on a group project, you can store files in your OneDrive and let other group members read and change the files. Anyone can access OneDrive using a web browser, even if they are using an Apple iPhone, for example, or an Xbox console. However, if you're using Windows 10 (or Windows 8 or 8.1), you can access OneDrive directly from File Explorer. If you are using Microsoft Office 2013 or Office 2016, a suite of productivity apps, you can save and open files directly from most Office apps.

When you move the pointer into the navigation pane, arrows appear next to some icons. A right-pointing arrow, or expand icon, indicates that a folder contains other folders that are not currently displayed in the navigation pane. Click the arrow to expand the folder and display its subfolders. (A **subfolder** is a folder contained in another folder.) A down-pointing arrow, or collapse icon, indicates the folder is expanded, and its subfolders are listed below the folder name. You can click a folder in the navigation pane to navigate directly to that folder and display its contents in the right pane.

Using the navigation pane to explore your computer usually involves clicking expand icons to expand objects and find the folder you want, and then clicking that folder to display its contents in the right pane. To display a list of all the folders on a drive, expand the This PC icon in the navigation pane, and then expand the icon for the drive, such as Local Disk (C:). The navigation pane shows the hierarchy of folders on the drive, so you can use it to find and manage your files and folders.

INSIGHT

Identifying Storage Devices

Each storage device you can access on your computer is associated with a letter. The first hard drive is drive C. (If you add other hard drives, they are usually drives D, E, and so on.) If you have a CD or DVD drive or a USB flash drive plugged in to a USB port, it usually has the next available letter in the alphabetic sequence. If you can access hard drives located on other computers in a network, those drives sometimes (although not always) have letters associated with them as well. Naming conventions for network drives vary. For example, the network drive on a typical computer might have the drive letter Z.

Now you're ready to use the navigation pane to find and open the Documents folder, a convenient place to store text files such as reports, assignments, and other documents. The Documents folder appears in the Quick access list and on This PC by default. You'll navigate to it in two ways.

To open the Documents folder:

1. In the navigation pane, click the **Documents** icon in the Quick access list to display the contents of the Documents folder in the right pane. See Figure 1-19. Your Documents folder might contain folders and files.

Figure 1-19 Contents of the Documents folder

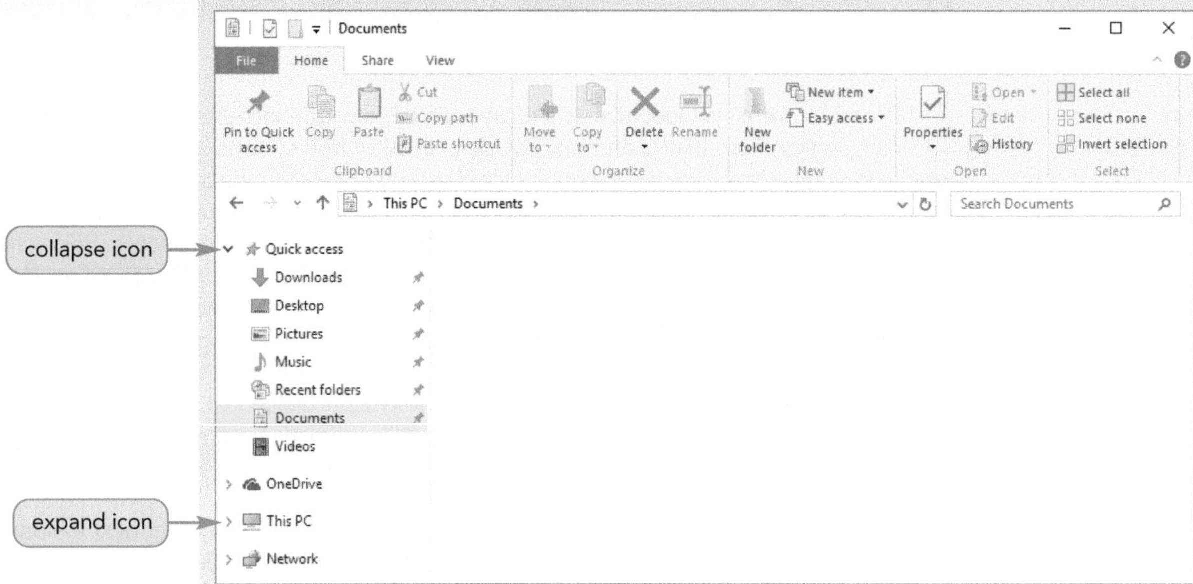

Trouble? If the Documents icon does not appear in the Quick access list, skip Step 1.

If you have opened many folders without opening the Documents folder, the Documents folder might not appear in the Quick access list. You can always open the folder using This PC.

2. If necessary, click the **expand** icon [>] next to This PC in the navigation pane to display locations on your computer. Note that the expand icon changes to a collapse icon [v].

Trouble? If the expand icon [>] does not appear next to This PC in the navigation pane, This PC is already expanded. Skip Step 2.

3. Click the **Pictures** folder to display its contents in the right pane, and then click the **Documents** folder below This PC in the navigation pane.

The Address bar in File Explorer provides handy shortcuts for navigating to locations on your computer. For example, you can use the Back button to return to the last location you visited. You can use it now to return to the Quick access list.

To return to the Quick access list:

1. Click the **Back** button [←] on the Address bar to return to your last location: the Pictures folder.
2. Click the **Close** button [X] to close File Explorer.

Getting Help

To get help on using Windows 10, you can use the Get Started app on your computer and Microsoft resources on the web. The Get Started app focuses on features new to Windows 10, including interacting with Cortana, working with apps, using File Explorer, and personalizing your computer.

To access a full library of Windows Help information, visit the How-to webpages for Windows on the Microsoft website. The webpages provide help articles, definitions, and step-by-step instructions for performing Windows tasks. You can also visit the Microsoft Community website to connect with other Windows users and experts to request answers to questions and find solutions to a wide range of problems.

Using the Get Started App

If you are familiar with earlier versions of Windows or want a quick tour of useful features in Windows 10, use the Get Started app.

To start the Get Started app:

1. Click the **Start** button on the taskbar to display the Start menu.
2. Click the **Get Started** tile in the right pane. The Get Started app opens and displays a list of categories and features on the left and an image or information on the right.

   Trouble? If the Get Started tile does not appear on your Start menu, click the All apps command, scroll down the list, and then click Get Started.
3. Click the **Maximize** button to maximize the Get Started window.
4. If necessary, click **Welcome** in the left pane to display the Get to know Windows 10 page. See Figure 1-20. The image on your Get to know Windows 10 page might be different.

Figure 1-20 Get Started window

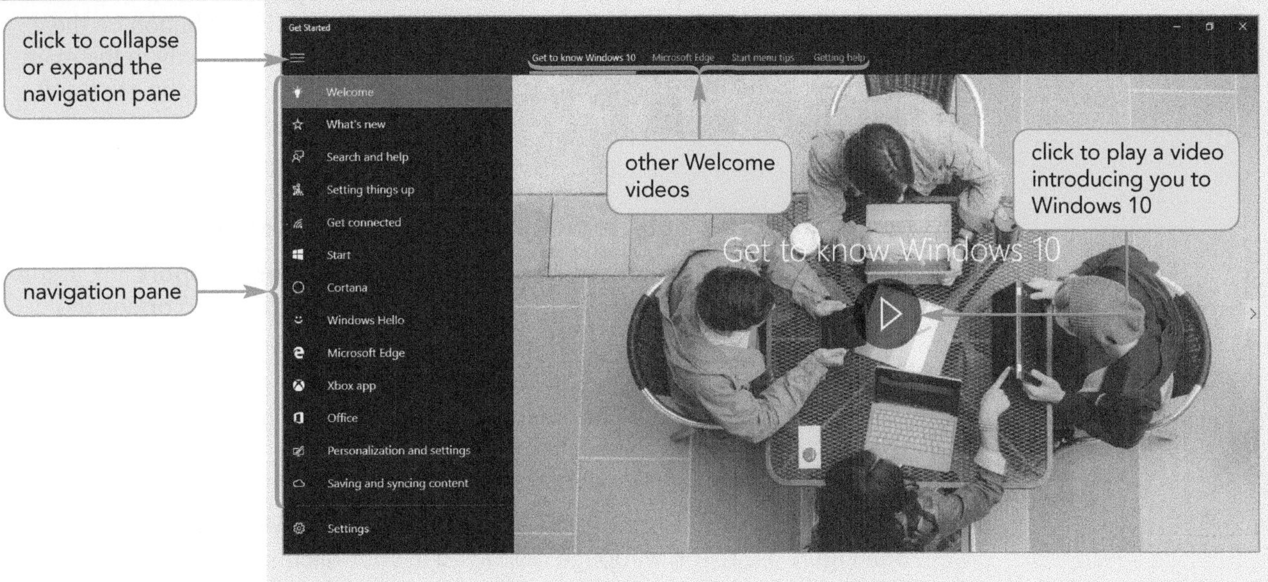

The Get Started window includes a navigation pane on the left and displays content on the right. When you select Welcome in the navigation pane, you can play one of four videos in the right pane. The Get to know Windows 10 page contains a video that you can play to learn about Windows 10 in general. You can also play videos to explore Microsoft Edge, to gain Start menu tips, and to learn about getting help.

For information about specific features, select an item in the navigation pane to display topic tiles or articles related to that feature. If topic tiles appear in the right pane, click one to display an article related to the topic. After you select an article or topic, a Back button appears on the title bar so you can return to the previous page you viewed.

To view Get Started topics:

1. Click **Search and help** in the navigation pane of the Get Started window. Tiles representing articles about searching and getting help appear in the right pane.
2. Click the **Search for help** tile. An article describing ways to get help appears in the right pane.
3. Scroll down to display the link to Windows support at windows.microsoft.com/support.

While the Get Started app provides an introduction to Windows 10, the Microsoft website includes forums, tutorials, articles, trending topics, and other helpful information about Windows 10.

Getting Help on the Microsoft Website

The Windows webpages on the Microsoft website provide a full range of help topics on using Windows 10. These topics are provided on the How-to webpages for Windows. Most How-to webpages include a link to the Microsoft Community website. If a How-to webpage does not answer your question, you can visit the Microsoft Community site and search for answers and solutions provided to other Windows users.

To access the Microsoft website, you can use **Microsoft Edge**, the default web browser provided with Windows 10. You start Microsoft Edge using its button on the taskbar or by clicking a webpage link in the Get Started app. To go directly to the main How-to page for Windows 10, enter windows.microsoft.com/support in the Microsoft Edge Address bar.

To find a Windows help topic on the Microsoft website:

1. In the Get Started app, click the **windows.microsoft.com/support** link at the bottom of the Search and help page. Microsoft Edge starts and opens the How-to page for Windows 10 on the Microsoft website.

   Trouble? If the windows.microsoft.com/support link does not appear in the Get Started app, click the **Microsoft Edge** button on the taskbar to open the Microsoft Edge browser, click the Address bar, type windows.microsoft.com/support, and then press the Enter key.

2. Click the **Maximize** button to maximize the Microsoft Edge window. See Figure 1-21. The webpage displayed in your Microsoft Edge window might differ.

Figure 1-21 **Windows 10 How-to webpage**

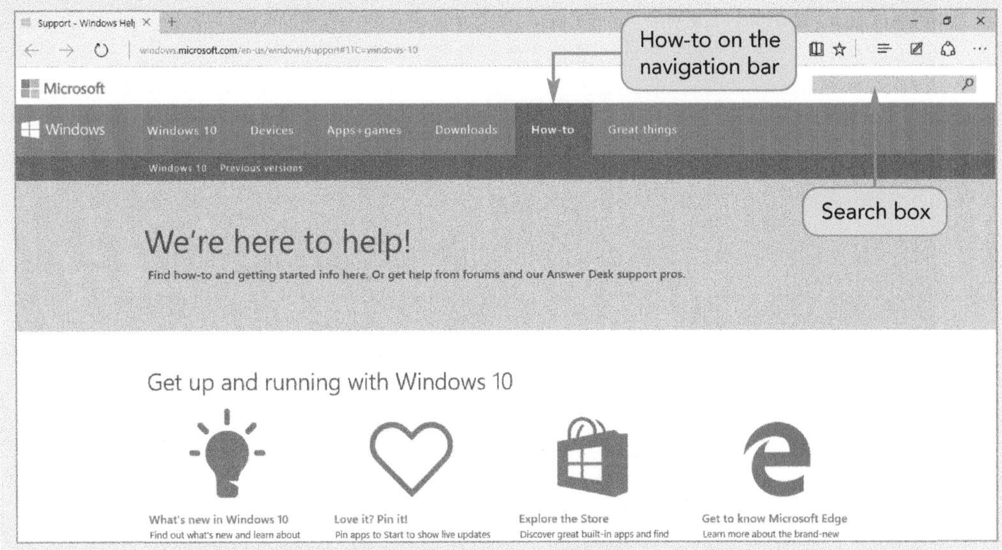

3. Scroll down to review the information on this webpage. In the Categories section, click the **Get started** link. A webpage opens listing Help topics related to new and popular features in Windows 10.

   Trouble? If the Get Started link is not listed, click any other link.

The Microsoft website also provides a Search box, a popular way to find answers to your Windows 10 questions.

Searching the Windows How-to Webpages

If you can't find the topic you need by clicking a link or browsing topics, or if you want to quickly find help information related to a particular topic, you can use the Search box on the Windows webpages. Ashley provides a typical example. Suppose you want to know how to close Windows 10, but you don't know if Windows refers to this as exiting, quitting, closing, or shutting down. You can search the Windows How-to webpages to find just the right topic.

To search the How-to webpages for information on exiting Windows 10:

1. Click the **Search** box at the top of the Windows How-to webpage. A blinking insertion point appears.

2. Type **shut down** and then press the **Enter** key. A list of How-to webpages containing the words "shut down" appears in the search results. See Figure 1-22. (Your results might differ.)

   Trouble? If a message appears at the bottom of the browser window informing you that only secure content is displayed, click the **Close** button ☒ to close the message.

TIP

You can also use the Search the web and Windows box on the taskbar to search for information on the web.

Figure 1-22 How-to search results

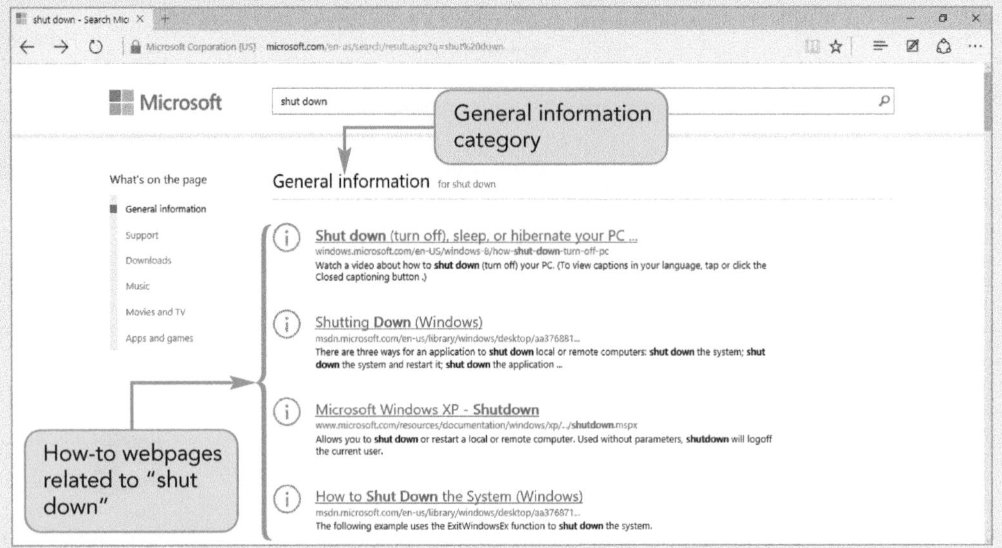

3. Click the **Shut down (turn off), sleep, or hibernate your PC** link. The instructions and a video demonstration appear in the Shut down (turn off), sleep, or hibernate your PC webpage.

   If this topic did not answer your question, you could scroll down to the "Need more help?" section and then click the community forums link. Doing so opens the Microsoft Community webpage where you can search for answers to your questions.

4. Click the **Close** button [X] to close Microsoft Edge, and then close the Get Started app.

Now that you know how to find help for using Windows 10, Ashley reminds you to use it when you need to perform a new task or want a reminder about how to complete a procedure.

Turning Off Windows 10

TIP

Shutting down does not automatically save your work, so be sure to save your files before selecting the Shut down or Restart option.

When you're finished working in Windows 10, you should always turn it off properly. Doing so saves energy, preserves your data and settings, and makes sure your computer starts quickly the next time you use it.

You can turn off Windows 10 using the Power command on the Start menu. When you click the Power command, you can choose the Sleep, Shut down, or Restart option. If you choose the Sleep option, Windows saves your work and then turns down the power to your display and computer, a condition called **sleep**. A light on your computer case blinks or changes color to indicate that the computer is sleeping. Because Windows saves your work, you do not need to close apps or files before your computer goes to sleep. To wake a computer, you typically press the hardware power button on the computer case. Some computer manufacturers might set the computer to wake when you press a key or move the mouse. After you wake a computer, the screen looks exactly as it did when you put your computer to sleep.

If you choose the **Shut down** option, your computer closes all open programs, including Windows itself, and then completely turns off your computer. Shutting down doesn't save your work, so you must save your files first.

If you select the Restart option, your computer shuts down and then immediately restarts, which you might need to do after installing new programs or hardware.

Decision Making: Sign out, Sleep, or Shut Down?

If you are using a computer on the job, your organization probably has a policy about what to do when you're finished working on the computer. If it does not, deciding on the best approach depends on who uses the computer and how long it will be idle. Keep the following guidelines in mind as you make your decision:

- Sign out—If another person might use your computer shortly, sign out of Windows to protect your data and prepare the computer for someone else to use. To sign out of Windows 10, click your user icon on the Start menu and then click Sign out.
- Sleep—By default, Windows 10 is set to sleep after 15–30 minutes of idle time, depending on whether you are using a mobile or desktop computer. If you will be away from the computer for more than 15 minutes but less than a day, you can generally let the computer go to sleep on its own.
- Shut down—If your computer is plugged in to a power outlet and you don't plan to use the computer for more than a day, such as over the weekend, you save wear and tear on your electronic components and conserve energy by turning the computer off. You should also turn off the computer when it is susceptible to electrical damage, such as during a lightning storm, and when you need to install new hardware or disconnect the computer from a power source. If your mobile computer is running on battery power only and you don't plan to use it for more than a few hours, you should also turn it off to save your battery charge.

Ashley suggests that you compare putting your computer to sleep and shutting down Windows 10.

To turn off Windows 10:

1. Click the **Start** button on the taskbar to display the Start menu.
2. Click **Power** to display the Power menu. See Figure 1-23.

Figure 1-23 **Power options**

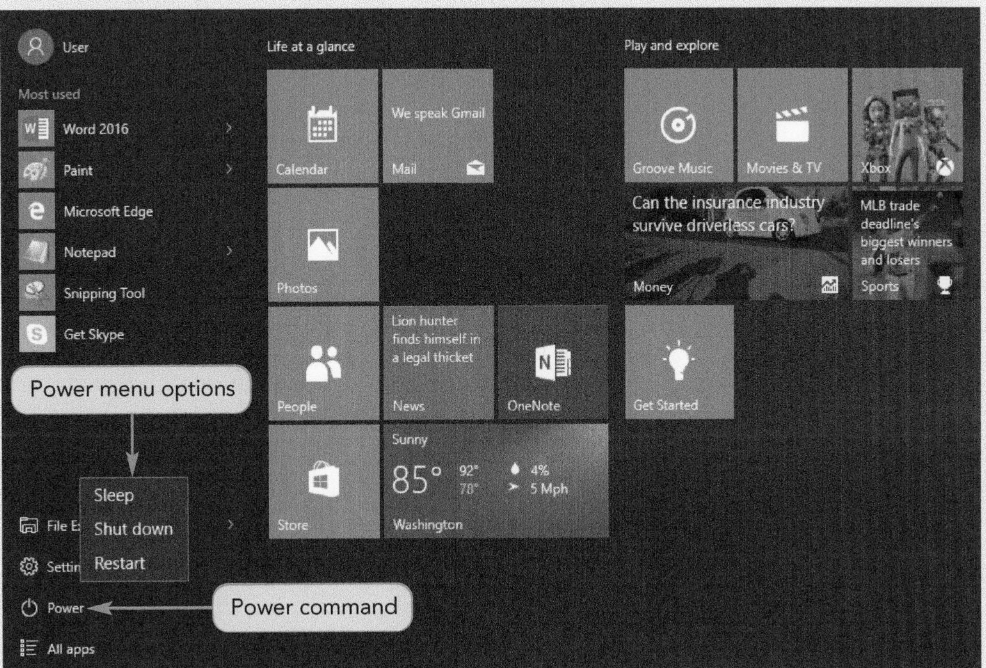

3. Click **Sleep**. Windows 10 saves your work and then puts the computer to sleep. The light in the hardware power button changes color or blinks to indicate the computer is in a sleep state.

   Trouble? If a Sleep option does not appear when you click the Power command, your computer might be set to go to sleep only automatically. Click Shut down on the Power menu, and skip the remaining steps.

4. If the light in the hardware power button changes color or is now blinking, press the hardware power button to wake up the computer. If necessary, clear the lock screen and enter your password. Otherwise, move the mouse or press a key to wake the computer.
5. Click the **Start** button on the taskbar to display the Start menu.

   Trouble? If you are instructed to sign out instead of shut down, click your user icon on the Start menu, and then click Sign out. Skip Step 6.

6. Click **Power** and then click **Shut down**. Windows 10 turns off the computer.

   Trouble? If the Power button displays the Update and shut down option instead of Shut down, click Update and shut down.

In this session, you learned how to use File Explorer to navigate your computer. You also learned how to change the view of the contents of the File Explorer window. Finally, you learned how to get help when you need it and how to turn off Windows 10. With Ashley's help, you should feel comfortable with the basics of Windows 10 and well prepared to demonstrate the fundamentals of using this operating system.

REVIEW

Session 1.2 Quick Check

1. You use ____________ to keep track of where your files are stored and to organize your files.
2. Describe the difference between Details view and Large icons view.
3. In the File Explorer window, what happens when you click the expand icon next to a folder in the navigation pane?
4. In the File Explorer window, what appears in the right pane when you click a folder icon in the navigation pane?
5. The __________ app focuses on features new to Windows 10.
6. What is Microsoft Edge?
7. How would you search for information about shutting down Windows 10 on the Microsoft website?
8. What Power option(s) save(s) your work before turning down the power to the computer?

PRACTICE

Review Assignments

There are no Data Files needed for the Review Assignments.

The day before your first Windows 10 training session with For Pet's Sake volunteers, Ashley Cramer offers to observe your tour of the operating system and help you fine-tune your session. You'll start working on the desktop with no apps open. Complete the following steps, recording your answers to any questions according to your instructor's preferences:

1. Start Windows 10 and sign in, if necessary.
2. Record the names and descriptions of each object on the desktop, using the mouse to point to objects as necessary to display ScreenTips.
3. Click the Start button. How many menu commands appear in the left pane of the Start menu?
4. Start the Calendar app.
5. Start Paint and maximize the Paint window. How many apps are running now?
6. Which app is active? How do you know?
7. Minimize the Paint window and then open the Recycle Bin window. Record the number of items it contains, and then drag and resize the Recycle Bin window so that you can see both it and the Calendar window.
8. Close Paint and Calendar. What actions did you take to close each app?
9. Maximize the Recycle Bin window and then click the Home tab. Which buttons are active (not gray)? Use any button on the Home tab to open a dialog box. What dialog box did you open? What do you think this dialog box is used for? Click the Cancel button to close the dialog box, and then close the Recycle Bin window.
10. Start File Explorer. Open the Pictures folder from the navigation pane. List the contents of the Pictures folder. Open a folder in the Pictures library. Explain how you opened the folder and describe its contents.
11. Open This PC from the navigation pane. Change the view of the items displayed in the right pane of the File Explorer window. What view did you select and how did your selection change the appearance of the items? Close File Explorer.
12. Start the Get Started app. Explain how you started the app.
13. Use the Get Started app to learn something new about Windows 10. What did you learn? How did you find this topic?
14. Find information about personalizing your computer. How can you open the Personalization window to change the background picture on the desktop?
15. Find information about Microsoft Edge. Describe one new feature in Microsoft Edge.
16. Close the Get Started app.
17. Turn off Windows 10 by using the Sleep command, shutting down, or signing out.

APPLY

Case Problem 1

There are no Data Files needed for this Case Problem.

Brandenburg Design Peter Brandenburg is the owner of Brandenburg Design, a graphics design studio in Bloomington, Indiana. Peter hired you to train employees on using their new Windows 10 computers productively. He asks you to show his employees how to determine the contents of their computers, especially media apps. Complete the following steps:

1. Start Windows 10 and sign in, if necessary.
2. Open the Start menu and then examine the tiles in the right pane. Use one to start an app that plays music or videos or displays photos. Which app did you start?
3. Start another media app. Which app did you start?
4. Use the Search the web and Windows box to search for "windows media" apps installed on your computer. Name one app you found.
5. Start an app you found in Step 4. Which app did you start? Is it a Windows app or a desktop app? How can you tell?
6. Start an app you could use to take photos with the camera on your computer. (If asked, do not allow the app to access your location.) Which app did you start? Is it a Windows app or a desktop app?
7. Find apps you can use to record or recognize voice. Which apps did you find?
8. Close all open apps.
9. Start File Explorer, and then navigate to a folder that contains files. Which folder did you open? View the files in Details view. What size is the largest file? (*Hint:* If there are no folders with files on your computer, display the contents of This PC.)
10. Change to Large icons view, and then point to a file to display a ScreenTip. What type of file did you select? What details are provided in the ScreenTip? Close File Explorer.
11. Open the Get Started app, and then find and read a topic about Windows Hello. Explain how to setup Windows Hello.
12. Close all open windows.

CHALLENGE

Case Problem 2

There are no Data Files needed for this Case Problem.

Tools of the Trade After earning a degree in business management and working as a prep cook in a few local restaurants, Erika Alston opened a store called Tools of the Trade in Chicago, Illinois. The store supplies restaurants, cafeterias, and other food service facilities with everything they need from teaspoons to freezers. So that she can concentrate on building her business, Erika hired you to help her perform office tasks. She asks you to start by teaching her the basics of using her computer, which runs Windows 10. She especially wants to know which applications are installed on her computer and what they do. Complete the following steps:

1. Write down the Windows apps listed on the Start menu.
2. Start one of the apps and then describe what it does. Close the app.
3. Use the Windows webpages to search for How-to information on getting apps for your PC. How can you pin an app so its tile appears in the right pane of the Start menu?
4. **Explore** Open the Start menu, select the All apps command, scroll down the list to the W category, and then click the Windows Accessories folder to display its apps. List the apps in the Windows Accessories folder.

5. Use the Windows webpages to search for information on one of the apps you examined in the previous step, such as Notepad or the Snipping Tool. List all the How-to topics related to the application you researched in the previous step. How many general information topics are displayed in the results? Select one of these topics and review the Help information. Describe the purpose of the app.

Explore 6. Use the Start menu to start any app you haven't worked with before. Use the Windows webpages to find answers to frequently asked questions (FAQs) about the app. List two FAQs for the app you selected. If no topics provide answers to FAQs, select a general help topic about the app and then list two tasks you can perform with the app.

Explore 7. Use the Search the web and Windows box to learn how to draw a shape in Paint. Describe what you did to find this information and the results of your actions.

8. Close all open windows.

CHALLENGE

Case Problem 3

There are no Data Files needed for this Case Problem.

Jordan & Phipps Real Estate Alicia Phipps recently joined the Jordan Real Estate firm in Roswell, Georgia, to create a new firm called Jordan & Phipps Real Estate. The firm works with commercial and residential buyers and sellers. Alicia uses her Windows 10 laptop to create listings, contracts, reports, and other documents as required to complete real estate transactions. She uses File Explorer to work with files, but suspects she is not taking full advantage of its features. As a new assistant at Jordan & Phipps, you will be responsible for showing Alicia around the File Explorer window and demonstrating how to customize its appearance. Complete the following steps:

1. Start File Explorer. Click each tab on the ribbon to find out the kind of commands it provides. Write down any commands that seem related to changing the appearance of the folder window.
2. Display the Quick access list, if necessary, and then switch to Large icons view.

Explore 3. Change the view to Content view. (*Hint:* Click the View tab, and then click an option in the Layout group.) Describe the differences between Large icons view and Content view.

4. Open the Pictures folder, select a folder or file in the Pictures folder, and then describe any changes in the ribbon.

Explore 5. Examine the buttons on the Home tab. How can you add a new file to the folder window using a button on the Home tab?

Explore 6. Select a command on the View tab that displays a pane showing the details of the selected folder. What command did you select?

Explore 7. Use a button on the View tab to close the navigation pane. What actions did you perform?

Explore 8. Click the Up one level button next to the Address bar. (*Hint:* Point to a button to display its name in a ScreenTip.) What is now displayed in the File Explorer window?

Explore 9. Close the pane showing the details of the selected folder, and then redisplay the navigation pane. (*Hint:* Perform Steps 6 and 7 again.)

Explore 10. Close File Explorer, and then use the Search the web and Windows box to search for information about changing folder options. Explain how to change folder and search options using the Folder Options dialog box.

11. Close all open windows.

RESEARCH

Case Problem 4

There are no Data Files needed for this Case Problem.

Irving Personal Trainers After earning their certifications as personal trainers specializing in sports medicine, Gabe and Stacy Irving decided to start a service called Irving Personal Trainers. They work with people in their homes to help them meet physical goals through exercise and proper nutrition. They have been using Windows 10 on laptops to schedule client appointments and track client progress, but recently purchased tablet computers to use when they are working with clients face to face. They hired you as a consultant to help them use and maintain their computers. Because Gabe and Stacy learned to use Windows 10 on laptop computers, they anticipate that they might have trouble adapting to tablets. Gabe asks you to help them troubleshoot by researching the skills and techniques they need to use Windows 10 on a tablet. Complete the following:

1. Use the Search the web and Windows box to find information about Tablet mode. What Tablet mode settings can you select?
2. Use the Windows webpages on the Microsoft website to obtain more information about Tablet Mode in Windows 10. Explain how to turn Tablet Mode on and off.
3. Search for information on the touch keyboard, and then watch a video that shows how to use it. Explain how to display the touch keyboard if the computer is using Tablet Mode.
4. Visit the Microsoft Community website and search for information about Tablet Mode in Windows 10. Identify a common Tablet Mode problem discussed on the website.
5. Write one to two paragraphs for Gabe and Stacy explaining the basics of using Windows 10 on a tablet and what problems they might encounter.

MODULE 2

Organizing Your Files

Managing Files and Folders in Windows 10

WINDOWS

OBJECTIVES

Session 2.1
- Develop file management strategies
- Plan the organization of your files and folders
- Find files and folders quickly
- Create folders
- Copy and move files and folders

Session 2.2
- Name and delete files and folders
- Work with new files
- Sort and group files
- Customize a folder window
- Compress and extract files

Case | *Miami Trolleys*

After moving to Miami, Florida, after college, Diego and Anita Marino started Miami Trolleys, a sightseeing company that provides guided tours of Miami on a hop-on, hop-off trolley. As marketing manager, Diego is in charge of creating resources that describe the tours and sights in Miami. He hired you to help him develop marketing materials and use computer tools to organize photos, illustrations, and text documents to promote the business. For your first task, Diego asks you to organize the files on his new computer. Although he has only a few files, he wants to use a logical organization to help him find his work as he stores more files and folders on the computer.

In this module, you'll work with Diego to devise a strategy for managing files. You'll learn how Windows 10 organizes files and folders, and you'll examine Windows 10 file management tools. You'll create folders and organize files within them. You'll also use techniques to display the information you need in folder windows, and explore options for working with compressed files.

STARTING DATA FILES

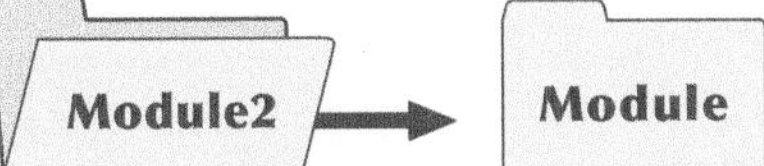

Module

Budget.txt
City Guide.rtf
Edison.jpg
Logo.png
Miami Beach.jpg
Ocean Drive.jpg
Trolley Tours.rtf
Trolley.jpg

Review

Background.png
Calendar.rtf
Events.xlsx
Skyline.jpg
Walking.rtf
Welcome.jpg

Case1

Advanced Classes.rtf
Beginner Classes.rtf
Designers.txt
Detail.jpg
Intermediate Classes.rtf
Kids Classes.rtf
Lampshade.jpg
Modern.jpg
Round.jpg
Studio.rtf

Case2

Estimate Tips.txt
Estimate01.xlsx
Estimate02.xlsx
Estimate03.xlsx
Planner01.xlsx
Planner02.xlsx
Planner03.xlsx
Project Plans.txt

Case3

Checklist.docx
Client Chart.pdf
Clients.accdb
Clients.pptx
Training.pptx

Session 2.1 Visual Overview:

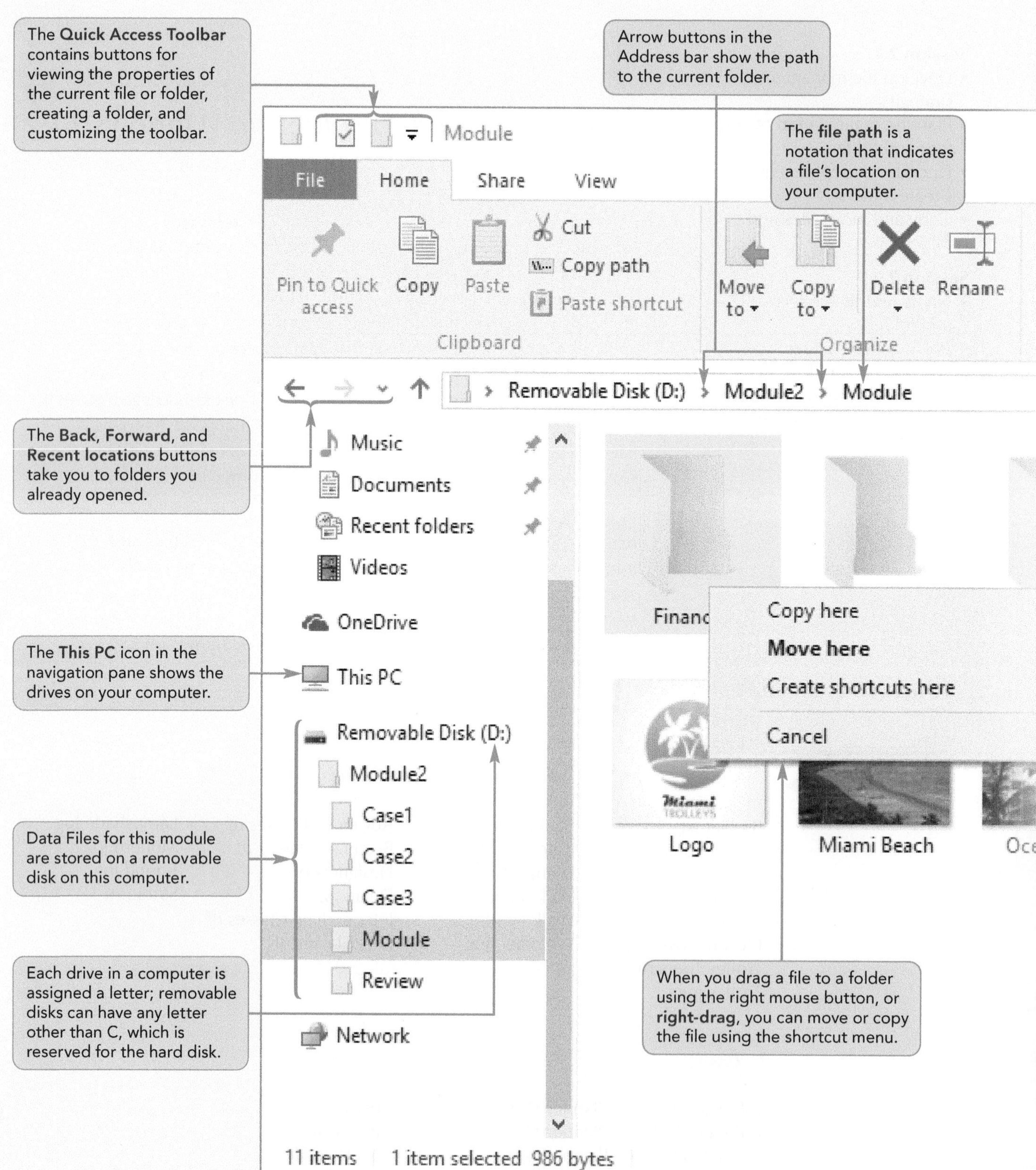
The **Quick Access Toolbar** contains buttons for viewing the properties of the current file or folder, creating a folder, and customizing the toolbar.
Arrow buttons in the Address bar show the path to the current folder.
The **file path** is a notation that indicates a file's location on your computer.
Module
File
Home
Share
View
Pin to Quick access
Copy
Paste
Cut
Copy path
Paste shortcut
Clipboard
Move to
Copy to
Delete
Rename
Organize
Removable Disk (D:)
Module2
Module
The **Back**, **Forward**, and **Recent locations** buttons take you to folders you already opened.
Music
Documents
Recent folders
Videos
OneDrive
The **This PC** icon in the navigation pane shows the drives on your computer.
This PC
Removable Disk (D:)
Module2
Case1
Case2
Case3
Module
Review
Network
Data Files for this module are stored on a removable disk on this computer.
Each drive in a computer is assigned a letter; removable disks can have any letter other than C, which is reserved for the hard disk.
Copy here
Move here
Create shortcuts here
Cancel
Logo
Miami Beach
When you drag a file to a folder using the right mouse button, or **right-drag**, you can move or copy the file using the shortcut menu.
11 items
1 item selected 986 bytes

©iStock.com/Meinzahn, ©iStock.com/Betelgejze, ©iStock.com/bosenok, ©iStock.com/Vladone, ©iStock.com/Ivan Cholakov

Files in a Folder Window

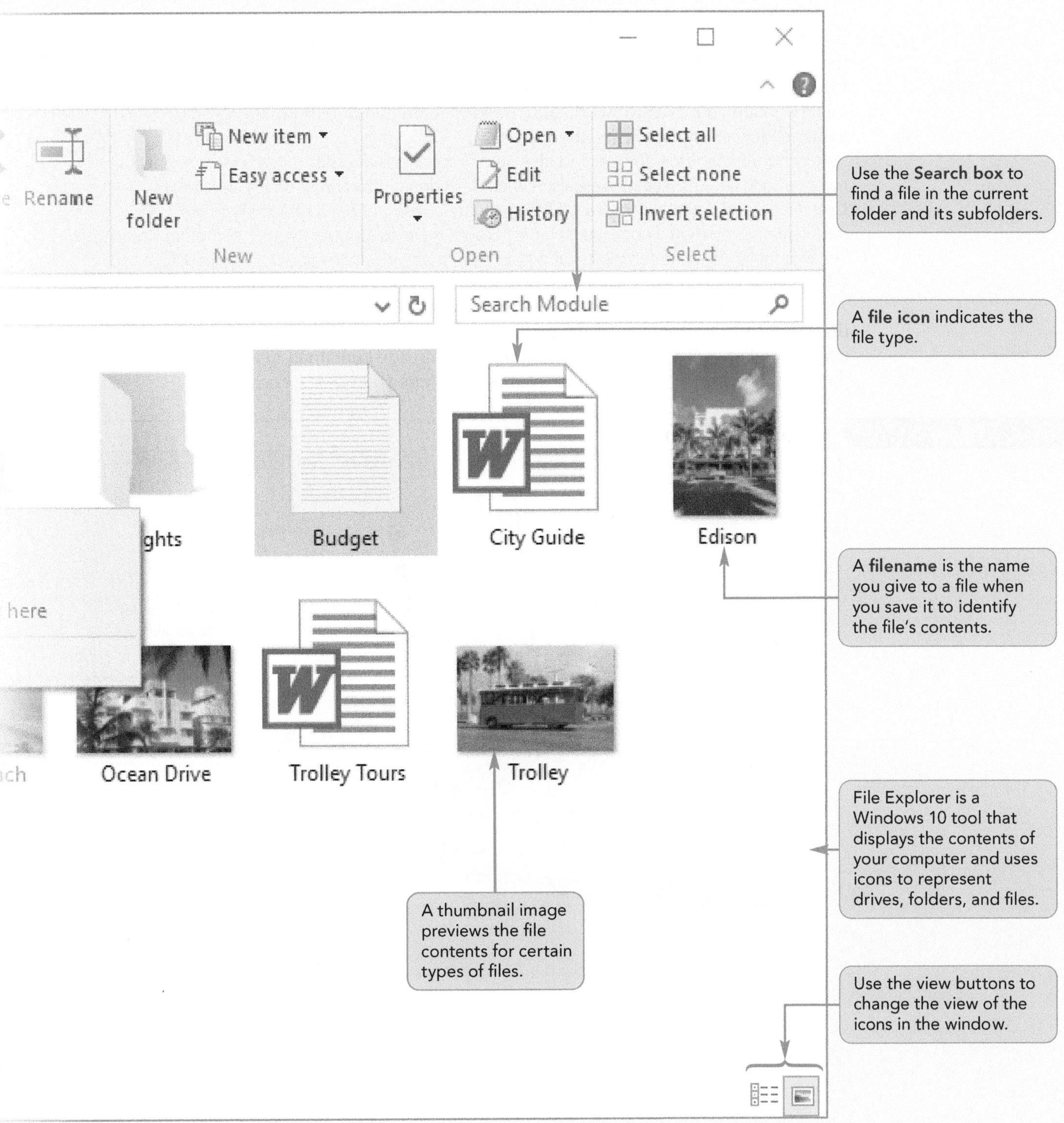
Rename
New folder
New item
Easy access
New
Properties
Open
Edit
History
Open
Select all
Select none
Invert selection
Select
Search Module
Budget
City Guide
Edison
Ocean Drive
Trolley Tours
Trolley
Use the **Search box** to find a file in the current folder and its subfolders.
A **file icon** indicates the file type.
A **filename** is the name you give to a file when you save it to identify the file's contents.
File Explorer is a Windows 10 tool that displays the contents of your computer and uses icons to represent drives, folders, and files.
A thumbnail image previews the file contents for certain types of files.
Use the view buttons to change the view of the icons in the window.

Preparing to Manage Your Files

Knowing how to save, locate, and organize electronic files makes you more productive when you are working with a computer. After you create a file, you can open it and edit the file's contents, print the file, and save it again—usually with the same application you used to create it. You organize files by storing them in folders. You need to organize files and folders so that you can find them easily and work efficiently.

A file cabinet is a common metaphor for computer file organization. A computer is like a file cabinet that uses a drawer as a storage device, or **disk**. Each disk contains folders that hold documents, or files. To make it easy to retrieve files, you arrange them logically into folders. For example, one folder might contain financial data, another might contain your creative work, and another could contain information you're gathering for an upcoming vacation.

A computer can store folders and files on different types of disks, ranging from removable media—such as **USB flash drives** (also called flash drives, thumbnail drives, or simply USB drives) and digital video discs (DVDs)—to **hard disks**, or fixed disks, which are permanently stored on a computer. Hard disks are the most popular type of computer storage because they provide an economical way to store many gigabytes of data. (A **gigabyte**, or **GB**, is about 1 billion bytes, with each byte roughly equivalent to a character of data.)

To have your computer access a removable disk, you must insert the disk into a **drive**, which is a computer device that can retrieve and sometimes record data on a disk. See Figure 2-1. A computer's hard disk is already contained in a drive inside the computer, so you don't need to insert it each time you use the computer.

Figure 2-1 **Computer drives and disks**

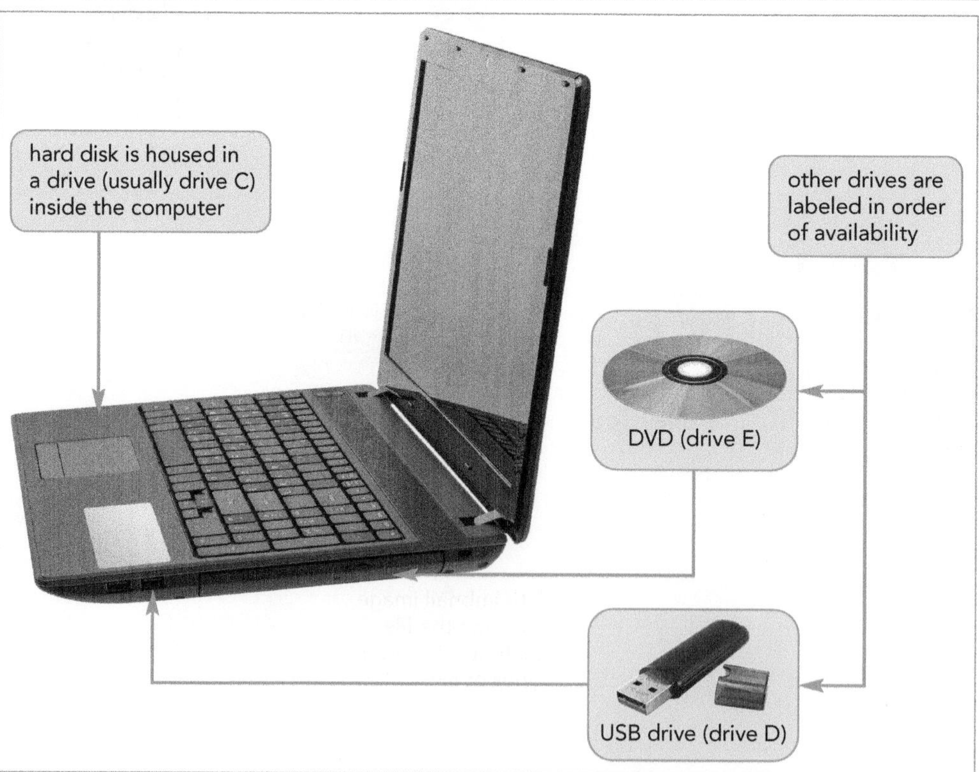

©iStock.com/Denis_Dryashkin, ©iStock.com/luminis, ©iStock.com/sassparela

A computer distinguishes one drive from another by assigning each a drive letter. As shown in the Session 2.1 Visual Overview, the hard disk in a computer is assigned to drive C. The remaining drives can have any other letters, but are usually assigned in the order that the drives were installed on the computer—so your USB drive might be drive D, drive E, or drive F.

If you are using a tablet or a recent-model laptop, it might not have drives for removable disks. Instead, you store files on the hard disk or in the **cloud**, a location on a large computer called a server, which you access through the Internet or other network. (A **network** is two or more computers connected together to share resources.) As a Windows 10 user, you probably have OneDrive, a Microsoft service that provides access to a server where you can store your files instead of using a hard disk or removable disk. Your school might also provide a cloud location for storing your files.

INSIGHT

Storing Files on OneDrive

OneDrive provides up to 15 GB of online storage space for your files by default. You can purchase additional storage space if you need it. Because these files are kept online, they take up no storage space on your computer and are available from any computer with an Internet connection, even those not running Windows. To protect the privacy of your files, you can designate which OneDrive users can access them: only you, you and some other users, or anyone. To use OneDrive, you need a free Microsoft account. (You can sign up for a Microsoft account at https://signup.live.com. If you have a Windows phone or use Outlook.com, Xbox Live, or Hotmail, you already have a Microsoft account.)

Understanding the Need for Organizing Files and Folders

Windows 10 stores thousands of files in many folders on the hard disk of your computer. Windows 10 needs these system files to display the desktop, use drives, and perform other operating system tasks. To keep the system stable and to find files quickly, Windows organizes the folders and files in a hierarchy, or **file system**. At the top of the hierarchy, Windows stores folders and important files that it needs when you turn on the computer. This location is called the **root directory** and is usually drive C (the hard disk). The term "root" refers to another popular metaphor for visualizing a file system—an upside-down tree, which reflects the file hierarchy that Windows uses. In Figure 2-2, the tree trunk corresponds to the root directory, the branches to the folders and subfolders, and the leaves to the files.

Figure 2-2 **Windows file hierarchy**

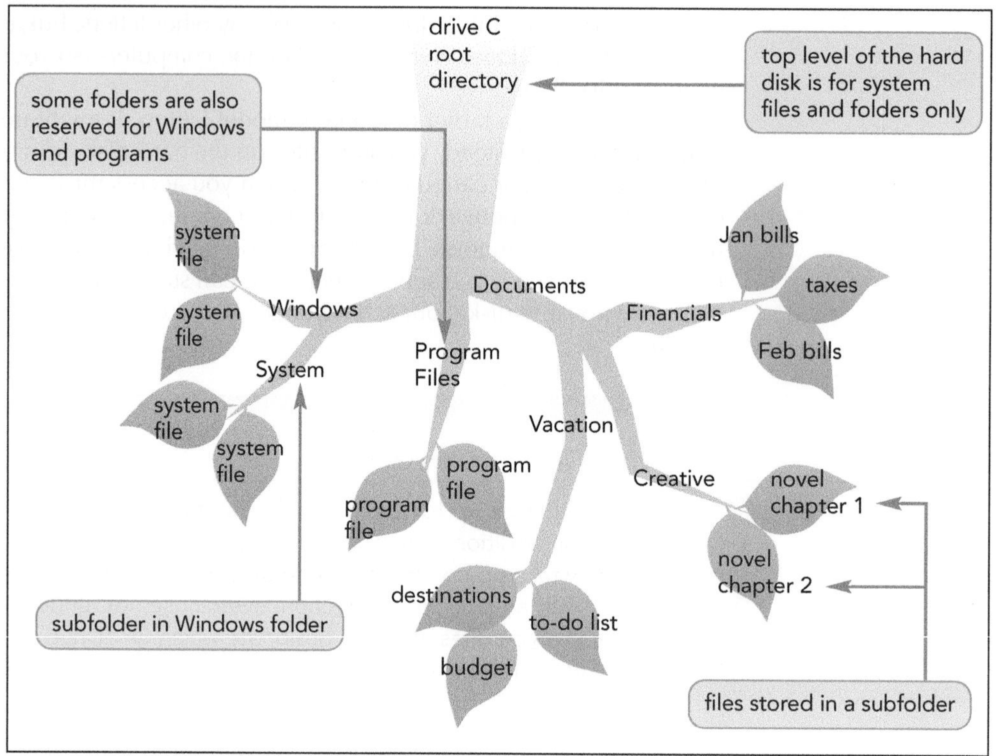

Note that some folders contain other folders. An effectively organized computer contains a few folders in the root directory, and those folders contain other folders, also called subfolders.

The root directory, or top level, of the hard disk is for system files and folders only. You should not store your own work in the root directory because your files could interfere with Windows or an application. (If you are working in a computer lab, you might not be allowed to access the root directory.)

Do not delete or move any files or folders from the root directory of the hard disk; doing so could disrupt the system so that you can't run or start the computer. In fact, you should not reorganize or change any folder that contains installed software because Windows 10 expects to find the files for specific applications within certain folders. If you reorganize or change these folders, Windows 10 can't locate and start the applications stored in those folders. Likewise, you should not make changes to the folder (usually named Windows) that contains the Windows 10 operating system.

Developing Strategies for Organizing Files and Folders

The type of disk you use to store files determines how you organize them. Figure 2-3 shows how you could organize files on a hard disk if you were taking a full semester of business classes. To duplicate this organization, you would open the main folder for your documents, create four folders—one each for the Basic Accounting, Computer Concepts, Management Skills, and Professional Writing courses—and then store the writing assignments you complete in the Professional Writing folder.

Figure 2-3 **Organizing folders and files on a hard disk**

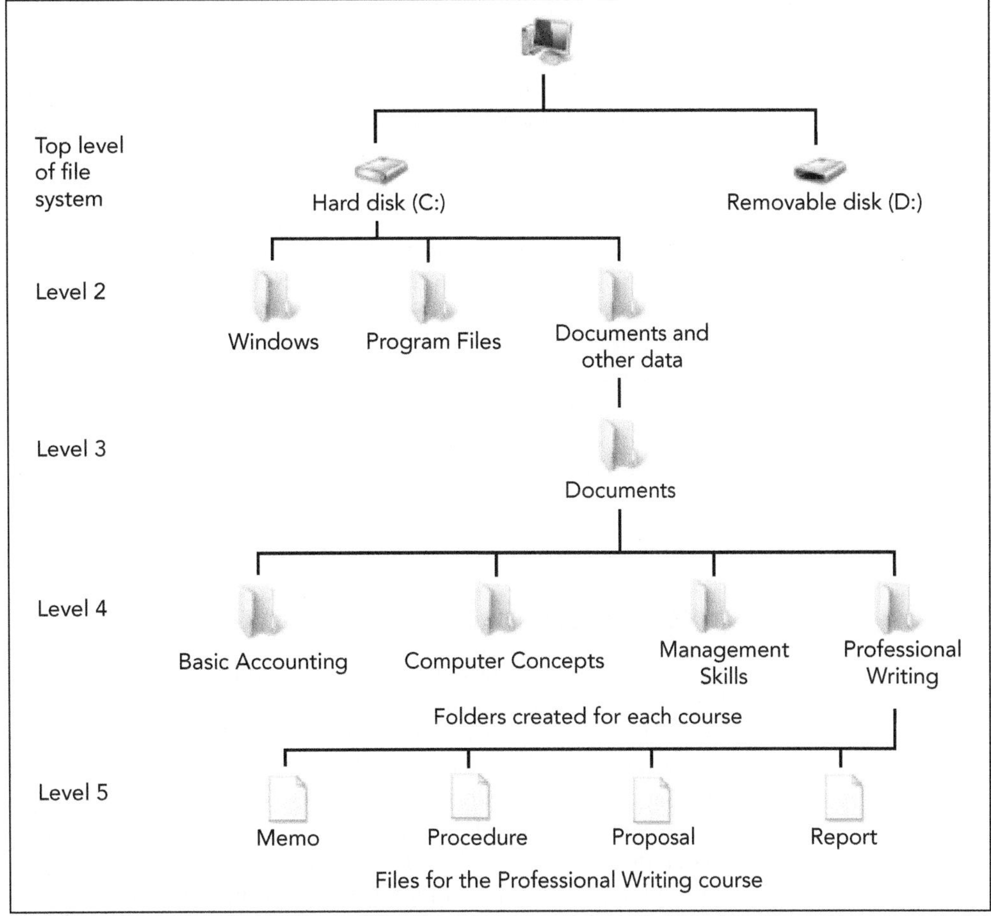

If you store your files on OneDrive or removable media, such as a USB drive, you can use a simpler organization because you do not have to account for system files. In general, the larger the medium, the more levels of folders you should use because large media can store more files and, therefore, need better organization. For example, OneDrive provides a collection of folders such as Documents, Favorites, Music, Pictures, and Public by default. If you were organizing your files on your 15 GB OneDrive, you could create folders in the top-level Documents folder for each course (Basic Accounting, Computer Concepts, Management Skills, and Professional Writing), and each of those folders could contain the appropriate files.

If you were organizing your files on a smaller removable disk, at the top level of the hierarchy you could create folders for each general category of documents you store—one each for Courses, Creative, Financials, and Vacation. The Courses folder could then include one folder for each course (Basic Accounting, Computer Concepts, Management Skills, and Professional Writing), and each of those folders could contain the appropriate files.

PROSKILLS

Decision Making: Determining Where to Store Files

When you create and save files on your computer's hard disk, you should store them in subfolders. The top level of the hard disk is off-limits for your files because they could interfere with system files. If you are working on your own computer, store your files within the Documents folder, which is where many applications save your files by default. When you use a computer on the job, your employer might assign a main folder to you for storing your work. In either case, if you simply store all your files in one folder, you will soon have trouble finding the files you want. Instead, you should create subfolders within a main folder to separate files in a way that makes sense for you.

Even if you store most of your files in the cloud, such as on OneDrive, or on removable media, such as USB drives, you still need to organize those files into folders and subfolders. Before you start creating folders in any location, you need to plan the organization you will use. Following your plan increases your efficiency because you don't have to pause and decide which folder to use when you save your files. A file organization plan also makes you more productive in your computer work—the next time you need a particular file, you'll know where to find it.

Exploring Files and Folders

To explore the files and folders on your computer in Windows 10, you use File Explorer. This tool displays the contents of your computer, using icons to represent drives, folders, and files. When you start File Explorer, it opens to show the contents of the **Quick access list**, which are the folders and files you used frequently and recently, making it easy to find the files you work with often.

A **folder window** refers to any File Explorer window that displays the contents of a folder, drive, or device. It is divided into two sections, called panes. The left pane is the navigation pane, which contains icons and links to locations that your computer can access. The right pane displays the contents of your folders and other locations. If you select a folder in the navigation pane, the contents of that folder appear in the right pane. To display the hierarchy of the folders and other locations on your computer, you select the This PC icon in the navigation pane, and then select the icon for a drive, such as Local Disk (C:) or Removable Disk (D:). If you have a Microsoft account, OneDrive appears as a location in the navigation pane. You can open and explore folders in any drive listed in the navigation pane.

If the navigation pane showed all the folders on your computer at once, it could be a very long list. Instead, you open drives and folders only when you want to see what they contain. If a folder contains undisplayed subfolders, an expand icon appears to the left of the folder icon. (The same is true for drives.) To view the folders contained in an object, you click the expand icon. A collapse icon then appears next to the folder icon; click the collapse icon to hide the folder's subfolders. To view the files contained in a folder, you click the folder icon, and the files appear in the right pane. See Figure 2-4.

Figure 2-4 Viewing files in a folder window

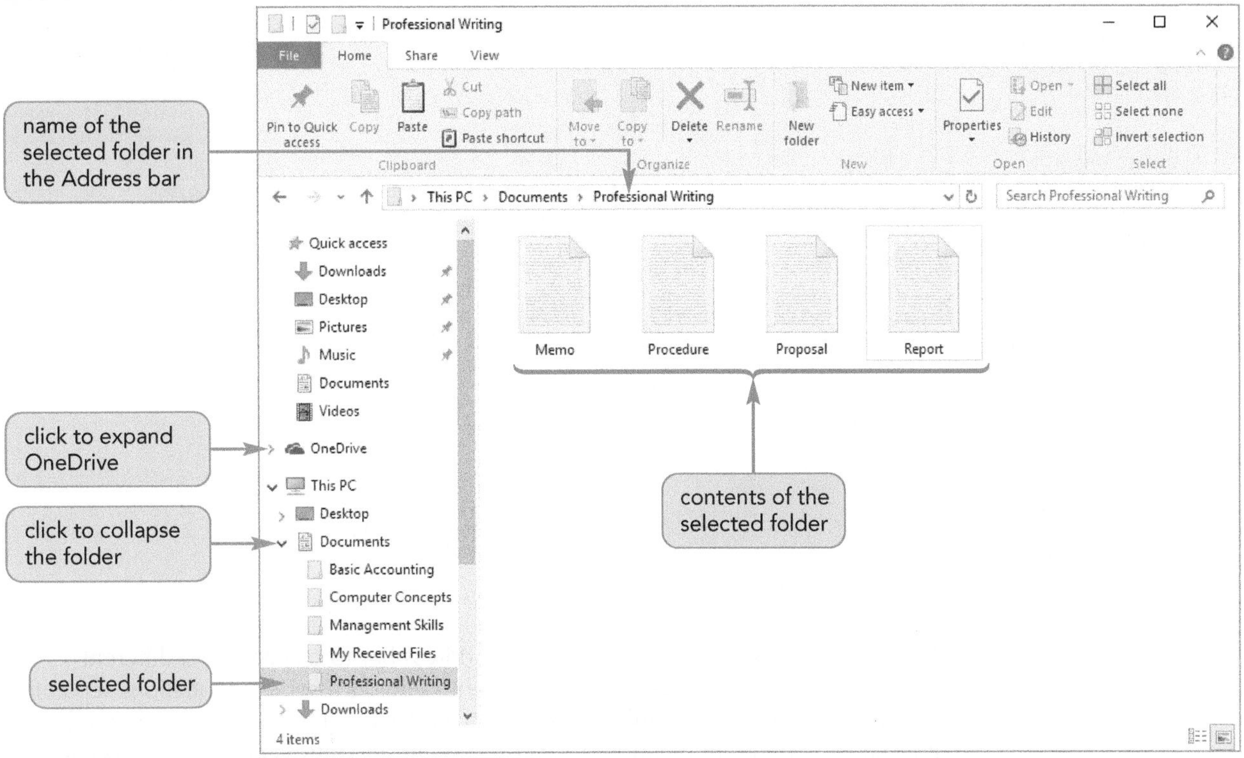

Using the navigation pane helps you explore your computer and orients you to your current location. As you move, copy, delete, and perform other tasks with the folders in the right pane of a folder window, you can refer to the navigation pane to see how your changes affect the overall organization.

In addition to using the navigation pane, you can explore your computer from a folder window in other ways. Use the following navigation techniques in any folder window and many dialog boxes:

- Opening drives and folders in the right pane—To view the contents of a drive or folder, double-click the drive or folder icon in the right pane of the folder window. For example, to view the contents of the Professional Writing folder shown in Figure 2-5, you double-click the Professional Writing folder in the right pane.

Figure 2-5 Viewing the contents of a folder

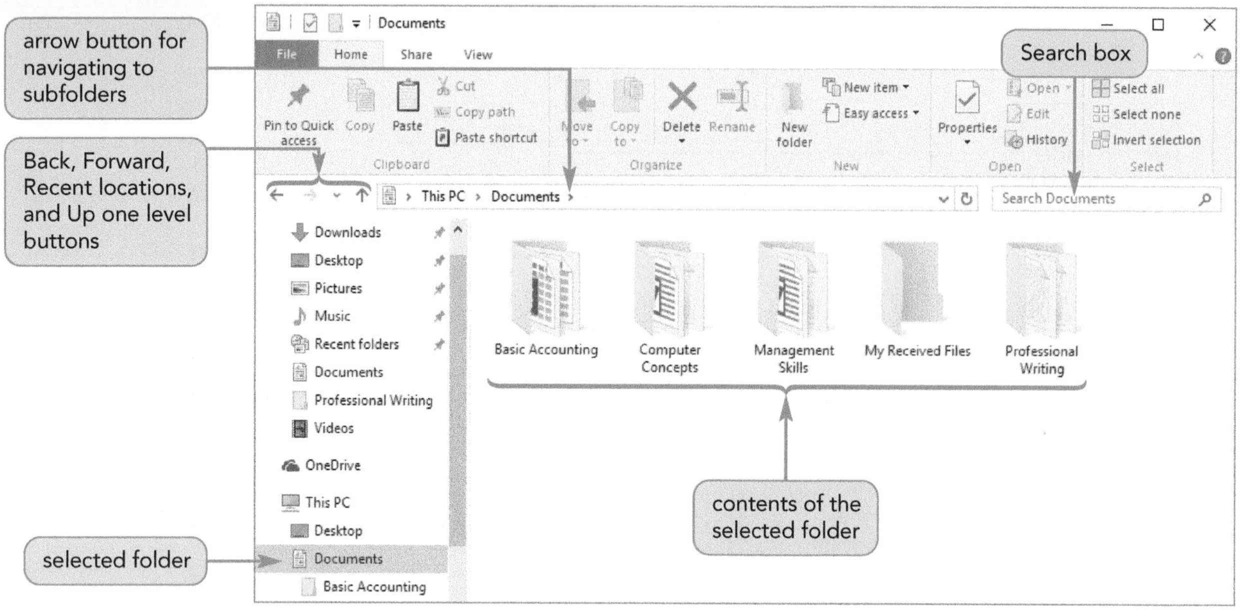

- Using the Address bar—You can use the Address bar to navigate to a different folder. The Address bar displays your current folder as a series of locations separated by arrow buttons. Click a folder name such as Documents or an arrow button to navigate to a different location. You'll explore these controls later in the module.
- Clicking the Back, Forward, Recent locations, and Up one level buttons—Use the Back, Forward, and Recent locations buttons to navigate to other folders you have already opened. After you use the Address bar to change folders, for example, you can use the Back button to return to the original folder. You can click the Recent locations button to navigate to a location you've visited recently. Use the Up one level button to navigate up to the folder containing the current folder. The ScreenTip for this button changes to reflect the folder to which you can navigate. For example, when you are working in a subfolder of the Documents folder, the ScreenTip is Up to "Documents."
- Using the Search box—To find a file or folder stored in the current folder or its subfolders, type a word or phrase in the Search box. The search begins as soon as you start typing. Windows finds files based on text in the filename, text within the file, and other characteristics of the file, such as **tags** (descriptive words or phrases you add to your files) or the author. For example, if you're looking for a document named September Income, you can type *Sept* in the Search box. Windows searches the current folder and its subfolders, and then displays any file whose filename contains a word starting with "Sept," including the September Income document.

Start your work with Diego by showing him how to navigate to the Documents folder using the Quick access list and the This PC icon.

To open the Documents folder:

1. Click the **File Explorer** button on the taskbar. The File Explorer window opens, displaying the contents of the Quick access list.
2. Click the **Documents** icon in the navigation pane to display its contents in the right pane. See Figure 2-6. The contents of your computer will differ.

   Trouble? If your window displays icons in a view different from the one shown in the figure, you can still explore files and folders. The same is true for all figures in this session.

TIP

When you are working in the navigation pane, you only need to click a folder or drive to open it, not double-click it.

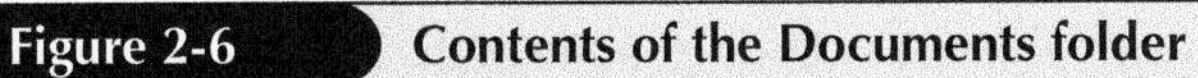

Figure 2-6 Contents of the Documents folder

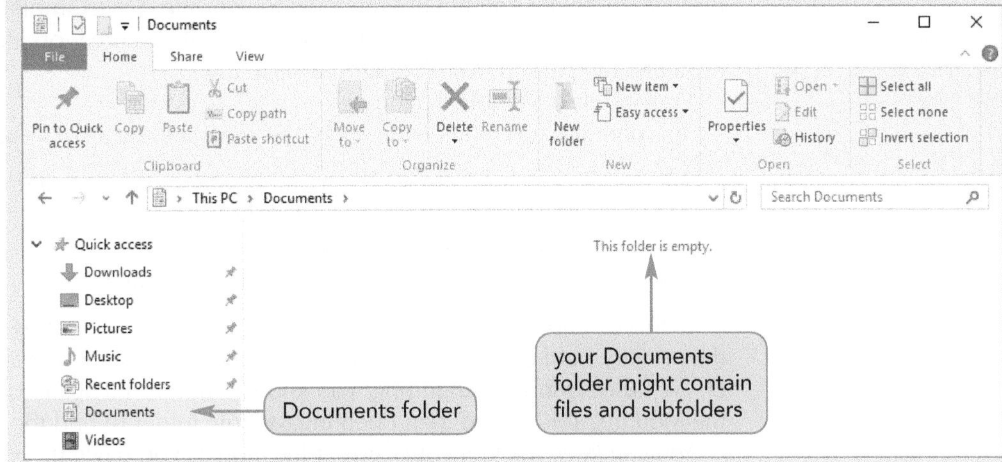
Documents
This folder is empty.
Documents folder
your Documents folder might contain files and subfolders

3. In the navigation pane of the open folder window, click the **This PC** icon. The right pane displays the devices and drives on the computer and the locations for storing your work files, including the Documents folder. See Figure 2-7.

Figure 2-7 Contents of This PC

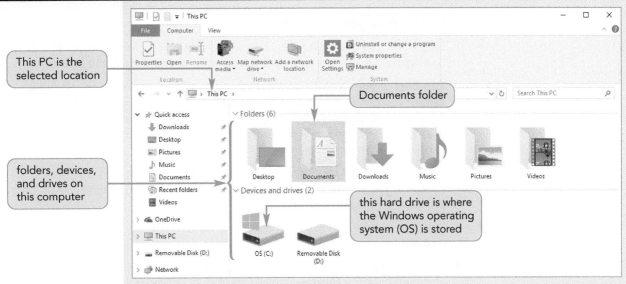

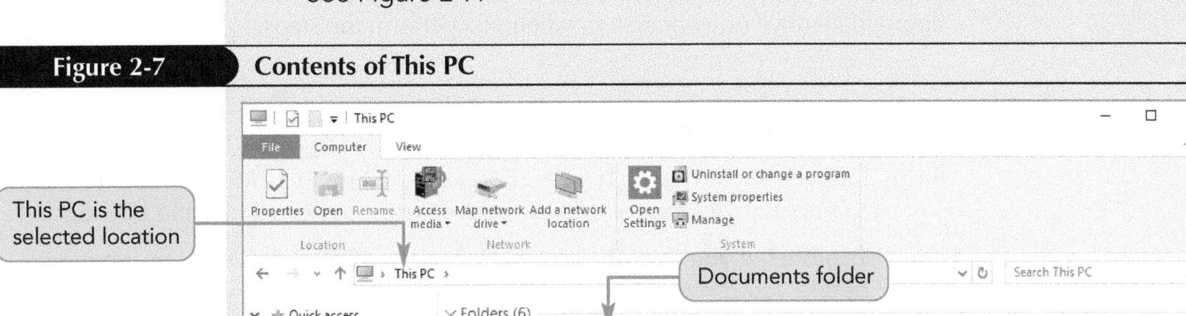
This PC is the selected location
Documents folder
folders, devices, and drives on this computer
this hard drive is where the Windows operating system (OS) is stored

4. In the right pane, double-click the **Documents** folder to display its contents.

The Documents folder is designed to store your files—the notes, reports, spreadsheets, presentations, and other files that you create, edit, and manipulate in an application. The Quick access list and This PC contain other folders that most users open frequently, such as the Pictures folder and the Music folder. Although the Pictures folder is designed to store graphics and the Music folder is designed to store music files, you can store graphics, music, or any other type of file in the Documents folder, especially if doing so makes it easier to find these files when you need them.

Navigating to Your Data Files

TIP

To display the file path in a folder window, click to the right of the text in the Address bar.

To navigate to the files you want, it helps to know the file path. The file path leads you through the folder and file organization to your file. For example, the Logo file is stored in the Module subfolder of the Module2 folder. If you are working on a USB drive, for example, the path to this file might be as follows:

D:\Module2\Module\Logo.png

This path has four parts, with each part separated by a backslash (\ ):

- D:—The drive name followed by a colon, which indicates a drive rather than a folder
- Module2—The top-level folder on drive D
- Module—A subfolder in the Module2 folder
- Logo.png—The full filename, including filename extension

In this example, drive D is the name for the USB drive. (If this file were stored on the primary hard disk, the drive name would be C.) If someone tells you to find the file D:\Module2\Module\Logo.png, you know you must navigate to your USB drive, open the Module2 folder, and then open the Module folder to find the Logo file.

You can keep track of your current location as you navigate between drives and folders using the Address bar, which displays the full file path using arrow buttons instead of backslashes. You can use the open folder window to navigate to the Data Files you need for the rest of this module. Before you perform the following steps, you need to know where you stored your Data Files, such as on a USB drive. The following steps assume that drive is Removable Disk (D:), a USB drive. If necessary, substitute the appropriate drive on your system when you perform the steps.

To navigate to your Data Files:

1. Make sure your computer can access your Data Files for this module. For example, if you are using a USB drive, insert the drive into the USB port.

   Trouble? If you don't have the starting Data Files, you need to get them before you can proceed. Your instructor will either give you the Data Files or ask you to obtain them from a specified location (such as a network drive). If you have any questions about the Data Files, see your instructor or technical support person for assistance.

2. In the open folder window, click the **expand** icon > next to the drive containing your Data Files, such as Removable Disk (D:). A list appears below the drive name showing the folders on that drive.

3. If the list of folders does not include the Module2 folder, continue clicking the **expand** icon > to navigate to the folder that contains the Module2 folder.

4. Click the **expand** icon > next to the Module2 folder to expand the folder, and then click the **Module2** folder so that its contents appear in the navigation pane and in the right pane of the folder window. The Module2 folder contains the Case1, Case2, Case3, Review, and Module folders, as shown in Figure 2-8. (Because Case Problem 4 does not require any files, the Module2 folder does not include a Case4 folder.) The other folders on your system might vary.

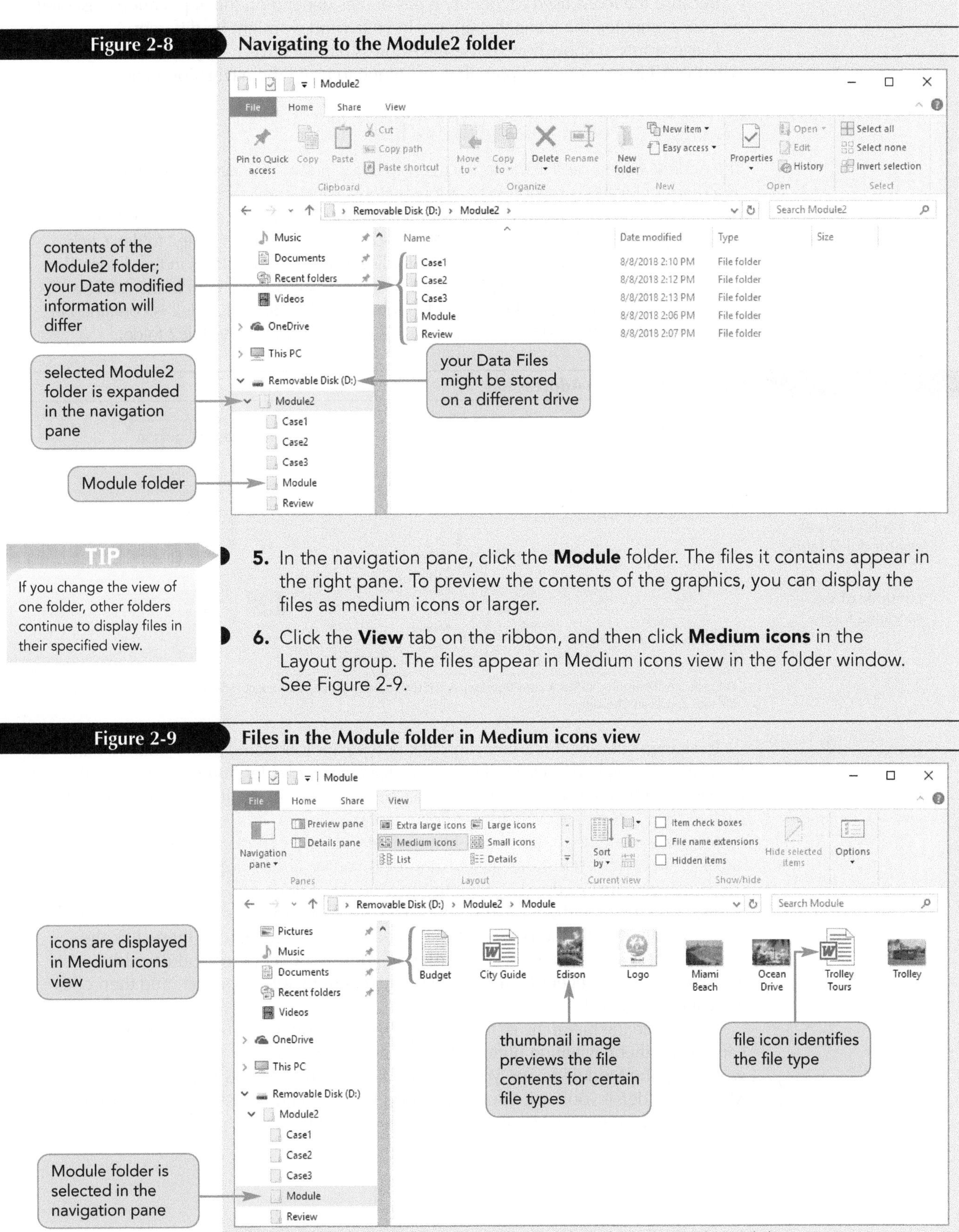

Figure 2-8 Navigating to the Module2 folder

contents of the Module2 folder; your Date modified information will differ
selected Module2 folder is expanded in the navigation pane
Module folder
your Data Files might be stored on a different drive

TIP

If you change the view of one folder, other folders continue to display files in their specified view.

5. In the navigation pane, click the **Module** folder. The files it contains appear in the right pane. To preview the contents of the graphics, you can display the files as medium icons or larger.
6. Click the **View** tab on the ribbon, and then click **Medium icons** in the Layout group. The files appear in Medium icons view in the folder window. See Figure 2-9.

Figure 2-9 Files in the Module folder in Medium icons view

icons are displayed in Medium icons view
thumbnail image previews the file contents for certain file types
file icon identifies the file type
Module folder is selected in the navigation pane

Because the icons used to identify types of files depend on the applications installed on your computer, the icons that appear in your window might be different.

Diego wants to know how to use the Address bar effectively, so you offer to navigate with the Address bar to compare that technique to using the navigation pane.

Navigating with the Address Bar

The Address bar, located at the top of every folder window, displays your current folder as a series of locations separated by arrow buttons. For example, in Figure 2-10, the Address bar shows the Module2 and Module folders separated by an arrow button, indicating that Module is the current folder and it's stored in the Module2 folder. Click the arrow button after the Module2 folder to display a list of subfolders in that folder. The same is true for any location displayed in the Address bar. The first item in the Address bar is Removable Disk (D:), the top level of the removable disk. Module2 is contained in Removable Disk (D:), and the Module folder is contained in the Module2 folder.

Figure 2-10 Navigating with the Address bar

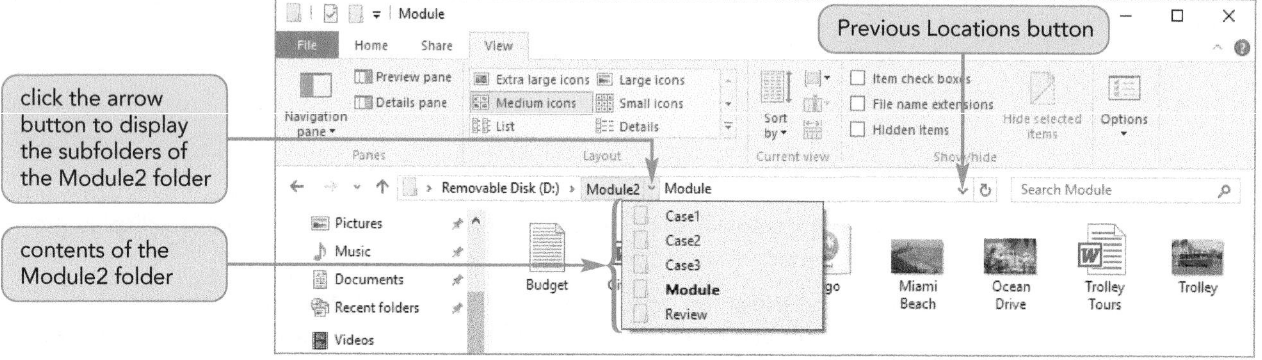

©iStock.com/Meinzahn, ©iStock.com/Betelgejze, ©iStock.com/bosenok, ©iStock.com/Vladone, ©iStock.com/Ivan Cholakov

TIP

To navigate to any location you visited in a folder window, click the Previous Locations button in the Address bar, and then click the location you want to visit.

To change your location, you can click or type a folder name in the Address bar. For example, you can click Module2 to navigate to that folder. You can also type the path to the folder you want, or type the name of a standard, built-in Windows folder, such as the Documents or Pictures folders.

After you navigate to a location by any method, you can click the Back, Forward, and Recent locations buttons to revisit folders you've already opened. For example, if you navigate first to drive D, then to the Module2 folder, and then to the Module folder, you can click the Back button to open your previous location, the Module2 folder. When you do, the Forward button becomes active. You can then click the Forward button to open the next location in your sequence, the Module folder. To navigate to any recent location, click the Recent locations button, and then click a location in the list.

To navigate the hierarchy of folders and drives on your computer, recall that you can use another navigation button: the Up one level button. For example, if you are working in the Module folder, you can click the Up one level button to navigate to the Module2 folder. If you click the Up one level button again, you navigate to the root directory of your removable disk, such as Removable Disk (D:).

To navigate using the Address bar and navigation buttons:

1. In the folder window displaying the contents of your Module folder, click the drive containing your Data Files, such as Removable Disk (D:), in the Address bar. The window displays the contents of the drive containing your Data Files.

   Trouble? If the drive containing your Data Files is not listed in the Address bar, click the first arrow button [>] in the Address bar, and then click Removable Disk (D:).

   Trouble? If the drive letter of your removable disk is different, substitute the correct drive letter for drive D for the remaining steps.

2. Click the **arrow** button [>] to the right of Removable Disk (D:) in the Address bar, and then click the name of the **Module2** folder.
3. Click the **Back** button [←] on the Address bar two times to return to the Module folder.
4. Click the **Recent locations** button [v] to display a list of locations you visited, and then click **Module2**. The subfolders in your Module2 folder appear in the right pane.

Leave the folder window open so that you can work with other file and folder tools.

Using the Search Box to Find Files

TIP

The name of the Search box reflects the location you are searching. If you select the Documents folder in the left pane, for example, the Search box name is Search Documents.

After you use a computer awhile, you're likely to have hundreds of files stored in various folders. If you know where you stored a file, it's easy to find it—you can use any navigation technique you like to navigate to that location and then scan the file list to find the file. Often, however, finding a file is more time consuming than that. You know that you stored a file somewhere in a standard folder such as Documents or Music, but finding the file might mean opening dozens of folders and scanning many long file lists. To save time, you can use the Search box to quickly find your file.

The Search box appears next to the Address bar in any folder window. To find a file in the current folder or any of its subfolders, you start typing text associated with the file. This search text can be part of the filename, text within the file, tags (keywords you associate with a file), or other file properties. By default, Windows searches for files by examining the names of the files displayed in the folder window and files in any subfolders. If it finds a file whose filename contains a word starting with the search text you specify, it displays that file in the folder window. For example, you can use the search text *guide* to find files named City Guide and Guide to Miami. If you are searching a hard drive, Windows also looks for files that contain a word starting with your search text. If it finds one, it displays that file in the folder window. For example, using *guide* as the search text also finds files containing words such as "guided" and "guidelines." If you are searching a removable drive, Windows searches filenames only by default. However, you can change settings to specify that you want to search other properties, including the contents. The following steps assume you are searching a removable drive.

Diego asks you to find a digital photo of a trolley on his computer. He knows he has at least one photo of a trolley. You can find this file by starting to type *trolley* in the Search box.

To use the Search box to find a file:

1. In the folder window displaying the contents of your Module2 folder, click the Search box.
2. Type **t** and then pause. Windows 10 examines the files in the Module2 folder and its subfolders, searching for a filename that includes a word starting with "t." The files in the Module2 folder that meet this criterion are displayed in the search results. You can continue typing to narrow the selection.
3. Type **ro** after the "t" so that the search text is now *tro*. Only two files have filenames that include a word beginning with "tro." See Figure 2-11. The first three letters in each filename are highlighted. Your files might appear in a different view.

   Trouble? If you are searching a hard drive, you see additional files that contain words beginning with "tro."

Figure 2-11 Searching for a file

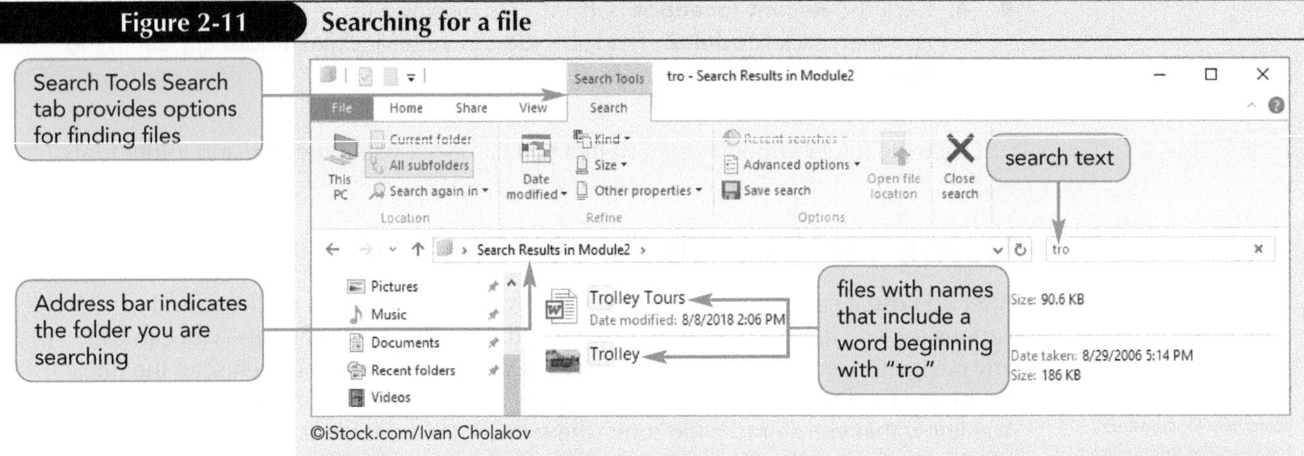

©iStock.com/Ivan Cholakov

When you click the Search box, the Search Tools Search tab appears with options you can use to find your files. You can choose to search the current folder or its subfolders. Clicking the Date modified button displays options such as "today," "yesterday," "two weeks ago," and "last year," which are especially helpful when you can't remember what you named the file, where you stored it, or when you created it.

Using the Search box in a folder window, you found a photo of a trolley for Diego—the Trolley image file.

Now that Diego is comfortable navigating a computer to find files, you're ready to show him how to manage his files and folders.

Managing Files and Folders

After you devise a plan for storing your files, you are ready to get organized by creating folders that will hold your files. You can do so using any folder window. In this module, you create folders in the Module folder, which is probably stored on a USB drive, not a hard drive. When you are working on your own computer, you usually create folders within the Documents folder and other standard folders, such as Music and Pictures. However, Edison, Logo, Miami Beach, Ocean Drive, and Trolley are all graphics files that Diego uses for marketing Miami Trolleys. The City Guide and Trolley Tours files contain descriptions of sights in Miami for customers. The Budget file relates to business finances.

One way to organize these files is to create three folders—one for graphics, one for sights, and another for the financial files. When you create a folder, you give it a name, preferably one that describes its contents. A folder name can have up to

255 characters. Any character is allowed, except / \ : * ? " < > and |. Considering these conventions, you could create three folders as follows:

- Marketing Graphics folder— Edison, Logo, Miami Beach, Ocean Drive, and Trolley files
- Sights folder—City Guide and Trolley Tours files
- Financial folder—Budget file

Before creating the folders, you show your plan to Diego. You point out that instead of creating a folder for the graphics files, he could store them in the Pictures folder that Windows 10 provides for photos, clip art, drawings, and other graphics. However, Diego wants to keep these marketing graphics files separate from any other files. He also thinks storing them in a folder along with the Sights and Financial folders will make it easier to find his business files later.

INSIGHT

Guidelines for Creating Folders

Keep the following guidelines in mind as you create folders:

- Keep folder names short and familiar. Long folder names can be more difficult to display in their entirety in folder windows, so use names that are short but clear. Choose names that will be meaningful later, such as project names or course numbers.
- Develop standards for naming folders. Use a consistent naming scheme that is clear to you, such as one that uses a project name as the name of the main folder, and includes step numbers in each subfolder name (for example, 01 Plan, 02 Approvals, 03 First Draft, and so on).
- Create subfolders to organize files. If a file list in a folder window is so long that you must scroll the window, consider organizing those files into subfolders.

Diego asks you to create the three new folders. After that, you'll move his files to the appropriate folders.

Creating Folders

You've already seen folder icons in the windows you've examined. Now, you'll create folders within the Module folder using the ribbon that appears in all File Explorer windows.

REFERENCE

Creating a Folder in a Folder Window

- In the navigation pane, click the drive or folder in which you want to create a folder.
- Click the Home tab and then click the New folder button in the New group, or click the New folder button on the Quick Access Toolbar.
- Type a name for the folder, and then press the Enter key.

or

- Right-click a drive or folder in the navigation pane, or right-click a blank area in the folder window, point to New, and then click Folder.
- Type a name for the folder, and then press the Enter key.

Now you can create three folders in your Module folder as you planned—the Marketing Graphics, Sights, and Financial folders. You create these folders in three ways: using the Home tab, shortcut menu, and Quick Access Toolbar.

To create folders:

1. Navigate to the **Module2 > Module** folder included with your Data Files.
2. Click the **Home** tab, if necessary, and then click the **New folder** button in the New group. A folder icon with the label "New folder" appears in the right pane. See Figure 2-12.

Figure 2-12 Creating a subfolder in the Module folder

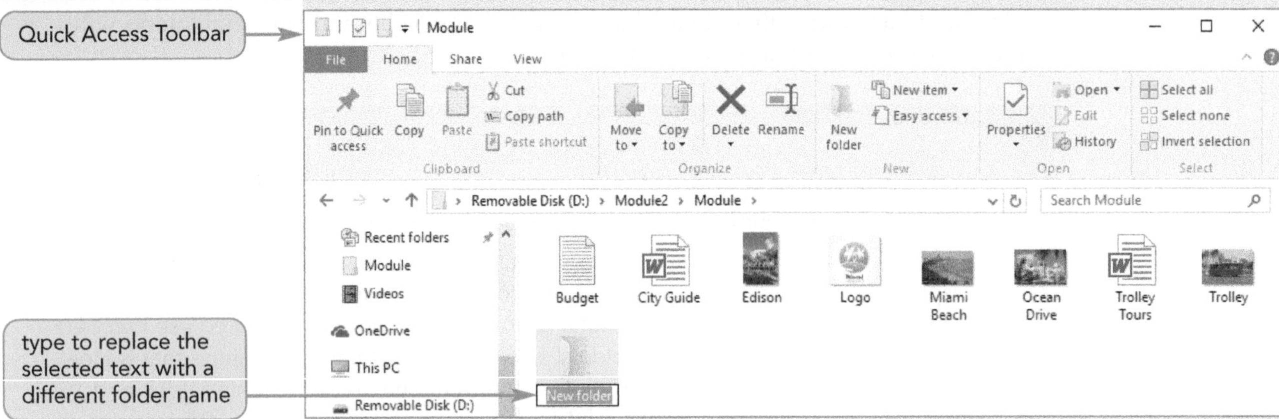

©iStock.com/Meinzahn, ©iStock.com/Betelgejze, ©iStock.com/bosenok, ©iStock.com/Vladone, ©iStock.com/Ivan Cholakov

TIP

When you first create a subfolder, it might appear at the end of the file list. When you finish naming the folder, all subfolders appear in the file list according to the sort order.

Trouble? If the "New folder" name is not selected, right-click the new folder, click Rename, and then continue with Step 3.

Windows uses "New folder" as a placeholder, and selects the text so that you can replace it immediately by typing a new name. You do not need to press the Backspace or Delete key to delete the text.

3. Type **Marketing Graphics** as the folder name, and then press the **Enter** key. The new folder is now named Marketing Graphics and is the selected item in the right pane. To create a second folder, you can use a shortcut menu.
4. Right-click a blank area in the right pane, point to **New** on the shortcut menu, and then click **Folder**. A folder icon appears in the right pane with the New folder text selected.
5. Type **Sights** as the name of the new folder, and then press the **Enter** key.
6. Click the **New folder** button on the Quick Access Toolbar, type **Financial**, and then press the **Enter** key to create and name the folder. The Module folder now contains three new subfolders.

After creating three folders, you're ready to organize your files by moving them into the appropriate folders.

Moving and Copying Files and Folders

If you want to place a file into a folder from another location, you can either move the file or copy it. **Moving** a file removes it from its current location and places it in a new location that you specify. **Copying** also places the file in a new location that you specify, but does not remove it from its current location. Windows 10 provides several techniques for moving and copying files. You can drag or right-drag a file with the mouse, use the Clipboard, or select the Move to or Copy to button in the Organize group on the Home tab on the File

Explorer ribbon. (The **Clipboard** is a temporary storage area for files and information that you copy or move from one place and plan to use somewhere else.) The same principles apply to folders: You can move and copy folders using a variety of methods.

REFERENCE

Moving a File or Folder in a Folder Window

- Right-drag the file or folder you want to move to the destination folder.
- Release the mouse button, and then click Move here on the shortcut menu.

or

- Right-click the file or folder you want to move to the destination folder, and then click Cut on the shortcut menu. (You can also click the file or folder and then press the Ctrl+X keys.)
- Navigate to and right-click the destination folder, and then click Paste on the shortcut menu. (You can also click the destination folder and then press the Ctrl+V keys.)

Diego suggests that you move some files from the Module folder to the appropriate subfolders. You'll start by moving the Budget file to the Financial folder using the right-drag technique, which you will learn next.

To move a file using the right mouse button:

1. Point to the **Budget** file in the right pane, and then press and hold the right mouse button.
2. With the right mouse button still pressed down, drag the **Budget** file to the **Financial** folder. When the Move to Financial ScreenTip appears, release the button. A shortcut menu opens as shown in the Session 2.1 Visual Overview.
3. With the left mouse button, click **Move here** on the shortcut menu. The Budget file is removed from the main Module folder and stored in the Financial subfolder.

   Trouble? If you released the mouse button before you dragged the Budget file all the way to the Financial folder and before seeing the Move to Financial ScreenTip, press the Esc key to close the shortcut menu, and then repeat Steps 1–3.

   Trouble? If you moved a file other than the Budget file, press the Ctrl+Z keys to undo the move, and then repeat Steps 1–3.
4. In the right pane, double-click the **Financial** folder. The Budget file is in the Financial folder.

   Trouble? If the Budget file does not appear in the Financial folder, you probably moved it to a different folder. Press the Ctrl+Z keys to undo the move, and then repeat Steps 1–4.
5. Click the **Back** button on the Address bar to return to the Module folder.

The advantage of moving a file or folder by dragging with the right mouse button is that you can efficiently complete your work with one action. However, this right-drag technique requires polished mouse skills so that you can drag the file comfortably. When you drag to move files, be sure to verify the destination by waiting for the Move to ScreenTip. Otherwise, you might move the file to an unintended folder and have trouble finding the file later.

Another way to move files and folders is to use the Clipboard. Although the Clipboard does not appear in a folder window, you can use it when working with files and folders. Select a file and use the Cut or Copy command to temporarily store the file on the Clipboard, and then use the Paste command to insert the file elsewhere. Although using the Clipboard takes more steps, some users find it easier than dragging with the right mouse button.

You'll move the City Guide file to the Sights folder next by using the Clipboard.

To move files using the Clipboard:

1. Right-click the **City Guide** file, and then click **Cut** on the shortcut menu. Although the file icon is still displayed in the folder window, Windows 10 removes the City Guide file from the Module folder and stores it on the Clipboard.
2. In the right pane, right-click the **Sights** folder, and then click **Paste** on the shortcut menu. Windows 10 pastes the City Guide file from the Clipboard to the Sights folder. The City Guide file icon no longer appears in the folder window.
3. In the navigation pane, click the **expand** icon > next to the Module folder, if necessary, to display its contents, and then click the **Sights** folder to view its contents in the right pane. The Sights folder now contains the City Guide file. See Figure 2-13.

TIP

As you navigate to folders, Windows displays the folders you use often in the Quick access list.

Figure 2-13 Moving a file

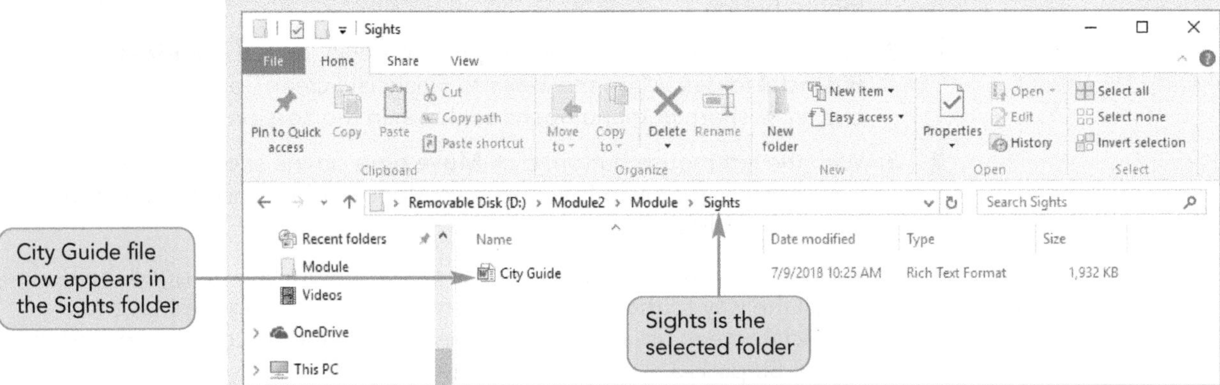

Next, you'll move the Trolley Tours file from the Module folder to the Sights folder.

4. Click the **Back** button ← on the Address bar to return to the Module folder, right-click the **Trolley Tours** file in the folder window, and then click **Cut** on the shortcut menu.
5. In the navigation pane, right-click the **Sights** folder, and then click **Paste** on the shortcut menu. The file is moved into the Sights folder.
6. Click the **Forward** button → on the Address bar to return to the Sights folder. The Sights folder now contains the City Guide and Trolley Tours files.

One way to save steps when moving or copying multiple files or folders is to select all the files and folders you want to move or copy, and then work with them as a group. You'll show Diego how to do that next.

Selecting Files and Folders

You can select multiple files or folders using several techniques, so you can choose the most convenient method for your current task. First, you open the folder that contains the files or folders you want to select. Next, select the files or folders using any one of the following methods:

- To select files or folders that are listed together in a folder window, click the first item, hold down the Shift key, click the last item, and then release the Shift key.
- To select files or folders that are listed together in a folder window without using the keyboard, drag the pointer to create a selection box around all the items you want to include.
- To select files or folders that are not listed together, hold down the Ctrl key, click each item you want to select, and then release the Ctrl key.
- To select all of the files or folders, click the Select all button in the Select group on the Home tab.
- To clear the selection of an item in a selected group, hold down the Ctrl key, click each item you want to remove from the selection, and then release the Ctrl key.
- To clear the entire selection, click a blank area of the folder window.

Copying Files and Folders

When you copy a file or folder, you make a duplicate of the original item. You can copy files or folders using techniques similar to the ones you use when moving them.

REFERENCE

Copying a File or Folder in a Folder Window

- Right-drag the file or folder you want to copy to the destination folder.
- Release the mouse button, and then click Copy here on the shortcut menu.

or

- Right-click the file or folder you want to copy to the destination folder, and then click Copy on the shortcut menu. (You can also click the file or folder and then press the Ctrl+C keys.)
- Navigate to and right-click the destination folder, and then click Paste on the shortcut menu. (You can also click the destination folder and then press the Ctrl+V keys.)

You'll copy the five graphics files from the Module folder to the Marketing Graphics folder now.

To copy files using the Clipboard:

1. Using any navigation technique you've learned, return to the Module folder window.
2. Click the **Edison** file, hold down the **Shift** key, click the **Trolley** file, and then release the **Shift** key. Five files are selected in the Module folder window.
3. Right-click the selected files, and then click **Copy** on the shortcut menu. Windows copies the files to the Clipboard.

4. Right-click the **Marketing Graphics** folder, and then click **Paste** on the shortcut menu.
5. Open the **Marketing Graphics** folder to verify it contains the five files you copied, and then return to the Module folder.

Now that you have copied files using the Copy and Paste commands, you can use the right-drag technique to copy the four photos to the Sights folder. As with moving files, you select the files, point to them, hold down the right mouse button, and then drag the file to a new location. However, when you release the mouse button, you click Copy here (instead of Move here) on the shortcut menu to copy the files.

To copy files:

1. Click the **Edison** file, hold down the **Ctrl** key, click the **Miami Beach** file, the **Ocean Drive** file, and the **Trolley** file, and then release the **Ctrl** key. Four files are selected in the Module folder window.
2. Right-drag the selected files from the Module folder to the Sights folder.
3. Release the mouse button, and then click **Copy here** on the shortcut menu.
4. Double-click the **Sights** folder to verify it contains the four photo files, and then return to the Module folder.

TIP

When you move or copy a folder, you move or copy all the files contained in the folder.

You can use another technique to copy or move a file or folder. You can drag the file or folder (using the left mouse button) to another location. Whether the file or folder is copied or moved depends on where you drag it. A ScreenTip appears when you drag a file to a new location—the ScreenTip indicates what happens when you release the mouse button. Figure 2-14 summarizes how to copy and move files and folders by dragging.

Figure 2-14 Dragging to move and copy files

Drag a File or Folder:	To:
Into a folder on the same drive	Move the file or folder to the destination folder
Into a folder on a different drive	Copy the file or folder to the destination folder

Although the copy and move techniques listed are common ways to copy and move files and folders, be sure you can anticipate what happens when you drag a file or folder.

REVIEW

Session 2.1 Quick Check

1. ____________ is a Windows 10 tool that displays the contents of your computer and uses icons to represent drives, folders, and files.
2. What is the purpose of a file path?
3. Explain why you should not store files in the root directory of a hard disk.
4. Explain how to use a folder window to navigate to a file in the following location: D:\Classes\Digital Literacy\Operating Systems.txt.
5. How can you access a file stored in the Documents folder on your OneDrive?
6. What is the difference between using the Cut and Copy commands when working with files?
7. Describe how to find files using the Search box.
8. What happens if you click the first file in a folder window, hold down the Ctrl key, click the last file, and then release the Ctrl key?

Session 2.2 Visual Overview:

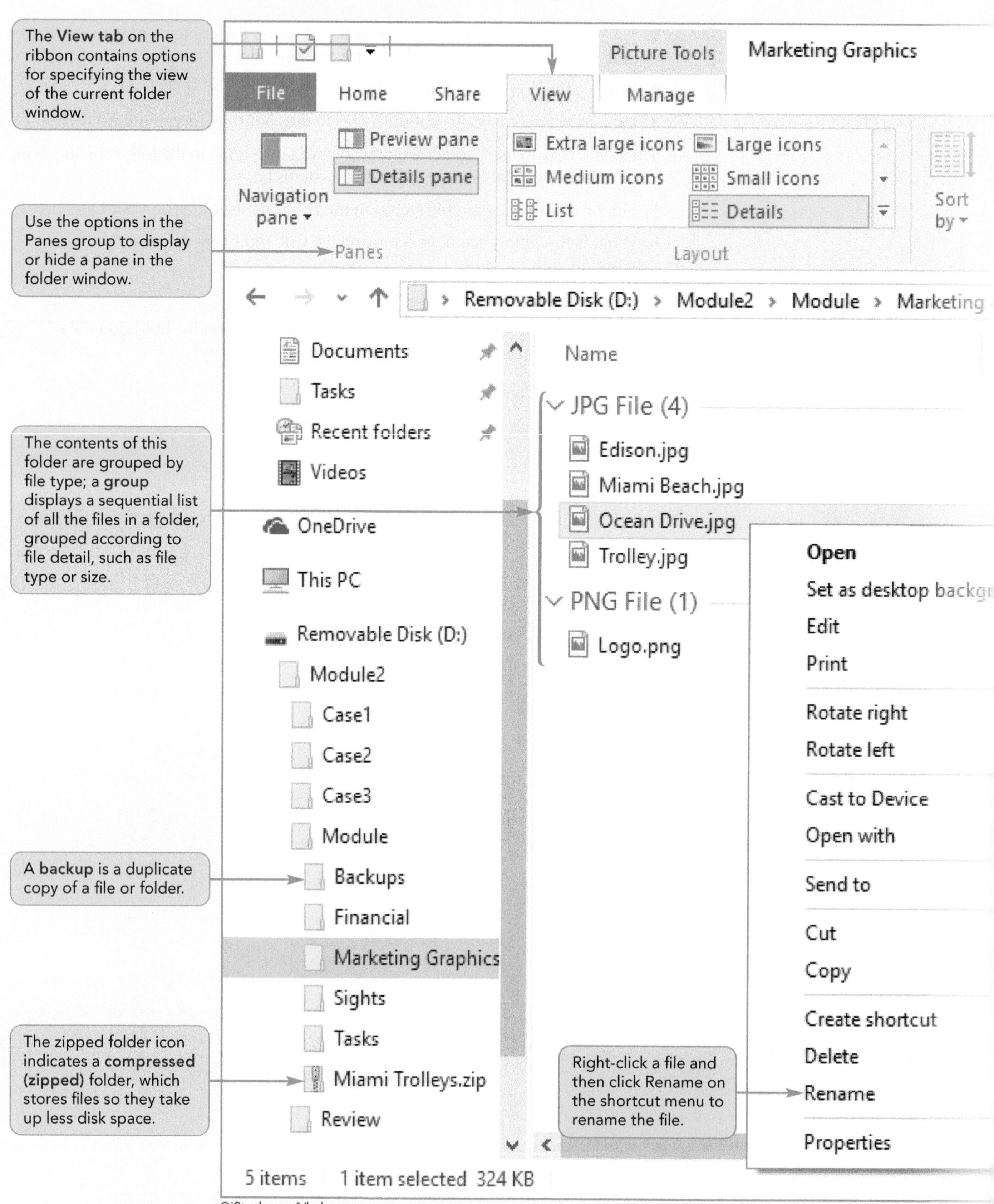

Customized Folder Window

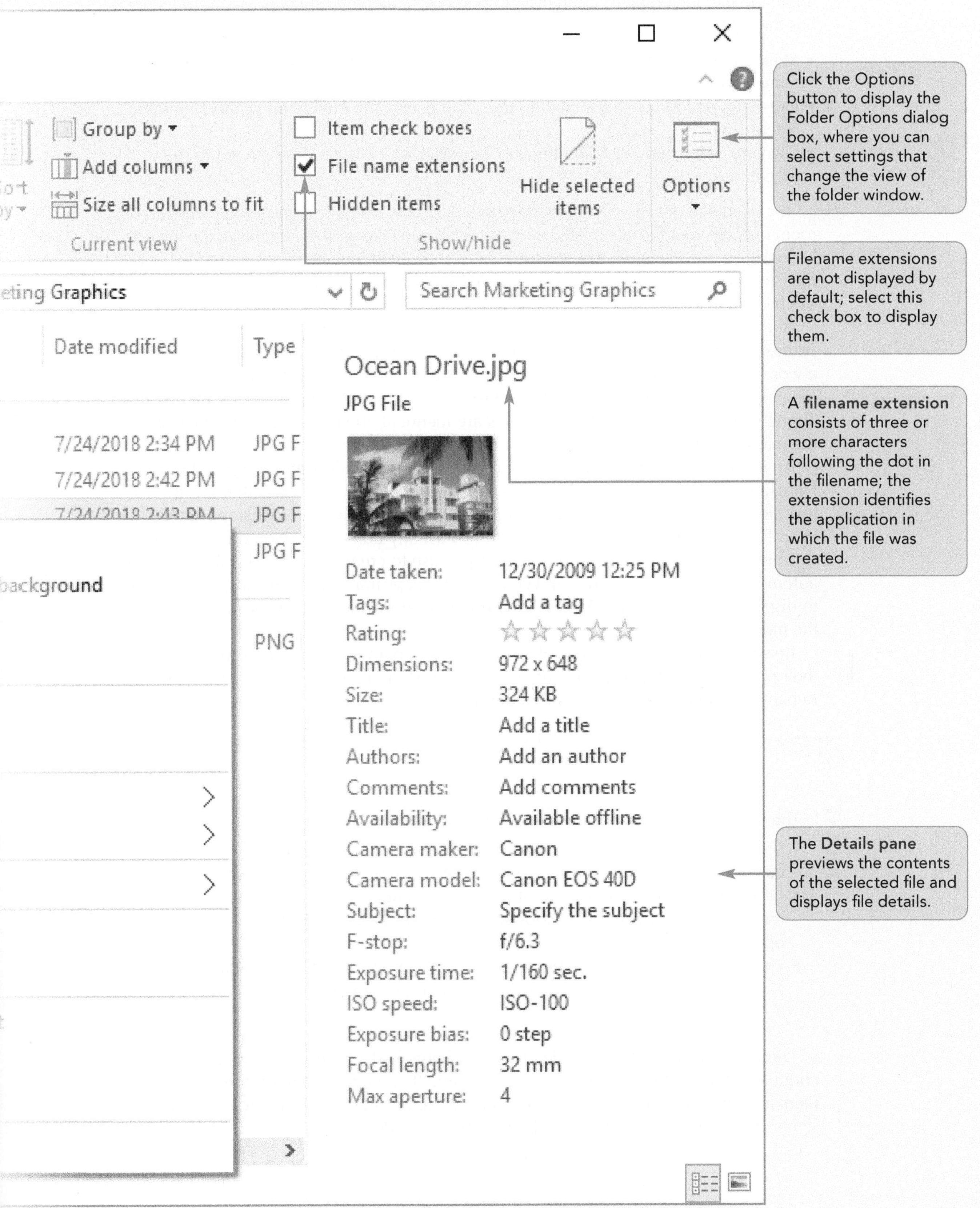

Click the Options button to display the Folder Options dialog box, where you can select settings that change the view of the folder window.

Filename extensions are not displayed by default; select this check box to display them.

A **filename extension** consists of three or more characters following the dot in the filename; the extension identifies the application in which the file was created.

The **Details pane** previews the contents of the selected file and displays file details.

Naming and Renaming Files and Folders

As you work with files, pay attention to filenames—they provide important information about the file, including its contents and purpose. A filename such as Miami Tours.docx has three parts:

- Main part of the filename—The name you provide when you create a file, and the name you associate with a file
- Dot—The period (.) that separates the main part of the filename from the filename extension
- Filename extension—Usually three or four characters that follow the dot in the filename

The main part of a filename can have up to 255 characters. This gives you plenty of room to name your file accurately enough so that you'll know the contents of the file just by looking at the filename. You can use spaces and certain punctuation symbols in your filenames. Like folder names, however, filenames cannot contain the symbols / \ : * ? " < > or | because these characters have special meanings in Windows 10.

A filename extension indicates the file type. For example, in the filename Miami Tours.docx, the extension .docx identifies the file as one created in Microsoft Word, a word-processing application. You might also have a file called Miami Tours.png—the .png extension identifies the file as one created in a graphics application such as Paint. Though the main parts of these filenames are identical, their extensions distinguish them as different files.

An extension also helps Windows identify what application should open the file. For example, the .txt extension in a file named Brochure.txt indicates that it is a text file and can be opened by applications associated with that extension, such as WordPad, Notepad, and Microsoft Word. You usually do not need to add extensions to your filenames because the application you use to create the file adds the extension automatically. However, although Windows 10 keeps track of extensions, it is not set to display them by default. (You will learn how to show filename extensions later in the module.)

Be sure to give your files and folders meaningful names that will help you remember their purpose and contents. You can, however, rename a file or folder by using the Rename command on the file's shortcut menu.

INSIGHT

Guidelines for Naming Files

The following are best practices for naming (or renaming) your files:

- Use common names. Avoid cryptic names that might make sense now but could cause confusion later, such as nonstandard abbreviations or imprecise names like Stuff18.
- Leave the filename extension as it is. Do not change the filename extension when renaming a file. If you do, Windows might not be able to find an application that can open the file.
- Find a comfortable balance between too short and too long. Use filenames that are long enough to be meaningful, but short enough to be read easily on the screen.

Diego notes that the City Guide file in the Sights folder could contain information about any city. He recommends that you rename that file to give it a more descriptive filename. The City Guide file was originally created to store text specifically about sights on Miami, so you'll rename the file Miami Guide.

To rename the City Guide file:

1. If you took a break after the previous session, make sure that a folder window is open, and then navigate to the **Module2** folder included with your Data Files. Click the **Module** folder in the left pane, and change to **Medium icons** view, if necessary.
2. Open the **Sights** folder to display its contents.
3. Right-click the **City Guide** file, and then click **Rename** on the shortcut menu. The filename is highlighted and a box appears around it.
4. Type **Miami Guide** and then press the **Enter** key. The file now appears with the new name.

   Trouble? If you make a mistake while typing and you haven't pressed the Enter key yet, press the Backspace key until you delete the mistake and then complete Step 4. If you've already pressed the Enter key, repeat Steps 3 and 4 to rename the file again.

   Trouble? If your computer is set to display filename extensions, a message might appear asking if you are sure you want to change the filename extension. Click the No button, and then repeat Steps 3 and 4.

TIP

To rename a file, you can also click the file, pause, click it again to select the filename, and then type to enter a new filename.

All the files that originally appeared in the Module folder are now stored in appropriate subfolders. You can streamline the organization of the Module folder by deleting the duplicate files you no longer need.

Deleting Files and Folders

TIP

In most cases, a file deleted from a USB drive does not go into the Recycle Bin. Instead, it is deleted permanently when Windows 10 removes its icon, and the file cannot be recovered.

You should periodically delete files and folders you no longer need so that your main folders and disks don't get cluttered. In a folder window, you delete a file or folder by deleting its icon. When you use File Explorer to delete a file from a hard disk, including a OneDrive file, Windows 10 removes the file from the folder but stores the file contents in the Recycle Bin. The Recycle Bin is an area on your hard disk that holds deleted files until you remove them permanently. When you delete a folder from the hard disk, the folder and all of its files are stored in the Recycle Bin. If you change your mind and want to retrieve a deleted file or folder, you can double-click the Recycle Bin icon on the desktop, right-click the file or folder you want to retrieve, and then click Restore on the shortcut menu. However, after you empty the Recycle Bin, you can no longer recover the files it contained.

REFERENCE

Deleting a File or Folder

- Click the file or folder you want to delete. (If you want to delete more than one file or folder, select them first.)
- Press the Delete key, and then click the Yes button.

or

- Right-click the file or folder you want to delete. (If you want to delete more than one file or folder, select them first.)
- Click Delete on the shortcut menu, and then click the Yes button.

Because you copied the Edison, Logo, Miami Beach, Ocean Drive, and Trolley files to the subfolders in the Module folder, you can safely delete the original files. As is true for moving, copying, and renaming files and folders, you can delete a file or folder in many ways, including using a shortcut menu or selecting one or more files and then pressing the Delete key or the Delete button in the Organize group on the Home tab on the File Explorer ribbon.

To delete files in the Module folder:

1. Use any technique you've learned to navigate to and display the **Module** folder.
2. Click **Edison**, hold down the **Shift** key, click **Trolley**, and then release the **Shift** key. All files in the Module folder are now selected. None of the subfolders should be selected.
3. Right-click the selected files, and then click **Delete** on the shortcut menu. Windows 10 might ask if you're sure you want to permanently delete these files.

   Trouble? If you are working with files on a hard disk, Windows does not ask if you want to permanently delete the files.
4. If necessary, click the **Yes** button.

Make sure you have copied the selected files to the Financial, Marketing Graphics, and Sights folders before completing this step.

So far, you've worked with files in folder windows, but you haven't viewed any file contents. To view a file's contents, you open the file. When you double-click a file in a folder window, Windows 10 starts the associated application and opens the file. You'll have a chance to try these techniques in the next section.

Working with New Files

The most common way to add files to a drive or folder is to create new files when you use an application. For example, you can create a text document in a word-processing application, a drawing in a graphics application, or a movie file in a video-editing application. When you are finished with a file, you must save it if you want to use the file again. To work with the file, you open it in an appropriate application; you can usually tell which applications can open a file by examining the filename extension or file icon.

Before you continue working with Diego's files, you decide to create a task list to summarize your remaining tasks. You'll create the task list file, save it, close it, and then reopen it to add some items to the list.

Creating a File

You create a file by starting an application and then saving the file in a folder on your computer. Some applications create a file when you open the application. When you open WordPad, for example, it starts with a blank page. This represents an empty (and unsaved) file. You type and format the document to create it. When you are finished, you save your work using the Save As dialog box, where you can select a location for the file and enter a filename that identifies the contents. By default, most applications save files in a folder such as Documents, Pictures, or Music, which makes it easy to find the files again later.

The task list you want to create is a simple text document, so you can create this file using Notepad, the basic text-editing application that Windows 10 provides.

To create a Notepad file:

1. Click the **Start** button to display the Start menu.
2. Type **notep** to insert "notep" in the Search the web and Windows box. The search results include Notepad, a desktop app.
3. Click **Notepad** in the search results. The Notepad application window opens on the desktop. See Figure 2-15.

Figure 2-15 **Creating a file**

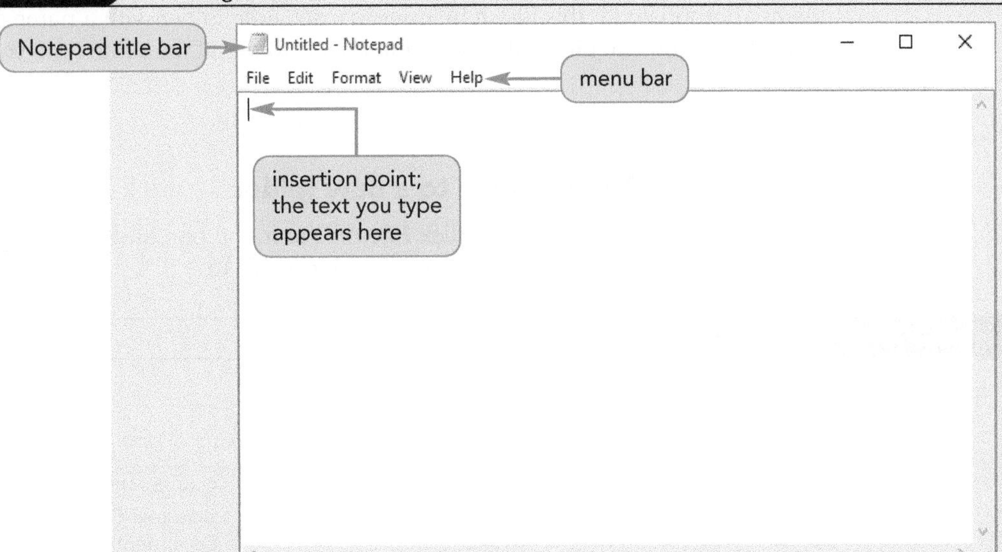

4. Type the following text in the Notepad window, pressing the **Enter** key at the end of each line, including the last line:

   To Do for Diego's Files

   1. Sort and filter files.

   2. Customize a folder window.

   3. Compress and extract files.

The Notepad title bar indicates that the name of this file is "Untitled." To give it a more descriptive name, preserve the contents, and store the file where you can find it later, you must save the file.

Saving a File

TIP

After you create a file, avoid cluttering the desktop by saving the file in a subfolder on your computer, not on the desktop.

As you are creating a file, you should save it frequently so you don't lose your work. When you save a new file, you use the Save As dialog box to specify a filename and a location for the file. When you open a file you've already created, you can use the application's Save command to save the file with the same name and location. If you want to save the file with a different name or in a different location, however, you use the Save As dialog box again to specify the new name or location. You can create a folder for the new file at the same time you save the file.

The Save As dialog box contains the same navigation tools found in a folder window, such as an Address bar, Search box, navigation pane, and right pane displaying folders and files. You can then specify the file location, for example, using the same navigation techniques that are available in all folder windows. In addition, the Save As dialog box always includes a File name box where you specify a filename, a Save as type list where you select a file type, and other controls for saving a file.

If the expanded Save As dialog box covers too much of your document or desktop, you can click the Hide Folders button to collapse the dialog box so it hides the navigation pane, right pane, and toolbar. (The Hide Folders button changes to the Browse Folders button when the dialog box is collapsed.) You can still navigate with the Back, Forward, Recent locations, and Up one level buttons; the Address bar; and the Search box, and you can still use the controls for saving a file, but you conserve screen space.

Now that you've created a task list, you need to save it. A good name for this document is Task List. However, none of the folders you've already created for Diego seems appropriate for this file. It belongs in a separate folder with a name such as Task Documents. You can create the Task Documents folder at the same time you save the Task List file.

To save the Notepad file to a new folder:

1. In the Notepad window, click **File** on the menu bar, and then click **Save As**. The Save As dialog box opens. See Figure 2-16.

Figure 2-16 Saving a new file

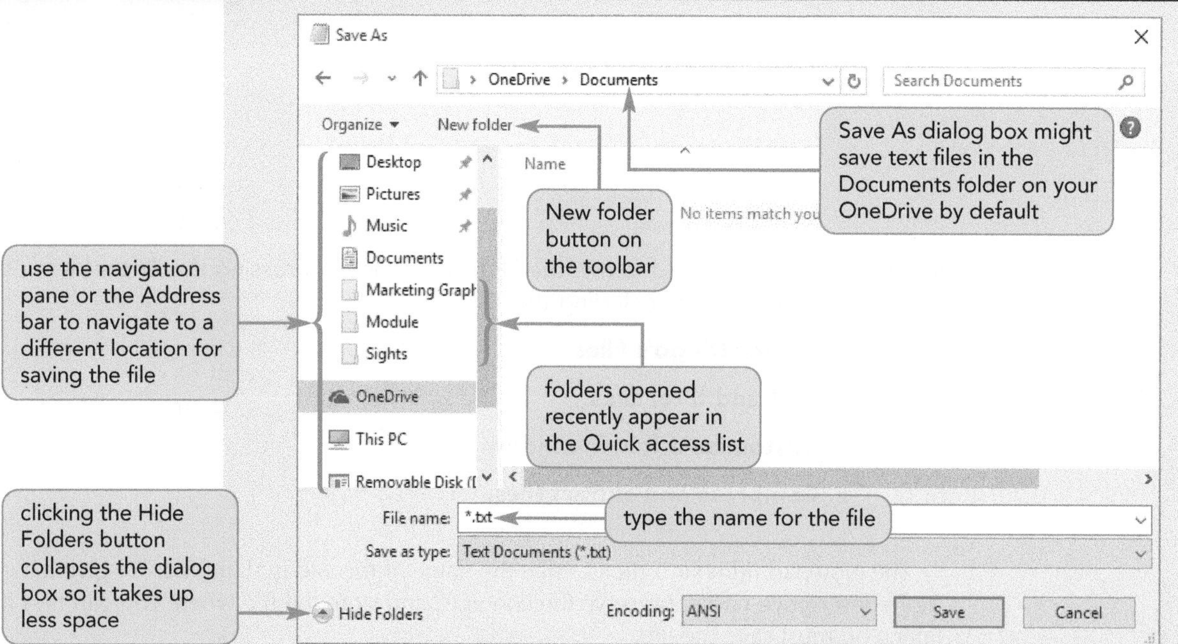
Save As
OneDrive > Documents
Search Documents
Organize
New folder
Desktop
Pictures
Music
Documents
Marketing Graph
Module
Sights
OneDrive
This PC
Removable Disk
Name
No items match you
File name: *.txt
Save as type: Text Documents (*.txt)
Hide Folders
Encoding: ANSI
Save
Cancel
Save As dialog box might save text files in the Documents folder on your OneDrive by default
New folder button on the toolbar
use the navigation pane or the Address bar to navigate to a different location for saving the file
folders opened recently appear in the Quick access list
type the name for the file
clicking the Hide Folders button collapses the dialog box so it takes up less space

TIP

Some Windows 10 applications, such as Microsoft Office, include OneDrive as a location for saving and opening files.

Trouble? If the navigation pane does not appear in the Save As dialog box, click the Browse Folders button.

Your computer might be set up to save Notepad files in the Documents folder on OneDrive or a different location, such as the Documents folder on This PC. You want to create a subfolder in the Module folder for this document.

2. In the Save As dialog box, use any technique you've learned to navigate to the **Module2 > Module** folder provided with your Data Files.
3. Click the **New folder** button on the toolbar in the Save As dialog box. A new folder appears in the Module folder, with the New folder name highlighted and ready for you to replace.

4. Type **Task Documents** as the name of the new folder, and then press the **Enter** key.
5. Double-click the **Task Documents** folder to open it. Now you are ready to specify a filename and save the task list file in the Task Documents folder.
6. Click the **File name** box to select the *.txt text, and then type **Task List**. Notepad will automatically provide a .txt extension to this filename, so you don't have to type it.
7. Click the **Save** button. Notepad saves the Task List file in the Task Documents folder. The new filename now appears in the Notepad title bar.
8. Click the **Close** button × to close Notepad.

Next, you can open the file to add another item to the task list.

Opening a File

If you want to open a file in a running application, you use the Open dialog box, which is a folder window with additional controls for opening a file, similar to the Save As dialog box. You use the application's Open command to access the Open dialog box, which you use to navigate to the file you want, select the file, and then open it. If the application you want to use is not running, you can open a file by double-clicking it in a folder window. The file usually opens in the application that you used to create or edit it. If it's a text file with a .txt extension, for example, it opens in a text editor, such as Notepad. If it's a text file with a .docx extension, it opens in Microsoft Word.

Not all documents work this way. Double-clicking a digital picture file usually opens a picture viewing app, which displays the picture. To edit the picture, you need to use a graphics editing application. When you need to specify an application to open a file, you can right-click the file, point to Open with on the shortcut menu, and then click the name of the app that you want to use.

To open and edit the Task List file:

1. In the right pane of the Module folder window, double-click the **Task Documents** folder.
2. Double-click the **Task List** file. Notepad starts and opens the Task List file.

   Trouble? If an application other than Notepad starts, such as WordPad, close the application, right-click the Task List file, point to Open with, and then click Notepad.
3. Press the **Ctrl+End** keys to move the insertion point to the end of the document, and then type **4. Restore system settings.**

   Because you want to save this file using the same name and location, you can use the Save command on the File menu to save your work this time.
4. Click **File** on the menu bar, and then click **Save**. Notepad saves the Task List file without opening the Save As dialog box because you are using the same name and location as the last time you saved the file.

As long as Notepad is still open, you can create another simple text file that describes the photos in the Sights folder.

To create and save another file:

1. Click **File** on the menu bar, and then click **New** to open a new, blank document.
2. Type the following text in the Notepad window, pressing the **Enter** key at the end of each line:

   Sights photos:

   Edison: Photo of the Edison hotel

   Miami Beach: Photo of Miami Beach and city skyline

   Ocean Drive: Photo of an art deco building on Ocean Drive

   Trolley: Photo of a company trolley
3. Click **File** on the menu bar, and then click **Save**. The Save As dialog box opens because this is the first time you are saving the file.
4. Navigate to the **Sights** folder in the Module folder.
5. Click in the **File name** box, and then type **Photo Descriptions**.
6. Click the **Save** button. Notepad saves the Photo Descriptions file in the Sights folder.
7. Click the **Close** button × to close Notepad. (Because Notepad only allows one file to be opened at a time, the application closed the first file for you when you created the new file.)

Now that you've organized Diego's files and then created and saved new folders and files, you're ready to refine the organization of the files.

Refining the Organization of Files

To refine the organization of your files, you can fine-tune the arrangement of your files and folders in a folder window. Changing the order of files in a list can often help you find files and identify those that share common features, such as two versions of the same file. One way to change the view is to sort your files. **Sorting** files and folders means listing them in a particular order, such as alphabetically by name or type, or chronologically by their modification date. You can also **filter** the contents of a folder to display only files and folders with certain characteristics, such as all those you modified yesterday. In short, sorting reorganizes all of the files and folders in a list, while filtering displays only those files and folders that share a characteristic you specify. Both actions change your view of the files and folders, not the items themselves.

Windows 10 provides another way to change the view of your files and folders—grouping. When you group your files by type, for example, Windows separates the files into several groups, such as Microsoft Word documents in one group and photo files in another group.

PROSKILLS

Problem Solving: Preventing Lost File Problems

Many computer users, even very experienced ones, fall into the trap of saving or moving a file to a folder and then forgetting where it's stored. You can prevent these types of lost file problems by managing your files systematically. To manage files so you know where to find them later, start by formulating a logical plan for organizing your files. Some people sketch a simple diagram of the file structure to help them visualize where to store files. Next, create the folders you need to store the files, and then move and copy your existing files into those folders. As you create files using applications, save them in an appropriate folder and use folder names and filenames that help you identify their contents. If possible, use a similar organization scheme in all of your folders. For example, if you organized the files for one project into subfolders such as Phase 1, Phase 2, Phase 3, and Follow Up, use the same organization for each project. To make it easier to find files, especially in a long file list, you can sort, filter, and group the files in a way that seems logical to you. Performing these basic management tasks helps you keep track of your files so you can easily find information when you need it.

You want to show Diego how to change the view of his files by sorting, filtering, and grouping so he can choose one view that makes the most sense for him or his current task.

Sorting and Filtering Files

TIP

To sort by a file detail that does not appear as a column heading, right-click any column heading and then select a file detail.

When you are working with a folder window in Details view, you can sort or filter the files using the column headings in the right pane of the window. To sort files by type, for example, click the Type column heading. You can sort files in ascending order (A to Z, 0 to 9, or earliest to latest date) or descending order (Z to A, 9 to 0, or latest to earliest date). To switch the order, click the column heading again.

Sorting is often an effective way to find a file or folder in a relatively short file list. By default, Windows 10 sorts the contents of a folder in ascending alphabetic order by filename, with any subfolders listed before the files. A file named April Marketing appears at the top of the list, and a file named Winter Expenses appears at the end. You can change the sort criterion to list files according to any other file characteristic.

If you are working with a longer file list, filtering the list might help you find the file you want. To filter the contents of a folder, you click the arrow button to the right of a column heading, and then click one or more file properties such as a specific filename, created or modified date, author, or file type. Windows displays only files and folders with those properties. For example, if you want to list only music files by a particular artist, you can filter by that artist's name.

Details view always includes column headings corresponding to file details. To sort files in other views that do not display column headings, you can right-click a blank area of the folder window, point to Sort by on the shortcut menu, and then click a file detail such as Type. (You cannot filter files in views without column headings.)

To sort and filter the files in the Sights folder:

1. Navigate to the Sights folder and then click the **Details** button on the status bar, if necessary, to switch to Details view.
2. Click the **Type** column heading to sort the files in ascending order according to file type. A sort arrow appears above the Type column heading label. The sort arrow points up to indicate the column is sorted in ascending order.

   Trouble? If the Type column does not appear in your folder window, right-click any column heading and then click Type. Then complete Step 3.

3. Click the **Type** column heading again to reverse the sort order. The sort arrow now points down, indicating the column is sorted in descending order.
4. Right-click any column heading to display a list of file details. Details with a check mark are displayed in the folder window. If the Date modified column heading does not appear in your folder window, click **Date modified** to display this column. Otherwise, click a blank area of the window. Your folder window should now display only the Name, Date modified, Type, and Size columns.

   Trouble? If your folder window contains columns other than Name, Date modified, Type, and Size, right-click any column heading, and then click the name of the column you want to remove from the folder window. The content of the column is not deleted; it is just no longer visible on-screen.
5. Click the **Date modified** column heading to sort the files in descending chronological order by the date they were modified. See Figure 2-17.

Figure 2-17 Sorting files by date

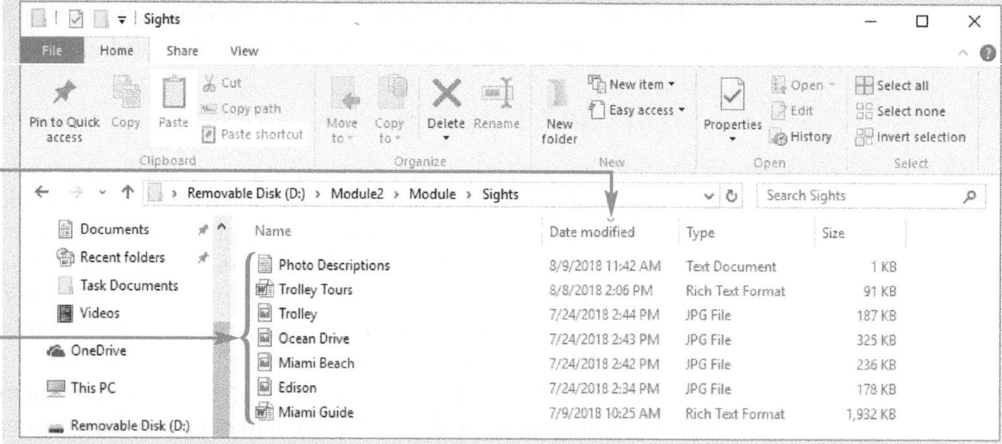

To compare sorting and filtering, you can filter the files by their modified date to display only the files you modified today.

TIP

When you sort files by Date modified with the most recent files on top, you can quickly find the files you modified recently.

6. Point to the **Date modified** column heading, and then click its **arrow** button to the right of the column heading to display a list of filtering options.

   Trouble? If the files are sorted in ascending order by Date modified, you clicked the sort arrow. Click the Date modified sort arrow again to sort the files in descending order, and then repeat Step 6.
7. Click the **Today** check box to select today's date. The folder window displays only the Photo Descriptions file. See Figure 2-18.

   Trouble? If you modified the Photo Descriptions file on a different date, click that date on the calendar.

   Trouble? If you clicked Today rather than the check box, skip Step 8.

Figure 2-18 **Filtering to display files modified today**

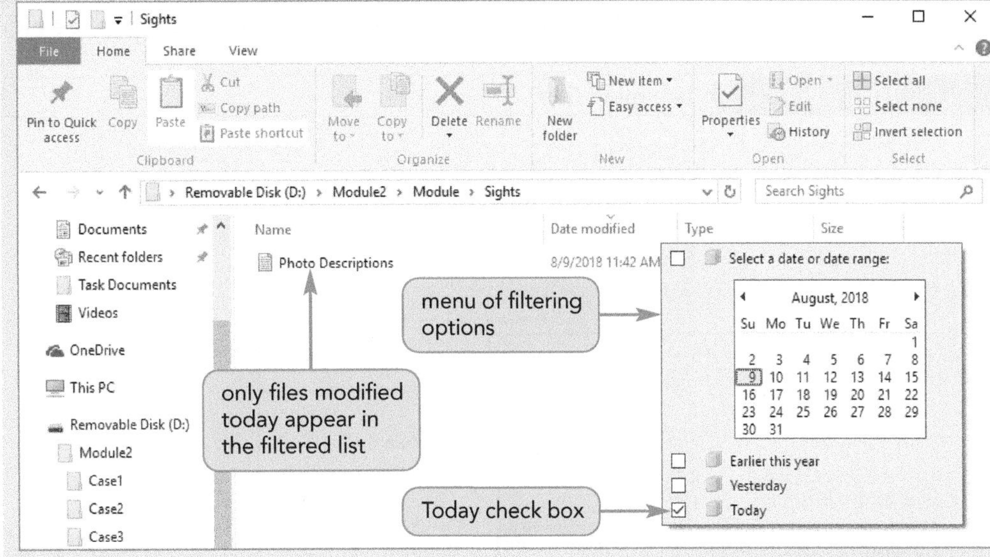

Note that you can filter by two or more properties by selecting the corresponding check boxes.

8. Click a blank area of the window to close the list. A check mark appears next to the Date modified column heading to indicate the file list is filtered by a Date modified detail.

Next, you can group the files in the Sights folder and compare this view to the views displayed when you sorted and filtered the files.

Grouping Files

To change your view of files and folders, you can group them—a technique that is especially effective when you are working with long file lists. You can group files according to any file detail such as Type or Authors. To group files by author, for example, you can right-click a blank area of the window, point to Group by, click More, and then click Authors. Windows divides the folder window into sections, with one section listing files you wrote, for example, and another section for files your colleague wrote.

Before grouping files, you must remove any filters you are using in the folder window. If you don't, you'll rearrange only the files that appear in the filtered list. After removing the filter, you'll group the files in the Sights folder by type using the Group by option in the Current view group on the View tab.

To remove the filter and group the files in the Sights folder:

1. In the Sights folder window, click the **check mark** on the Date modified column heading, and then click the **Today** check box (or the **Select a date or date range** check box if you selected a date on the calendar earlier) to clear the check box. Click a blank area of the folder window. The complete list of Sights files appears in the right pane.

2. Click the **View** tab on the ribbon, click the **Group by** button in the Current view group, and then click **Type**. Windows arranges all the files in the Sights folder into three groups, one for each file type. See Figure 2-19.

Figure 2-19 Grouping files

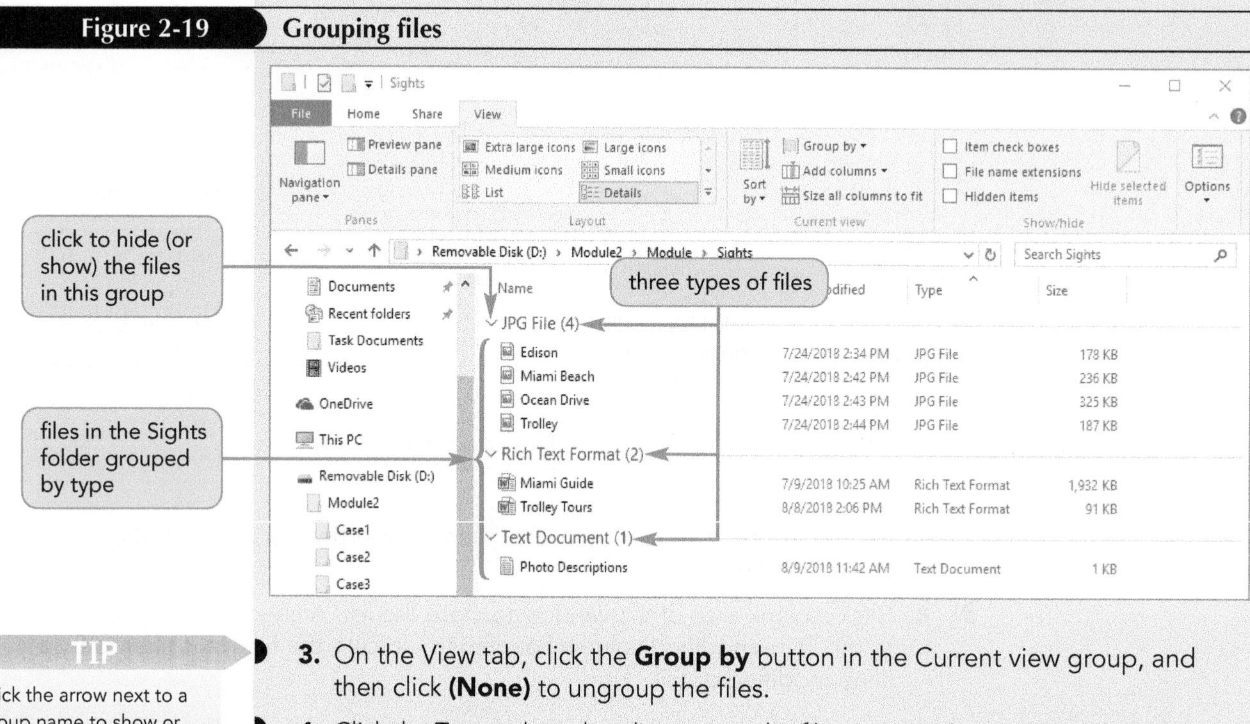

TIP

Click the arrow next to a group name to show or hide a group of files.

3. On the View tab, click the **Group by** button in the Current view group, and then click **(None)** to ungroup the files.
4. Click the **Type** column heading to sort the files in ascending order again by type.

Now that Diego knows how to sort, filter, and group files in a folder window, he mentions that he might want to hide or show elements of the folder window itself, such as the navigation pane. You'll show him how to customize the folder window next.

Customizing a Folder Window

As you learned earlier, you can change how you view your files and folders in a folder window, such as changing from large icons to a detailed list. You can make other changes to the layout of your folder windows. For example, you can hide the navigation pane to devote more space to file lists. The View tab includes options you can use to fine-tune the layout of a folder window. You have already used some options in the Current view and Layout groups. Figure 2-20 summarizes all the options on the View tab.

Figure 2-20 View tab options

Group	Option	Description
Panes	Navigation pane	Show or hide the navigation pane in this window only, and specify whether to expand the navigation pane to the open folder, show all folders, or show libraries, containers for built-in folders such as Documents and Pictures.
	Preview pane	Show or hide the Preview pane. When you select this option, you can preview the contents of a file without having to open an application.
	Details pane	Show or hide the Details pane. When you select this option, you display the most common properties associated with a selected file, such as the author of the file or its type.
Layout	View options	Select one of eight views for displaying the contents of the current folder: Extra large icons, Large icons, Medium icons, Small icons, List, Details, Tiles, Content.
Current view	Sort by	Select a file property to use for sorting, select ascending or descending sort order, and choose one or more columns to display in the current folder window.
	Group by	Group files by a file detail displayed in the current folder window.
	Add columns	Select a file detail to display as a column in the current folder window or choose a file detail not included in the list.
	Size all columns to fit	Change the width of all columns to fit the contents.
Show/ hide	Item check boxes	Show or hide check boxes next to files and folders; use the check boxes to select items.
	File name extensions	Show or hide the extensions for all files in the current folder window.
	Hidden items	Show or hide the files and folders marked as hidden.
	Hide selected items	Hide the selected files or folders.
	Options	Use the Folder Options dialog box to change settings for opening items, file and folder views, and searching.

You'll show Diego how to change the layout of a folder window, and then how to customize the appearance of the folder contents. Finally, you'll demonstrate how to add items to the navigation pane to suit the way he works.

Changing the Layout of a Folder Window

You can change the layout of a folder window by showing or hiding the navigation pane and either the Preview pane or the Details pane. The **Preview pane** appears on the right side of a folder window and displays the contents of a selected picture file and some other types of files. The Details pane also appears on the right and provides information about a selected file, such as the author and file type. Only one of these panes can be open in a folder window. Neither pane appears by default. Figure 2-21 shows a folder window with the Navigation and Preview panes open.

Figure 2-21 Folder window displaying the navigation and Preview panes

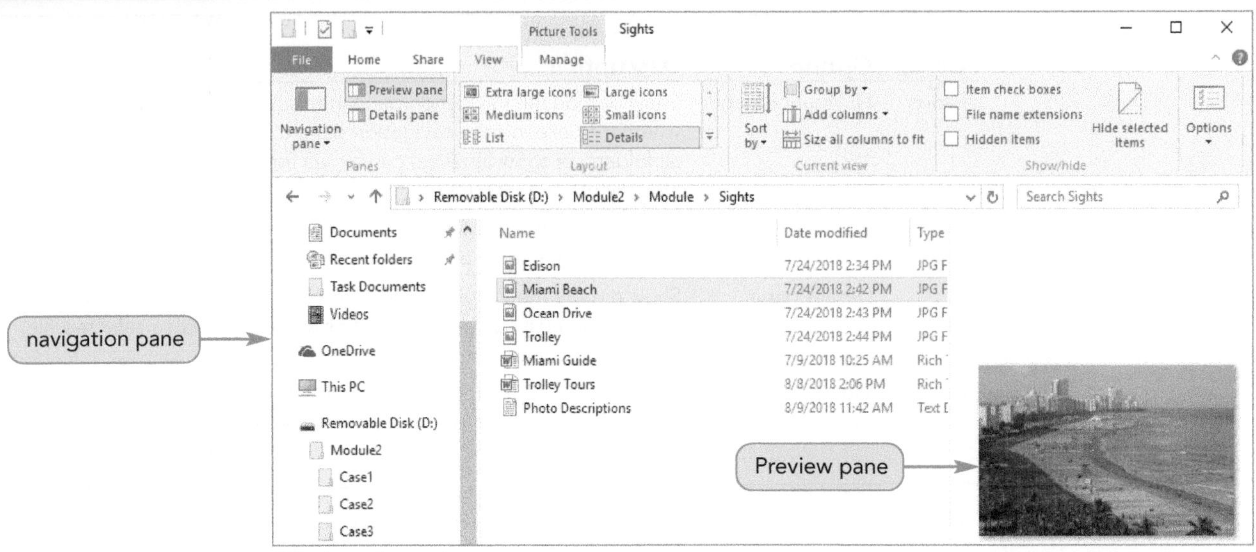

©iStock.com/bosenok

Diego wants to see if he likes having the Details pane in the folder window, so he asks you to display that pane. He is also curious about the Preview pane, so you'll open that for him first. The Sights folder window should currently be open in Details view, with files sorted according to type.

To change the layout of a folder window:

1. Click the **Edison** file to select it, click the **View** tab on the ribbon, if necessary, and then click the **Preview pane** button in the Panes group to display the Preview pane.
2. On the View tab, click the **Details pane** button in the Panes group to close the Preview pane and display the Details pane. See Figure 2-22. Your file details might vary.

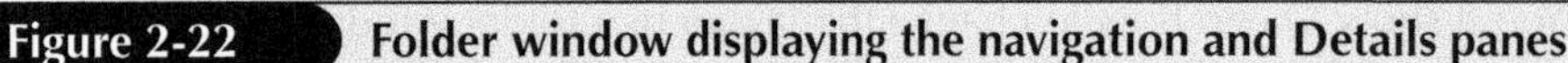

Figure 2-22 Folder window displaying the navigation and Details panes

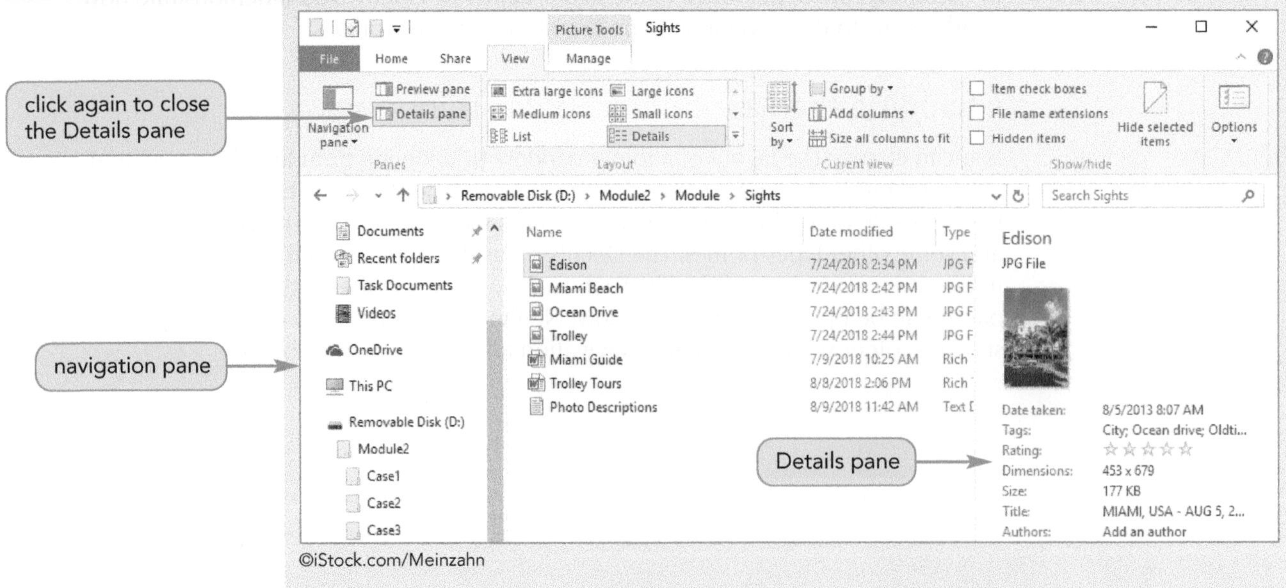

©iStock.com/Meinzahn

You can also use options in the Show/hide group on the View tab to customize the file list.

Customizing the File List

TIP

Windows hides filename extensions only for file types it can identify. If it can't identify the file type, Windows always displays the extension.

Although Windows 10 refers to a filename extension to identify a file's type, filename extensions are not displayed by default in a folder window. Windows hides the extensions to make filenames easier to read, especially for long filenames. If you prefer to display filename extensions, you can show them in all the folder windows (as you do in the following steps).

Another type of file not displayed by default in a folder window is a **hidden file**. Windows hides many types of files, including temporary files it creates before you save a document. It hides these files so that you do not become confused by temporary filenames, which are similar to the names of the files you save on your computer. By default, Windows 10 also hides system files, which are files the operating system needs to work properly. You should keep these files hidden unless a reliable expert, such as a technical support professional, instructs you to display them. Keep in mind that hidden files still take up space on your disk.

You use the options in the Show/hide group on the View tab to show and hide filename extensions in all windows. To show and hide hidden files, you use the Folder Options dialog box.

To show filename extensions:

1. On the View tab, click the **File name extensions** check box in the Show/hide group to insert a check mark so filename extensions appear in all windows. See Figure 2-23.

Figure 2-23 Folder window showing filename extensions

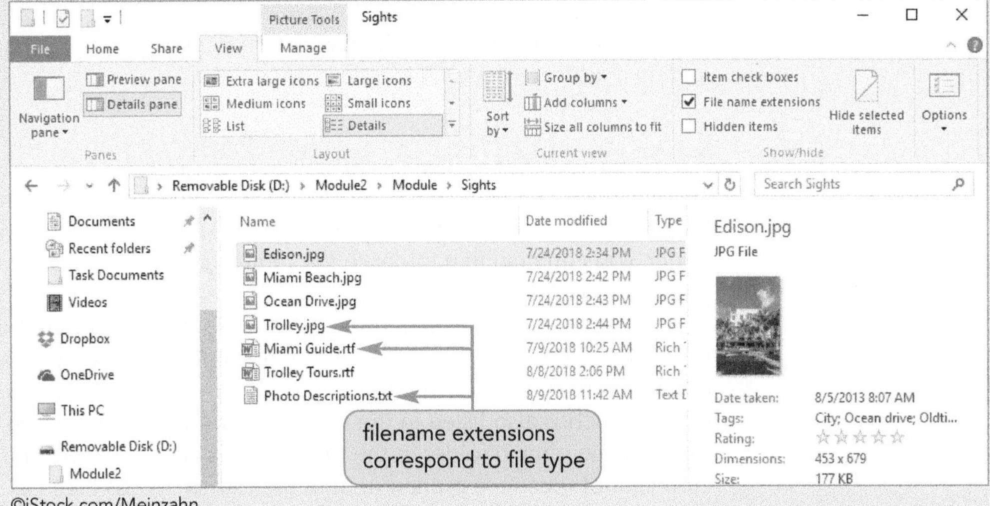
filename extensions correspond to file type

©iStock.com/Meinzahn

2. Click the **Options** button to open the Folder Options dialog box.
3. Click the **View** tab in the Folder Options dialog box. See Figure 2-24. The settings selected on the View tab of your Folder Options dialog box might differ.

TIP

To display This PC instead of the Quick access list when File Explorer opens, change the Open File Explorer to option on the General tab of the Folder Options dialog box to This PC.

Figure 2-24 Folder Options dialog box

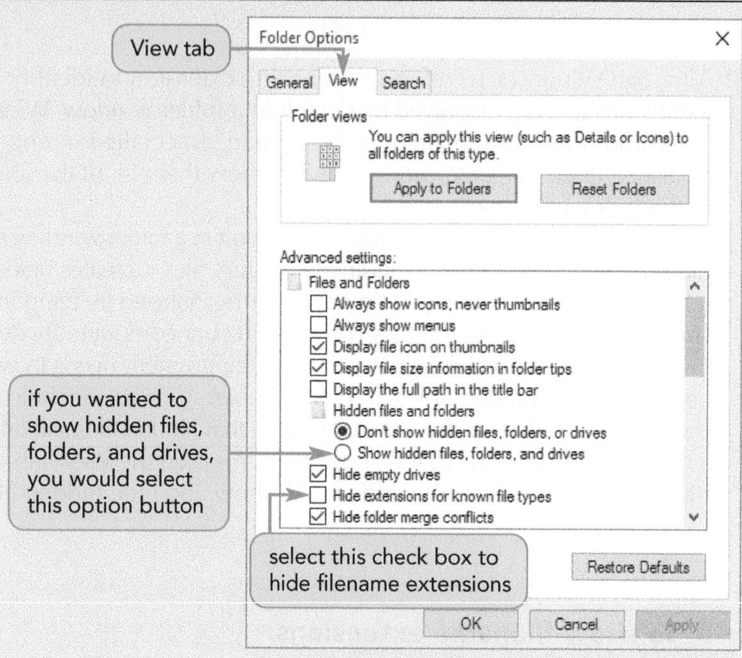

4. Click the **Hide extensions for known file types** check box to insert a check mark, and then click the **OK** button to hide the filename extensions again.

   Trouble? If the Hide extensions for known file types check box already contains a check mark, just close the dialog box.

Next, you can customize the navigation pane by changing its appearance and adding a folder to the Quick access list.

Customizing the Navigation Pane

You can customize the navigation pane by adding, renaming, and removing items in the Quick access list. For example, if you use the navigation pane to open a particular folder, you can drag that folder to the Quick access list to make it one of the locations you access often.

TIP

When you unpin a folder from the Quick access list, you remove it from the Quick access list only; you do not delete the folder itself.

To customize your navigation pane, you'll start by **pinning** the Task Documents folder to the Quick access list so it remains in the list, allowing you to access the folder quickly. Next, you'll rename the actual folder to distinguish it from the Documents folder, which is also listed in the navigation pane. When you do, Windows also renames the pinned folder in the Quick access list so the two names always match. (You cannot rename a pinned item in the Quick access list.) Later, when you restore the settings on your computer, you'll unpin the folder.

To customize the navigation pane:

1. Use any navigation method you've learned to display the folders in the Module folder. Scroll to the top of the navigation pane, if necessary.
2. Drag the **Task Documents** folder from the Module folder to the Quick access icon in the navigation pane. When the Pin to Quick access ScreenTip appears, release the mouse button to pin the Task Documents folder to the Quick access list. See Figure 2-25.

Figure 2-25 Task Documents folder pinned to the Quick access list

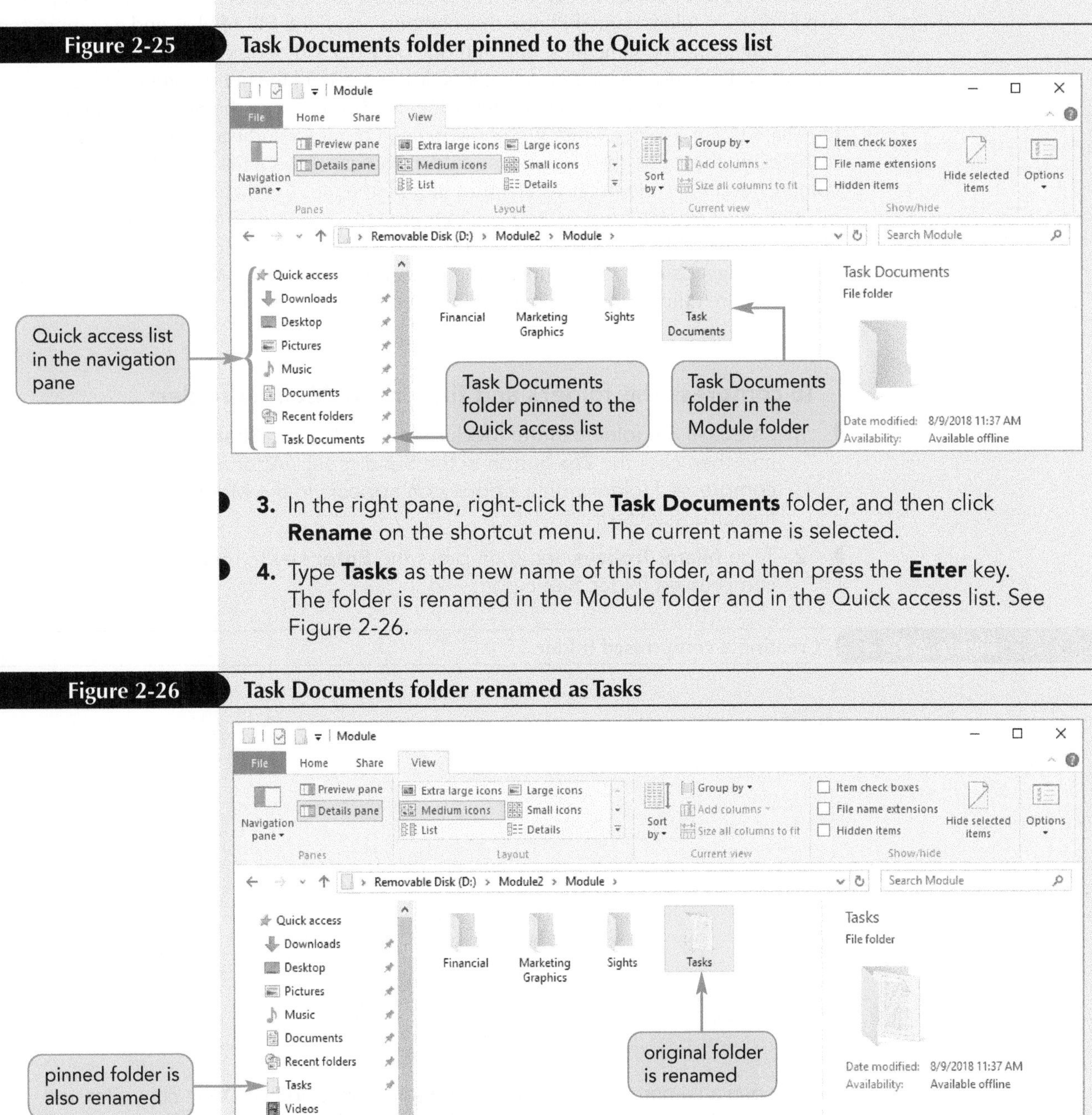

3. In the right pane, right-click the **Task Documents** folder, and then click **Rename** on the shortcut menu. The current name is selected.
4. Type **Tasks** as the new name of this folder, and then press the **Enter** key. The folder is renamed in the Module folder and in the Quick access list. See Figure 2-26.

Figure 2-26 Task Documents folder renamed as Tasks

Now that you've refined your file organization and customized the folder window, you are ready to show Diego two final tasks—compressing and extracting files.

Working with Compressed Files

If you transfer files from one location to another, such as from your hard disk to a removable disk or vice versa, or from one computer to another via email, you can store the files in a compressed (zipped) folder so that they take up less disk space. You can then transfer the files more quickly. If you or your email contacts can send and receive files only up to a certain size, compressing large files might make them small enough to send and receive. When you create a compressed folder using the Windows 10 compression tool, a zipper appears on the file folder icon.

You compress a folder so that the files it contains use less space on the disk. Compare two folders—a folder named Photos that contains about 8.6 MB of files, and a compressed folder containing the same files, but requiring only 6.5 MB of disk space. In this case, the compressed files use about 25 percent less disk space than the uncompressed files.

TIP

Another way to compress files is to select the files, right-click the selection, point to Send to on the shortcut menu, and then click Compressed (zipped) folder.

You can create a compressed folder using the Zip button in the Send group on the Share tab of a folder window. Then you can compress additional files or folders by dragging them into the compressed folder. You can open a file directly from a compressed folder, although you cannot modify the file. To edit and save a compressed file, you must extract it first. When you **extract** a file, you create an uncompressed copy of the file in a folder you specify. The original file remains in the compressed folder.

Diego suggests that you compress the files and folders in the Module folder so that you can more quickly transfer them to another location.

To compress the folders and files in the Module folder:

1. Select all the folders in the Module folder, click the **Share** tab on the ribbon, and then click the **Zip** button in the Send group. After a few moments, a new compressed folder with a zipper icon appears in the Module window with the filename selected.
2. Type **Miami Trolleys** and then press the **Enter** key to rename the compressed folder. See Figure 2-27.

Figure 2-27 Creating a compressed folder

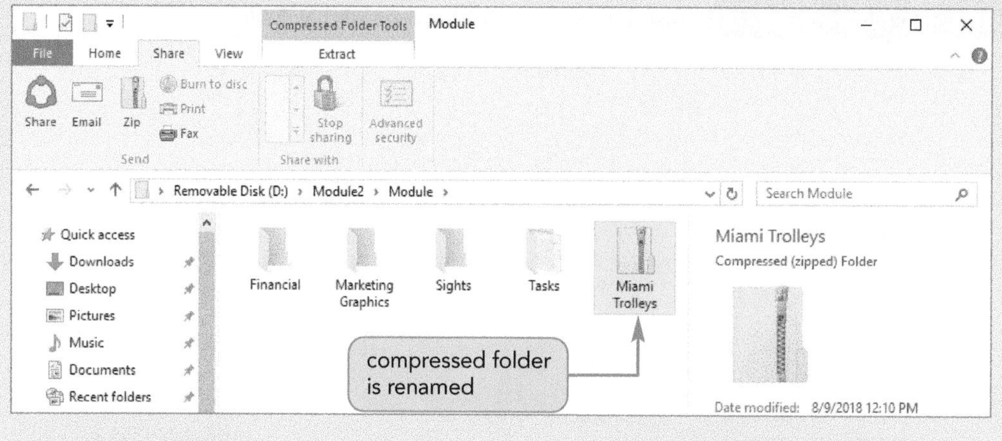

You open a compressed folder by double-clicking it. You can then copy files and folders from the opened compressed folder to other locations, although you cannot rename the files. More often, you extract all of the files in the compressed folder. Windows 10 then uncompresses and copies them to a location that you specify, preserving the files in their original folders as appropriate.

INSIGHT

Understanding Compressed File Types

Some types of files, such as JPG picture files (those with a .jpg or .jpeg filename extension), are already highly compressed. If you compress JPG (pronounced "jay peg") pictures into a folder, the total size of the compressed folder is about the same as the collection of uncompressed pictures. However, if you are transferring the files from one computer to another, such as by email, it's still a good idea to store the compressed files in a zipped folder to keep them together.

To extract the compressed files:

1. Click the **Compressed Folder Tools Extract** tab on the ribbon, and then click the **Extract all** button. The Extract Compressed (Zipped) Folders Wizard starts and opens the Select a Destination and Extract Files dialog box.
2. Press the **End** key to deselect the path in the box and move the insertion point to the end of the path, press the **Backspace** key as many times as necessary to delete the Miami Trolleys text, and then type **Backups**. The final three parts of the path in the box should be \Module2\Module\Backups. See Figure 2-28.

Figure 2-28 Extracting files from a compressed folder

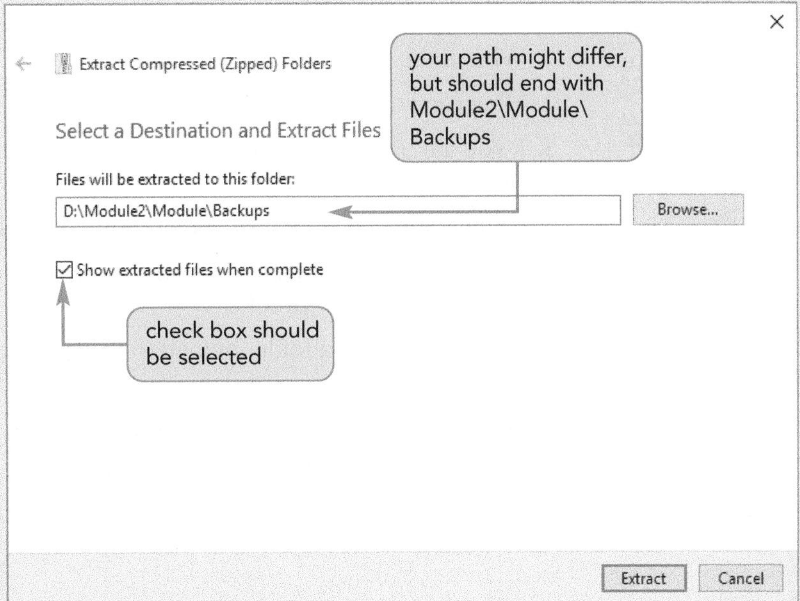

3. Make sure the Show extracted files when complete check box is checked, and then click the **Extract** button. Windows extracts the files and then opens the Backups folder, showing the Financial, Marketing Graphics, Sights, and Tasks folders.
4. Open each folder to make sure it contains the files you worked with in this module.
5. Close the Backups folder window, and then click a blank area of the Module folder window.

In this session, you renamed and deleted files according to your organization plan, and then created a file, saved it in a new folder, and opened and edited the file. Then you refined the organization of the files and folders, customized a folder window, and worked with compressed files. Before you end your Windows 10 session, you should restore your computer to its original settings.

Restoring Your Settings

If you are working in a computer lab or on a computer other than your own, complete the steps in this section to restore the original settings on the computer.

To restore your settings:

1. In the Module folder window, click the **View** tab, and then click the **Details pane** button in the Panes group to hide the Details pane in the folder window.
2. Right-click the **Tasks** folder in the Quick access list in the navigation pane, and then click **Unpin from Quick access**.
3. Close all open windows.

REVIEW

Session 2.2 Quick Check

1. What is the purpose of a filename extension?
2. How can you restore a file that you deleted from the hard disk?
3. If you are using Notepad to edit a text document named Project, how can you save it as a file named Project Steps?
4. Explain the difference between grouping and filtering files.
5. How is sorting a folder window by file type different when using Details view and Medium icons view?
6. What happens to a folder pinned to the Quick access list when you rename the original folder?
7. What is the purpose of compressing a folder?
8. Describe how to extract all the files from a compressed folder.

PRACTICE

Review Assignments

Data Files needed for the Review Assignments: Background.png, Calendar.rtf, Events.xlsx, Skyline.jpg, Walking.rtf, Welcome.jpg

Diego has saved a few files from his old computer on a removable disk. He gives you these files in a single, unorganized folder, and asks you to organize them logically into subfolders. He needs at least one subfolder for files related to a newsletter he is planning. Devise a plan for managing the files, and then create the subfolders you need. Next, rename, copy, move, and delete files, and perform other management tasks to make it easy for Diego to work with these files and folders. Complete the following steps:

1. Use File Explorer to navigate to and open the Module2 > Review folder provided with your Data Files. Examine the six files in this folder and consider possible ways to organize the files.
2. In the Review folder, create three folders: **Business**, **Newsletter**, and **Tours**.
3. To organize the files into the correct folders:
   - Move the Background and Calendar files from the Review folder to the Business folder.
   - Move the Events file to the Newsletter folder.
   - Move the Skyline, Walking, and Welcome files to the Tours folder.
4. Copy the Walking file in the Tours folder to the Newsletter folder.
5. Rename the Calendar file in the Business folder as **2018 Calendar**. Rename the Walking file in the Newsletter folder as **Walking Tours**.
6. Return to the Review folder and use the Search box to find a file whose filename begins with the text "back." Rename this file **Company Banner**.
7. Create a Notepad file that includes the following text:

   When to Visit Miami
   Nov - April: Perfect weather
   Dec - March: High season
   May - Sept: Hot and steamy
8. Save the Notepad file as **When to Go** in the Newsletter folder. Close the Notepad window.
9. Navigate to the Newsletter folder, open the When to Go file, and then add the following line to the end of the document: **Oct: Pleasant**.
10. Save the When to Go file with the same name and in the same location. Open a new document in Notepad, and then type the following text:

    Art Deco Hotels
    Cadillac Hotel
    McAlpin Hotel
11. Save the file as **Art Deco** in the Tours folder. Close Notepad.
12. Navigate to the Tours folder and then perform the following tasks:
    - Sort the files by Date modified. How many files appear in the folder window?
    - Filter the files by today's date (or the date you created the two text files). How many files appear in the folder window?
13. Remove the filter, and then group the files by type. How many types are displayed? How many files are displayed of each type?
14. Navigate to the Newsletter folder, and then display filename extensions in the folder window. Group the files by size. How many files are displayed of each type?
15. Change the layout of the folder window by displaying the Details pane, and then change the grouping to (None).
16. In the Review folder, add the Business folder to the Quick access list in the navigation pane. Rename the folder **MT Business**.

17. Open the MT Business folder, click the Company Banner.png file, and then press the Print Screen key to capture an image of the folder window. (*Hint:* Depending on the type of computer you are using, the Print Screen key might be labeled differently, for example, PrtScn.) Start Paint and then press the Ctrl+V keys to paste this image in a file. Save this file as **Review** in the Module2 > Review folder provided with your Data Files. Close Paint.
18. Restore your computer's settings by hiding the Details pane, hiding filename extensions in the folder window, and unpinning the MT Business folder from the Quick access list in the navigation pane.
19. Create a compressed (zipped) folder in the Review folder named **Miami** that contains all the files and folders in the Review folder.
20. Extract the contents of the Miami compressed folder to a new folder named **Miami Backups** in the Review folder. (*Hint:* The file path will end with \Module2\Review\Miami Backups.)
21. Close all open windows.

APPLY

Case Problem 1

See the Starting Data Files section at the beginning of this module for the list of Data Files needed for this Case Problem.

Art Glass Studio Shannon Beecher started the Art Glass Studio in Lake George, New York, to provide custom stained glass works for residential and commercial buildings. The business also holds classes on stained glass techniques for children and adults. Knowing you are multitalented, Shannon hired you to help her manage the front end of the studio and other parts of her growing business, including electronic business files. Your first task is to organize the files on her new Windows 10 computer. Complete the following steps:

1. In the Module2 > Case1 folder provided with your Data Files, create three folders: **Classes**, **Designs**, and **Marketing**.
2. Move the Advanced Classes, Beginner Classes, Intermediate Classes, and Kids Classes files from the Case1 folder to the Classes folder.
3. Rename the four files in the Classes folder by deleting the word Classes from each name.
4. Move the four JPG files from the Case1 folder to the Designs folder.
5. Copy the remaining two files to the Marketing folder. Also, copy the Designers file to the Designs folder.
6. Delete the Designers and Studio files from the Case1 folder.
7. Open the Recycle Bin folder by double-clicking the Recycle Bin icon on the desktop, and then display the window in Details view. Sort the contents of the Recycle Bin by filename in descending order.
8. Filter the files by their deletion date to display only the files you deleted today. (*Hint:* If you deleted files from the Case1 folder on a different date, click that date on the calendar.) Do the Designers and Studio files appear in the Recycle Bin folder? Explain why or why not. Remove the filter, and then close the Recycle Bin window.
9. Make a copy of the Designs folder in the Case1 folder. The name of the duplicate folder appears as Designs - Copy. Rename the Designs - Copy folder as **Sawyer Designs**.
10. Search for the Advanced file and then copy it to the Sawyer Designs folder. Rename this file **Sawyer Classes**.
11. Compress the four photo files in the Sawyer Designs folder in a new compressed folder named **Photos**, and then move the zipped Photos folder to the Case1 folder.
12. Close all open windows.

CHALLENGE

Case Problem 2

See the Starting Data Files section at the beginning of this module for the list of Data Files needed for this Case Problem.

Avant Web Design Dante Havens is the owner of Avant Web Design, a new website design company in Austin, Texas. You work as a part-time technology assistant at the company and spend some of your time organizing business files. Dante recently upgraded to Windows 10 and asks you to examine the folder structure and file system on his computer, and then begin organizing the files logically. Complete the following steps:

Explore 1. Open a folder window, click the OneDrive icon in the navigation pane, and then open and identify each folder that appears in the OneDrive folder window.
2. Examine the files in the Module2 > Case2 folder provided with your Data Files. Display the Details pane in the folder window and then select each file to display its details. Based on the filenames and the descriptions displayed in the Details pane, create an organization plan for the files.
3. In the Case2 folder, create the folders you need according to your plan.
4. Move the files from the Case2 folder to the subfolders you created.
5. Rename the spreadsheet files in each subfolder as follows. (*Hint:* If Microsoft Excel is not installed on your computer, Windows displays the .xlsx filename extension as you rename the files.)
   - Estimate01: **Websites**
   - Estimate02: **Costs**
   - Estimate03: **Trade Show**
   - Planner01: **Travel**
   - Planner02: **Kincaid**
   - Planner03: **Sorley**
6. Search for a file in the Case2 folder that contains "estimate" in its filename.
7. Open the text document you found, and then add the following tip at the end of the file: **Estimate technology separately**. Save and close the file.
8. Open the folder window for one of the subfolders you created.
9. Change the view of the folder window to Content. Press the Print Screen key to capture an image of the folder window. (*Hint:* Depending on the type of computer you are using, the Print Screen key might be labeled differently, for example, PrtScn.) Start Paint and then press the Ctrl+V keys to paste this image in a file. Save the image as **Content View** in the Module2 > Case2 folder provided with your Data Files. Close Paint.

Explore 10. In one of the Case2 subfolders, compress all Excel workbooks (that is, all .xlsx files) in a new compressed folder named **Spreadsheets** in the Case2 folder. (*Hint:* After you create the compressed folder, move it to the Case2 folder.)
11. Restore your settings by hiding the Details pane.
12. Close all open windows.

CHALLENGE

Case Problem 3

Data Files needed for this Case Problem: Checklist.docx, Client Chart.pdf, Clients.accdb, Clients.pptx, Training.pptx

Tamada Consulting Haruki Tamada founded Tamada Consulting to help small businesses in Tacoma, Washington, grow and prosper. Haruki recently installed Windows 10 on the company's computers, and now finds that he cannot open some files with any installed application. You offer to help him identify the file types and organize the files. Complete the following:

1. Examine the files in the Module2 > Case3 folder provided with your Data Files. In the Case3 folder, create the subfolders you need to organize the files.
2. Use the View tab on the ribbon to display the filename extensions for all of these files. List the filename extensions not already discussed in this module.
3. **Explore** Use your favorite search engine to find information about each file type you listed in Step 2. For example, search for PDF files to learn what type of application can open files with a .pdf extension.
4. Move the files from the Case3 folder to the subfolders you created.
5. Open the Checklist file in an application, read the contents, and then close the application. Based on the contents of the Checklist file, move it to a different folder, if necessary.
6. **Explore** Open the Checklist file in its new location. Type your name at the beginning of the file, and then use the Save As dialog box to save the file as a different type, such as .rtf or .txt, but using the same location. (*Hint:* Click the Save as type arrow, and then click a file type.) Close the application.
7. Double-click any other file in a Case3 subfolder and describe what happens.
8. **Explore** If an application did not start when you double-clicked the file in Step 7, right-click the file, and then click Open with. If you are connected to the Internet, look for an app in the Windows Store that might open this file. Go to the Windows Store and scroll through apps, looking for one that might open the file. Return to the desktop. Describe what you found.
9. Close all open windows.

RESEARCH

Case Problem 4

There are no Data Files needed for this Case Problem.

Business-Centric Brenda Lindauer owns Business-Centric, a corporate training firm in Minneapolis, Minnesota. Brenda and her staff use Windows 10 laptop and tablet computers when they meet with clients to record their training needs. You are working as a technology intern to teach the staff about using their computers efficiently. One common problem is losing versions of files they have created for clients. Brenda asks you to research this problem so the staff can avoid losing files in Windows 10. Complete the following:

1. Windows 10 provides a feature called File History, which will be very helpful to the company employees. Search Windows websites to find information on File History. What is the purpose of this feature?
2. Search the Windows 10 How-to webpages to learn how to use OneDrive to back up files.
3. Search the Windows 10 How-to webpages to find topics about restoring (or recovering) files. Which Windows 10 tools let you restore (or recover) files?
4. Search the Windows 10 How-to webpages to learn about system image backups. What is a system image and why would you create one?

MODULE 3

Personalizing Your Windows Environment

Changing Desktop Settings

WINDOWS

OBJECTIVES

Session 3.1
- Explore the Settings app and the Control Panel
- Customize the desktop and lock screen
- Change display settings
- Personalize desktop icons
- Create desktop shortcuts

Session 3.2
- Modify the taskbar
- Use taskbar tools
- Personalize the Start menu
- Pin items to the Start menu
- Change the user account picture

Case | *Crafted Quilts*

Crafted Quilts is a business based in Springfield, Massachusetts, that sells custom quilts directly to customers through a website and a retail store. Rachel Shearer started the company with Mai Vang about two years ago. Mai now travels throughout the United States to find antique quilts and to contract with quilters, while Rachel runs the website and manages the store in Springfield.

You have been working as the office manager for Crafted Quilts for a few months, providing general assistance to Rachel, Mai, and the staff. Rachel recently upgraded the office computers to Windows 10, and now she asks you to customize those computers so that everyone can access frequently used apps, important files, and computer resources. She also wants the desktop to reflect the image of Crafted Quilts. You will start by personalizing Rachel's computer so she can approve the changes. Later, she will apply the changes to the other office computers.

STARTING DATA FILES

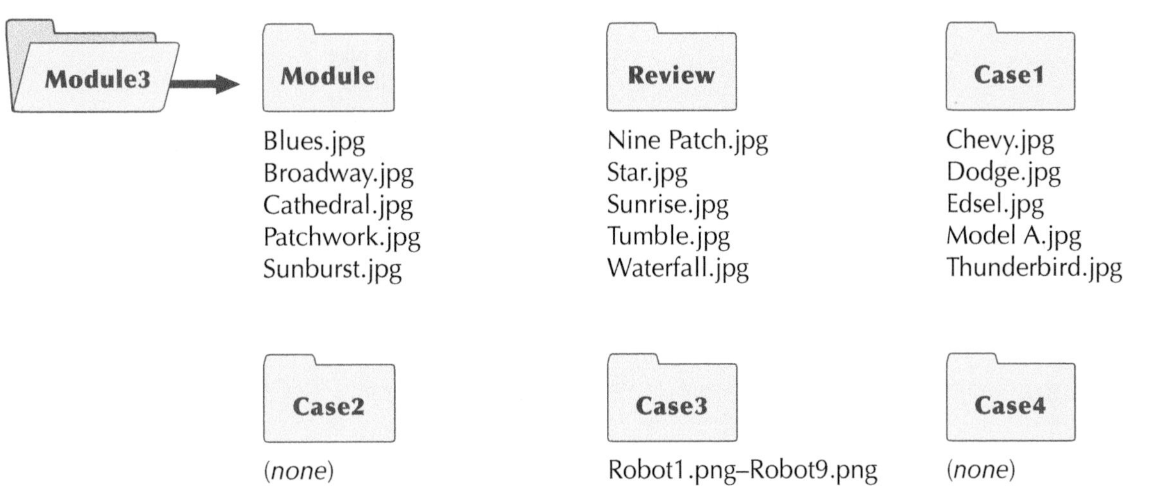

Session 3.1 Visual Overview:

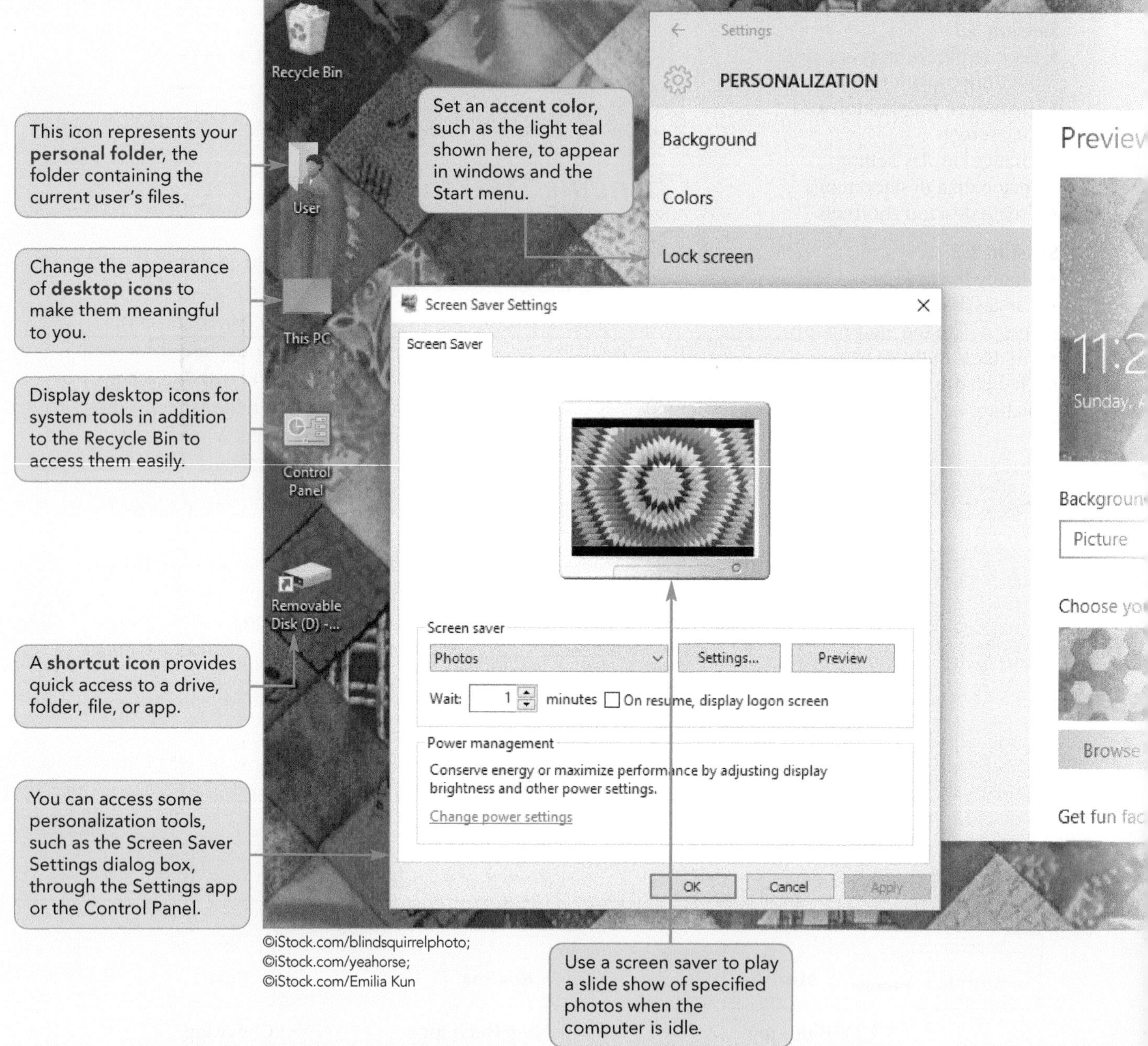
This icon represents your **personal folder**, the folder containing the current user's files.
Change the appearance of **desktop icons** to make them meaningful to you.
Display desktop icons for system tools in addition to the Recycle Bin to access them easily.
A **shortcut icon** provides quick access to a drive, folder, file, or app.
You can access some personalization tools, such as the Screen Saver Settings dialog box, through the Settings app or the Control Panel.
Set an **accent color**, such as the light teal shown here, to appear in windows and the Start menu.
Use a screen saver to play a slide show of specified photos when the computer is idle.
Recycle Bin
User
This PC
Control Panel
Removable Disk (D) -...
Settings
PERSONALIZATION
Background
Colors
Lock screen
Screen Saver Settings
Screen Saver
Screen saver
Photos
Settings...
Preview
Wait: 1 minutes On resume, display logon screen
Power management
Conserve energy or maximize performance by adjusting display brightness and other power settings.
Change power settings
OK
Cancel
Apply

©iStock.com/blindsquirrelphoto;
©iStock.com/yeahorse;
©iStock.com/Emilia Kun

Customized Desktop

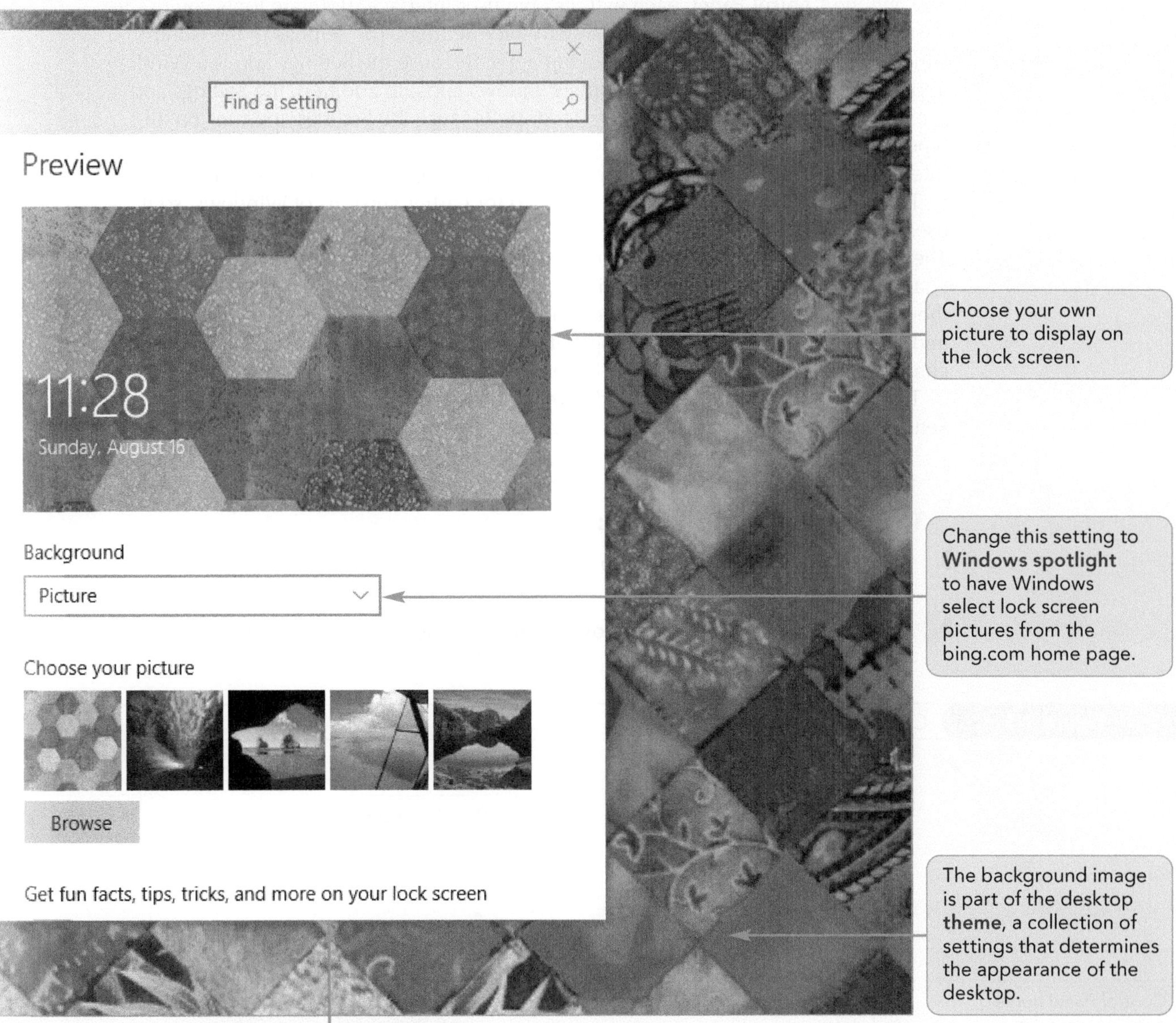

Choose your own picture to display on the lock screen.

Change this setting to **Windows spotlight** to have Windows select lock screen pictures from the bing.com home page.

The background image is part of the desktop **theme**, a collection of settings that determines the appearance of the desktop.

The Personalization window is part of the **Settings app**, a Windows app for changing system settings.

Changing Windows Settings

Windows 10 provides two ways to customize your computer's settings: the Settings app and the **Control Panel**, each with its own user interface. Both are tools you use to customize the computer and select system-wide settings. The settings in the Control Panel affect only the desktop and desktop apps. Because the Settings app is a Windows app, it includes settings that affect only Windows apps. In addition, the Settings app provides settings for customizing the desktop. Because the Settings app runs on all types of Windows devices, including tablets and phones, it provides a touch-friendly interface, so you change many settings using a fingertip if you have a touchscreen.

The Control Panel was originally designed for earlier versions of Windows, so it uses a design familiar to users of desktop and laptop computers without touchscreens. The Control Panel provides access to traditional dialog boxes that let you select or change the **properties**, or characteristics, of an object. For example, you can change the picture displayed for the Recycle Bin icon on the desktop. Both the Control Panel and the Settings app organize settings into similar categories, allowing you to easily change the way Windows looks and behaves to better suit the way you work.

To become acquainted with the difference between the Control Panel and the Settings app, you'll open their main windows, beginning with the Control Panel.

To open the Control Panel:

1. Click the **Start** button to display the Start menu, and then type **Control Panel** to search for the app.
2. In the search results, click **Control Panel** to open the Control Panel home page. See Figure 3-1.

Figure 3-1 Control Panel home page

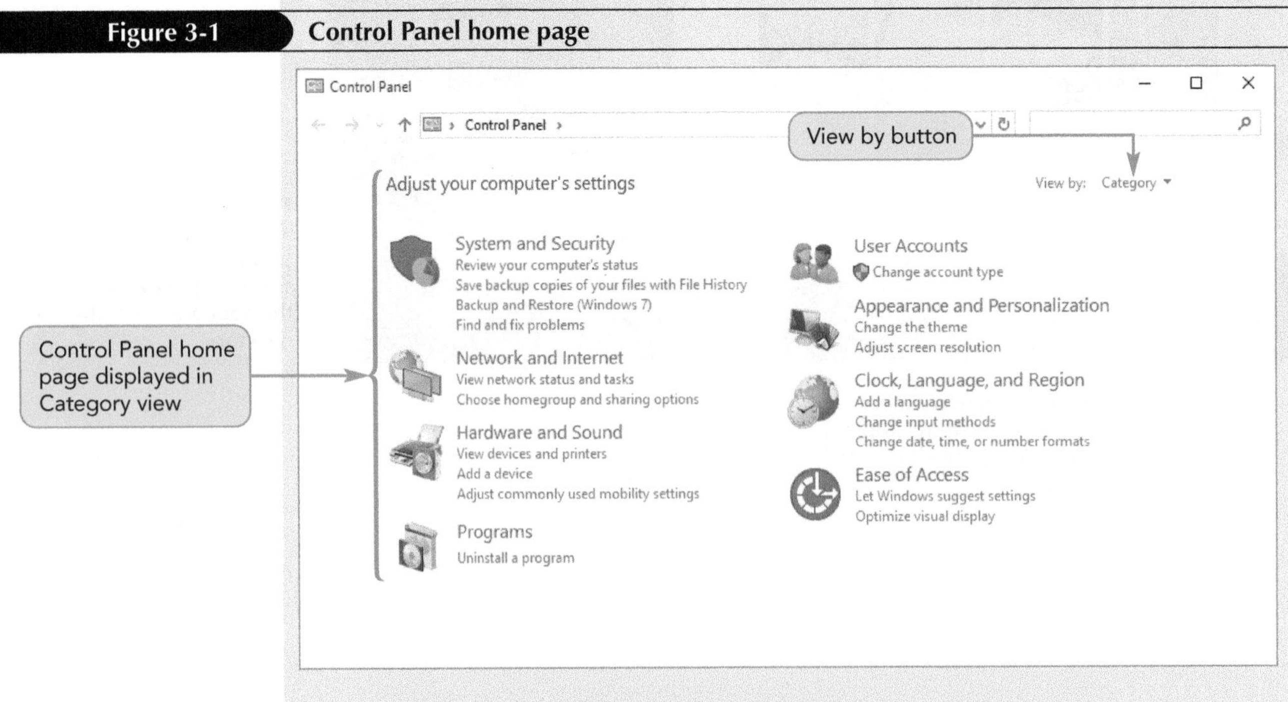

Trouble? If your window doesn't look like the one in the figure, click the View by button, and then click Category.

Trouble? If your icons look slightly different from those in the figure, Microsoft updated the icons, which it does from time to time. The appearance of the icons does not affect the way the Control Panel works.

By default, the Control Panel home page displays tools in Category view, which groups similar tools into eight categories. See Figure 3-2.

Figure 3-2 Control Panel categories

Control Panel Category	Typical Tasks
System and Security	Schedule maintenance checks, increase the space on your hard disk, maintain Windows security settings, and keep Windows up to date.
Network and Internet	Set Internet options, view network status, and set up a homegroup to share files and perform other network tasks.
Hardware and Sound	Change the sounds on your computer, and change the settings for your printer, keyboard, mouse, camera, and other hardware.
Programs	Install and uninstall programs and Windows features, and set options for default settings and programs.
User Accounts	Change user account settings and set email options.
Appearance and Personalization	Change the appearance of desktop items, apply a theme or screen saver, and customize the Start menu and taskbar.
Clock, Language, and Region	Change the date, time, and time zone; the language you use on your computer; and the format for numbers, currencies, dates, and times.
Ease of Access	Change computer settings for vision, hearing, and mobility.

For most of the customization settings you change in this module, you can use the Settings app, so you can begin your work for Crafted Quilts by closing the Control Panel, starting the Settings app, and then examining its categories of settings.

To start the Settings app:

1. Close the Control Panel window.
2. Click the **Start** button ⊞ to display the Start menu, and then click **Settings** to start the Settings app. See Figure 3-3.

Figure 3-3 Settings app

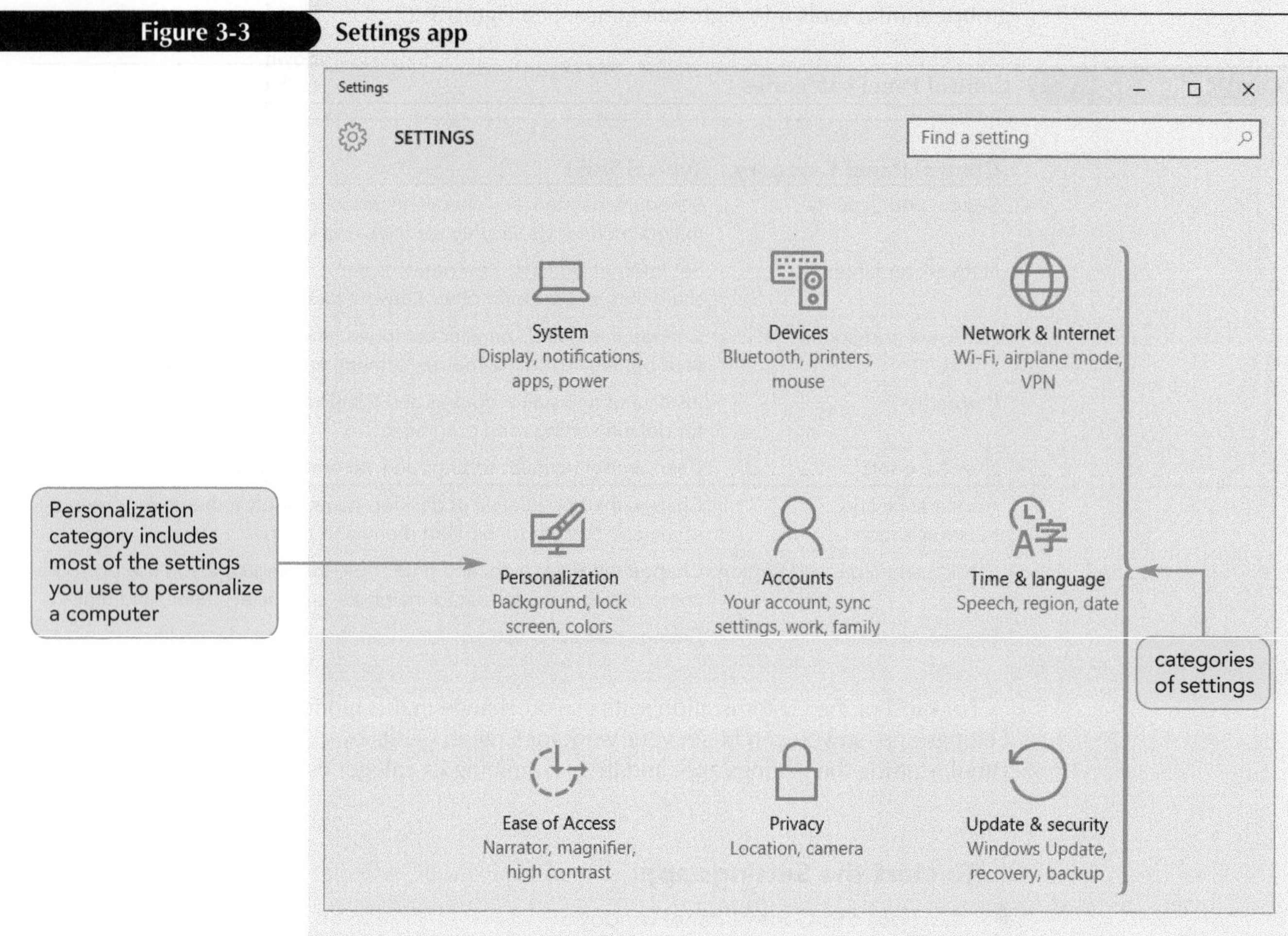

The main screen of the Settings app is also called the Settings home page. It lists nine categories of settings you can change in Windows. Figure 3-4 describes these categories.

Figure 3-4 Settings app categories

Category	Change Settings for:
System	Display, notifications, apps, power, and system
Devices	Printers and scanners, connected devices, Bluetooth devices, and mouse and touchpad, typing, and AutoPlay behavior
Network & Internet	Wi-Fi, airplane mode, data usage, and network connections
Personalization	Desktop background, system colors, lock screen, themes, and Start menu
Accounts	User accounts, sign-in options, and synchronizing with other Windows devices
Time & language	Date, time, time zone, and the language you use on your computer
Ease of Access	Vision, hearing, and mobility features
Privacy	Privacy options related to location, camera, microphone, Windows apps, and devices
Update & security	Windows updates and computer and data protection

Some of the categories in the Settings app, such as the Ease of Access category, provide the same type of settings as the Control Panel but use a Windows app interface. Other categories, such as Personalization, let you change settings using the Control Panel but are included in the Settings app for convenience.

To change a particular setting, you can select a category to open a category window, which lists the settings you can change. For example, you can open the Personalization window to change the desktop background or to set a theme.

To open the Personalization window:

1. On the Settings home page, click **Personalization**. The Personalization window opens, showing the settings related to personalizing your computer's appearance. See Figure 3-5. Your current settings and options might differ.

Figure 3-5 **Personalization window**

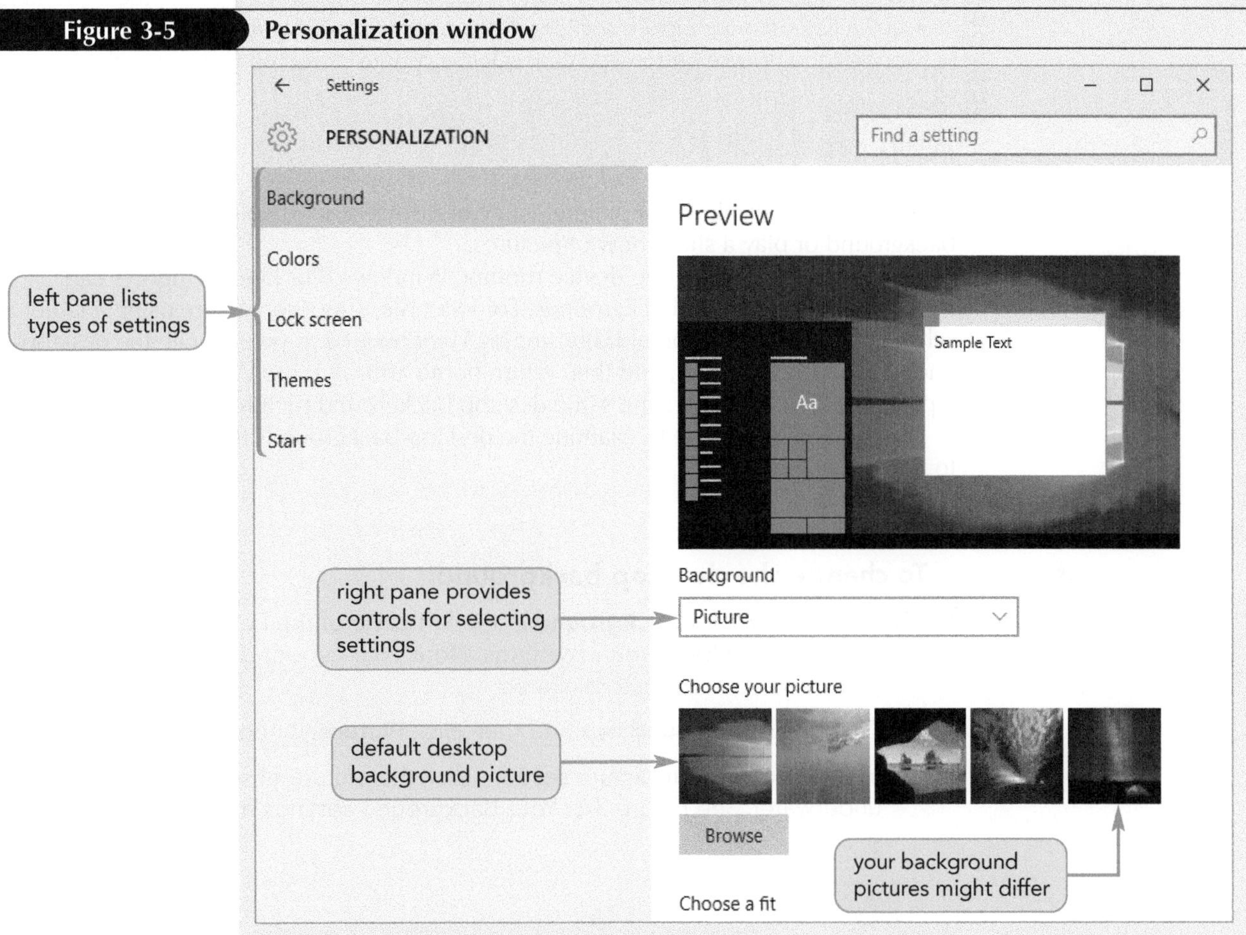

The Personalization window, like the other category windows in the Settings app, lists types of settings in the left pane. The right pane is a panel with controls for changing the selected type of setting. Background is selected by default. You use the Background settings in the right pane to change the picture displayed on the desktop background and set other background options.

While Mai is on a buying trip, you'll work with Rachel to customize her computer. She wants the office computers to reflect the image of Crafted Quilts, and she'd like the desktop itself to be more appealing to her and her employees. You'll work with the Settings app to personalize Rachel's desktop.

Changing the Desktop Background

TIP

To display any picture saved on your computer as your desktop background, right-click the picture and then click Set as desktop background.

You can change the desktop background, or its **wallpaper**, to display one of the pictures that Windows provides, or you can select your own picture to use as wallpaper. When you change the background, you are not placing a new object on the desktop; you are only changing its appearance. You can also determine how you want to position the picture—resized to fill the screen, resized to fit the screen, stretched across the screen (which might distort the picture), tiled (repeated across the screen), or centered. If you center the picture on the screen, you can select a color to frame the background picture.

REFERENCE

Changing the Desktop Picture

- Click the Start button and then click Settings.
- Click Personalization and then click Picture in the Background box in the right pane.
- In the Choose your picture section, click a picture to display as the desktop background, or click the Browse button and then select a picture stored on your computer.

In addition to displaying a picture, you can display a solid color as the desktop background or play a slide show of pictures.

If you have more than one device running Windows 8 or later, Windows can synchronize the desktop backgrounds. For example, suppose you are using a tablet at school and a laptop at home, both running Windows 10. If you change the desktop background on the tablet, and then return home and sign into Windows 10 on your laptop, the laptop displays the same desktop background picture as the tablet.

You and Rachel decide to examine the desktop backgrounds that Windows provides to find a suitable picture.

To change the desktop background:

1. If necessary, click **Background** in the left pane of the Personalization window to display the Background settings. Note your current desktop background picture so you can restore it later.
2. Click the **Background** box and then click **Picture**, if necessary.
3. In the Choose your picture section, click the picture of someone swimming underwater. See Figure 3-6. Your Background settings might differ.

Figure 3-6 **Background settings**

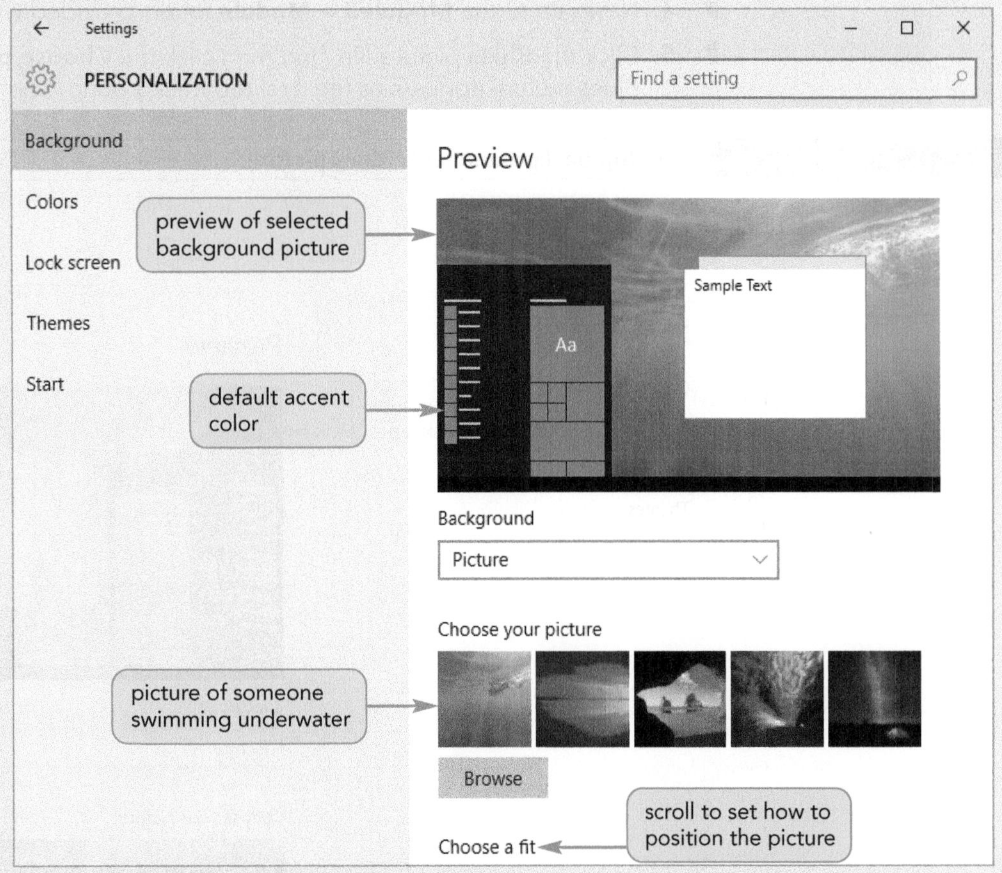

Trouble? If the picture of someone swimming underwater isn't available, choose any picture other than the current one.

4. Minimize the Personalization window to see the new background picture.

After examining the desktop, Rachel doesn't think the underwater picture is right for her business. However, she didn't notice other more appropriate pictures in the Choose your picture section of the Background settings. She does have a picture of a quilt that she often uses in promotional materials. You offer to show her how to use that picture as the desktop background.

To use a different picture as the desktop background:

1. Make sure your computer can access your Data Files for this module. For example, if you are using a USB flash drive, insert the drive into the USB port.

   Trouble? If you don't have the starting Data Files, you need to get them before you can proceed. Your instructor will either give you the Data Files or ask you to obtain them from a specified location (such as a network drive). If you have any questions about the Data Files, see your instructor or technical support person for assistance.

2. Click the **Settings** button on the taskbar to restore the Personalization window.

3. Click the **Browse** button to open the Open dialog box.
4. Navigate to the **Module3 > Module** folder provided with your Data Files.
5. Click the **Blues** picture file, and then click the **Choose picture** button. The Blues picture appears as the desktop background. See Figure 3-7.

Figure 3-7 **Desktop background with Blues picture**

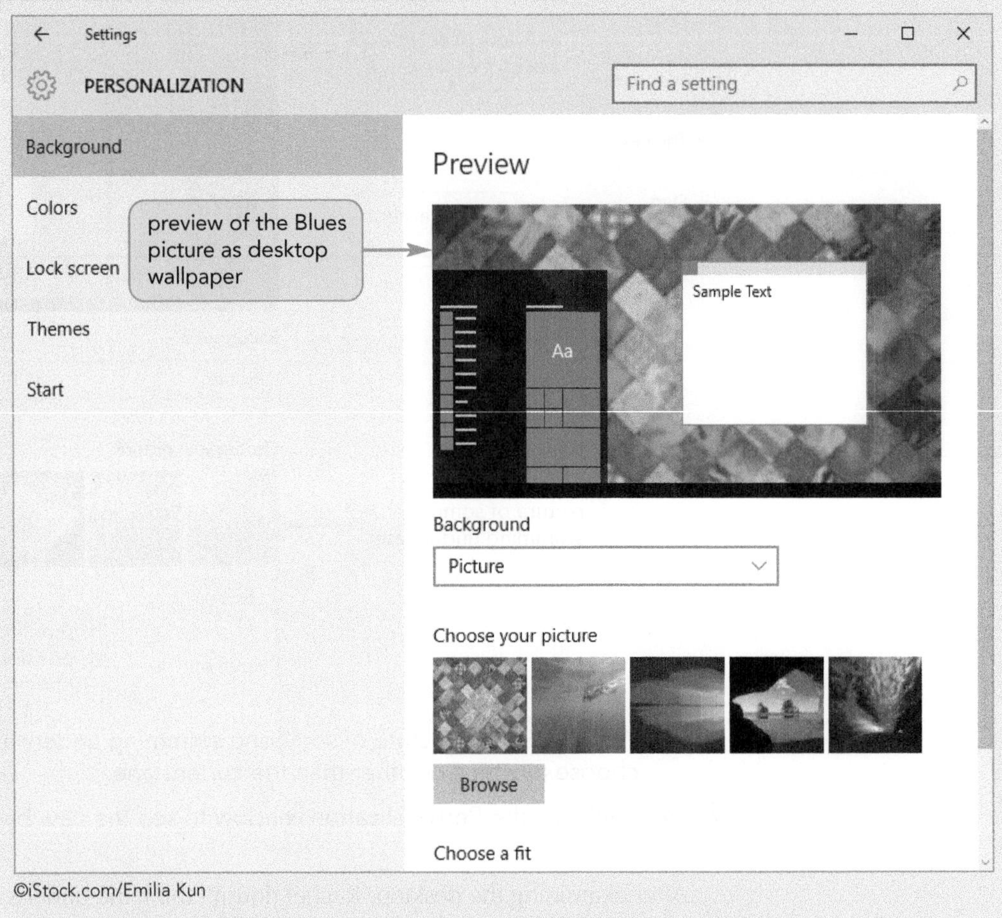

©iStock.com/Emilia Kun

Rachel likes the new picture but comments that she would prefer more colorful windows, preferably using a color that coordinates with the background picture. You'll show her how to change the colors of the desktop.

Changing Desktop Colors

Besides changing the desktop background, you can use the Colors settings in the Personalization window to set the accent, or contrasting, color of windows and the Start menu. Windows uses the accent color in several places to create contrast or visual interest. For example, Windows apps use the accent color for icons and the highlight bar that indicates a selection. The Start menu uses the accent color as a background for icons and tiles.

You can select an accent color from a palette of almost 50 colors or let Windows select an accent color from the background picture.

By default, the Start menu, taskbar, and action center are semitransparent and black. (The **action center** is a panel that keeps track of your notifications.) You can change the Colors settings so that these items show the selected accent color and are opaque rather than transparent.

Rachel wants all the Crafted Quilts computers to apply an accent color to the icons and highlight bar in Windows apps and as a background for icons and tiles on the Start menu.

To change the accent color:

1. In the Personalization window, click **Colors** in the left pane to display the Colors settings. See Figure 3-8. Note the current accent color so you can restore it later.

Figure 3-8 Colors settings

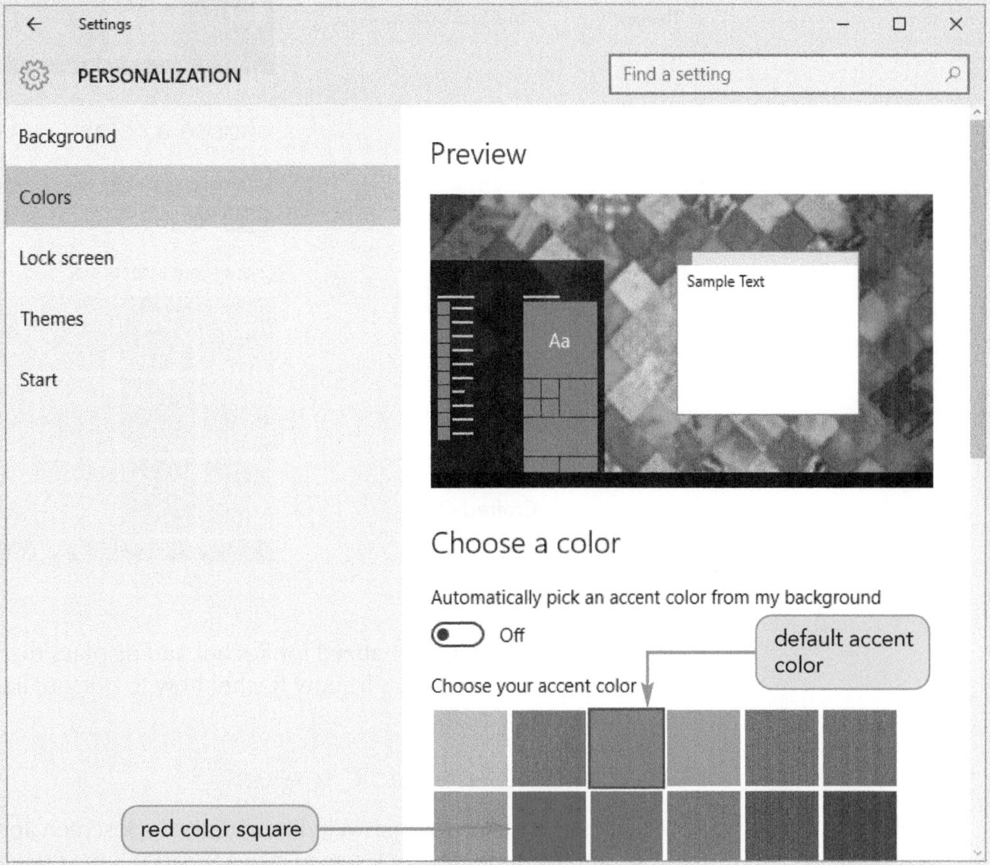

©iStock.com/Emilia Kun

2. Click the **red square**, which is in the second column and second row of the accent color palette. The Settings icon and highlight bar change to red.
3. On the Choose a color slider, drag the **slider button** from Off to On. Windows changes the red accent color to one it finds in the Blues background picture.

   Rachel wants all of the Crafted Quilts computers to use the same accent color, so you'll show her how to select a different one from the color palette.
4. On the Choose a color slider, drag the **slider button** from On to Off, and then click the **teal** color square, the color square in the fourth column and third row of the palette. See Figure 3-9.

Figure 3-9 New accent color

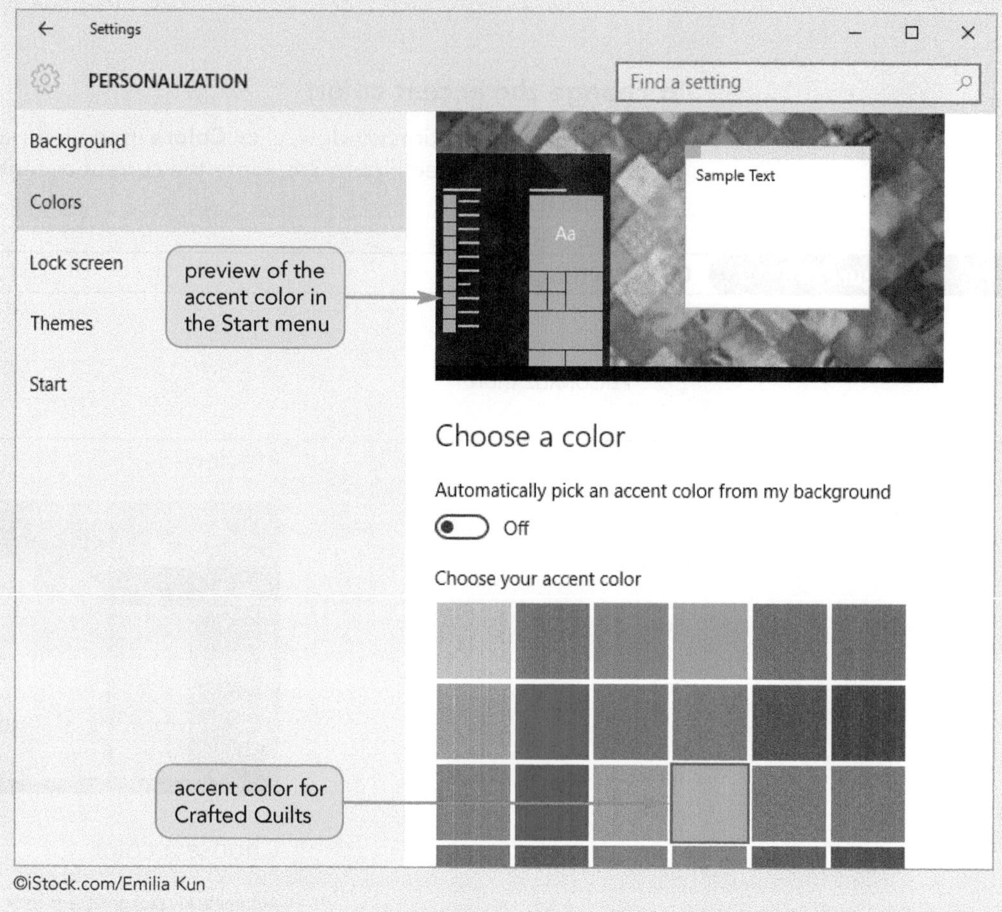

©iStock.com/Emilia Kun

The desktop is now personalized for Rachel and displays the Blues quilt picture and coordinated accent color. You'll show Rachel how to personalize the Windows lock screen next.

Personalizing the Lock Screen

Recall that shortly after you start Windows 10, the lock screen appears to display a picture, the date, and the time. The lock screen also appears when you wake your computer from sleep or hibernation. By default, the lock screen displays Windows spotlight pictures, which are photos from the bing.com home page. (Bing.com is a website you use to search the Internet and is owned by Microsoft.) The lock screen also displays facts, tips, and links related to Windows. You can personalize the lock screen by clicking a link to vote for pictures you like. Windows will select pictures based on your votes and display them on the lock screen.

REFERENCE

Changing the Lock Screen Picture

- Click the Start button and then click Settings.
- Click Personalization, and then in the left pane, click Lock screen.
- Click the Background box, and then click a picture to display as the desktop background, or click the Browse button and then select a picture stored on your computer.

You can also set the lock screen background to display a picture of your choice or play a slide show of pictures. If you want to display a single picture, you can choose one of the built-in lock screen pictures, which are different from the desktop pictures, or you can choose one of your own. For a slide show, select the Pictures folder on your computer to display pictures stored in that folder or add a different Pictures folder, such as the one stored on your OneDrive.

By default, Windows also displays facts, tips, and links on the lock screen pictures and slide shows you select, though you can change this setting to display the pictures only. In addition, you can select apps to provide helpful information on the lock screen. For example, you can display details about today's appointments stored in the Calendar app or a brief overview of the weather in your location.

Instead of using the Windows spotlight images, Rachel wants to display a picture of a different quilt on the lock screen.

To change the lock screen picture:

1. In the Personalization window, click **Lock screen** in the left pane to display the Lock screen settings. See Figure 3-10. Your lock screen picture will differ. Note the current settings so you can restore them later.

Figure 3-10 Lock screen settings

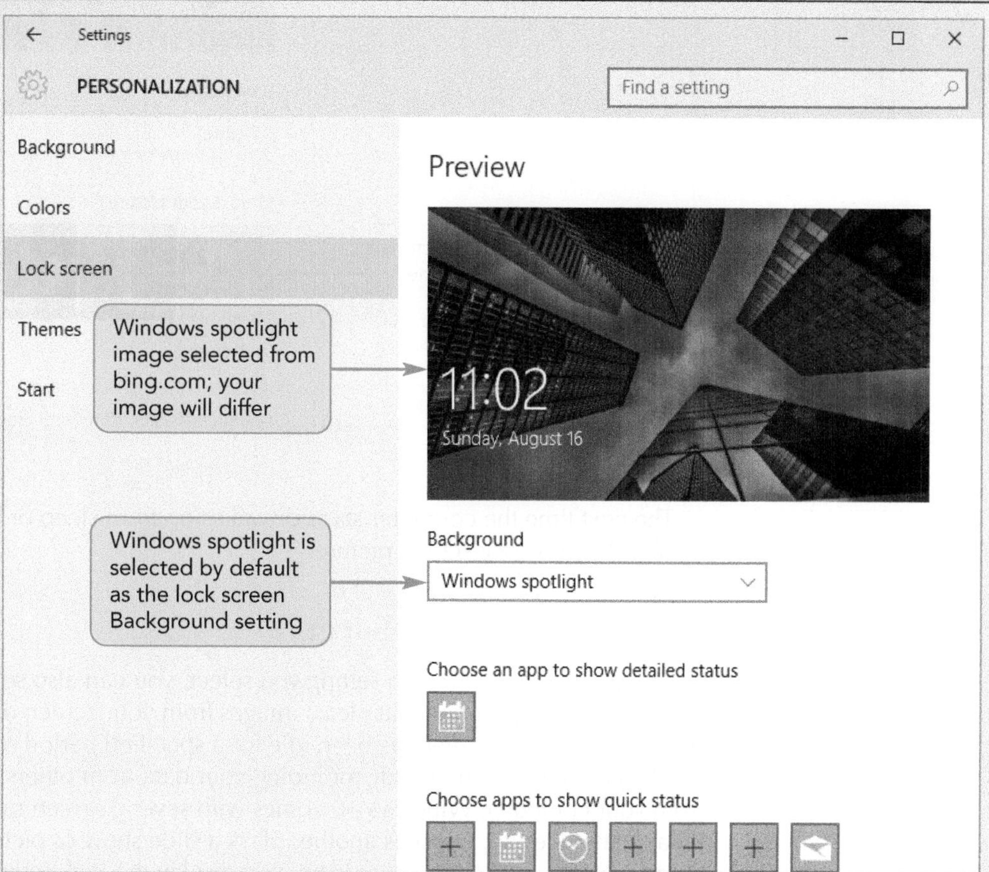

2. Click the **Background** box and then click **Picture** to display the options for using a Picture as the lock screen background.
3. Click the **Browse** button to open the Open dialog box so you can select a lock screen picture.

4. If necessary, navigate to the **Module3 > Module** folder provided with your Data Files.
5. Click the **Patchwork** picture file, and then click the **Choose picture** button. The Patchwork picture appears as the lock screen background. See Figure 3-11.

Figure 3-11 **Personalized lock screen picture**

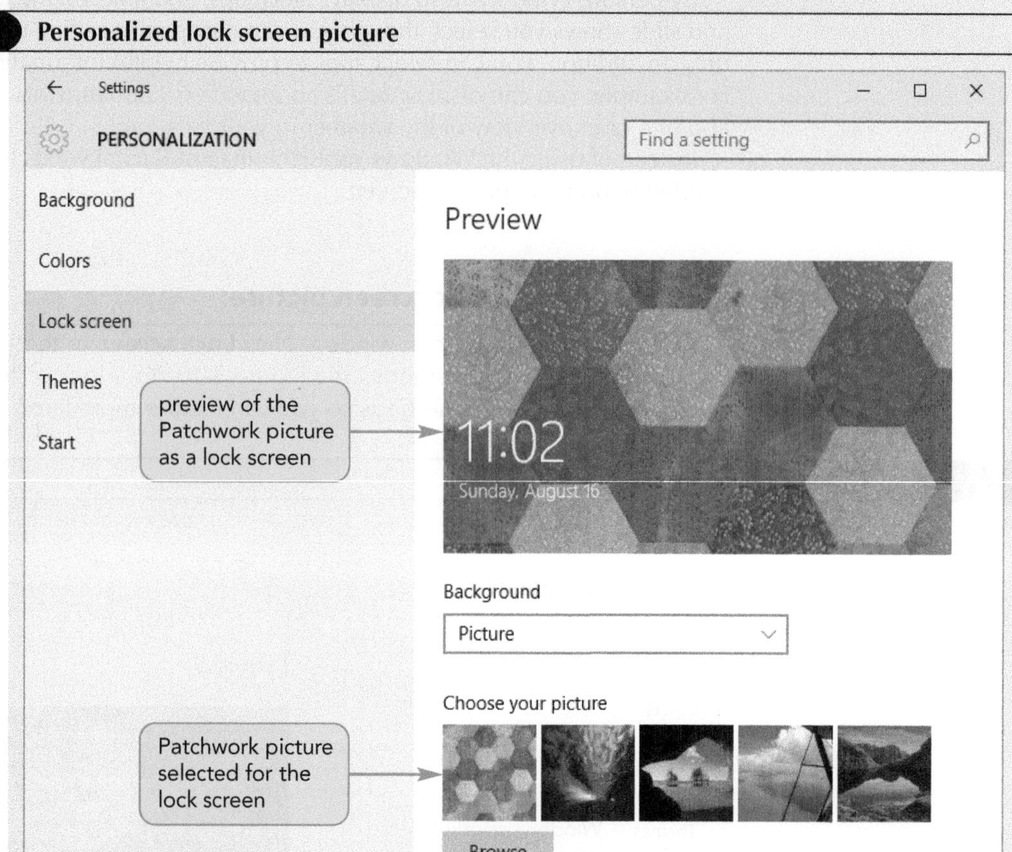

©iStock.com/yeahorse

The next time the computer starts or wakes up from sleep or hibernation, it will display the new lock screen picture.

Activating a Screen Saver

No matter which lock screen setting you select, you can also set your computer to use a screen saver, a program that clears images from your screen or displays a moving design after the computer has been idle for a specified period of time. Screen savers can be entertaining and handy for hiding your data from others if you step away from your computer. Windows 10 comes with several screen savers. Some show an animated design, whereas another plays a slide show of pictures stored on your computer. When a screen saver is on, you display the lock screen by moving your mouse or pressing a key. You can then return to the desktop the way you normally do.

You can select how long you want the computer to sit idle before the screen saver starts. Most users find settings between 3 and 10 minutes to be the most convenient. You set up a screen saver and specify the idle time using the options in the Screen Saver Settings dialog box.

INSIGHT

Using a Screen Saver for Security

To enhance the security of your computer and prevent unauthorized people from accessing your files, take advantage of a security setting available in the Screen Saver Settings dialog box. To have the screen saver request your user name and password before displaying your desktop, select the check box in this dialog box labeled "On resume, display logon screen." This means that only you and other people who know your user name and password can work with your desktop and files.

Rachel wants to examine the screen savers that Windows provides and then choose the most appropriate one for her organization.

To activate a screen saver:

TIP

To open the Screen Saver Settings dialog box from the Control Panel home page, click Appearance and Personalization, and then click Change screen saver in the Personalization category.

1. Scroll the Lock screen settings, if necessary, to click the **Screen saver settings** link at the bottom of the Personalization window. The Screen Saver Settings dialog box opens. See Figure 3-12. Note the name of the current screen saver so you can restore it later.

   Trouble? If the Screen Saver Settings dialog box opens behind the Personalization window, click the title bar of the dialog box or click the Screen Saver Settings taskbar button to make it the active window.

Figure 3-12 **Screen Saver Settings dialog box**

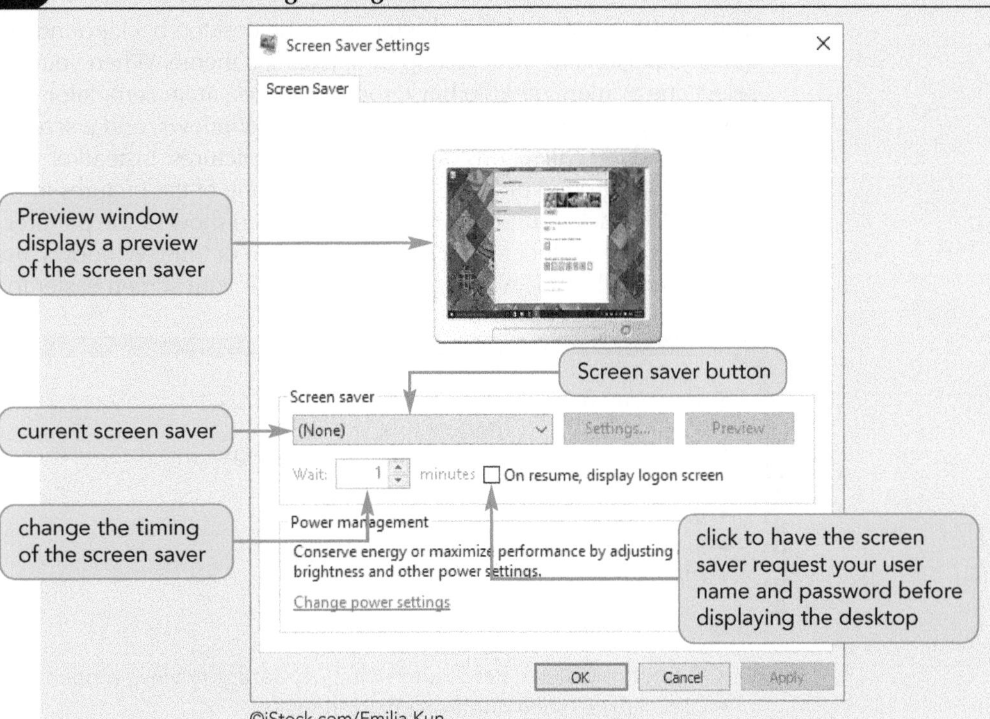

©iStock.com/Emilia Kun

2. Click the **Screen saver** button to display the screen savers installed on your computer.
3. Click **Ribbons**. The animated screen saver plays in the Preview window. Rachel likes that screen saver, but it's not appropriate for her company. You suggest the Photos screen saver, which plays a slide show of the pictures and videos stored in the Pictures folder by default.

4. Click the **Screen saver** button, and then click **Photos**. By default, the preview window plays a slide show of the graphics files stored in the Pictures folder, if any.
5. To display pictures of quilts, click the **Settings** button to open the Photos Screen Saver Settings dialog box. You use this dialog box to specify which files to include in the slide show and to select other settings, such as the slide show speed.
6. Click the **Browse** button. The Browse For Folder dialog box opens.
7. Navigate to the **Module3 > Module** folder provided with your Data Files, and then click the **OK** button to indicate you want to include all the pictures in the Module folder in the screen saver slide show.
8. Click the **Save** button to close the Photos Screen Saver Settings dialog box. Now only the pictures in the Module3 > Module folder appear in the Preview window.
9. Click the **OK** button to close the Screen Saver Settings dialog box.

After your computer is idle for a minute or so, the screen saver will start, playing a slide show of the photos.

Now that Rachel has personalized the desktop, lock screen, and screen saver, you'll show her how to save these settings as a theme.

Selecting Themes

Instead of selecting individual settings for the desktop background and screen saver, you can also personalize the desktop by selecting a theme. When you select a theme, you select one or more desktop background pictures, an accent color, a collection of sounds to signal system tasks, such as shutting down Windows, and a screen saver. Windows themes include collections of high-resolution pictures. Instead of working with separate desktop background pictures, you can select one of the pictures in a theme to display as the desktop background, or you can play a slide show of the pictures and switch from one picture to another after a specified amount of time. Windows also provides a few high-contrast themes, which make the items on your screen easier to see.

REFERENCE

Selecting a Theme

- Click the Start button and then click Settings.
- Click Personalization.
- In the left pane, click Themes.
- In the right pane, click Theme settings.
- Click a theme.

or

- Open the Control Panel and switch to Category view, if necessary.
- Click Appearance and Personalization.
- Click Personalization.
- Click a theme.

Rachel asks you to show her a few desktop themes to see if one would be suitable for Crafted Quilts.

To change the theme:

1. In the Personalization window, click **Themes** in the left pane.
2. Click **Theme settings** in the right pane to open the Control Panel's Personalization window, which lists many types of themes. See Figure 3-13. Your Personalization window might differ.

Figure 3-13 Themes in the Control Panel Personalization window

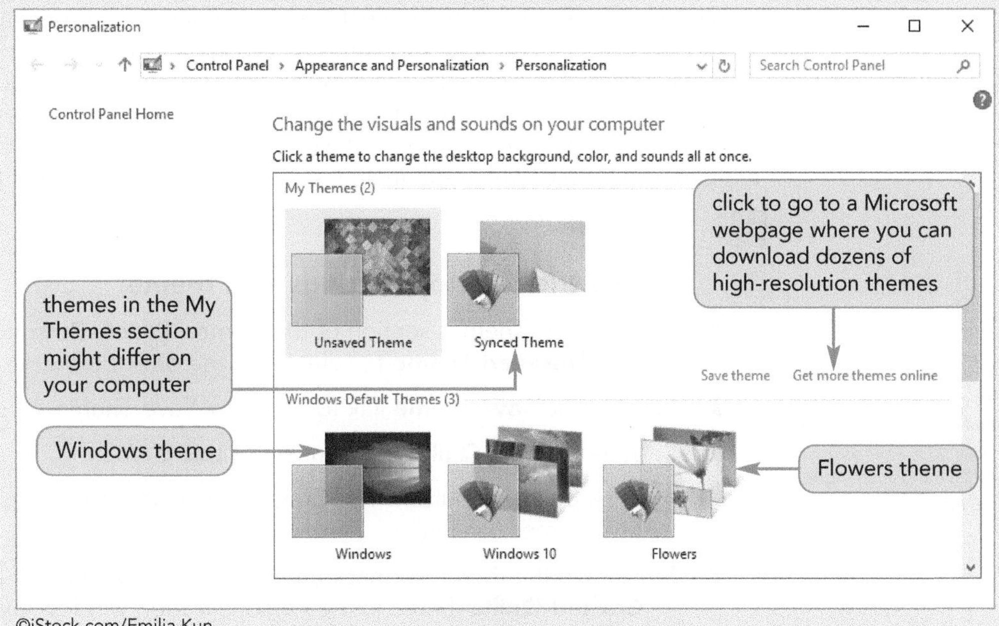

©iStock.com/Emilia Kun

3. If necessary, scroll the themes, and then click **Flowers**. The desktop background changes to a picture of a large flower, the taskbar and window borders change color, and a sound plays (if your speakers are turned on). Minimize the Control Panel's Personalization window to see more of the picture, and then restore the window.

   Trouble? If the Flowers theme does not appear in your Personalization window, select any other theme that displays photos.

The Control Panel's Personalization window includes a Get more themes online link, which you can click to start a browser and visit a Microsoft webpage listing themes organized into categories such as Featured, Animals, and Natural wonders. To use an online theme, click the Download link for the theme. When the download is finished, the browser displays a message in which you can click the Open button to add the theme to the Control Panel's Personalization window.

The Flowers theme is not as suitable for Crafted Quilts as the Blues quilt background picture and teal accent color. Windows is keeping track of your customized settings in case you want to save them as a new theme.

Saving Themes

After personalizing the desktop, you can save the settings as a theme. If you save the current settings as a theme, you can apply all of the changes—the Blues picture desktop background, the teal accent color, and the screen saver—at the same time, without selecting the individual settings again. By default, Windows stores the theme files in a system folder. You can create your own theme file—called a **theme pack**—that you can store in a folder of your choice, and then share that theme with other people running Windows 8 or later on their computers. Although you cannot move or copy a theme from a system folder, you can move or copy a theme pack.

If you change settings that affect the desktop appearance, sounds, or screen saver, Windows records the changes in a theme called Unsaved Theme. For example, if you select the Flowers theme and then change the accent color to blue, Windows records that change in the Unsaved Theme. If you want to switch themes but return to the Flowers theme with the blue accent color, you can save the Unsaved Theme as Blue Flowers, for example. The original Flowers theme remains unchanged.

You will save the desktop settings you created for Rachel as a theme and a theme pack, both called Crafted Quilts. Rachel will use the theme pack and the photos in the Module folder to apply the Crafted Quilts theme to other office computers. Before saving a theme, you must select the one you want to save. In this case, you select the Unsaved Theme, which still includes all the settings customized for Rachel.

TIP

The Unsaved Theme stores any changes you make to the current theme settings in case you want to save those changes as a new theme.

To save the desktop settings as a theme:

1. In the My Themes section of the Control Panel's Personalization window, click **Unsaved Theme** to select it as the desktop theme.
2. Click the **Save theme** link to open the Save Theme As dialog box.
3. Type **Crafted Quilts** as the name of this theme.
4. Click the **Save** button. The Crafted Quilts theme now appears in the My Themes section.
5. To save the theme so that others at Crafted Quilts can use it, right-click the **Crafted Quilts** theme in the Personalization window, and then click **Save theme for sharing** on the shortcut menu.
6. In the Save Theme Pack As dialog box, navigate to the **Module3 > Module** folder provided with your Data Files.
7. Click in the **File name** box, if necessary, and then type **Crafted Quilts**. Note that the Save as type is Desktop Theme Pack (*.deskthemepack).
8. Click the **Save** button. Windows saves the Crafted Quilts theme pack file in the Module folder.
9. Close the Personalization windows for the Control Panel and the Settings app.

Next, you can explore the display properties that affect the sharpness of the images on your desktop.

Changing Display Settings

After working with the properties for the desktop background, theme, and screen saver, you're ready to explore the properties that affect the computer display itself. For example, you can set the size of the desktop and choose whether to use more than one display. Windows selects the best settings, including screen resolution and orientation, based on your display hardware. **Screen resolution** is the number of horizontal and vertical pixels on a display screen, which determines the clarity of the text and images on your screen. (A **pixel**, short for "picture element," is an individual point of color.) At higher resolutions, items appear sharper and smaller, so more items fit on the screen. At lower resolutions, fewer items fit on the screen, but they are larger and easier to see. At very low resolutions, however, images might have jagged edges. Selecting the best settings for your display enhances your Windows experience.

INSIGHT

Selecting the Best Settings for Your Display

Laptop and desktop computers have a standard or widescreen liquid crystal display (LCD) screen. Settings for standard LCD display screens typically differ from those for widescreen displays. However, all LCD screens show the sharpest images and clearest text at a particular resolution, which is called their **native resolution**. Screen resolution is measured horizontally and vertically in pixels. For example, many 19-inch standard LCD screens have a native resolution of 1280 × 1024. A 22-inch widescreen LCD screen usually has a native resolution of 1680 × 1050. You can change the resolution to a lower setting, such as 1024 × 768, to make the on-screen objects larger, although the text might not be as clear as text displayed at the native resolution. If you are using a standard display screen, be sure to select a resolution with an aspect ratio of 4:3, such as 1024 × 768. (An **aspect ratio** is the ratio of the width to the height.) If you are using a widescreen display, select a resolution with an aspect ratio of 16:9 or 16:10, such as 1366 × 768.

Changing the Screen Resolution

In the Settings app, you use the Advanced Display Settings window to change the screen resolution. The Resolution box lists the available resolutions for your display screen. Select a setting to increase or decrease the resolution, or sharpness, of the desktop image. You will change the screen resolution from its current setting to 1024 × 768, if that setting is not already selected, and then back to its original setting.

To change the screen resolution:

1. Right-click the **desktop** and then click **Display settings** on the shortcut menu to open the System window in the Settings app with Display selected in the left pane.
2. Scroll down, if necessary, and then click the **Advanced display settings** link to open the Advanced Display Settings window. Note the original setting in the Resolution box so you can restore it later.
3. Click the **Resolution** box to list the settings available for your display. See Figure 3-14. Your settings might differ.

Figure 3-14 Changing the screen resolution

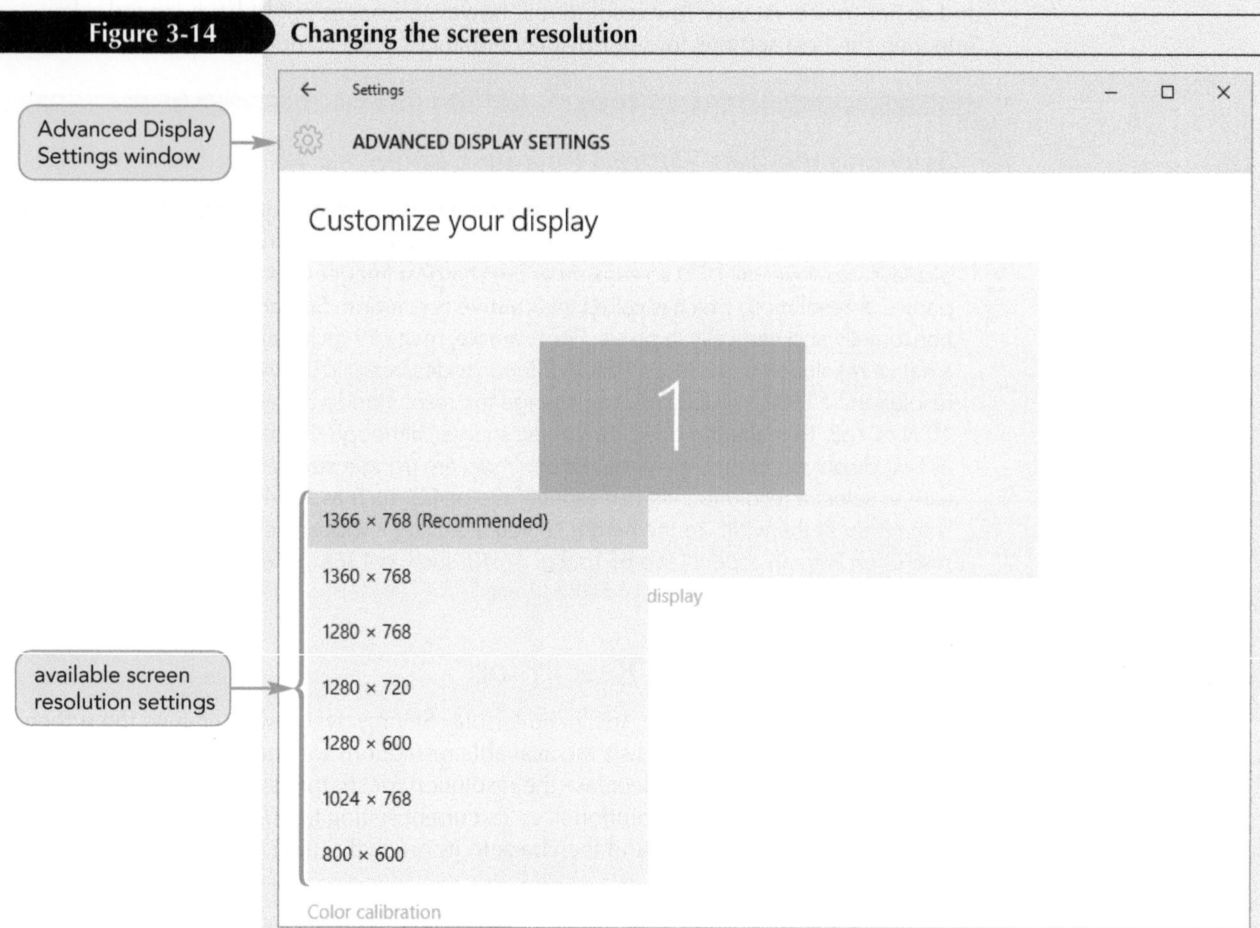

4. Click the **1024 × 768** resolution, if possible.

   Trouble? If your Resolution settings do not include the 1024 × 768 resolution, choose a different resolution.

5. Click the **Apply** button to select the new screen resolution.
6. When Windows asks you to confirm the change, click the **Keep changes** button to change the screen resolution, and then minimize the Advanced Display Settings window to view the change to the desktop.
7. To return to the original resolution, display the Advanced Display Settings window again, click the **Resolution** box, click the original resolution, such as 1366 × 768, click the **Apply** button, and then click the **Keep changes** button.

If you select a screen resolution recommended for your display but find the text and objects are now too large or small, you can adjust the size of the text and objects.

Changing the Size of Text and Objects

Without adjusting your screen resolution, you can change the size of the text and objects, such as icons on your screen. This means you can increase or decrease the size of text and objects while maintaining the native resolution of your monitor. For example, if you use a low screen resolution, such as 1024 × 768, you can make text and objects smaller to display more information on the screen. Conversely, if you use a high resolution, you can make text and objects easier to see by making them larger while retaining the sharpness of the high resolution.

Rachel's computer uses the 100% setting, which is the default for her display. You'll view the other settings to see if they would improve the appearance of her desktop.

To view the display settings:

1. In the Advanced Display Settings window, click the **Back** button [←] to return to the System window with the Display category selected.
2. On the Change the size of text, apps, and other items slider, drag the **slider button** to 125%.

   Trouble? If the 125% setting is already selected, drag to the 100% setting.
3. Click the **Apply** button to apply the new setting. The text and objects in the Display window are larger and easy to see, but they take up too much space.

   Trouble? If a window opens requesting you to sign in again for the best experience, click the Sign out later button.
4. On the Change the size of text, apps, and other items slider, drag the **slider button** to your original setting, such as 100% (Recommended), and then click the **Apply** button.

   Trouble? If a window opens requesting you to sign in again for the best experience, click the Sign out later button.
5. Close the System window.

Personalizing Desktop Icons

As you know, the desktop displays a background picture, the Recycle Bin icon, and the taskbar by default. Your desktop might also include other icons installed by your computer manufacturer or your school.

Because the desktop provides your first view of the computer and its contents, it should contain the items you want to access when you start your computer. You can place icons on the desktop that represent objects you want to access quickly or frequently, such as Windows tools, drives, programs, and documents. Windows provides desktop icons for system tools, such as the Recycle Bin and This PC. You can add or remove these icons according to your work preferences. Figure 3-15 shows the types of icons you can include on the desktop and the objects they represent.

Figure 3-15 **Types of desktop icons**

Icon	Description
	This PC icon
	Control Panel icon
	Document shortcut icon
	Drive shortcut icon
	Folder shortcut icon
	Network icon
	Program shortcut icon (such as Paint)
	Recycle Bin icon (full and empty)
	User folder icon

Besides the built-in desktop icons for system tools, you can use shortcuts to start an app or access an object. Double-clicking a shortcut on the desktop opens its associated file, folder, device, or app. When you delete a shortcut or desktop icon, you delete only the icon—the file or resource it represents remains in its original location. You typically create shortcuts on the desktop (or elsewhere, such as in a folder) to locations, files, and devices that you use often.

PROSKILLS

Problem Solving: Simplifying Tasks with Shortcuts

If you work with many devices, apps, or folders, it might be difficult to access all of these resources efficiently. One way to solve this problem is to add shortcuts to the desktop. Shortcut icons can simplify tasks you perform regularly. For example, you can create a shortcut icon for a USB drive and then drag files to the shortcut icon to copy them to the removable disk. You also can create a shortcut icon for a desktop app you use often, such as Paint, and then double-click the icon to start the app. Some apps add a shortcut icon to the desktop when you install the app. If you work with a particular folder often, you can add a desktop shortcut to the folder. That way, you can double-click the folder shortcut to open the folder without navigating many folder windows.

You'll show Rachel how to add icons to the desktop for system tools she uses often and how to create a shortcut icon on the desktop to a USB drive.

Adding Icons to the Desktop

Windows provides five standard icons that you can display on the desktop. Besides the Recycle Bin, which appears on the desktop by default, you can display the This PC icon (also called the Computer icon) to provide easy access to the This PC window and therefore the drives and devices connected to your computer. If you display the desktop icon for your personal folder (that is, the folder containing the current user's files), you can quickly find and open the folders containing your documents. Having the Network icon on the desktop gives you access to a window that lists the shared computers and other devices on your network. You can also add the Control Panel icon to the desktop and then use that desktop app to change the way Windows looks and behaves.

Rachel mentions that the Windows tools she plans to use most frequently are her personal folder, This PC, and the Control Panel. You'll add these icons to Rachel's desktop.

To display standard desktop icons:

1. Right-click a blank area of the **desktop**, and then click **Personalize** on the shortcut menu. The Settings app starts and opens the Personalization window.
2. In the left pane, click **Themes**.
3. In the Related Settings section of the right pane, click **Desktop icon settings**. The Desktop Icon Settings dialog box opens. See Figure 3-16. The Recycle Bin check box is already selected, indicating that Windows is displaying the Recycle Bin icon on the desktop.

TIP

Note that the Recycle Bin icon has two appearances: one when it is empty, and another when it contains deleted items.

Figure 3-16 Desktop Icon Settings dialog box

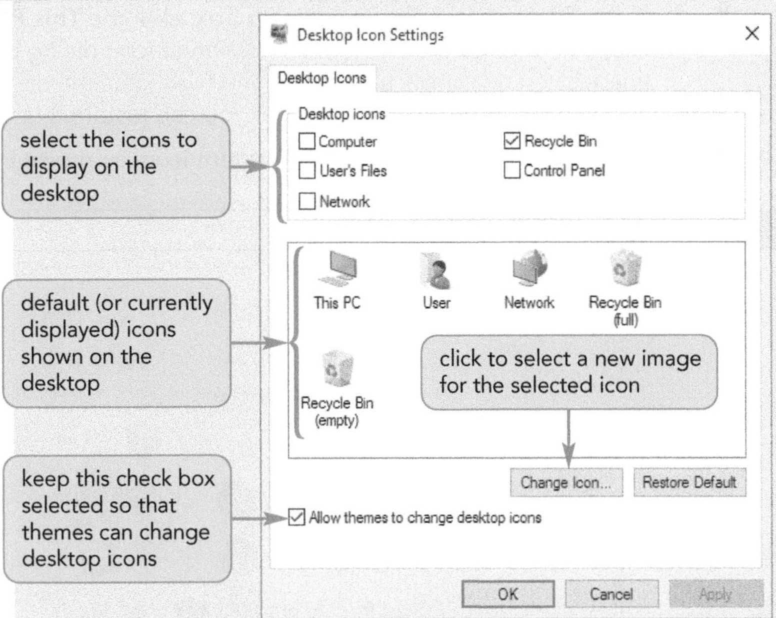

Trouble? If you are working in a computer lab, you might not be able to open the Desktop Icon Settings dialog box. In that case, read but do not perform the remaining steps in this section and the next section.

Trouble? If the settings in your Desktop Icon Settings dialog box differ from those in the figure, note the current options so you can restore them later, and then change the options so only the Recycle Bin check box is selected.

4. Click the **Computer**, **User's Files**, and **Control Panel** check boxes.
5. Click the **Apply** button to apply the changes but keep the Desktop Icon Settings dialog box open, and then drag the dialog box to the middle of the desktop so you can see the icons for your personal folder, This PC, and the Control Panel on the left side of the desktop.

Some themes include customized desktop icons. If the Allow themes to change desktop icons check box is checked (which it is by default) in the Desktop Icon Settings dialog box, the icons change when you select a new theme. If you want the desktop icons to always keep their appearance, click to remove the check mark from the check box.

Now that you've added desktop icons for Rachel, you can customize their appearance according to her preferences.

Changing the Appearance of Desktop Icons

You can change the images displayed on the desktop icons using the Change Icon dialog box, which you open from the Desktop Icon Settings dialog box. Change the image to suit your preferences or to display a more accurate image. For example, the This PC icon shows an image of a desktop computer. If you work on a different type of computer, you might want to change this image to match your computer type.

Because Rachel works on an all-in-one computer, with the computer and display screen built in to the same case, she wants to change the image for the This PC icon on the desktop.

To change the image of the This PC icon:

1. In the Desktop Icon Settings dialog box, click the **This PC** icon, and then click the **Change Icon** button. The Change Icon dialog box opens to display images you can apply to the icon and highlights the current image. Note the image used for the This PC icon so you can restore it later.
2. Click the icon directly below the current icon, as shown in Figure 3-17.

Figure 3-17 Changing the default This PC icon

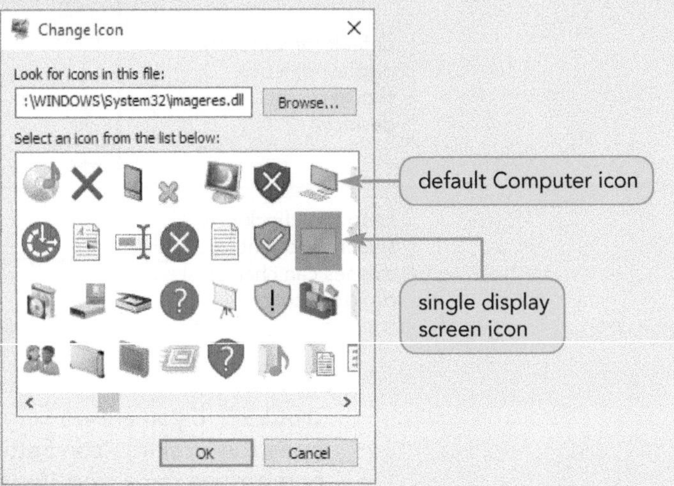

Trouble? If the computer display image shown in the figure does not appear in your Change Icon dialog box, click any other suitable image.

3. Click the **OK** button to close the Change Icon dialog box.
4. Click the **OK** button to close the Desktop Icon Settings dialog box, and then close the Personalization window. The This PC icon on the desktop now appears as a single display screen.

The standard Windows desktop icons provide quick access to common Windows tools. These are standard tools that Windows provides to simplify or enhance your computer work. However, other items you access often (such as documents, folders, and drives) might be different from the items other users access often. In addition, the folders you use frequently one week might differ from those you use frequently the next week. To personalize your desktop to provide quick access to these items, you can create and use shortcuts.

Creating Desktop Shortcuts

On the desktop, you can create shortcuts to access drives, documents, files, apps, or other computer resources, such as a network folder. For example, you can easily open a document from the desktop by creating a shortcut icon for the document. A shortcut icon for a document works much the same way as a document icon does in a folder window—you can double-click the shortcut icon to open the document in the appropriate program. However, a shortcut icon is only a link to the actual document. If you move the icon, you move only the shortcut, not the document itself. One advantage of using shortcut icons is that if your desktop becomes cluttered, you can delete the shortcut icons without affecting the original documents.

You can also create shortcut icons for the folders, drives, and devices on your computer. This way, you can access your local hard disk, for example, directly from the desktop, instead of having to open a folder window and then navigate to the hard disk.

Windows provides several ways of creating shortcuts on the desktop. Figure 3-18 summarizes the techniques you can use to create shortcuts. The one you choose is a matter of personal preference.

Figure 3-18 **Methods for creating shortcuts**

Method	Description
Drag (for drives and devices only)	To create a drive shortcut on the desktop, use a folder window to locate the drive icon, and then drag the icon to the desktop.
Right-drag	Use a folder window to locate and select an icon, hold down the right mouse button, and then drag the icon to a new location. Release the mouse button and click Create shortcuts here on the shortcut menu.
Right-click, Create shortcut	Use a folder window to locate an icon, right-click the icon, click Create shortcut on the shortcut menu, and then drag the shortcut icon to a new location.
Right-click, Send to	To create a shortcut on the desktop, use a folder window to locate an icon, right-click the icon, point to Send to, and then click Desktop (create shortcut).

Next, you'll create a shortcut to a USB drive on the desktop. You could use any technique for creating shortcuts, but you'll use the drag method because it involves the fewest steps.

Creating a Shortcut to a Drive

TIP

You can rename a shortcut icon the same way you rename a folder.

To create a shortcut to a drive, you can open the This PC window and then drag the drive icon from the window to the desktop. Windows creates a shortcut icon that looks like a drive icon with a shortcut arrow and includes an appropriate label, such as Removable (D) – Shortcut. If you drag a document icon from a folder window to the desktop, you move the actual document from its original location to the desktop. However, you cannot move a drive, a program, or another computer resource—its location is fixed during installation. Therefore, when you drag a drive icon to the desktop, you automatically create a shortcut.

When you create a shortcut to a USB drive, you can insert the drive in a USB port and then double-click the shortcut to view your Data Files. You can move or copy documents to the drive without having to open a separate folder window.

Rachel regularly copies files from her computer to a USB drive and wants to use a shortcut to simplify the task. You'll show her how to create a shortcut to a USB drive on her desktop.

To create a shortcut to a USB drive:

1. If necessary, insert the USB drive containing your Data Files into a USB port on your computer.
2. Double-click the **This PC** icon on the desktop. If necessary, move or resize the This PC window so you can see the icons along the left side of the desktop. You need to see both the desktop icons and the This PC window to drag effectively.

3. Point to the **Removable Disk (D:)** icon in the This PC window, press and hold the left mouse button, and then drag the **Removable Disk (D:)** icon from the This PC window to an empty area of the desktop.

   Trouble? If your USB drive has a name other than Removable Disk (D:), substitute the appropriate name and drive on your system as you perform the steps.

4. Release the mouse button. A shortcut labeled Removable Disk (D) – Shortcut now appears on the desktop. Click the desktop to deselect the shortcut icon. See Figure 3-19. Your shortcut icon might appear in a different part of the desktop.

Figure 3-19 Shortcut to a removable disk

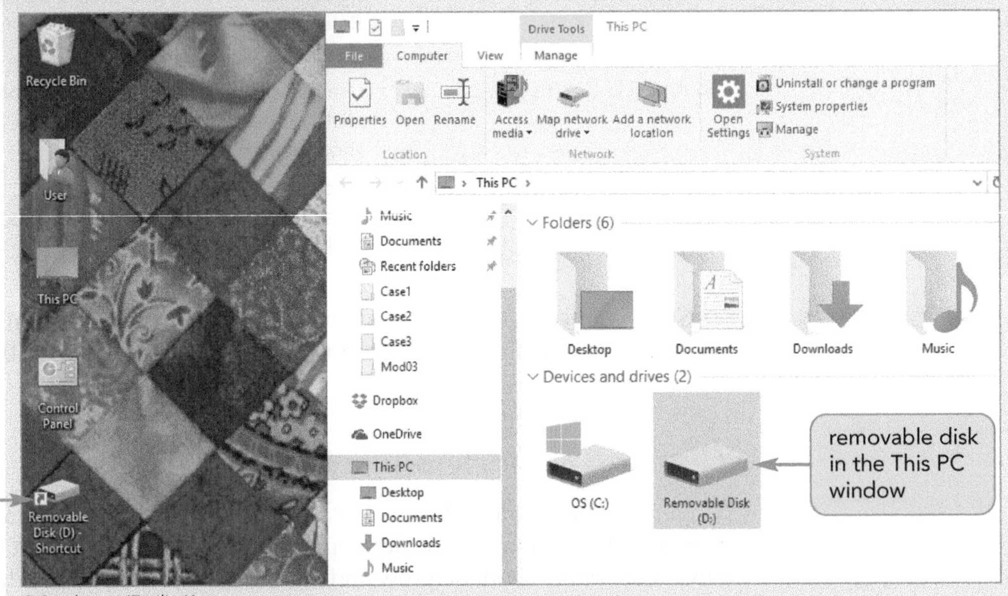

©iStock.com/Emilia Kun

   Trouble? If you dragged with the right mouse button instead of the left, a shortcut menu appears when you release the mouse button. Click Create shortcuts here to add the Removable Disk (D) – Shortcut to the desktop.

5. Point to the **Removable Disk (D) – Shortcut** icon to view its ScreenTip, which indicates the permanent location of the drive on your computer.

Rachel wants to copy a picture of a freeform quilt from the Module3 > Module folder on the USB drive to a new folder in the Pictures folder. She expects Mai to send her other pictures of freeform quilts, and she wants them to be available in a central location. Use the shortcut on the desktop to copy the file from the Module3 > Module folder on the USB drive to a new folder in the Pictures folder.

To use the removable disk shortcut:

1. In the navigation pane of the This PC window, click **Pictures** to display the contents of the Pictures folder.
2. In the New group on the Home tab, click the **New folder** button to create a folder in the Pictures folder.

3. Type **Freeform Quilts** as the name of the new folder, and then press the **Enter** key.
4. Double-click the **Freeform Quilts** folder to open it.
5. Double-click the **Removable Disk (D) – Shortcut** icon on the desktop. A new window opens showing the contents of the USB drive.
6. Navigate to the **Module3 > Module** folder provided with your Data Files. Arrange the windows to display the right panes of both windows on the desktop.
7. Drag the **Broadway** file from the Module folder to the right pane of the Freeform Quilts folder window. Because you are dragging a file from a removable disk to a folder on a hard drive, Windows copies the Broadway file rather than moving it to the Module folder.
8. Close all open windows.

Using a shortcut to a drive saves a few steps when you want to make backup copies of files or transfer files from one computer to another.

REVIEW

Session 3.1 Quick Check

1. How are the Settings app and the Control Panel similar? How are they different?
2. Name two places where the Settings app uses the current accent color.
3. How can you use Windows spotlight to personalize the lock screen?
4. What is the advantage of saving personalization settings as a theme?
5. Explain the difference between low- and high-screen resolutions.
6. What happens when you double-click a shortcut on the desktop?
7. If you display the desktop icon for your _______________, you can quickly find and open the folders containing your documents.
8. Which screen saver do you select in the Screen Saver Settings dialog box to play a slide show of pictures as a screen saver?

Session 3.2 Visual Overview:

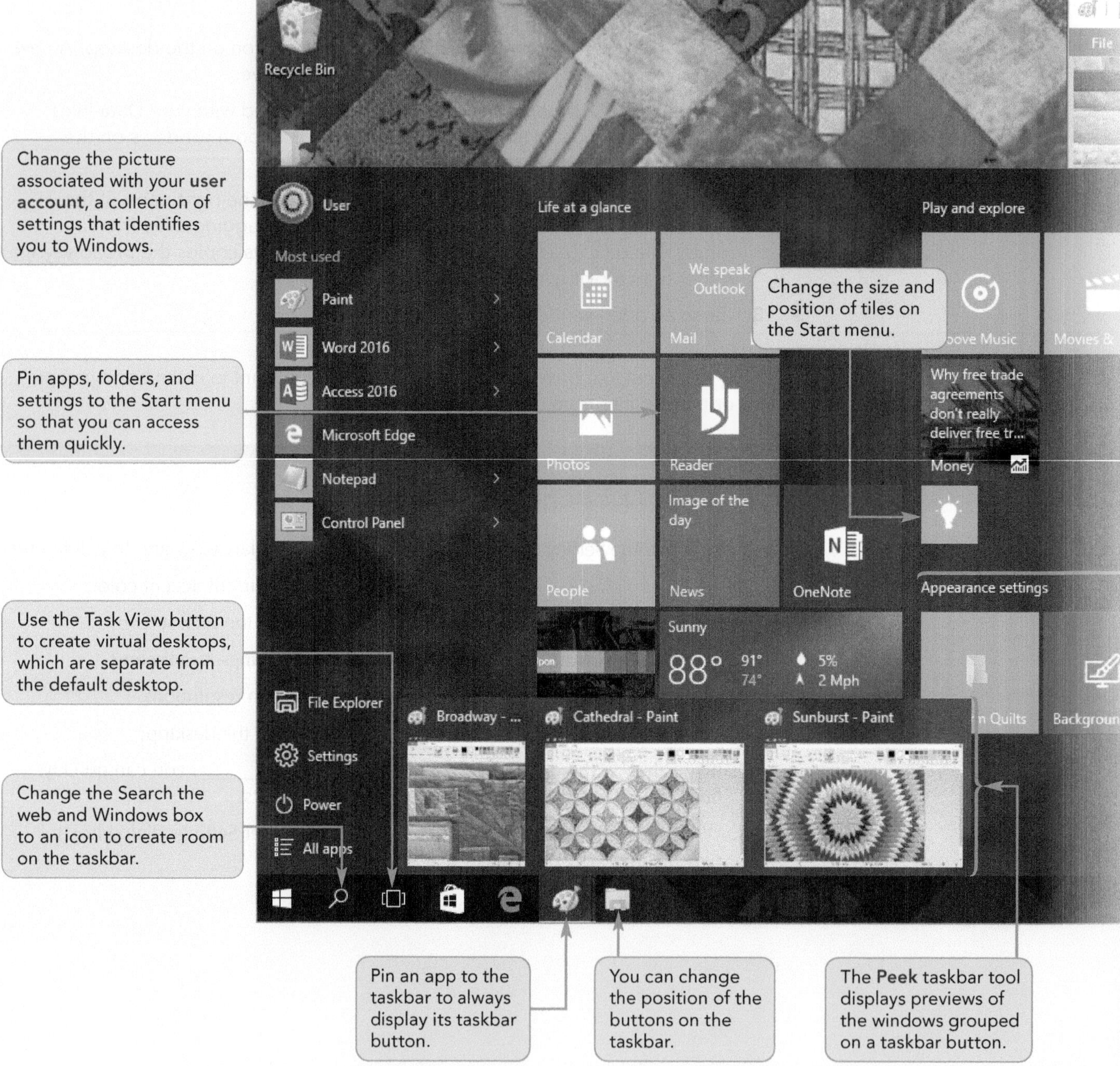
Change the picture associated with your **user account**, a collection of settings that identifies you to Windows.
Pin apps, folders, and settings to the Start menu so that you can access them quickly.
Use the Task View button to create virtual desktops, which are separate from the default desktop.
Change the Search the web and Windows box to an icon to create room on the taskbar.
Change the size and position of tiles on the Start menu.
Pin an app to the taskbar to always display its taskbar button.
You can change the position of the buttons on the taskbar.
The **Peek** taskbar tool displays previews of the windows grouped on a taskbar button.
Recycle Bin
User
Most used
Paint
Word 2016
Access 2016
Microsoft Edge
Notepad
Control Panel
File Explorer
Settings
Power
All apps
Life at a glance
Play and explore
Calendar
Mail
Photos
Reader
People
News
OneNote
Money
Appearance settings
Background
Broadway - ...
Cathedral - Paint
Sunburst - Paint

©iStock.com/blindsquirrelphoto; ©iStock.com/dmfoss; ©iStock.com/Jewelee; ©iStock.com/Emilia Kun

Personalized Start Menu and Taskbar

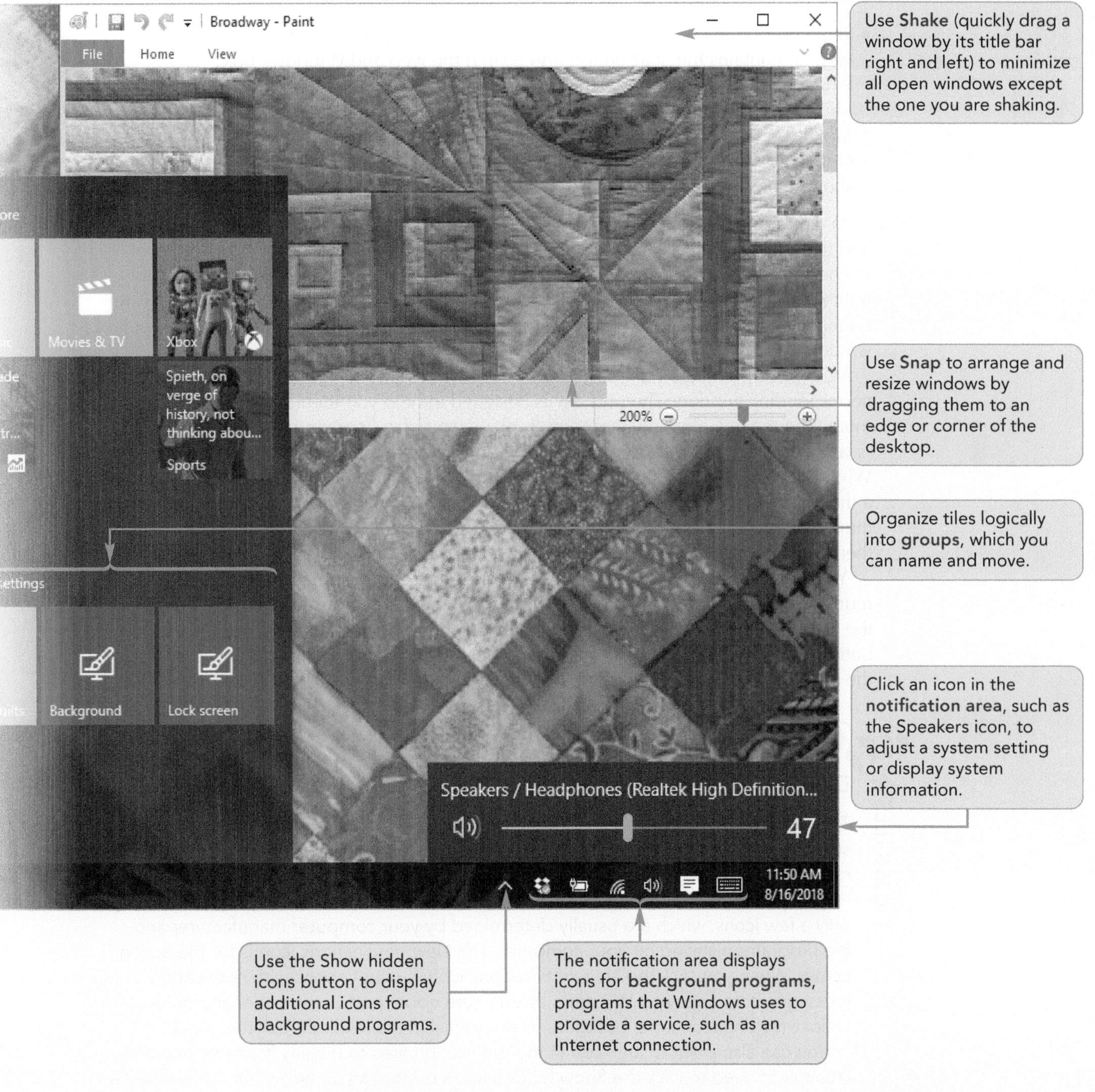

Use **Shake** (quickly drag a window by its title bar right and left) to minimize all open windows except the one you are shaking.

Use **Snap** to arrange and resize windows by dragging them to an edge or corner of the desktop.

Organize tiles logically into **groups**, which you can name and move.

Click an icon in the **notification area**, such as the Speakers icon, to adjust a system setting or display system information.

Use the Show hidden icons button to display additional icons for background programs.

The notification area displays icons for **background programs**, programs that Windows uses to provide a service, such as an Internet connection.

Modifying the Taskbar

As you know, the bar that appears by default at the bottom of the desktop is the taskbar. In Windows 10, the taskbar is divided into the following four sections:

- Start and Cortana search area: This section, which begins at the left side of the taskbar, contains the Start button and Search the web and Windows box.
- Pinned items: This section contains the Task View, File Explorer, Windows Store, and Microsoft Edge icons by default.
- Middle section: This section displays taskbar buttons for desktop apps currently running.
- Notification area: On the right side of the taskbar is the notification area, this section shows icons for system tools and the current date and time.

In the middle section of the taskbar, Windows displays buttons for each Windows and desktop app that is running. Each button is identified by an icon, not a text label, to conserve space. If you open another file in one of these apps, Windows groups the buttons for that app into a single button. A few windows might be grouped on the Paint button, for example. The Paint icon would appear on top, and the outlines of the open windows would be stacked behind it.

When you point to a taskbar button, Windows displays a thumbnail preview of the corresponding window. The preview is designed to help you identify a window by more than the title alone. If a window is playing a video or an animation, the video or animation also plays in the preview. When you point to a grouped taskbar button, Windows arranges the thumbnail previews in a row above the taskbar. You can click a thumbnail to open a window. Recall that to close a window, you can point to a thumbnail until a Close button appears in the upper-right corner of the thumbnail, and then you click the Close button.

You can personalize the taskbar to suit your preferences. For example, you can reorder the taskbar buttons by dragging them to a new location. You can also change the appearance of taskbar buttons by displaying button labels and specifying when buttons should be grouped together. To further customize the taskbar, you can change the size and position of the taskbar or hide it altogether.

PROSKILLS

Decision Making: Monitoring the Notification Area

The icons in the notification area of the taskbar let you access certain computer settings, such as the system time. The icons also communicate the status of programs running in the background. Background programs are those programs that Windows runs to provide a service, such as an Internet connection. The notification area displays only a few icons, which are usually determined by your computer manufacturer and the programs installed on your computer. The New notifications icon is for the action center. When you click the New notifications icon, a panel opens with notification messages from apps and Windows listed in the upper part of the panel and quick actions (settings for some background programs) in the lower part of the panel.

You can also point to any icon in the notification area to display its status or name. (You might need to click the Show hidden icons button (an up arrow) on the taskbar to display all of the icons in the notification area.) For example, if you're having trouble hearing sounds on your computer, point to the speaker icon to determine whether you need to turn up the volume. (The name of the speaker icon varies depending on the hardware manufacturer.)

Now you can personalize the taskbar on Rachel's computer. You'll start by showing her how to pin items to the taskbar.

Pinning Apps to the Taskbar

Task View, File Explorer, Windows Store, and Microsoft Edge are pinned to the taskbar by default. If you use another Windows or desktop app often, you can also pin that app to the taskbar. Pinning an app to the taskbar increases your efficiency because the pinned app is always visible as you work on the desktop, and you can start the app with a single click. (You need to double-click desktop shortcut icons for programs.) You can rearrange the buttons for pinned and running apps on the taskbar to suit your preferences.

REFERENCE

Pinning Apps to the Taskbar

- If the app is already running, right-click the taskbar button, and then click Pin this program to taskbar on the shortcut menu.

or

- If the app is not running, open the Start menu, locate and right-click the app's tile or command on the Start menu or All apps menu, and then click Pin to taskbar on the shortcut menu.

Because Rachel frequently uses Paint, you suggest that she pin Paint to the taskbar.

To pin Paint to the taskbar:

1. Click the **Start** button to display the Start menu, and then click **Paint**.

   Trouble? If Paint does not appear on the Start menu, type "Paint" in the Search the web and Windows box, and then click Paint in the search results.

2. Right-click the **Paint** button on the taskbar, and then click **Pin this program to taskbar** on the shortcut menu.

3. To confirm that Paint is pinned to the taskbar, close the Paint window. The Paint button remains on the taskbar.

   Trouble? If a dialog box appears asking if you want to save changes to an image, click the Don't Save button.

TIP

You can use the same technique to pin Windows apps to the taskbar.

In addition to starting an app from the taskbar, you can use a pinned item to open favorite and recent files from that program. To do so, you use a **Jump List**, a list of recently or frequently opened files, folders, or websites. When you right-clicked the Paint button in the previous steps, you displayed the Paint Jump List at the top of the shortcut menu. If you opened any picture files in Paint, such as the Broadway quilt picture, one or more of them might have appeared on the Jump List. To make sure you can always access one of those files, you can pin it to the Jump List. To open a pinned file, right-click the Paint button on the taskbar to display the Jump List, and then click the recent or favorite file you want to open in Paint.

Rachel plans to use the picture of the Broadway quilt often, so you'll show her how to pin the file to the Paint Jump List and then open the file from the taskbar. First, you'll open two files in Paint to make sure you have pictures to display in the Jump List.

To pin a file to the Paint Jump List:

1. Click the **Paint** button on the taskbar, click the **File** tab on the ribbon, and then click **Open** to open the Open dialog box.
2. Navigate to the **Module3 > Module** folder provided with your Data Files, and then double-click the **Blues** picture to open it. Next, open a second picture in Paint.
3. Click the **File** tab, click **Open** to open the Open dialog box, and then double-click the **Broadway** picture to open it.
4. Close Paint. Now you are certain to see recent files in the Paint Jump List.
5. Right-click the **Paint** button on the taskbar to display the Jump List.
6. Point to **Broadway**, and then click the **Pin to this list** icon to pin the Broadway picture file to the Jump List. See Figure 3-20. The items in your Paint Jump List might differ.

Figure 3-20 File pinned to the Paint Jump List

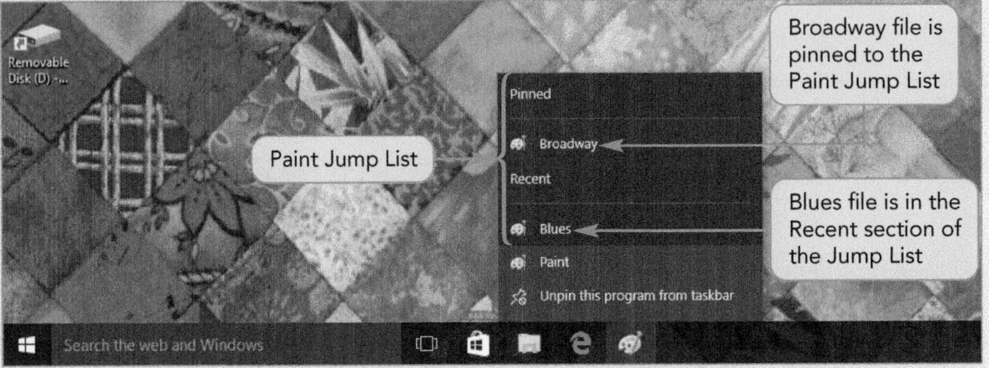

©iStock.com/Emilia Kun

7. To open the Broadway file in Paint, click **Broadway** on the Jump List. Paint starts and opens the Broadway picture file.
8. Close the Paint window.

TIP

To unpin a file, open the Jump List, point to the filename, and then click the Unpin from this list icon.

Rachel mentions that she would also like to adjust the position of the taskbar buttons. She uses the File Explorer button frequently, so she asks you to move the File Explorer button to the right of the Paint button for easy access.

To move a taskbar button:

1. Point to the **File Explorer** button on the taskbar, and then drag it to the right.
2. When the File Explorer button appears to the right of the Paint button, release the mouse button. See Figure 3-21.

Figure 3-21 Moving a taskbar button

File Explorer is now to the right of the Paint button
Search the web and Windows

©iStock.com/Emilia Kun

You can move any taskbar button, even those for programs that are not pinned to the taskbar. When you do, you move the entire button group so the open files remain grouped on a program button.

The taskbar is starting to look cluttered with buttons and icons. To create room for other items, you can change the Search the web and Windows box to an icon.

To change the Search the web and Windows box to an icon:

TIP

You can also use the taskbar shortcut menu to hide or show the Task View button.

1. Right-click a blank area of the taskbar, and then point to **Search** on the shortcut menu to display a list of options for the Search the web and Windows box. You can hide the box, show an icon instead of the box, or continue showing the box.

   Trouble? If Cortana is activated on your computer, point to Cortana on the shortcut menu instead of Search.

2. Click **Show search icon** on the menu to display an icon instead of a box. All of the icons on the taskbar move to the left. See Figure 3-22.

Figure 3-22 Search icon on the taskbar

icon displayed instead of a box

©iStock.com/Emilia Kun

   Trouble? If Cortana is activated on your computer, click Show Cortana icon instead of Show search icon. The Cortana icon appears on the taskbar instead of the search icon.

Now that you've shown Rachel how to customize the icons on the taskbar, you'll show her how to change the taskbar itself.

Setting Taskbar Properties

You can set taskbar properties using the Taskbar and Start Menu Properties dialog box. Using this dialog box, you can increase the amount of screen space available for open windows by hiding the taskbar. In this case, the taskbar is not closed, removed, or minimized, but instead hidden under the border of the desktop or the app windows open on the desktop. The taskbar still remains active and accessible—you can point to the area of your screen where the taskbar would be located to redisplay the taskbar when you need to use it.

You can also use the Taskbar and Start Menu Properties dialog box to determine whether to display small icons on the taskbar, group similar taskbar buttons, and change the location of the taskbar to another position on the screen.

You'll show Rachel how to increase the amount of screen space on the desktop by hiding the taskbar and using small icons.

To set taskbar properties:

1. Right-click a blank area on the taskbar, and then click **Properties** on the shortcut menu. The Taskbar and Start Menu Properties dialog box opens. See Figure 3-23. Your settings might differ.

Figure 3-23 Taskbar and Start Menu Properties dialog box

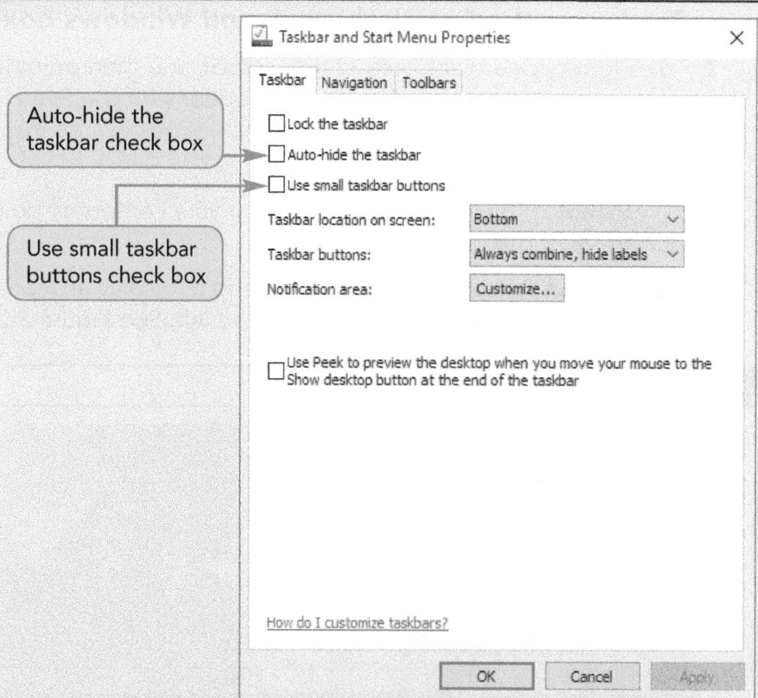

Note the options currently selected in this dialog box so you can restore them later.

2. Click to select the **Auto-hide the taskbar** check box, and then click the **Apply** button. Windows hides the taskbar.
3. Point to the bottom of the desktop to redisplay the taskbar. Pointing away from the taskbar hides it again.

4. In the Taskbar and Start Menu Properties dialog box, click the **Auto-hide the taskbar** check box to remove the check mark, and then click the **Apply** button. The taskbar appears in its default position at the bottom of the desktop.
5. Click to select the **Use small taskbar buttons** check box, and then click the **Apply** button. The taskbar icons shrink and the height of the taskbar decreases accordingly.
6. Click the **Use small taskbar buttons** check box to remove the check mark, and then click the **Apply** button to display the taskbar icons at their default size.
7. Make sure the options in the Taskbar and Start Menu Properties dialog box are in their original state, and then click the **OK** button to close the dialog box.

Managing the Desktop with Taskbar Tools

Windows 10 includes three taskbar tools you can use to manage the windows on your desktop: Snap, Peek, and Shake. You can also use the Task View button on the taskbar to create and use virtual desktops, which are desktops you can add to the Windows user interface, separate from the default desktop.

Arranging Windows with Snap

With Snap, you can drag the title bar of an open window to the top of the desktop to maximize the window. To restore the window to its original size, drag the title bar away from the top of the desktop. You can also use Snap to arrange two windows side by side and arrange four windows in each corner of the desktop. You can also use a feature called **Snap Assist** to list the thumbnails of open windows as you snap a window into place. Instead of dragging, you can click the thumbnail you want to snap into an empty part of the desktop.

To use Snap, you first turn on the feature in the Settings app. Your screen resolution must also be high enough (at least 1366 × 768) to snap windows. Turning on Snap activates two other settings. One adjusts the size of the snapped windows so they each take up an equal amount of the desktop. The other setting turns on Snap Assist. You can turn on Snap, but turn off the other two settings according to your preferences.

To turn on Snap:

1. Click the **Start** button to display the Start menu, and then click **Settings** to start the Settings app.
2. Click **System** to display the System settings.
3. In the left pane, click **Multitasking** to display multitasking features, including Snap, in the right pane.
4. If the first slider is set to Off, click the **slider button** to change the Snap from Off to On. By default, you also activate the other two Snap settings. See Figure 3-24.

TIP

To find the Snap settings quickly, you can start the Settings app and then type "Snap" in the Find a setting box.

Figure 3-24 **Turning on Snap**

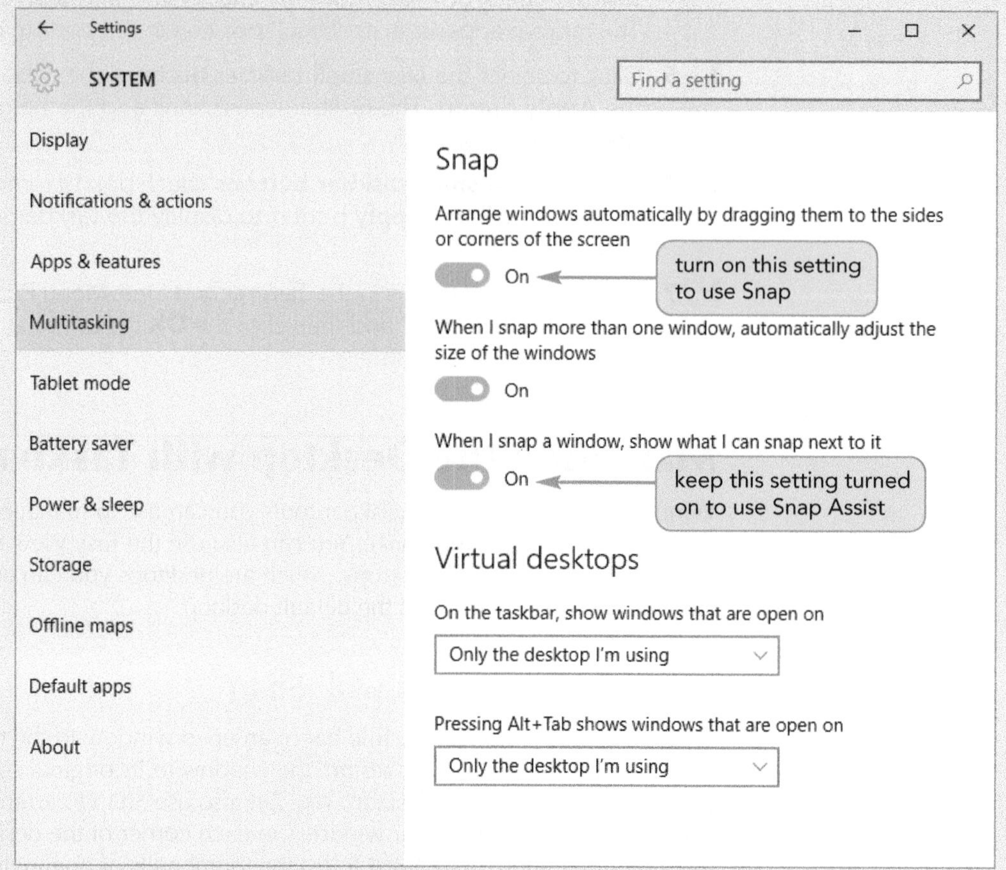

Trouble? If the Snap settings are unavailable, your screen resolution might be too low to use Snap. Read but do not perform the next two series of steps.

Rachel sometimes needs to work with two windows open as she examines images and manages her files and folders. You offer to show her how to quickly arrange windows side by side using Snap and Snap Assist. The System window is already open. You'll open the Broadway picture in Paint and then snap the windows.

To arrange windows side by side with Snap:

1. Right-click the **Paint** button on the taskbar to display its Jump List, and then click **Broadway** to open the Broadway picture in Paint.

   Trouble? If the Paint window opens as maximized, click the Restore Down button to resize the window.

2. Click the **title bar** of the Paint window, and then drag it to the left side of the desktop until a translucent outline of the window appears. Make sure the outline takes up half of the desktop.

3. Release the mouse button to snap the Paint window to the left side of the desktop and display a thumbnail of the System window. See Figure 3-25.

Figure 3-25 **Arranging windows with Snap and Snap Assist**

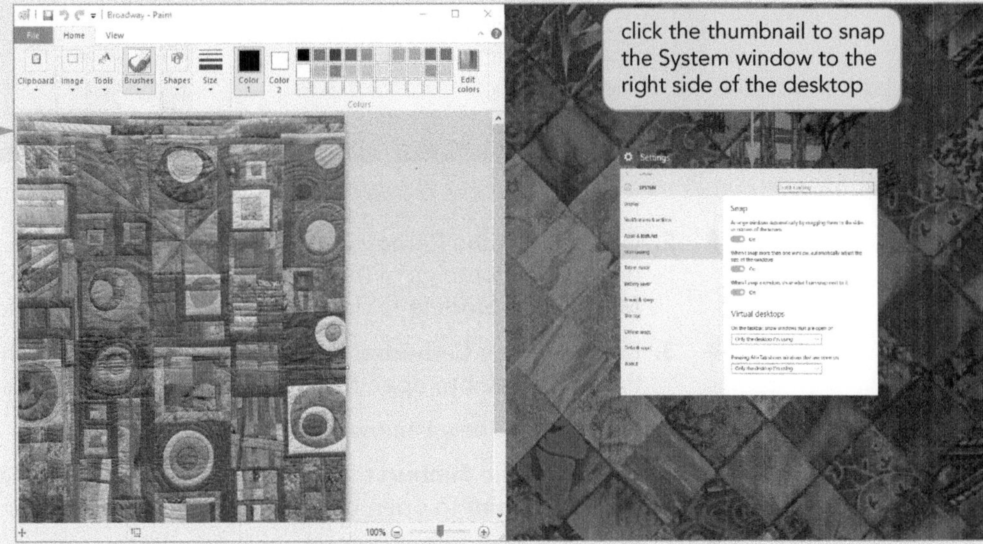
Paint is snapped to the left side of the desktop
click the thumbnail to snap the System window to the right side of the desktop

©iStock.com/Emilia Kun; ©iStock.com/dmfoss

Trouble? If the Paint window is maximized, you dragged the window to the upper-center part of the desktop. Click the Restore Down button and then repeat Steps 2 and 3.

4. Click the **thumbnail** of the System window to snap it to the right side of the desktop.

Instead of arranging windows side by side, you can arrange up to four windows in each corner of the desktop. If your screen resolution is higher than 1366 × 768, you can snap one window to a corner of the desktop and then use Snap Assist to display thumbnails of the remaining windows to snap.

Keeping Track of Windows with Peek

Peek helps you manage open windows. To quickly minimize all open windows, you click the Show desktop button on the far right side of the taskbar. To preview open windows without leaving your current window, you point to a taskbar button to display thumbnails of open files, and then point to a thumbnail. Any open windows fade to reveal the selected window and then reappear when you move the pointer away from the thumbnail. To open the window you're previewing, you click the thumbnail.

When Rachel has many windows open, she often has to stop working with a document or an image to manage those windows. For example, she might open a few more image files and then decide to copy other files to a USB drive. She'd like to quickly view the desktop to verify that it contains a shortcut to the removable disk so she can copy the files using the shortcut icon. She also wants to know how to briefly display a particular window to view its contents. You'll show her how to use Peek to perform both tasks.

To use Peek:

1. Click the **Show desktop** button on the far right side of the taskbar (to the right of the date and time) to minimize all of the open windows. See Figure 3-26.

Figure 3-26 Displaying the desktop with Peek

©iStock.com/Emilia Kun

2. Double-click the **Removable Disk (D)** shortcut icon on the desktop to display the contents of the removable disk, and then navigate to the **Module3 > Module** folder provided with your Data Files.
3. Right-click the **Cathedral** file, point to **Open with** on the shortcut menu, and then click **Paint** to open the Cathedral picture file in Paint.
4. Minimize the new Paint window.
5. Right-click the **Sunburst** file, point to **Open with** on the shortcut menu, and then click **Paint** to open the Sunburst picture file in Paint.
6. Minimize the new Paint window.
7. Point to the **Paint** button on the taskbar to display thumbnail previews of the three pictures open in Paint. See Figure 3-27.

Figure 3-27 Previewing windows with Peek

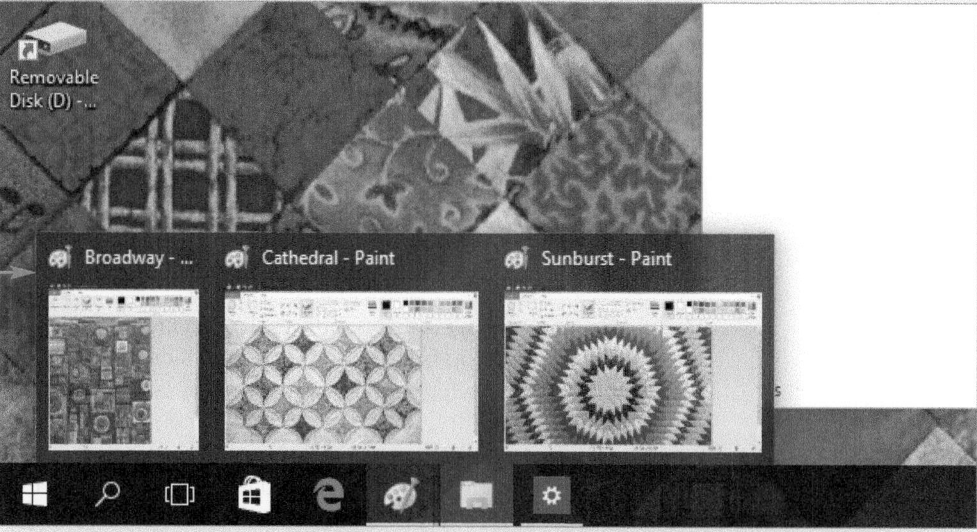

©iStock.com/Emilia Kun; ©iStock.com/dmfoss; ©iStock.com/Jewelee; ©iStock.com/blindsquirrelphoto

Trouble? If a list of filenames appears instead of thumbnails when you point to the Paint taskbar button, the thumbnails feature is probably disabled on your computer. Read but do not perform Steps 8 and 9.

TIP

To restore the desktop when you're previewing a window, move the pointer away from the thumbnail.

8. To preview the Sunburst picture, point to the **Sunburst** thumbnail. The File Explorer window fades so that the Sunburst window is the only one open on the desktop.
9. Click the **Sunburst** thumbnail to display the Sunburst picture in Paint and make it the active window. The File Explorer window is also redisplayed, but it is not the active window.

Minimizing and Restoring Windows with Shake

Shake is another handy tool for managing windows. Use Shake to quickly minimize all open windows on the desktop except the one you want to focus on—you don't have to minimize the windows one by one. Click and hold the title bar of the window you want to keep open, and then shake it by quickly dragging the window to the right and left. When you do, you minimize all of the other open windows. To restore the minimized windows, shake the open window again.

Rachel mentions that when she needs to focus on the contents of a window, she likes to minimize all of the other open windows. You suggest she use Shake to do so.

To use Shake:

1. Point to the **Paint** button on the taskbar, and then click the **Broadway** thumbnail to open the Broadway picture in Paint.
2. Point to the **Paint** button on the taskbar again, and then click the **Cathedral** thumbnail to open the Cathedral picture in Paint.
3. Point to the **title bar** of the Cathedral window, hold down the mouse button, and then quickly drag the window about an inch to the right and left to shake it. The Cathedral window remains open while all of the other open windows are minimized.
4. To restore the minimized windows, shake the **Cathedral** window again.
5. Click the **Show desktop** button on the far right side of the taskbar to minimize all open windows.

You have used the taskbar to manage open windows. Next, you'll learn how to use the taskbar to manage multiple desktops.

Using Virtual Desktops

If your desktop quickly becomes cluttered or you want to keep certain apps open or pinned to the taskbar depending on your task, you can create one or more virtual desktops. For example, you might use the default desktop for work-related tasks and open apps such as Calendar, WordPad, and File Explorer. At the end of the day or during a break, you can switch to a second desktop and catch up on the weather or explore the Windows Store. If an app is open on one desktop but you need it in a different one, you can move the window from one desktop to another.

Rachel thinks virtual desktops will help her be more productive, so you'll show her how to create and use a second desktop. First, you'll open a window on the default desktop so you can easily distinguish between the default and virtual desktops.

To use a virtual desktop:

1. Point to the **Paint** button on the taskbar, and then click **Cathedral** to display the Cathedral picture in a Paint window on the default desktop.
2. Click the **Task View** button on the taskbar, and then click **New desktop** in the lower-right corner of the desktop. Desktop 2 opens as a duplicate of Desktop 1 (the default desktop) except that Desktop 2 does not include any open apps. See Figure 3-28.

Figure 3-28 New virtual desktop

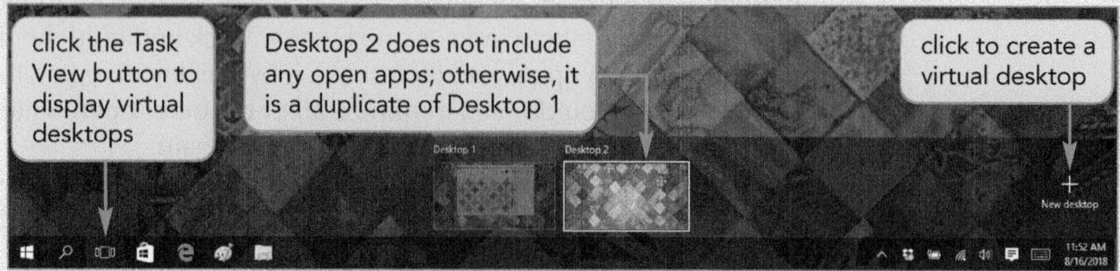

©iStock.com/Emilia Kun; ©iStock.com/Jewelee

3. Click the **Desktop 2** thumbnail to switch to Desktop 2.
4. Click the **Start** button and then click **Weather** to start the Weather app and open its window on Desktop 2.
5. Click the **Task View** button and then right-click the **Weather** thumbnail on the desktop.
6. Point to **Move to** on the shortcut menu, and then click **Desktop 1** to move the Weather window to the default desktop. The Weather window no longer appears on Desktop 2.
7. Point to the **Desktop 1** thumbnail to display the windows open on the default desktop: Weather, three Paint windows, and one File Explorer window.
8. Point to the **Desktop 2** thumbnail to display a Close button on the thumbnail, and then click the **Close** button to close Desktop 2.
9. Click a blank area of the desktop, and then close all open windows.

Besides customizing the taskbar to suit your preferences and work habits, you can do the same to the Start menu.

Personalizing the Start Menu

Most of the items on the Start menu are created for you by Windows 10 or by the apps you install. Windows 10 personalizes the left pane of the Start menu as you work to show the apps you use most frequently. However, you can also determine the content and appearance of your Start menu. For example, you can pin tiles for apps, settings, and folders to the Start menu and organize the Start menu to use it most effectively. Because the Start menu is the gateway to the apps on your computer, it should display the apps you use most often, organized in a way that makes sense for how you work.

To personalize the Start menu, you can add tiles for apps you use often and remove tiles for the apps you don't use. Like the shortcut icons on the desktop, each tile is a shortcut, providing a quick way to perform an action such as starting an app. Besides shortcuts for apps, you can add shortcuts for folders such as the Documents folder and settings such as the Background settings.

The Start menu initially contains two groups of tiles by default: a Life at a glance group, for apps you are likely to use every day, and a Play and explore group for entertainment apps. If you add a new tile or drag one near the bottom of the right pane in the Start menu, you can create a new group. For example, you might want to pin a few settings to the Start menu and organize them into a Settings group.

If the Start menu becomes cluttered with tiles, you can display it as a full-screen menu. To do so, start the Settings app, select Personalization, select the Start category, and then turn on the "Use Start full screen" setting. Because the Start menu background is transparent by default, you can still see the desktop when you display the Start menu full screen.

PROSKILLS

Problem Solving: Adding Apps to Work Productively

In addition to the default apps that come with Windows 10, you can purchase and install apps using the Windows Store, a Microsoft website accessible from the taskbar and Start menu. The Windows Store provides apps created by Microsoft and other developers. It organizes apps by categories, such as Social, Productivity, Tools, and Security. If you're looking for a specific app, you can use Cortana or the Search the web and Windows tool to search for the app by name. Most of the default apps are designed for entertainment and connecting with your contacts. The Windows Store includes Windows and desktop apps to help you work productively, such as dictionaries, eBook readers, antivirus software, and even the latest version of Microsoft Office. Signing in to Windows 10 makes you eligible to purchase, download, and install apps from the Windows Store. Microsoft and other developers frequently post new apps in the Windows Store, so you should visit the site occasionally to see whether new productivity apps are available.

Rachel wants to change the Start menu on her computer to include a tile for a new Windows app and for settings she uses often. You'll show her how to pin these items as tiles on the Start menu.

Pinning Tiles on the Start Menu

To pin an app, setting, folder, or device on the Start menu, you find the command or icon for the item, right-click it, and then select the Pin to Start command. The tiles on the Start menu are pinned items because they remain on the Start menu until you unpin them. When you unpin an item, Windows removes the tile from the Start menu, but it doesn't remove the app from your computer.

REFERENCE

Pinning an App on the Start Menu

- Click the Start button and then click All apps.
- Right-click an app in the All apps list, and then click Pin to Start on the shortcut menu.

Rachel mentions that she often receives reports and other documents as **PDF files**, which are files in the Portable Document Format. Reader is a Windows app that lets you read and navigate PDF documents. Because Rachel thinks she will use Reader often, she wants to add a tile for the app to the Start menu. She also plans to use the Background settings and the Lock screen settings often, and she wants quick access to the Freeform Quilts folder.

You'll show Rachel how to pin tiles for Reader, Background settings, Lock screen settings, and the Freeform Quilts folder on the Start menu.

To pin Reader on the Start menu:

1. Click the **Start** button ⊞ to display the Start menu, and then click **All apps** to display an alphabetic list of apps installed on your computer.
2. Click a letter, such as A, to collapse the All apps list, click **R**, and then right-click **Reader** to display its shortcut menu. See Figure 3-29. Your All apps list might contain different apps.

Figure 3-29 Pinning an app to the Start menu

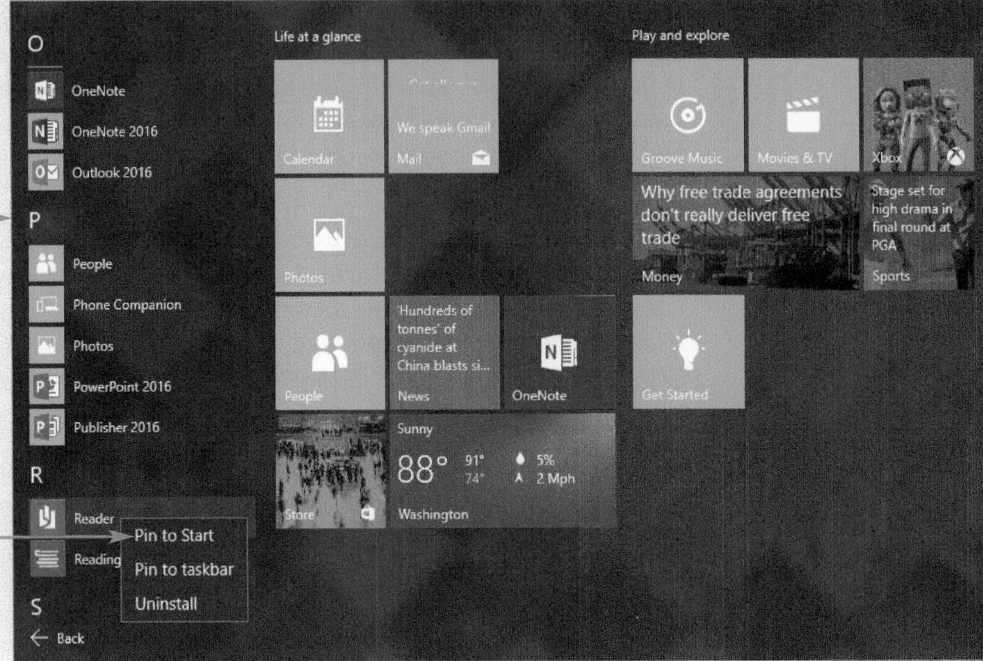

©iStock.com/Emilia Kun

TIP

If you drag an icon from the All apps list to the Start menu, you remove the app from the All apps list and pin that app to the Start menu.

3. Click **Pin to Start** on the shortcut menu. A Reader tile appears on the Start menu while a Reader icon remains on the All apps list.

   Trouble? If the Reader app is not installed on your computer, right-click any other app that does not appear in the right pane, such as the Reading List app, and then click Pin to Start on the shortcut menu.

You can also pin apps to the taskbar the same way: right-click the app on the All apps list, and then click Pin to taskbar on the shortcut menu.

Next, you can add tiles for the Background and Lock screen settings to the Start menu.

To pin the Background and Lock screen settings to the Start menu:

1. At the bottom of the All apps list, click the **Back** button to return to the Start menu, and then click **Settings** to start the Settings app.
2. Click **Personalization** to open the Personalization window, which includes the Background and Lock screen settings.
3. In the left pane, right-click **Background** and then click **Pin to Start** on the shortcut menu.
4. Right-click **Lock screen** in the left pane, and then click **Pin to Start** on the shortcut menu.
5. Close the Personalization window, and then click the **Start** button to display the Start menu with the new pinned tiles. See Figure 3-30.

Figure 3-30 Settings pinned to the Start menu

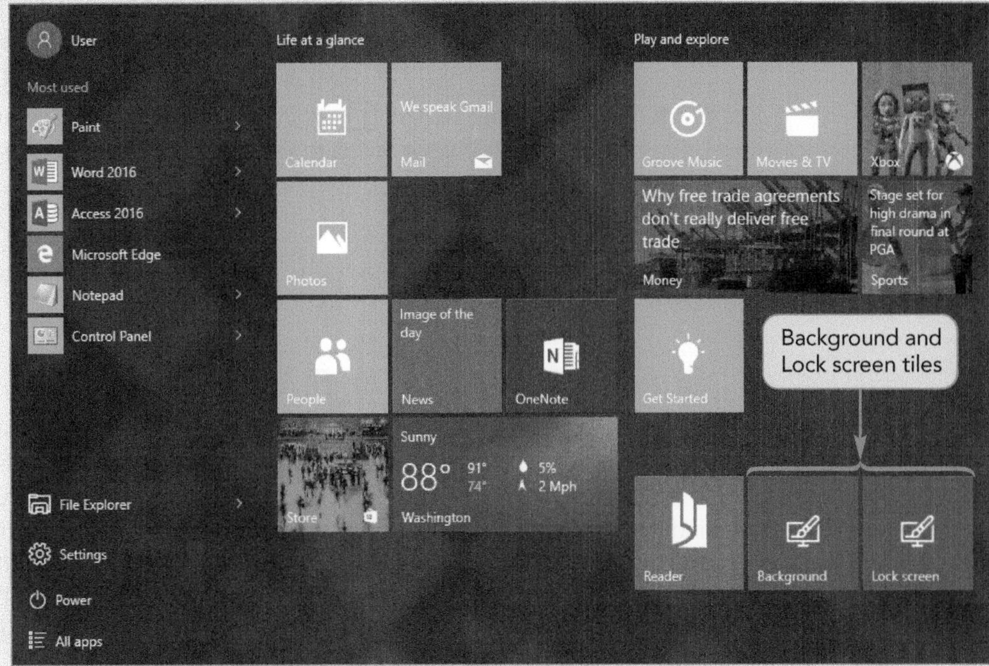

©iStock.com/Emilia Kun

6. Click a blank area on the desktop to close the Start menu.

The last tile to add to the Start menu for Rachel is one for the Freeform Quilts folder.

To pin the Freeform Quilts folder to the Start menu:

1. Click the **File Explorer** button on the taskbar, and then display the contents of the Pictures folder.
2. Right-click the **Freeform Quilts** folder, and then click **Pin to Start** on the shortcut menu.
3. Close the File Explorer window.

You can test the four new tiles on the Start menu to make sure each opens the appropriate app, settings, or folder.

To test the new tiles on the Start menu:

1. Click the **Start** button to display the Start menu with four new tiles.
2. Click the **Reader** tile on the Start menu to start Reader. When the app starts, it might display a document explaining how to convert PDF files into Word documents or it might display a Browse button, which you can click to find a PDF file to open.
3. Close the Reader window, and then click the **Start** button to display the Start menu again.

4. Click the **Background** tile on the Start menu. The Personalization window opens and displays the Background settings.
5. Click the **Start** button and then click the **Lock screen** tile. The Personalization window changes to display the Lock screen settings.
6. Click the **Start** button again, scroll down, if necessary, and then click the **Freeform Quilts** tile to open the folder window on the desktop.
7. Close all open windows.

Now that you've pinned apps to the Start menu, you can organize them to make the tiles easier to find.

Organizing Tiles on the Start Menu

If you continue to pin items to the Start menu, you will eventually have an unmanageable number of tiles on the Start menu. One way to organize tiles is by grouping them so that similar tiles appear together. You can assign a name to the group, which helps you quickly find the tile you want. Another way to organize the tiles is to modify their appearance. For example, you can reduce the size of tiles to fit more on the Start menu and turn live tiles on or off. If you're not using a tile, you can remove it from the Start menu, which helps to keep the Start menu uncluttered. You can still use the All apps list or the Search the web and Windows tool to start and use the app.

You pinned four new tiles on the Start menu for Reader, Background settings, Lock screen settings, and the Freeform Quilts folder. All of these new tiles appear together in their own group. You can start organizing the tiles by moving the Reader tile into one of the default groups, such as the Life at a glance group. Next, you can create a group for the Freeform Quilts, Background, and Lock screen tiles. Rachel plans to occasionally update the appearance settings on the company computers and will use these tiles when she does.

To organize the new tiles on the Start menu:

1. Click the **Start** button to display the Start menu.
2. Drag the **Reader** tile to a blank area in the Life at a glance group of tiles. The other three new tiles remain together in a group, which you can name to identify them.
3. Point above the three new tiles until "Name group" appears, and then click **Name group** to display a box for naming the group. See Figure 3-31.

Figure 3-31 Naming a group of tiles

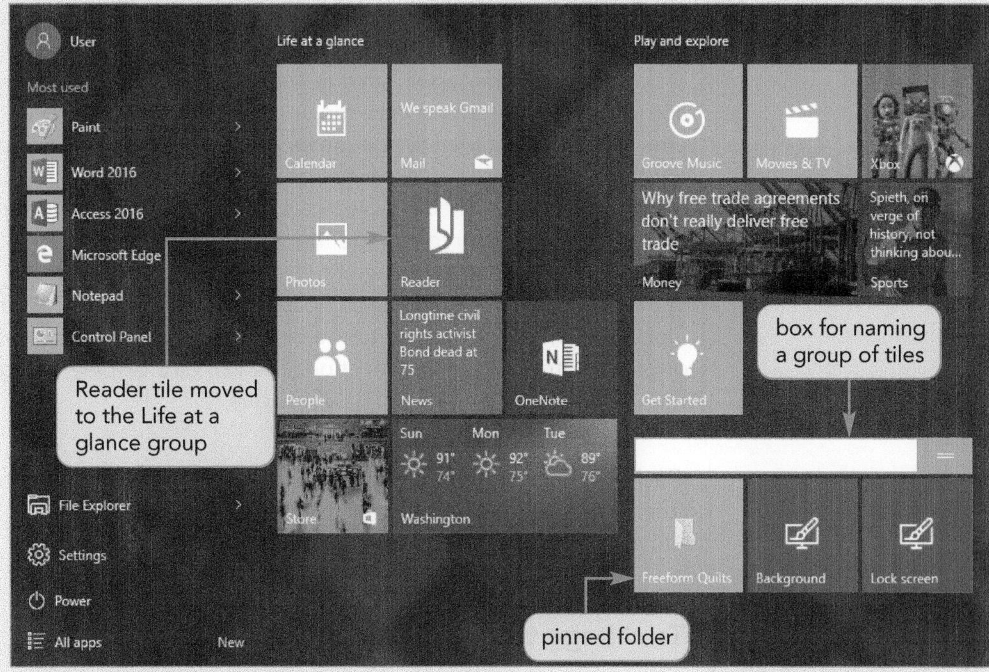

©iStock.com/Emilia Kun

TIP

To rename a group, click the group name to display the box, and then replace the text.

4. Type **Appearance settings** and then press the **Enter** key to name the group.

To keep your Start menu clean and uncluttered, you can remove tiles to display only those you use often. To remove a tile, right-click it, and then click Unpin from Start on the shortcut menu. Keep in mind that when you remove a tile, you are only unpinning the item, not deleting an app or a folder.

Modifying Tiles on the Start Menu

Besides rearranging, grouping, and removing the tiles on the Start menu, you can also change their size. For example, if you need to scroll to display tiles, you can reduce the size of large tiles to display more tiles in the same space. You can display tiles as small, medium, wide, or large. You can also modify tiles by making them live tiles, which change to display the contents or updated information for an app. For example, if you make the Photos tile a live tile, it displays a slide show of photos and other images.

INSIGHT

Turning on Live Tiles

Some tiles on the Start menu are live tiles by default—they display the latest information from apps including Store, News, Weather, Money, and Sports. To turn on live tiles for other apps, such as Mail, People, and Photos, you need to set up an account or add information to the app. For example, after you use Mail to set up an email account, the Mail tile becomes a live tile and displays recent email messages. For the People app, you need to add contact information, including pictures. If a live tile becomes too distracting, you can right-click the tile and then click Turn live tile off on the shortcut menu to change the tile to a static one.

To display images in the live Photos tile, first make sure you have stored photos in a location the Photos app can access, such as the Pictures folder in This PC or on OneDrive, or add a location to the Photos app. You can then have the Photos tile display photos from your collection. You can also display a single photo in the Photos tile instead of a changing series of images.

Rachel asks you to reduce the size of a tile so she can see how to display more tiles on the Start menu. She also wants to display the Broadway quilt picture in the Photos tile to see if she likes the result.

To change the size of Start menu tiles:

TIP

To change the size of the Start menu itself, drag its top or right border.

1. On the Start menu, right-click the **Money** tile, point to **Resize** on the shortcut menu, and then click **Medium** to change its size setting from Wide to Medium.

   Trouble? If the size setting for the Money tile is already Medium, keep the setting by clicking Medium as instructed in Step 1.

2. Right-click the **Get Started** tile, point to **Resize** on the shortcut menu, and then click **Small** to change its size. See Figure 3-32.

Figure 3-32 Changing the size of tiles

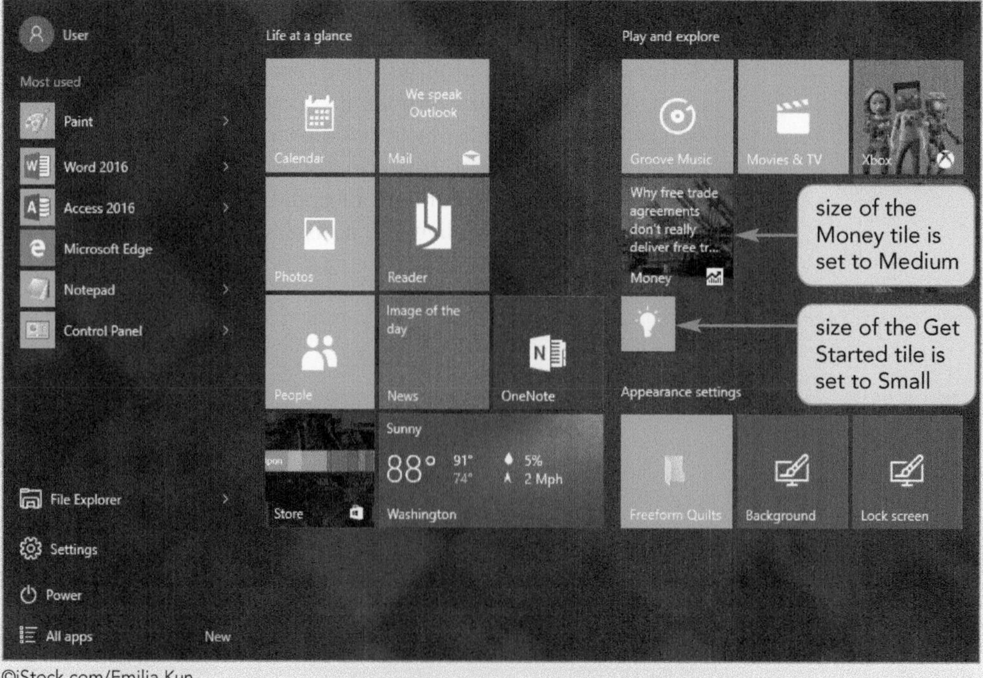

©iStock.com/Emilia Kun

Next, you can start the Photos app to select the Freeform Quilts folder as a source for photos to display in the tile and make the Photos tile a live tile on the Start menu.

To make the Photos tile a live tile:

1. Right-click the **Photos** tile, point to **More**, and then click **Turn live tile on** on the shortcut menu.

   Trouble? If the Turn live tile off option appears on the shortcut menu instead of the Turn live tile on option, the Photos tile is already a live tile. Skip Step 1.
2. Click the **Photos** tile to start the Photos app, which might display a collection or album of photos stored on your computer or in your OneDrive.
3. In the upper-left corner of the Photos window, click the **Menu** button to display a list of options.
4. Click **Settings** on the Photos menu to display the settings for the app. See Figure 3-33.

Figure 3-33 Settings for the Photos app

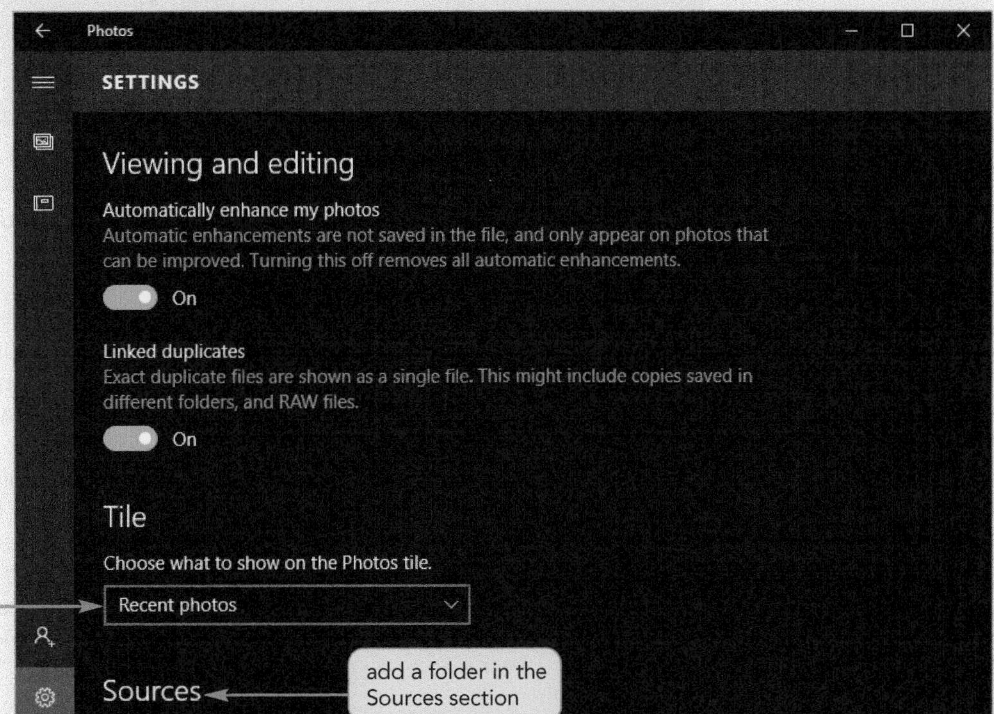

5. In the Sources section, click the **Add a folder** button to open the Select folder dialog box.
6. Navigate to the **Pictures > Freeform Quilts** folder, and then click the **Add this folder to Pictures** button to add this folder as a source of pictures to display on the Photos tile on the Start menu.
7. Close the Photos app and then open the Start menu. The Photos tile becomes a live tile displaying photos from the sources listed in the Photos app, including the Broadway quilt photo, which might take a few seconds. See Figure 3-34.

Figure 3-34 Live Photos tile

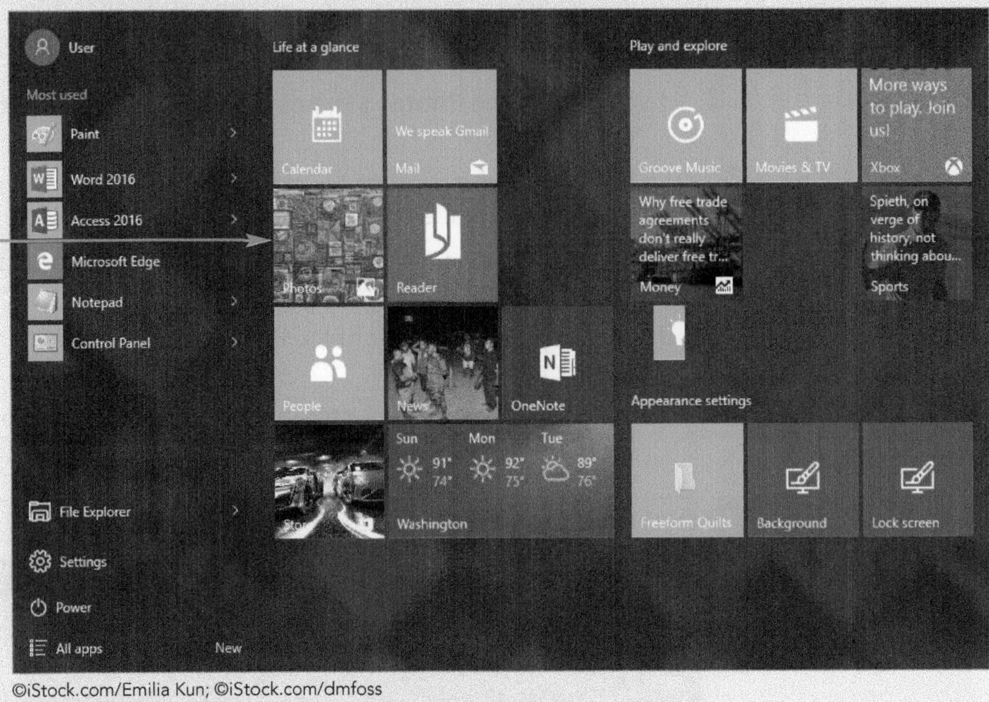

©iStock.com/Emilia Kun; ©iStock.com/dmfoss

Now the live Photos tile reflects the mission of the Crafted Quilts organization.

Changing the User Picture

Windows displays a generic icon as the default user account picture, but you can change this picture to display a photo of yourself or anything else that identifies you. If your computer includes a built-in camera, you can use the camera to take a photo and display it as your user account picture. Otherwise, you can use any image file stored in a location your computer can access, such as the Pictures folder. Your user picture represents your user account, which is a collection of information specifying how you can use the computer and its apps and includes appearance settings such as your Start menu background and color.

Rachel wants to use the photo of a Sunburst quilt as her user picture. You'll show her how to replace the generic user icon on the Start menu with a more meaningful photo.

To change the user account picture:

1. Click the **user icon** on the Start menu, and then click **Change account settings** on the shortcut menu to open the Accounts window displaying settings for your user account. See Figure 3-35. Your account information will differ.

Figure 3-35 Changing the account picture

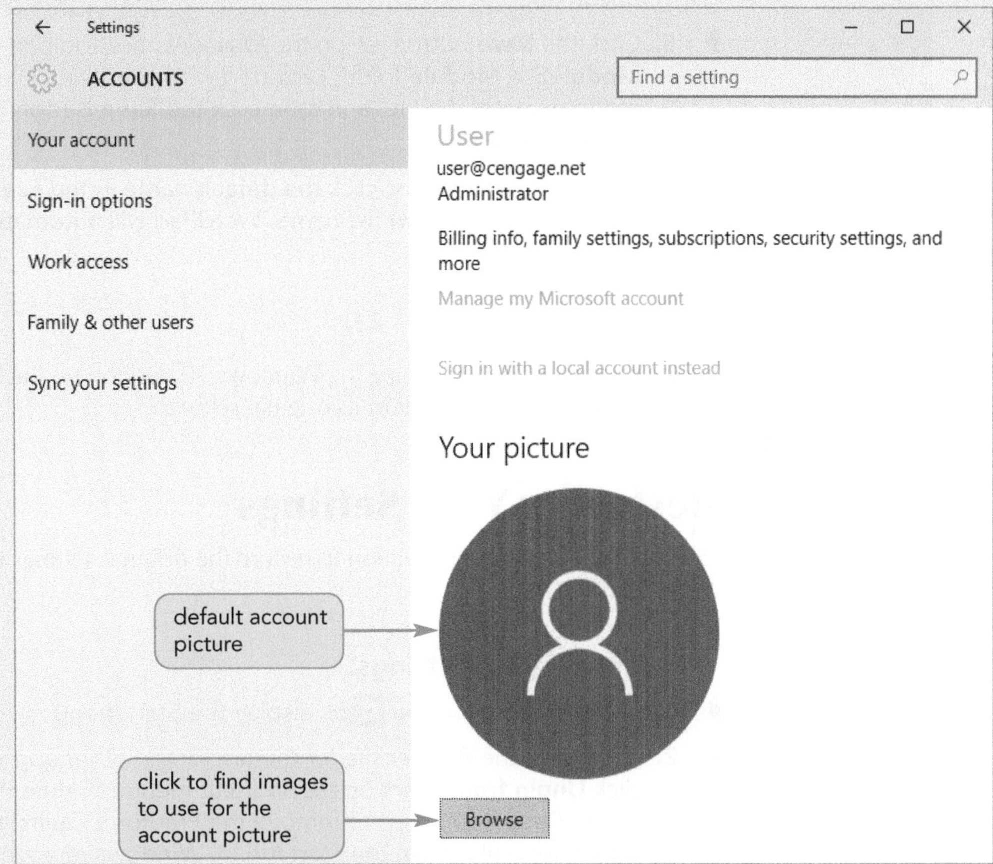

2. Click the **Browse** button to open the Open dialog box, and then navigate to the **Module3 > Module** folder.
3. Click the **Sunburst** file to select it.
4. Click the **Choose picture** button to select the Sunburst picture as the account picture.
5. Close the Accounts window and then open the Start menu, which now includes the new account picture.

To create an image of the Start menu that displays many of the changes you made, you can take a screenshot of the Start menu. Rachel can use that image for reference as she customizes the other Crafted Quilts computers.

TIP

You can also press the Windows+Print Screen keys to create a screenshot named Screenshot (1), for example, which Windows stores in a folder named Screenshots in the Pictures folder.

To create a screenshot of the Start menu:

1. Press the **Print Screen** key to capture an image of the Start menu and save the image on the Clipboard. Depending on the type of computer you are using, the Print Screen key might be labeled differently (for example, PrtScn).
2. Click the **All apps** icon on the Start menu, scroll the list, click **Windows Accessories**, and then click **WordPad** to start WordPad and open a new, blank document.
3. Type your name followed by **Customized Start menu**, and then press the **Enter** key.

4. Press the **Ctrl+V** keys to paste the Start menu image into the new WordPad document.
5. Click the **Save** button on the Quick Access Toolbar, navigate to the **Module3 > Module** folder provided with your Data Files, type **Start menu** as the name of the file, and then click the **Save** button to save the file in the Module folder.

   Trouble? If necessary, click the default name in the File name box to select it before typing a new file name. WordPad will automatically add the file extension .rtf.
6. Close WordPad.

You've finished personalizing the Windows 10 desktop on Rachel's computer, so you should restore your computer to its original settings.

Restoring Your Settings

Complete the steps in this section to restore the original settings on your computer.

To restore your settings:

1. Click the **Start** button to display the Start menu.
2. Right-click the **Reader** tile (or the tile for the other app you pinned), and then click **Unpin from Start** on the shortcut menu to unpin the app from the Start menu. Repeat this step to remove the Freeform Quilts, Background, and Lock screen tiles from the Start menu. Windows removes the group name when you remove the tiles.
3. Right-click the **Money** tile on the Start menu, point to **Resize** on the shortcut menu, and then click your original size setting. Right-click the **Get Started** tile on the Start menu, point to **Resize** on the shortcut menu, and then click your original size setting.
4. Right-click the **Photos** tile on the Start menu, and then click **Turn live tile off** on the shortcut menu.
5. Click the **user icon** on the Start menu, click **Change account settings** to open the Accounts window, and then click your original user picture.

   Trouble? If you were using the original generic user picture that appeared when you installed Windows, and this picture is not provided in the Accounts window, click the Browse button and then enter C:\ProgramData\Microsoft\User Account Pictures in the Address bar of the Open dialog box to navigate to the location of the generic pictures. Click the user picture, and then click the Choose picture button.
6. Click the **Start** button and then click the **Photos** tile to start the app. In the Photos window, click **Settings**. In the Sources section, click the **Close** button for the Pictures > Freeform Quilts folder, click the **Remove Folder** button, and then close the Photos app.

7. Right-click the **desktop**, and then click **Personalize** on the shortcut menu to display the Personalization settings. In the left pane, click **Themes**. In the right pane, click **Theme settings**, and then click your original theme, such as **Windows**, to restore your original desktop background, window color, screen saver (which might be "None"), and desktop icons.
8. Right-click the **Crafted Quilts** theme, and then click **Delete theme** on the shortcut menu. If necessary, click the **Yes** button to confirm the deletion. Close the Control Panel's Personalization window.
9. In the right pane of the Personalization window for the Settings app, click **Desktop icon settings**. Click the check boxes to restore the original settings. By default, only the Recycle Bin appears on the desktop. Click the **OK** button to close the Desktop Icon Settings dialog box.
10. In the left pane of the Personalization window, click **Lock screen**, click the original lock screen picture, click the **Background** box, and then click your original background setting. Close the Personalization window.
11. Open the Pictures folder, and then move the **Freeform Quilts** folder to the **Module3 > Module** folder provided with your Data Files. Close all open windows.
12. Click the desktop **shortcut icon** that you created in this module, and then press the **Delete** key to delete the shortcut. If necessary, click the **Yes** button to confirm the deletion.
13. Right-click the **Paint** button on the taskbar, point to **Broadway**, and then click the **Unpin from this list** icon.
14. On the Paint shortcut menu, click **Unpin this program from taskbar**.
15. Drag the **File Explorer** button on the taskbar to its original location to the left of the Microsoft Edge button on the taskbar.
16. Right-click the **Search the web and Windows** button on the taskbar, point to **Search** on the shortcut menu, and then click **Show search box** to redisplay the Search the web and Windows box on the taskbar.

    Trouble? If you have activated Cortana, point to Cortana on the shortcut menu, and then click Show search box.

REVIEW

Session 3.2 Quick Check

1. How do you change the position of taskbar buttons?
2. Why would you pin a file to a taskbar button's Jump List?
3. You can use a feature called ____________ to list the thumbnails of open windows as you snap a window into place.
4. How can you quickly minimize all open windows on the desktop?
5. Explain how to create a virtual desktop.
6. Name two ways you can change the appearance of a tile on the Start menu.
7. What can you do with the Reader app?
8. Explain how to personalize the user icon on the Start menu.

PRACTICE

Review Assignments

See the Starting Data Files section at the beginning of this module for a list of Data Files needed for the Review Assignments.

Crafted Quilts keeps a computer in its conference area for any staff member to use when needed. Rachel asks you to customize that computer so it is appropriate for the company. Rachel recently received photographs of new quilts that Mai found and wants to make the photos available to staff members to use in promotional materials for an upcoming quilt show. As you perform the following steps, note the original settings of the desktop and other items so you can restore them later. Complete the following steps:

1. Change the desktop theme to any other theme that displays photographs.
2. Change the lock screen to display the Star picture in the Module3 > Review folder provided with your Data Files.
3. Change the screen saver to play a slide show of the pictures in the Module3 > Review folder.
4. Change the desktop icon settings on your computer to display the This PC and Control Panel icons in addition to the default Recycle Bin icon. Change the image for the This PC icon so that it displays any other appropriate image.
5. With the USB drive or other removable media containing your Data Files in the appropriate drive, create a shortcut to this drive on the desktop. Use **Review Removable Disk Shortcut** as the name of the shortcut.
6. Use the Review Removable Disk Shortcut on the desktop to copy the five picture files in the Module3 > Review folder provided with your Data Files to a new folder in the Pictures folder. Use **Classic Quilts** as the name of the new folder.
7. Complete the following steps to open and work with Paint:
   - Use Paint to open the Tumble picture in the Classic Quilts folder, and then pin Paint to the taskbar.
   - Pin the Tumble picture file to the Paint Jump List.
   - Close the File Explorer and Personalization windows.
8. Use Snap to align the Paint window on the right side of the desktop.
9. Move the Paint button so it appears directly to the right of the Task View button.
10. Open the Screen Saver Settings dialog box again. (*Hint*: Double-click the Control Panel shortcut icon on the desktop, click Appearance and Personalization, and then click Change screen saver in the Personalization category.) Close the Control Panel window, and then position the Screen Saver Settings dialog box to the left of the Paint window.
11. Press the Print Screen key to capture an image of the desktop. In Paint, open a new file. (*Hint*: Click File on the menu bar, and then click New.) Press the Ctrl+V keys to paste the image in the Paint file. Save the file as **Review Desktop XY**, where XY are your initials, in the Module3 > Review folder provided with your Data Files. Close Paint and the Screen Saver Settings dialog box.
12. Pin the following items to the Start menu:
    - Maps app
    - Classic Quilts folder (which you created in Step 6)
    - Themes settings
13. Complete the following tasks on the Start menu:
    - If the Maps tile is a live tile, turn the live tile off.
    - Resize the Maps tile to the Large setting.
    - Arrange the Themes and Classic Quilts tiles directly to the right of the Maps tile.
    - Use **Quilt Show** as the name of the new group of tiles.
14. Change the user picture to display one of the pictures stored in the Classic Quilts folder.

15. Complete the following tasks to create a screenshot of your Start menu:
    - Display the Start menu, scroll to show the entire Quilt Show group, and then press the Print Screen key to capture an image of the Start menu.
    - Start Paint, and then press the Ctrl+V keys to paste the image in the Paint file.
    - Save the file as **Review Start XY**, where XY are your initials, in the Module3 > Review folder provided with your Data Files.
    - Close Paint.
16. Complete the following tasks to restore the settings on your computer:
    - Make the Maps tile on the Start menu a live tile.
    - Unpin the Maps, Themes, and Classic Quilts files from the Start menu.
    - Restore the default image for the user picture.
    - Change the desktop theme to its original theme, which is Windows by default.
    - Display the original set of icons on the desktop.
    - Unpin the Tumble picture file from the Paint Jump List, and then unpin Paint from the taskbar.
    - Delete the Classic Quilts folder in the Pictures folder.
    - Delete the Review Removable Disk Shortcut icon from the desktop.
17. Close any open windows.

APPLY

Case Problem 1

See the Starting Data Files section at the beginning of this module for a list of Data Files needed for this Case Problem.

Retro Motors Chad Bachman started Retro Motors as a place for classic car enthusiasts to buy and sell their cars. When he is not traveling to auto shows and private dealers to test drive vintage vehicles, Chad manages 10 employees in a showroom and office in Tempe, Arizona. He has hired you to help him run the office. Because he just installed Windows 10, he asks you to personalize the Start menu and desktop on his computer to focus on tools he can use in his business. As you perform the following steps, note the original settings of the Start menu and desktop so you can restore them later. Complete the following steps:

1. Change the desktop theme to any other theme (including an online theme) that seems appropriate for Retro Motors. (*Hint*: If you choose an online theme, click the Open button when the download is complete to add the theme to the Control Panel's Personalization window.) Close Microsoft Edge or other browser, if necessary. Close the Control Panel's Personalization window.
2. Complete the following tasks to add desktop icons to the desktop:
    - Change the desktop icon settings on your computer to display the Computer, Network, and Control Panel icons in addition to the default Recycle Bin icon.
    - Change the image for the Network icon so that it displays any other appropriate image.
3. Change the accent color to orange (first square in the color palette).
4. Insert the USB drive or other removable media containing your Data Files in the appropriate drive, and then create a shortcut to this drive on the desktop. Use **Case1 Removable Disk Shortcut** as the name of the shortcut.
5. Use the Case1 Removable Disk Shortcut on the desktop to copy the five picture files in the Module3 > Case1 folder provided with your Data Files to a new folder in the Pictures folder. Use **Retro** as the name of the new folder.
6. Complete the following tasks to customize the Start menu:
    - Unpin the News and Xbox tiles.
    - Pin the Calculator and Camera apps.
    - Pin the Retro folder (which you created in Step 5).

- Resize the Calculator and Camera tiles to the Wide setting, and then stack them on top of one another.
- Name the group containing the Calculator, Camera, and Retro tiles as **Business**.
- Change the user picture to display one of the pictures stored in the Pictures > Retro folder.

7. Display the Start menu, scroll down to display the entire Business group, and then press the Print Screen key to capture an image of the Start menu. Start Paint and then press the Ctrl+V keys to paste the image in the Paint file. Save the file as **Case1 Start XY**, where XY are your initials, in the Module3 > Case1 folder provided with your Data Files.
8. Complete the following tasks to set up a screen saver:
   - Open the Screen Saver Settings dialog box, and select the Photos screen saver.
   - Change the settings so the screen saver displays pictures from the Retro folder.
   - Move the dialog box so that some or all of the desktop items are clearly visible.
   - Use a taskbar tool to minimize other open windows.
9. Press the Print Screen key to capture an image of the desktop. Make Paint the active window, and then press the Ctrl+V keys to paste the image in the Paint file. Save the file as **Case1 Desktop XY**, where XY are your initials, in the Module3 > Case1 folder provided with your Data Files.
10. Complete the following tasks to restore the settings on your computer:
    - Close the Screen Saver Settings dialog box without saving your changes.
    - Unpin the Calculator, Camera, and Retro tiles from the Start menu.
    - Pin the News and Xbox apps to the Start menu, and then drag each to its original group.
    - Restore the default image for the user picture.
    - Restore the original theme, which is Windows by default.
    - If you downloaded a theme from the Microsoft website, delete the theme. (*Hint*: Right-click the theme, click Delete theme on the shortcut menu, and then click the Yes button.)
    - Display the original set of icons on the desktop (which is only the Recycle Bin icon by default).
    - Delete the Retro folder in the Pictures folder.
    - Delete the Case1 Removable Disk Shortcut icon from the desktop.
11. Close any open windows.

CHALLENGE

Case Problem 2

There are no Data Files needed for this Case Problem.

Clarity Weather Services Kiera and Will Moore own Clarity Weather Services, a company in Bethesda, Maryland, that provides weather information to businesses that need accurate, constantly updated forecasts. You are the office manager for the company and work with the staff and clients to help them use the company's resources. After installing Windows 10 on all of the office computers, Kiera asks you to personalize the desktop on her computer to reflect the company image. As you perform the following steps, note the original settings of the Start menu and desktop so you can restore them later. Complete the following steps:

1. Change the desktop theme to any other theme (including an online theme) that seems appropriate for Clarity Weather Services. (*Hint*: If you choose an online theme, click the Open button when the download is complete to add the theme to the Control Panel's Personalization window.) Close Microsoft Edge or other browser, if necessary. Close the Control Panel's Personalization window.
2. Complete the following tasks to add desktop icons to the desktop:
   - Change the desktop icon settings on your computer to display the This PC and Network icons in addition to the default Recycle Bin icon.
   - Change the image for the Recycle Bin (full) icon so that it displays a picture of a folder with contents.
   - Change the image for the Recycle Bin (empty) icon so that it displays a picture of a folder with no contents.

3. Change the accent color to one Windows picks from the desktop background picture.

Explore 4. Show the color on the Start menu, taskbar, and action center. (*Hint*: In the Colors category of the Personalization window, use a slider in the Choose a color section.)

5. Save the current desktop settings as a theme for sharing. Name the theme **Clarity**, and store it in the Case2 folder.

Explore 6. Pin the Weather app to the taskbar.

Explore 7. In the Lock screen category of the Personalization window, show detailed status for the Weather app. (*Hint*: Use a button in the "Choose an app to show detailed status" section.)

8. Change the screen saver to Mystify. Leave the Personalization window open, but close any other open windows.
9. Create a virtual desktop and then switch to it. Open the Weather app on the new desktop.
10. Switch to Desktop 1 and then display thumbnail images of both desktops.
11. Press the Print Screen key to capture an image of the desktops. Start Paint on Desktop 1, and then press the Ctrl+V keys to paste the image in the Paint file. Save the file as **Case2 Desktop XY**, where XY are your initials, in the Module3 > Case2 folder provided with your Data Files.
12. Complete the following tasks to work with the two desktops:
    - Close the Screen Saver Settings dialog box on Desktop 1.
    - Move the Weather app from Desktop 2 to Desktop 1.
    - Close Desktop 2.
13. Snap the Weather app to the right side of the desktop, and then snap the Personalization window to the left side of the desktop.

Explore 14. Complete the following steps to customize the Start menu:
- Pin the following items to the Start menu: Alarms & Clock app, Cortana app, and File Explorer. (*Hint*: Use the File Explorer command on the Start menu.)
- Move each new tile into a blank space in the Life at a glance group.

15. With the Start menu open, press the Print Screen key to capture an image of the Start menu. Start Paint, and then press the Ctrl+V keys to paste the image in the Paint file. Save the file as **Case2 Start XY**, where XY are your initials, in the Module3 > Case2 folder provided with your Data Files. Close Paint.
16. Complete the following tasks to restore the settings on your computer:
    - Unsnap the two windows on the desktop. (*Hint*: Drag the title bar of each window.)
    - Unpin the Alarms & Clock, Cortana, and File Explorer tiles from the Start menu.
    - Unpin the Weather app from the taskbar, and then close the Weather window.
    - Restore the original app used to show detailed status on the Lock screen.
    - Restore the original screen saver.
    - Restore the original theme, which is Windows by default.
    - If you downloaded a theme from the Microsoft website, delete the theme. (*Hint*: Right-click the theme, click Delete theme on the shortcut menu, and then click the Yes button.)
    - Display the original set of icons on the desktop (which is only the Recycle Bin icon by default).
    - Restore the default images for the Recycle Bin icons.
    - Turn off the setting that shows color on the Start menu, taskbar, and action center.
17. Close any open windows.

CHALLENGE

Case Problem 3

See the Starting Data Files section at the beginning of this module for a list of Data Files needed for this Case Problem.

Pottery Works Allison Markos is the manager of Pottery Works in Asheville, North Carolina. Allison provides clay and studio space in which customers can sculpt clay or choose a piece of pottery and then paint or glaze it. Allison finishes the piece by firing it in a kiln. For inspiration, Allison provides sample designs. The most popular of these are robot pictures that customers paint on plates and other pottery with flat surfaces. Allison recently hired you as an assistant to provide customer service and general back-office support. She has a visual impairment and asks you to customize her computer so she can use it more effectively. As you perform the following steps, note the original settings of the desktop and other items so you can restore them later. Complete the following steps:

1. Insert the USB drive or other removable media containing your Data Files in the appropriate drive, and then create a shortcut to this drive on the desktop. Use **Case3 Removable Disk Shortcut** as the name of the shortcut.
2. Use the Case3 Removable Disk Shortcut on the desktop to copy the nine picture files in the Module3 > Case3 folder provided with your Data Files to a new folder in the Pictures folder. Use **Robots** as the name of the new folder.
3. Pin the following items to the Start menu: Paint app, Ease of Access settings, Display settings, Personalization settings, and the Robots folder.
4. **Explore** Complete the following steps to use the Personalization tile to change the desktop background:
   - Play a slide show on the desktop background.
   - Choose the Robots folder (which you created in Step 2) as the source of the pictures.
   - Change the picture every minute.
   - Choose the Fit setting for the desktop pictures.
5. **Explore** Display the Start menu as a full-screen menu. (*Hint*: Use the Start category of settings in the Personalization window.) Close the Personalization window.
6. Complete the following tasks to rearrange the tiles on the Start menu:
   - Unpin two medium tiles from the Start menu. (Note which tiles you remove so you can pin them later.)
   - Resize two medium tiles in the Life at a glance group to large. (Note which tiles you resize so you can restore them to their original size later.)
   - Move tiles in the Life at a glance group into blank spaces in the group. (Note the original configuration so you can restore it later.)
   - Rename the new group, which contains the Paint, Ease of Access, Display, Personalization, and Robots tiles, as **Pottery Works**.
7. With the Start menu open, press the Print Screen key to capture an image of the desktop. Start Paint, and then press the Ctrl+V keys to paste the image in the Paint file. Save the file as **Case3 Start XY**, where XY are your initials, in the Module3 > Case3 folder provided with your Data Files.
8. **Explore** Complete the following tasks to make the taskbar easier for Allison to use:
   - Pin Paint to the taskbar.
   - Use Paint to open three pictures of your choice in the Robots folder. Pin each picture to the Paint Jump List, and then minimize the Paint window.
   - If necessary, unlock the taskbar. (*Hint*: Right-click the taskbar and if the Lock the taskbar option is checked, click Lock the taskbar to deselect the option.)
   - Increase the height of the taskbar to make it about twice its original height. (*Hint*: Drag the top of the taskbar to resize it.)
   - Use the Ease of Access tile on the Start menu to display the Ease of Access settings.
   - Turn on Magnifier.

- When the Magnifier icon appears, increase the magnification to 200%. (*Hint*: Click the Magnifier icon, if necessary, to display the Magnifier title bar and toolbar, and then click the Zoom In button.)
- Right-click the Paint button to display its Jump List.

Explore 9. Press the Print Screen key to capture an image of the desktop. Reduce the magnification to 100%. (*Hint*: Click the Magnifier icon, and then click the Zoom out button.)

10. Make Paint the active window, and then press the Ctrl+V keys to paste the image in the Paint file. Save the file as **Case3 Desktop XY**, where XY are your initials, in the Module3 > Case3 folder provided with your Data Files. Minimize the Paint window.

Explore 11. Turn off the Magnifier, and then close the Ease of Access window.

12. Change the desktop icon settings on your computer to display the This PC and Control Panel icons.

Explore 13. Use the desktop shortcut menu to change the view of the desktop so it displays large icons. (*Hint*: Right-click the desktop, point to View, and then click Large icons.)

14. Press the Print Screen key to capture an image of the desktop. Make Paint the active window, and then press the Ctrl+V keys to paste the image in the Paint file. Save the file as **Case3 Icons XY**, where XY are your initials, in the Module3 > Case3 folder provided with your Data Files. Close Paint.
15. Complete the following tasks to restore the settings on your computer:
    - Delete the Case3 Removable Disk Shortcut icon from the desktop.
    - Change the view of the desktop so it displays Medium icons.
    - Display the original set of icons on the desktop, which is only the Recycle Bin by default.
    - Change the taskbar to its original height.
    - Restore the original theme, which is Windows by default.
    - Unpin the three robot pictures from the Paint Jump List, and then unpin Paint from the taskbar.
    - Unpin the Paint, Ease of Access, Display, Personalization, and Robots tiles from the Start menu.
    - Resize the two large tiles in the Life at a glance group to medium.
    - Pin the two tiles you removed from the Start menu.
    - Return all the tiles to their original positions.
    - Turn off the setting that displays the Start menu full screen.
    - Delete the Robots folder in the Pictures folder.
16. Close all open windows.

CREATE

Case Problem 4

There are no Data Files needed for this Case Problem.

Choi Graphics After training to be a graphic designer, Jin Choi decided to start his own company in Santa Clara, California, providing illustrations and animations to electronic game companies. Jin recently upgraded all of the computers at Choi Graphics to Windows 10 and then hired you to manage the office. After working with a client in San Jose, Jin shows you a screenshot of that client's Start menu and another of his desktop. See Figure 3-36. He thinks the design of the Start menu and desktop would be appropriate for the computers at Choi Graphics, and he asks you to create something similar on your computer.

Figure 3-36 Model Start menu and desktop for Choi Graphics

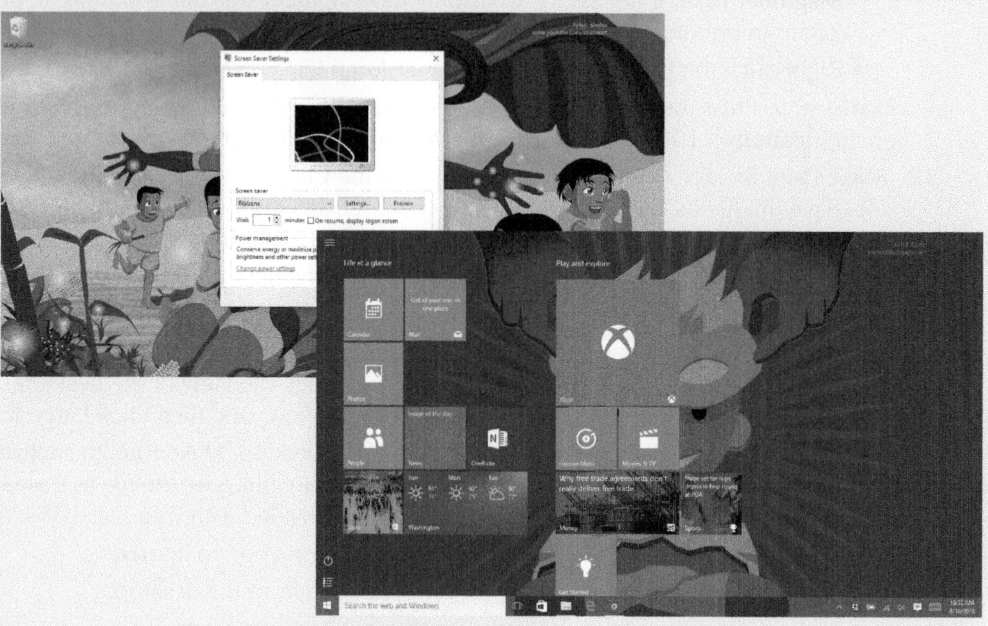

1. Complete the following steps to customize the desktop:
   - Download an online theme in the Art (illustrative) or Games category. The one shown in the figure is called "Giving Heroes." (*Hint*: If you choose an online theme, click the Open button when the download is complete to add the theme to the Control Panel's Personalization window.)
   - Set Windows to automatically pick an accent color from the desktop background.
   - Choose the Ribbons screen saver.
   - Minimize the Personalization window, if necessary.
2. Capture an image of the desktop with the Screen Saver Settings dialog box open, and then save the image in a Paint file named **Case4 Desktop XY**, where XY are your initials, in the Module3 > Case4 folder provided with your Data Files.

Explore 3. Complete the following steps to customize the Start menu:
   - Display the Start menu full screen. (*Hint*: Use the Start category of settings in the Personalization window.)
   - Show color on the Start menu, taskbar, and action center. (*Hint*: In the Colors category of the Personalization window, use a slider in the Choose a color section.)
   - Resize the Xbox tile to the Large setting.
4. Capture an image of the Start menu, and then save the image in a Paint file named **Case4 Start XY**, where XY are your initials, in the Module3 > Case4 folder provided with your Data Files.
5. Restore the original settings, and then close all open windows.

MODULE 4

Working with the Internet and Email

Communicating with Others

WINDOWS

OBJECTIVES

Session 4.1
- Open, view, and navigate webpages in Microsoft Edge
- Find online information with Cortana
- Annotate webpages
- Read and revisit webpages
- Organize links to your favorite webpages

Session 4.2
- Explain how email works
- Send, receive, reply to, and delete email with Mail
- Attach a file to an email message
- Add a contact using People
- Create appointments with Calendar

Case | *Step Up*

Kent Arneson is the director of Step Up in Salt Lake City, Utah, a career coaching agency that provides job counseling services to recent graduates, residents returning to the workforce, and professionals interested in changing careers. Step Up focuses on opportunities in Salt Lake City and surrounding areas and offers workshops on general career development topics. One of the organization's most popular workshops teaches participants how to research jobs and find reliable, up-to-date occupation information. Although Kent has been focused on running the company, he wants to teach a few workshops to keep in touch with clients. He is also organizing a three-day conference on career opportunities in Salt Lake City for people from out of state. In preparation, he wants to learn about using online resources to find quick answers to questions about living and working in Salt Lake City. As his project assistant, you regularly use Microsoft Edge to gather information for Step Up on the World Wide Web. You also use the Windows 10 Mail app to exchange email with Step Up's clients. Kent has asked you to get him up to speed on using these apps.

In this module, you'll explore how the Internet and the web work and use Microsoft Edge to visit and organize webpages. You'll examine email technology and use Mail to send, receive, and reply to email messages. You'll also use two Windows apps to manage your contacts and your schedule.

STARTING DATA FILES

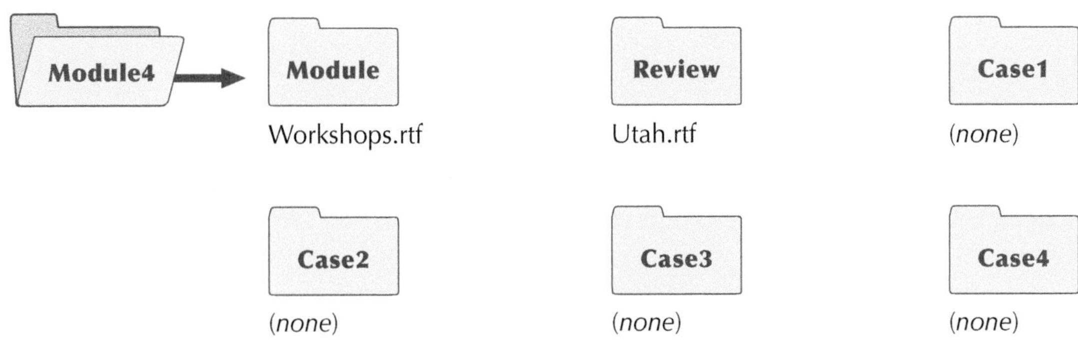

Session 4.1 Visual Overview:

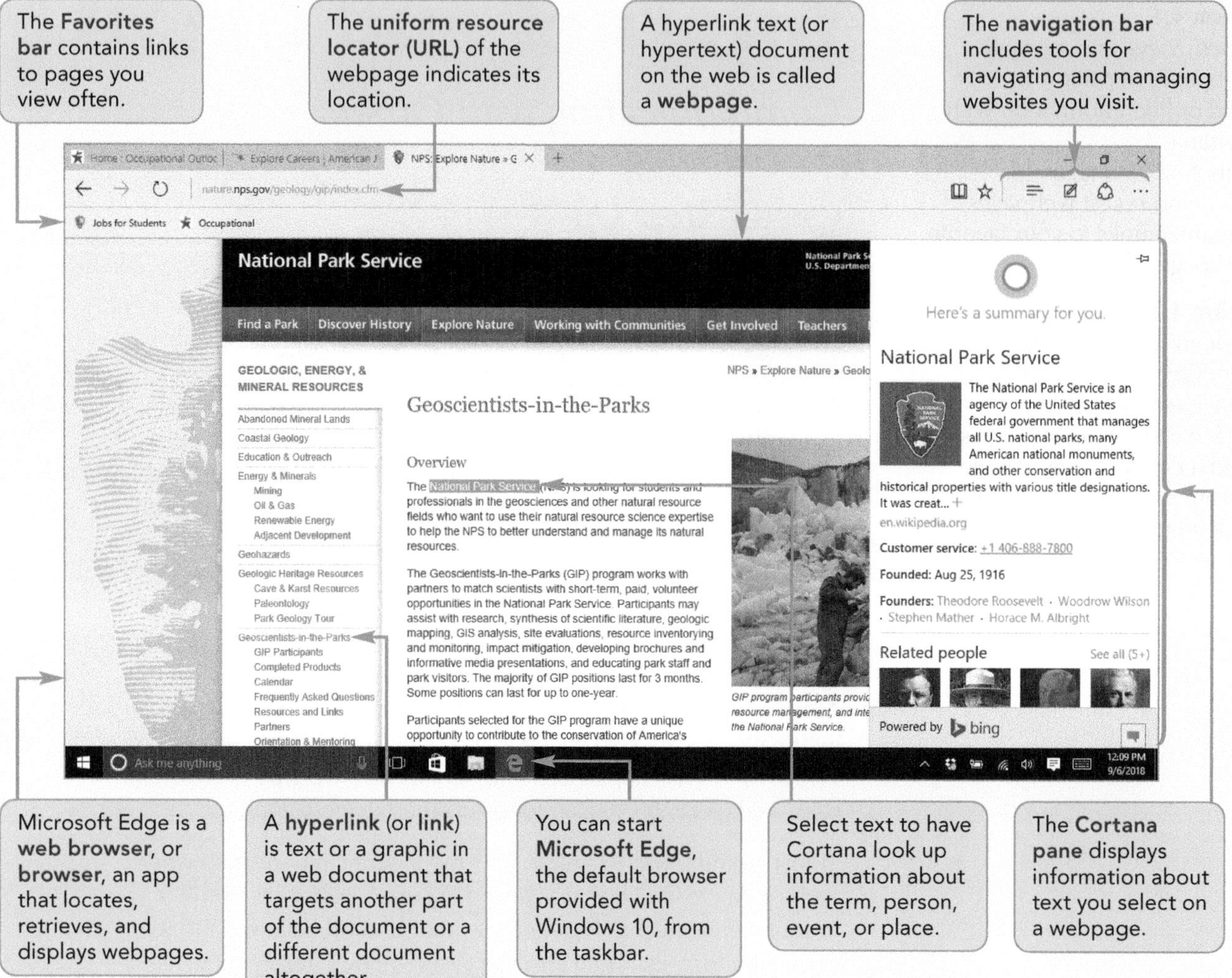

The **Favorites bar** contains links to pages you view often.
The **uniform resource locator (URL)** of the webpage indicates its location.
A hyperlink text (or hypertext) document on the web is called a **webpage**.
The **navigation bar** includes tools for navigating and managing websites you visit.
Microsoft Edge is a **web browser**, or **browser**, an app that locates, retrieves, and displays webpages.
A **hyperlink** (or **link**) is text or a graphic in a web document that targets another part of the document or a different document altogether.
You can start **Microsoft Edge**, the default browser provided with Windows 10, from the taskbar.
Select text to have Cortana look up information about the term, person, event, or place.
The **Cortana pane** displays information about text you select on a webpage.
National Park Service
Geoscientists-in-the-Parks
Here's a summary for you.

Courtesy of the National Park Service

Microsoft Edge

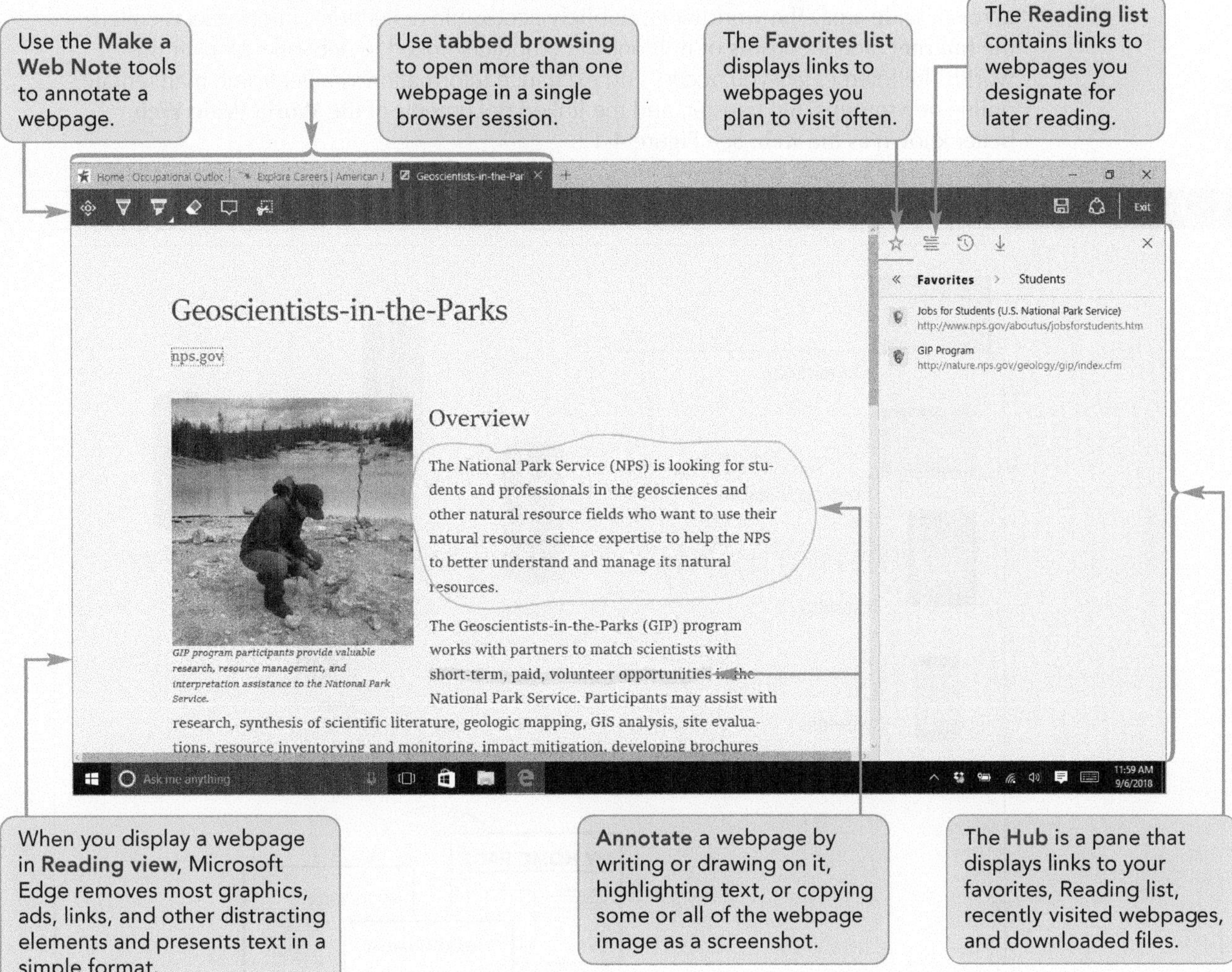

Use the Make a Web Note tools to annotate a webpage.
Use tabbed browsing to open more than one webpage in a single browser session.
The Favorites list displays links to webpages you plan to visit often.
The Reading list contains links to webpages you designate for later reading.
Favorites
Students
Jobs for Students (U.S. National Park Service)
http://www.nps.gov/aboutus/jobsforstudents.htm
GIP Program
http://nature.nps.gov/geology/gip/index.cfm
Geoscientists-in-the-Parks
nps.gov
Overview
The National Park Service (NPS) is looking for students and professionals in the geosciences and other natural resource fields who want to use their natural resource science expertise to help the NPS to better understand and manage its natural resources.
The Geoscientists-in-the-Parks (GIP) program works with partners to match scientists with short-term, paid, volunteer opportunities in the National Park Service. Participants may assist with research, synthesis of scientific literature, geologic mapping, GIS analysis, site evaluations, resource inventorying and monitoring, impact mitigation, developing brochures
GIP program participants provide valuable research, resource management, and interpretation assistance to the National Park Service.
When you display a webpage in Reading view, Microsoft Edge removes most graphics, ads, links, and other distracting elements and presents text in a simple format.
Annotate a webpage by writing or drawing on it, highlighting text, or copying some or all of the webpage image as a screenshot.
The Hub is a pane that displays links to your favorites, Reading list, recently visited webpages, and downloaded files.

Exploring the Internet and the Web

When you connect two or more computers to exchange information and resources, they form a network. You can connect networks to each other to share information across a wide area. The worldwide, publicly accessible collection of networks is called the **Internet**, and it consists of millions of computers linked to networks all over the world. The Internet lets you access and exchange information via electronic mail (email), online newsgroups, file transfer, and the linked documents of the **World Wide Web**, better known as the **web**. See Figure 4-1.

Figure 4-1 Connecting computers to the Internet

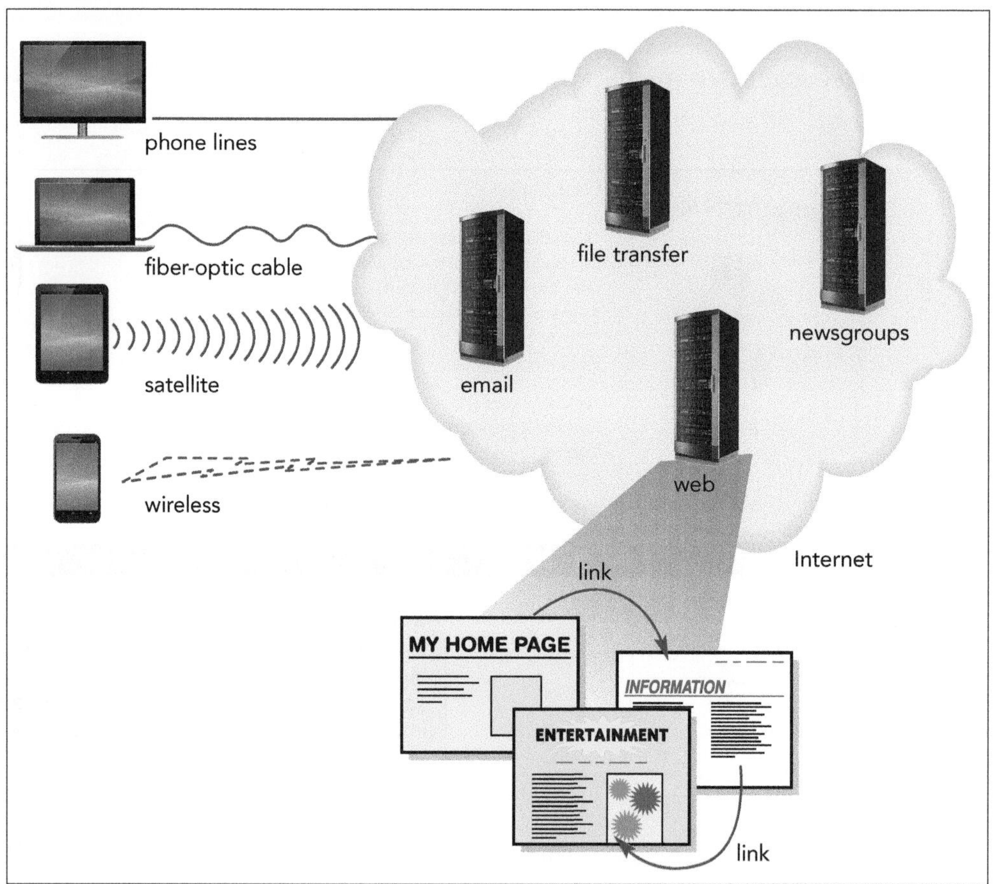

©iStock.com/CostinT, ©iStock.com/scanrail

The web is a service that you access via the Internet. While the Internet is a collection of networks connected by communication media such as fiber-optic cables and wireless connections, the web is a collection of documents connected by hyperlinks. You click a link to display the targeted information. For example, as shown in Figure 4-2, you can click links on the first Library of Congress web document to display related documents.

Figure 4-2 **Library of Congress webpage with links to other webpages**

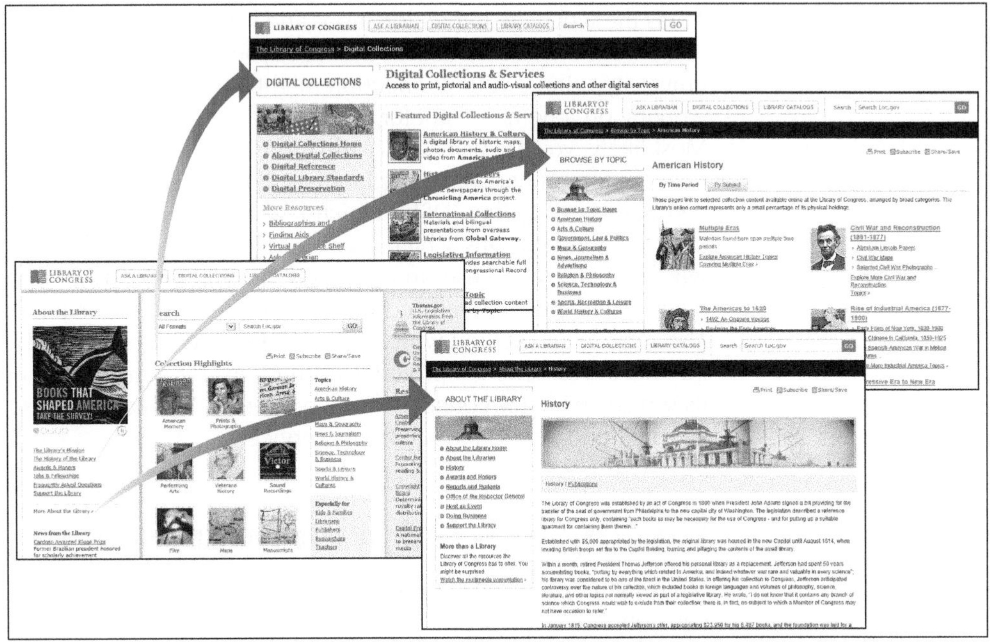

Courtesy of the Library of Congress

Webpages are stored on Internet computers called **web servers**. A **website** is a collection of webpages that have a common theme or focus, such as all pages containing information about the Library of Congress. The web is appealing because it generally displays up-to-date information in a colorful, lively format that can use images, text, sound, video, and animation.

When you want to find information on the web, you typically use a **search engine**, which is a program that conducts searches to retrieve webpages. To work with a search engine, you enter a word or an expression as the search criteria. The search engine lists links to webpages that fit your criteria. General search engines include Google and Bing.

A popular innovation in web technology is called **cloud computing**, which refers to providing and using computer tools, such as software, via the Internet (or the cloud). With cloud computing you can use your web browser to access and work with software. You do not need to purchase and install a complete app. Instead, you use the software services you need for free or for a usage fee. For example, when you use a web mapping service, such as MapQuest or Google Maps, to find directions from one location to another, you are using cloud computing. The software and data for the maps are not stored on your computer—they're on the cloud at the mapping service's website. This software is known as a **web app**. For example, Microsoft Office Online is a suite of web apps provided on the cloud as simplified versions of the programs provided in Microsoft Office, such as Word and Excel.

Using Web Browsers

You use a web browser, or browser, to visit websites around the world; interact with webpages by clicking links; view multimedia documents; transfer files, images, videos, and sounds to and from your computer; conduct searches for specific topics; and run programs on other computers. The browser included with Windows 10 is called Microsoft Edge.

When you attempt to view a webpage, your browser locates and retrieves the document from the web server and displays its contents on your computer. The server stores the webpage in one location, and browsers anywhere in the world can display it.

For your browser to access the web, you must have an Internet connection. In a university setting, your connection might come from your campus network. If you are working on a home computer, you have a few options for connecting to the Internet. Most likely, you are using a **broadband connection**, a high-capacity, high-speed medium for connecting to the Internet. Popular broadband technologies include a **digital subscriber line (DSL)**, which is a high-speed connection through your telephone line, and **digital cable**, which uses a cable modem attached to cable television lines. A **wireless connection** uses infrared light or radio-frequency signals to communicate with devices that are physically connected to a network or the Internet. Home connections also require an account with an **Internet service provider (ISP)**, a company that sells Internet access. The ISP provides instructions for connecting your computer to one of its servers, which is connected to the Internet. You can then use your browser to visit websites and access other Internet services.

Getting Started with Microsoft Edge

Microsoft Edge (or Edge for short) is the default web browser in Windows 10 and lets you communicate, access, and share information on the web. Microsoft Edge has a clean, modern design that lets you focus on webpage content instead of browser controls. As a Windows app, it can run on a variety of Windows 10 devices ranging from desktops and laptops to tablets and smartphones. Because it integrates with other Windows 10 apps such as Cortana, Microsoft Edge does not run on earlier versions of Windows. To maintain compatibility with older websites, Windows 10 still includes Internet Explorer, the default browser provided with earlier versions of Windows.

When you start Microsoft Edge, it opens to a **home page**, which is the webpage that a browser is set to open at startup. The default home page for Microsoft Edge is the Start page, which displays a changing gallery of personalized news images, weather information, sports, and games collected from websites. Your computer manufacturer or school might have set up a different home page.

Your first task in showing Kent how to research career information for Step Up clients is to start Edge. You must be connected to the Internet to perform all of the steps in this session. Mute your speakers, if necessary, so the sounds that certain webpages play do not disturb others.

To start Microsoft Edge:

1. Click the **Microsoft Edge** button on the taskbar. Microsoft Edge opens to its home page.

   Trouble? If a Network Connection dialog box opens, enter your user name and password, and then click the Connect button. If you do not know your user name or password, ask your instructor or technical support person for help. You must have an Internet connection to complete the steps in this module.

2. Click the **Maximize** button to maximize the Microsoft Edge window, if necessary. Figure 4-3 shows the Start page in Microsoft Edge. Your Start page will differ, or you might have a different home page.

TIP

To change the home page, start Microsoft Edge, click the More button, click Settings, and then select an option in the Open with section.

Figure 4-3 Microsoft Edge default home page

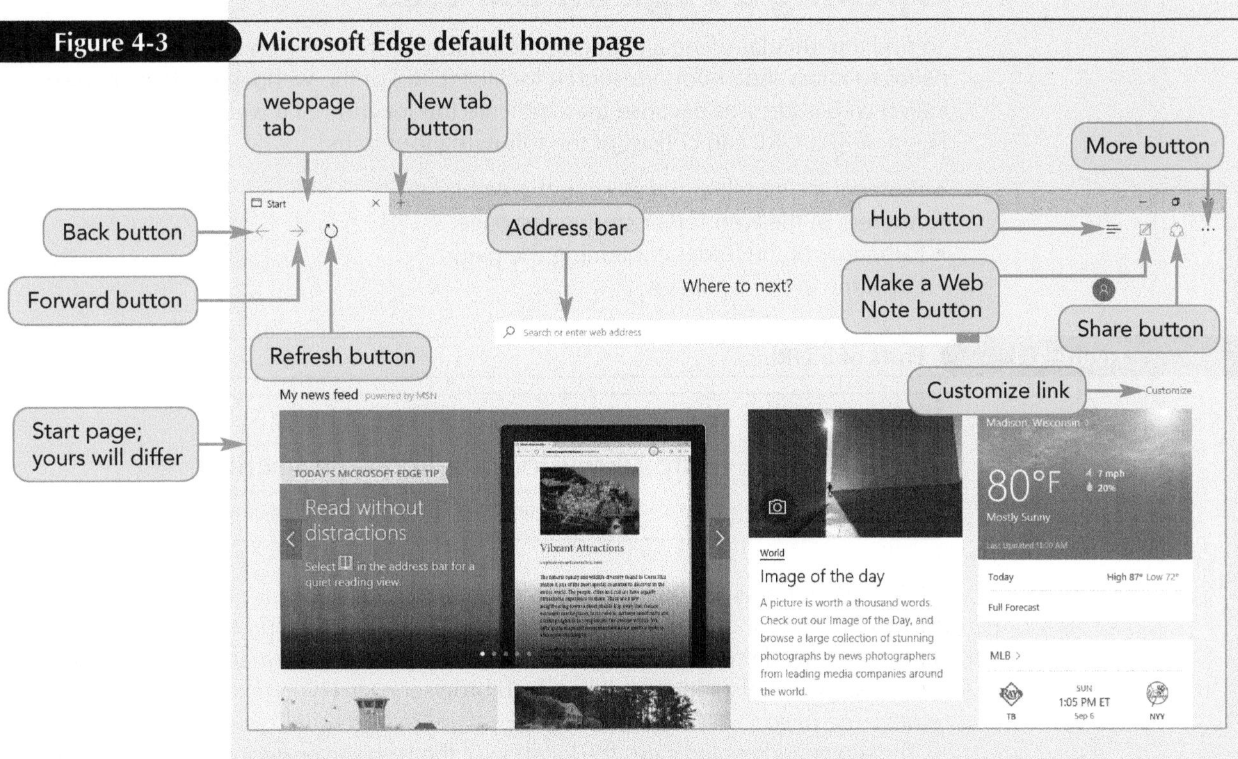

When you start Microsoft Edge, it displays a navigation area at the top of the window. The navigation area includes the following tools:

- Tabs—Display the webpages you open on separate tabs so you can switch from one webpage to another.
- Back and Forward buttons—Browse to the previous or next webpage in a sequence of opened pages.
- Refresh button—Refresh the contents of the webpage.
- Hub button—Access webpages you've identified as favorites and view other personalized information, such as your browsing history.
- Make a Web Note button—Click this button to use a pointing device, stylus, or fingertip to write and draw directly on a webpage. (A **stylus** is a pen-shaped digital tool for selecting and entering information on a touchscreen.) The Make a Web Note button is not active on the Start page.
- Share button—Share webpages with others through apps such as Mail. The Share button is not active on the Start page.
- More button—Manage the current webpage, and select settings for Microsoft Edge. For example, you can click the More button, and then click New window to open the current webpage in a new window.
- Address bar—View the address of the webpage; you can also type the address of a webpage you want to visit.

The main part of the Start page displays your **news feed**, a collection of live headlines, images, and information from six categories of websites: autos, entertainment, lifestyle, money, news, and sports. You can click the Customize link on the Start page to display websites from fewer than six categories, such as only news and sports.

Now you're ready to use Microsoft Edge to open and view a webpage.

Opening a Page on the Web

To find a particular webpage among the billions stored on web servers, your browser needs to know the uniform resource locator (URL) of the webpage. URLs are also called web addresses because they indicate the location of a webpage. As shown in Figure 4-4, a URL can consist of the following four parts:

- Protocol to use when transferring the webpage
- Address of the web server storing the page
- Pathname of the folder containing the page
- Filename of the webpage

Figure 4-4 **Parts of a URL**

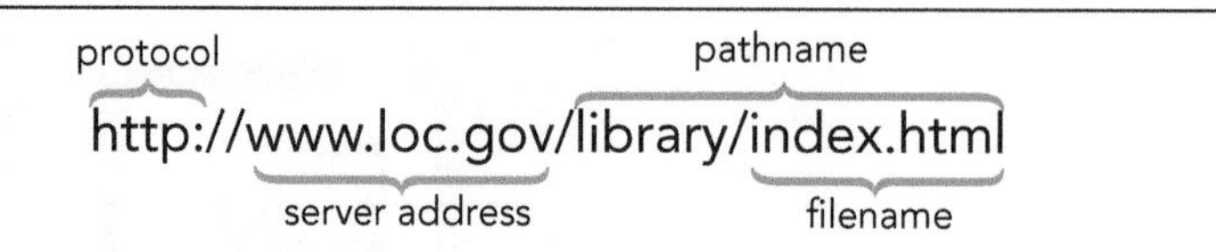

The URL for most webpages starts with http, which stands for **Hypertext Transfer Protocol**, the most common way to transfer information around the web. (A **protocol** is a standardized procedure computers use to exchange information.) When the URL for a webpage starts with http://, the web browser uses Hypertext Transfer Protocol to retrieve the page.

The server address indicates the location of the web server storing the webpage. In www.loc.gov, the www indicates that the server is a web server, loc is the name the Library of Congress chose for this website, and .gov means that a government entity runs the web server. Other common types of web servers in the United States are .com (commercial), .net (network service providers or resources), .org (not-for-profit organizations), and .edu (educational institutions). The server address in a URL corresponds to an Internet Protocol (IP) address, which identifies every computer on the Internet. An **IP address** is a unique number that consists of four sets of numbers from 0 to 255 separated by periods, or dots, as in 216.35.148.4. Although computers can use IP addresses easily, they are difficult for people to remember, so domain names were created. A **domain name** identifies one or more IP addresses, such as loc.gov. URLs use the domain name in the server address part of the URL to identify a particular website.

In addition, each file stored on a web server has a unique pathname, just like files stored on a disk. The pathname in a URL includes the names of the folders containing the file, the filename, and its extension. A common filename extension for webpages is .html, sometimes shortened to .htm. For example, the pathname might be library/index.html, which specifies a file named index.html stored in a folder named library.

Not all URLs include a pathname. If you don't specify a pathname or filename in a URL, most web browsers open a file named index.html or index.htm, which is the default name for a website's main page.

Opening a Webpage Using a URL

One way to open a webpage in Microsoft Edge is to enter a URL in the Address bar. You can often find URLs in advertisements, in informational materials, and on the web so that you can gain quick access to specific information.

In most cases, URLs are not case sensitive, so you can enter a URL using all lowercase or all uppercase text. However, if the web server storing a webpage uses the UNIX operating system, the URL might be case sensitive. For mixed-case URLs, it's safer to enter them using the mixed case exactly as printed.

The first webpage you want to open for Kent is the home page of the U.S. Bureau of Labor Statistics, which provides information about employment throughout the United States.

To open a page on the web using a URL:

1. Click in the **Address bar**. On the Start page, the Address bar displays "Search or enter web address." Microsoft Edge removes this text when you begin to type a web address. If Microsoft Edge is using a home page other than the Start page, clicking the Address bar selects the current web address. If the contents of the Address bar are not selected, drag to select the entire address.
2. Type **bls.gov** in the Address bar. As you type, Microsoft Edge displays the names of other webpages you've opened that have URLs starting with the same characters, a feature called **AutoComplete**. Also, you can omit the http:// and www when you type a web address. Edge recognizes the entry in the Address bar as a URL.
3. Press the **Enter** key. Edge opens the main, or home, page for the Bureau of Labor Statistics website. See Figure 4-5.

   Trouble? If the home page of the Bureau of Labor Statistics website does not open, you might have typed the URL incorrectly. Repeat Steps 1–3, making sure that the URL in the Address bar matches the URL in Step 2. If you still receive an error message, ask your instructor or technical support person for help.

Figure 4-5 **Opening the Bureau of Labor Statistics home page**

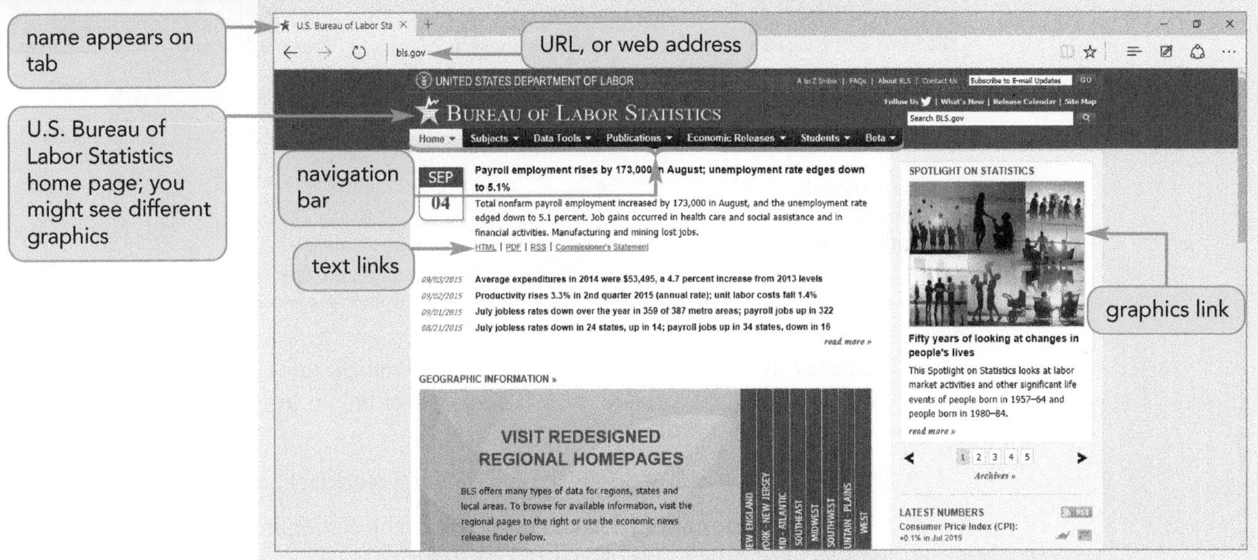

Because web content changes frequently, the webpages you open might differ from the figures in this module.

A home page on the web can have at least two meanings. It can be the webpage a browser is set to open by default, and it can also be the main page for a website that provides links to other webpages with related information.

Navigating with Links

The home page for a typical website includes plenty of links to help you navigate to its webpages, and those pages also include links you can click to navigate from one page to another. Links can be text, images, or a combination of both. Text links are usually colored and underlined, though the exact style can vary from one website to another.

To determine whether something on a webpage is a link, point to it. If the pointer changes to a pointing-hand pointer, the text or image is a link you can click to open a webpage. A ScreenTip displaying the URL of the link appears at the bottom of the window.

Step Up's clients are interested in the outlook for particular occupations so they can pursue jobs in fields that are expected to grow or be in high demand. For example, many clients are interested in the technology field and often ask about jobs as a computer support specialist. You'll show Kent how to find the occupational outlook for computer support specialists on the Bureau of Labor Statistics website.

To navigate a website using links:

1. Point to **Publications** in the site's navigation bar. The pointer changes to a pointing-hand pointer and a menu of links in the Publications category appears below the navigation bar. See Figure 4-6.

Figure 4-6 Pointing to a link

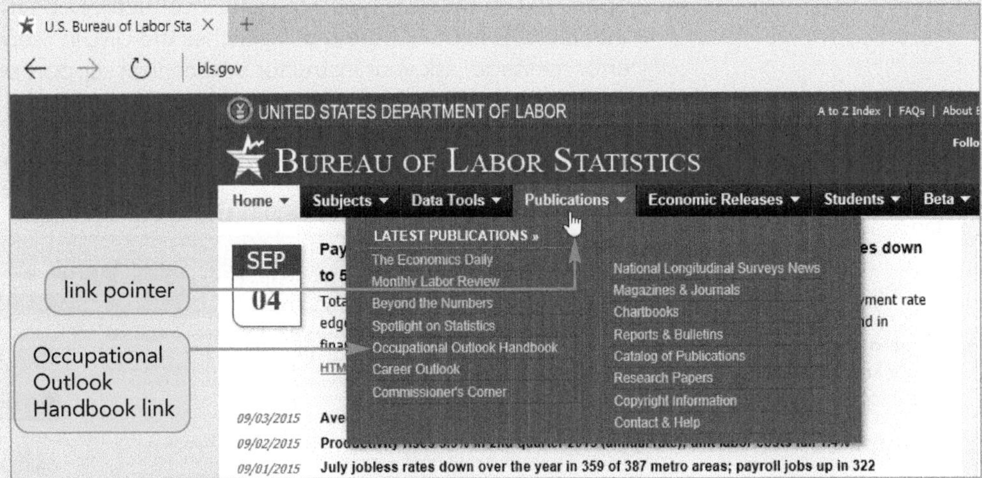

Trouble? If the current Bureau of Labor Statistics home page does not include a Publications link, point to any other link in the navigation bar and substitute that link when you perform Step 2.

Trouble? If a window opens asking for your feedback, close the window.

2. Click **Occupational Outlook Handbook** in the Publications menu to open the Occupational Outlook Handbook webpage.
3. In the OCCUPATION GROUPS list on the left, click **Computer and Information Technology** to open the Computer and Information Technology Occupations page, which lists occupations, summarizes the jobs, identifies the education required for an entry-level position, and provides the median pay in a recent year.

   Trouble? If the webpage does not include a Computer and Information Technology link, read but do not perform the remaining steps in this section.
4. Scroll to display the Computer Support Specialists link. See Figure 4-7. The webpage you opened might look different.

Figure 4-7 **Computer and Information Technology Occupations webpage**

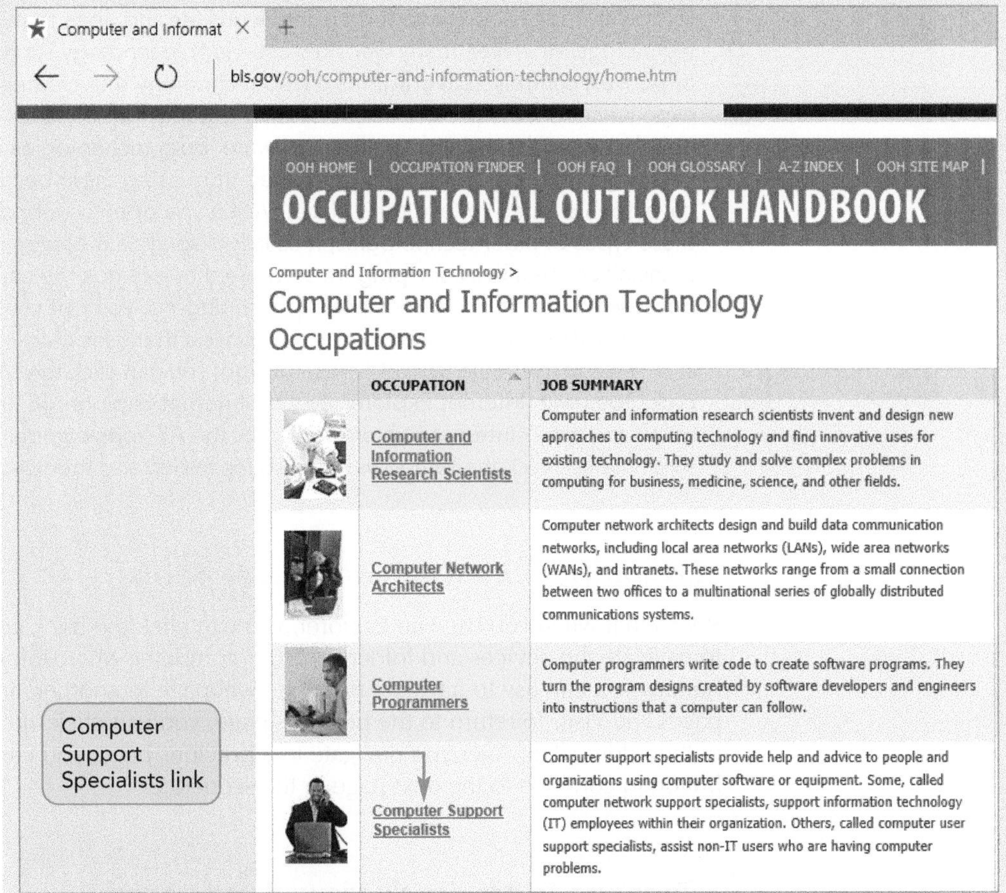

5. Click the **Computer Support Specialists** link to open the Computer Support Specialists page, which provides detailed information about the occupation.

Besides clicking links to navigate from one webpage to another, you can use tools that Edge provides.

INSIGHT

Displaying Webpages in Internet Explorer

Microsoft Edge is designed for modern websites and apps that use contemporary technology. However, many websites use older technology such as Silverlight videos or ActiveX controls. (**Silverlight** is a web technology that creates interactive media experiences. **ActiveX controls** are small programs that enhance your browsing activities or help with tasks such as installing software. Both technologies are **deprecated**, meaning that developers are discouraged from using them because newer technologies have been created to take their place.) When you open a webpage that depends on these types of older technologies, it usually displays a message indicating that you need to install or use a **browser plug-in**, software that extends the capabilities of a browser. Because Microsoft Edge does not support plug-ins, you can use Internet Explorer in Windows 10 when you need to visit a webpage that uses plug-ins. If you encounter such a webpage while using Microsoft Edge, you can click the More button and then click Open with Internet Explorer. To start Internet Explorer on its own, open the Start menu and type "Internet Explorer," or click the All apps command on the Start menu, scroll the list, click the Windows Accessories folder, and then click Internet Explorer.

Navigating with Microsoft Edge Tools

Recall that when you use File Explorer, you can click the Back and Forward buttons to navigate the devices and folders on your computer. Microsoft Edge includes similar buttons you can use to navigate from one webpage to another, and it keeps track of the pages you visit. To return to the previous page, you can click the Back button to the left of the Address bar. After you navigate to a previous page, you can click the Forward button to continue to the next page in the sequence.

To return to previously viewed webpages:

1. To the left of the Address bar, click the **Back** button ← to return to the Computer and Information Technology Occupations page.
2. Click the **Forward** button → to return to the Computer Support Specialists page.

   Trouble? If you opened different webpages in the previous set of steps, substitute the names of the pages as appropriate in Steps 1 and 2.

Next, you want to show Kent how to use tabs to open other webpages without closing the Computer Support Specialists page.

Managing Webpages in Microsoft Edge

If you want to open a new webpage without closing the one you're currently viewing, you can use tabbed browsing to open more than one webpage at a time. To use tabbed browsing, you open a tab for each new page you want to view. You can open a new tab in three ways: click the New tab button at the top of the Microsoft Edge window, press the Ctrl key as you click a link on a webpage, or right-click the link and then click Open in new tab on the shortcut menu. You can then switch from one webpage to another by clicking the tabs at the top of the Microsoft Edge window. Each tab displays the title of its webpage so you can quickly identify the page you want to display. To close a tab, you click its Close tab button.

Now that you've explored a few pages on the Bureau of Labor Statistics website, you can compare that information to information on the American Job Center website, which provides resources for job seekers and people who want to explore career options. You'll show Kent how to open a new tab in Microsoft Edge and then use it to open the American Job Center home page.

TIP

To customize the New tab, click the Customize link, and then choose whether you want the New tab to display top sites and your news feed, top sites only, or a blank page.

To open other webpages on new tabs:

1. Click the **New tab** button at the top of the Microsoft Edge window to open the New tab, which provides an Address bar and tiles representing popular websites.
2. Click in the **Address bar**, type **jobcenter.usa.gov**, and then press the **Enter** key. The American Job Center home page opens on the new tab. See Figure 4-8. The webpage you open might look different.

Figure 4-8 American Job Center home page

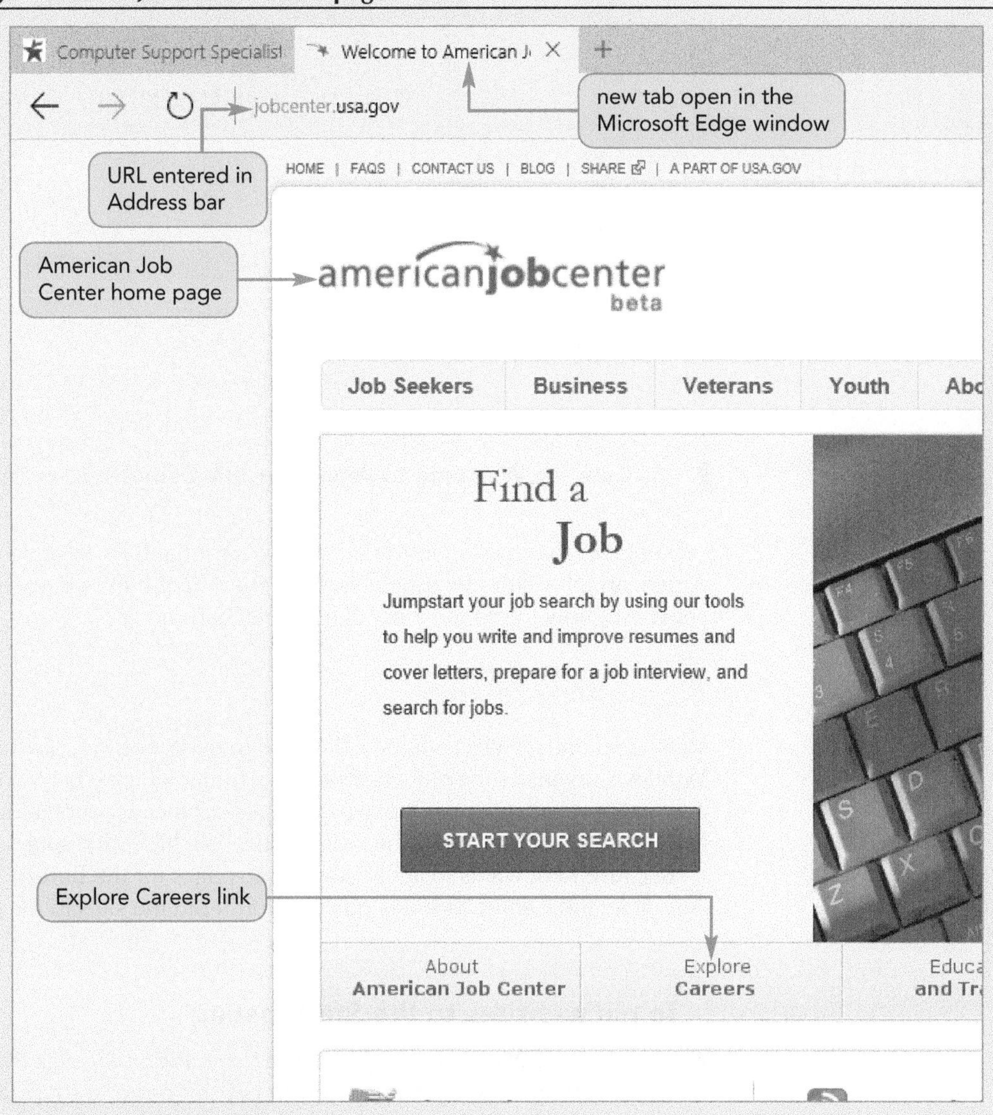

3. Right-click the **Explore Careers** link on the webpage, and then click **Open in new tab** on the shortcut menu. The Explore Careers webpage opens in a new tab, although the page is not visible yet. You need to display the tab for that page.

   Trouble? If the Explore Careers link does not appear on the current webpage, right-click a different link on the page.

4. Click the **Explore Careers** tab to display the webpage. Now three tabs are displayed in Microsoft Edge for the open webpages. See Figure 4-9.

Figure 4-9 **Tabs for the open webpages**

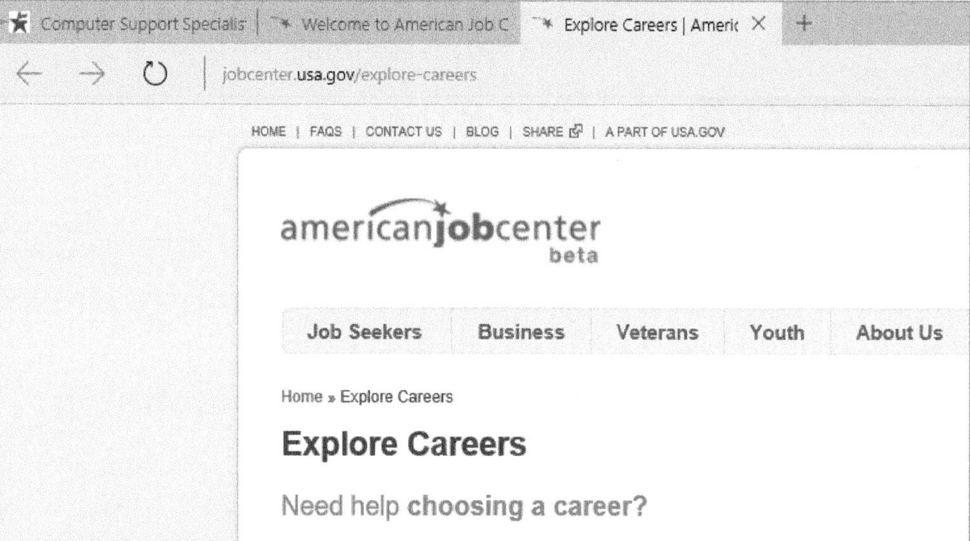

TIP

Point to an undisplayed tab to see a thumbnail of the webpage.

5. Click the **Welcome to American Job Center** tab to display that webpage.

Kent will return often to the home pages for the Bureau of Labor Statistics and American Job Center websites. To make it easy for him to reopen the webpages, you'll show him how to pin the webpages to the Start menu.

Pinning Webpages

When you find a website that you'll return to often, you can pin the site to the Start menu. Windows organizes the pinned sites into a group, which you can name. If you have an account on a website that displays messages or other account information, such as Twitter or Facebook, you can make the pinned site a live tile so it displays messages on the tile.

Because Kent wants to access the home pages for the Bureau of Labor Statistics and American Job Center websites quickly, you'll pin the sites to the Start menu.

To pin websites to the Start menu:

1. Click the **More** button ··· in the navigation bar, click **Pin this page to Start**, and then click the **Yes** button to pin the page to the Start menu.
2. Click the **Computer Support Specialists** tab to display its webpage. Kent wants to pin the home page for the Bureau of Labor Statistics to the Start menu, so you need to open the home page in a new tab.

3. Press and hold the **Ctrl** key, and then click the **Bureau of Labor Statistics** link at the top of the webpage to open the Bureau of Labor Statistics home page in a new tab.
4. Click the **U.S. Bureau of Labor Statistics** tab to display the webpage.
5. Click the **More** button in the navigation bar, click **Pin this page to Start**, and then click the **Yes** button to pin the page to the Start menu.
6. Click the **Close** button to close Microsoft Edge. When a dialog box opens asking if you want to close all tabs, click the **Close all** button.

   Trouble? If a dialog box asking if you want to close all tabs does not open, someone has already selected the Always close all tabs check box. All tabs close when you close Microsoft Edge.

7. Click the **Start** button to display the Start menu, which now includes the two tiles for the pinned sites. See Figure 4-10. The tiles on your Start menu might appear in a different place.

Figure 4-10 Pinned sites on the Start menu

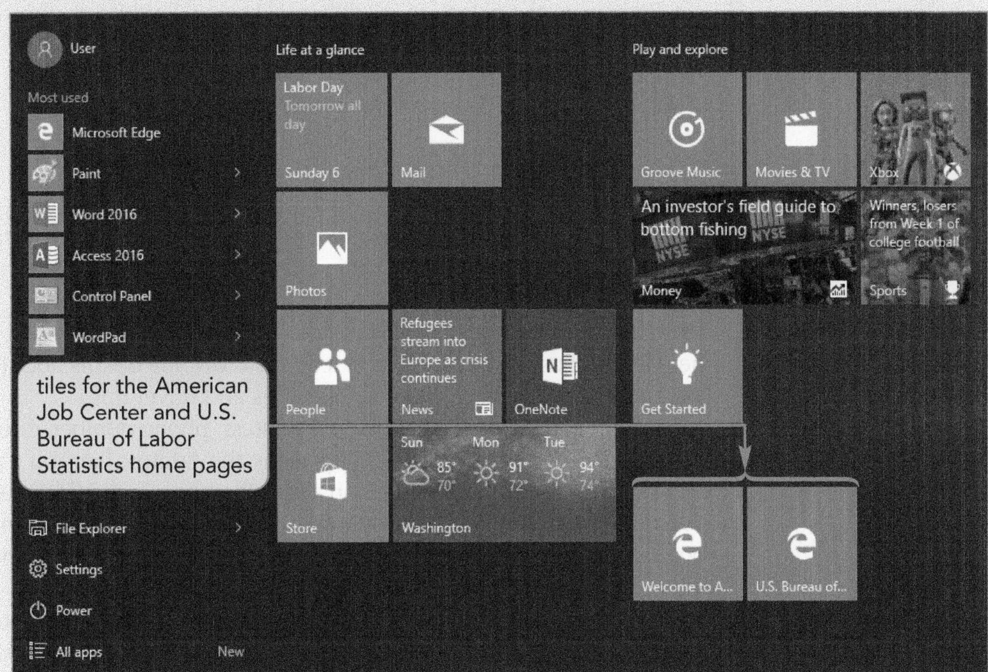

Trouble? If you can't see the two tiles for the pinned sites, you might need to scroll the Start menu.

8. Click the **Welcome to American Job Center** tile to open the site in Microsoft Edge.
9. Click the **Start** button and then click the **U.S. Bureau of Labor Statistics** tile to open the home page for the Bureau of Labor Statistics website on a new tab.

Now that Kent knows the basics of opening and navigating webpages, he wants to learn how to search for a webpage. You'll show him how to use Cortana without leaving Microsoft Edge to find webpages.

Using Cortana to Find Online Information

TIP

Cortana provides instant results for calculations, conversions, definitions, flight information, stocks, sports scores, trivia, weather, time, and some restaurant information.

Recall that Cortana is an electronic personal assistant designed to help you find files, search the web, keep track of information, and answer your questions. Cortana is integrated with Microsoft Edge to find answers and information on the web. When you enter a search term or ask a question in the Address bar, Edge displays search suggestions, search terms you've used before, and in some cases, the result or answer from Cortana, saving you the extra step of navigating to a search engine. For example, if you enter "Salt Lake City weather" in the Address bar, Cortana opens a highlighted bar below the Address bar to display the current weather conditions in Salt Lake City, Utah. Because the answer appears as you are typing the search term, the answer is called an instant result.

REFERENCE

Using Cortana to Find Online Information

- In Microsoft Edge, enter a question about weather, sports, finance, or other category in the Cortana Notebook to display instant results.

or

- Select text on a webpage.
- Right-click the selection, and then click Ask Cortana on the shortcut menu.

or

- Click the Cortana icon in the Address bar.

You can also use Cortana to learn more about a topic displayed on a webpage. Right-click a word, link, or selected text, and then click Ask Cortana to find out more information about the topic. Cortana opens a pane called the Cortana pane in Microsoft Edge to display the results so you don't have to leave the current webpage. For example, if you're viewing a webpage about things to do in Salt Lake City, you can select text on the page and use the Ask Cortana feature to display details about the Arches National Park, including opening and closing times and travel tips.

For some webpages that contain an address, phone number, or other location information, the Cortana icon appears in the Address bar. You can click the icon to have Cortana display detailed information about the place in the Cortana pane. For example, if you visit the website for a restaurant, Cortana displays a map identifying the restaurant's location, lists reviews, shows photos, provides the restaurant's phone number and hours, and presents links to directions and menus.

Cortana is turned off by default. If you have a Microsoft account, you can activate Cortana, which involves agreeing to let it collect information about you. If you use more than one Windows device, Cortana uses the information you provide to keep the devices in sync.

In the following steps, you activate Cortana if you haven't already activated it.

To activate Cortana:

1. Click in the **Search the web and Windows** box on the taskbar. Cortana opens and displays some of the tasks it can do for you. See Figure 4-11.

   Trouble? If your taskbar has an Ask me anything box instead of a Search the web and Windows box, Cortana is already activated. Skip ahead to the "To find an instant result" steps on the next page.

   Trouble? If your screen does not match the one in Figure 4-11, click the Try Cortana button in the left pane.

Figure 4-11 Activating Cortana

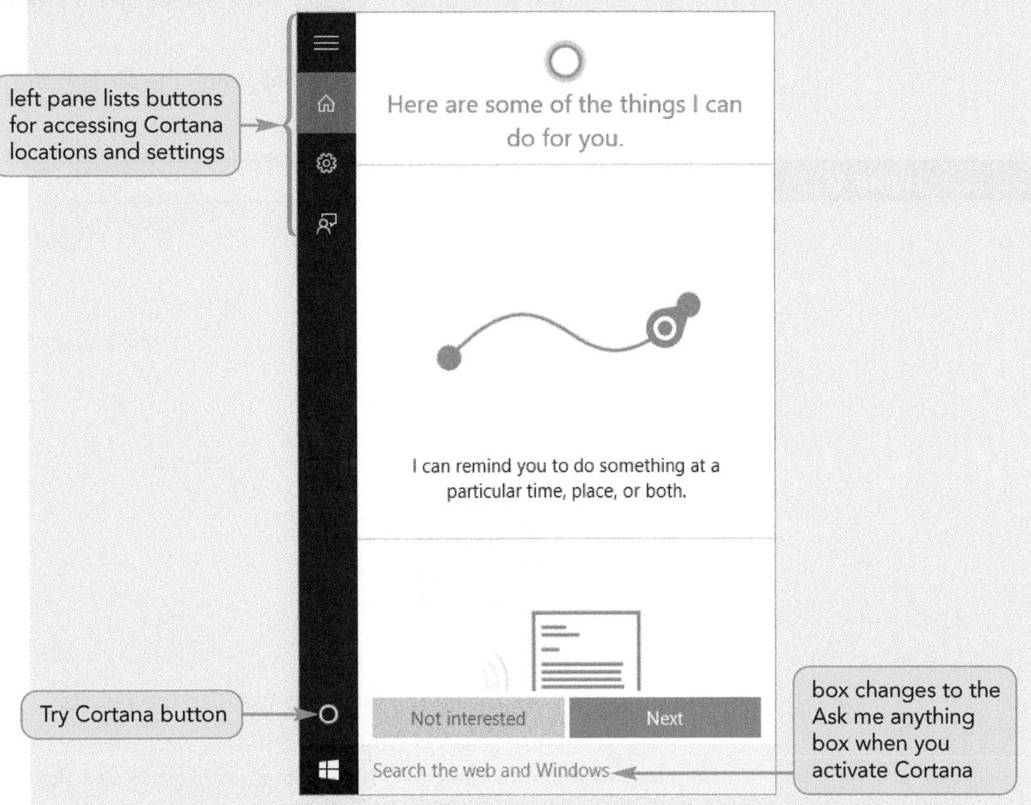
left pane lists buttons for accessing Cortana locations and settings
Here are some of the things I can do for you.
I can remind you to do something at a particular time, place, or both.
Not interested
Next
Try Cortana button
Search the web and Windows
box changes to the Ask me anything box when you activate Cortana

2. Click the **Next** button. A notice appears explaining that Cortana will collect and use information and store it in its Notebook. (Recall that the Notebook keeps track of what you like, such as your interests and favorite places, and what you want it to do, such as display reminders or information that might interest you.)
3. Click the **I agree** button. Cortana asks for a name to use when addressing you.
4. Type your first name and then click the **Next** button. Cortana displays a few starter interests, webpages, and search text that might suit you based on information in your Microsoft account.
5. Click the **Got it** button. Cortana stores the webpage information and search text in your Notebook.

Step Up is organizing a conference on job opportunities in Salt Lake City to attract people to the area from out of state. Kent is planning an event at the conference center to welcome participants the day they arrive. Many of the conference participants will fly through Denver on their way to Salt Lake City, and Kent wants to track the flights to check their status. You'll show him how to use Microsoft Edge and Cortana to find the status of a popular flight as an instant result.

To find an instant result:

1. Click the **New tab** button + at the top of the Microsoft Edge window to open the New tab.
2. In the Address bar, type **frontier 579** to search for the status of Frontier Airline's flight 579. Cortana displays the current status of the flight. See Figure 4-12.

Trouble? If you pressed the Enter key after typing the text in the Address bar, click the Back button ← and then repeat Step 2, making sure you do not press the Enter key.

Trouble? If no flight information appears, the flight number has probably changed. Continue to Step 3.

Figure 4-12 Instant search results

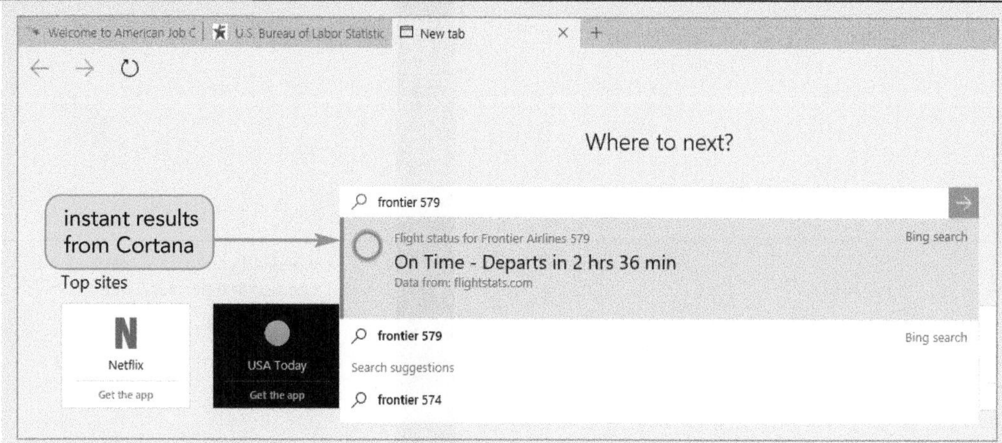

3. Click a blank spot on the New tab to close the results.

Kent knows that many people considering a move to Salt Lake City want to know about nearby outdoor activities. In fact, Utah has five national parks, many of them near Salt Lake City. You'll show Kent how to find a webpage about Utah's national parks and then use Cortana to display details about one of the parks.

To find a webpage and display details about a topic:

1. On the New tab, select the text in the Address bar, and then type **utah national park** to display search suggestions for the text you entered. See Figure 4-13.

Figure 4-13 Search suggestions on the New tab

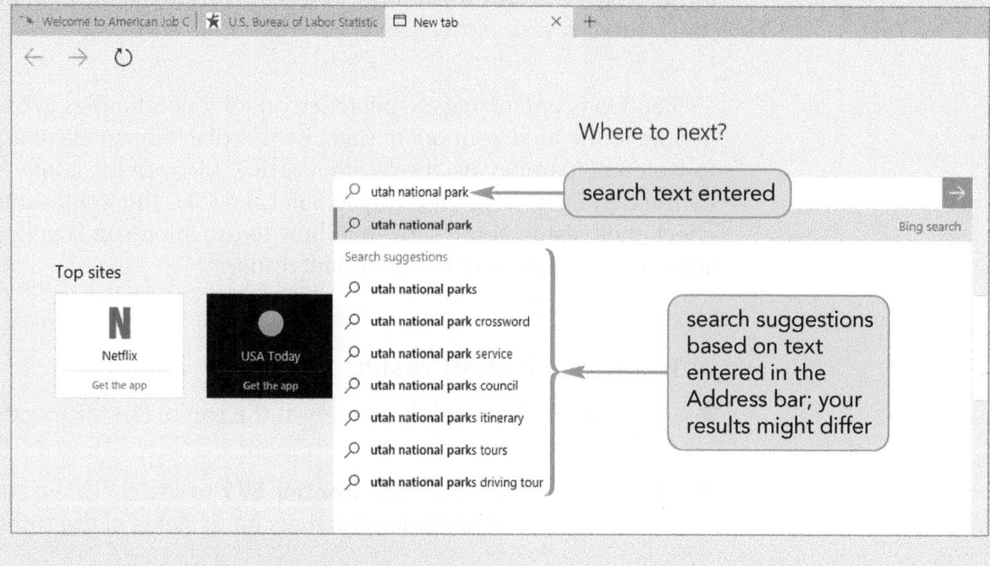

2. In the search suggestions, click **utah national park service** to display the search results in Bing, the Microsoft search engine.

   Trouble? If "utah national park service" does not appear in the search results, continue typing to add "service" to the search text, and then press the Enter key.

3. Scroll as necessary to display a result from the U.S. National Park Service, and then click that result. For example, click **Utah (U.S. National Park Service)**. (The specific wording of your result might vary.) A webpage on the National Park Service website (nps.gov) opens displaying information about the national parks in Utah.

   Trouble? If "Utah (U.S. National Park Service)" does not appear in the search results, type "nps.gov/state/ut/index.htm" in the Address bar, and then press the Enter key.

4. Scroll as necessary to display information about Bryce Canyon, right-click the **Bryce Canyon** link, and then click **Ask Cortana** on the shortcut menu. The Cortana pane opens on the right side of the Microsoft Edge window to display information about Bryce Canyon National Park, including photos, a map, and a description. See Figure 4-14.

Figure 4-14 **Cortana providing details about a webpage topic**

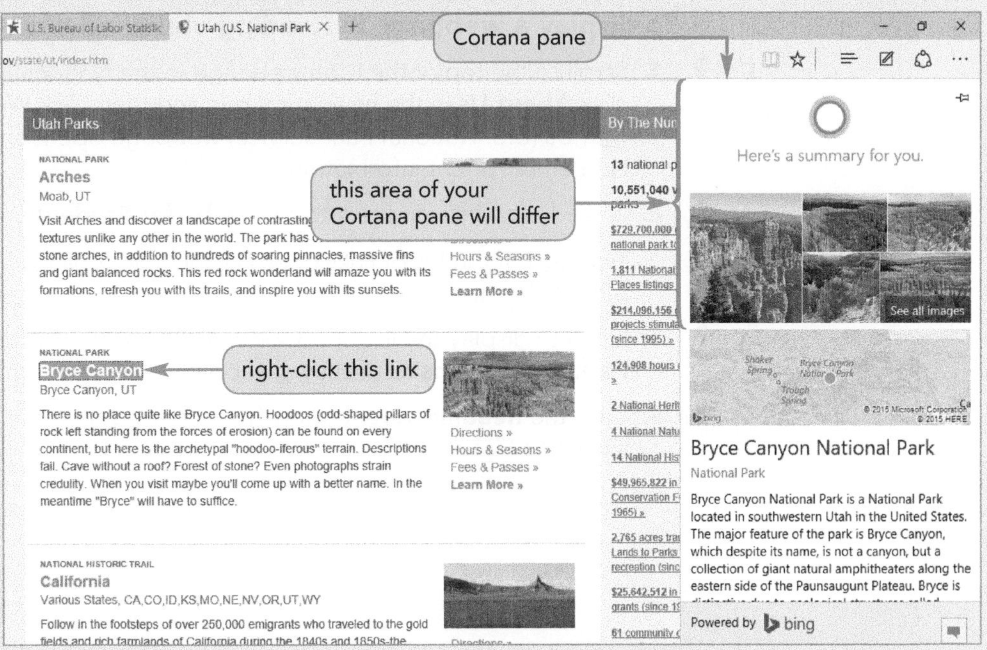

5. Scroll down to review the information, and then click a blank area of the webpage to close the Cortana pane.

The National Park Service (NPS) often employs people living in Salt Lake City and other parts of Utah, especially students looking for summer jobs and internships. Kent wants to explore employment resources on the NPS website next. As he does, you'll show him how to use two popular features in Microsoft Edge: Reading view and Make a Web Note.

Reading and Annotating Webpages

When you find a webpage containing information you want to focus on, you can use the Reading view button on the Address bar to switch to Reading view, which removes most graphics, ads, links, and other distracting elements and presents webpage text in a simple format. Reading view is especially helpful when you are browsing information-rich webpages, such as articles or studies, and pages that are cluttered with extra, nonessential content. You can also set your preferences for how the webpage appears in Reading view. For example, you can display the page with a light or dark background and change the size of the text.

Microsoft Edge can display many, but not all, webpages in Reading view. If the Reading view button on the Address bar is active—that is, it is no longer grayed, or dimmed, and displays a ScreenTip when you point to it—you can display the current webpage in Reading view.

On pages containing information you want to refer to quickly, you can use the Make a Web Note button to annotate the webpage by writing or drawing on it, highlighting text, or copying some or all of the webpage image as a screenshot. You can also save the annotated webpage and share it with others.

Kent thinks he will use Reading view frequently because he is often distracted by graphics, ads, and other extraneous information when viewing webpages. As you look for student employment information on the National Parks Service website, you'll show Kent how to use Reading view and set his preferences for using it.

To display a webpage in Reading view and change settings:

1. Scroll to the top of the Utah webpage in the National Park Service website, click **About Us** in the navigation bar, and then click **Work With Us**. The Work with Us (U.S. National Park Service) webpage opens showing an overview of NPS employment information.
2. In the list of links on the left, click **Jobs for Students**.

   Trouble? If the list of links does not include Jobs for Students, click any other link in the list.
3. Scroll to display the list of opportunities, and then click **Geoscientists-in-the-Parks Internships** to display a webpage describing this program.
4. Click the **Reading view** button on the Address bar to switch to Reading view. See Figure 4-15.

Figure 4-15 **Webpage in Reading view**

page appears with most of the graphics and links removed

your page in Reading view might display a photo or differ in other ways

Reading view button

Geoscientists-in-the-Parks

nps.gov

Overview

The National Park Service (NPS) is looking for students and professionals in the geosciences and other natural resource fields who want to use their natural resource science expertise to help the NPS to better understand and manage its natural resources.

The Geoscientists-in-the-Parks (GIP) program works with partners to match college students and recent graduates age 18 - 35 years old with short-term, paid, internships with the National Park Service. Participants may assist with research, synthesis of scientific literature, geologic mapping, GIS analysis, site evaluations, resource inventorying and monitoring, impact mitigation, developing brochures and informative media presentations, and educating park staff and park visitors.GIP positions can last from 3 months to one-year.

Participants selected for the GIP program have a unique opportunity to contribute to the conservation of America's national parks.

Parks benefit from a participant's knowledge and skills in geological or other natural

5. Click the **More** button ··· in the navigation bar, and then click **Settings** to display the Settings pane.
6. Scroll to display the Reading section, click the **Reading view style** box to display the styles, and then click **Dark**. The webpage appears with a black background and white text.
7. Click the **Reading view font size** box, and then click **Large** to change the font size of the webpage text. See Figure 4-16.

Figure 4-16 **Changing Reading view settings**

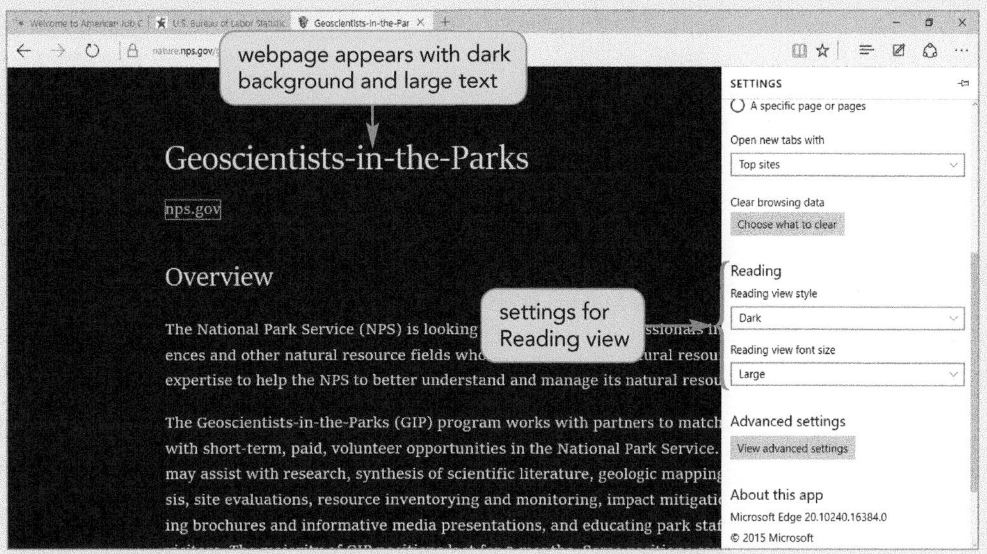

The current settings might work well in sunny conditions, but you might not need them in normal indoor lighting. For now, you can return the settings to their defaults.

8. In the Settings pane, click the **Reading view style** box, and then click **Default**.
9. Click the **Reading view font size** box, and then click **Medium**.
10. Click a blank spot on the webpage to close the Settings pane.

Now you can show Kent how to use annotations on the current webpage. He wants to highlight information of interest to potential applicants.

To annotate a webpage:

1. Click the **Make a Web Note** button to display the Make a Web Note tools at the top of the webpage. The Pan tool is active by default, allowing you to drag the webpage to display content out of view. Panning is typically more useful on a regular webpage than one in Reading view.
2. Click the **Pen** button on the toolbar, and then drag to draw a circle around the first paragraph after the "Overview" heading. Release the mouse button when the circle is complete.
3. Click the **Highlighter** button on the toolbar, and then drag to highlight **short-term, paid, internships** in the next paragraph. See Figure 4-17.

TIP

You can display options for the Pen and Highlighter tool, including colors and sizes, by right-clicking the Pen or Highlighter button.

Figure 4-17 Annotated webpage

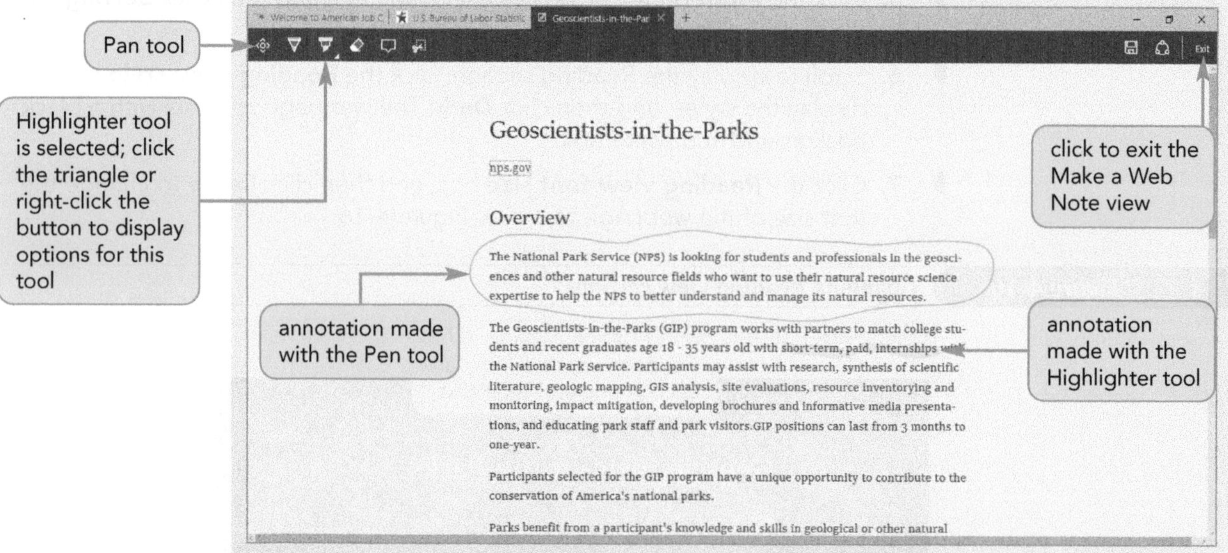
Pan tool
Highlighter tool is selected; click the triangle or right-click the button to display options for this tool
annotation made with the Pen tool
click to exit the Make a Web Note view
annotation made with the Highlighter tool
Geoscientists-in-the-Parks
nps.gov
Overview
The National Park Service (NPS) is looking for students and professionals in the geosciences and other natural resource fields who want to use their natural resource science expertise to help the NPS to better understand and manage its natural resources.
The Geoscientists-in-the-Parks (GIP) program works with partners to match college students and recent graduates age 18 - 35 years old with short-term, paid, internships with the National Park Service. Participants may assist with research, synthesis of scientific literature, geologic mapping, GIS analysis, site evaluations, resource inventorying and monitoring, impact mitigation, developing brochures and informative media presentations, and educating park staff and park visitors.GIP positions can last from 3 months to one-year.
Participants selected for the GIP program have a unique opportunity to contribute to the conservation of America's national parks.
Parks benefit from a participant's knowledge and skills in geological or other natural

The Make a Web Note toolbar includes three other buttons you can use to annotate a webpage. Use the Eraser tool to erase a mark you made with the Pen or Highlighter tool. (Be aware that the Eraser removes all the annotation marks). Select the Add a typed note button to write a short note, which you can leave open or collapse so the note appears only as a numbered icon. Select the Clip button to take a screenshot of some or all of the webpage and store the image temporarily on the Clipboard. You can then start an app such as Paint to paste the image in a new file and save it.

Now that you've annotated the webpage for Kent, he wants to save the annotations. You can do so by saving it to the Microsoft Edge Reading list, which is part of the Hub. The next section explains both of these features.

Using the Hub to Revisit Webpages

Microsoft Edge provides a central location for tracking, storing, and finding webpages you've already visited and files you downloaded from websites. This feature is called the Hub, a pane that displays links to webpages you've identified as your favorites (your Favorites list), webpages you've designated for reading later (your Reading list), webpages you visited recently (the **History list**), and a list of files you downloaded recently.

Creating a Reading List

Both the Favorites list and the Reading list provide quick access to webpages you want to revisit. The difference between the two tools is how you plan to use the webpages. Use the Favorites list for webpages you plan to return to often. For example, if you frequently use an online dictionary while preparing assignments or reports, add the home page of the online dictionary to your Favorites list. Use the Reading list for webpages you plan to return to once or twice so you can read the information at a convenient time. For example, if you are reading an in-depth article on a news site but don't have time to finish it, save the article to your Reading list so you can finish it later.

You can add annotated webpages to the Favorites list or the Reading list. When you do, Microsoft Edge saves the annotations along with the webpage. (You can also send the annotated webpage to OneNote, a Windows app for collecting and organizing your digital information.) Edge removes the annotations when you close the webpage, so you lose the annotations if you don't save them.

You'll show Kent how to save the current webpage, including annotations, to the Reading list.

To save an annotated webpage to the Reading list:

1. Click the **Save Web Note** button on the toolbar to display a list of places you can save the annotated webpage.
2. If necessary, click **Reading list** to display an image of the page and a box where you can enter a name. See Figure 4-18.

Figure 4-18 Adding a webpage to the Reading list

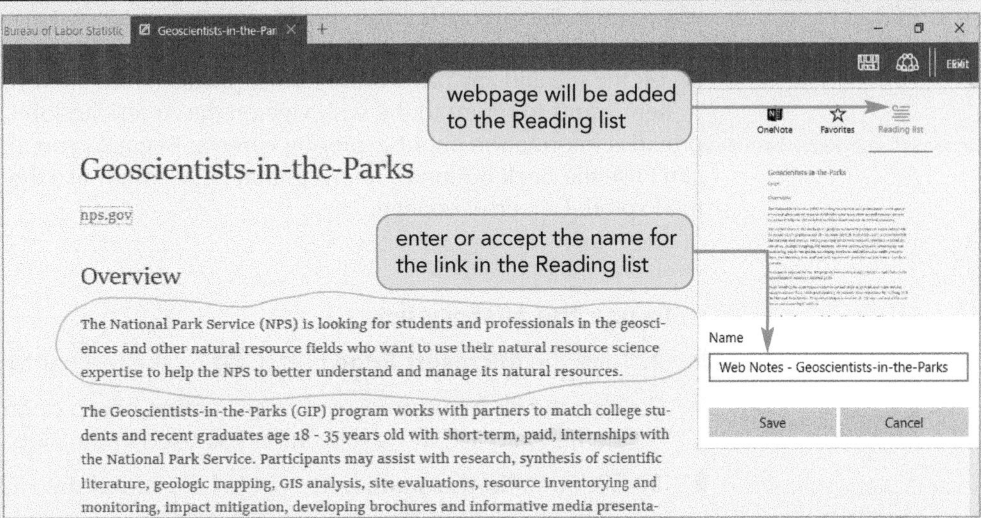
Bureau of Labor Statistic
Geoscientists-in-the-Par
Exit
webpage will be added to the Reading list
OneNote
Favorites
Reading list
Geoscientists-in-the-Parks
nps.gov
enter or accept the name for the link in the Reading list
Overview
The National Park Service (NPS) is looking for students and professionals in the geosciences and other natural resource fields who want to use their natural resource science expertise to help the NPS to better understand and manage its natural resources.
The Geoscientists-in-the-Parks (GIP) program works with partners to match college students and recent graduates age 18 - 35 years old with short-term, paid, internships with the National Park Service. Participants may assist with research, synthesis of scientific literature, geologic mapping, GIS analysis, site evaluations, resource inventorying and monitoring, impact mitigation, developing brochures and informative media presenta-
Name
Web Notes - Geoscientists-in-the-Parks
Save
Cancel

The suggested name is short and accurate, so you can accept it as the name to use in the Reading list.

TIP

You can add a webpage to the Reading list with or without annotations and save it in Reading view or regular webpage view.

3. Click the **Save** button to add the webpage and its annotations to the Reading list.
4. Click **Exit** on the toolbar to exit the Make a Web Note view and return to the current webpage without annotations.

   To make sure that Microsoft Edge saved a link to the annotated page, you can display the Reading list in the Hub.

5. Click the **Hub** button in the navigation bar, and then click the **Reading list** button to display the contents of the Reading list. See Figure 4-19.

Figure 4-19 Reading list

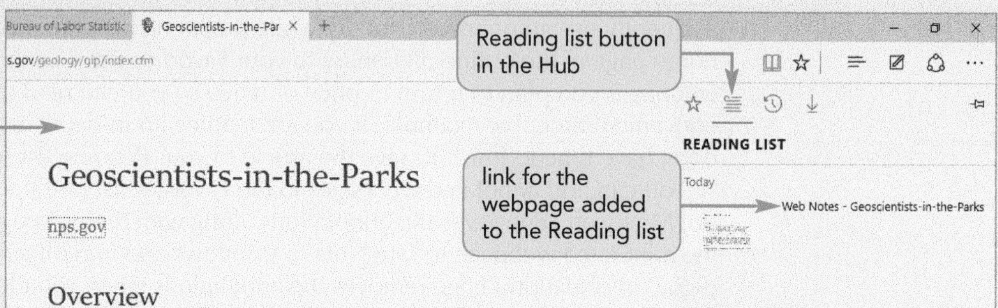

6. Click a blank area of the webpage to close the Reading list.
7. Click the **Close** button to close Microsoft Edge. When a dialog box opens asking if you want to close all tabs, click the **Close all** button.

Another way to revisit a webpage you've already opened is to use the History list.

Using the History List

To open any webpage you've recently visited, you can use the History list, which is available in the Hub. The History list includes the websites you visited today, last week, and up to three weeks ago by default. You can also clear all history, which removes all the webpages in the History list. You should clear the History list after you visit websites that use confidential information, such as banking sites, so that unauthorized users cannot access the site and any passwords or other private information you might have entered.

Kent wants to return to the webpage on the American Job Center website that provides information about exploring careers. Because you already closed Edge, you can't use the Back button to return to that page. You'll use the History list to revisit the Explore Careers webpage.

To use the History list:

1. Click the **Microsoft Edge** button on the taskbar to start Microsoft Edge.
2. Click the **Hub** button in the navigation bar to open the Hub and display the Reading list, the last location you used in the Hub.
3. Click the **Pin this pane** button at the top of the Hub to keep the Hub open on the right side of the Edge window.

   Trouble? If the Pin this pane button does not appear in your Hub, the Hub is already pinned to the Microsoft Edge window. Skip Step 3.

Be sure to pin the Hub to the Edge window so you can work with its features efficiently.

4. Click the **History** button to display the History list. See Figure 4-20.

Figure 4-20 Displaying the History list

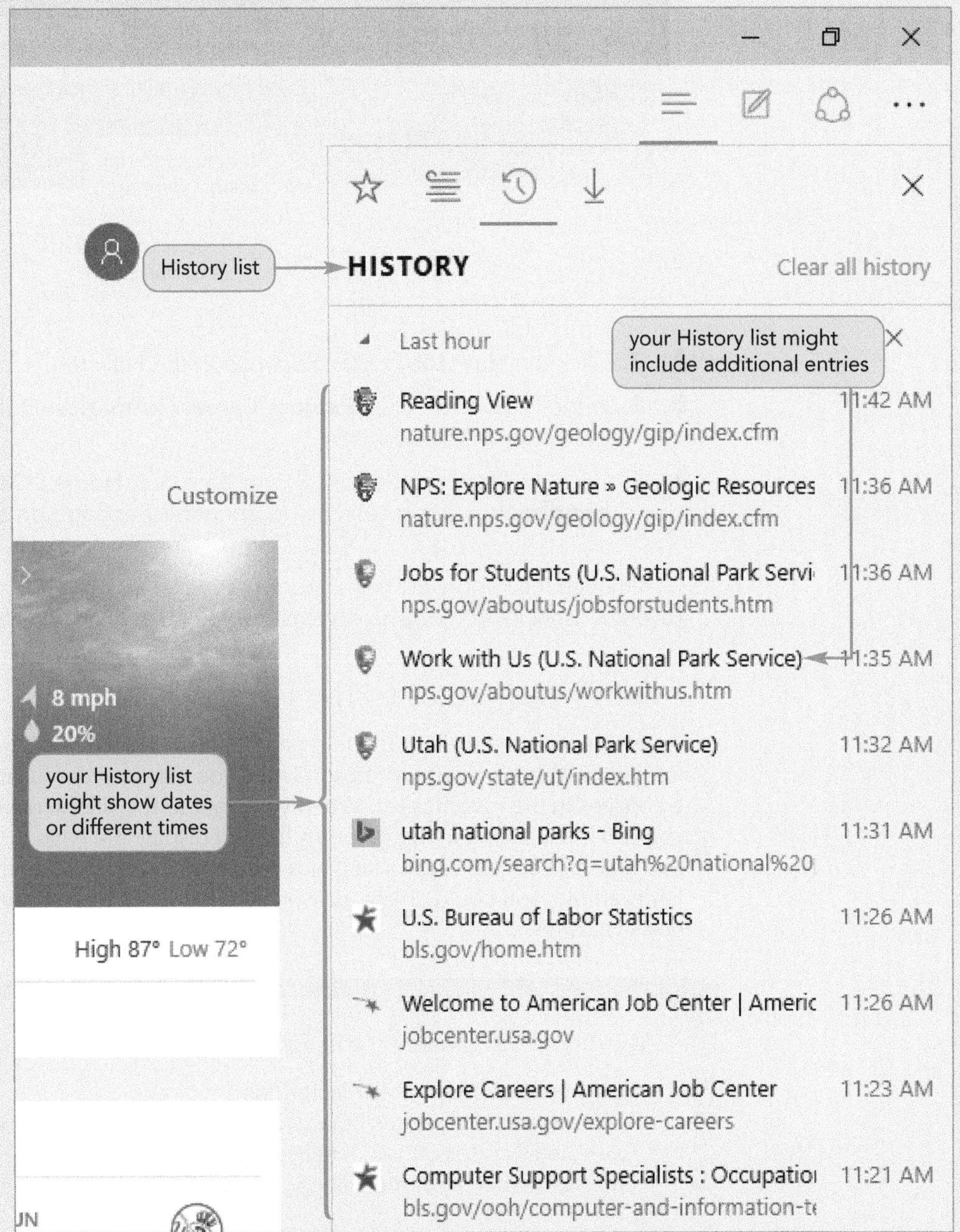

5. If necessary, click **Last hour** or click **Today** in the History list to expand the list and display the most recent webpages you've visited.

6. Click **Jobs for Students (U.S. National Park Service)**. The corresponding webpage opens in Edge. See Figure 4-21.

Figure 4-21 **Revisiting a webpage from the History list**

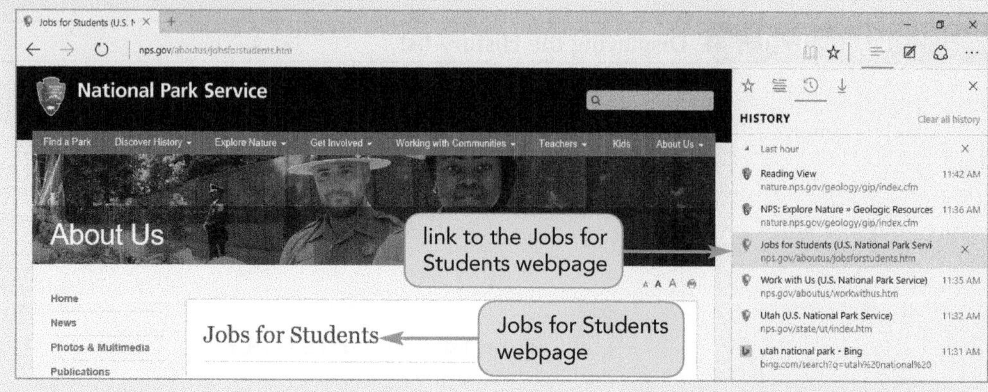

7. Click the **New tab** button [+] to open the New tab.
8. In the History list, click **Explore Careers | American Job Center** to open that webpage on the new tab.
9. Click the **New tab** button [+] and then click **Home : Occupational Outlook Handbook** in the History list to open the webpage on a new tab.

Although the History list helps you access webpages you opened recently, the Favorites list helps you organize webpages you open often, which you'll show Kent next.

Adding Webpages to the Favorites List

As you explore the web, you'll find pages that are your favorites—those you visit frequently. When you use Microsoft Edge, you can save the location of your favorite webpages in the Favorites list. When you want to revisit one of your favorite webpages, you can click its link in the Favorites list and display the page in your browser. As you add links or your list of favorite pages grows, you can organize the links into folders. For example, you could create a Favorites folder for travel websites and another for news websites.

REFERENCE

Adding a Webpage to the Favorites List

- Open the webpage in Microsoft Edge.
- Click the Add to favorites or reading list button in the Address bar.
- Click the Favorites button, if necessary.
- Enter a new name for the webpage and select a folder, if necessary.
- Click the Add button.

To add a webpage to the Favorites list, you access the page in Microsoft Edge, and then you use the Add to favorites or reading list button in the Address bar. By default, Microsoft Edge adds the new page to the end of the Favorites list. If you organize the webpages into folders, you can add a webpage to one of the folders. You can store the page using the title of the webpage as its name, or you can change the name so it is more descriptive or meaningful to you.

If you created favorites in another browser such as Internet Explorer or Chrome, you can import the favorites to Microsoft Edge. You do so by using the Import favorites link in the Favorites list to display a list of browsers installed on the computer. Select the browser with the favorites you want to import to have Microsoft Edge add them to the Favorites list.

TIP

To display the Favorites bar, click the More button in the navigation bar, click Settings, click the View favorites settings button, and then click the slider button for the Show the favorites bar setting from Off to On.

The Favorites list includes one folder at first: the Favorites Bar folder. This folder is for links you want to display on the Favorites Bar, a separate location for links to webpages you visit often. Microsoft Edge does not display the Favorites bar by default. If you change a setting to display it, the Favorites bar appears as a horizontal bar below the navigation bar.

The three open webpages provide the kind of information Kent will refer to often when preparing workshops for Step Up. You'll add the pages to the Favorites list.

If you are working on a school network, you might not be able to change the content of the Favorites list. In that case, read the following steps and examine the figures, but do not perform the steps.

To add webpages to the Favorites list:

1. With the Occupational Outlook Handbook page displayed in Microsoft Edge, click the **Add to favorites or reading list** button ☆ on the Address bar. A window opens where you choose to add a link to the Favorites list or the Reading list.

   Trouble? If you clicked the Favorites button in the Hub, the History list switched to the Favorites list. Click the Add to favorites or reading list button ☆ in the Address bar above the Hub to add a webpage to the Favorites list.

2. Click the **Favorites** button in the window to indicate that you want to add a link to the Favorites list. The Name box displays the name of the webpage, and the Save in box displays the location, such as "Favorites" for the Favorites list. If you wanted to save the link in a folder, you could click the Create new folder link and enter a folder name. In the Name box, you can change the name of the webpage, but the default name here makes the page easy to identify.

3. With Home Occupational Outlook Handbook displayed in the Name box, click the **Add** button to add the webpage to the Favorites list. The Add to favorites or reading list button is yellow, indicating that the webpage is a favorite.

4. Click the **Explore Careers | American Job Center** tab to display the webpage, and then click the **Add to favorites or reading list** button ☆ on the Address bar.

5. Click the **Add** button to add the webpage to the Favorites list using the name suggested in the Name box.

   Kent wants to keep the Jobs for Students link separate from the others in the Favorites list, so you'll create a folder as you add the webpage to the Favorites list.

6. Click the **Jobs for Students (U.S. National Park Service)** tab, and then click the **Add to favorites or reading list** button ☆ on the Address bar.

7. Click the **Create new folder** link, and then type **Students** as the folder name.

8. Click the **Add** button to add a link to the webpage to the Students folder in the Favorites list. See Figure 4-22.

Figure 4-22 Links to webpages in the Favorites list

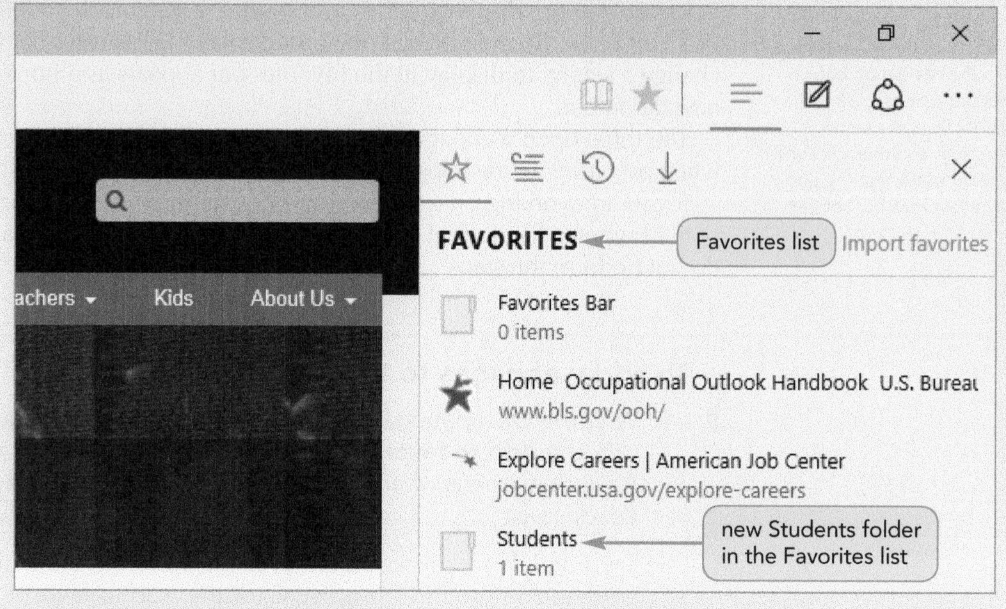

Kent realizes that many students will be interested in the NPS Geoscientists-in-the-Parks program and now wants to add that page to the Favorites list. You'll use the History list to open the page on a new tab, and then save a link to the webpage in the Students folder in the Favorites list.

To add a webpage to a folder in the Favorites list:

1. Click the **New tab** button at the top of the Microsoft Edge window to open the New tab.
2. In the Hub, click the **History** button to display the History list.
3. Click the **Geoscientists-in-the-Parks** link to open the Geoscientists-in-the-Parks webpage on the new tab.
4. Click the **Add to favorites or reading list** button in the Address bar to display the window for adding the webpage to the Favorites list.

   You can rename the webpage and add it to the Students folder at the same time.
5. In the Name box, type **GIP Program** to rename the link.
6. Click the **Save in** box, click **Students**, and then click the **Add** button to add the GIP Program link to the Students folder.
7. In the Hub pane, click the **Favorites** button to display the Favorites list.
8. Click the **Students** folder to display the links you saved as favorites.

TIP

To add a link to the Favorites bar instead of the Favorites list, select the Favorites Bar folder as the Save in location.

Next, you can organize the Favorites list to make the links easy to find.

Organizing the Favorites List

As you add more items to the Favorites list, you can organize its links by renaming or deleting some links and moving others to new folders. Using folders is an excellent way to organize your favorite webpages.

REFERENCE

Organizing the Favorites List

- Click the Hub button and then click the Favorites button to open the Favorites list.
- To move a link into a new folder, right-click the link and then click Create new folder on the shortcut menu. Type the folder name and then press the Enter key.
- To move a link into a Favorites folder, drag the link to the folder.
- To remove a link or folder from the Favorites list, right-click the item and then click Delete on the shortcut menu.
- To rename a link or folder, right-click the item and then click Rename on the shortcut menu. Type the name and then press the Enter key.

Kent sees the value of storing related links in a folder and now wants to move the links to the Explore Careers and Occupational Outlook Handbook webpages into a folder. He also wants to rename a link to shorten it.

To organize the Favorites list:

1. Click the **Favorites** button to return to the main Favorites list.
2. Right-click the **Home Occupational Outlook Handbook U.S. Bureau of Labor Statistics** link, and then click **Rename** on the shortcut menu.
3. Type **Occupational Outlook Handbook** as the new name, and then press the **Enter** key.
4. Right-click the **Explore Careers American Job Center** link, and then click **Create new folder** on the shortcut menu. A new folder appears in the Favorites list with the placeholder name, New folder, selected.
5. Type **U.S. Gov** as the new folder name, and then press the **Enter** key.
6. Drag the **Occupational Outlook Handbook** link to the U.S. Gov folder to move the link.
7. Drag the **Explore Careers American Job Center** link to the U.S. Gov folder to move the link.
8. Click the **U.S. Gov** folder in the Favorites list to verify that both links are now stored in the folder, and then click **Favorites** to return to the main Favorites list.

Now the Favorites list is organized so that Kent can easily access his favorite webpages.

INSIGHT

Using the Downloads List

In addition to the Favorites list, Reading list, and History list, the Hub includes a Downloads list. Many websites provide files you can download to your computer. For example, you can visit the Downloads webpage on the Microsoft website to download desktop themes. Microsoft Edge keeps track of the downloaded files in the Downloads list. If you need to access a downloaded file, you can display the Downloads list and then click a filename to open the file or run an installation program. You can also click the Open folder link in the Downloads list to display the file in File Explorer so you can move or delete it. (By default, Microsoft Edge saves downloaded files in the Downloads folder.) To remove a filename from the Downloads list, click the Clear button for the file. Clearing a filename from the Downloads list does not delete the downloaded file.

Printing and Saving Webpage Content

If you find a page on the web and want to refer to it when you don't have computer access, you can print the webpage. Sometimes, webpages include a Printer-Friendly Format link or other similar link for printing a webpage, indicating that the website formats the page for a standard size sheet of paper before printing. However, not all webpages provide such an option. Therefore, you should preview the page before you print it to see how it will look when printed. To print a webpage in Microsoft Edge, click the More button in the navigation bar, and then click Print to open the Print dialog box, which displays a preview of how the content will appear on the printed page. If the webpage requires more than a single page to print, you can view each page before printing. Click the Print button to print the webpage.

PROSKILLS

Decision Making: Determining Whether to Save Webpage Content

Using a browser, you can easily save webpage content on your computer, including the graphic images displayed on the page, files the webpage provides (such as text or music files), and the webpage itself. However, doing so is not always legal or ethical. Before you save any webpage content on your computer, you need to determine whether you have the legal right to do so. This consideration is especially important when you want to save and use images, video, and other media for work projects because commercial use of such content is often prohibited.

Web content such as software, video, music, and images is easy to copy in its digital form. However, if this material is protected by copyright, you usually are not allowed to copy or share it unless you receive permission from the owner. The term **copyright** refers to the originator's exclusive legal right to reproduce, publish, or sell works he or she creates. If you copy someone else's work without giving that person credit, you are committing plagiarism, and you may also be violating copyright laws.

Before you copy or save content from websites that you visit, you need to find out if and how you can use the materials. If you want to use material you find on a website, first get permission from the owner of the site. Often, websites include links to their copyright and permission-request information on their main pages. Even if you think the information or material you found is not copyrighted, you should always request permission to use it and give credit to any website that you use in your work or school projects.

Kent does not want to print or save any information you found for Step Up because he can access it quickly using Edge tools. You can exit Edge.

To close the Hub and exit Edge:

1. Click the **Close this pane** button ☒ in the upper-right corner of the Favorites list to close the Hub.
2. Click the **Close** button ☒ on the Microsoft Edge title bar.
3. Click the **Close all** button in the dialog box to close all tabs.

So far, you have learned about the structure of the Internet and the web and how to use Microsoft Edge to open, navigate, and organize webpages. In the next session, you'll use another service the Internet provides—email.

REVIEW

Session 4.1 Quick Check

1. A(n) _____________ is a program that locates, retrieves, and displays webpages.
2. What are two definitions for the term "home page"?
3. What is the purpose of a webpage tab?
4. How can you use Cortana to learn more about a topic you find on a webpage?
5. When you find a webpage containing information you want to focus on, you can switch to _____________, which removes most graphics, ads, links, and other distracting elements and presents text in a simple format.
6. Explain how to draw a circle around a paragraph on a webpage.
7. What is the difference between the Reading list and the Favorites list?
8. What is the difference between the History list and the Favorites list?

Session 4.2 Visual Overview:

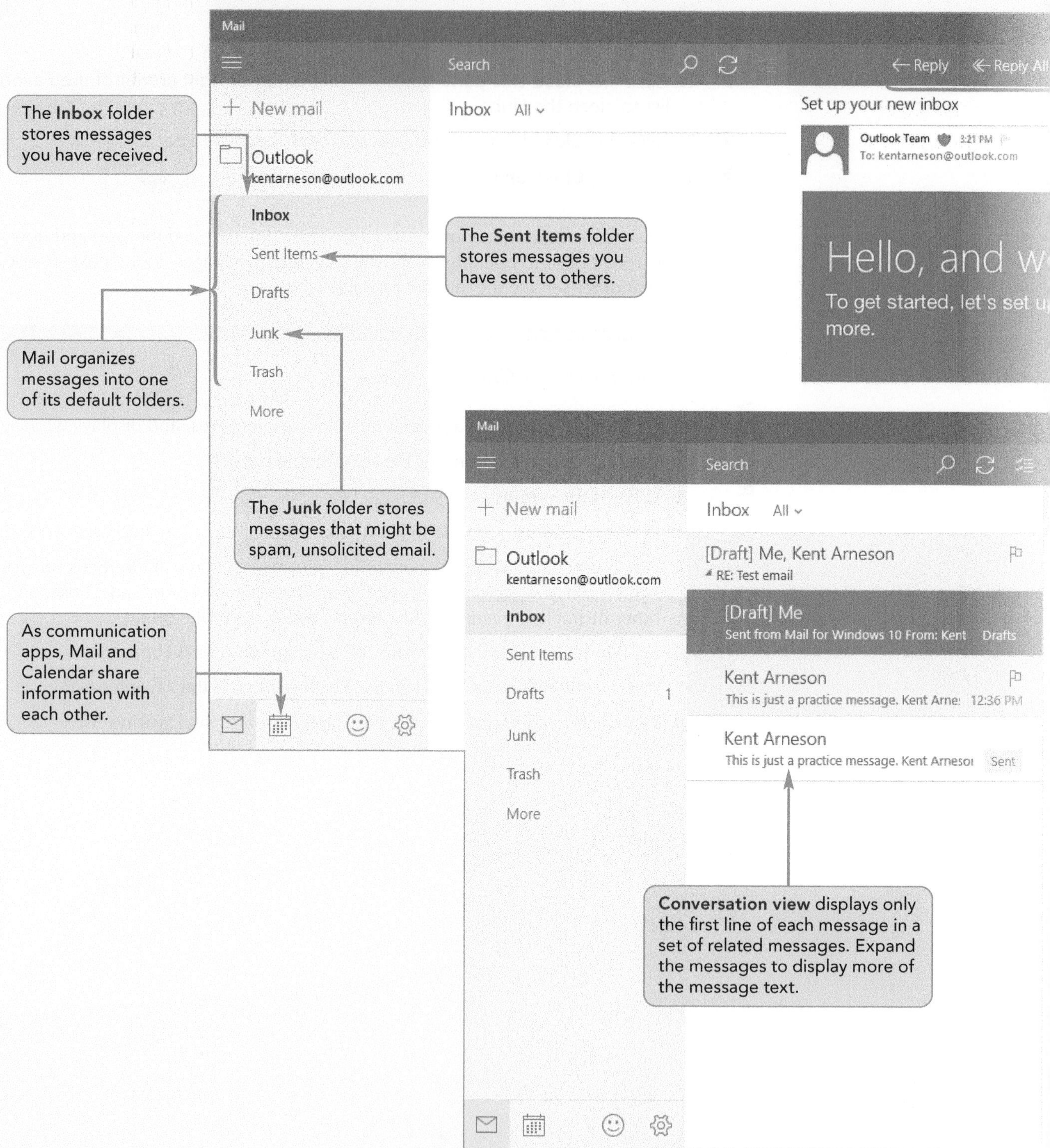
The Inbox folder stores messages you have received.
Mail organizes messages into one of its default folders.
The Sent Items folder stores messages you have sent to others.
The Junk folder stores messages that might be spam, unsolicited email.
As communication apps, Mail and Calendar share information with each other.
Conversation view displays only the first line of each message in a set of related messages. Expand the messages to display more of the message text.
Mail
Search
Reply
Reply All
New mail
Inbox
All
Outlook
kentarneson@outlook.com
Inbox
Sent Items
Drafts
Junk
Trash
More
Set up your new inbox
Outlook Team
3:21 PM
To: kentarneson@outlook.com
Hello, and w
To get started, let's set u
more.
[Draft] Me, Kent Arneson
RE: Test email
[Draft] Me
Sent from Mail for Windows 10 From: Kent
Drafts
1
Kent Arneson
This is just a practice message. Kent Arne:
12:36 PM
Kent Arneson
This is just a practice message. Kent Arnesoı
Sent

Windows 10 Mail App

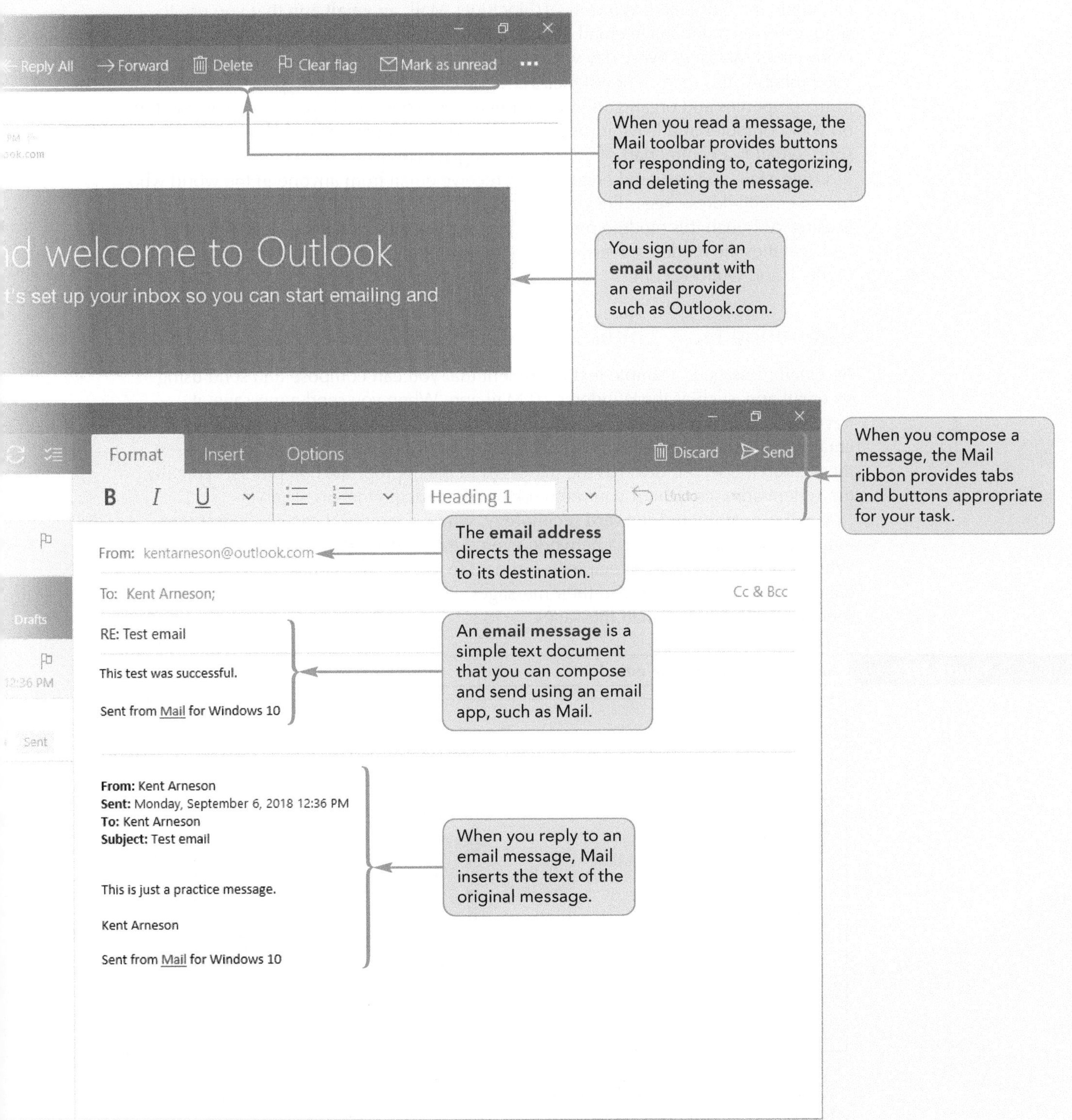
Reply All
Forward
Delete
Clear flag
Mark as unread
When you read a message, the Mail toolbar provides buttons for responding to, categorizing, and deleting the message.
nd welcome to Outlook
t's set up your inbox so you can start emailing and
You sign up for an **email account** with an email provider such as Outlook.com.
Format
Insert
Options
Discard
Send
Heading 1
Undo
When you compose a message, the Mail ribbon provides tabs and buttons appropriate for your task.
The **email address** directs the message to its destination.
From: kentarneson@outlook.com
To: Kent Arneson;
Cc & Bcc
Drafts
12:36 PM
Sent
RE: Test email
This test was successful.
Sent from Mail for Windows 10
An **email message** is a simple text document that you can compose and send using an email app, such as Mail.
From: Kent Arneson
Sent: Monday, September 6, 2018 12:36 PM
To: Kent Arneson
Subject: Test email
This is just a practice message.
Kent Arneson
Sent from Mail for Windows 10
When you reply to an email message, Mail inserts the text of the original message.

Getting Started with Mail

As you learned, the web is a service that the Internet provides. Another service is electronic mail, or email. Windows 10 includes Mail, an **email app** that you use to send, receive, and manage email. If you're like most computer users, you exchange many email messages every day with friends, family, colleagues, and other contacts. You probably also receive newsletters, coupons, offers, and other types of messages from companies and organizations. You might start your email app as soon as you turn on your computer and leave it running until you shut down at the end of the day. In short, email is a central part of your computing activities.

Using Mail, you can send email to and receive email from anyone in the world who has an email address, regardless of the operating system or type of computer the person is using. Although this module provides steps for using the Mail app, the concepts and activities the module covers apply to any email application, including Microsoft Outlook and Outlook.com.

Examining How Email Works

An email message is a simple text document that you can compose and send using an email app, such as the Windows 10 Mail app. When you send a message, it travels from your computer, through a network, and arrives at a computer called an **email server**. The email server stores the email messages until the recipients request them. Then the server forwards the messages to the appropriate computers. Typically, the system administrator of your network or ISP manages the email server.

Email uses **store-and-forward technology**, which means you can send messages to anyone on the Internet or a network, even if a recipient's computer isn't turned on. When it's convenient, your recipients connect to the Internet or network and use their email apps to receive and read their messages. Figure 4-23 illustrates the process of sending and receiving email messages.

Figure 4-23 **Sending and receiving email**

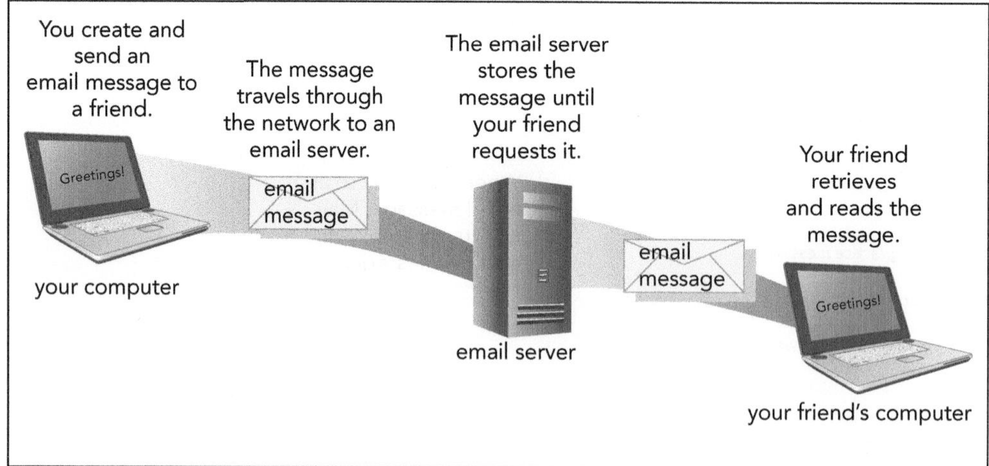

To send and receive email, you must be able to access an email server on the network. If your computer is part of a network at a college or university, for example, you sign in to the network to access its services. An email server provides mail services to faculty, staff, and students who have access to the network. When someone sends you a message, it is stored on your email server until you sign in to the network and use an email app to check your mail. The email server then transfers new messages to your electronic mailbox. You use an email app to open, read, print, delete, reply to, forward, and save the mail.

If your computer is not part of a network, you can access an email server on the Internet. To do so, you open an email account with a service that provides Internet access. For example, email accounts are included as part of the subscription fee for most ISPs. Email accounts are also provided free of charge by advertiser-supported websites, such as Outlook.com and Google. After you establish an email account, you can connect to the Internet to send and receive your email messages.

Addressing Email

Just as you must address a piece of ordinary mail, you need to supply an address for an email message. The email address you enter directs the message to its destination. Your email address is included in the message as the return address so your recipients can easily respond to your message. Anyone who has an email address can send and receive electronic mail. If you work for a company or attend a school that provides email, a system administrator probably assigns an email address to you. Other times, you create your own email address, though it must follow a particular format. See Figure 4-24.

Figure 4-24 **Typical format of an email address**

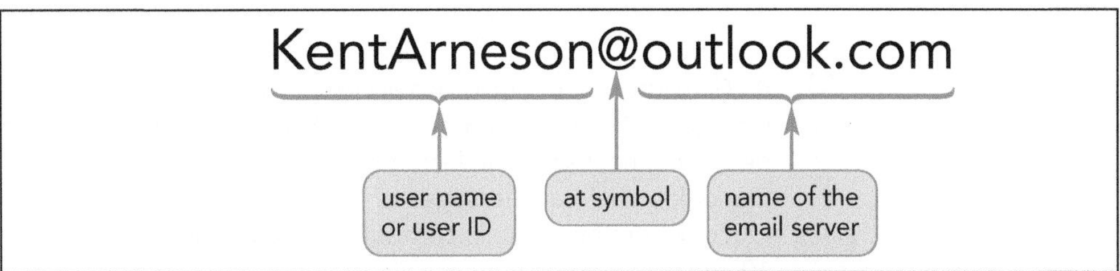

The **user name**, or **user ID**, is the name entered when your email account is set up. The @ symbol (read as "at sign") signifies that the email server name is provided next. For example, "KentArneson" is the user name and "outlook.com" is the email server.

The easiest way to learn a person's email address is to ask the person what it is. You can also look up an email address in a network or Internet directory. Most businesses and schools publish a directory listing email addresses of people who have email accounts on their network. Many websites also provide email directories for people with email accounts on the Internet, such as Yahoo! People Search at people.yahoo.com.

When you sign up for an email account, you can send your new email address to friends, colleagues, and clients. If your email address changes, such as when you change email services, you can subscribe to an email forwarding service so you don't miss any mail sent to your old address.

Setting Up Mail

To use email, you need an Internet connection, an email app, and an email address. Make sure you have an Internet connection and email address before performing the steps in this section. Having an email address means you have an email account, which is space on an email server reserved for your messages. You set up an account with an email service provider, which can be an ISP, an employer or school, or a web service such as Outlook.com or Gmail.

You can set up the following types of email accounts in Mail:

- Outlook—Microsoft offers Outlook.com as a free web-based email service.
- Exchange—This type of account can be an Exchange or Office 365 account (also offered by Microsoft). Organizations such as a business or school typically offer Exchange accounts, which reside on an Exchange server. Home users usually do not have Exchange accounts.

- Google—Google provides Gmail, a free web-based email service.
- YahooMail—Yahoo provides YahooMail, a free web-based email service.
- iCloud—Apple provides iCloud, a free web-based email service.
- Other account—Accounts provided by ISPs, including Post Office Protocol (POP) accounts and Internet Message Access Protocol (IMAP) accounts.

If you already have one of these types of email accounts, you can set up Mail to send and receive email by starting Mail and then entering the user name and password you use for the account. If you use more than one of these email accounts, you can add them to Mail.

If you do not have any of these types of email accounts, you can set up a free Outlook.com or Gmail account. To set up an Outlook.com account, use a browser to go to Outlook.com. Sign up for a Microsoft account by providing your name and other information and then selecting an account name (which is the same as a user name) and a password. You can also set up a Gmail account in a similar way. Use a browser to go to mail.google.com, provide your name and other information, and then select a user name and password.

INSIGHT

Using a Microsoft Account

A Microsoft account provides access to online services such as OneDrive for file storage and Outlook.com for email. You can sign in to a Microsoft account on any device connected to the Internet. When you do, you can read and respond to your Outlook.com email messages or access files stored on OneDrive. If you access Outlook.com on a public computer, for example, and then return to your Windows 10 home computer, your email messages and responses also appear in Mail. Your Microsoft account synchronizes Outlook.com and Mail so your messages are up to date in either place.

Kent has an Outlook.com account, but he hasn't set up Mail to use it yet. Because this is the first time you're starting Mail on his Windows 10 computer, you'll show Kent how to set up Mail to use his Outlook.com account. The following steps assume that you have a Microsoft account.

To set up Mail:

1. Click the **Start** button to display the Start menu.
2. Click the **Mail** tile to start the Mail app. The Mail app starts and opens the Welcome window.

   Trouble? If a dialog box opens asking if you want Mail to be your default mail program, click the Yes button only if you are using your own computer and want to use Mail as your mail program. If you are using a school or institutional computer, click the No button or ask your technical support person for assistance.
3. Click the **Get started** button to display the Accounts window.
4. If the Accounts window displays an email account you want to use in Mail, click the account name and then click the **Ready to go** button. You can skip the remaining steps. Otherwise, click the **Add account** button to display the Choose an account window in which you select an account type.

5. Click an account type, such as **Outlook.com**. The Add your Microsoft account window opens.

   Trouble? If you select an account type other than Outlook.com, the remaining steps might differ. Follow the on-screen instructions to finish setting up your email account.

   Trouble? If you want to use a Microsoft account but don't have one, click the No account? Create one! link, and then follow the on-screen instructions to set up the account.

6. Click in the **Email or phone** box, and then enter the email address or phone number for your Microsoft account.
7. Click in the **Password** box, and then enter the password for the account.
8. Click the **Sign in** button. If this is the first time you are signing in to Mail, the app connects to your Outlook.com account and displays messages received in that account.

Now you can show Kent how to send and receive email.

Sending and Receiving Email Using Mail

You can use the Mail app to compose, send, and receive email messages. After you set up an email account, you're ready to start using Mail to manage your email.

To start Mail:

1. Start Mail if necessary (click the **Mail** tile on the Start menu), and then maximize the window. Figure 4-25 shows the Mail window. The email account shown in the figures in this module belongs to Kent Arneson. Your screens will look different from the figures. For example, the background color or design might differ.

Figure 4-25 Mail app

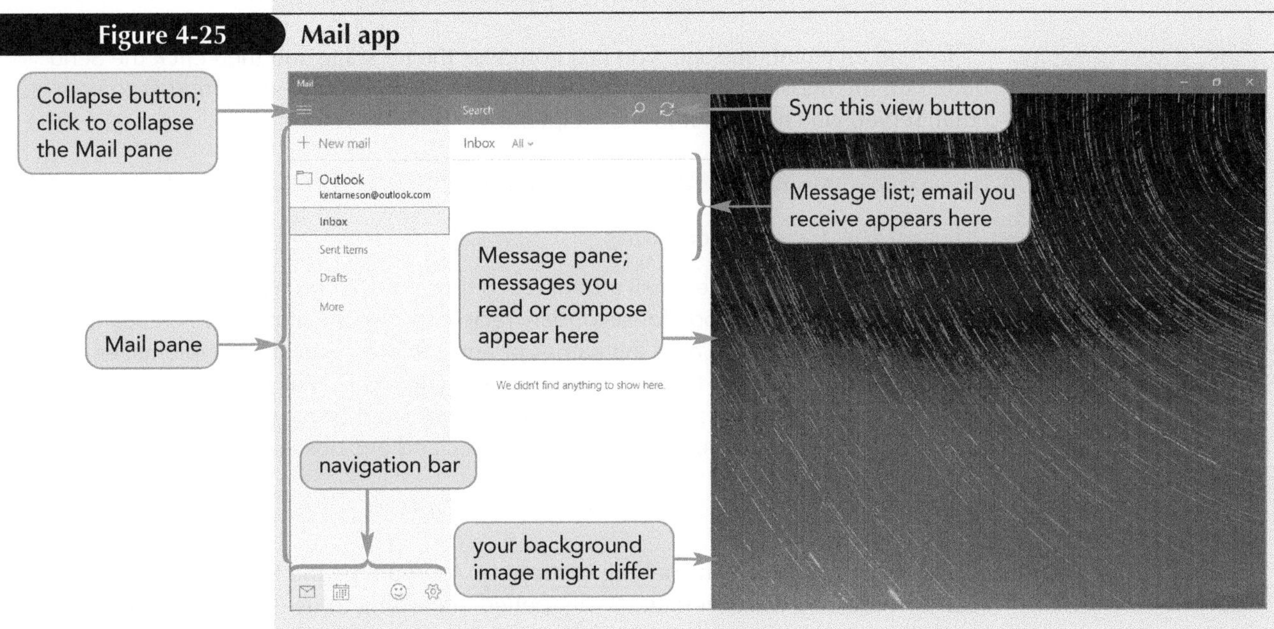

The Mail app includes the following tools and components:

TIP

You can display the Junk and Trash (or Deleted Items) folders in the Mail pane by clicking the More link, right-clicking an unpinned folder, and then clicking Add to Favorites.

- Mail pane—This part of the Mail window lists your email accounts at the top followed by the default Mail folders, including the Inbox, Sent Items, and Drafts folders. These folders are pinned to the Mail pane as favorites so that they are always available in that pane. Click the More link in the Mail pane to pin additional folders as favorites, including Junk and Trash. (Your folder might be called Deleted Items, depending on the type of email account.) Mail organizes your email into these folders automatically.
- Message list—This area displays the email messages you have sent or received.
- Message pane—This area displays the email message you are composing or reading.
- Navigation bar—The navigation bar provides buttons for starting the Calendar app, providing feedback, and displaying settings.

Creating and Sending Email Messages

An email message uses a format similar to a standard memo, which typically includes Date, To, and Subject lines, followed by the content of the message. The To box indicates who will receive the message. The Subject line, although optional, alerts the recipient to the topic of the message. You should always include a Subject line because people often delete messages without reading them if they do not contain subjects. Finally, the message area contains the content of your message. You can also include additional information, such as a Cc line, which indicates who will receive a copy of the message. Mail automatically supplies the date you send the message (as set in your computer's clock).

REFERENCE

Creating and Sending an Email Message

- Click the New mail button in the Mail pane.
- Enter the email address of the recipient in the To box.
- Click in the Subject box, and then type the subject of the message.
- Click in the message area, and then type the content of the message.
- Click the Send button.

To send an email message, you first compose the message and then click the Send button on the message window. Mail sends the message from your computer to your email server, which routes it to the recipient.

INSIGHT

Using the Cc and Bcc Lines

In the To box, restrict the email addresses to those of your primary recipients. Use the Cc (courtesy copy) box for secondary recipients who should receive a copy of the message. If you want to hide the names or email addresses of any recipients, enter their email addresses in the Bcc (blind courtesy copy) box. Mail sends individual copies of the message to each person listed in the Bcc box but displays only the recipient's and sender's email addresses. To display the Cc and Bcc boxes, click the Cc & Bcc link in the message window.

Mail includes a built-in spelling dictionary. As you type the text of a message, Mail corrects any words it flags as misspelled according to its dictionary. When a red line appears under a word, it means that the word is not in Mail's spelling dictionary.

You can right-click the word to display a shortcut menu of spelling suggestions and an option to add the word to the dictionary.

TIP

To personalize the appearance of the Mail app, click the Settings button in the navigation bar, and then click Personalization.

When you create or reply to an email message, Mail inserts a signature line by default. A **signature line** identifies the sender of the message. You can change the signature line to include your name, for example, by clicking the Settings button at the bottom of the Mail pane, clicking Options on the Settings menu, and then changing the text in the Signature box.

Now you can show Kent how to create and send an email message using Mail by sending a practice email to yourself.

To create and send an email message:

1. Click the **New mail** button in the Mail pane. The window for composing a new message opens. See Figure 4-26. Maximize the Mail window, if necessary.

Figure 4-26 Composing a new message

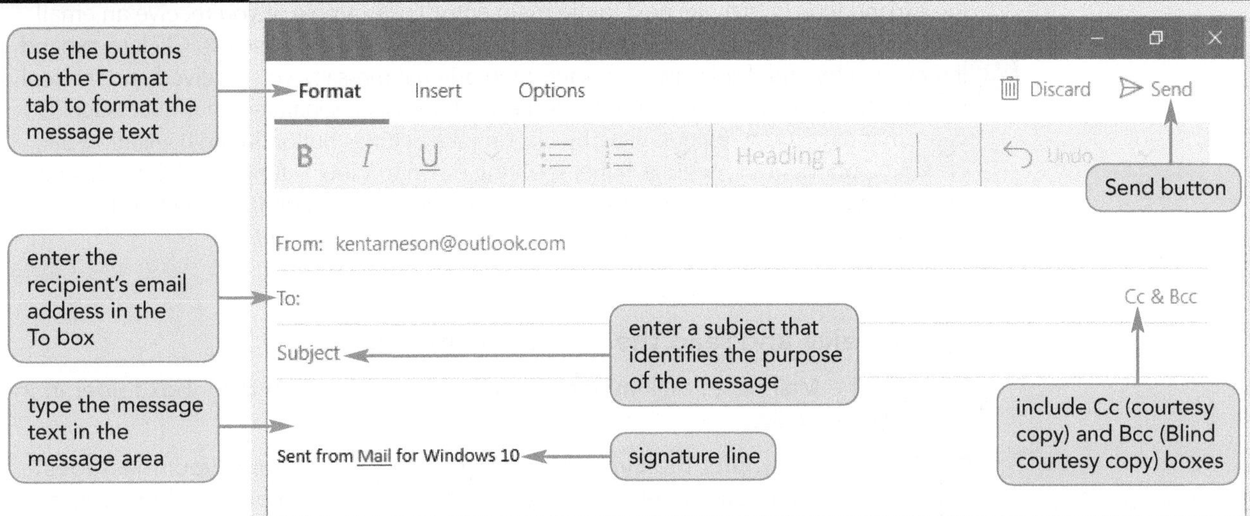

TIP

Mail might suggest the complete email address (or a list of possible email addresses) after you type a few characters in the To box.

2. Type your email address in the To box. When you finish, Mail converts the email address to the display name, such as Kent Arneson, and adds a semicolon after the name in case you need to enter another email address.

   Trouble? If you're not sure what email address you should enter, check with your instructor or technical support person.

3. Click in the **Subject** box, and then type **Test email** as the subject.
4. Click in the message area, and then type **This is just a practice message.** as the message content.
5. Press the **Enter** key twice, and then type your name.
6. Click the **Send** button on the toolbar. Mail sends the message to your email server and then places a copy of the sent message in the Sent Items folder. To make sure your message has been sent, you can open the Sent Items folder to see all of the messages you have sent.
7. In the Mail pane, click **Sent Items**. Your message appears in the Message list.

   Trouble? If your message does not appear in the Message list, and you entered your email address correctly in the original message, then Mail is not configured to send messages immediately. In that case, click the Sync this view button on the toolbar to send your message, which Mail saved in the Drafts folder.

When you composed the new message, you might have noticed that the window displayed the Format tab, Insert tab, and Options tab on the Mail ribbon. Use the tabs and buttons for formatting the text, inserting content such as tables and pictures, and using options such as checking the spelling.

Receiving and Reading Email Messages

Mail automatically checks to see if you've received email whenever you start the program and periodically after that. (Every 30 minutes is the default.) Mail also checks for received email when you click the Sync this view button on the toolbar. Email you receive appears in your Inbox. By default, the Inbox shows the **message header** for each message, which includes the name of the sender, the subject, the first line of the message, and the date or time you received the message. Mail you have received but have not read yet appears in bold. To read a message, you click the message in the list to open the message window.

By default, Mail displays messages in Conversation view, which collapses related messages into a single entry in the message list. To display all of the related messages, click the expand icon (a triangle) next to the main entry. For example, if you receive an email message and then reply to it, one main entry appears in the message list. Click to expand the main entry and display two messages: the original message you received and the reply you sent to that message. If you prefer to list each message separately in the message list, you can turn off Conversation view by clicking the Settings button in the navigation bar, clicking Options in the Settings pane, scrolling down to View Settings, and then clicking the slider button for the Show messages arranged by conversation from On to Off.

You'll show Kent how to read the email message you just sent.

TIP

If your computer is using a screen resolution of 1366 x 768 or higher, you can snap the Mail app to the screen so that it stays open as you work with other apps.

To receive and read the Test email message:

1. In the Mail pane, click **Inbox** to display the contents of the Inbox folder in the Message list.
2. If necessary, click the **Sync this view** button to retrieve your messages from your email server, route them to your Inbox, and display them in the Message list. Your Inbox folder might contain additional email messages from other people.

   Trouble? If the message you sent doesn't appear in the Inbox, wait a few minutes, and then click the Sync this view button again.
3. If necessary, click the **Test email** message to display the message. See Figure 4-27.

Figure 4-27 Reading a message

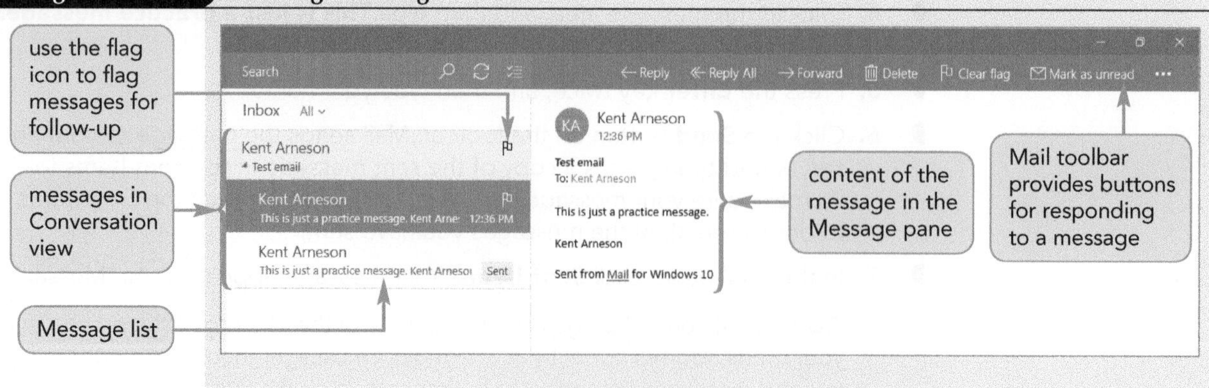

The flag icons on each message are for setting a reminder to follow up on the message. When you click a flag icon, it turns red by default, making it easy to find the message.

Next, you'll show Kent how to perform another common email task—responding to the messages you receive.

Responding to Email Messages

Some of the email you receive might ask you to provide information, answer questions, or confirm decisions. Instead of creating a new email message, you can reply directly to a message that you receive. When you reply to a message, Mail inserts the email address of the sender and the subject into the proper places in the message window and includes the text of the original message.

You can respond to messages by using the Reply or Reply all command. If the original message was sent to more than one person, use the Reply command to respond to only the original sender. Use the Reply all command to respond to all other recipients as well. Use the Reply all command carefully so that the only messages people receive from you are those they need to read. You can also use the Forward command to create a message with the original message text, and then you can send the message to someone other than the original senders.

You will show Kent how to reply to an email message.

To reply to the Test email message:

1. With the Test email message displayed in the Mail window, click the **Reply** button on the toolbar. The window displays the text of the original message, inserts the email address of the original recipient in the To box, and displays RE: before the original subject text. It also marks the reply message you are writing as a draft because it's in progress. See Figure 4-28.

Figure 4-28 Replying to a message

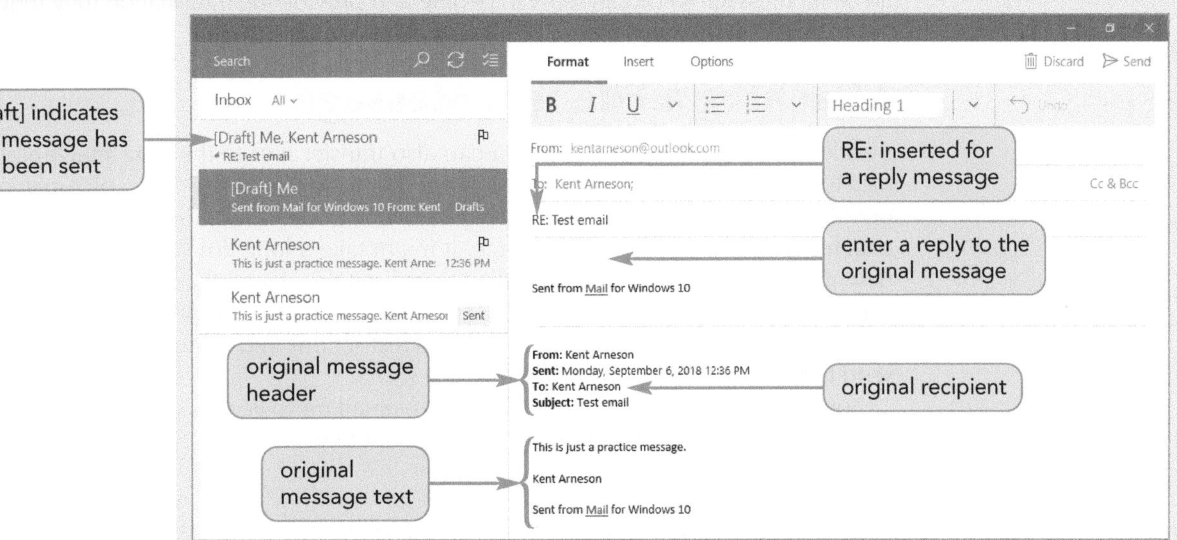

2. In the message area, type **This test was successful.** and then click the **Send** button on the toolbar.

3. When the RE: Test email message appears in your Inbox, click it, if necessary, to display the content of the four related messages: the original message with the "This is just a practice message." text, the copy of that message that appears in the Sent Items list, the reply with the "This test was successful." text, and the copy of the reply that appears in the Sent Items list. See Figure 4-29.

   Trouble? If the message doesn't appear in the Inbox folder, click the Sync this view button.

Figure 4-29 **Displaying the contents of related messages**

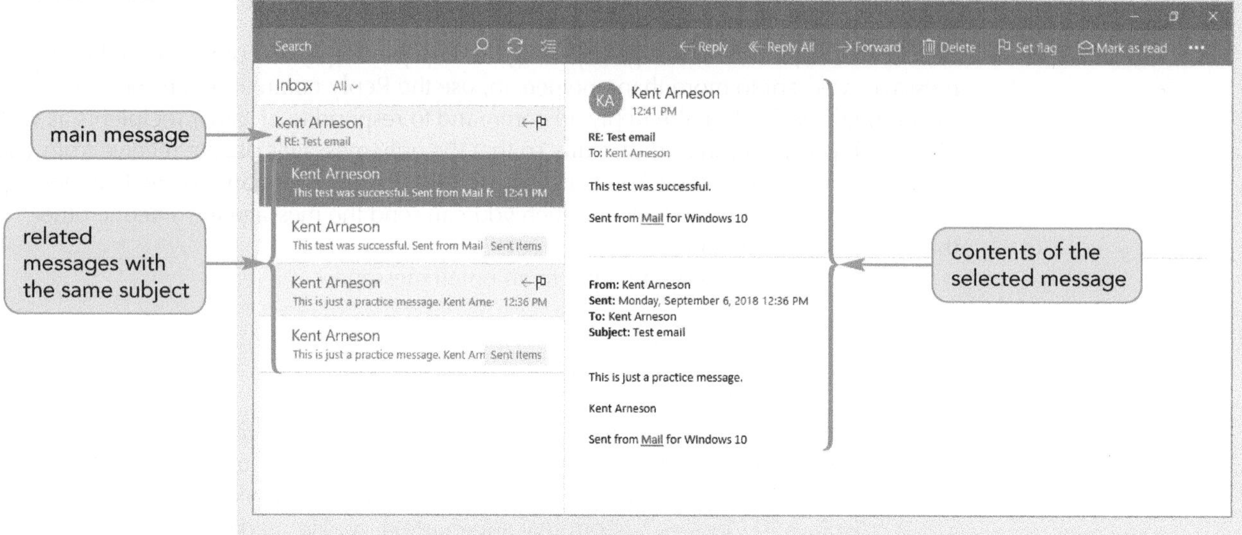

Kent mentions that clients often request a list of upcoming career information workshops, which he stores in a Word document. You'll show him how to attach a file to an email message so he can reply to people and provide the information they request.

Attaching a File to a Message

Besides sending email to others, you can also transfer files to them by attaching the files to messages. You can send any kind of file, including documents, pictures, music, or videos. Check the size of the files you attach before you send a message. If you attach a large file to an email message, it might take a long time for your recipient to download your message. Most email servers limit the size of the files you can attach; some allow files no larger than 3 MB. Check with your correspondents before sending large file attachments to find out about size restrictions and set up a convenient time to send the attachment.

You'll show Kent how to send and open an email message that includes an attachment. As before, you'll create a test message and send it to yourself.

To create and send a message with an attachment:

1. Make sure your computer can access your Data Files for this module. For example, if you are using a USB drive, insert the drive into the USB port.
2. In the Mail pane, click the **New mail** button.
3. Type your email address in the To box.

4. Click in the **Subject** box, and then type **Workshop list you requested** as the message subject.
5. Click in the message area, click the **Insert** tab on the Mail ribbon, and then click the **Attach** button to display the Open dialog box.
6. Navigate to the **Module4 > Module** folder provided with your Data Files, click the **Workshops** file, and then click the **Open** button. Mail attaches the file to the message and displays the filename and size next to the file icon.
7. In the message area, type **This is a test email message with a file attachment.**
8. Click the **Send** button on the toolbar.
9. If necessary, click the **Sync this view** button on the toolbar to send and receive the message.

When you receive a message that contains an attachment, you can choose to save or open the attached file. You should open files only after scanning them with antivirus software. Some people spread harmful software, called viruses, in email attachments. Before you open the file, you need to make sure the app used to create the attachment is installed on your computer. If it's not, you can sometimes use a text editor, such as WordPad or Notepad, to open and read the attached file.

To receive and open a message with an attachment:

1. When the Workshop list you requested message appears in your Inbox, click the message to expand it, and then click the first message below it, which is the message you received, to display the entire message.
2. Right-click the **Workshops.rtf** file icon to display a shortcut menu, which lets you open or save the attachment.
3. Click **Open** on the shortcut menu. The file opens in a desktop word-processing program, such as Word or WordPad. You could save the document now if necessary.
4. Close the word-processing program.

PROSKILLS

Written Communication: Observing Email Etiquette

Because email is a widespread form of communication, you should follow standard guidelines and common sense when using it. For example, use language appropriate for the purpose of your message and your recipients. Following are a few guidelines to keep in mind when you are composing email messages so that you can communicate effectively, without offending or annoying your correspondents:

- Be concise and direct. As a courtesy to your correspondents and to make sure your message is read, get right to the point and keep your messages short.
- Include your response first. When you reply to an email, you can include text from the original message. If you do, make sure that your response is at the top of the message so your recipients can find it easily. If you respond to questions or insert comments in the original message, use a contrasting font color so your recipients can identify your additions.
- Don't email sensitive or confidential information. Email is not private, and your recipients can forward your message to others, either intentionally or accidentally. Be professional in your tone and careful about what you say to and about others.
- Avoid abbreviations. Although you should strive to be brief, don't overcompensate by using nonstandard abbreviations. Stick to the abbreviations that are common in business writing, such as FYI and ASAP.
- Don't use all capital letters. Using all capital letters, as in "SEND ME THE REPORT TODAY," can be difficult to read and misconstrued as shouting.
- Check your spelling and grammar. The accuracy and quality of your writing in an email message is as important as in any piece of communication you send. Use the spelling tool available in your email app, and proofread for grammatical accuracy.

Kent might want to delete the email messages he's read. You'll show him how to do so next.

Deleting Email Messages

TIP

To delete several messages at once, select the first message in the Message list, and then press and hold the Delete key to delete a series of other messages.

After you read and respond to your messages, you can delete any message you no longer need. When you delete a message, it moves to the Trash folder (also called the Deleted Items folder in some types of accounts). Messages remain in the Trash folder until you delete them. You can delete a message by selecting the message and then clicking the Delete button on the toolbar, by pointing to the message and then clicking the Delete this item icon, or by right-clicking the message and then clicking Delete on the shortcut menu. If the Trash (or Deleted Items) folder isn't listed in the Mail pane, click the More button and then click Trash.

To select messages before you delete them or perform any other task with them, you can click the Enter selection mode button on the toolbar to display a check box next to each message. You click the check box to select the corresponding message. If you have only one or two messages, you can point to a message to display a Delete this item icon, and then click the icon to delete the message.

To delete the Test email messages:

1. Point to the main message in the Message list, and then click the **Delete this item** icon to delete the message. A Delete message and icon appear briefly at the bottom of the Mail window, and the message is moved to the Trash or Deleted Items folder.

INSIGHT

Dealing with Junk Email

Junk email, or **spam**, is unsolicited email, often containing advertisements, fraudulent schemes, or legitimate offers. Mail includes a junk email filter that analyzes the content of the email messages you receive and moves suspicious messages to the Junk folder, where you can examine and manage them as necessary. To reduce the amount of junk email you receive, avoid posting your email address on websites or other public areas of the Internet. If a website requests your email address, read its privacy statement to make sure it doesn't disclose your email address to others. Finally, never respond to junk email—you're likely to receive even more spam. Be sure to open your Junk folder often to review the messages it contains, and then delete the spam messages, which are often from senders you don't recognize.

You're finished working with Mail for now, so you can close the app. You should also delete the test email messages you worked with in this session.

To delete messages and close Mail:

1. Point to the message in the message list for the Inbox, and then click the **Delete this item** icon to delete the message.
2. In the Mail pane, click **Sent Items**.
3. Point to the main messages in the message list, and then click the **Delete this item** icon to delete each message.
4. Click the **Close** button to close Mail.

Two Windows apps are designed for use with Mail: People and Calendar. You'll explore the People app next.

Adding Information to the People App

Another communication app in Windows 10 is the People app, which you use to keep track of your contacts, including email correspondents. You can also use People on its own to save information about people and organizations. In addition to storing email addresses, you can store related information such as street addresses, home phone numbers, and personal information, such as anniversaries and birthdays. When you create an email message to someone stored in the People app, Mail suggests the complete email address after you type a few characters in the To box.

REFERENCE

Adding a Contact in People

- Click the Start button and then click the People tile.
- Click the Add button in the Contacts pane.
- Enter contact information.
- Click the Save button.

You can add contact information to People by importing the information from an email app or from social networking sites where you maintain contacts, such as Google, LinkedIn, and Twitter. If you import the same contact information from two or more sources, the People app detects the duplicate contacts and combines them into a single entry called a linked contact. You can also create a new contact and then enter as much information as you want about that contact, including a photo.

If you import contact information from your accounts on social networking sites, People maintains a connection to those accounts so it can display updated contact information. If the People tile is a live tile on the Start menu, it also displays updated information as it becomes available.

If you have more than one account set up in the Mail app, you must choose an account in which you want to save your new contacts the first time you start People. For example, the accounts might include your Microsoft account and an Outlook.com account. If you choose the Microsoft account, you can access the contacts on any device for which you sign in using a Microsoft account. The name of the window you use to add a contact reflects the account you select. For example, the window might appear with the title New Outlook Contact.

Kent doesn't want to import his contacts from other services, so you'll show him how to use People to add a new contact.

To add a contact:

1. Click the **Start** button to display the Start menu, and then click the **People** tile to start the People app.

   Trouble? If the People tile does not appear on your Start menu, type "People" in the Ask me anything box after you click the Start button, and then click the People app in the results.

2. If this is the first time you are starting the People app, a window opens listing sources of contacts, such as your Microsoft account. Click the account in which you want to store your contacts.
3. Click the **Add** button in the Contacts pane to display a window for adding a new contact. The type of online account you are using, such as Outlook, appears in the Save to box.
4. Click in the **Name** box, if necessary, and then type **Kent Arneson**.
5. Click in the **Mobile phone** box, and then type **(801) 555-1100**. To change the box label, click the Phone down arrow to display the Change label menu, and then click the label you want—for example, Work.
6. Click in the **Personal email** box, and then type **KentArneson@outlook.com**. You can change the type of email from Personal to Work, for example, by clicking the Personal email arrow to display the Change label menu.
7. Click **Other** to display the Add a field menu with a list of other contact details, and then click **Company** to add the Company box to the window.
8. Type **Step Up** in the Company box.
9. Click the **Save** button on the toolbar in the upper-right part of the window.
10. If the contact information for Kent Arneson does not appear in the right pane, click **Kent Arneson** in the Contacts pane to display his contact information. See Figure 4-30.

TIP

You can click the Add a field button (plus icon) below a box to enter phone numbers, email addresses, addresses, or other information for a contact.

Figure 4-30 New contact in People

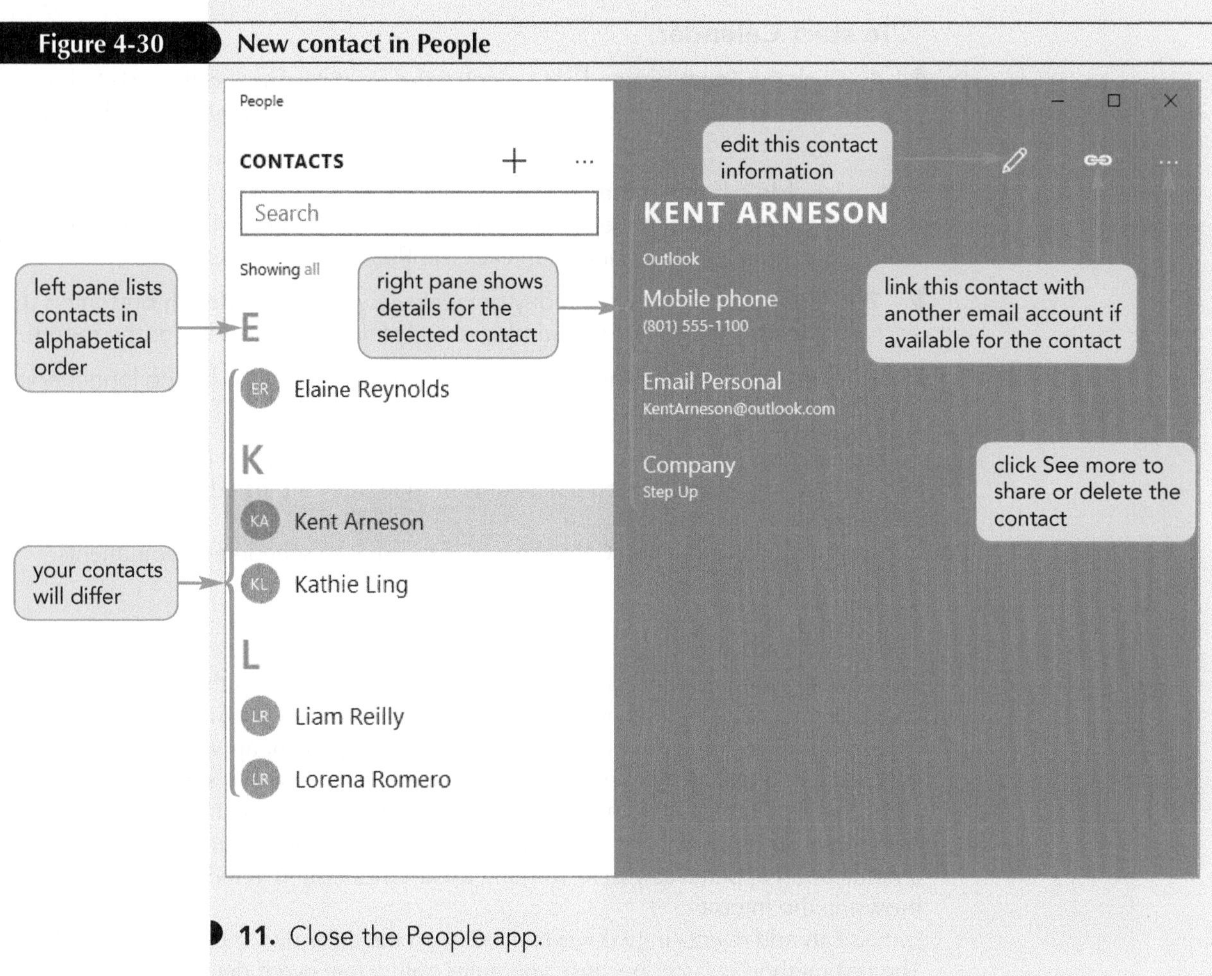

11. Close the People app.

Next, you want to help Kent manage his schedule with the Calendar app.

Managing Your Schedule with Calendar

Calendar is another app that works with Mail. You use it to schedule appointments, track tasks, and stay on top of deadlines. Calendar also lets you schedule recurring events, such as weekly staff meetings, and set reminders so you don't miss an important appointment. When you schedule an event, Calendar blocks out the time in your schedule, helping you avoid scheduling conflicts. If the event is a meeting, you can invite contacts stored in the People app to attend the meeting. You can also adjust the Calendar view to display scheduled events in the Day, Week, or Month format. The Day format shows you the events for today and tomorrow.

Calendar actually includes more than one calendar. The Main calendar displays your user name and is designed for scheduling all of your appointments and events. Other calendars include Birthday, Personal, Holidays, and Work. If you want to keep your personal appointments separate from work events, for example, you can maintain two calendars—Personal and Work. On the Birthday calendar, add birthdays of your contacts and other people. Calendar will remind you about the upcoming birthday in a notification message as you are working anywhere in Windows 10. The same is true for the Holidays calendar. If you list national and personal holidays in the calendar, Calendar will remind you about each one.

Because Kent works so often at his computer, he is ready to use an electronic calendar. You'll show him how to start Calendar.

TIP

When you're working in the Mail app, click the Calendar button in the navigation bar to start the Calendar app.

To start Calendar:

1. Click the **Start** button to display the Start menu, and then click the **Calendar** tile. The Calendar app opens, showing a calendar for the current day, week, or month.

   Trouble? If this is the first time you are starting Calendar, a Welcome screen appears. Click the Get started button to display a list of email accounts. Click your email account and then click the Ready to go button.

2. If the calendar shows the day or week view, click the **Month** button on the toolbar at the top of the window to display your schedule for the month.
3. If necessary, widen the window until the horizontal scroll bar no longer appears.

The first time you start Calendar, a window opens asking you to add your email accounts. If you already entered accounts in Mail, they are listed in this window for confirmation.

Now that you've opened Calendar, you can use it to schedule appointments.

Scheduling Appointments

In Calendar, you can schedule appointments such as meetings that occur for part of a day. You can also schedule events that last 24 hours or longer. An appointment appears as a colored block in your calendar, while a day-long event appears in a banner at the beginning of a day. When you schedule appointments, you can specify that they are recurring, such as training that takes place once per week, meetings scheduled once per month, or birthdays and other annual events. If you set a reminder for an event, a notification appears as you're working on another task in Windows 10, such as browsing the Internet.

You can add events in two ways: directly on the calendar or using the Details pane. The first method is faster because you enter only a few event details. However, you cannot select settings such as status, reminders, and recurrence. To select those settings and enter more event details, click the New event button to collapse the left pane and open the Details pane.

The first appointment Kent wants to schedule is for a staff meeting later today, which is usually 30 minutes long. He wants to be reminded about the meeting 30 minutes before it begins so he has time to prepare.

To schedule an appointment:

1. In the left pane, click today's date, if necessary, to select it, and then click the **New event** button. The left pane collapses and a Details pane opens on the right, displaying the details you can enter for the new appointment, such as the name, location, and start time.
2. In the Event name box, type **Staff meeting** as the event name.
3. Click in the **Location** box, and then type **West conference room**.
4. Click the **arrow button** for the Start time, and then click a time about two hours from now, such as **1:30 pm**.

   Trouble? If the Start time box is gray and unavailable, click the All day check box to remove the checkmark, and then perform Step 4.

TIP

To invite people to an event or meeting, use the People pane.

5. Click in the **Event description** box, and then type **Check the status of accounts and workshops.** to enter a description.
6. Click the **Reminder** box on the toolbar, and then click **30 minutes** on the menu to set the reminder time. You can accept the current selection for the Calendar box. See Figure 4-31.

Figure 4-31 Scheduling an appointment

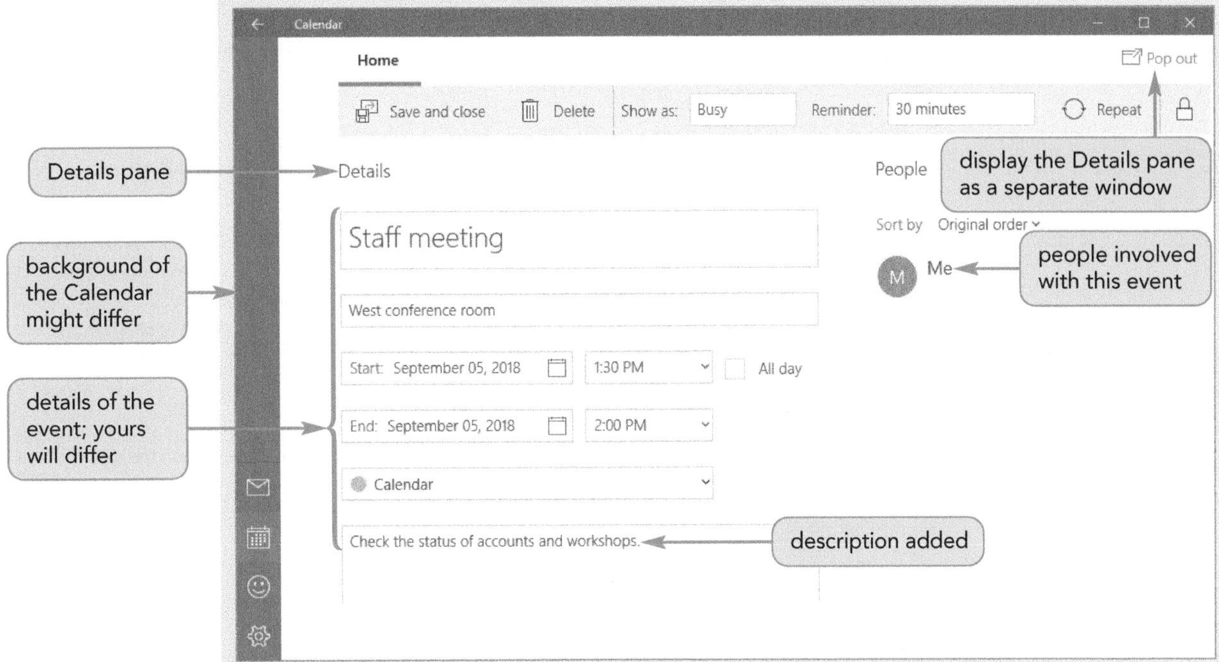

7. Click the **Save and close** button on the toolbar. The calendar in the right pane displays an entry for the event.
8. Close the Calendar app.

TIP

To edit an appointment already scheduled in the Calendar, double-click the appointment.

You've created an appointment for Kent's weekly staff meeting. Recall that when you set options for the lock screen, you could choose an app to show its detailed status on the lock screen. By default, the Calendar app shows your appointment details on your lock screen so you see them as soon as you turn on your computer or return to it after being away awhile. You can verify that the lock screen shows details from the Calendar app using the Settings app, which you've used in previous modules.

To display Calendar details on the lock screen:

1. Click the **Start** button to display the Start menu, and then click **Settings** to start the Settings app.
2. Click **Personalization** to display the Personalization window.
3. In the left pane, click **Lock screen** to display the settings for the lock screen.
4. Scroll down to the Lock screen apps section. In the Choose an app to show detailed status section, click an icon to display apps that can show detailed information on the lock screen. See Figure 4-32.

Figure 4-32 **Selecting Calendar as a lock screen app**

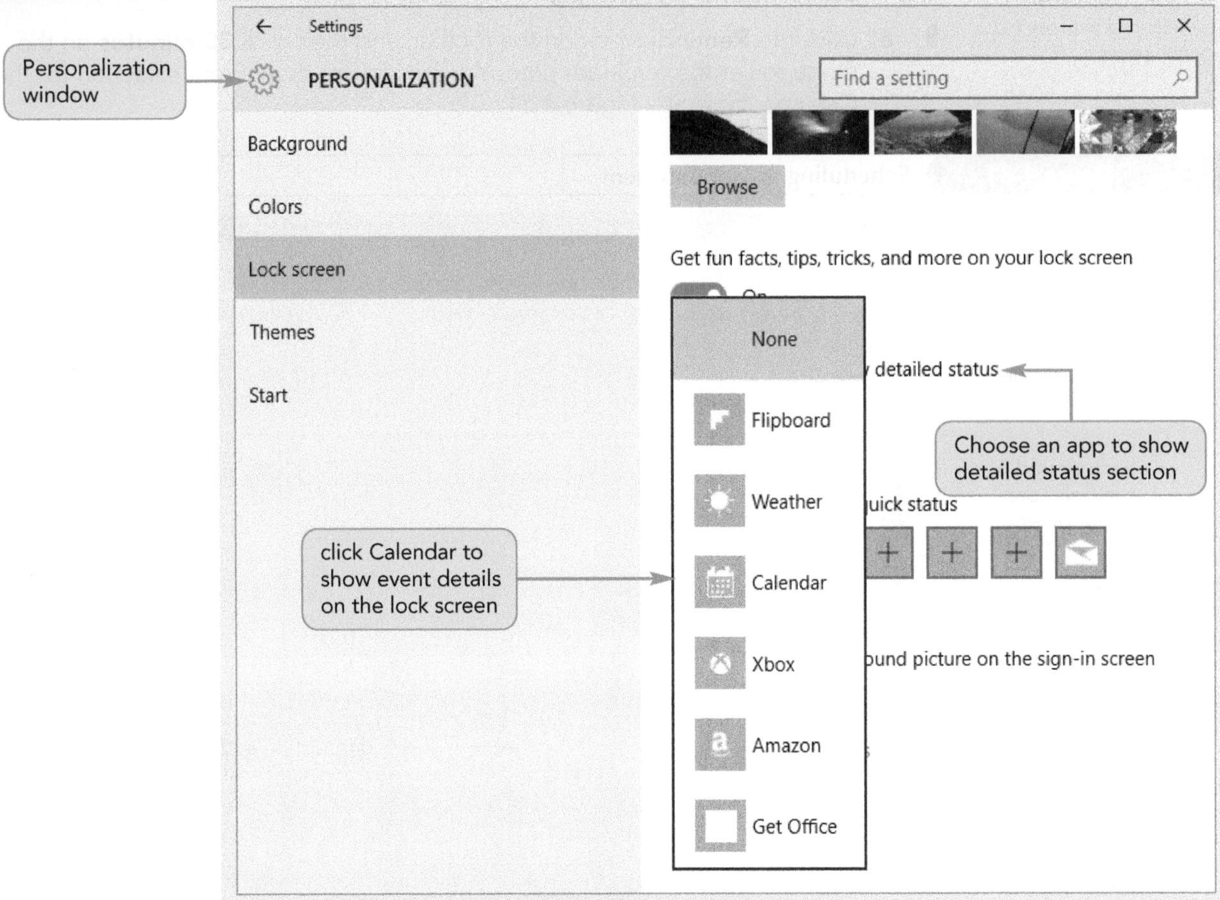

5. If Calendar is not selected, click **Calendar** and then close the Personalization window.
6. Hold down the **Windows** key and then press the **L** key to display the lock screen. Today's event appears on the lock screen. Press the **Enter** key and then sign in to Windows the way you usually do.

Now that you've finished exploring the Internet and email on Kent's computer, you should restore the computer to its original settings.

Restoring Your Settings

If you are working in a computer lab or using a computer other than your own, complete the steps in this section to restore the original settings on the computer.

To restore your settings:

1. Start Microsoft Edge, click the **Hub** button in the navigation bar, click the **History** button, click **Clear all history**, click the **Browsing history** check box to select it (if necessary), deselect the other check boxes, and then click the **Clear** button.

2. Click the **Hub** button and then click the **Favorites** button to display the Favorites list.
3. Right-click the **U.S. Gov** folder, and then click **Delete** on the shortcut menu to delete the folder.
4. Right-click the **Students** folder in the Favorites list, and then click **Delete** on the shortcut menu to delete the folder.
5. Click the **Reading list** button to display the contents of the Reading list.
6. Right-click the first link in the Reading list, and then click **Delete** on the shortcut menu to delete the link.
7. Close Microsoft Edge.
8. Click the **Start** button to display the Start menu, right-click the **Welcome to American Job Center** tile, and then click **Unpin from Start** to remove the tile from the Start menu.
9. Right-click the **U.S. Bureau of Labor Statistics** tile, and then click **Unpin from Start** to remove the tile from the Start menu.
10. Start Mail, click the **No** button if a message appears asking if you want to set Mail as your default email app, click **Trash** (or **Deleted Items**) in the Mail pane or click **More** and then click **Trash** (or **Deleted Items**). Click the first message, and then hold down the **Delete** key to delete all the messages. Close the Mail app.
11. Click the **Start** button and then click the **People** tile (or search for it using the Ask me anything box). Right-click **Kent Arneson** in the list of contacts, click **Delete** on the shortcut menu, and then click the **Delete** button to confirm. Close the People app.
12. Click the **Start** button and then click the **Calendar** tile. Right-click the appointment you added to the calendar, and then click **Delete** on the shortcut menu. Close the Calendar app.
13. Close all apps and windows.

REVIEW

Session 4.2 Quick Check

1. Before you can have an email address, you must sign up for an email ____________ with an email service.
2. Where does Mail display the email messages you have sent or received?
3. Identify the user name and the email server name in the following email address: CoraPatel@mymail.net.
4. When composing an email message, what information do you enter in the To box?
5. The ____________ for an email message includes the name of the sender, the subject, the first line of the message, and the date or time you received the message.
6. If you set a reminder for a scheduled event, how does Calendar remind you?
7. Describe how the Mail app and the People app can work together.

PRACTICE

Review Assignments

Data File needed for the Review Assignments: Utah.rtf

You already showed Kent how to conduct research on career development resources to prepare for his workshops at Step Up. He also needs information about the attractions of Utah for out-of-state people thinking of relocating to Salt Lake City. He is interested in information about state parks, especially the activities and attractions for visitors. You'll use Microsoft Edge to research information for Kent. Complete the following steps:

1. Start Microsoft Edge and then use the Address bar to search for websites with information about Utah state parks.
2. Open the first webpage listed on a new tab. Explore the webpage and then click any link that might provide more information about activities or things to do in the state parks.
3. Pin the webpage about Utah state park activities to the Start menu.
4. Return to the search results to find a link to another webpage about Utah state parks. Open that webpage on a new tab.
5. Explore the new webpage and then click any link that might provide more information about activities or things to do in the state parks. Pin the second webpage about Utah state park activities to the Start menu.
6. Return to the search results, and then open any other webpage on a new tab. If the Reading view button is available, keep the webpage open. If the Reading view button is not available, close the tab, return to the search results, and then open a different webpage on a new tab.
7. When you find a webpage available in Reading view, switch to Reading view, and then scroll to display all of its information.
8. Use a Make a Web Note tool to highlight a heading or other text on the page.
9. Display the Start menu, scroll if necessary to display the pinned tiles, and then press the Print Screen key to capture an image of the screen. Start Paint, paste the screen image in a new file, and then save the file as **Reading view** in the Module4 > Review folder provided with your Data Files.
10. Exit from Make a Web Note and Reading view.
11. Return to the search results, and then search for information about Bear Lake state park. Find a webpage about Bear Lake state park, open it on a new tab, and then display the webpage.
12. Display the Favorites bar in the Microsoft Edge window. (*Hint*: Click the More button, click Settings, click the View favorites settings button, and then click the slider button for the Show the favorites bar setting from Off to On.)
13. Add the webpage about Bear Lake state park to the Favorites bar. (*Hint*: As you are creating the favorite, click the Save in box and then click Favorites Bar.)
14. Ask Cortana about Bear Lake state park.
15. Press the Print Screen key to capture an image of the Microsoft Edge window. In Paint, paste the screen image in a new file, and then save the file as **Bear Lake** in the Module4 > Review folder provided with your Data Files.
16. Close Paint and Microsoft Edge.
17. Start Mail and create an email message. Enter your email address and your instructor's email address in the To box and **Utah state parks** in the Subject box.
18. In the message area, write a message describing one activity or attraction Kent should mention to out-of-state visitors, based on your research.
19. Attach the **Utah** file from the Module4 > Review folder to the message, and then send the message.
20. Add your email address and your instructor's email address to the People app.
21. Add an appointment to the Calendar for a 30-minute meeting with Kent today to discuss his upcoming presentation.

22. Complete the following tasks to restore your computer to its original settings:
    - In Microsoft Edge, clear the History list, remove the webpage you added to the Favorites bar (*Hint*: Right-click the link and then click Delete on the shortcut menu), and then hide the Favorites bar.
    - Close Microsoft Edge.
    - On the Start menu, delete the tiles for the pinned webpages.
    - In Mail, delete the emails you sent and received, and then delete the messages from the Trash (or the Deleted Items) folder.
    - In People, delete yourself and your instructor from the contacts list.
    - In Calendar, delete the appointment you created.
23. Close all open windows and apps.

APPLY

Case Problem 1

There are no Data Files needed for this Case Problem.

Wild Weather Joseph Lafleur is the publisher of *Wild Weather*, a magazine for students interested in weather and meteorology, in Lincoln, Nebraska. Joseph runs a summer school program on tornadoes, which is especially popular with students in all grades. He wants to take advantage of the tornado information posted on the web by national weather organizations and use it in his program. Recently, Joseph hired you to help administer the program. He asks you to find online information about tornados, especially information involving students. Complete the following steps:

1. Start Microsoft Edge and then go to the home page for the National Oceanic and Atmospheric Administration website at **noaa.gov**.
2. Using the tools on this page, look for information about tornados. (*Hint*: You might need to search for this information.) Open one of the pages you found.
3. On a new tab, open the National Weather Service webpage at **weather.gov**.
4. On a new tab, use the Address bar to search for **Smithsonian tornados**, and then open the first webpage in the search results.
5. On a new tab, use the Address bar to search for **JetStream weather school**, and then open the first webpage in the search results.
6. Pin the Favorites list to the Microsoft Edge window, and then add the four webpages to the Favorites list in a new folder named **Tornados**.
7. Display the favorites in the Tornados folder.
8. On one of the webpages, use the Make a Web Note tool to circle basic information about tornados, such as the definition of a tornado or when tornados are likely to occur.
9. Press the Print Screen key to capture an image of the screen. Start Paint, paste the screen image in a new file, and then save the file as **Tornados** in the Module4 > Case1 folder provided with your Data Files.
10. Exit from the Make a Web Note view.
11. Display the JetStream webpage and then add it to the Reading list with the name Microsoft Edge suggests.
12. Display the Smithsonian tornado webpage, and then add it to the Reading list with the name Microsoft Edge suggests.
13. Display the Smithsonian tornado webpage in Reading view.

Explore 14. Use Cortana and the Address bar to define "tornado." (*Hint*: Type **define tornado** in the Address bar without pressing the Enter key to have Cortana display the definition.)

15. Press the Print Screen key to capture an image of the screen. Start Paint, paste the screen image in a new file, and then save the file as **Definition** in the Module4 > Case1 folder provided with your Data Files.

16. Exit from Reading view.
17. On the open webpages, look for information about tornado warnings. Ask Cortana to display information about a tornado warning.
18. Press the Print Screen key to capture an image of the screen. Start Paint, paste the screen image in a new file, and then save the file as **Warning** in the Module4 > Case1 folder provided with your Data Files.
19. Close Microsoft Edge and Paint.
20. Start Mail and create an email message. Enter your email address and your instructor's email address in the To box, and enter **Ideas for tornado program** as the subject of the message.
21. In the message area, write a message describing the tornado information provided on one of the webpages you found. Send the message.
22. Restore your computer by completing the following tasks:
    - In Microsoft Edge, clear the History list, delete the Tornados folder you added to the Favorites list, and then delete the links in the Reading list. Close Microsoft Edge.
    - In Mail, delete the email you sent, and then delete the messages from the Trash (or Deleted Items) folder.
23. Close all open windows and apps.

APPLY

Case Problem 2

There are no Data Files needed for this Case Problem.

Artifact Phoebe Carver owns a shop called Artifact in Harrisburg, Pennsylvania. The shop acquires rights to reproduce archaeological artifacts from museums and universities. Phoebe and her staff create replicas of figurines, statues, plaques, coins, and other objects found at archaeological sites. Phoebe is expanding her offerings of fossils and miniature replicas of dinosaurs. She recently hired you as a research assistant and wants you to focus on learning about the dinosaur collections at American natural history museums, which you can do by using Microsoft Edge. Complete the following steps:

1. Start Microsoft Edge, and then go to the Smithsonian National Museum of Natural History website at **mnh.si.edu**.
2. On additional tabs, open the home pages for the following websites:
    - Field Museum: **fieldmuseum.org**
    - American Museum of Natural History: **amnh.org**
3. Use the links on each website and the tools available in Microsoft Edge to find information on dinosaurs or dinosaur exhibits.
4. Pin the three dinosaur webpages to the Start menu.
5. Open the Start menu, and then press the Print Screen key to capture an image of the screen. Start Paint, paste the screen image in a new file, and then save the file as **Dinosaurs** in the Module4 > Case2 folder provided with your Data Files.
6. Display the home page for the Smithsonian National Museum of Natural History.
7. Use the links on the website and Microsoft Edge tools to find information about location and hours at the museum. (*Hint*: Look for a "Plan Your Visit" link.)
8. Add the page you found to the Reading list using the name that Microsoft Edge suggests. Pin the Hub to the Microsoft Edge window.
9. Return to the Field Museum home page. (*Hint*: Use the History list.) Use the navigation bar to explore the Science topic. Find a page that shows images of fossils, and then add the page to the Reading list using the name that Microsoft Edge suggests.
10. On the American Museum of Natural History website, find a page showing information about dinosaur discoveries. Display the page in Reading view.

Explore 11. Send the webpage to your instructor by sharing it with Mail. (*Hint*: Click the Share button in the Microsoft Edge navigation bar, and then click Mail.)

12. Add the Dinosaur Discoveries page to the Reading list.
13. Press the Print Screen key to capture an image of the desktop. In Paint, paste the screen image in a new file, and then save the file as **Reading List** in the Module4 > Case2 folder provided with your Data Files.
14. Close Reading view. On any open webpage, find the name of a dinosaur—for example microraptor. Ask Cortana to find information about the dinosaur you found.
15. Press the Print Screen key to capture an image of the desktop. In Paint, paste the screen image in a new file, and then save the file as **Cortana** in the Module4 > Case2 folder provided with your Data Files.
16. Restore your computer by completing the following tasks:
    - In Microsoft Edge, clear the History list and then delete the links you added to the Reading list.
    - Unpin the tiles from the Start menu.
    - Close Microsoft Edge.
    - In Mail, delete the email you sent, and then empty the Trash (or Deleted Items) folder.
17. Close all open windows and apps.

CHALLENGE

Case Problem 3

There are no Data Files needed for this Case Problem.

Concierge Atlanta Belinda Washington started Concierge Atlanta to provide personal assistant services to companies, residents, and visitors in Atlanta, Georgia. Belinda and her staff make restaurant reservations, secure tickets to events, organize travel, order gifts, and perform other personal services. Belinda recently hired you as a junior concierge and asked you to begin by researching requested information on the Internet. Complete the following steps:

1. Start Microsoft Edge, and then use the Address bar to search for information about the best restaurants in Atlanta.

Explore 2. Find a restaurant listed as one of the top ten restaurants in Atlanta and then go to the home page of the restaurant's website. Use the Make a Web Note tools to capture an image of the restaurant's hours and copy it to the Clipboard. Start Paint, paste the screen image in a new file, and then save the file as **Hours** in the Module4 > Case3 folder provided with your Data Files.

3. Exit Make a Web Note view, and then navigate the restaurant's website to display a menu.
4. Use the Make a Web Note tools to highlight a menu item that sounds appealing to you.
5. Save the annotated menu page in the Reading list using the name Microsoft Edge suggests, and then exit Make a Web Note view.

Explore 6. Navigate to a webpage that displays the name of the restaurant. If Cortana appears in the Address bar, click the Cortana icon to display information about the restaurant.

If Cortana does not appear in the Address bar, select the name of the restaurant and then ask Cortana to display information about it.

7. Press the Print Screen key to capture an image of the desktop. In Paint, paste the screen image in a new file, and then save the file as **Restaurant** in the Module4 > Case3 folder provided with your Data Files.
8. Use the Address bar to search for a calendar of classical music events in Atlanta. Select an event that appeals to you, and then add the details to the Calendar app.

Explore 9. Switch to Day view, and then navigate to the day and time of the event. (*Hint*: Click the date in the left pane, and then scroll the right pane.)

10. Add the webpage to the Reading list using the name that Microsoft Edge suggests.
11. Arrange the Calendar window over the Microsoft Edge window so the Reading list is visible, and then press the Print Screen key to capture an image of the screen. Start Paint, paste the screen image in a new file, and then save the file as **Calendar** in the Module4 > Case3 folder provided with your Data Files.
12. Minimize the Calendar window, and then use the Address bar to search for information about the Georgia Aquarium. Open the home page of the Georgia Aquarium, and then click a link to display webpages about experiencing the aquarium.

Explore 13. Find a description of a tour, and then use the Share button in the navigation bar to send an email message about the tour to your instructor.

Explore 14. On the Georgia Aquarium website, find a video or webcam displaying images of the wildlife at the aquarium. Display the webpage in Internet Explorer. (*Hint*: Click the button in the navigation bar to find the appropriate command.)

15. When the Internet Explorer window opens, maximize the window, and then press the Print Screen key to capture an image of the screen. Start Paint, paste the screen image in a new file, and then save the file as **Internet Explorer** in the Module4 > Case3 folder provided with your Data Files.
16. Close Internet Explorer.
17. Restore your computer by completing the following tasks:
    - In Microsoft Edge, clear the History list, and then delete the links in the Reading list.
    - Close Microsoft Edge.
    - In Calendar, remove the event you added. (*Hint*: Click the event and then click the Delete button on the toolbar.)
    - Close Calendar.
    - In Mail, delete the email you sent, and then empty the Trash (or Deleted Items) folder.
18. Close all open windows and apps.

CHALLENGE

Case Problem 4

There are no Data Files needed for this Case Problem.

WLAX Boosters WLAX Boosters is an organization in Chestnut Hill, Massachusetts, that supports and promotes women's lacrosse teams at colleges and universities in the United States. Jen Dickerson, the director of the organization, recently hired you as a part-time assistant. You help Jen write the monthly newsletter and organize promotional events. Jen wants you to visit college websites periodically to make sure the colleges are promoting their women's lacrosse teams. Complete the following steps:

1. Start Microsoft Edge and go to the home page for the National College Athletics Association (NCAA) website at ncaa.com, and then find the webpage for women's lacrosse.
2. Display the current rankings in NCAA women's lacrosse.
3. On additional tabs, open the following webpages:
    - Maryland Terrapins Athletics home page: umterps.com
    - University of North Carolina Tar Heels Official Athletic home page: goheels.com
    - Syracuse University Athletics home page: cuse.com
4. On each of the three university athletic home pages, explore links to find a webpage for women's lacrosse. (*Hint*: Look for a Sports link on each page.)
5. Click links and use Microsoft Edge tools to find at least one webpage from each site that shows the schedule for the recent or upcoming season.
6. Pin the three webpages you found to the Start menu.

Explore 7. Use a link on one of the university sport webpages to print that school's schedule.

Explore 8. Use a link to email a schedule to yourself. Start Mail and display the Inbox with the message you received containing a link to the schedule.

9. Display the Start menu and then press the Print Screen key to capture an image of the screen. Start Paint, paste the screen image in a new file, and then save the file as **Schedule** in the Module4 > Case4 folder provided with your Data Files.

10. From the ncaa.com page, navigate to **ncaapublications.com**, the home page for NCAA manuals, rule books, scorebooks, and other publications.

11. Point to the COMPLIMENTARY link, and then click Records Books to display a list of NCAA record books. Find a publication appropriate for WLAX Boosters, and then click the link to the publication.

Explore 12. Use the links on the page to download a free PDF of the publication. When the download is finished, right-click the webpage, and then click Save As on the shortcut menu. Save the webpage as a PDF file named **NCAA** in the Module4 > Case4 folder provided with your Data Files. (Recall that PDFs, or Portable Document Format files, contain text and images that you can often download from a website and read with Windows Reader.) Close the webpage with the download.

13. In Mail, create an email message addressed to you and your instructor. Enter **NCAA publication** as the subject.

14. In the message area, write a message identifying the type of publication you downloaded, such as a rule book.

15. Attach the NCAA file to the message, and then send the message.

Explore 16. On the website for any of the three colleges, find a webpage showing the results of a recent season. Share the results with OneNote. (*Hint*: Click the Share button in the navigation bar).

Explore 17. Start OneNote from the Start menu, and then display the information you shared from the women's lacrosse website. Press the Print Screen key to capture an image of the screen. Start Paint, paste the screen image in a new file, and then save the file as **OneNote** in the Module4 > Case4 folder provided with your Data Files.

18. Restore your computer by completing the following tasks:
    - In Microsoft Edge, clear the History list.
    - On the Start menu, delete the tiles for the pinned webpages.
    - In Mail, delete the emails you sent and received, and then empty the Trash (or Deleted Items) folder.
    - In the left pane of OneNote, right-click the page containing the link to lacrosse results, and then click Delete Page on the shortcut menu. Click the Delete Page button to confirm you want to delete the page.

19. Close all open windows and apps.

MODULE 5

Protecting Your Computer

Managing Computer Security

OBJECTIVES

Session 5.1
- Manage Windows Firewall
- Set up Windows Update
- Protect your computer from viruses and other malicious software
- Use Windows Defender to protect against spyware
- Examine Mail security

Session 5.2
- Manage Microsoft Edge security
- Protect privacy with InPrivate Browsing
- Set up user accounts
- Control access to your computer
- Examine other built-in security features

Case | *Snap Home Automation*

A few years ago, Lamar Jefferson founded Snap Home Automation in Santa Clara, California. Snap Home Automation (or Snap for short) designs and installs systems that keep homes safe, manage energy consumption, and control electronic devices using a smartphone. Snap works with homeowners and businesses throughout California and other parts of the West Coast. Recently, Lamar has become concerned with the security of Snap's computers. Many of Lamar's system designers work at client sites using mobile computers, including laptops and tablets, running Windows 10. Although the designers can access the Internet with their computers, they can't usually connect to the Snap network, where an administrator oversees security. Instead, they must take advantage of the security tools in Windows 10 to prevent problems stemming from viruses, spyware, and other types of harmful software. Lamar hired you to support the system design staff. One of your first duties is to investigate the security features in Windows 10 and show Lamar how to use them to address security threats.

In this module, you'll explore the security tools in the Control Panel's System and Security category, including Windows Firewall, and those provided through the Settings app, including Windows Update and Windows Defender. You'll learn how to set up Windows 10 to work with antivirus software and how to implement other security measures, including setting up user accounts. You will also examine Microsoft Edge security settings so that you can use the Internet safely.

STARTING DATA FILES

There are no starting Data Files needed for this module.

Session 5.1 Visual Overview:

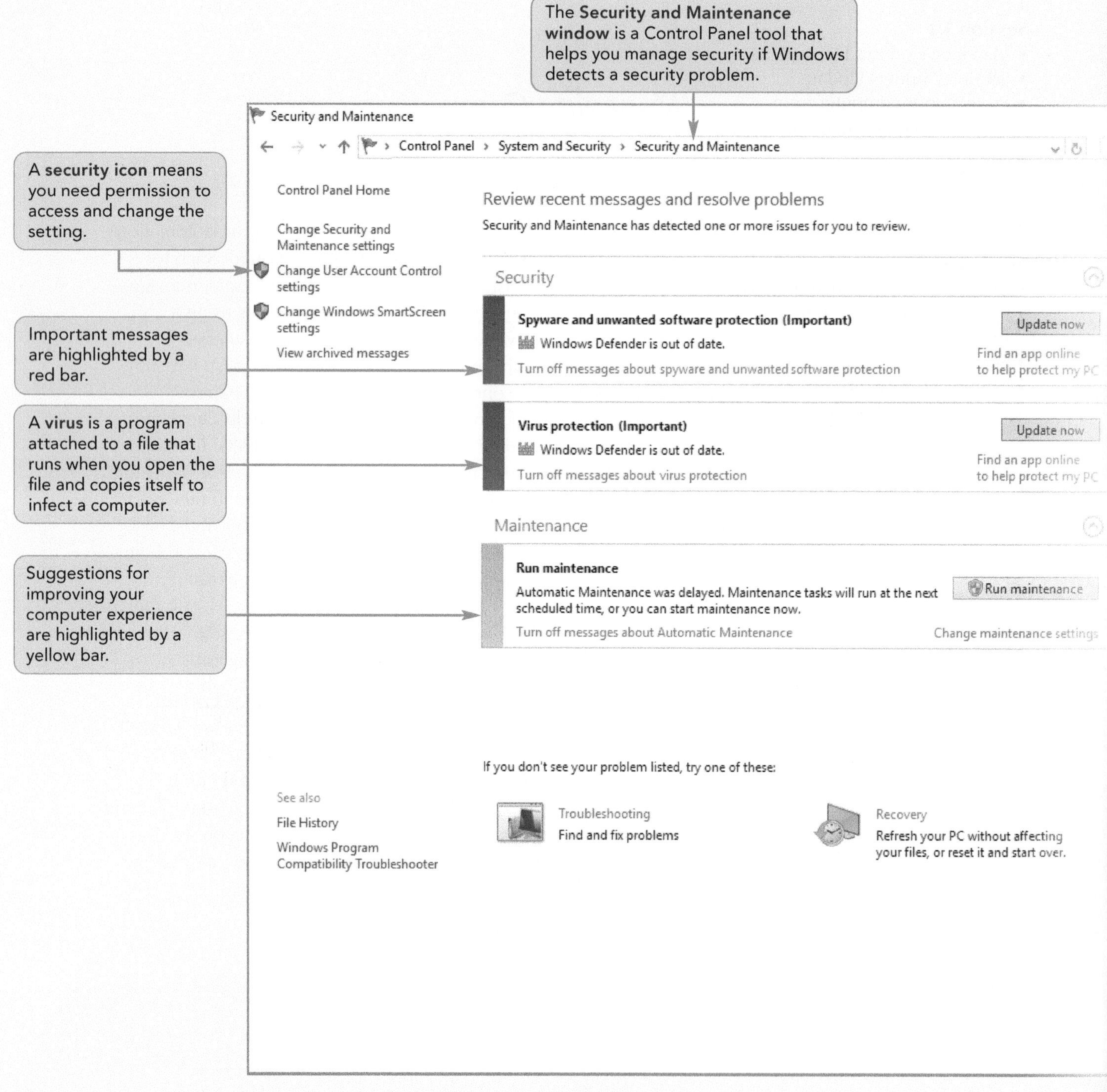
The **Security and Maintenance window** is a Control Panel tool that helps you manage security if Windows detects a security problem.
A **security icon** means you need permission to access and change the setting.
Important messages are highlighted by a red bar.
A **virus** is a program attached to a file that runs when you open the file and copies itself to infect a computer.
Suggestions for improving your computer experience are highlighted by a yellow bar.
Security and Maintenance
Control Panel > System and Security > Security and Maintenance
Control Panel Home
Change Security and Maintenance settings
Change User Account Control settings
Change Windows SmartScreen settings
View archived messages
Review recent messages and resolve problems
Security and Maintenance has detected one or more issues for you to review.
Security
Spyware and unwanted software protection (Important)
Windows Defender is out of date.
Turn off messages about spyware and unwanted software protection
Update now
Find an app online to help protect my PC
Virus protection (Important)
Windows Defender is out of date.
Turn off messages about virus protection
Update now
Find an app online to help protect my PC
Maintenance
Run maintenance
Automatic Maintenance was delayed. Maintenance tasks will run at the next scheduled time, or you can start maintenance now.
Turn off messages about Automatic Maintenance
Run maintenance
Change maintenance settings
If you don't see your problem listed, try one of these:
See also
File History
Windows Program Compatibility Troubleshooter
Troubleshooting
Find and fix problems
Recovery
Refresh your PC without affecting your files, or reset it and start over.

Windows 10 Security Tools

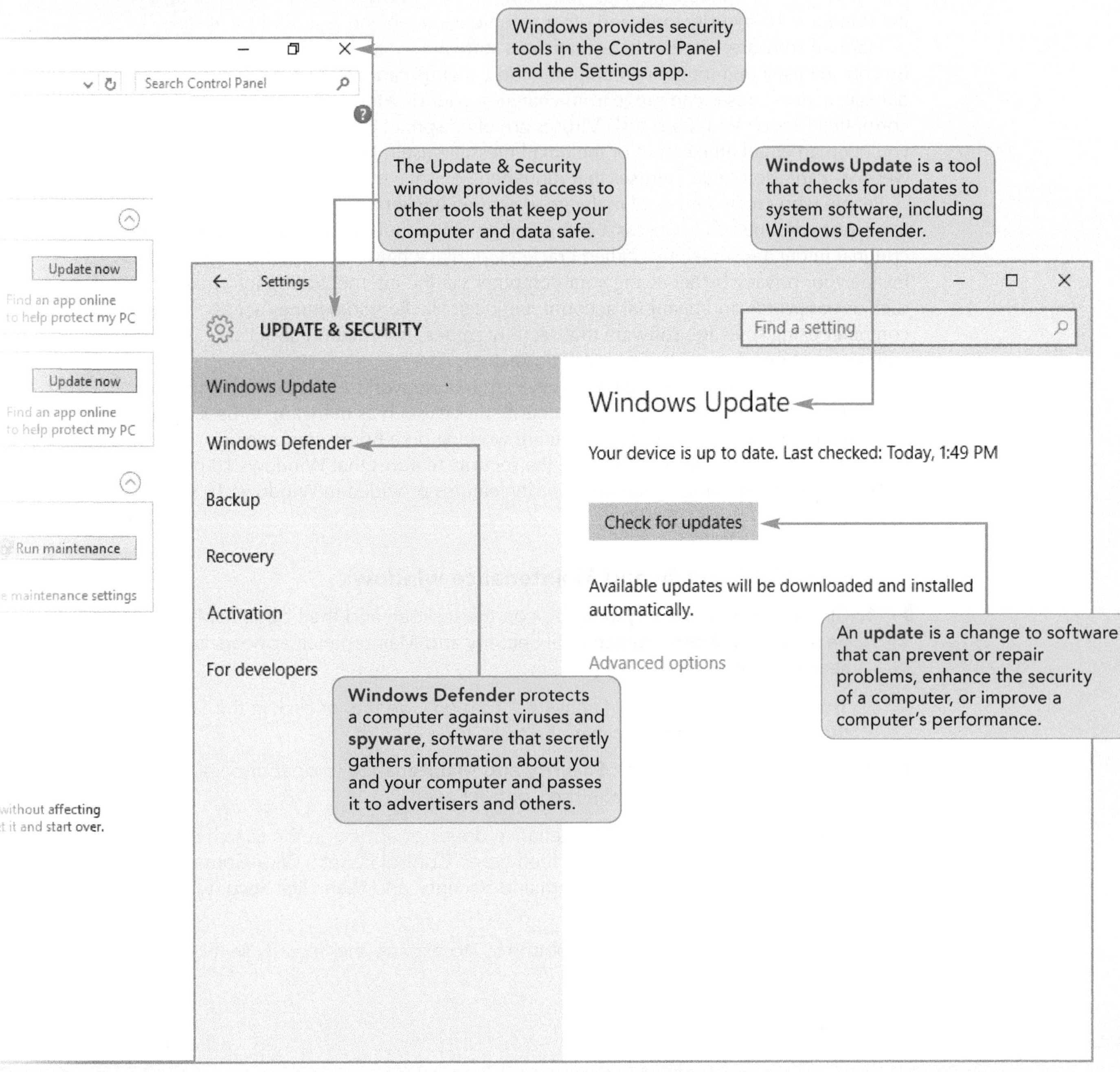
Windows provides security tools in the Control Panel and the Settings app.
Search Control Panel
The Update & Security window provides access to other tools that keep your computer and data safe.
Windows Update is a tool that checks for updates to system software, including Windows Defender.
Update now
Find an app online to help protect my PC
Update now
Find an app online to help protect my PC
Run maintenance
maintenance settings
without affecting
et it and start over.
Settings
UPDATE & SECURITY
Find a setting
Windows Update
Windows Defender
Backup
Recovery
Activation
For developers
Windows Update
Your device is up to date. Last checked: Today, 1:49 PM
Check for updates
Available updates will be downloaded and installed automatically.
Advanced options
An **update** is a change to software that can prevent or repair problems, enhance the security of a computer, or improve a computer's performance.
Windows Defender protects a computer against viruses and **spyware**, software that secretly gathers information about you and your computer and passes it to advertisers and others.

Using Windows 10 Security Tools

Windows 10 provides security tools that help to keep your computer safe from threats such as harmful software, unsolicited email, and invasions of your privacy. When you connect to the Internet, send and receive email, or share your computer or files with others, your computer is vulnerable to harm from people who might attempt to steal your personal information, damage your files, or interrupt your work. You should use the Windows 10 security tools and other techniques to defend against these threats.

Harmful software, referred to as **malicious software**, or **malware**, includes viruses. By copying itself and triggering computer code, a virus can infect your computer. The damage a virus causes can range from changing your desktop settings to deleting or corrupting files on your hard disk. Viruses are often spread by email and run when you open an email attachment or the email message itself. Files you download from websites can also contain viruses that run when you save the files on your computer.

People who create and send malware are called **hackers**, a generic term that refers to anyone who intends to access a computer system without permission. (Hackers with criminal intent are sometimes called **crackers**, or black hat hackers.) Hackers can also invade your privacy by accessing your computer via the Internet to find information such as passwords and financial account numbers. Hackers sometimes access your computer using spyware, software that secretly gathers information about you and your computer actions, including sensitive information.

If you are working on a computer connected to a network, a network administrator probably defends the network against security threats such as malware, viruses, spyware, and hackers. Otherwise, if you are working on a home computer, for example, you should take advantage of the security features that Windows 10 provides.

You'll start by showing Lamar the security features provided in Windows 10.

To open the Security and Maintenance window:

1. Click in the **Ask me anything** box on the taskbar, and then begin typing **Security and Maintenance** until Security and Maintenance appears in the search results.

   Trouble? If Cortana is not activated, turn on Cortana, or click in the Search the web and Windows box on the taskbar.

2. In the search results, click **Security and Maintenance** to open the Security and Maintenance window in the Control Panel.

   Trouble? If Security and Maintenance does not appear in the search results, delete the text you typed, and then type "Control Panel." Click Control Panel in the search results, click System and Security, and then click Security and Maintenance.

3. If necessary, click the **expand** button to expand the Security section, as shown in Figure 5-1.

Figure 5-1 **Security and Maintenance window**

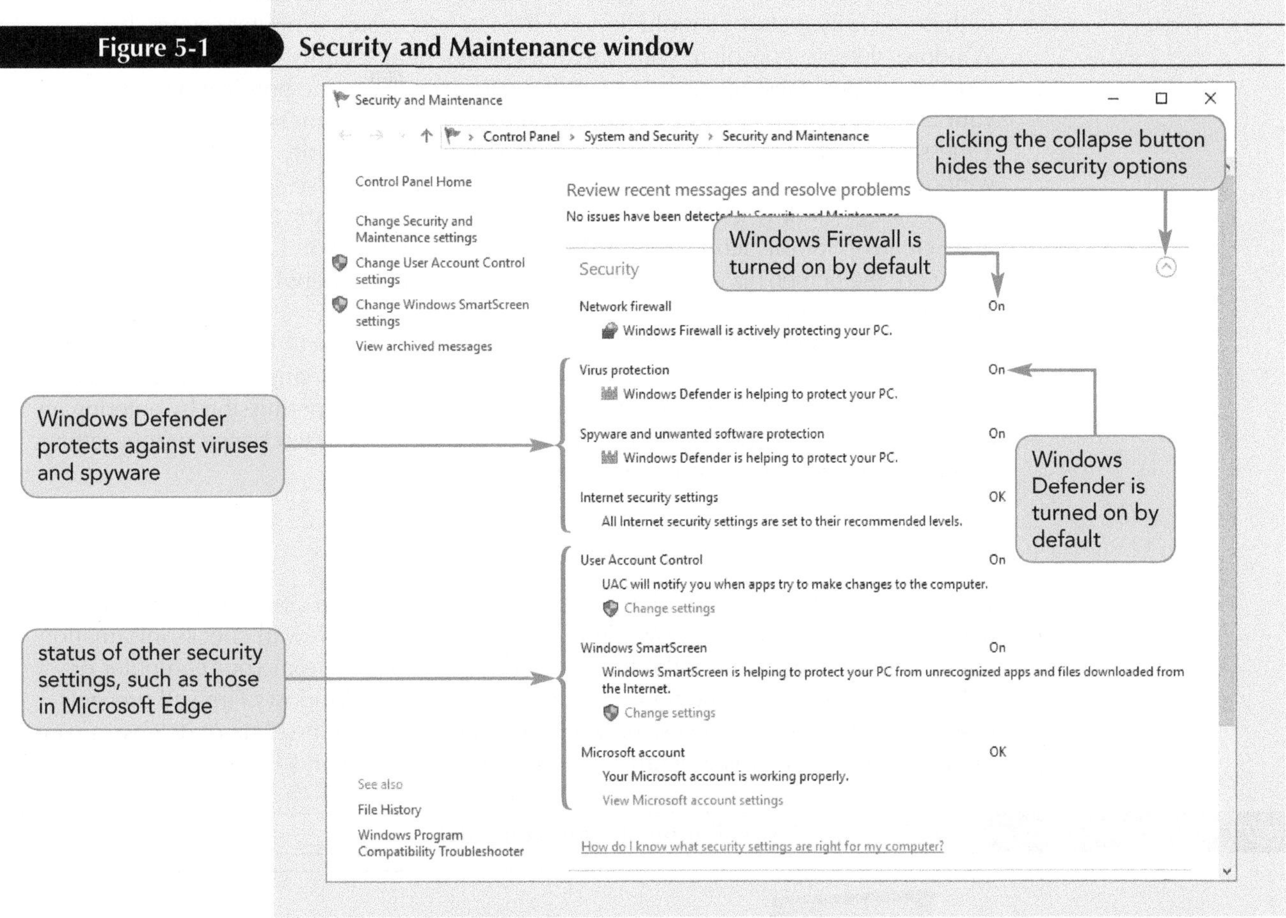

Figure 5-2 describes the security features listed in the Security and Maintenance window.

Figure 5-2 **Security features**

Security Feature	Description
Network firewall	This feature uses Windows Firewall by default to monitor and restrict communication with the Internet, which helps protect your computer from hackers. Before an app can send or receive information via the Internet, Windows Firewall must allow it to do so.
Virus protection	Antivirus software is your best protection against viruses, worms, and other types of harmful software. If you have antivirus software, Windows reminds you to use it regularly to scan your computer for virus infections and to monitor email. If you do not have antivirus software, Windows Defender runs automatically to defend your computer against malware.
Spyware and unwanted software protection	Antispyware software, such as Windows Defender, prevents some types of malware from infecting your system.
Internet security settings	Security and Maintenance checks that your web browser is using appropriate security settings to block malware from being installed on your system when you visit websites.
User Account Control (UAC)	This service displays a dialog box requesting your permission to install software or open programs that could harm your computer.
Windows SmartScreen	This tool protects your computer from unrecognized apps and files you download from the Internet.
Microsoft account	This tool keeps track of your account settings and alerts you if an unauthorized user tries to change them.

Most of the features listed in Figure 5-1 and Figure 5-2 are considered essential–all of these security features should be turned on to keep your computer secure. If Windows detects a problem with one of these essential security features, Windows displays an **alert message** near the Notifications icon in the notification area of your taskbar. For example, you might see the following alert message, "Solve PC issues: 1 message." You can click the alert message to open the Security and Maintenance window and find out how to address the problem. You can also see if the Security and Maintenance window lists any new messages by pointing to the Notifications icon. The ScreenTip for this icon changes depending on whether you have new notifications. If you do, the ScreenTip appears as "New notifications." Otherwise, the ScreenTip appears as "No new notifications."

Some features display a security icon next to the Change settings link (as shown in the Session 5.1 Visual Overview). This icon indicates that you might need permission to access and change the setting. You indicate that you have permission by entering an administrator password. Requiring a user to enter a password to change system settings is another way to protect your computer.

Managing Windows Firewall

Windows Firewall is software that serves as a barrier between your computer and a network or the Internet. As shown in Figure 5-3, Windows Firewall checks information coming from the network or the Internet and either blocks it from your computer or allows it to pass, depending on your settings. In this way, Windows Firewall prevents unauthorized users from accessing your computer and is the first line of defense against malware. Many antivirus programs include a firewall that works in a similar way.

Figure 5-3 **How Windows Firewall protects your computer**

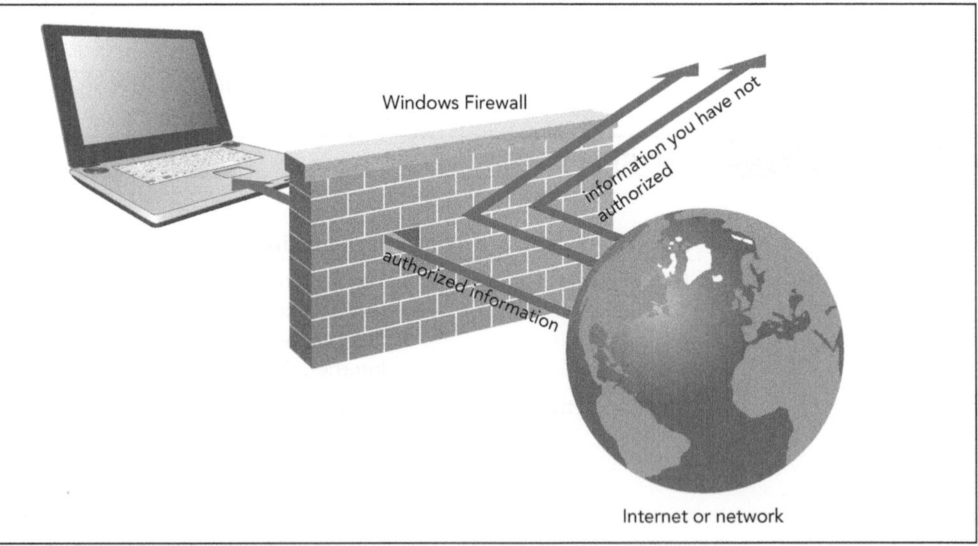

A firewall defends against malware trying to gain access to your computer by monitoring your network and Internet connections. However, a firewall does not scan email, so it cannot detect viruses sent in email messages (a common way to spread viruses). Neither can a firewall detect viruses in files you download from the web. Furthermore, a firewall can't protect you from email scams, called **phishing**, that try to deceive you into revealing private information such as passwords. To protect against viruses in email and downloaded files, use antivirus software. To minimize phishing attempts, use the Windows SmartScreen Filter. (Both topics are covered later in this module.)

Windows Firewall is turned on by default, so it doesn't allow communications with most programs via the Internet or a network. However, your computer manufacturer or someone else might turn off Windows Firewall, so you should verify that it is running. Typically, Windows Firewall is turned off only if another firewall, which might be provided by other security software or your network, is protecting your computer.

Using Windows Firewall, you can customize four settings for each type of network location, including **private networks**, which are those you use at home or work involving people and devices you trust, and **public networks**, those in public places such as airports and libraries. You'll show Lamar how to find these Windows Firewall settings.

To turn on Windows Firewall:

1. In the Security and Maintenance window, click **System and Security** in the Address bar to display the System and Security window.
2. Click **Windows Firewall** to open the Windows Firewall window.
3. If necessary, click the **expand** icons to expand the Private networks and the Guest or public networks sections. See Figure 5-4.

Figure 5-4 Windows Firewall window

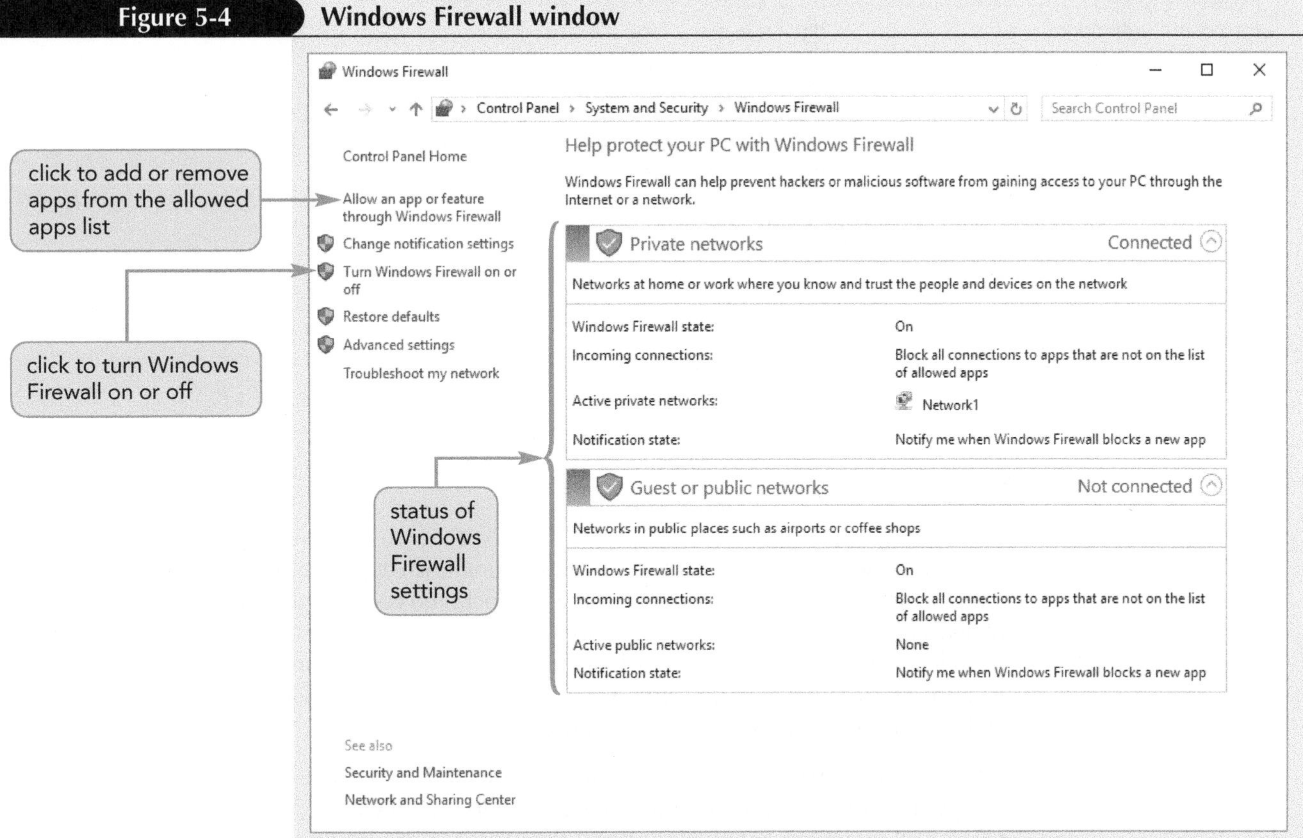

Trouble? If a different firewall is installed on your computer and is managing the firewall settings, your Windows Firewall window will look different from the figure, and you might not be able to expand the sections or change the settings. In that case, read but do not perform Steps 4–6.

4. Click the **Turn Windows Firewall on or off** link in the left pane.

   Trouble? If a User Account Control dialog box opens requesting an administrator password or your permission to continue, make sure you have permission to change Windows Firewall settings (check with your instructor, if necessary), and then enter the password or click the Yes button.

5. In the Customize Settings window, click the first **Turn on Windows Firewall** option button (the one for Private network settings) if it is not already selected. See Figure 5-5.

Figure 5-5 Customize Settings window

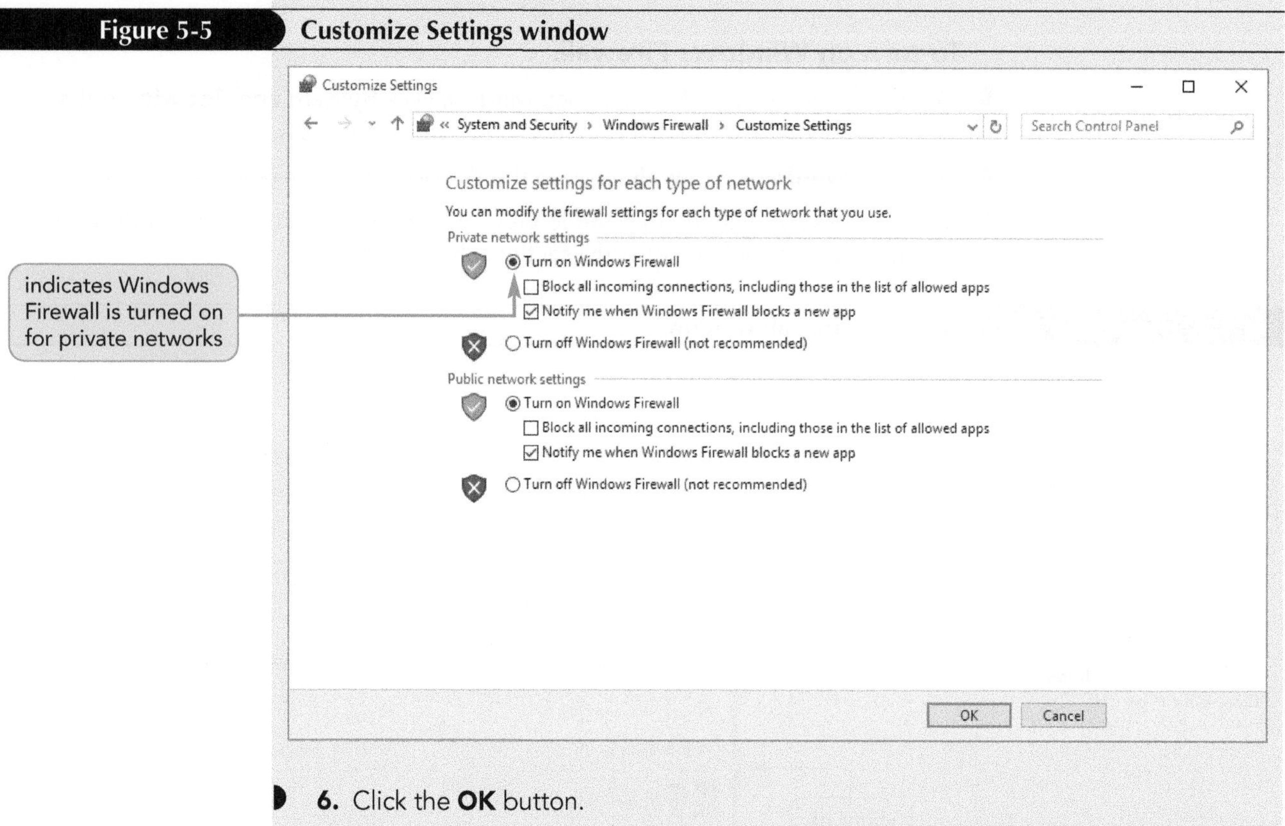

6. Click the **OK** button.

When Windows Firewall is turned on and an unknown app tries to connect to your computer from the Internet, Windows Firewall blocks the connection. Instead of turning off Windows Firewall every time you want to use a blocked app, you can customize the firewall by adding apps to its allowed list so that it maintains a level of security that's right for you.

In the Customize Settings window, you can specify the following firewall settings for each type of network location that you use:

- Turn on Windows Firewall—This setting is selected by default, meaning that most apps are blocked from communicating through the firewall.
- Block all incoming connections, including those in the list of allowed apps—When you connect to a public network, such as in a hotel or an airport, you might want to select this setting. Windows blocks all apps, even those in the allowed apps list.
- Notify me when Windows Firewall blocks a new app—When you select this check box, Windows Firewall informs you when it blocks a new app, giving you the option of adding the app to the allowed apps list.
- Turn off Windows Firewall (not recommended)—The only time you should select this setting is when another firewall is running on your computer.

Lamar often sets up entertainment networks in client homes so they can play their favorite music and videos in any room, even those that don't have a computer. To provide this service, he uses Windows Media Player, an app you can use to store, organize, and play media files such as music and videos. By default, Windows Media Player is blocked from sending or receiving media on a network. You'll show Lamar how to add the Windows Media Player app to the allowed programs list so he can use and test this app on the entertainment networks he sets up.

If you are performing the following steps in a computer lab, you might not be able to change the allowed apps. Check with your instructor or technical support person to determine whether you can specify Windows Media Player as an allowed app in Windows Firewall. If you cannot, read but do not perform the following steps.

To add an app to the allowed apps list:

1. In the left pane of the Windows Firewall window, click the **Allow an app or feature through Windows Firewall** link to open the Allowed apps window.

   Trouble? If the Allow an app or feature through Windows Firewall link is inactive in the Windows Firewall window, click the Back button to return to the System and Security window, and then click the Allow an app or feature through Windows Firewall link.

   Trouble? If a dialog box opens requesting an administrator password or your permission to continue, make sure you have permission to change the Windows Firewall settings (check with your instructor, if necessary), and then enter the password or click the Yes button.

2. Scroll the list, which is sorted alphabetically, to display the Windows Media Player check box. See Figure 5-6. Your apps might differ.

Figure 5-6 Allowed apps window

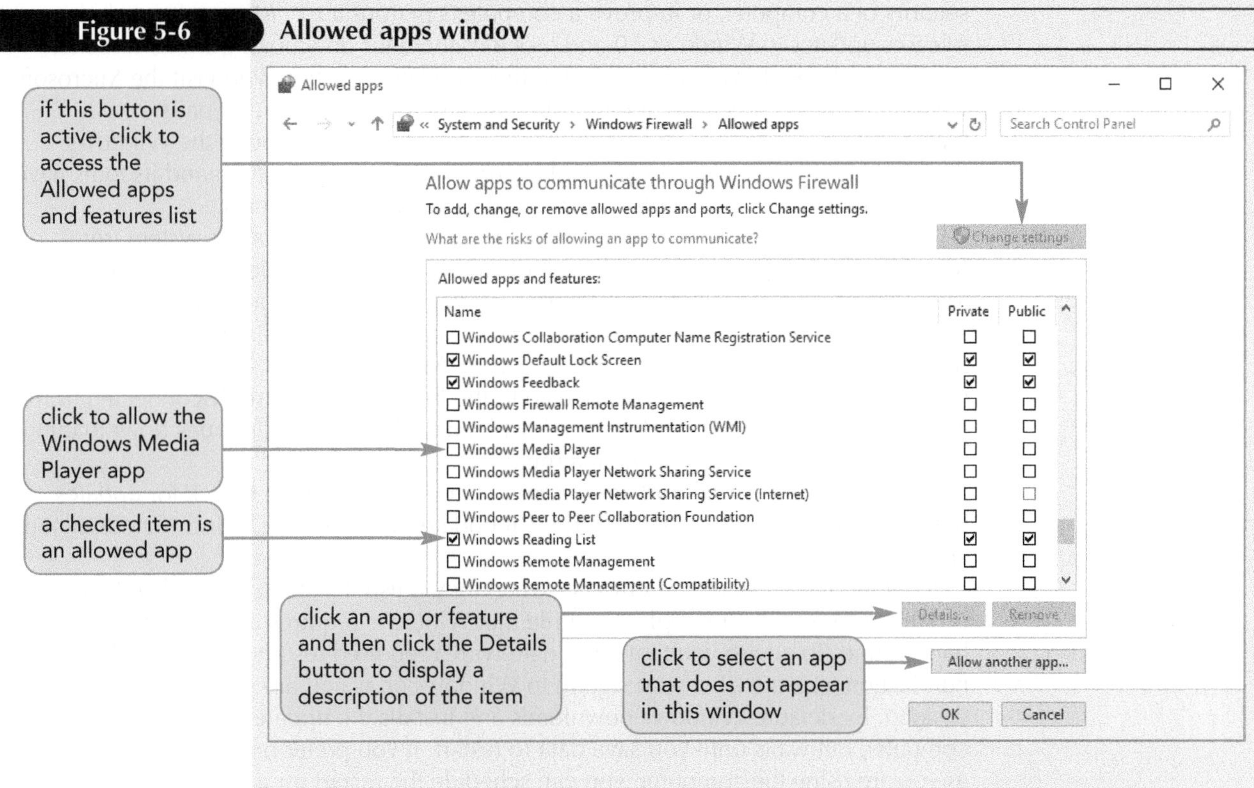

3. Click the **Windows Media Player** check box to select it. A checkmark appears in the Private column, indicating that Lamar will be able to connect to the device within a private network.

   Trouble? If you cannot select an app in the list, click the Change settings button, and then repeat Step 4.

   Trouble? If you are not allowed to change the allowed apps in Windows Firewall, click the Cancel button in the Allowed apps window, and then skip Step 5.

   Trouble? If Private is not selected, click the check box in the Private column to insert a checkmark, and then click the check box in the Public column to remove the checkmark, if necessary.

4. Click the **OK** button to add Windows Media Player to the allowed apps list for private networks and to return to the Windows Firewall window.
5. Click the **Back** button [←] to return to the System and Security window, and then minimize it.

Keep in mind that when you add an app to the Windows Firewall allowed apps list, you are making your computer easier for apps to access and therefore more vulnerable to malware infection. You should allow an app only when you really need it, and never allow an app that you don't recognize—it could be a virus or a worm. Finally, be sure to remove an app from the allowed apps list when you no longer need it.

Setting Up Windows Update

An **update** is a change to software that can prevent or repair problems, enhance the security of a computer, or improve a computer's performance. Microsoft regularly releases updates to Windows 10 and provides them for download from its website. You can look for, download, and install these updates any time you visit the Microsoft website. However, because updates often include critical security repairs and enhancements, Microsoft also makes them available to you through the Windows Update feature. Windows Update makes sure your operating system and its tools have the most recent software improvements and security enhancements.

Windows Update periodically checks for updates to the operating system from Microsoft, including security updates, critical updates, and service packs. (When Microsoft combines many updates in one package, the collection of updates is called a **service pack** and is often abbreviated as **SP**.) If an update is available, Windows Update downloads the software and installs it for you. Windows downloads the updates in the background as long as you're connected to the Internet. If you are disconnected from the Internet before Windows finishes downloading, Windows continues downloading the next time you connect to the Internet.

You can also check for updates yourself at any time using the Check for updates button in the Windows Update window. If updates are available, Windows downloads and installs them.

Some updates restart the computer when they finish installing the updated files, usually because they are replacing a file that Windows requires and runs in the background. To advise you that an update with a required restart is scheduled, a notification appears when you sign in to Windows or as you are working on the desktop. By default, Windows downloads and installs the update as you work on your computer, but waits until you save data to restart. If you prefer not to be interrupted as you are using the computer, you can schedule the restart for a more convenient time. If you are using a version of Windows other than Windows Home, you can defer downloading and installing the update until a later date that you specify.

To view your current update status and settings for Windows Update, you open the Update & Security window in the Settings app. You can also use this window to access advanced options and review your update history.

Windows 10 updates automatically because Microsoft offers Windows as a Service rather than a software package. The Windows-as-a-Service approach means that after you install Windows on a device, Microsoft keeps it up to date for as long as the device is running. One reason that Microsoft adopted this approach is to keep Windows secure from hackers.

INSIGHT

Windows Update and Metered Internet Connections

A **metered Internet connection** is one for which your ISP sets a limit on the amount of data your device sends and receives. If you exceed the limit, you might be charged extra for the data usage or your connection speed might be slower until the end of the billing cycle. Metered Internet connections are common on mobile devices such as cell phones. If you are using a metered Internet connection, Windows Update downloads only priority updates, which are those Microsoft considers necessary to maintain the security and reliability of Windows. If you access the Internet through a mobile broadband network, which provides high-speed Internet access for cell phones and other portable devices, Windows sets your Internet connection to metered by default. If you are using a different type of network with a metered connection, you can set your computer to use a metered connection. To check the setting, start the Settings app and then select Network & Internet. With Wi-Fi selected in the right pane, click Advanced options in the right pane. In the Metered connection section, click the slider button to turn on the Set as metered connection setting.

Although Lamar will update automatically most of the time, he wants to know how to schedule a restart after an update has been downloaded and installed. He sometimes keeps his computer running all night to test systems that he is about to install. After Windows notifies him about an update, he can schedule a restart so it doesn't interrupt his testing.

As you perform the following steps, note your original settings so you can restore them later.

TIP

To check for updates manually, click the Check for updates button in the right pane.

To set up Windows Update:

1. Click the **Start** button to display the Start menu, and then click **Settings** to start the Settings app.
2. In the Settings home page, click **Update & security**. The Update & Security window opens with Windows Update selected in the left pane. See Figure 5-7. Your settings might differ.

Figure 5-7 Update & Security window

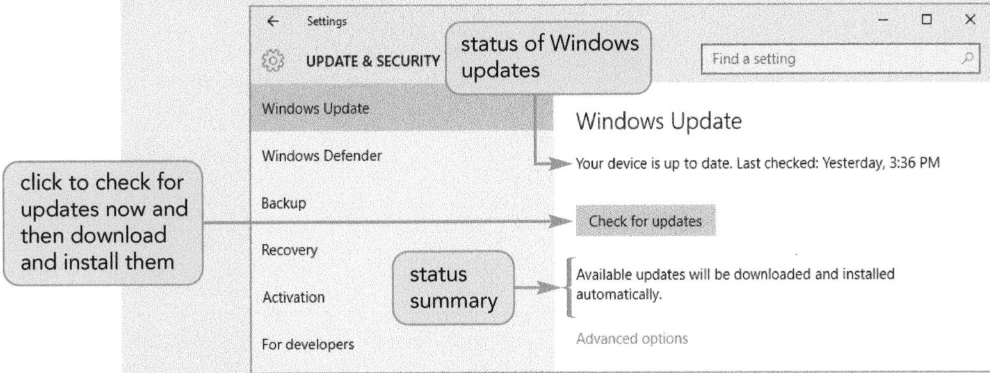

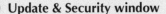

3. In the right pane, click the **Advanced options** link. The Advanced Options window opens. See Figure 5-8.

Figure 5-8 Advanced Options window

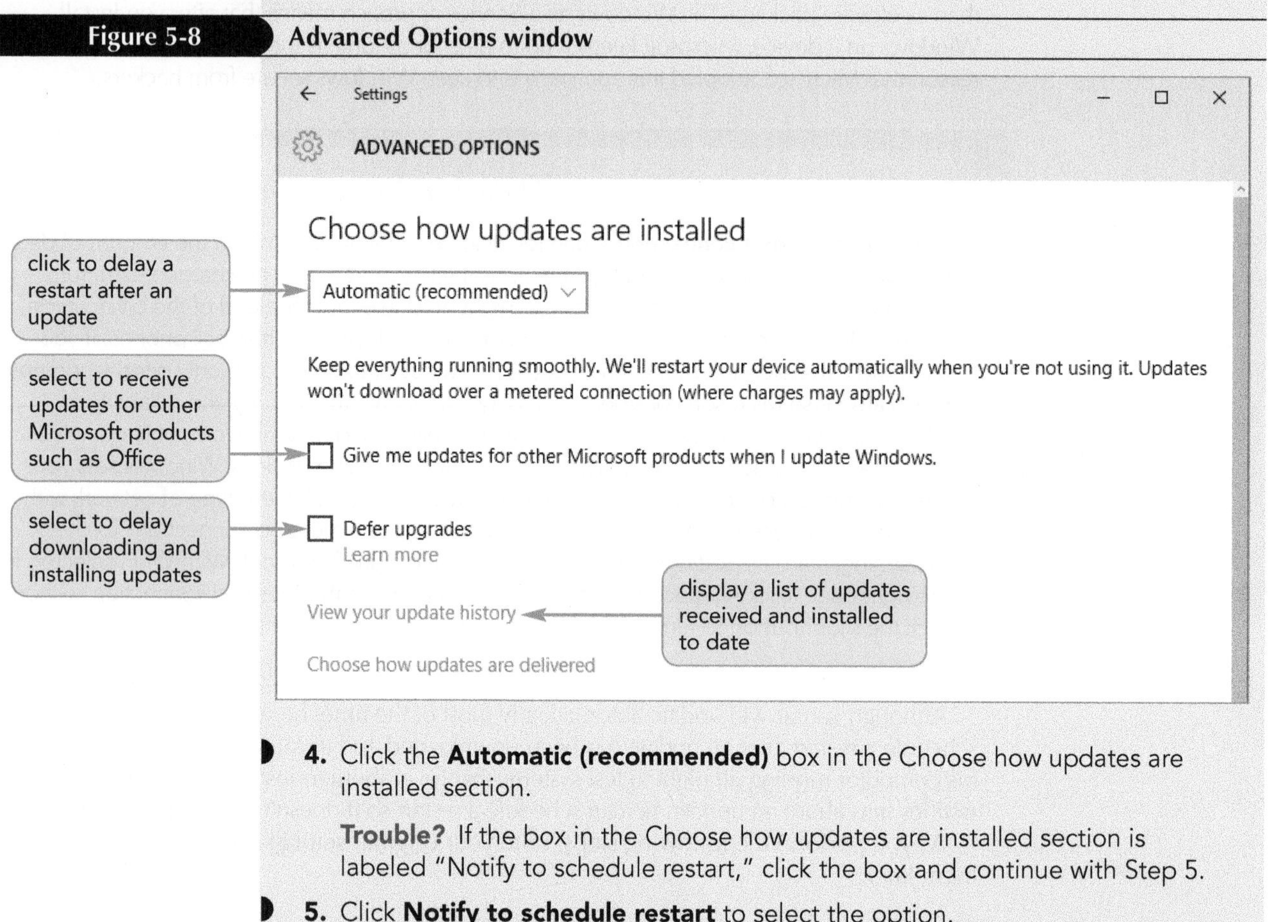

4. Click the **Automatic (recommended)** box in the Choose how updates are installed section.

   Trouble? If the box in the Choose how updates are installed section is labeled "Notify to schedule restart," click the box and continue with Step 5.

5. Click **Notify to schedule restart** to select the option.

The next time an update with a required restart is available, open the Update & security window to view your options. Windows indicates an update is ready and that it will restart the computer when you usually don't use it, such as at 3:30 am. As shown in Figure 5-9, you can click the Select a restart time option button to select the date and time of the restart.

Figure 5-9 Selecting a restart time

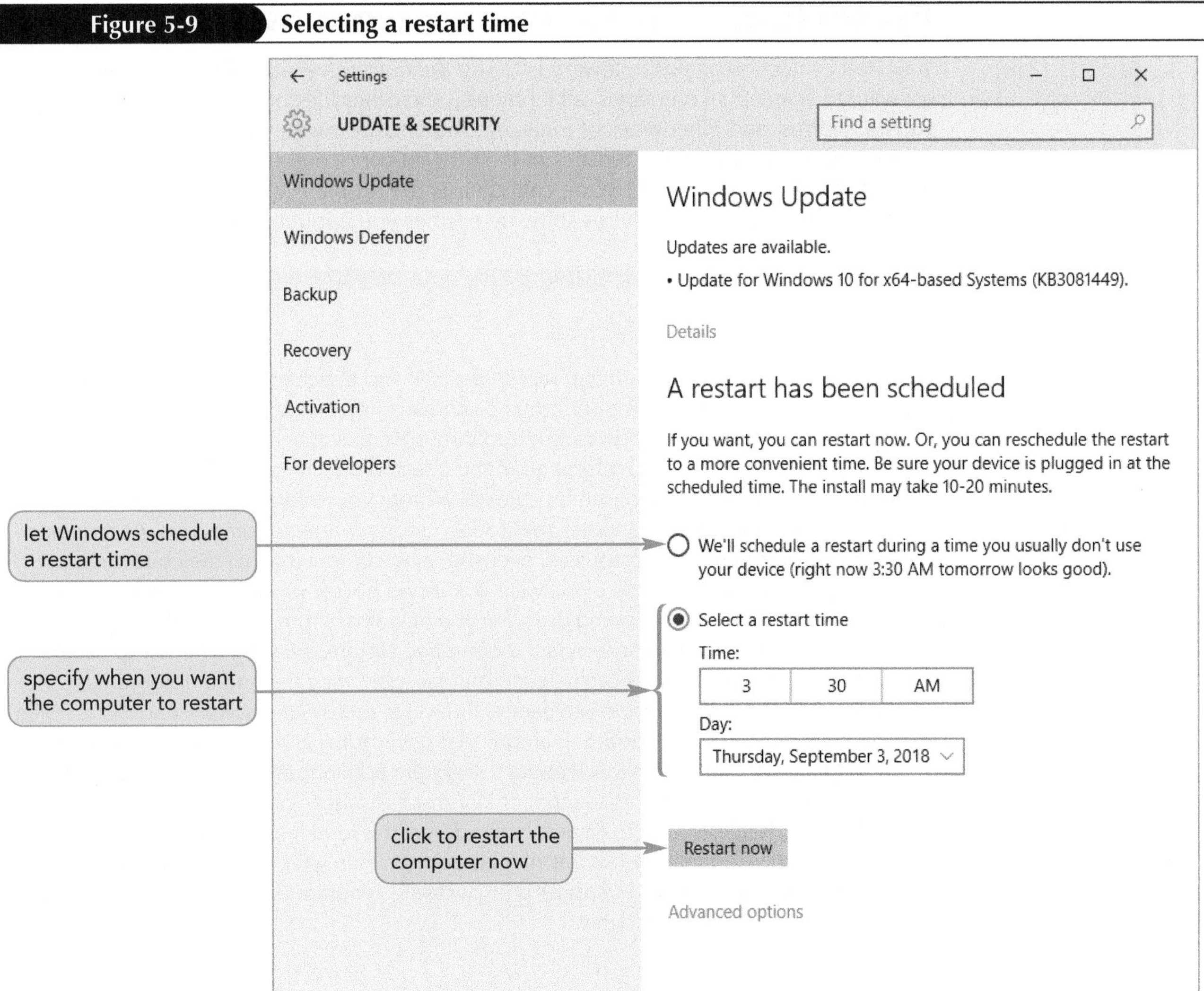

Windows also keeps track of the updates it installed. You can display the list of updates to determine whether the update was successfully installed. If it wasn't, you can try to install it again. If you or a technical support specialist suspects a problem with an update, you can also uninstall the update to see if that solves the problem. You'll show Lamar how to display the update history on his computer.

To view your update history:

1. In the Advanced Options window, click the **View your update history** link to display the View Your Update History window, which lists recent updates. The Update history list includes the name of the update, whether it was installed successfully, and when the installation was attempted or completed.
2. Click the **Back** button [←] to return to the Advanced Options window.
3. Click the **Back** button [←] again to return to the Update & Security window, and then close the window.

Now that you know Lamar's copy of Windows 10 is up to date, you can turn to protecting his computer from viruses and other types of malware.

Protecting Your Computer from Malware

Your best protection against malware is to use the current version of your antivirus software to scan email messages, attachments, and other files on your computer for viruses, worms, and other types of malware. Antivirus software locates a virus by comparing identifying characteristics of the files on your computer to the characteristics of a list of known viruses, which are called **virus definitions**. When it finds a virus, or any type of malware, the antivirus software notifies you about the virus.

INSIGHT

Recognizing Types of Malware

Recall that a virus is a program that replicates itself and attaches to files or programs, usually affects your computer's performance and stability, and sometimes damages or removes files. Viruses are often transmitted through email attachments or downloaded files, but they don't spread until you open the infected attachment or file. In contrast, a **worm** is harmful computer code that spreads without your interaction. A worm slips from one network connection to another, replicating itself on network computers. As it does, a worm consumes network resources, overwhelming computers until they become slow or unresponsive. Another type of malware is a **Trojan horse**, which hides inside another program, such as a photo-viewing program you download from the web. When you install the program, the Trojan horse infects the operating system, allowing a hacker to access your computer. Trojan horses can't spread on their own; they depend on programs, including viruses and worms, to proliferate. If hackers access your system through a Trojan horse, they might install a **rootkit**, malware that gains administrator-level, or root-level, access to a computer or network without the system administrators or users detecting its presence. Hackers use rootkits to monitor keystrokes (to learn passwords, for example), modify files, disable or alter tools that might detect the rootkit, and attack other devices on the network. Common symptoms of malware are when your computer runs much slower than normal, messages appear unexpectedly, programs start or close on their own, or Windows shuts down suddenly.

When you buy a new computer, most likely it comes with antivirus software already installed as a trial version so you can test it for a limited time. (Look for the antivirus software on the All apps list.) Windows Defender is automatically installed with Windows 10 to make sure the computer is protected from malware. To determine whether you should continue running the preinstalled antivirus software or Windows Defender, you should compare their features and read reviews from security experts to learn how well each app protects against viruses, spyware, Trojan horses, rootkits, and other malware.

Windows 10 can detect whether you have antivirus software installed on your computer. If you do not, Windows runs Windows Defender to protect your computer from malware. If you have antivirus software installed on your computer but the subscription has expired, Windows reminds you to renew the subscription, activate Windows Defender, or select another antivirus program from the Windows Store. If you have antivirus software installed and it's up to date, do not also run Windows Defender to scan for viruses because only one antivirus app should be running on your computer at any time.

Most vendors of antivirus software offer fee-based subscription services that provide regular updates for current virus definitions. You can refer to the antivirus software's help system to learn how to run the software and receive regular updates, or you can use the Security and Maintenance window to check for updates. Besides Windows Defender, Windows recognizes most types of antivirus software and displays their status in the Security and Maintenance window. In most cases, you can use the

Security and Maintenance window to determine whether your antivirus software needs to be updated and then run the updating program. Windows Update keeps Windows Defender and its virus definitions up to date. Keeping the virus definition list current helps to protect your computer from new attacks. If your list of viruses is out of date, your computer is vulnerable to new threats.

Although Lamar is certain that antivirus software is installed on his computer, he asks you to make sure it is up to date and that virus scanning is turned on.

To check for virus protection on your computer:

1. In the Control Panel, open the System and Security window, and then click **Security and Maintenance** to return to the Security and Maintenance window. If necessary, click **Security** to expand the Security section.
2. Examine the settings in the Virus protection section, which should report if an installed antivirus program is protecting your computer. In Figure 5-10, the Security and Maintenance window reports that the antivirus program is out of date.

   Trouble? If the Security and Maintenance window reports that your virus protection is up to date and is protecting your computer, skip Step 3.

Figure 5-10 Antivirus software needs to be updated

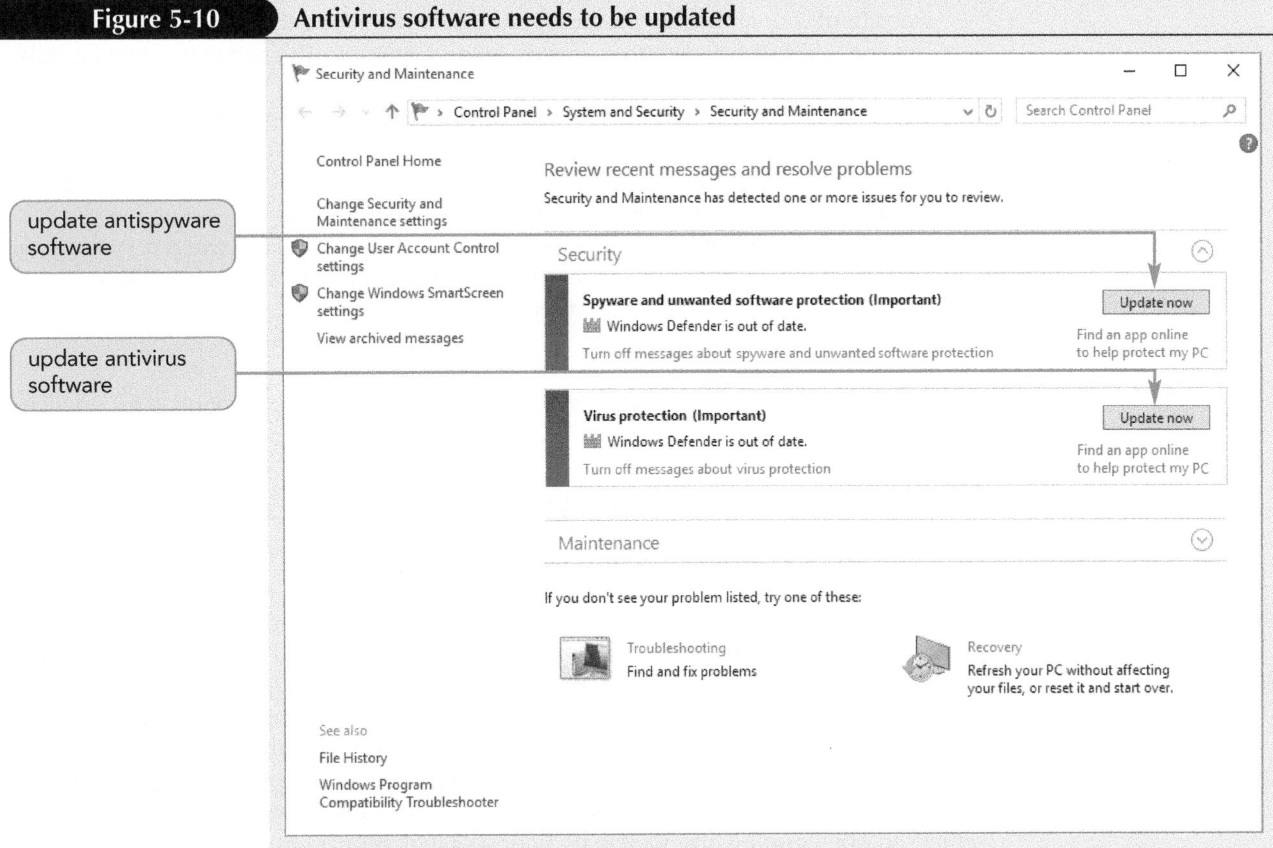

3. If necessary, click the **Update now** button. Your antivirus software starts and checks for updates on its manufacturer's website. When it is finished updating, close the antivirus software window, if necessary.
4. Close the Security and Maintenance window.

PROSKILLS

Problem Solving: Avoiding and Removing Viruses

One of the most difficult computer problems to solve is removing a virus from your system. To avoid this problem, you can defend against viruses in the following ways so that they do not infect your computer:

- Do not open unexpected email attachments. If the message containing the attachment is from a trusted source, send an email to that person asking about the file and what it contains.
- Regularly scan your hard drive with an antivirus program. Most antivirus software includes an option to schedule a complete system scan. You only need to make sure your computer is turned on to perform the scan.
- Set your antivirus program to scan all incoming email.
- Keep your antivirus software up to date. New viruses are introduced frequently, and your antivirus software needs to use the latest virus definitions to protect your computer.
- Create backups of your work files periodically. Viruses can corrupt or destroy data files, which are the most valuable files on your computer.

When you notice symptoms such as your computer running slowly or turning off on its own, suspect a virus. You can try to remove a virus in the following ways:

- Update your antivirus software. Look for an update feature that connects with the website of your antivirus software developer to download the latest virus definitions.
- Use the antivirus software to scan your entire computer. The software might be able to remove the virus for you or identify the virus by name.
- Use an online scanner. If your antivirus software does not find or report a virus, visit the Microsoft website (www.microsoft.com) and search for "Windows security software providers." In the search results, look for a link to vendors that provide free online virus scanners to help you find and remove the virus.
- Search for instructions on removing the virus. If your antivirus software or online scanner identifies but does not remove the virus, search an antivirus vendor's website to find information about removing the virus.

Another security concern is spyware, which can also affect your computing experience.

Defending Against Spyware

TIP

Before installing any software from a website, read the license agreement. Do not install software that requires you to accept pop-up ads or to let the program send data about you to the software publisher.

Spyware can install itself or run on your computer without your consent or control. It's called spyware because it monitors your computing actions, usually while you are online, to collect information about you. Spyware can change system settings, interrupt programs, and slow your computer's performance. Spyware might infect your computer when you visit a certain website or download a free program, such as a screen saver or search toolbar. Less frequently, spyware is distributed along with other programs on a CD, DVD, or other type of removable media. Spyware might also pass information about your web browsing habits to advertisers, who use it to improve their products or websites. Other times, a special type of spyware called **adware** changes your browser settings to open **pop-up ads**, which are windows that appear while you are viewing a webpage and advertise a product or service. Pop-up ads interrupt your online activities and can be difficult to close; they can also be vehicles for additional spyware or other types of malware.

Because spyware can download, install, and run on your computer without your knowledge or consent, it's often difficult to know if spyware is infecting your computer. If you are experiencing any of the following symptoms, they are most likely due to spyware:

- New toolbars, links, or favorites appear in your web browser unexpectedly.
- Your home page, pointer, or search engine changes without your consent.
- When you enter a URL for a website, such as a search engine, you go to a different website without notice.
- Pop-up ads interrupt you, even when you're not on the Internet.
- Your computer suddenly restarts or runs slowly.

Be sure to scan your computer with a program, such as Windows Defender, to detect and remove any spyware on your computer.

Scanning Your Computer with Windows Defender

To protect your computer against spyware, you can run an up-to-date **antispyware** (or **antimalware**) **program**, such as Windows Defender, to check for both spyware and viruses. Windows Defender helps prevent malware from installing itself and running on your computer, and it periodically scans your computer to detect and remove malware.

REFERENCE

Performing a Quick Scan with Windows Defender

- Click in the Ask me anything box or the Search the web and Windows box, and then type Windows Defender.
- Click Windows Defender in the search results.
- Click the Quick option button on the Home tab.
- Click the Scan now button.

You need to keep the malware definitions in the antimalware up to date. Windows Defender refers to the definitions to determine whether software it detects is a virus or spyware. When you update your computer, Windows Update installs any new virus and spyware definitions. You can also set Windows Defender to check for updated definitions before scanning your computer.

You'll show Lamar how to start Windows Defender and scan for malware. You can run a quick scan, a full system scan, or a custom scan. A quick scan checks the locations on your computer that spyware is most likely to infect. A full scan checks all your files and programs, but it takes longer and can make your computer run slowly. With a custom scan, you select the locations you want Windows Defender to check.

TIP

You can find Windows Defender in the Windows System category in the All apps list or in the Update & security window from the Settings home page.

To start Windows Defender and perform a quick scan:

1. Click in the **Ask me anything** box on the taskbar, type **Windows Defender**, and then click **Windows Defender** in the search results. The Windows Defender window opens on the desktop. See Figure 5-11, which shows that Windows Defender is up to date. Your settings might differ.

   Trouble? If Windows Defender is turned off, click the Turn on button.

Figure 5-11 Windows Defender

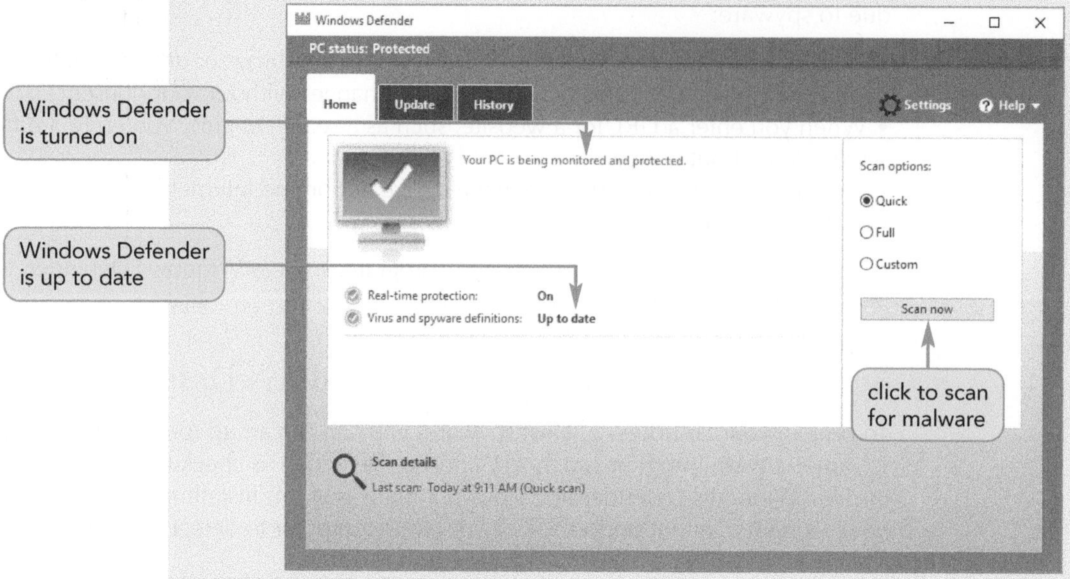

2. If the virus and spyware definitions are not up to date, click the **Update** tab, and then click the **Update** button. Windows Defender checks for program and malware definition updates, downloads and installs any updates, and then reports the update status.
3. If necessary, click the **Home** tab, click the **Quick** option button (if necessary), and then click the **Scan now** button. Windows Defender scans your computer, displaying first its progress and then the results of the scan. Depending on the number of programs on your computer, your scan might take a few minutes. Wait for the scan to finish and for Windows Defender to display the results before continuing.

TIP

Most antivirus programs quarantine suspicious files so you can choose to restore or delete them.

If Windows Defender finds suspicious files, it alerts you that these files have been **quarantined**, which means Windows Defender moved them to another location on your computer to safely segregate them from other files. Quarantined files cannot run, so they cannot harm your computer. You can review all quarantined files to determine what to do with them. Open the History page in Windows Defender, click the Quarantined items option button, and then click the View details button to display a list of quarantined files. The file list includes the filename, alert level, and date of quarantine. The alert level can help you decide whether to remove or restore a file. Remove files with a Severe or High alert level. If you do not recognize or trust the publisher of files with Medium or Low alert levels, search the web for information on those files to determine whether it is safe to restore them.

Windows Defender occasionally identifies a file as potential malware when the computer actually needs the file. If your computer has experienced problems since quarantining those files, go to the Microsoft Support webpage (https://support.microsoft.com) to contact a Microsoft support person and determine what to do with the files. If you haven't had any computer problems since Windows Defender quarantined the files, you can remove the files or leave them in the quarantine location.

To remove a quarantined file:

1. In the Windows Defender window, click the **History** tab to display the History page, click the **Quarantined items** option button, if necessary, and then click the **View details** button to display details about quarantined items. See Figure 5-12.

   Trouble? If a dialog box opens requesting an administrator password or your permission to continue, enter the password and then click the Yes button.

   Trouble? If Windows Defender did not quarantine any items after its quick scan, or if you do not have permission to work with quarantined items, read but do not perform Step 2.

Figure 5-12 Quarantined item in Windows Defender

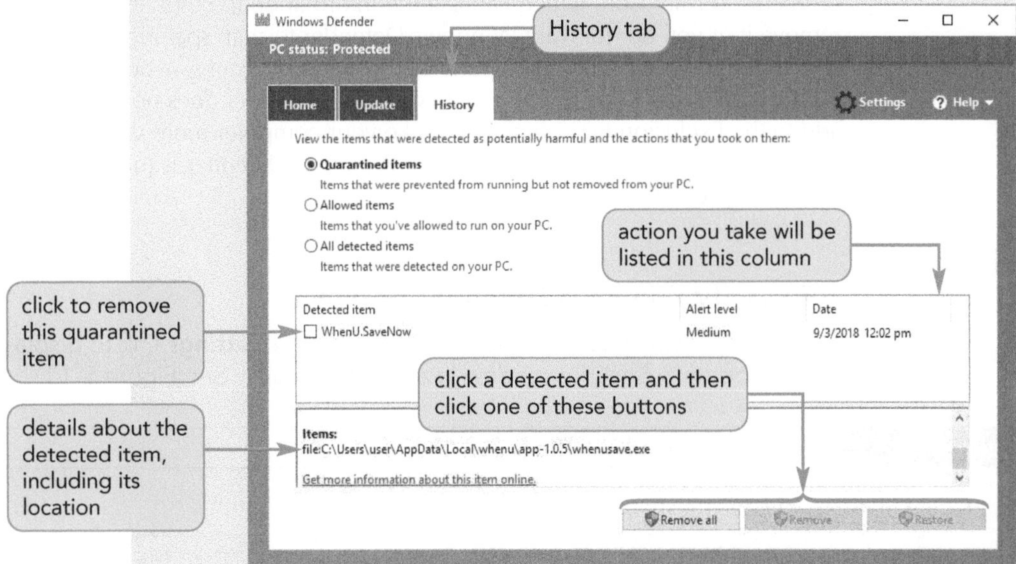

The quarantined item, WhenU.SaveNow, has a Medium alert level. Lamar does not recognize the publisher of this program, so you will remove it.

2. In the Quarantined items list, click **WhenU.SaveNow** (or another item with a Severe, High, or Medium alert level and a publisher you do not recognize), and then click the **Remove** button.

   Trouble? If a dialog box opens requesting an administrator password or your permission to continue, enter the password or click the Yes button.

Now that you've scanned Lamar's computer and handled the items Windows Defender found, you can set an option to make sure Windows Defender runs effectively and then learn how to turn Windows Defender on and off.

Setting Windows Defender Options

To turn Windows Defender on or off, you use an option in the Settings app. If you have been using Windows Defender and then install different antimalware software, you should turn Windows Defender off so it doesn't interfere with the other antivirus or antispyware program. If you remove other antimalware software or do not renew an antimalware subscription, Windows Defender runs automatically. To make sure your computer is being protected, you can verify Windows Defender's status in the Settings app and make sure it is set to use **Real-time protection**. This setting is selected by default, which means Windows Defender is set to constantly monitor your computer for virus and spyware activity. Windows Defender then alerts you when suspicious software attempts to install itself or to run on your computer, and notifies you when programs try to change important Windows settings. As with a scan, when Windows Defender detects suspicious software using Real-time protection, it assigns an alert level to the software and then displays a dialog box where you can choose one of the following actions:

- Quarantine—Quarantine the software. Windows Defender prevents the software from running and allows you to restore it or remove it from your computer.
- Remove—Permanently delete the software from your computer.
- Allow—Add the software to a list of allowed items so the software can run on your computer. Windows Defender does not alert you to risks that the software might pose to your privacy or your computer unless you remove the program from the Allowed items list.

Other Windows Defender settings you can select include **Cloud-based protection**. When this option is turned on, Windows sends information about potential security problems to Microsoft, which can use the information to better identify malware and remove it. If you do not want Windows Defender to scan specific files, folders, file types, or processes—which are parts of computer programs—you can add that item to the **Exclusion list**. Keep in mind that Windows Defender does not scan any item you add to the Exclusion list, which can make your computer more vulnerable to malware.

You'll show Lamar how to make sure Windows Defender is turned on and using Real-time protection.

To verify Windows Defender options:

1. In the Windows Defender window, click the **Settings** link to display the Update & Security window in the Settings app. See Figure 5-13.

Figure 5-13 Windows Defender settings

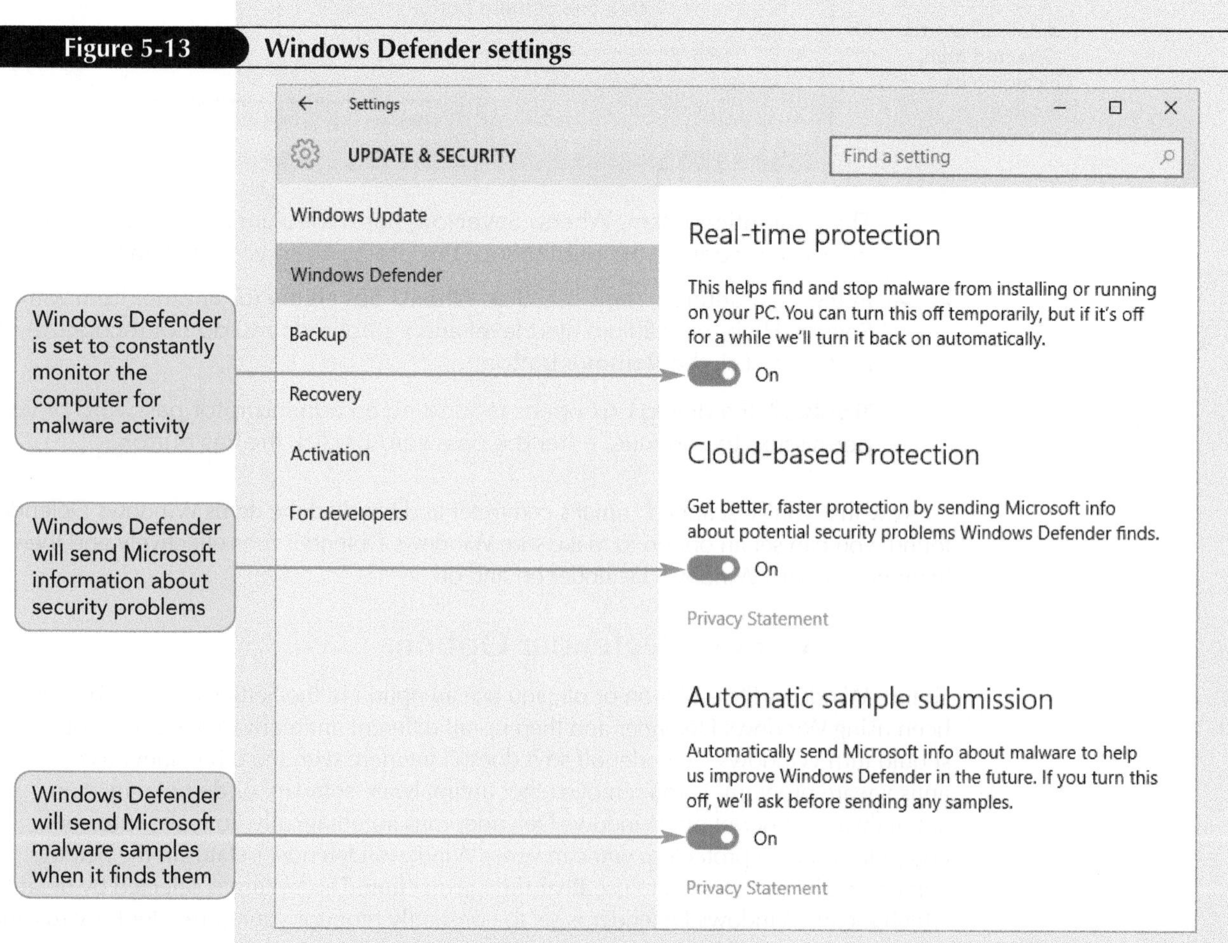
Settings
UPDATE & SECURITY
Find a setting
Windows Update
Windows Defender
Backup
Recovery
Activation
For developers
Real-time protection
This helps find and stop malware from installing or running on your PC. You can turn this off temporarily, but if it's off for a while we'll turn it back on automatically.
On
Cloud-based Protection
Get better, faster protection by sending Microsoft info about potential security problems Windows Defender finds.
On
Privacy Statement
Automatic sample submission
Automatically send Microsoft info about malware to help us improve Windows Defender in the future. If you turn this off, we'll ask before sending any samples.
On
Privacy Statement
Windows Defender is set to constantly monitor the computer for malware activity
Windows Defender will send Microsoft information about security problems
Windows Defender will send Microsoft malware samples when it finds them

2. In the Real-time protection section, click the **slider button**, if necessary, to change the Windows Defender setting from Off to On.
3. Scroll down to view the other settings.
4. Close all open windows.

Defending Against Email Viruses

TIP

Viewing a picture in a junk email message might validate your email address and result in your receiving more junk email.

An annoying and potentially dangerous type of privacy invasion is **spam**, or junk email, messages offering products and services that are sometimes fake or misleading. Some users receive thousands of spam messages a day; the volume alone makes spam a nuisance. In addition, spam can be a vehicle for malware. Communicating via email is one of the most popular activities on the Internet, and email is the most common way for computer viruses to spread. Viruses and other security threats are often contained in email attachments, especially files with filename extensions such as .exe, .bat, and .js.

To help prevent spam and potentially offensive material, Mail does not download graphics with messages sent in HTML format. People sending spam (called **spammers**) often use graphics to access your email address. Spammers can also take advantage of vulnerabilities in your computer to use it to send spam to other computers without your permission, a practice known as an **email relay**. This lets spammers work without being detected and can seriously downgrade the performance of your computer.

Phishing (pronounced *fishing*) is an attempt to deceive you into revealing personal or financial information when you respond to an email message or visit a website. A typical phishing scam starts with an email message that looks like an official notice from a trusted person or business, such as a bank, credit card company, or reputable online merchant. The email message asks you to reply with sensitive information, such as an account number or password, or directs you to a fraudulent website that requests this information. Phishers often use the information for identity theft.

To combat these threats, Mail blocks email attachments, graphics, and website links that might be harmful, notifying you when it does. Mail also helps prevent spammers from using your computer for email relays, and catches obvious spam messages and moves them to the built-in Junk folder.

REVIEW

Session 5.1 Quick Check

1. What is Windows Firewall?
2. Harmful software is called malicious software or ___________.
3. Why might you want to view your update history?
4. What is a virus definition?
5. How do you use Windows Defender to check only the locations on your computer that spyware is most likely to infect?
6. If Windows Defender finds files that might be spyware, it _____________ the files, which means it moves them to another location on your computer and prevents them from running until you remove or restore the files.
7. What is phishing?

Session 5.2 Visual Overview:

If a website is safe for an online transaction, the website name is green and a lock icon appears in the Address bar.

If the InPrivate button appears next to the tabs, InPrivate Browsing is in effect.

InPrivate Browsing opens a separate Microsoft Edge window for private browsing.

The **Pop-up Blocker** limits most pop-up windows and displays a notification when it blocks a pop-up.

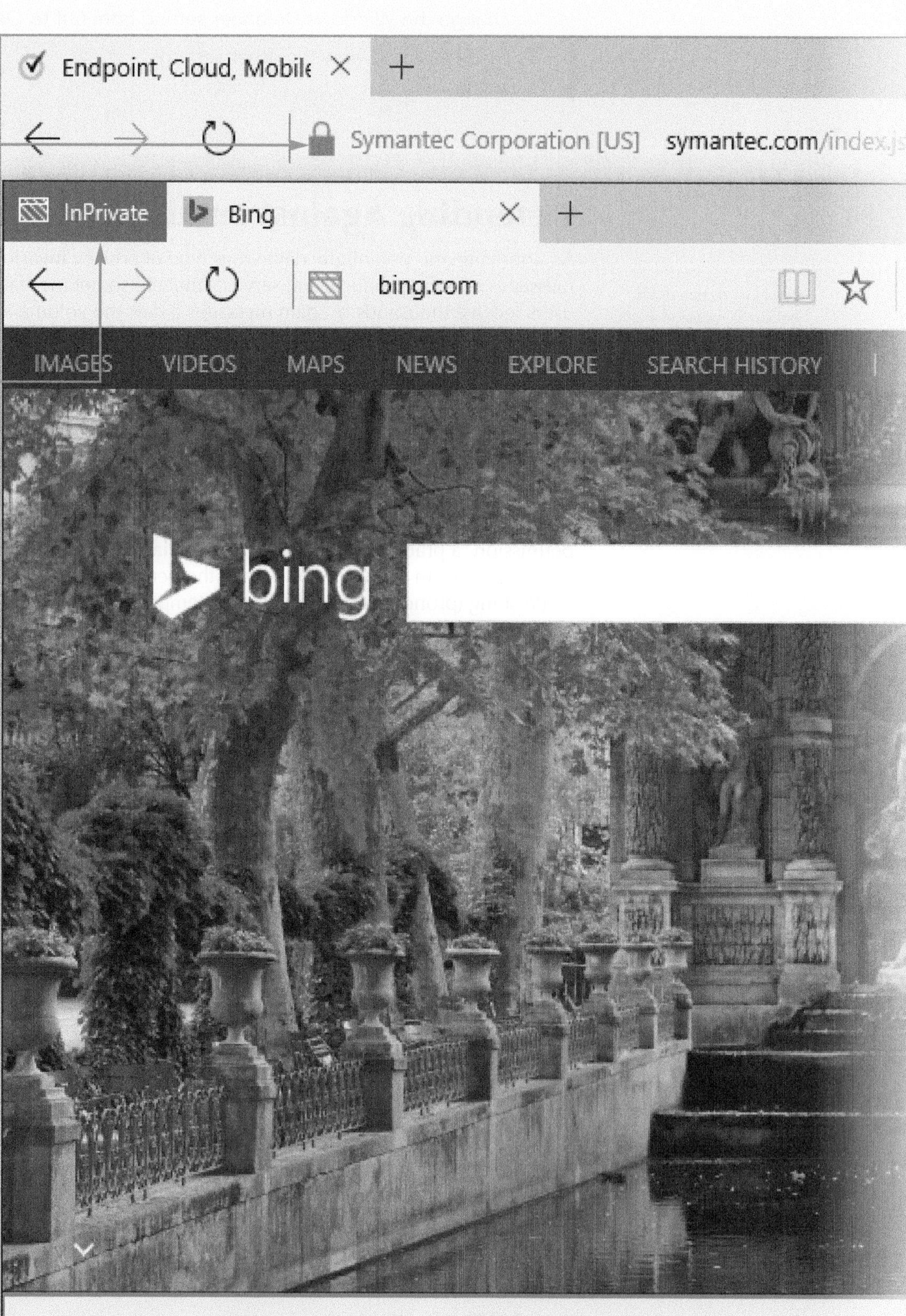

Microsoft Edge Security Features

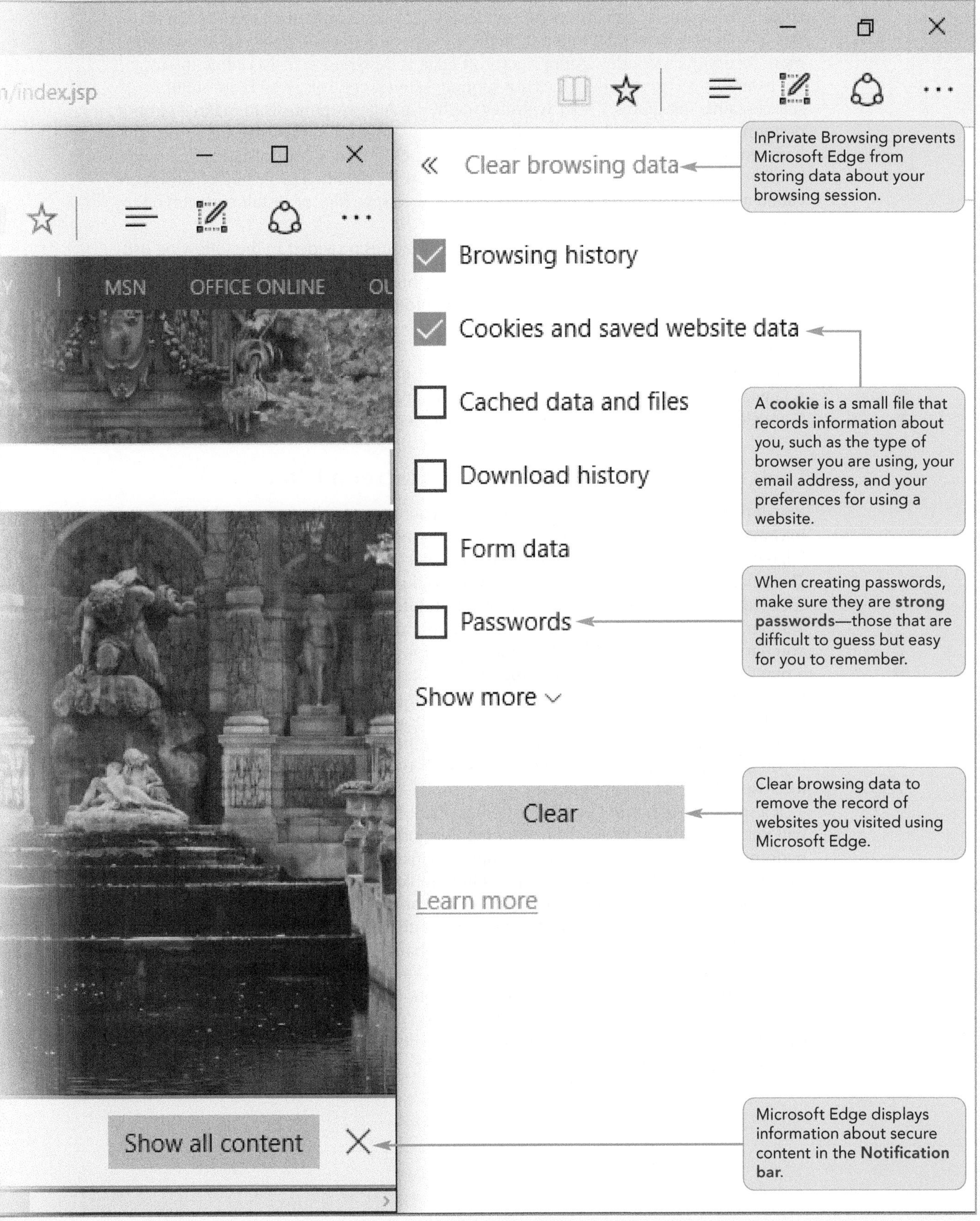
n/index.jsp
Clear browsing data
InPrivate Browsing prevents Microsoft Edge from storing data about your browsing session.
MSN
OFFICE ONLINE
Browsing history
Cookies and saved website data
Cached data and files
Download history
Form data
Passwords
A cookie is a small file that records information about you, such as the type of browser you are using, your email address, and your preferences for using a website.
When creating passwords, make sure they are strong passwords—those that are difficult to guess but easy for you to remember.
Show more
Clear
Clear browsing data to remove the record of websites you visited using Microsoft Edge.
Learn more
Show all content
Microsoft Edge displays information about secure content in the Notification bar.

Managing Microsoft Edge Security

Your computer is most vulnerable to security threats when you are connected to the Internet. You should therefore take advantage of the security settings in Microsoft Edge to help protect your computer by identifying viruses and other security threats that are circulated over the Internet, making your computer and personal information more secure. As a Windows app, Microsoft Edge is designed to resist online threats. For example, Microsoft Edge does not support ActiveX controls, which are small, self-contained programs. Older websites might use ActiveX controls to make it easier to perform tasks, such as submitting information to websites. Other ActiveX controls can harm your computer and files. Microsoft Edge blocks ActiveX controls and similar types of add-on or plug-in programs. Microsoft Edge always runs in a protected environment called a **sandbox** to guard against websites trying to save files or install malware on your computer.

In addition, Microsoft Edge uses the security features provided in the following list:

- SmartScreen Filter—This feature helps detect online scams, such as websites that try to trick you into revealing financial account information. The SmartScreen Filter also helps detect and block unknown and potentially malicious programs in files that you download from websites.
- Pop-up Blocker—This tool allows you to limit or block most pop-up windows.
- Digital signatures—Microsoft Edge can detect and display **digital signatures**, which are electronic security marks added to files to verify their authenticity.

Checking Websites with the SmartScreen Filter

Recall that phishing is an attempt to deceive you into revealing personal or financial information when you respond to an email message or visit a website. Microsoft Edge can protect you from online scams by detecting possible phishing websites. The SmartScreen Filter helps to protect you from phishing attacks, online fraud, and spoofed websites. (A **spoofed website** is a fraudulent site posing as a legitimate one.) The SmartScreen Filter operates in the background to analyze a website you visit by comparing its address to a list of reported phishing and malicious software websites, a practice called **reputation checking**. If the SmartScreen Filter finds that the website you're visiting is on the list of known malware or phishing sites, Microsoft Edge does not display the suspicious website. Instead, it shows a blocking webpage where you can choose to bypass the blocked website and go to your home page instead. If you are certain the blocked website is safe, you can continue to the site, though Microsoft does not recommend it.

If a spoofed site has not been reported as possibly malicious, the SmartScreen Filter will not detect it as a site to avoid. Commonly spoofed websites are those where you perform financial transactions, such as online banking or shopping sites. They often use phony web addresses to mislead you into thinking you are visiting a legitimate site. When you visit a site that requests personal or financial information, look in the Address bar for the web address. Microsoft Edge displays the true domain you are visiting. For example, you might do your online banking at an Accounts webpage with the address www.bank.com/accounts. If you visit the Accounts webpage but notice that the Address bar displays the address www.phony.com/accounts, you are visiting a spoofed site and should close the webpage, and then report it as a possible phishing site. The Microsoft support team will investigate the site and add it to the list of known phishing sites as appropriate.

INSIGHT

Protecting Yourself from Phishing Attempts

In addition to using the SmartScreen Filter, use the following guidelines to protect yourself from online phishing:

- Never provide personal information in an email, an instant message, or a pop-up window.
- Do not click links in email and instant messages from senders you do not know or trust. Even messages that seem to be from friends and family can be faked. Therefore, check with the sender to make sure he or she actually sent the message (especially if the message contains only a link to a website).
- Only use websites that provide privacy statements or indicate how they use your personal information.

The SmartScreen Filter is turned on by default so that it checks websites and files automatically as you browse. You'll show Lamar how to make sure the SmartScreen Filter is protecting his computer when it is connected to the Internet.

To turn on the SmartScreen Filter in Microsoft Edge:

1. Click the **Microsoft Edge** button on the taskbar to start the browser.
2. Click the **More** button in the navigation bar, and then click **Settings** to display the Settings pane.
3. Scroll the Settings pane and then click the **View advanced settings** button in the Advanced settings section to display the Advanced settings options.
4. Scroll the Advanced settings options to display a section titled Help protect me from malicious sites and downloads with SmartScreen Filter. See Figure 5-14. This option is turned on by default.

TIP

You can also set SmartScreen Filter options by clicking Change Windows SmartScreen settings in the left pane of the Security and Maintenance window.

Figure 5-14 SmartScreen Filter setting in Microsoft Edge

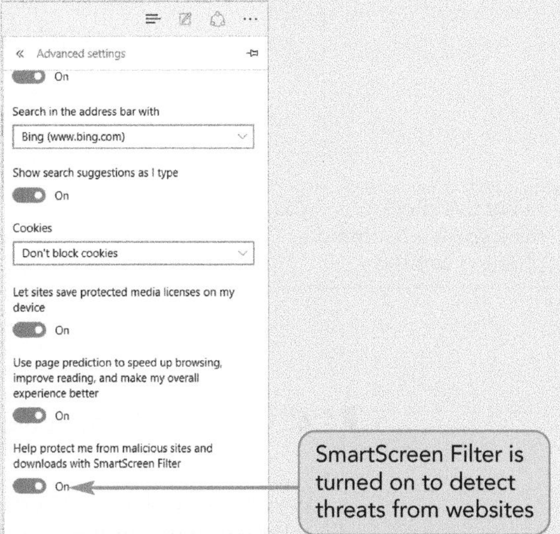

5. If SmartScreen Filter is not turned on, click the **slider button** to change the setting from Off to On.

If you want to check an individual website to determine whether it has been reported as a potentially unsafe site, you must switch to Internet Explorer. You can also report websites to Microsoft using Internet Explorer. You'll show Lamar how to perform both tasks.

To check and report a website:

1. Click a blank area of the Start page (or a webpage), click in the **Address bar**, type **microsoft.com**, and then press the **Enter** key to go to the Microsoft website.
2. To switch to Internet Explorer, click the **More** button in the navigation bar, and then click **Open with Internet Explorer**.
3. Maximize the Internet Explorer window, if necessary, click the **Tools** button in the navigation bar, point to **Safety**, and then click **Check this website**. The SmartScreen Filter dialog box opens and explains that the site has not been reported to Microsoft for containing threats. The message tells you to check the address to make sure it is a site you trust, and if you suspect that the site it unsafe, you can report it to Microsoft.

   Trouble? If the SmartScreen Filter dialog box does not open, you or another user chose not to display the message again. Skip Step 4.
4. Click the **OK** button to close the SmartScreen Filter dialog box.
5. To see how to report a possible phishing site, click the **Tools** button in the navigation bar, point to **Safety**, and then click **Report unsafe website**. The Microsoft Report a website webpage opens so you can report information about the website. See Figure 5-15.

Figure 5-15 Microsoft Report a website webpage

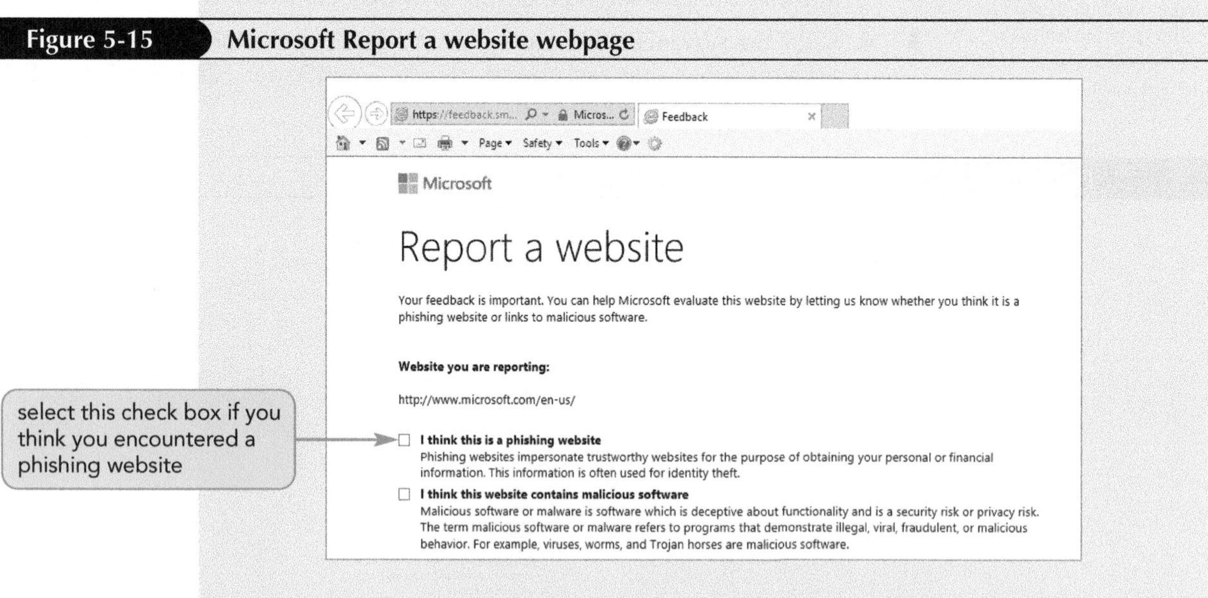

6. Close the Microsoft Report a website webpage and Internet Explorer.

As you visit websites, Microsoft Edge checks their certificates. A **certificate** is a digital document (similar to a digital signature) that verifies the security of a website you visit. Microsoft Edge can detect certificate errors, which are signs that you are visiting a phishing site or one that uses spyware or other malware. If Microsoft Edge detects a certificate error or other security problem, it identifies the problem type in the Address bar. For example, a certificate error message might appear in the Address bar. You can click the error message to learn about the problem. See Figure 5-16.

Figure 5-16 Security message in Microsoft Edge

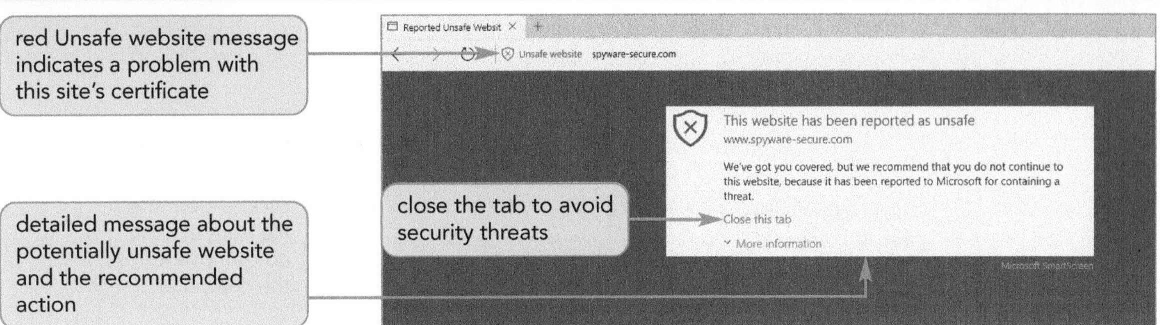

The color of the website message in the Address bar also indicates the type of error or problem. Red means the certificate is out of date, is invalid, or has an error. Yellow signals that the certificate cannot be verified, which sometimes happens with a suspected phishing site. White means the certificate is normal, and green indicates sites that have high security, such as those for financial transactions.

Downloading Files Safely

The SmartScreen Filter also works with the Microsoft Edge Downloads list to manage downloaded files. Recall that you can click the Downloads button in the Hub to list the files you download from the Internet, keep track of where they're stored on your computer, and pause, open, run, delete, or save the downloaded files. The SmartScreen Filter analyzes files you want to download similar to how it analyzes websites. When you select a file to download from a website, the SmartScreen filter refers to a list of files known to be malicious. If the file you want to download is on that list, the SmartScreen Filter blocks the download and explains the file is unsafe. If the file is not on the list of malicious files, the SmartScreen Filter refers to a list (kept by Microsoft) of programs downloaded by a significant number of other Microsoft Edge and Internet Explorer users. The SmartScreen Filter displays an Open file – Security Warning dialog box to notify you if the file is not on the list of commonly downloaded files. In that case, you should not open or install the file unless you trust its publisher and the website that provided the file. You can use the Downloads list to delete the program or run it if you know the file is safe.

If you download a file and find that it is unsafe, such as a file quarantined after a scan, you can right-click the file in the Downloads list, and then click Report that this download is unsafe on the shortcut menu to report the file to Microsoft, which adds the file to the SmartScreen Filter list of malicious files.

You'll show Lamar how to use Microsoft Edge to display a list of downloaded files. Lamar also wants to know where the Downloads list stores downloaded files on his computer. If he suspects a downloaded file contains malicious software, he can quickly find the file and delete it using File Explorer. He can also use the Downloads list to test, delete, and report suspicious files.

To display and locate downloaded files:

1. Click the **Hub** button in the navigation bar, and then click the **Downloads** button to display the Downloads list. See Figure 5-17. The list of downloaded files on your computer will differ.

Figure 5-17 Downloads list

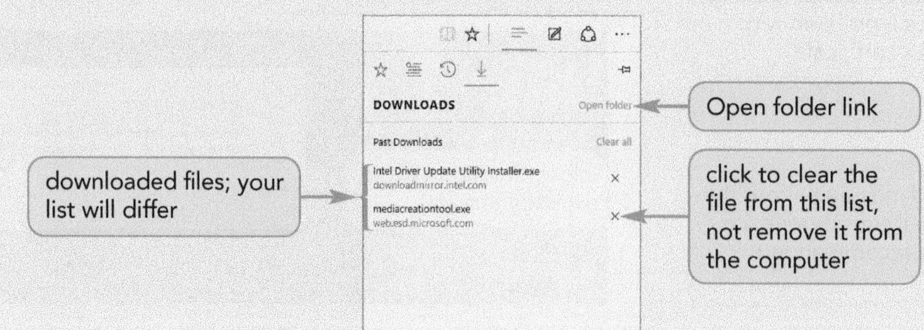

2. Click the **Open folder** link to open the folder window displaying the location of the downloaded files. By default, Windows 10 uses the Downloads folder for downloaded files.
3. Close the Downloads folder window.

If you want to remove all downloaded files in the Downloads list, you can click the Clear all link in the Downloads list. To remove a single file, click its Clear button. Removing the file from the Downloads list does not delete the file from your computer. You must navigate to the Downloads folder and then delete the file to remove it from your computer.

Blocking Malware

To install or run programs on your computer, hackers often take advantage of web programming tools, such as scripts, that are designed to enhance your online experience. A **script** is programming code that performs a series of commands and can be embedded in a webpage. For example, a website designer might use a script to verify that you've completed all the necessary fields in an online form. In contrast, hackers use scripts on a webpage to automatically download programs to your computer that can collect and transmit information about you without your knowledge or authorization.

A common way for hackers to distribute adware and spyware is to include the malware with other content or programs. If the files lack digital signatures, meaning the files are unverified, Microsoft Edge blocks them and displays a message that only secure content is shown. Recall that a digital signature is an electronic security mark that can be added to files, similar to a certificate added to websites. A digital signature identifies the publisher of a file and verifies that the file has not changed since it was signed.

INSIGHT

Digital Signatures

Microsoft Edge and other programs, including Windows 10, can detect whether a file has a digital signature. A file without a valid digital signature might not be from the stated source or might have been tampered with (possibly by a virus) since it was published. Avoid opening an unsigned file unless you know for certain who created it and whether the contents are safe to open. However, even a valid digital signature does not guarantee that the contents of the file are harmless. When you download a file, determine whether to trust its contents based on the identity of the publisher and the site providing the file.

To protect against malicious scripts and unsafe content, Microsoft Edge runs in a protected environment that makes it difficult for hackers to install malware on your computer. If a webpage tries to install any type of software or run a script, Microsoft Edge displays a dialog box warning you about the attempt. If you trust the program, you can allow it to run once or always. If you are not familiar with the program or don't want to run it, you can deny it once or always.

Next, you'll show Lamar how to use the Pop-up Blocker to limit or block most pop-up windows when he visits websites.

Blocking Pop-Up Windows

A pop-up ad is a small web browser window that appears when you visit a website and advertises a product or service. Many legitimate advertisers use pop-up ads because they effectively get your attention and provide information or services that might interest you. However, some pop-up ads are annoying because they repeatedly interrupt your online activities, are difficult to close, or display objectionable content. Other pop-up ads are dangerous because they can download spyware or **hijack** your browser—meaning they seize control of the browser, opening many more new windows each time you close one pop-up window until you have to close your browser or restart your computer.

To avoid the nuisance and danger of pop-up ads, Microsoft Edge includes the Pop-up Blocker, which warns you about or blocks pop-up ads. The Pop-up Blocker is turned on by default, meaning that Microsoft Edge blocks most pop-up windows. Not all pop-up windows are ads. If a pop-up window opens as soon as you visit a website, it probably contains an ad. However, many websites use pop-up windows to display tools such as calendars or verification notices. For example, if you visit a travel website to make flight or hotel reservations, the site might provide a calendar in a pop-up window so you can select your travel dates. If you click a link or button to open the pop-up window, Microsoft Edge does not block it by default. However, it does block pop-up windows that appear automatically if you have not clicked a link or button.

Lamar has had problems with pop-up ads before, so he wants to verify that Microsoft Edge is blocking pop-ups.

To verify the pop-up settings in Microsoft Edge:

1. In Microsoft Edge, click the **More** button ... in the navigation bar, and then click **Settings** to display the Settings pane.
2. Scroll the Settings pane, and then click the **View advanced settings** button. See Figure 5-18.

Figure 5-18 **Block pop-ups setting**

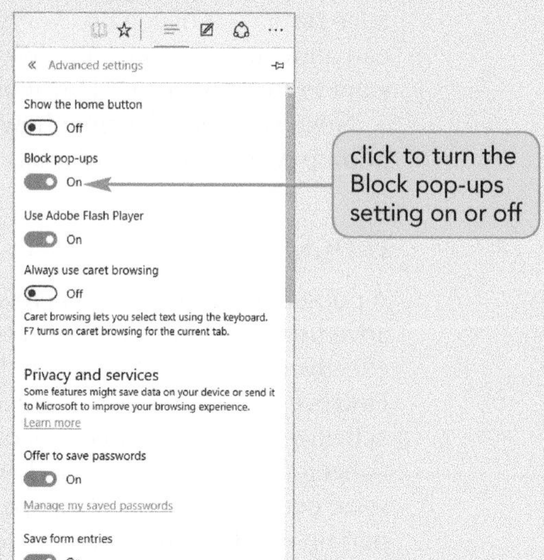

Trouble? If the Block pop-ups setting is turned off, then click the slider button to change the setting from Off to On.

3. Leave the Settings pane open for the next set of steps.

Now that you have explored the security settings in Microsoft Edge, you can turn your attention to its privacy settings.

Selecting Microsoft Edge Privacy Settings

In addition to security protection, Microsoft Edge includes the following tools and features to protect your privacy:

- Privacy settings and alerts—These settings specify how to handle identifying information when you're online and alert you when a website you're visiting doesn't meet your criteria.
- InPrivate Browsing—This feature helps prevent Microsoft Edge from storing data about your browsing session by opening a separate InPrivate Browsing Microsoft Edge window to keep your browsing actions private.
- Do Not Track requests—This feature helps prevent website content providers from collecting information about sites you visit.
- Secure connections—Microsoft Edge informs you when it is using a secure connection to communicate with websites that handle sensitive personal information.

REFERENCE

Selecting Privacy Settings

- In Microsoft Edge, click the More button.
- Click Settings.
- Click the View advanced settings button.
- Scroll to the Privacy and services section, and then change the settings using the slider buttons.

One privacy concern is cookies, which many websites store on your computer when you visit them. A cookie is a small file that records information about you, such as the type of browser you are using, your email address, and your preferences for using a website. Like other web tools, cookies can enhance your online experience by helping trusted websites customize their service to you. However, they can also pose a security risk—hackers can retrieve cookies to search for private information such as passwords, or use cookies to track the websites you visit. In Microsoft Edge, you can specify privacy settings to either allow websites to save cookies on your computer or prevent them from doing so.

One way to protect your privacy with Microsoft Edge is to block cookies on some or all of the websites you visit. You should be selective about which websites you allow to store cookies on your computer. Blocking all cookies keeps your website visits private but might also limit your experience or prove annoying. Allowing all cookies might compromise your privacy. Some users find that the Block only third party cookies setting provides a good balance because it allows most **first-party cookies**, which are generated from the websites you visit and contain information the website reuses when you return. For example, to keep track of products you add to an electronic shopping cart or wish list, a website saves a first-party cookie on your computer. In contrast, this setting blocks most **third-party cookies**, which are generated from website advertisers, who might use them to track your web use for marketing purposes.

Lamar often visits his business clients' websites for research as he prepares to develop automation systems for them. He wants to protect the privacy of Snap Home Automation and his clients by blocking third-party cookies.

As you perform the following steps, note your original settings so you can restore them later.

To change privacy settings for saving cookies:

1. Scroll the list of Advanced settings, and then click the box in the Cookies section to display options for blocking and allowing cookies. See Figure 5-19.

Figure 5-19 **Blocking or allowing cookies**

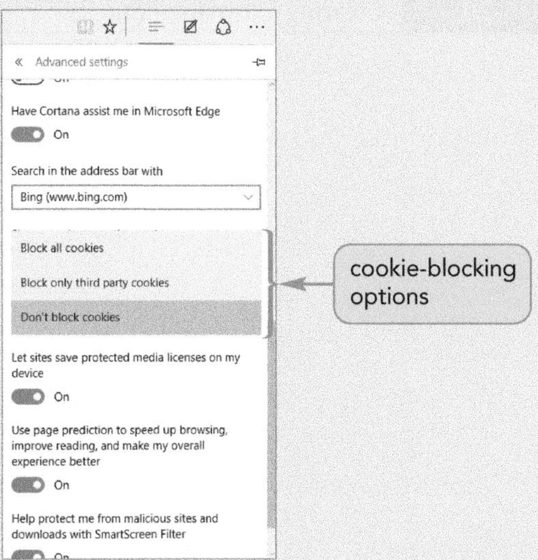

Trouble? If you are working in a computer lab, you might not have permission to change the Privacy and services settings. In that case, read but do not perform Step 2.

2. Click **Block only third party cookies**. When you select this setting, Microsoft Edge blocks cookies except for some first-party cookies and those created by websites you identify.
3. Click a blank area of the webpage to close the Settings pane.

Microsoft Edge will block most cookies except for first-party cookies on Lamar's computer from now on. However, if websites stored cookies on his computer before you changed the privacy setting, they will remain there until you delete them. You can delete cookies by clearing your browsing history. In addition to cookies, Microsoft Edge stores cached data and files, form data, a history of the websites you've visited, information you've entered in the Address bar, and web passwords you've saved. **Cached data and files** are copies of webpages, images, and other media that Microsoft Edge stores on your computer so it can download content faster the next time you visit a website. Microsoft Edge also stores media licenses, pop-up exceptions, and permissions you've granted to websites. Usually, maintaining this history information improves your web browsing because it can fill in information that you would otherwise have to retype. If you have particular privacy concerns, however, such as when you are using a public computer, you can clear some or all of your browsing history to delete this information.

Lamar wants to delete all of the cookies and the list of websites he has visited.

To clear cookies and your browsing history:

1. Click the **Hub** button in the navigation bar, and then click the **History** button, if necessary, to display the History list.
2. Click the **Clear all history** link to display a list of browsing information you can clear.
3. Click the **Show more** button, if necessary, to display the complete list. See Figure 5-20. Your settings might differ.

Figure 5-20 Clearing browsing data

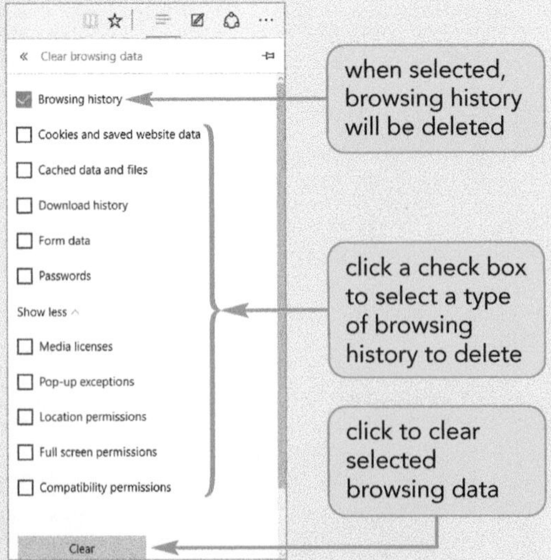

Trouble? If you are working in a computer lab, you might not have permission to clear your browsing history. In that case, read but do not perform Steps 4–6.

TIP

Deleting all of your browsing history does not delete your Favorites list or Reading list.

4. If necessary, click the **Browsing history** check box to insert a check mark and indicate you want to delete the list of websites you have visited.
5. If necessary, click the **Cookies and saved website data** check box to insert a checkmark and indicate you want to delete all of the cookies stored on your computer.
6. Click the **Clear** button to delete cookies and your browsing history. It takes a few moments for Microsoft Edge to clear the browsing history and cookies.
7. When Microsoft Edge is finished, click a blank area of the webpage to close the Hub.

Another privacy feature of Microsoft Edge is InPrivate Browsing, which you'll explore next.

Protecting Your Privacy with InPrivate Browsing

If you want to keep information about your web browsing private, you can use InPrivate Browsing. This feature prevents Microsoft Edge from storing data about your browsing session. If you are searching online for a gift, for example, or want to prevent another user from retracing your steps to a website containing your financial information, use InPrivate Browsing to hide the history of the webpages you visited. When you do, Microsoft Edge opens a new window and displays InPrivate on the title bar. As you work in the InPrivate window, Microsoft Edge protects your privacy. To end your InPrivate Browsing session, close the browser window.

Keep in mind that InPrivate Browsing does not make you anonymous on the Internet. Websites might still be able to identify you through your web address. They can still record and save any forms you complete and selections you make. You will show Lamar how an InPrivate Browsing session works.

To turn on InPrivate Browsing:

1. Click the **More** button ··· in the navigation bar, and then click **New InPrivate window** to start an InPrivate Browsing session. Maximize the window, if necessary. See Figure 5-21.

Figure 5-21 InPrivate window

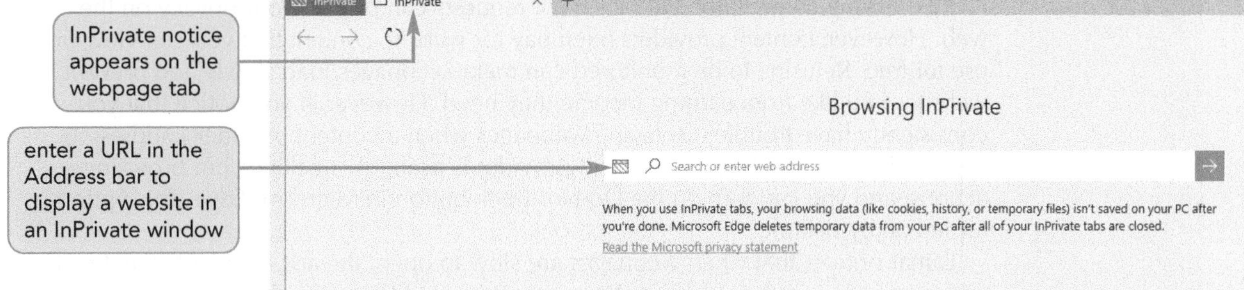
InPrivate
InPrivate
InPrivate notice appears on the webpage tab
Browsing InPrivate
enter a URL in the Address bar to display a website in an InPrivate window
Search or enter web address
When you use InPrivate tabs, your browsing data (like cookies, history, or temporary files) isn't saved on your PC after you're done. Microsoft Edge deletes temporary data from your PC after all of your InPrivate tabs are closed.
Read the Microsoft privacy statement

2. Click in the **Address bar**, type **www.whitehouse.gov**, and then press the **Enter** key. The home page for the White House website appears in the InPrivate browser window.

3. Point to the **Briefing Room** link near the top of the page, and then click the **Your Weekly Address** link in the From the Press Office section.

   Trouble? If the Your Weekly Address link does not appear on the webpage you are viewing, click any other link.

4. Click the **Hub** button in the navigation bar, and then click the **History** button, if necessary, to display the History list. Note that the White House webpages you visited during your InPrivate Browsing session are not included in the History list. When you close the InPrivate window, the list of recent webpages in the regular Microsoft Edge window will not include any of the White House pages either.
5. Close the InPrivate window.
6. Click the **Hub** button in the navigation bar, and then click the **History** button, if necessary, to display the History list. Expand the list to show the webpages you visited in the last hour or today, which includes pages you visited recently except for those you visited during your InPrivate Browsing session.
7. Click a blank area of the webpage to close the Hub.

Microsoft Edge includes another privacy feature—Do Not Track requests—which you'll learn about next.

Requesting Tracking Protection

Many webpages use content such as ads, maps, or web analysis tools that count the number of visitors to the website. This content is typically supplied by other websites called content providers or third-party websites. When you visit a website with third-party content, information that identifies your computer is sent to the content provider. For example, the content provider can learn your browser type, operating system, web address, and screen resolution. If you visit many websites that the same content provider uses, the content provider can create a profile of your browsing preferences. The profile can be used to target ads that are likely to appeal to you, for example.

Web tracking tools, such as visitor counters, sometimes appear as visible content, but not always. For example, **web beacons** are transparent images that invisibly track website usage. Web analysis tools often contain scripts that can track information such as the pages you visit and the selections you make. To control the information sent to content providers, you can have Microsoft Edge send Do Not Track requests to the websites.

By blocking content, the Do Not Track requests can protect your privacy on the web. However, content providers often pay for website content that you can view or use for free. Refusing to be monitored can make webpages load slowly and prevent websites you like from earning income they need. However, if you notice that you consistently have trouble displaying webpages when a content provider's address appears in the status bar, that content provider is probably tracking your browsing actions, and you can turn on the Do Not Track option in Microsoft Edge. This option is turned off by default.

Lamar notices that when webpages are slow to open, the ads.doubleclick.net web address appears in the status bar. You suggest he set Microsoft Edge to send Do Not Track requests to see if that improves his browsing experience.

To send Do Not Track requests:

1. Click the **More** button [···] in the navigation bar, and then click **Settings** to display the Settings pane.
2. Scroll the Settings pane and then click the **View advanced settings** button in the Advanced settings section to display the Advanced settings options.
3. Scroll the list of Advanced settings, if necessary, and then click the **slider button** for the Send Do Not Track requests setting from Off to On.
4. Click a blank area of the webpage to close the Advanced settings.
5. Close Microsoft Edge.

Besides using the security tools provided in Microsoft Edge, use common sense when visiting websites, especially when sharing private information.

PROSKILLS

Decision Making: Deciding Whether to Trust a Website

Your decision about whether to trust a website should be based on who publishes the website, what information the publisher wants from you, and what you want from the site. To make your web browsing more efficient and productive, consider the following guidelines when deciding whether to trust a website with confidential information:

- Ensure you have a secure connection to the website. Look in the Address bar for a website address that begins with "https" rather than "http." Also, look for a security icon such as a padlock in the Address bar or status bar, which indicates that the website is secure.
- Confirm that you are familiar with the organization that sponsors the website. If you are a satisfied customer of a business that provides products in a physical location, you can probably trust its website. Read the website's privacy or terms of use statement to make sure you are comfortable with the terms. Avoid websites that require you to accept email offers or advertising from the website.
- Check to see if the website is certified by an Internet trust organization. An Internet trust organization verifies that a website has a privacy statement and gives you a choice about how it uses your information. Approved websites display one or more privacy certification seals, usually on their home page or order forms. However, unscrupulous websites sometimes fraudulently display these trust logos. You can contact the trust organization to see if the website is registered with it. Reputable trust organizations include TRUSTe (www.truste.com), the Better Business Bureau or BBBOnLine (www.bbb.org/online), and webTrust (www.webtrust.org). On the website of each trust organization, you can display a list of certified websites.
- Stay away from sites that unnecessarily request confidential personal information. Provide personal or confidential information such as credit card numbers only when necessary and only on a secure form. Make sure you are using a secure connection when completing the form. Also, look for a message explaining that your information will be encrypted for security.
- Avoid sites that use untrustworthy ways to contact you. Untrustworthy websites are often referred to you through an email message from someone you don't know. Stay away from websites making offers that seem too good to be true.

Now that you have thoroughly explored the privacy and security settings in Microsoft Edge, you can show Lamar another way to protect his company's computers—by using user accounts.

Setting Up User Accounts

In Windows, a **user account** is a collection of information that indicates the files and folders you can access, the types of changes you can make to the computer, and your preferred appearance settings (such as your desktop background or color scheme). If you have a user account on a computer that you share with other people, you can maintain your own files and settings separate from the other users.

REFERENCE

Setting Up a User Account

- Click the Start button and then click Settings.
- Click Accounts.
- In the left pane, click Family & other users.
- In the right pane, click the Add someone else to this PC button.
- Click the I don't have this person's sign-in information link.
- Click the Add a user without a Microsoft account link.
- Enter a user name, password, and password hint, and then click the Next button.

You can create two types of accounts in Windows 10:

- **Microsoft account**—This type of account provides access to Microsoft cloud computing services, such as Outlook.com for email, OneDrive for file storage, and Xbox for games. With this type of user account, you can use Windows 10 and some Windows apps to access files and other data stored in your online Microsoft account. For example, if you keep albums of photos on your OneDrive, you can use the Photos app to display those photos on your PC. If you run Windows 10 on more than one PC, you can also **synchronize**, or **sync**, (that is, to make sure data on the two devices match) your settings, preferences, and some apps so that all your PCs are set up the same way. The advantage of a Microsoft account is that you provide one user name and one password to connect to the cloud and to sync settings. Most likely, you created a Microsoft account when you set up Windows 10.
- **Local-only user account**—This type of account accesses only resources on your computer. If you want to allow family members or other people to use your computer occasionally, you can set up a local-only user account for those users.

In addition, a Microsoft account or a local-only user account is a Standard account or an Administrator account, which determines how much control the user has over the computer:

- **Standard account**—A Standard account is designed for everyday computing and can protect your computer and data by preventing users from changing settings that affect all users. To make changes such as installing software or changing security settings, Windows requests permission or a password for an Administrator account. Microsoft recommends that every regular user on a computer have a Standard account.
- **Administrator account**—An Administrator account is created when Windows 10 is installed and provides full access to the computer. The administrator can access the files of any user, install software, and change any settings. The intention is that when you install Windows 10, you first sign in to the computer as the administrator, and then create a Standard user account for yourself and for each person who will use the computer.

When you install Windows 10, the setup program guides you through the steps of creating an Administrator account. During that process, you choose whether you want to use your Microsoft account or a local-only user account as the Administrator account. If you don't have a Microsoft account, you can create one as you install Windows.

After completing the installation, you can set up Standard accounts using the Settings app. Any accounts you create after the initial Administrator account are Standard accounts by default. Standard accounts can be Microsoft or local-only user accounts.

Selecting a User Name and Password

When you create an Administrator account or a Standard account, Windows asks for your user credentials, which are a user name and a password. If you have a Microsoft account, you can provide the user name and password you use for that account. If you don't have a Microsoft account, you can create one as you set up a new Administrator or Standard account. To use a Microsoft account, you provide your email address and a password as your user credentials.

INSIGHT

Synchronizing Accounts

If you use your Microsoft account credentials for your user account on a Windows 10 laptop, for example, you can synchronize settings, preferences, and some apps that you use on other computers, such as a Windows 10 tablet. No matter which computer you use, the desktop will look the same and you'll have access to the same apps.

Before you can synchronize accounts, you need to trust each computer you use. (**Trusting** a computer means you verify that you have an account on that computer.) To trust a computer, open the Settings app and then select Accounts. With Your account selected in the left pane, click the Verify link in the right pane. (If the Verify link does not appear, the PC is already a trusted device in your Microsoft account.) Enter the password to your Microsoft account, and then click the OK button. Choose how you want to receive a security code for verification, such as a text or email message, and then click the Next button. Wait to receive the security code, enter it, and then click the Submit button. The PC is now a trusted device and will sync settings and data automatically.

If you set up a new Administrator or Standard account as a local-only user account, you must provide a user name, but the password is optional. However, Microsoft strongly recommends that you use a password for all accounts, which is one of the most effective ways you can keep your computer secure. When your computer is protected with a password, only someone who knows the password can sign in to Windows.

A **text password** is a series of letters, numbers, spaces, and symbols that you provide to access your files, applications, and other resources on the computer. Windows passwords are case sensitive, so LaJffson18 is different from lajffson18. Passwords strengthen computer security because they help to make sure that no one can access the computer unless he or she is authorized to do so. Therefore, you should not give your passwords to others or write them in a place where others can see them.

When creating a text password, make sure you devise a strong password—one that is difficult to guess but easy for you to remember. Strong text passwords have the following characteristics:

- Contain at least eight characters
- Do not include your user name, real name, or company name
- Are not words you can find in the dictionary
- Are significantly different from your previous passwords
- Contain characters from each of the following categories: uppercase letters, lowercase letters, numbers, and symbols (not including spaces)

For any account that has a text password, you can also set up a four-digit **personal information number (PIN)**, a picture password, or Windows Hello to protect the account. Similar to a PIN you use for banking transactions, you can use a PIN for a

Windows account as a fast way to sign in. (Keep in mind, however, that a PIN does not meet the requirements for a strong password.)

A **picture password** involves an image and gestures, and is easiest to provide on a touchscreen device. You select a photo or another graphic stored in a location your computer can access, and then draw three gestures (that is, circles, lines, and taps or clicks) on the picture to create a password. You must remember the size, position, and direction of the gestures and the order you make them so you can repeat the gestures to gain access to your account.

If your device has a fingerprint reader or a high-quality camera, you can sign in using **Windows Hello**, a feature that accepts a fingerprint or facial scan instead of a password. When you set up Windows Hello, you might be asked to enter a PIN to associate with your fingerprint or facial scan. Windows Hello is a form of **biometric security**, a way to verify your identity based on physical characteristics. Microsoft considers Windows Hello the most secure way to sign in to Windows.

At times, Windows requests your text password or fingerprint or facial scan, such as when you want to change system settings. At other times, you can use a PIN or picture password, such as to sign in to your account.

Creating a Local-Only User Account

Lamar has a Microsoft Administrator account on his PC, but wants to set up a separate Standard account on the same computer to prevent anyone from using it to change system settings or install unauthorized software. He can then let his assistants use his PC by signing in to the Standard account when they are working at a client site. Because he also wants to prevent his assistants from downloading and installing apps from the Windows Store, he wants the Standard account to be a local-only user account, which means it is restricted to his PC only.

To create a Standard local-only user account on Lamar's computer, you provide a user name and password. You can also set up a PIN so he can sign in quickly and create a picture password as an alternate method for signing in to Windows. He also wants to investigate Windows Hello to determine whether the camera on his PC is compatible with this feature.

You must be signed in using an Administrator account to perform the following steps. If you do not have access to an Administrator account, read but do not perform the following steps.

To create a Standard local-only user account:

1. Click the **Start** button to display the Start menu, and then click **Settings** to start the Settings app.
2. Click **Accounts** in the Settings home page to display the Accounts window, which includes your account information.

   Trouble? If a message appears on your account screen about trusting the PC, disregard the message. You don't need to sync settings now.
3. In the left pane, click **Family & other users** to display options for setting up accounts for your family or other people. See Figure 5-22.

Figure 5-22 Family and other users settings

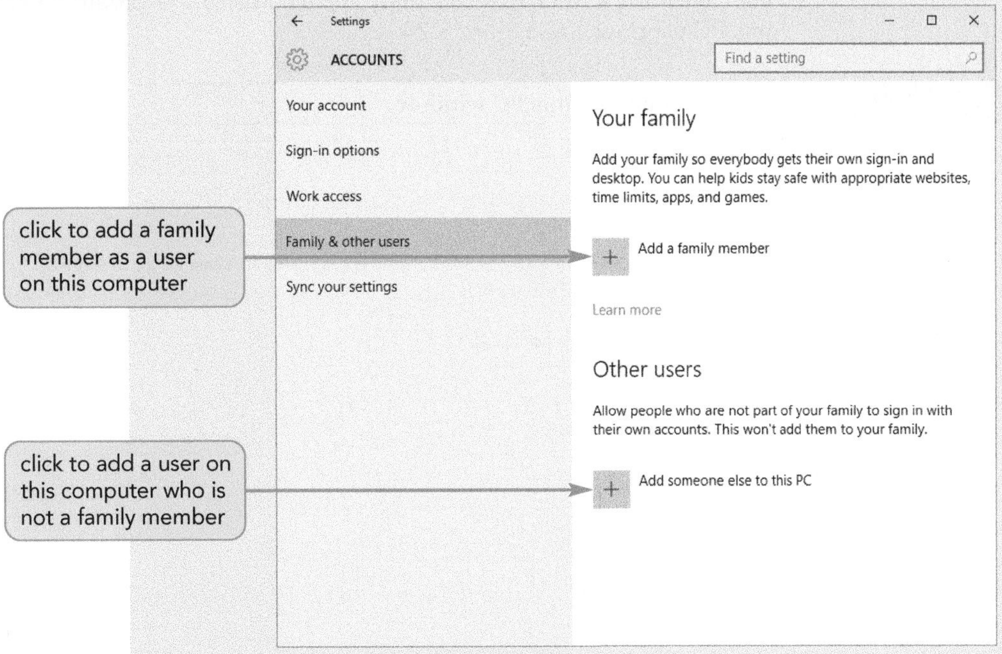

click to add a family member as a user on this computer
click to add a user on this computer who is not a family member
Settings
ACCOUNTS
Find a setting
Your account
Sign-in options
Work access
Family & other users
Sync your settings
Your family
Add your family so everybody gets their own sign-in and desktop. You can help kids stay safe with appropriate websites, time limits, apps, and games.
Add a family member
Learn more
Other users
Allow people who are not part of your family to sign in with their own accounts. This won't add them to your family.
Add someone else to this PC

4. Click the **Add someone else to this PC** button to display a window asking how this person will sign in. See Figure 5-23.

Figure 5-23 Choosing how the new user will sign in

click this link to set up a local-user account
How will this person sign in?
Enter the email address or phone number of the person you want to add. If they use Windows, Office, Outlook.com, OneDrive, Skype, or Xbox, enter the email or phone number they use to sign in.
Email or phone
I don't have this person's sign-in information
Privacy statement
Next
Cancel

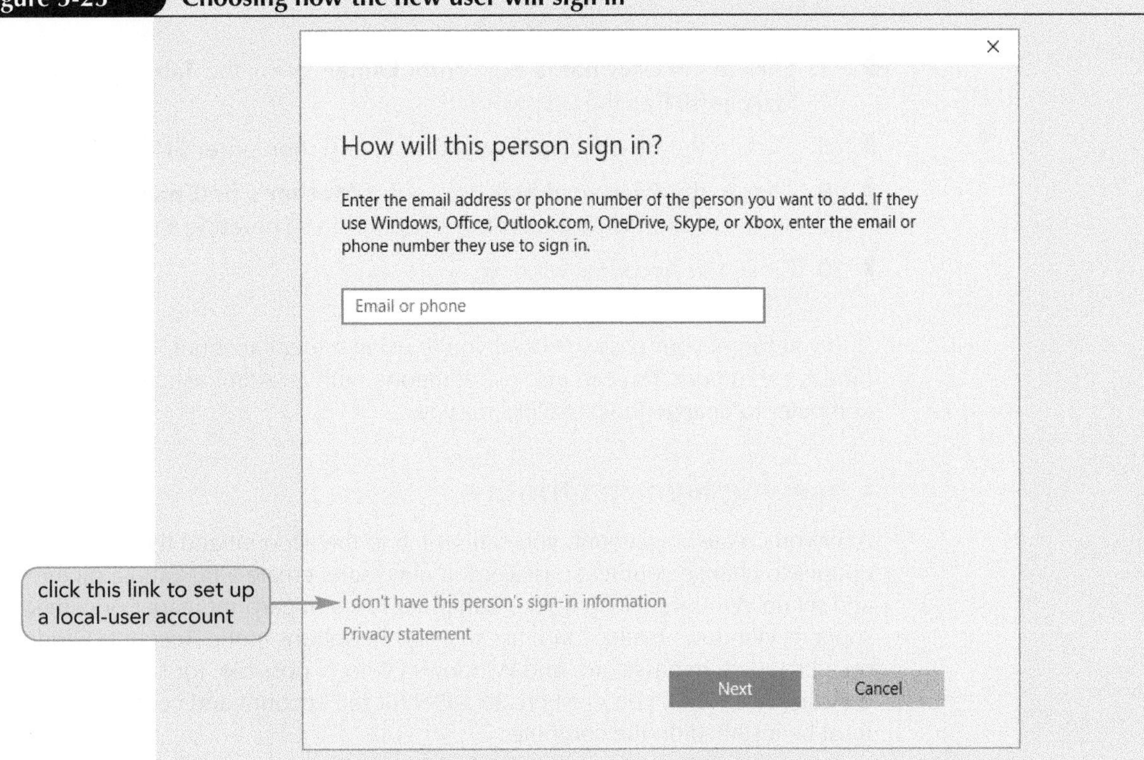

5. Click the **I don't have this person's sign-in information** link to continue creating a local-only user account.

6. Near the bottom of the Let's create your account window, click the **Add a user without a Microsoft account** link to display the Create an account for this PC window. See Figure 5-24.

Figure 5-24 Create an account for this PC window

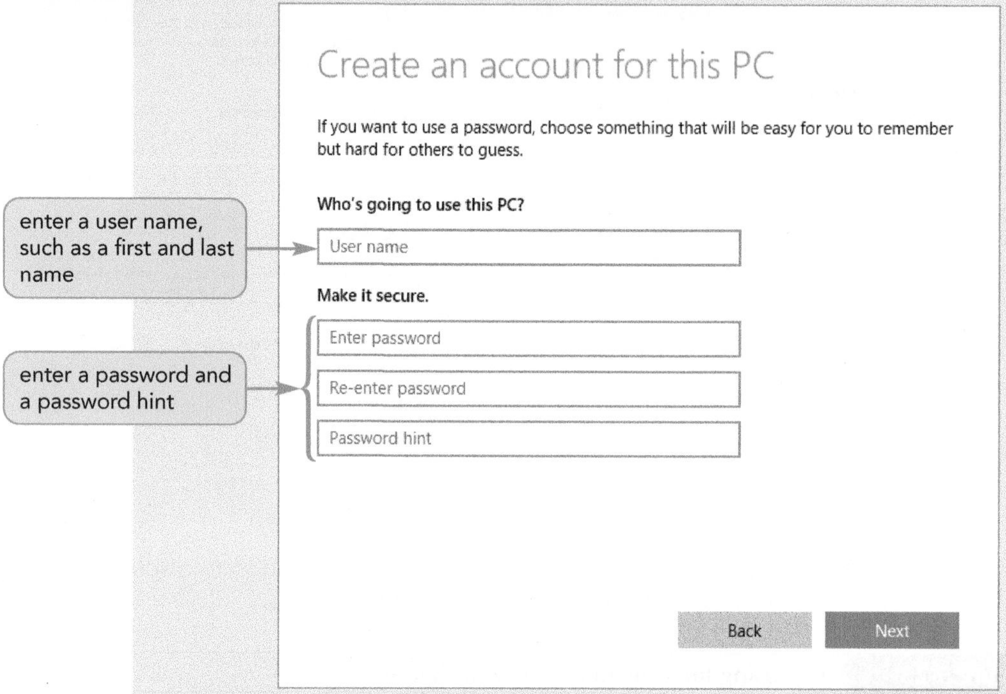

7. Click in the **User name** box, enter **Lamar**, press the **Tab** key, and then enter **SHA_jeff01** as the password.
8. Click in the **Re-enter password** box, and then enter **SHA_jeff01** again.
9. Click in the **Password hint** box, enter **Mother's first name** as the password hint, and then click the **Next** button to finish creating the account.
10. Close the Accounts window.

If you forget your password and you're using a local account, use your password hint as a reminder. You can also ask someone with an Administrator account on your computer to change the password for you.

Changing Sign-in Options

After you create an account, you can switch to the account and then change the sign-in options to change your text password, if necessary, create a PIN and a picture password, and set up Windows Hello if your computer has a fingerprint reader or camera that supports Windows Hello. You'll use the sign-in options in the Accounts window to set up a PIN, picture password, and Windows Hello, if possible, for Lamar. Before setting up Windows Hello, you must create a PIN for the account and compatible hardware must be installed on the computer.

To switch accounts:

1. Click the **Start** button to display the Start menu.
2. Click the **user icon** at the top of the Start menu, and then click **Lamar** to switch to the new account. Windows signs out of your account and displays the sign-in screen.
3. Type **SHA_jeff01** in the Password box, and then press the **Enter** key to sign in. Windows takes a few minutes to set up the new account.

Next, you can create a PIN. Lamar wants to use 5412 as the PIN, the date he founded the company.

To create a PIN:

1. On the desktop for the new account, click the **Start** button to display the Start menu, click **Settings** to start the Settings app, and then click **Accounts** to display the Accounts window for the Lamar account.
2. In the left pane, click **Sign-in options** to display the sign-in options in the right pane.
3. In the PIN section, click the **Add** button to display a window where you verify your account password.
4. Type **SHA_jeff01** in the Password box, and then click the **OK** button to verify the password. The Set up a PIN window opens. See Figure 5-25.

Figure 5-25 Create a PIN

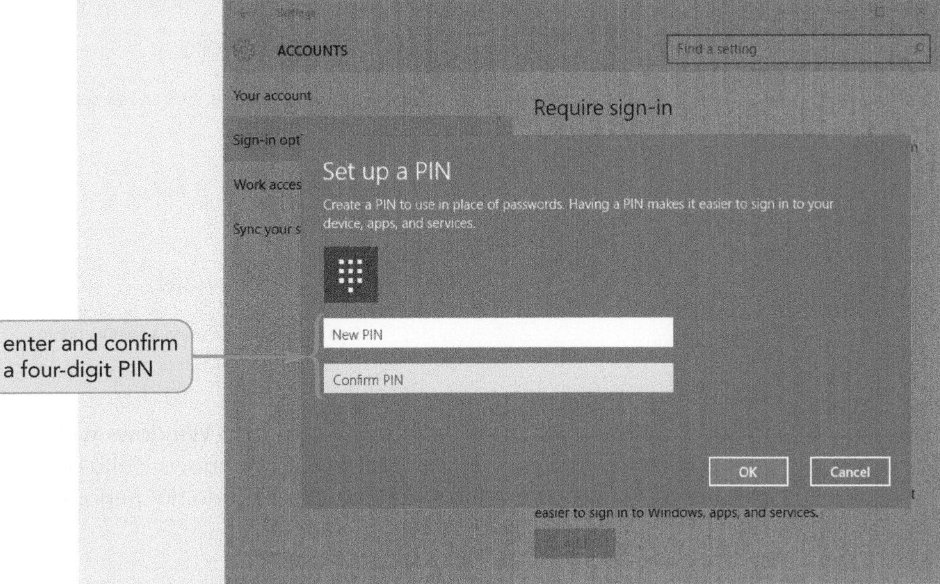

5. Enter **5412** in the New PIN box.

6. Click in the **Confirm PIN** box, type **5412**, and then click the **OK** button to create the PIN.

   If your computer is equipped with the hardware required for Windows Hello, the Windows Hello options are now available in the Accounts window. Scroll to display the Windows Hello option. See Figure 5-26. The computer in this figure has a fingerprint reader. If your computer has a camera compatible with Windows Hello, the Windows Hello option is different.

   Trouble? If the Windows Hello option does not appear in the Accounts window, your computer does not have the hardware required to use Windows Hello.

Figure 5-26 **Windows Hello option for fingerprint verification**

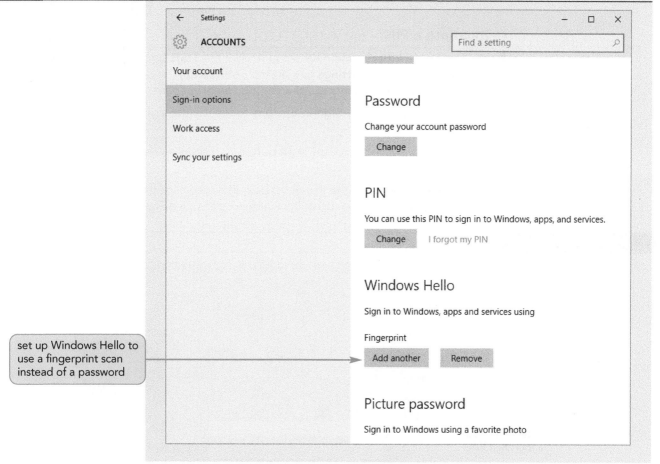

Next, you can set up Windows Hello to sign in to Windows with a fingerprint scan. If your computer has a camera compatible with Windows Hello or does not have hardware that works with Windows Hello, read but do not perform the following steps.

To set up Windows Hello:

1. In the Windows Hello section of the Accounts window, click the **Add another** button below the Fingerprint text to display the Windows Hello setup window, which introduces Windows Hello.
2. Click the **Get started** button to display a window requesting your PIN to verify your identity.

3. In the PIN box, type **5412** to display a window showing how to scan your index finger on the fingerprint reader for your computer.
4. Follow the on-screen instructions to scan your fingerprint a few times so that Windows recognizes it. See Figure 5-27.

Figure 5-27 Scanning your fingerprint

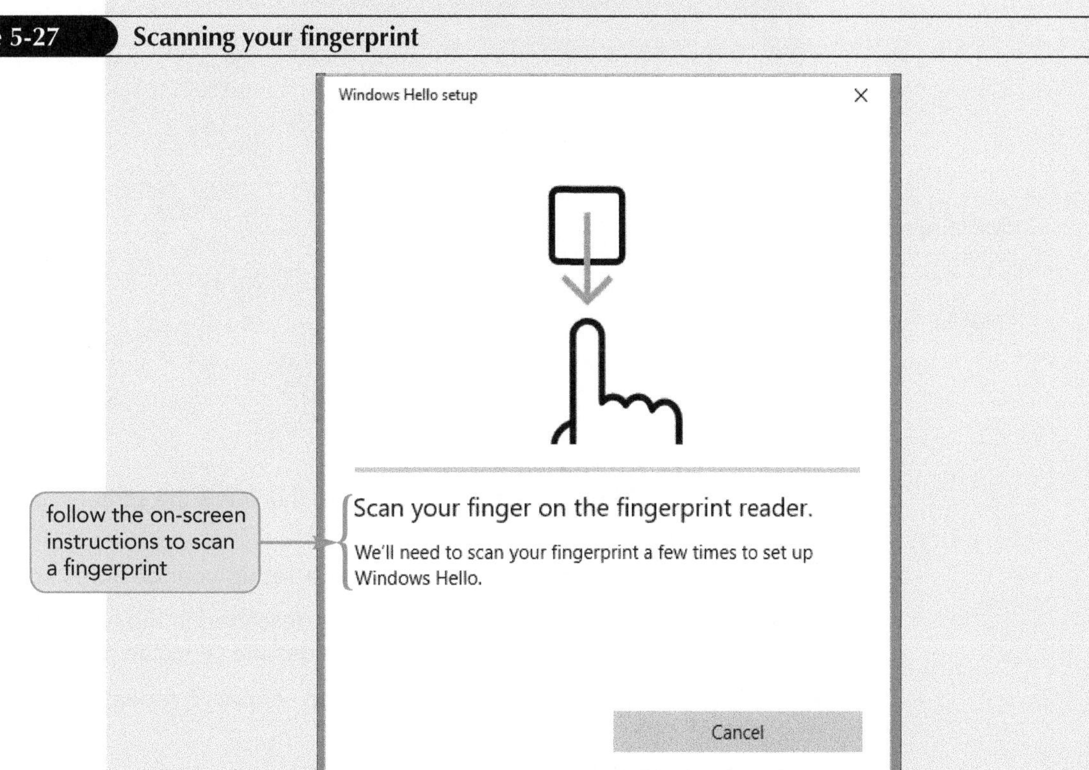
Windows Hello setup
Scan your finger on the fingerprint reader.
We'll need to scan your fingerprint a few times to set up Windows Hello.
Cancel
follow the on-screen instructions to scan a fingerprint

5. When the All set! window opens, click the **Close** button.

The next time you sign into the Lamar account, you can do so with a fingerprint scan. Next, you can create a picture password for Lamar's account. First, you'll take a screenshot of the Bing home page and then use that image for the picture password.

To create a picture password:

1. Start Microsoft Edge, maximize the window, and then navigate to the Bing website at **www.bing.com**.
2. When the Bing home page is displayed, press the **Print Screen** key to capture an image of the screen, and then close Microsoft Edge.
3. Start Paint.
4. Press the **Ctrl+V** keys to paste the screen image in a new Paint file.
5. Click the **Save** button on the Quick Access Toolbar, and then save the screen image as a PNG file named **Bing** in the Pictures folder. Close Paint.
6. In the Accounts window, click the **Add** button in the Picture password section.
7. Type **SHA_jeff01** in the Password box, and then click the **OK** button to verify the password and display the Picture password window. See Figure 5-28.

Figure 5-28 Picture password window

8. Click the **Choose picture** button, and then click the screenshot you saved in the Pictures folder.
9. Click the **Use this picture** button. The Set up your gestures screen appears.
10. Draw three gestures on the picture as described in the left pane of the screen. Select objects on the picture and use gestures you can remember easily.
11. When the Confirm your gestures screen appears, repeat the gestures in the same order you used in Step 10.

    Trouble? If the "Something's not right" message appears, click the Try again button and repeat Step 11, carefully redrawing the gestures you created. If you are still having trouble, click the Start over button and repeat Steps 10 and 11, but make sure you use simple gestures (for example, draw a line under a word or picture) and note their placement on the screen.
12. Click the **Finish** button, and then close the Accounts window.

To perform the remaining steps in the module, you need to sign out of the Standard account and sign in with your original (that is, Administrator) account.

To switch accounts:

1. Click the **Start** button to display the Start menu, click the **Lamar** user icon, and then click your user name. Windows signs out of your account and displays the sign-in screen.
2. Enter your password and then press the **Enter** key.

Now you and Lamar can show all of the Snap Home Automation employees how to create accounts and passwords on their computers.

Controlling Access to Your Computer

One way to manage access to your computer is to take advantage of **User Account Control (UAC)**, a feature that is turned on by default and can help prevent unauthorized changes to your computer. As you performed previous steps in this module, you might have seen UAC at work, asking for permission by providing an administrator password before performing actions that could affect your computer's settings. A User Account Control dialog box usually opens when a program or an action is about to start. The dialog box requests an administrator password as permission to start the program. By notifying you, UAC can help prevent malware from installing itself on or changing your computer without permission. Make sure the name of the action or program in the User Account Control dialog box is one that you intended to start. The dialog box indicates whether the program or action is part of Windows, is not part of Windows, is unidentified, or is blocked by the administrator. The dialog box also indicates whether the program has a digital certificate. If you are working on a computer on which you've set up an Administrator account and one or more Standard accounts, the User Account Control dialog box asks for an administrator password so that software can be installed only with the administrator's knowledge or permission.

The UAC feature is turned on by default and should not be turned off. You'll show Lamar how to make sure UAC is turned on for all of the Snap computers.

To verify that User Account Control is turned on:

1. Click in the **Ask me anything** box on the taskbar, type **Security and Maintenance**, and then click **Security and Maintenance** in the search results to open the Security and Maintenance window in the Control Panel.
2. Click the **Change User Account Control settings** link. The User Account Control Settings window opens. See Figure 5-29.

Figure 5-29 User Account Control Settings window

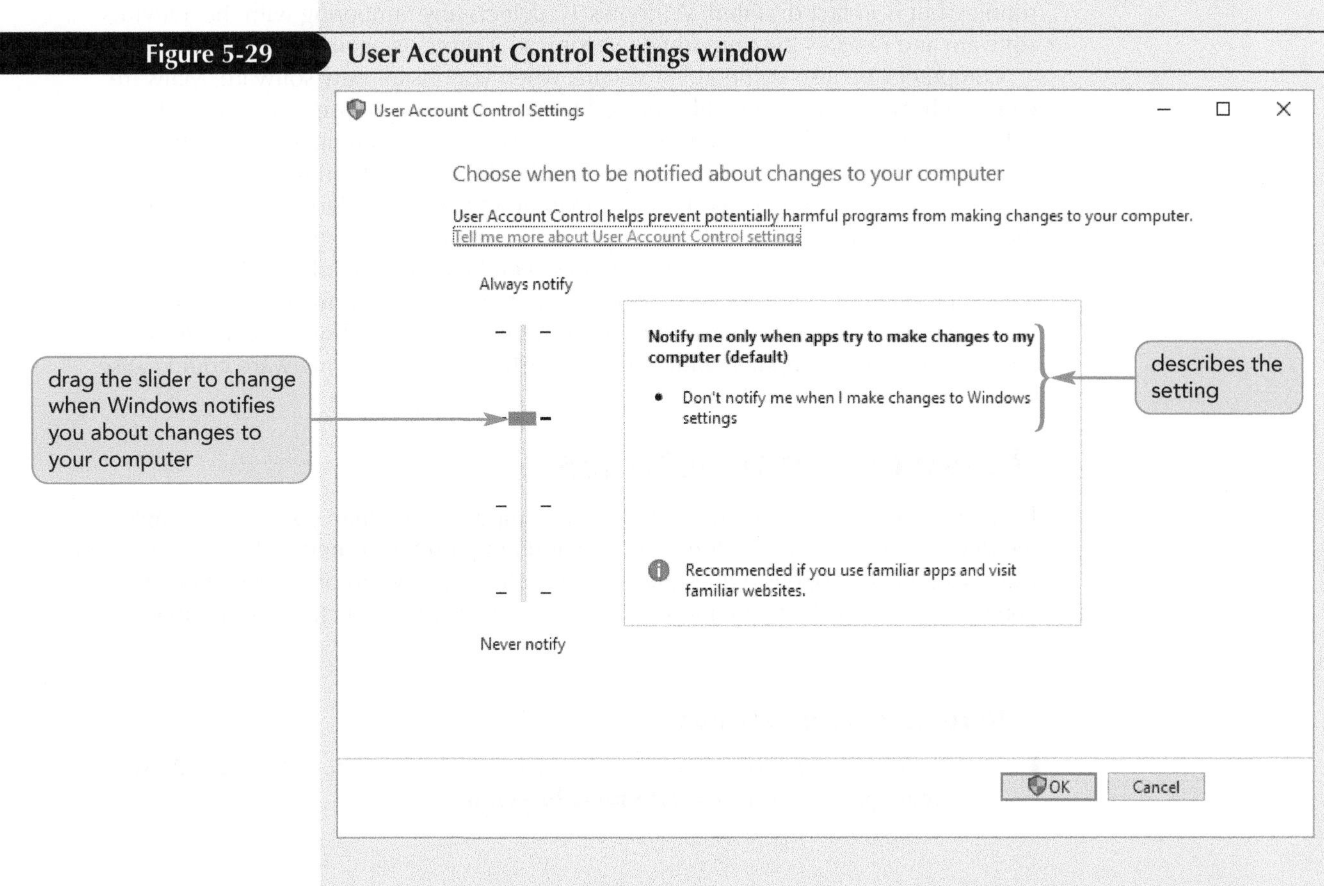

3. Drag the slider up and down to examine each setting, drag the slider to the **Notify me only when apps try to make changes to my computer (default)** setting, and then click the **OK** button.

   Trouble? If a User Account Control dialog box opens asking if you want to allow the program to make changes to this computer, click the Yes button.

Besides controlling access to your computer with passwords and UAC, you should be aware of security features that Windows provides at startup when installing apps.

Startup and App Security Features

Besides the tools and features covered so far in this module, Windows provides behind-the-scenes security protections that don't require your intervention. One of these is a boot method called **Unified Extensible Firmware Interface (UEFI)**.

When you turn on the power to a computer, it performs a series of steps and checks as it loads the operating system and prepares for you to use it. This startup process is called **booting** the computer. A computer with UEFI boots faster and in a more secure way than previous methods. Some malware is designed to start as the operating system loads. The computer is vulnerable at this point because antivirus software hasn't started yet. Rootkits in particular can interfere with operating system files and start before antivirus software can detect them. The Secure Boot feature in UEFI makes Windows 10 resistant to this type of malware. **Secure Boot** can detect when a file has interfered with the operating system and prevent that file from loading so it doesn't interfere with the operating system again.

After the operating system loads, the next application that starts is antivirus software. Malware sometimes tampers with antivirus software as it loads so it appears to be running but is in fact disabled. Windows 10 detects any tampering with the antivirus software and restores the unmodified version so it protects against malware.

Computers are also vulnerable to attack when you install new software. Malware can attach itself to legitimate files posted for download on websites, for example. When you download a new app, you might also be downloading a virus or worm. This scenario is very unlikely with apps you download from the Windows Store. Microsoft rigorously screens apps posted for download on the Windows Store to make sure they are free from malware. Microsoft provides a digital signature to verify the app is safe, and Windows tools such as the SmartScreen Filter and Windows Defender read the digital signature to make sure the file was not intercepted and changed during the download. Windows 10 also runs apps so they have only limited access to other resources on your computer, which minimizes the damage any malware could cause.

Restoring Your Settings

If you are working in a computer lab or on a computer other than your own, complete the steps in this section to restore the original settings on the computer. If a User Account Control dialog box opens requesting an Administrator password or confirmation after you perform any of the following steps, enter the password or click the Yes button.

To restore your settings:

1. Display the Control Panel home page in Category view, click **System and Security**, and then click **Windows Firewall**.

2. In the left pane of the Windows Firewall window, click the **Allow an app or feature through Windows Firewall** link, and then click the **Change settings** button.
3. Click the **Windows Media Player** check box to remove the check mark, and then click the **OK** button.
4. Start the Settings app, click **Update & security**, and then click the **Advanced options** link. Click the **Notify to schedule restart** button, and then click **Automatic (recommended)**. Close the Advanced Options window.
5. Start Microsoft Edge, click the **More** button [...] in the navigation bar, and then click **Settings** to display the Settings pane. Click the **View advanced settings** button and then click the **slider button** to turn the Send Do Not Track requests setting from On to Off.
6. In the Cookies section, click the **Block only third party cookies** box, and then click your original setting.
7. Click the **chevron** button [«] at the top of the Advanced settings pane to display the Settings pane, and then click the **Choose what to clear** button to display the list of browsing data you can clear. Click the check boxes as necessary to restore the original settings. Close Microsoft Edge.
8. In the Windows Firewall window, return to the Control Panel home page, click **User Accounts**, and then click **Remove user accounts**. Click the **Lamar** icon for the local user account you created, click **Delete the account**, click the **Delete Files** button, and then click the **Delete Account** button. Click the **Yes** button to confirm you want to remove the account. Close the Control Panel window.
9. Close all open windows.

REVIEW

Session 5.2 Quick Check

1. A(n) ____________ is an electronic security mark added to a file to verify its authenticity.
2. Explain how the SmartScreen Filter uses reputation checking to find potentially harmful websites.
3. How can you check an individual website to determine whether it has been reported as a potentially unsafe site?
4. What happens when you remove a file from the Downloads list in Microsoft Edge?
5. What threats do some pop-up ads pose?
6. A(n) ____________ is a collection of information that indicates the files and folders you can access, the types of changes you can make to the computer, and your preferred appearance settings.
7. In Microsoft Edge, you can use ____________ to hide the history of the webpages you visited.
8. What is Windows Hello?

PRACTICE

Review Assignments

There are no Data Files needed for the Review Assignments.

Lamar recently bought a new Windows 10 computer for you to share with Christie Chen, one of his project managers. Christie often transfers photos of client homes and businesses to her computer using a wireless camera. She is also preparing to visit a client in Oakland, California, and is concerned about the security of her computer during the visit. You'll show Christie how to keep the new computer secure. Complete the following steps, noting your original settings so you can restore them later:

1. Open the Windows Firewall window, and then perform the following tasks:
   a. Choose to allow an app through Windows Firewall.
   b. Change the settings to add Wireless Portable Devices to the allowed apps list on private networks.
   c. If the Allowed apps window is maximized, click the Restore Down button to resize it.
2. Start the Settings app, and then display the Advanced Options window for Windows Update. Display your update history.
3. Arrange the Allowed apps window and the View Your Update History window to display the setting you changed for Windows Firewall. Press the Print Screen key to capture an image of the screen. Open Paint or WordPad, and then press the Ctrl+V keys to paste the image in a new file. Save the file as **Review Settings** in the Module5 > Review folder provided with your Data Files.
4. Close all open windows. Start Windows Defender and then use it to perform a quick scan on your computer.
5. With the Windows Defender window open on your desktop and displaying the scan results, press the Print Screen key to capture an image of the window. Open Paint or WordPad, and then press the Ctrl+V keys to paste the image in a new file. Save the file as **Defender** in the Module5 > Review folder provided with your Data Files. Close all open windows.
6. In Microsoft Edge, open a webpage in your Favorites list or go to the home page of a popular search engine, such as Google (www.google.com) or Bing (www.bing.com). Open the webpage with Internet Explorer, and then arrange the Internet Explorer and Microsoft Edge windows side by side. In Internet Explorer, use the SmartScreen Filter to verify this website is not a phishing website.
7. Make sure the Pop-up Blocker in Microsoft Edge is turned on, and then visit a website that uses pop-up windows such as www.movies.com. Enter a search term (for example, spider man) to display a Notification bar explaining that only secure content is displayed. Press the Print Screen key to capture an image of the desktop. Open Paint or WordPad, and then press the Ctrl+V keys to paste the image in a new file. Save the file as **Blocked** in the Module5 > Review folder provided with your Data Files.
8. Close the Notification bar in Microsoft Edge, close the SmartScreen Filter dialog box in Internet Explorer, and then close Internet Explorer.
9. In Microsoft Edge, turn on InPrivate Browsing and then perform the following tasks:
   a. Visit the California state website at www.ca.gov.
   b. Click the Visit & Play tab.
   c. Click the Activities & Events link.
10. In the original Microsoft Edge window you used in Step 7 (that is, the movie website), pin the Hub to the window, display the History list, and then click the Last hour or the Today link, if necessary, to display websites you visited today except for those visited during your InPrivate Browsing session.

11. Perform the following tasks to capture an image of the windows:
    a. Resize the InPrivate Browsing window so it appears next to the window displaying the History list.
    b. Press the Print Screen key to capture an image of the desktop.
    c. Open Paint or WordPad, and then press the Ctrl+V keys to paste the image in a new file.
    d. Save the file as **InPrivate** in the Module5 > Review folder provided with your Data Files.
    e. Close all open windows.
12. Create a PIN for your user account using **6695** as the number.
13. With the Set up a PIN window open, press the Print Screen key to capture an image of the screen. Open Paint or WordPad, and then press the Ctrl+V keys to paste the image in a new file. Save the file as **Pin** in the Module5 > Review folder provided with your Data Files.
14. To restore the settings on your computer, remove Wireless Portable Devices from the Windows Firewall allowed apps list.
15. Close all open windows.

APPLY

Case Problem 1

There are no Data Files needed for this Case Problem.

Rockwell Accounting Nicole Rockwell runs a small business in Windsor, Connecticut, called Rockwell Accounting, which helps small businesses manage their finances and plan for growth. Nicole uses a laptop computer running Windows 10 to create most of her business plans and other documents, which she develops while visiting clients. She is concerned about maintaining security as she researches competitors for her clients. In particular, she has experienced problems with pop-up ads and spyware and wants to know how to block pop-ups in Microsoft Edge. You'll help her use the Windows 10 security settings to protect her computer. Complete the following steps, noting your original settings so you can restore them later:

1. Open the Windows Firewall window, and then add File and Printer Sharing to the Windows Firewall allowed apps list for private and public networks. Leave the Allowed apps window open.
2. Start Windows Defender and then use it to perform a quick scan on your computer.
3. Arrange all windows to show the settings you changed, and then press the Print Screen key to capture an image of the desktop. Open Paint or WordPad, and then press the Ctrl+V keys to paste the image in a new file. Save the file as **File Security** in the Module5 > Case1 folder provided with your Data Files. Close all open windows.
4. In Microsoft Edge, display the pop-ups setting, and then set Microsoft Edge to block pop-ups, if necessary. Press the Print Screen key to capture an image of the dialog box. Open Paint or WordPad, and then press the Ctrl+V keys to paste the image in a new file. Save the file as **Popups** in the Module5 > Case1 folder provided with your Data Files.
5. Set Microsoft Edge to clear browsing data for your browsing history, cookies, and saved website data. Press the Print Screen key to capture an image of the window. Open Paint or WordPad, and then press the Ctrl+V keys to paste the image in a new file. Save the file as **Browsing** in the Module5 > Case1 folder provided with your Data Files. Close Microsoft Edge.
6. Start a Windows app and then capture the screen. Save the image as a file named **Windows App** in the Pictures folder. Close the Windows app.
7. Create a picture password for your user account using the Windows App picture. Enter the required three gestures.
8. Before you confirm the three gestures, press the Print Screen key to capture an image of the screen. Open Paint or WordPad, and then press the Ctrl+V keys to paste the image in a new file. Save the file as **PicPassword** in the Module5 > Case1 folder provided with your Data Files. Confirm the gestures and then close the Picture password window.

9. Restore the settings on your computer. Remove File and Printer Sharing from the Windows Firewall allowed apps list. Change the Pop-up Blocker setting to its default setting, if necessary. Remove the picture password from your user account, and then delete the Windows App file from the Pictures folder.
10. Close all open windows.

CHALLENGE

Case Problem 2

There are no Data Files needed for this Case Problem.

Shorewood Health Center Kelly Robson is the director of the Shorewood Health Center, a clinic in Shorewood, Wisconsin. The Shorewood Health Center has three mobile walk-in clinics that Shorewood residents can visit to receive flu shots and vaccinations, and request other health services. Because the Health Center computers are not part of the municipal network, Kelly uses Remote Desktop to connect to other computers in the city, and regularly uses Microsoft Edge to run the organization. She has experienced problems with spyware and viruses, and wants to know when to trust websites she visits. You'll help her use the Windows 10 security settings to protect her computer. Complete the following steps, noting your original settings so you can restore them later:

1. Change the settings to add Windows Remote Management to the Windows Firewall allowed apps list for private and public networks. Capture an image of the Allowed apps window, and then save it in a Paint file named **Firewall** in the Module5 > Case2 folder provided with your Data Files.
2. **Explore** In Windows Update, check for updates. When Windows Update finishes checking, capture an image of the Update & Security window, and save it as a Paint file named **Update Check** in the Module5 > Case2 folder provided with your Data Files. Close all open windows.
3. In Microsoft Edge, open a webpage in your Favorites list or go to the home page of a popular search engine, such as Google (www.google.com) or Bing (www.bing.com). Open the webpage with Internet Explorer and then maximize the Internet Explorer window. Use the SmartScreen Filter to verify this website is not a phishing website. Capture an image of the Internet Explorer window and SmartScreen Filter dialog box, and then save it in a Paint file named **Filter** in the Module5 > Case2 folder provided with your Data Files.
4. **Explore** Close the SmartScreen Filter dialog box, click the Tools button in the navigation bar, and then click Internet options to open the Internet Options dialog box. On the General tab in the Browsing history section, click the Delete button to display the browsing data you can delete in Internet Explorer. Capture an image of the dialog box, and then save the image as a Paint file named **Delete** in the Module5 > Case2 folder provided with your Data Files.
5. **Explore** Click the Cancel button to close the Delete Browsing History dialog box. Click the Privacy tab, and then click the Advanced button to open the Advanced Privacy Settings. Change the settings to accept all first-party cookies and prompt you for all third-party cookies. Capture an image of the dialog box, and then save the image as a Paint file named **IE Cookies** in the Module5 > Case2 folder provided with your Data Files.
6. Click the Cancel button to close the Advanced Privacy Settings dialog box, close the Internet Options dialog box, and then close Internet Explorer. Close Microsoft Edge.
7. **Explore** Open the Control Panel and then display a window that lets you change your account type. Start the Settings app and then use it to display your account information. With both windows open, capture an image of the desktop, and then save the image as a Paint file named **Accounts** in the Module5 > Case2 folder provided with your Data Files.
8. Restore the settings on your computer. Remove Windows Remote Management from the Windows Firewall allowed programs list. Change the Advanced Privacy Settings for accepting all first-party cookies and prompting you for all third-party cookies to their original settings.
9. Delete browsing history and close all open windows.

CHALLENGE

Case Problem 3

There are no Data Files needed for this Case Problem.

Beowulf Books Cliff Gervase owns Beowulf Books in Oxford, Mississippi, and has designed the bookstore as a casual gathering place for the neighborhood. Besides selling books and hosting readings, Cliff offers Internet connections and computers to customers who want to use them. His school-age son often visits him in the bookstore and uses the computers to do homework. Cliff is particularly concerned about the security of the computers when customers access the Internet and check email. You'll help him use the Windows 10 security settings to protect a public computer. Complete the following steps, noting your original settings so you can restore them later:

Explore 1. In Windows Firewall, block all incoming connections for private and public networks. (*Hint*: Select options in the Customize Settings window.)

Explore 2. Set Windows Defender to perform a custom scan of your removable disk or any disk other than your hard disk. Keep the Windows Defender dialog box open showing the drive you selected to scan.

3. Capture an image of the screen. Save the image as a Paint file named **Scan** in the Module5 > Case3 folder provided with your Data Files. Close all open windows.

Explore 4. In Microsoft Edge, start an InPrivate Browsing session. Select options to clear browsing data that includes passwords, media licenses, and location permissions. Clear any other selected options. Capture an image of the desktop, and then save it as a Paint file named **Private** in the Module5 > Case3 folder provided with your Data Files.

5. Clear browsing history and then close all open windows.

Explore 6. Start Mail. Use the Settings button to display the Trust Center settings. Capture an image of the desktop, and then save it in a Paint file named **Trust** in the Module5 > Case3 folder provided with your Data Files. Close Mail.

Explore 7. Begin to set up an account for a family member. (*Hint*: Open the Accounts window in the Settings app, select Family & other users, and then click the Add a family member button.)

8. With the Add a child or an adult dialog box open on the desktop, capture an image of the desktop, and then save it as a Paint file named **Family** in the Module5 > Case3 folder provided with your Data Files. Click the Cancel button to close the dialog box, and then close the Settings app.

9. Restore the settings on your computer. Restore the original settings in Windows Firewall so you are not blocking all incoming connections. Restore Windows Defender to scan using its original settings.

10. Close all open windows.

RESEARCH

Case Problem 4

There are no Data Files needed for this Case Problem.

Rodriguez Engineering Paco Rodriguez is the president of Rodriguez Engineering, a firm in Towson, Maryland, that performs environmental clean-up on building sites. Paco wants to protect the computers his staff uses against security threats. To do so, he first wants to understand who typically attacks computers and their data. He also wants to learn more about the types of attacks people use to access computers, and how much damage such attacks have caused. He asks you to research these topics and report your findings. Complete the following steps:

1. Use your favorite search engine to find information about the types of people behind attacks on desktop computers. (Attacks on networks are in a separate category.) Search for information about the following types of attackers:
   a. White hat hackers
   b. Black hat hackers
   c. Blue hat hackers
   d. Script kiddies
2. Use your favorite search engine to find information about the techniques attackers use to exploit a computer. Search for information about the following types of techniques:
   a. Smurf attacks
   b. Password cracking
   c. Social engineering
   d. Spoofing or phishing attacks
   e. Vulnerability scanners
3. Use a word processor to summarize your findings in one or two pages. Be sure to define any new terms and cite the websites where you found your information. Save the document as an RTF file named **Attacks**.
4. Clear browsing history and then close all open windows.

MODULE 6

Searching for Information

Finding Apps, Settings, Files, and Information

OBJECTIVES

Session 6.1
- Develop search strategies
- Find information on your computer using Cortana
- Search for apps and settings
- Find files by name, type, and category
- Filter the search results

Session 6.2
- Use Boolean filters in advanced searches
- Search the web using Cortana and Microsoft Edge
- Use search engines
- Narrow searches using advanced search features
- Add a search engine to Microsoft Edge

Case | *Ithaca Imports*

A few years ago, Howard Brandt opened Ithaca Imports, a shop in Ithaca, New York, that imports prints, crafts, and other artistic goods from around the world. The shop then sells pieces to gift shops, home décor stores, and the general public. Recently, Howard received a shipment of prints of European paintings and photos of sculptures, which he wants to post on the shop's website. He hired you to assist him with the website and at the shop. Your duties include taking digital photos of the imports, organizing them logically, and finding items to feature on the website to keep it up to date.

In this module, you'll learn how to develop strategies for finding apps, data, files, folders, and settings on your computer and the web and to use the Windows 10 search tools in that pursuit. You'll refine your searches by using advanced techniques such as Boolean filters and multiple criteria. You'll also learn how to apply these search strategies when using Cortana to find information on your computer and when using Microsoft Edge to find information on the web.

STARTING DATA FILES

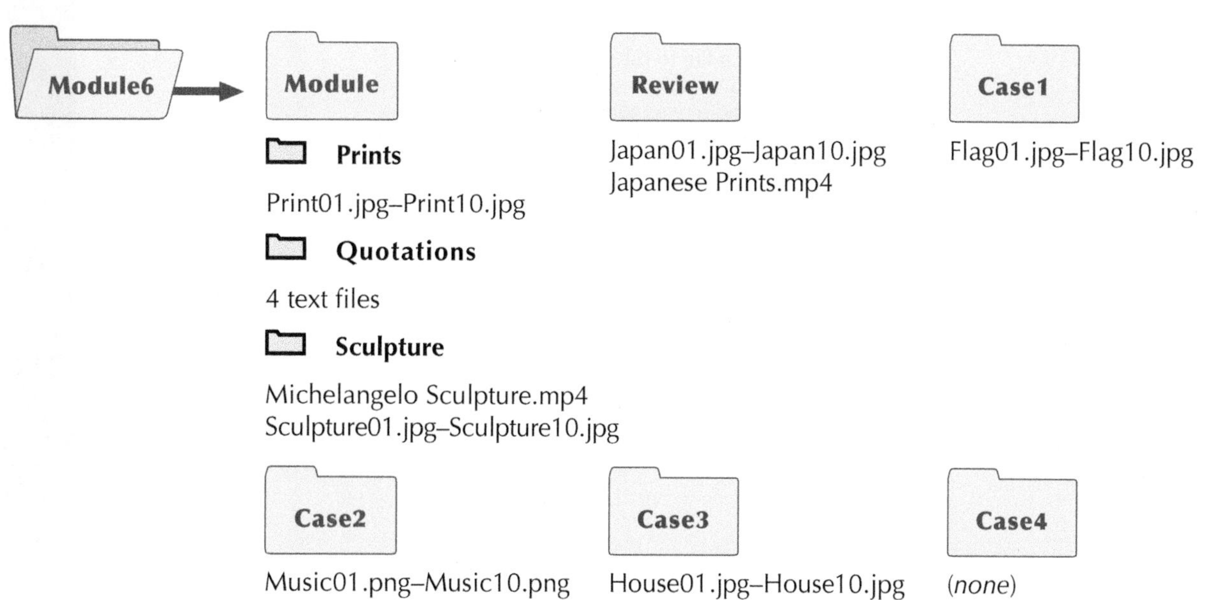

Session 6.1 Visual Overview:

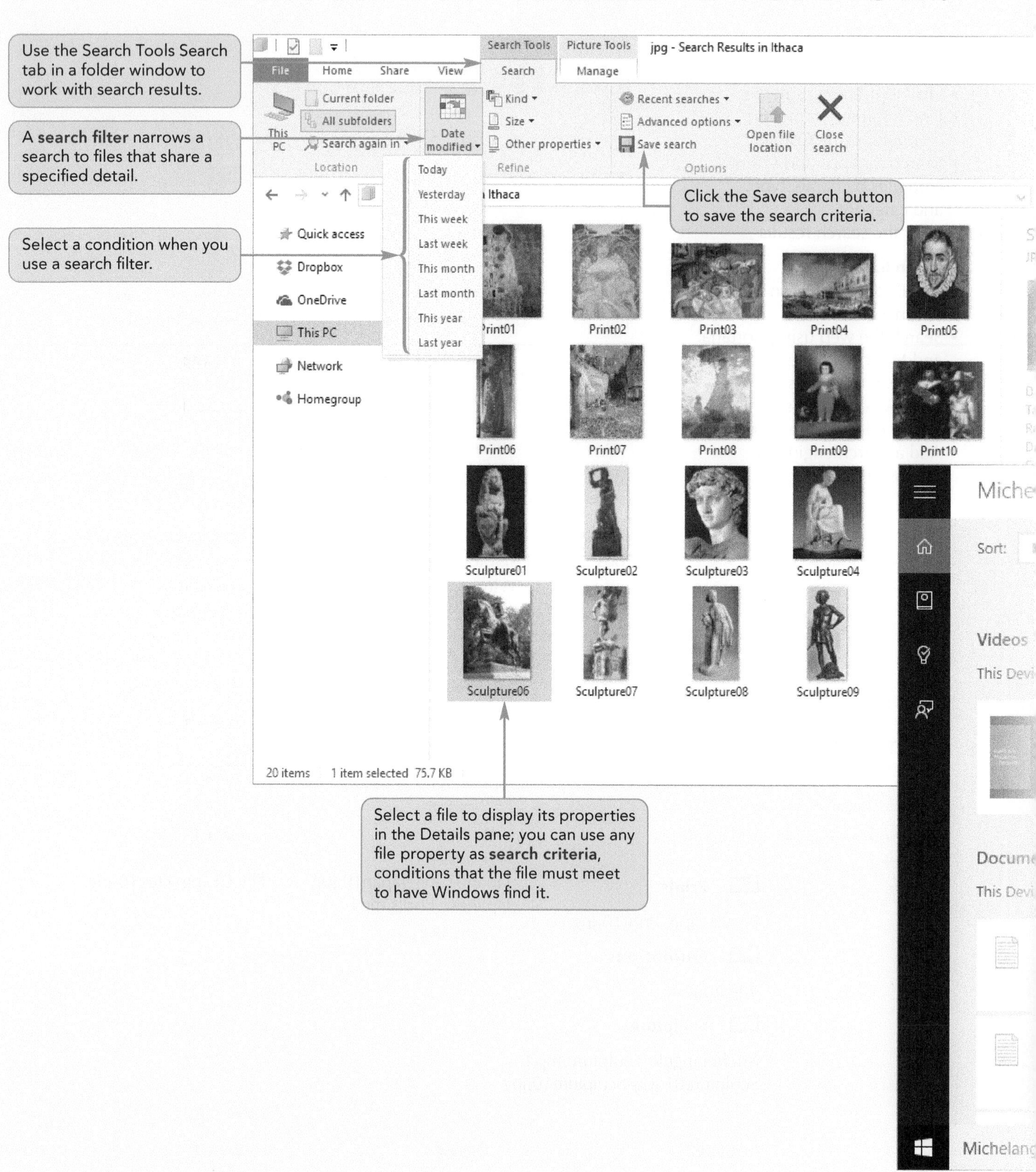

Searching for Files

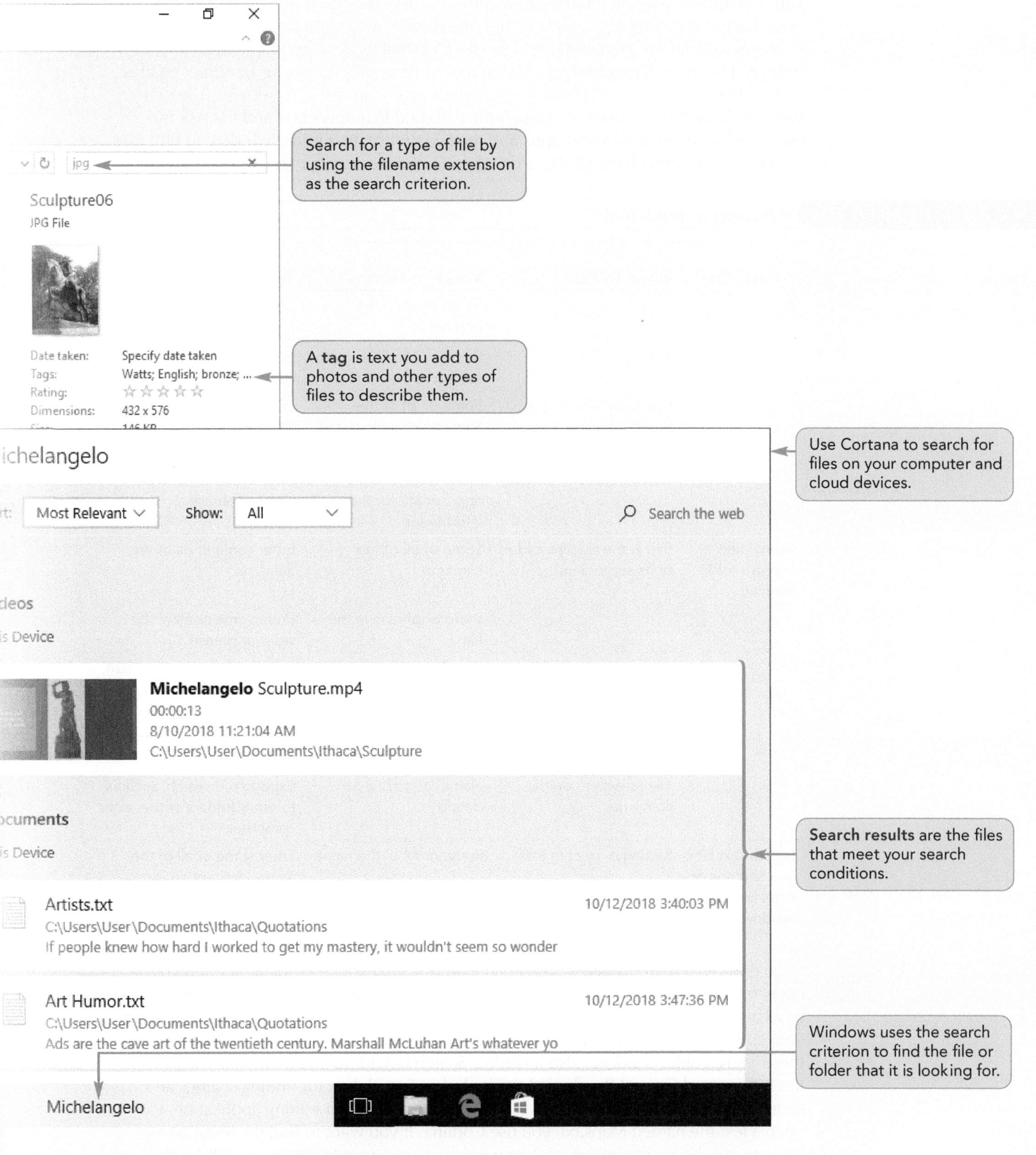
jpg
Sculpture06
JPG File
Date taken: Specify date taken
Tags: Watts; English; bronze; ...
Rating:
Dimensions: 432 x 576
Search for a type of file by using the filename extension as the search criterion.
A tag is text you add to photos and other types of files to describe them.
Most Relevant
Show: All
Search the web
Use Cortana to search for files on your computer and cloud devices.
Michelangelo Sculpture.mp4
00:00:13
8/10/2018 11:21:04 AM
C:\Users\User\Documents\Ithaca\Sculpture
Artists.txt
10/12/2018 3:40:03 PM
C:\Users\User\Documents\Ithaca\Quotations
If people knew how hard I worked to get my mastery, it wouldn't seem so wonder
Art Humor.txt
10/12/2018 3:47:36 PM
C:\Users\User\Documents\Ithaca\Quotations
Ads are the cave art of the twentieth century. Marshall McLuhan Art's whatever yo
Search results are the files that meet your search conditions.
Windows uses the search criterion to find the file or folder that it is looking for.
Michelangelo

Developing Search Strategies

As you install apps and store data on your computer, the number of files and folders you have grows, making it harder to locate a particular item. Using an efficient organization scheme helps you find files and folders when you need them. Knowing your way around the Start menu and the desktop makes it easier to find apps and settings. However, if pinpointing an item means browsing dozens or hundreds of files and folders, or if you don't know where to look, you can use a Windows 10 search tool. You have already used the Search the web and Windows box and the Ask me anything box (Cortana) to find apps and the Search box in a folder window to find files. Figure 6-1 offers recommendations on when to choose one search tool over another.

Figure 6-1 **Choosing a search tool**

Search Tool	What to Find	What You Know	Technique to Use
Cortana	App	Some or all of the app name	Enter some or all of the app name
	Setting	Some or all of the setting name	Enter some or all of the setting name
	File anywhere on the computer, including system files	Some or all of the filename or a file detail	Enter some or all of the filename or enter a detail, an operator, and a filter
	Information on the web	Word or phrase appropriate for the information	Enter some or all of the word or phrase
Search text box in a folder window	File in the current folder or its subfolders	Some or all of the filename	Enter some or all of the filename
		Word or phrase in the file	Enter some or all of the word or phrase
		Details listed below the Search text box	Select a detail, such as size, and then select a filter, such as Large
		Details not listed below the Search text box	Enter a detail, an operator, and a filter
	File anywhere on the computer	Name, contents, or details	Expand the search, such as to other folders or the entire computer
Search text box in a Settings or Control Panel window	Setting or system tool	Some or all of the name	Enter some or all of the name, description, or keyword

To develop a search strategy, you need to know what you are looking for and you need to have some information about the item. Start by identifying what you want to find or what task you want to perform. Cortana can help you find apps, settings, and files on your computer and information on the web, so you can use Cortana to search for any of these items. Folder windows also include a Search box to help you find files. Likewise, the Settings and Control Panel windows include a Search box for finding settings and system tools. For example, if you want to start Notepad, a text-editing application, to open a text file named Maps.txt, you use Cortana. If you want to find the Maps.txt file, you can use the Search box in a folder window. If you want to set the default app for displaying maps, you can use Cortana or the Search box in the Settings window.

Next, you need to identify what you already know about the item you want to find. This information becomes your search criteria, which are conditions that the app, setting, or file must meet to have Windows find it. These conditions help you define and narrow your search so you can quickly find the item you want. For example, if you are searching for an app and using "explore" as the search condition, Windows locates and displays every app that matches that condition—in other words, all apps whose names contain a word starting with "explore," such as Internet Explorer and File Explorer. Note that case doesn't matter—you could type explore, Explore, or even EXPLORE to include Internet Explorer and File Explorer in the search results.

When you know what you want to find and what information you have about the item, you can choose the search tool that best fits your needs, and then use search criteria that are most likely to find the item. For example, suppose you want to find a photo that you took last New Year's Eve and stored somewhere in the Pictures folder. Because you know the location of the photo, you can use the Search box in the Pictures folder window. You also know when you took the photo, so you can search for files created on 12/31/2017.

Using Cortana to Search for Apps and Information

You have already used the Search the web and Windows box to find apps installed on your computer. After you activated Cortana, the label for this box became "Ask me anything." This module uses Cortana as a major search tool in Windows 10, and therefore assumes that you have already activated Cortana, which was covered in an earlier module. If you have not activated Cortana, you will be able to perform some, but not all, of the steps in this module. Some of the explanations that refer to Cortana do not apply to the Search the web and Windows box.

If you want to find an app, click the Start button or the Ask me anything box and start typing the name of the app. The text appears in the search box on the taskbar. As you type, Cortana displays a pane with the search results, which are separated into categories, such as apps installed on your computer, apps available in the Windows Store, settings, folders, websites, and files. Files might be further categorized as music, photos, videos, or documents. For example, if you click in the Ask me anything box and begin to type *photo*, the results include apps whose names contain a word starting with the text you typed, including Photos, an app that comes with Windows 10, and Photo Editor, which is available in the Windows Store. The results might also include settings for choosing a default photo viewer, a folder named Vacation Photos, and a file named American photography.docx.

The search results display the name and icon associated with the item so you can identify it. For some items, Cortana also displays the source or location. For example, when Windows apps that come with Windows 10, such as Calendar and Weather, are displayed in the search results, they include the text "Trusted Windows Store app." This notation indicates that they are available in the Windows Store and have been verified as safe apps by their vendor.

When the item you want appears in the search results, you can stop typing and then click the item to access it. For example, you can click an app's name to start the app, click a document name to open it in its default app, or click a setting to open it in the Settings app or Control Panel.

Howard often works with an art dealer in Amsterdam, the Netherlands, to buy and sell prints of artwork. He needs a quick way to convert the price of a print from U.S. dollars to euros when he's selling a print, and to convert from euros to U.S. dollars when he's buying a print. He asks you to find tools on his Windows 10 computer that let him perform these tasks.

You know that one app Howard can use to convert currencies is the Calculator app. You'll show him how to use Cortana to find the Calculator app.

To search for an app:

1. Click in the **Ask me anything** box, and then type **cal** to search for apps whose name contains a word starting with "cal." See Figure 6-2. Your search results will differ but should include the Calculator app.

Figure 6-2 App search results

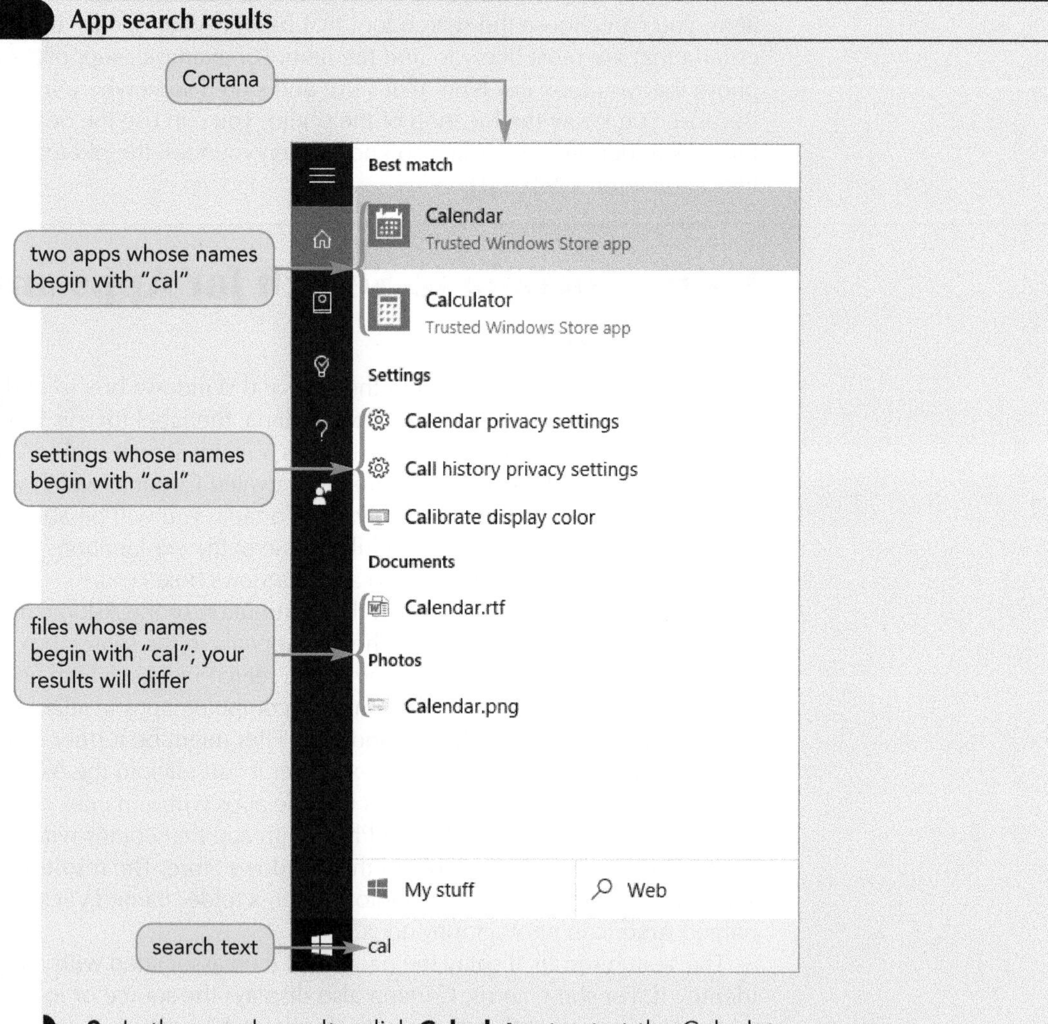

2. In the search results, click **Calculator** to start the Calculator program.

Howard has a print that he usually sells for $25 and wants to calculate the cost in euros. Before he can do that, he needs to know how many euros are equivalent to $1. You'll show him how to use Cortana to find up-to-date currency information.

To use Cortana to search for information:

1. Click in the **Ask me anything box**, and then type **$1 is how many euros**. Cortana retrieves the latest currency conversion information from the web and then displays the results. See Figure 6-3. Your results might differ.

   Trouble? If you pressed the Enter key, your browser probably opened. Close the browser and then repeat Step 1, making sure not to press the Enter key.

Figure 6-3 Cortana displaying currency conversion

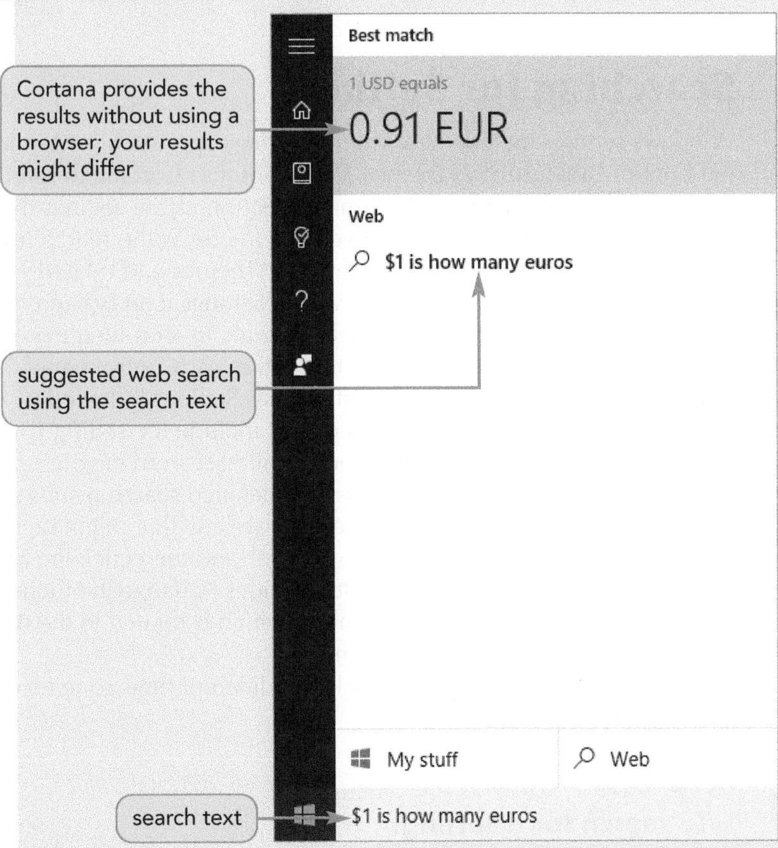

2. Click a blank area of the desktop to close the search results.

Now you and Howard know that $1 currently equals 0.91 euros. You'll use the Calculator to determine the cost in euros of the $25 print.

To use the Calculator to convert dollars to euros:

1. Click in the Calculator window to make it the active program, if necessary.
2. Type **25*.91** and then press the **Enter** key to display the results: 22.75.
3. Click the **Close** button [X] to close the Calculator app.

TIP

Instead of typing the equation, you can use the Calculator keypad.

Howard wonders if Cortana could do the complete conversion so he doesn't need to use the Calculator app. You'll use Cortana again to find how many euros equal $25.

To use Cortana to find more detailed information:

1. Click in the **Ask me anything box**, and then type **$25 equals how many euros**. Cortana retrieves the latest currency conversion information from the web, performs the calculation, and then displays the results: 22.67 EUR. Your results might differ.
2. Click a blank area of the desktop to close the search results.

Besides converting between euros and dollars, Howard wants to display a clock that shows the current time in Amsterdam. You'll use Cortana to look for such a tool on Howard's computer.

Searching for Settings

Windows settings include items in the Settings app, such as Windows Update, and in the Control Panel, such as themes. When you use Cortana to search for settings, the search results begin with the Best match section, those settings that include the search text in their name. For example, if you use *theme* as the search text, the Best match section includes "Change the theme" and "Themes and related settings." In the search results, a Settings app item appears with a Settings icon and identifies its location as "System settings." A Control Panel tool with an icon identifying the tool, such as the Personalization icon, identifies its location as "Control panel."

After the Best match section, Cortana lists Settings followed by other items such as Folders, Files, or Store. If the results do not include the setting you want, you can click the My stuff button to conduct a more detailed search on your computer and other connected drives, such as OneDrive. The detailed search results are also organized into categories, including Settings. The settings are any that might be related to your search term. For example, if you search for "theme" and then click the My stuff button, the Settings category in the search results includes "Change the theme," as in the original results, and "Choose your accent color," which is related to the theme but does not include the word "theme" in its name.

To find a tool that displays a clock in a different time zone for Howard, you can use *clock* as the search text.

To search for a setting:

1. Click in the **Ask me anything box**, and then type **clock** to search for apps, settings, files, and web search terms that contain the word "clock," which is bold in the search results. See Figure 6-4. Your results might differ.

Figure 6-4 Searching for a setting

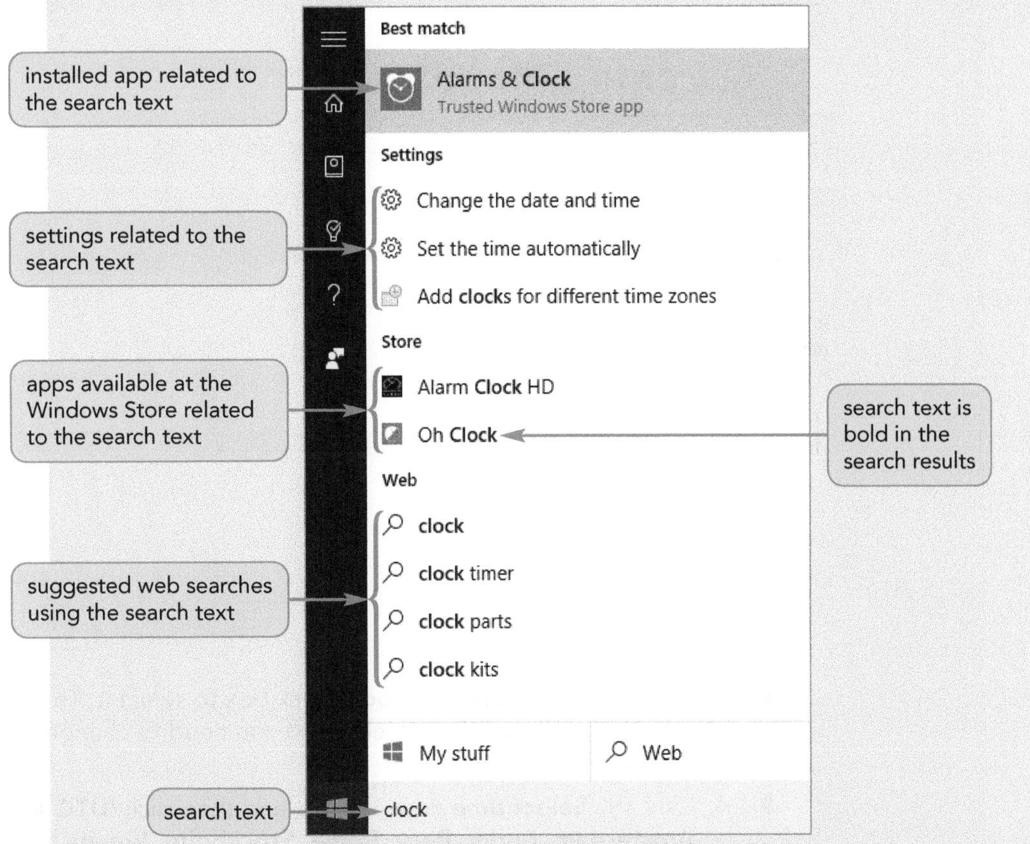

The results include an app in the Best match section, a few settings in the Settings section, followed by apps at the Store and popular search terms containing the word "clock." The "Add clocks for different time zones" setting seems the most promising.

2. Click **Add clocks for different time zones** to display the Date and Time dialog box, which is open to the Additional Clocks tab. See Figure 6-5.

Figure 6-5 Date and Time dialog box

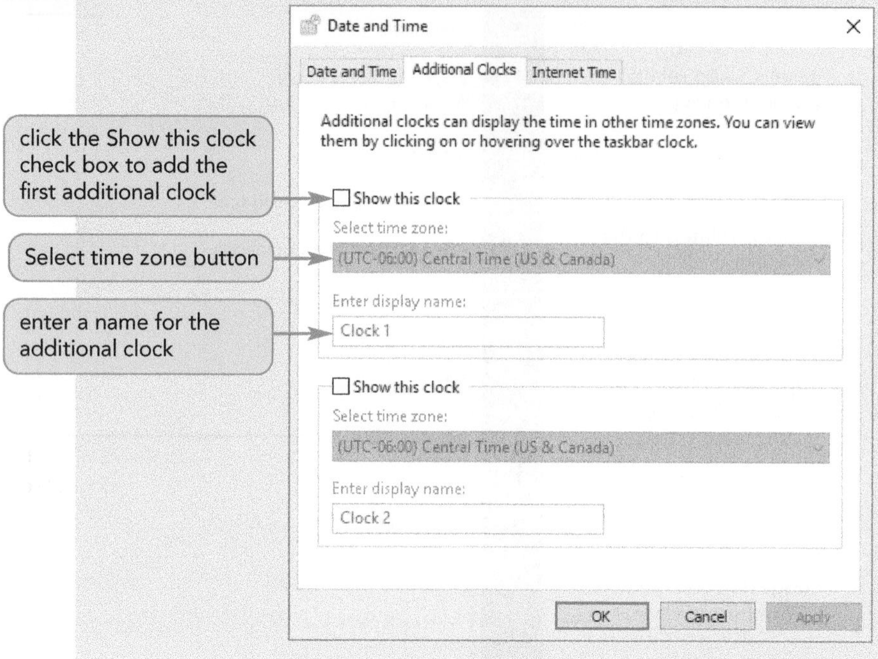

3. Click the first **Show this clock** check box to select it. The current time zone is selected for the additional clock, so you need to change it to show the time zone in Amsterdam.
4. Click the **Select time zone** button, and then click **(UTC + 01:00) Amsterdam, Berlin, Bern, Rome, Stockholm, Vienna** to select the time zone for Amsterdam.
5. Select the text in the Enter display name box, and then type **Amsterdam** to name the clock.
6. Click the **OK** button to close the Date and Time dialog box.
7. Point to the date and time control in the notification area of the taskbar to display the local time and the current time in Amsterdam.

Howard is confident he will use the additional clock frequently when communicating with the art dealer in Amsterdam.

To try the same search with a different tool, you can use the Search box in the Settings app.

To search in the Settings app:

1. Click the **Start** button and then click **Settings** to open the Settings app.
2. Click in the **Find a setting** box, and then type **clock** to search for settings related to the search text. The Search Results window displays a few settings, including "Add clocks for different time zones."
3. Close the Search Results window.

Searching the Control Panel works in the same way—you open the Control Panel window and then enter search text in the Search box. Now you can use more than one method to find settings when you need them.

Searching for Files

You can search for files using Cortana or the Search box in a folder window. Cortana looks for files stored anywhere on your computer or locations in the cloud you use to store files, such as OneDrive. The Search box looks for files in the current folder or one of its subfolders. The tool you choose depends on your current task. If you are working on the desktop or in an app, use Cortana. If you are working in a folder window, use the Search box.

When you search for files using either tool, you can conduct a basic search or an advanced search. If you use text from the filename or the file contents as search criteria, you are conducting a basic search. If you use other properties such as tags or file size as search criteria, you are conducting an advanced search. The other properties you can use as search criteria include any detail you can display as a column in a folder window. (Recall that you can display additional columns in a folder window by right-clicking any column heading, and then clicking a detail on the shortcut menu. If the detail you want to display does not appear on the shortcut menu, click More to open the Choose Details dialog box.) Figure 6-6 describes common criteria you can use when you conduct basic and advanced searches to find a file.

Figure 6-6 Typical search criteria

File Property	Description	What to Find	Search Criterion
Basic Searches			
Filename	All or part of the filename	File named April sales.docx	Apr or sales
File type	Filename extension	All of your photos	jpg
Contents	Text the file contains	File that uses "European Paintings" as a heading	European Paintings
Advanced Searches			
Date	Date the file was modified, created, or accessed	Document edited on May 15, 2018	datemodified:5/15/2018
Size	Size of the file	Files larger than 3 MB	size>3 MB
Tag	Word or phrase in the file properties	Photo with "winter," "vacation," and "ski" as tags	tag:winter vacation ski
Author	Name of the person who created the file	Document that Howard created	author:Howard

When you combine criteria, such as to find a file named Agenda that you created last Monday, you are also conducting an advanced search. You'll learn how to combine search criteria later in the module.

Finding Files by Name and Contents

Suppose you want to start working with a spreadsheet file named Poster Prices as soon as you sign in to Windows. Click in the Ask me anything box and then start typing a word in the filename, such as "poster," to display files on your hard disk with filenames or contents that include a word beginning with the letters you typed. Performing this type of basic search using Cortana or a folder window is the most common way to find files on a Windows 10 computer.

A sales clerk for Ithaca Imports created a short video that showcases prints of Michelangelo's sculpture. Howard knows this video is stored somewhere on his computer, but isn't sure of the exact location or the complete filename. He does know that the filename includes the word "Michelangelo." You'll show him how to use Cortana to find the file.

First, however, you'll copy the Data Files for this module to the Documents folder on your hard disk. The Module6 > Module folder includes three subfolders: Prints, Quotations, and Sculpture. The Prints folder includes images of paintings, and the Sculpture folder contains files related to the shop's collection of prints showing sculpture. The Quotations folder contains text documents of quotations from authors, artists, and other people on various subjects. Howard likes to include at least one quotation on the shop's website.

To copy files and search for files by name:

1. Open File Explorer, open the Documents folder, and then create a folder named **Ithaca** in the Documents folder.
2. If necessary, insert the USB flash drive containing your Data Files into a USB port on your computer.
3. Right-click the **File Explorer** button on the taskbar, and then click **File Explorer** to open a second folder window. Display the contents of the Module6 > Module folder provided with your Data Files. Copy the **Prints**, **Quotations**, and **Sculpture** folders from the Module folder to the Ithaca folder.

Be sure to copy the folders to the subfolder of the Documents folder so you can search for files and contents.

4. Close the Module folder window (the second window displaying the USB flash drive), but leave the Ithaca folder window open.
5. Click in the **Ask me anything** box, and then type **michela** to search for files and other items with a name starting with the text "michela," the first few letters in "Michelangelo." See Figure 6-7. Your results might differ.

   Trouble? If the Michelangelo Sculpture.mp4 file doesn't appear in the search results, click in a blank area in the folder window, and then make sure the contents of the Ithaca folder are displayed in the right pane of the File Explorer window before repeating Step 5.

Figure 6-7 Using Cortana to find files

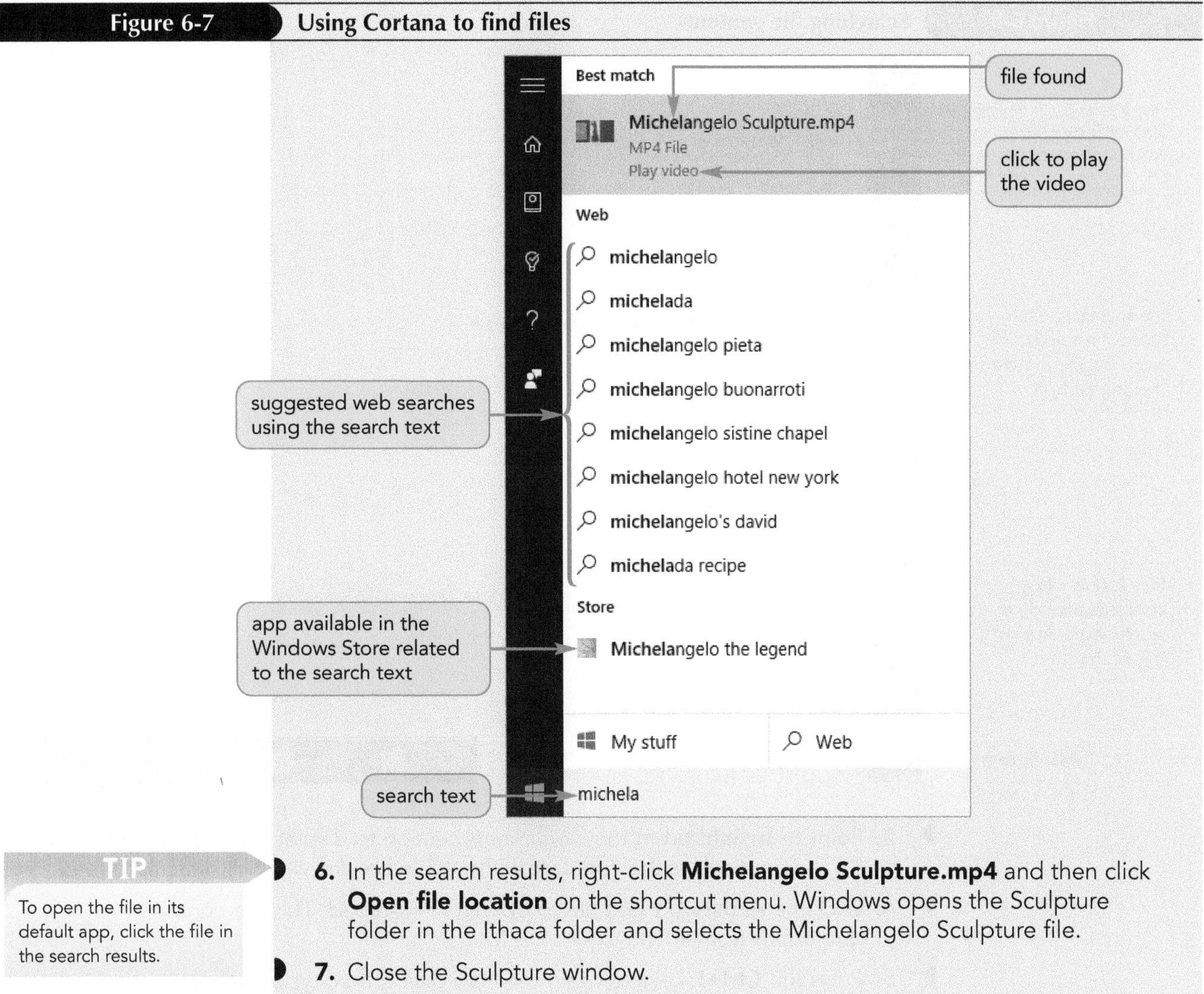

TIP

To open the file in its default app, click the file in the search results.

6. In the search results, right-click **Michelangelo Sculpture.mp4** and then click **Open file location** on the shortcut menu. Windows opens the Sculpture folder in the Ithaca folder and selects the Michelangelo Sculpture file.
7. Close the Sculpture window.

Howard plans to provide the Michelangelo Sculpture video on the Ithaca Imports website. When he does, he wants to include a quotation by or about Michelangelo. If one of the text files in the Quotations folder had a filename containing a word that starts with "michela," the text file would have appeared in the previous search results. To find a quotation by or about Michelangelo, you need to search the file contents. You can use Cortana to search file contents by using the My stuff button.

To search for files by contents:

1. Click in the **Ask me anything** box, and then type **michela** to conduct the same search as in the previous steps.
2. Click the **My stuff** button to display files whose filenames or contents include a word starting with "michela." See Figure 6-8.

Figure 6-8 Searching file contents

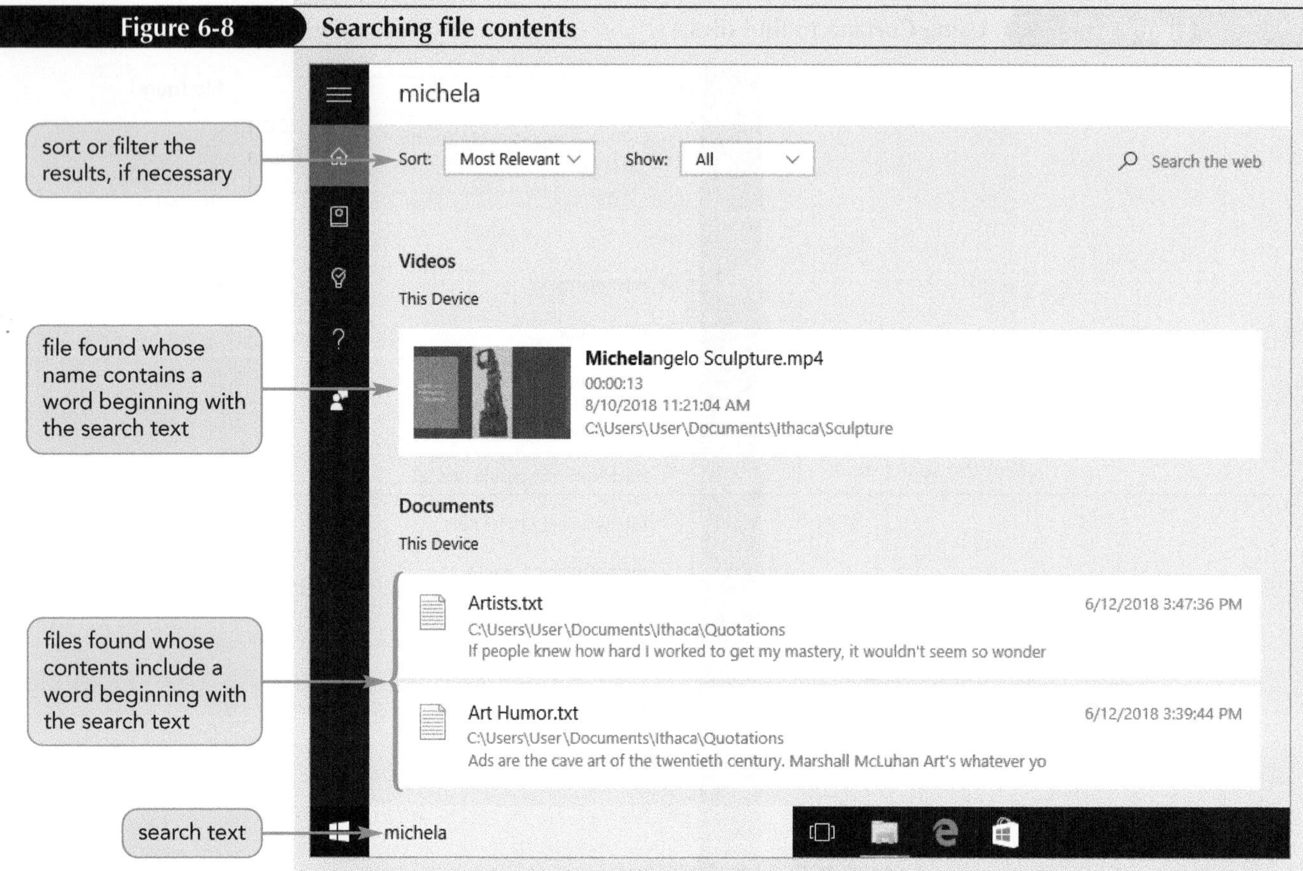

3. Point to **Artists.txt** in the Documents section to display the file contents. The ScreenTip displays the contents without line breaks, which is difficult to read.
4. Click the **Artists.txt** text file to open it in Notepad. This file contains quotations from artists.
5. Press the **Ctrl+F** keys to open the Find dialog box, type **michela** in the Find what box, and then click the **Find Next** button. Notepad selects the first instance of "michela" in the Artists file, the name "Michelangelo" following a quotation about carving marble. This quotation is perfect for Howard's needs. When he's ready, he can return to the Artists file in the Quotations folder to copy and paste the quotation on the Ithaca Imports website.
6. Close the Find dialog box and then close Notepad.

Although the Artists and Art Humor filenames do not include a word starting with "michela," the file contents do. When you search files stored on a hard disk, Windows includes the file contents in the search. However, if you search files stored on a removable disk, such as a USB drive, Windows searches only the filenames, not the contents, by default.

Searching by File Type

Using the Search box in a folder window to find files based on their filenames and contents is similar to using Cortana. You type text in the Search box, and Windows displays only those files in the current folder or its subfolders that match the criterion—files whose contents or filename include a word starting with the text you typed.

You can also use a filename extension as the search criterion to find files by type. For example, you could enter *jpg* to find files with a .jpg extension (image files called JPGs, pronounced *Jay Peg*), which are usually photo files. When you search for files by type, you can enter the filename extension on its own (*jpg*) or use an asterisk and a dot before the filename extension (**.jpg*). In this case, the asterisk is a **wildcard**, a symbol that stands for one or more unspecified characters in the search criterion.

Using a wildcard is a good idea if you want to search for certain types of files, such as those with a DOC extension. Suppose some of your filenames include words that start with the extension text, such as "Doctor Visit," "June Docket," or "Howard Docs." In this case, using a wildcard and a dot makes it clear that you are searching by filename extension only and produces more accurate search results.

Howard is creating webpages and printed marketing materials that feature prints of notable European paintings and sculptures in the shop's collection. He has been taking photos of these prints and saving the photos on his computer. First, he wants to know how many photos of paintings and sculpture he has saved. Because all of these photos are stored in two subfolders, you can provide the information Howard wants by conducting a basic search in a folder window using the filename extension .jpg as the search criterion.

To search for files by type:

1. In the File Explorer window, display the contents of the Ithaca folder in the Documents folder, if necessary.
2. Click in the **Search Ithaca** box, and then type **jpg**. Windows displays only the files with a .jpg extension in the search results.
3. If necessary, click the **Large Icons** button in the status bar to display the search results in Large icons view. See Figure 6-9. Your files might appear in a different order. Note that the status bar indicates that the search results include 20 files.

Figure 6-9 Searching for files with a .jpg filename extension

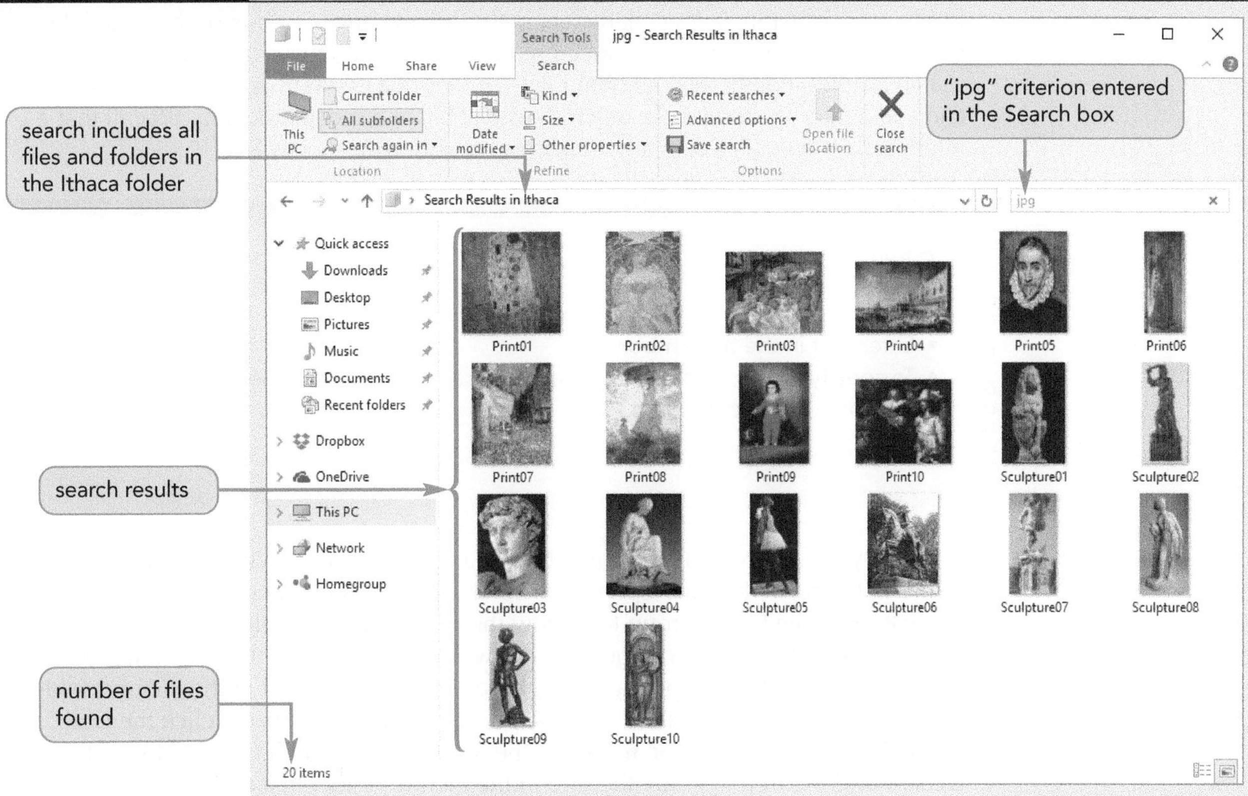

search includes all files and folders in the Ithaca folder

"jpg" criterion entered in the Search box

search results

number of files found

PROSKILLS

Decision Making: Searching vs. Sorting, Filtering, or Grouping

Recall that instead of using the Search box, you can often quickly find files by sorting, filtering, or grouping files using the column headings or the View menu in a folder window. The method you choose depends on the number of files you want to search, the location of the files, and their names. For example, suppose you need to find JPG files. If you want to search the current folder and its subfolders, use the Search box—the other options find files only in the current folder.

If you're searching a single folder, the Search box is also preferable if the folder contains similar filenames (because sorting would list many files that start with the same text) or many types of files (because grouping would produce many groups). If you want to find a particular file in a very large folder, it is often easier to use the Search box rather than dealing with a long file list; however, if the folder doesn't contain too many files, then sorting, grouping, or filtering is usually a more efficient method.

Now that you found the number of photos Howard took of paintings and sculpture, he wants you to research the items so he can provide accurate information in the webpages and printed brochure. Some of the JPG files you found have filenames starting with "Print" followed by a number, such as Print01 and Print02. The other JPG files have filenames starting with "Sculpture" followed by a number. Howard set his digital camera to assign these names so he could take the photos quickly. The camera used Print01 for the first photo Howard took of a print and then automatically added 1 to the number each time he took another photo until he finished photographing the prints. The camera used the same process to name the sculpture photos. Although this filenaming scheme worked well to save the photo files quickly, it poses challenges for your research because the filenames do not reveal anything about the content except that they show paintings or sculpture.

Filtering the Search Results by Size

Besides simply typing a few characters in the Ask me anything box or the Search box, you can also conduct more advanced searches using Cortana or a folder window. To search for files modified on a certain date or files of a certain size, for example, you can add a filter to narrow a search to files that share a specified detail. (Recall that a filter displays only files with a certain characteristic you specify.)

REFERENCE

Filtering Search Results

- Open the folder or drive you want to search.
- Enter text in the Search box.
- To specify a filter, click a button in the Refine group on the Search Tools Search tab, and then click a criterion.

When you enter text in the Search box of a folder window, Windows displays the results in the right pane and opens the Search Tools Search tab on the ribbon. You use the buttons in the Refine group to narrow the results. For example, if you are searching the Pictures folder for photos you took last week, you can click the Search box in the Pictures folder and then type jpg to display all the photos stored in the Pictures folder. To narrow the results to display only the photos you took last week, click the Date modified button in the Refine group on the Search Tools Search tab, and then click Last week. Windows displays only the files in the Pictures folder that meet your criteria.

When you select a search filter, Windows automatically adds a file property name, a colon, and the criterion to the Search box. The file property name is shorthand for the detail you want to use to narrow the search. The criterion determines how to narrow the search. For example, when you click the Date modified button on the Search Tools Search tab and then click Last week, Windows inserts "datemodified:last week" in the Search box.

To conduct an advanced search using Cortana, you use more natural language. For example, to find photos you took last week, enter *find photos from last week* in the Ask me anything box, and then click the My stuff button. Cortana searches files on your hard disk and other connected drives, such as OneDrive.

Howard photographed one of the prints using a high resolution, which makes the image sharp and clear even when printed. He wants to use this photo in a printed brochure. However, he can't recall which photo has the high resolution. He mentions that high-resolution images are usually large files, often more than 1 MB in storage size. You can use this information to find the file Howard wants. Conducting a basic search using the jpg extension as the search text finds all the JPG files in the Prints and Sculpture folders. To narrow the search to large files only, you'll refine the results.

To narrow a search using a search filter:

1. In the folder window displaying the results of the previous search, click the **Search Tools Search** tab, if necessary, and then in the Refine group, click the **Size** button to display a list of size options. See Figure 6-10.

   Trouble? If the folder window open on the desktop does not display the results of the previous search, type "jpg" in the Search box.

Figure 6-10 Selecting a search filter

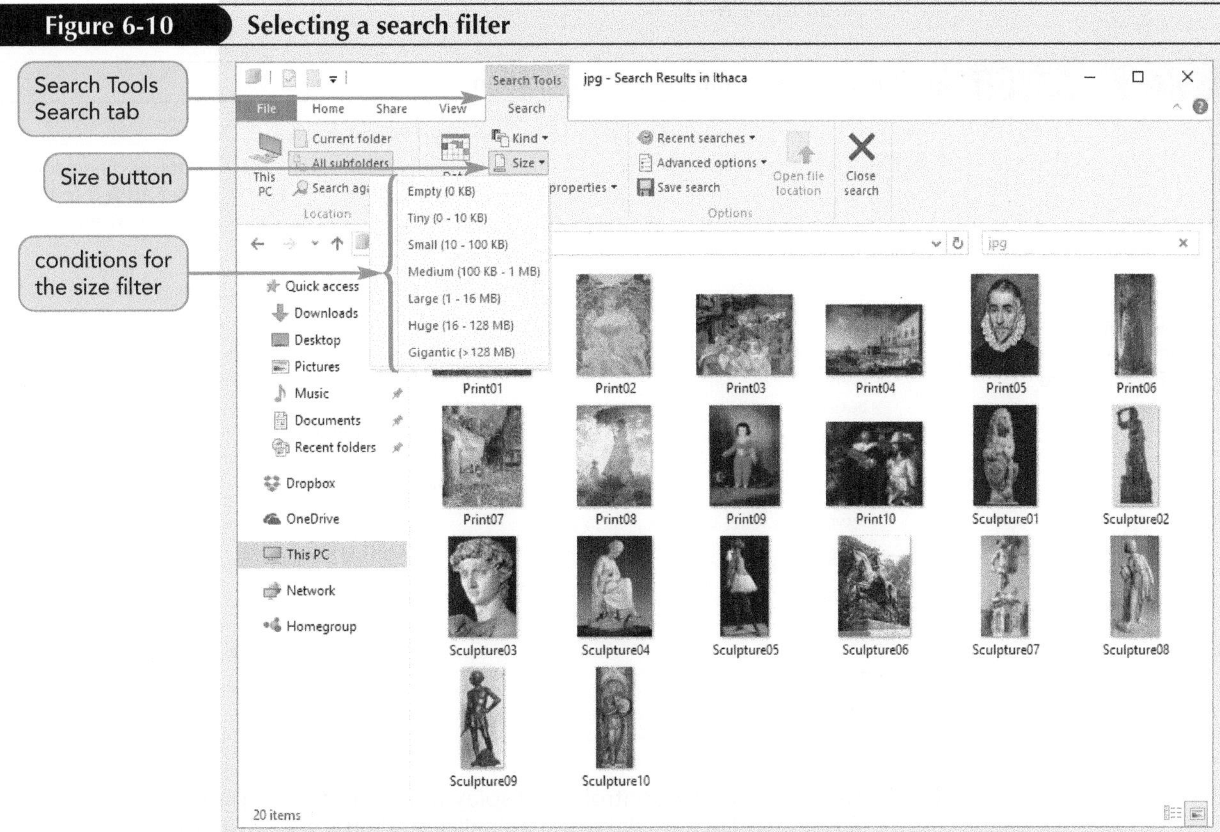

2. Click **Large (1–16 MB)** in the Size options list. Windows reduces the search results to files that meet both criteria—large JPG files.

Only one file meets the search criteria: Print07, which is a high-resolution photo of a Van Gogh painting of a café at night.

Filtering Search Results by Date Modified

Howard usually photographs an imported item as soon as he receives it. On the shop's website, Howard wants you to display photos of imported items he acquired recently, which are those photos taken after August 31, 2018. To find these files, you can start with the same criterion you used to find all the JPG files, and then narrow the results by specifying the date condition. When you use the Date modified button in the Refine group on the Search Tools Search tab, you can select only predefined options such as Today, This week, or Last year. To use a specific date, you select one of these criteria and then click the Search box to display a calendar where you can select a date or date range.

To find JPG files taken after August 31, 2018:

1. In the folder window, click the **Back** button until you return to the Ithaca window.
2. Click in the **Search** box and then type **jpg**. Windows displays all the JPG files in the search results.
3. In the Refine group on the Search tab, click the **Date modified** button, and then click **Today** to select a date option. No results appear, so you need to modify the date further.
4. Click in the text "today" in the Search box to display a calendar control. See Figure 6-11.

TIP

Click in the Search box to display a list of recently used search text.

Figure 6-11 Using a date modified search condition

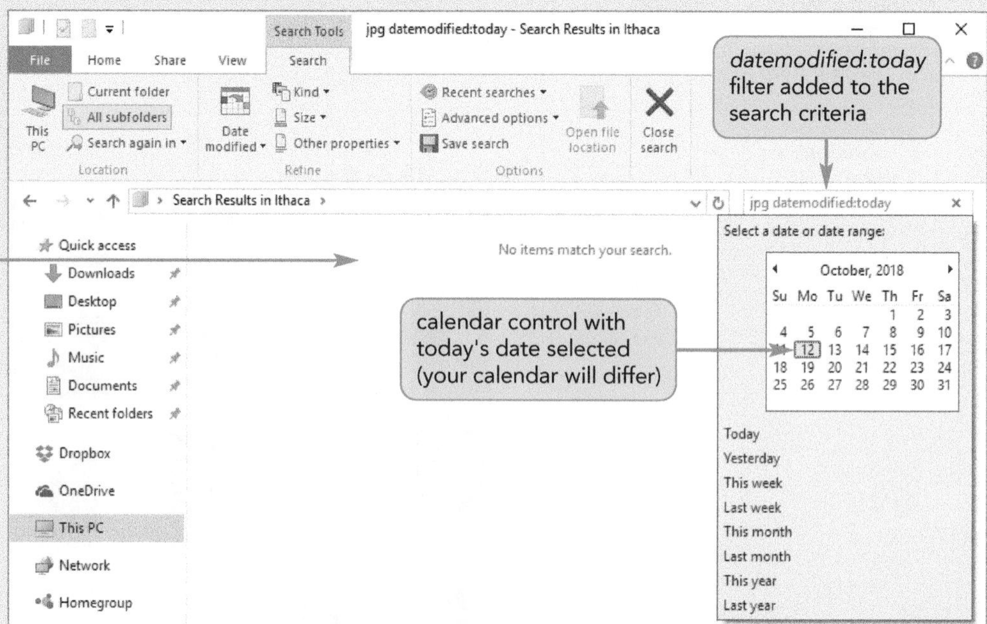

5. Use the calendar controls to display the August 2018 page. To change the month (and eventually the date), click the left arrow and right arrow buttons. When the calendar page for August, 2018 appears, click **31**.

No files appear in the search results because no files in the Ithaca folder were modified on August 31, 2018. You want to find files that were modified after that date. To do so, you use the greater than (>) operator. You can use the greater than operator with any property in the Search box. For example, to find files that are larger than 500 KB, enter *size:>500KB*. (You can include a space after the colon or omit it—the space does not affect the search results.) You can also use the less than (<) operator in the same way. To find files less than 500 KB, enter *size:<500KB*. To find files modified after August 31, 2018, you use the greater than operator to enter *datemodified:>8/31/2018* in the Search box.

To modify the search criteria:

1. Click in the **Search** box.
2. Move the insertion point after the colon (:) in datemodified, and then type >. Seven files appear in the search results.

To make sure you find the files you need or to expand a search, you should examine the search results.

Examining the Search Results

After you enter search criteria using the Search box, Windows filters the view of the folder window to display files that meet your criteria. These are your search results. Figure 6-12 shows the results of the search performed in the preceding set of steps—JPG files modified after August 31, 2018.

Figure 6-12 **Search results**

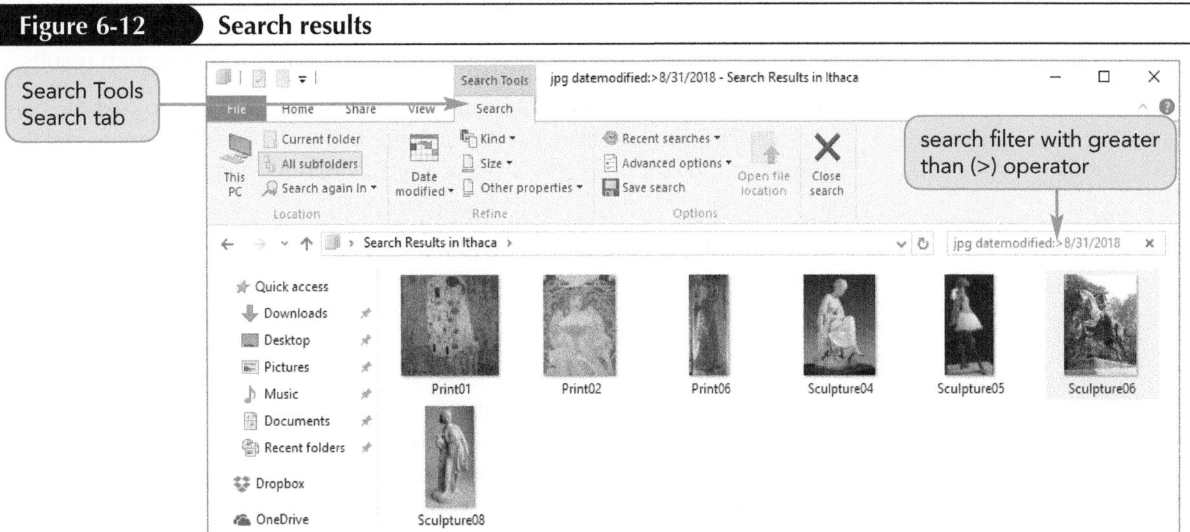

Search results windows provide extra tools and information to help you work with the files you found. The title bar displays the search criteria. In Details view, the search results display the name, location, date modified, size, and other available properties of each file. If the results include text files, they preview their first two lines of text to help you identify the file contents.

Besides the buttons in the Refine group, the Search Tools Search tab contains other groups of controls to help you find the files or information you need. The Location group and Options group provide other search tools that you can use to broaden or narrow your search. Using the buttons in the Location group, you can change the default search location on your computer (that is, the current folder and all of its subfolders), or you can search the Internet using your default web browser (such as Microsoft Edge) and search engine, which is a program (such as Google or Bing) a website uses to conduct the search using keywords. The Recent searches button in the Options group stores a history of the criteria for your last eight searches. The Advanced options button in this group allows you to change how Windows uses the criteria entered to search for files using an exact match setting, for example. To speed up a search, you can set Windows to search an indexed location, such as the Documents folder or Pictures folder on your hard disk, so Windows searches the file contents. (An **indexed location** is one or more folders that Windows indexes so it can search them quickly. Folders and other locations that contain your personal files—not system files—are indexed locations.) The Save search button provides access to tools for saving the criteria and folder location of a search. Use the Open file location button to open the location of the selected file.

Howard occasionally works with files stored on a removable disk, so you want to show him how to search filenames and contents in that location.

To search for files on a removable disk:

1. If necessary, insert the USB flash drive containing your Data Files into a USB port on your computer.
2. Navigate to and display the contents of the **Module6 > Module** folder on the USB flash drive.
3. Type **michela** in the Search box to display folders and files with names that contain a word beginning with **michela**.
4. In the Options group on the Search Tools Search tab, click the **Advanced options** button and then click **File contents** under the In non-indexed locations section (which includes a USB drive). Windows adds the two text files that contain a word beginning with "michela" to the search results.

   Trouble? If File contents is already selected, a JPG and two text files are already displayed in the results for Step 3. Do not click File contents; this will deselect the option. Press the Esc key to close the list of advanced options.

In addition to the extra tools provided in a search results window, you can use the standard folder window tools to open, move, copy, rename, or delete a file.

Saving a Search

If you conduct a successful search that you are likely to conduct again, especially one that uses two or more criteria, you might want to save the search. Saving a search preserves your original criteria and folder location so you can perform the search again without reconstructing the criteria. By default, Windows saves the search in the Searches folder, which is stored in your personal folder (the one whose name is the same as your user name). You can double-click a saved search to use the same criteria in a new search. The search results display the most current files that match the original conditions, so the results might differ from other times when you conducted the same search.

To save a search and perform it again:

TIP

Click in the Search box to display the recent searches, and then click jpg datemodified:>8/31/2016.

1. In the search results window, click the **Back** button [←] to navigate back to the results of the jpg datemodified:>8/31/2018 search.

   Trouble? If a new folder window opened when you inserted the USB drive containing your Data Files, close that window and return to the one showing the results of the jpg datemodified:>8/31/2018 search.

2. Click the **Save search** button in the Options group on the Search Tools Search tab. The Save As dialog box opens, providing jpg datemodified8-31-2018 as the filename. (Windows doesn't include the colon and greater than symbol because they are not allowed in filenames; Windows also replaces any forward slashes with dashes for the same reason.) See Figure 6-13.

Figure 6-13 Saving a search

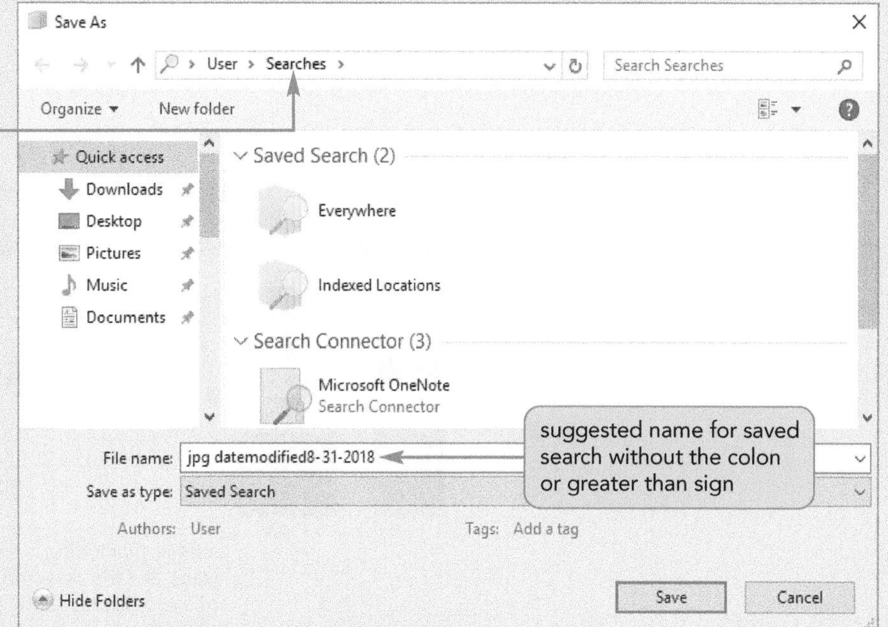

Be sure to save the search so you can use it again.

3. Change the filename to **JPG Sept**, and then click the **Save** button to save the search in the Searches folder.
4. To view the saved search, click **Searches** in the Address bar of the folder window. The JPG Sept search appears in the Saved Search list.
5. To test the search, double-click **JPG Sept**. Windows conducts the search again and finds the JPG files modified after August 31, 2018.

Howard asks if using tags would help him find and identify files. In fact, one of the most useful properties when searching for files is a file tag, which is one or more descriptive words you store with a file to help identify its purpose or contents. You are sure that adding tags to the photo files would save you and Howard a lot of time when searching for photos. You'll show him how to do so next.

Using Tags and Other Properties

As you know, properties are characteristics of files, such as names and sizes. When you create or modify a file, you automatically set some file properties, including the filename, location, and date created or modified. You can add other properties later, including tags, ratings, titles, and authors. Tags are often the most useful properties because they make finding similar files easier.

To add properties to a file, you can use the Details pane in a folder window or the file's Properties dialog box. (You can use the Details pane to add or modify the properties of only some types of files, such as Microsoft Office documents, but not TXT or RTF files.) As you recall, to open the Details pane in a folder window, you click the Details pane button in the Panes group on the View tab. Figure 6-14 shows the Details pane when the Print01 file is selected in the Prints folder.

Figure 6-14 **File properties in the Details pane**

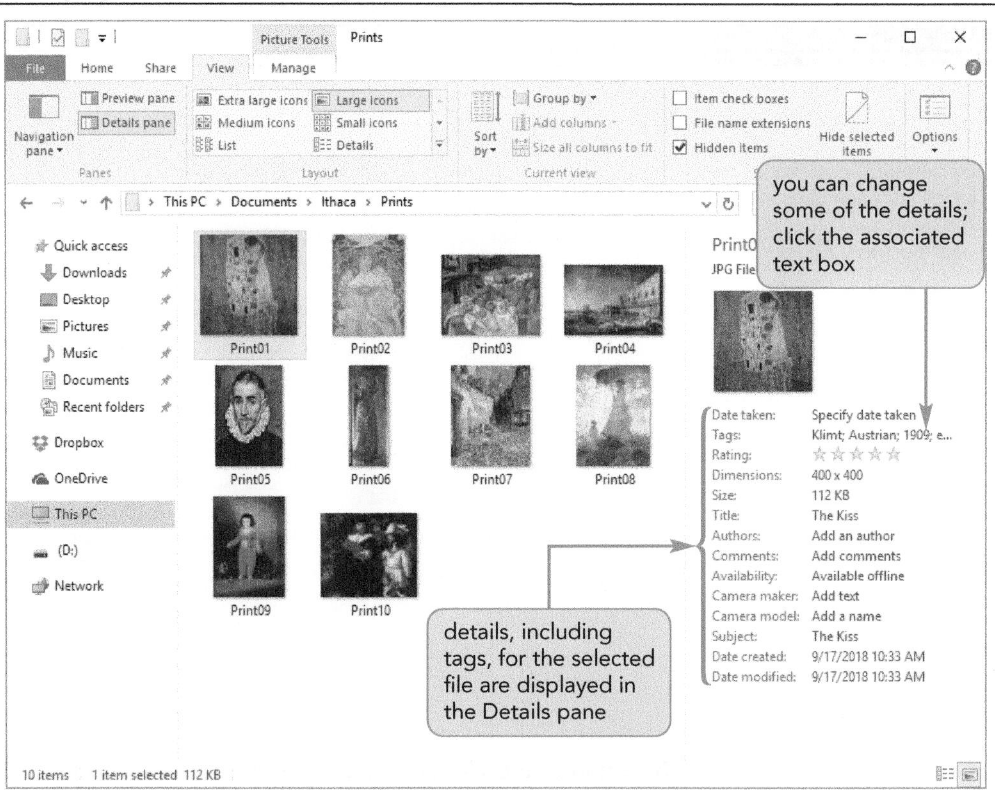

Properties you can add using the Details pane vary by file type. For photos, you can specify date taken, tags, and other properties by using the appropriate box in the Details pane. You can also rate photos by clicking a star in a series of five stars. If you click the first star, you apply a one-star rating. If you click the fourth star, you apply a four-star rating.

If you want to specify file properties other than the ones that appear in the Details pane by default, you can open the Properties dialog box for a file. To do so, you right-click the file and then click Properties on the shortcut menu. On the Details tab, you can add or modify dozens of properties. Figure 6-15 shows the Properties dialog box for the Print01 file.

Figure 6-15 **File details in the Properties dialog box**

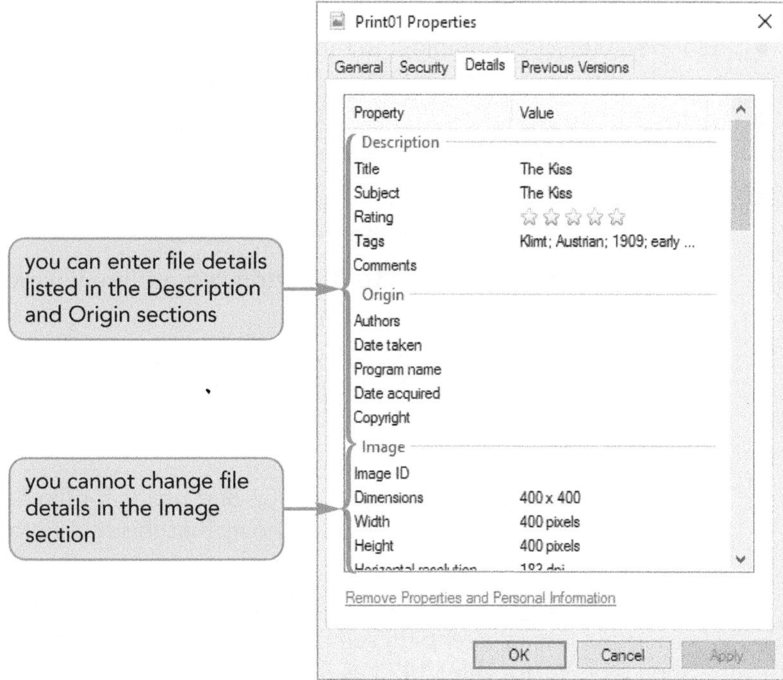

Adding Tags to Files

You can add a tag to a file by using the Save As dialog box when you save the file, or by using the Details pane or the file's Properties dialog box after you save the file. To use the Details pane, you select the file, click the Tags box in the Details pane, and then type a word or phrase that will help you find the file later. To add more than one tag, separate each word or phrase with a semicolon (;). For example, if you have a photo of yourself on the peak of the Blackrock Mountain in Virginia, you could use Blackrock; mountain; Virginia as tags.

REFERENCE

Adding Tags to Files

- In a folder window, click the file to which you want to add a tag.
- In the Panes group on the View tab, click the Details pane button to display the Details pane.
- Click the Tags box in the Details pane, and then type a tag. To enter another tag, type a semicolon (;) and then type the next tag.
- Click the Save button on the Details pane.

Howard has already added tags to some of the photo files in the Prints and Sculpture folders, but two recent files still need tags. Howard asks you to add descriptive tags to these files.

To add tags to files:

1. Open the Sculpture folder in the Documents > Ithaca folder on your hard disk, and then switch to Details view. Maximize the window, if necessary.
2. Click the **View** tab on the ribbon, and then in the Panes group, click the **Details pane** button to display the Details pane.
3. Display the Tags column, if necessary, by right-clicking any column heading and then clicking **Tags** on the shortcut menu.
4. Click the **Size all columns to fit** button in the Current view group to display all of the columns in the window.
5. Click each file in the file list to examine its properties in the Details pane. Note that Michelangelo Sculpture, Sculpture09, and Sculpture10 do not have any tags. Michelangelo Sculpture is a video, so it's easy to identify that file without tags.
6. Click **Sculpture09** to display its image and boxes for file details, such as Tags, in the Details pane. Howard knows that this sculpture is called *David* and the sculptor is Verrocchio.
7. Click in the **Tags box** in the Details pane, and then type **David** as the first tag. Windows inserts an ending semicolon for you. Click after the ; (semicolon), and then type **Verrocchio; 1473** as the second and third tags. See Figure 6-16.

Figure 6-16 **Adding tags to a file**

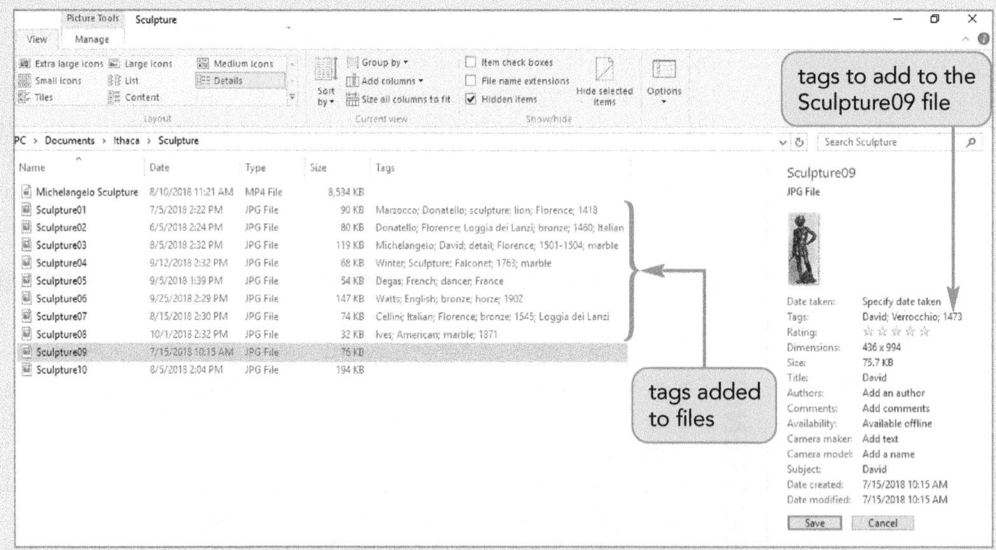

8. Click the **Save** button in the Details pane. Windows saves the tags you added. Because you modified the file by adding a tag, the date in the Date column changes to today's date.
9. Click the **Sculpture10** file, add the tags **Sibyl; Ghiberti; 1425**, and then click the **Save** button. Note that after you save a tag in one file, that tag appears in the list of suggested tags for other files.
10. Close all open windows.

TIP

If Windows suggests tags as you begin to type, click the tag you want.

When entering multiple tags, you don't need to click after the semicolon automatically entered; it is replaced as you type a series of tags.

INSIGHT

Selecting Tags for Files

To create tags that will help you find files later, keep the following guidelines in mind:

- Include the obvious. Use words or phrases that describe the overall purpose or content of the file. For photo files, use tags that list the people in the picture, the location of the photo, and the occasion. For documents, describe the type of document, such as a proposal or report, and its subject.
- Consider the sample tags. If you are working with files on a hard disk, you can find typical tags by typing a letter in the Tags box in the Details pane. For example, type *p* to find sample tags that start with the letter *p*, such as people, pet owners, pets, and photography.
- Use complete words and phrases. Avoid abbreviations and codes because you might not remember them later. Assign complete words or use phrases to be as clear as possible. Feel free to use text that appears in the filename; doing so might help you find other related files with the same tag but a different filename.

You've already explored many ways to search for files on your computer. You conducted basic searches by searching filenames and contents. You also conducted advanced searches by using properties to filter the search results. In the next session, you'll build on these techniques by searching tags and combining criteria using shorthand notation and Boolean filters. You'll apply these new skills to search for information in Windows 10 apps and on the Internet.

REVIEW

Session 6.1 Quick Check

1. What are search criteria?
2. Name two ways you can search for settings.
3. When you use Cortana to search for apps, what does the notation "Trusted Windows Store app" mean in the search results?
4. You can use Cortana to search file contents by using the ____________ button.
5. Explain how to search for DOCX files in a folder window.
6. How can you search for files larger than 1 MB in a folder window?
7. Why might you want to save a search?

Session 6.2 Visual Overview:

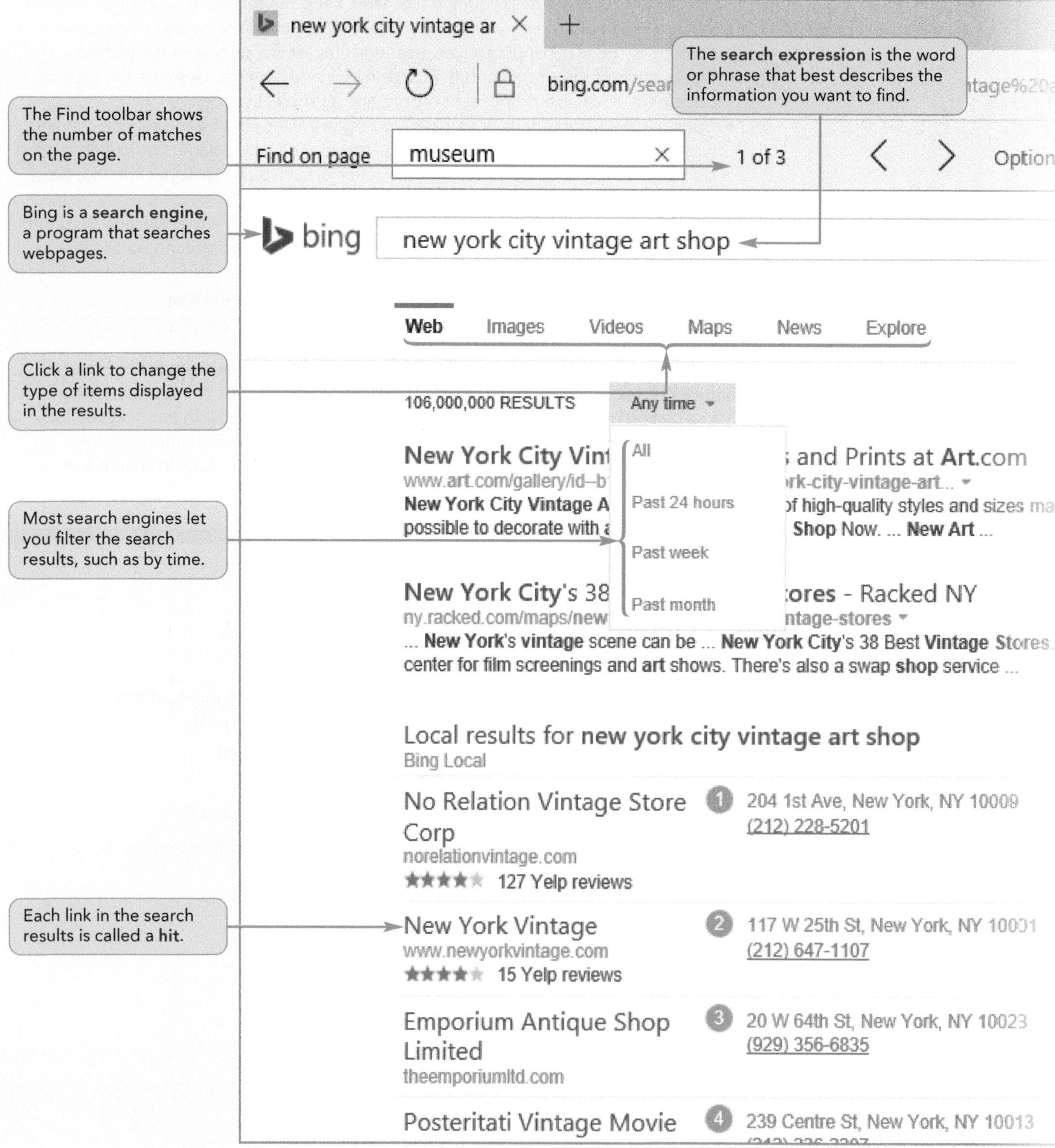

new york city vintage ar
bing.com/sear
The search expression is the word or phrase that best describes the information you want to find.
The Find toolbar shows the number of matches on the page.
Find on page
museum
1 of 3
Options
Bing is a search engine, a program that searches webpages.
bing
new york city vintage art shop
Web
Images
Videos
Maps
News
Explore
Click a link to change the type of items displayed in the results.
106,000,000 RESULTS
Any time
All
Past 24 hours
Past week
Past month
Most search engines let you filter the search results, such as by time.
New York City Vint
www.art.com/gallery/id--b
New York City Vintage A
possible to decorate with
and Prints at Art.com
rk-city-vintage-art...
of high-quality styles and sizes mak
Shop Now. ... New Art ...
New York City's 38
ny.racked.com/maps/new
ores - Racked NY
ntage-stores
... New York's vintage scene can be ... New York City's 38 Best Vintage Stores
center for film screenings and art shows. There's also a swap shop service ...
Local results for new york city vintage art shop
Bing Local
No Relation Vintage Store Corp
norelationvintage.com
127 Yelp reviews
204 1st Ave, New York, NY 10009
(212) 228-5201
Each link in the search results is called a hit.
New York Vintage
www.newyorkvintage.com
15 Yelp reviews
117 W 25th St, New York, NY 10001
(212) 647-1107
Emporium Antique Shop Limited
theemporiumltd.com
20 W 64th St, New York, NY 10023
(929) 356-6835
Posteritati Vintage Movie
239 Centre St, New York, NY 10013

Searching the Internet

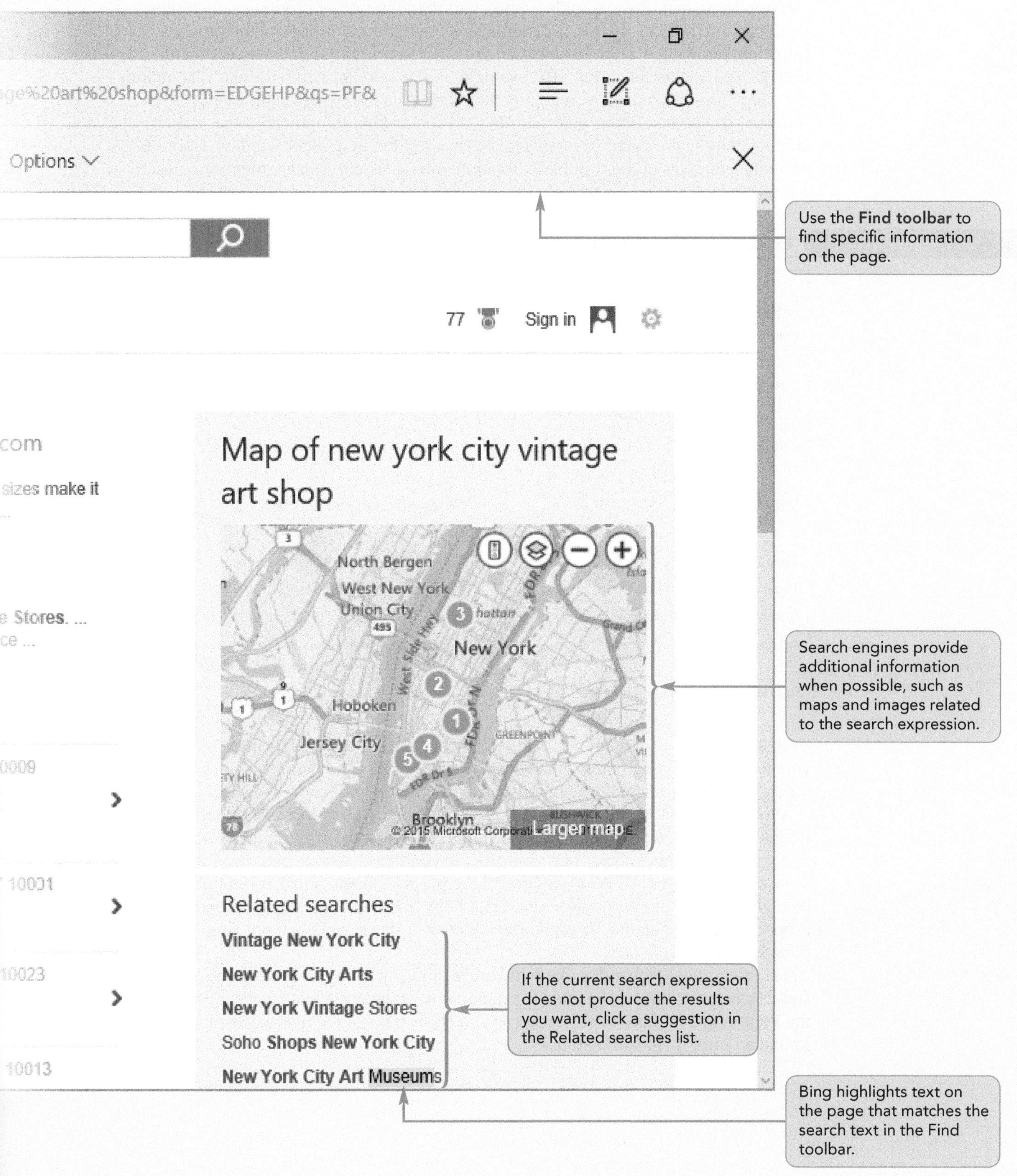

Use the **Find toolbar** to find specific information on the page.

Search engines provide additional information when possible, such as maps and images related to the search expression.

If the current search expression does not produce the results you want, click a suggestion in the Related searches list.

Bing highlights text on the page that matches the search text in the Find toolbar.

Using Advanced Search Criteria

In addition to searching for files using common properties such as file type or size, you can use the Search box in a folder window to search for other properties, including tags, title, and subject. To use any property as a criterion, you specify the property using the following shorthand notation: *property name:criterion*. (You can include or omit the space after the colon.) For example, if you want to search for files that include the word "Ithaca" as a tag, you could enter *tag:ithaca*. (The properties are not case sensitive, so you could also enter *Tag:Ithaca*.) The properties you can use as search criteria include any detail you can display as a column in a folder window. Figure 6-17 provides examples of the shorthand notation you can use to specify file properties as search criteria.

Figure 6-17 **Examples of using file properties as search criteria**

Property	Example	Finds
Name	Name:city	Files and folders with names that contain a word beginning with "city"
Date modified	DateModified:10/28/2018	Files and folders modified on October 28, 2018
	DateModified:<10/28/2018	Files and folders modified before October 28, 2018
Date created	DateCreated:>10/28/2018	Files and folders created after October 28, 2018
	DateCreated:2018	Files and folders created during the year 2018
Size	Size:200KB	Files with a size of 200 KB
	Size:>1MB	Files larger than 1 MB
Type	Type:docx	Files with a .docx filename extension
Tags	Tag:French	Files that include "French" as a tag
Authors	Author:Howard	Files that specify "Howard" as the author
Artists	Artist:Elvis	Files that specify artists with "Elvis" in their names, such as Elvis Presley and Elvis Costello
Rating	Rating:4 stars	Files with a rating of four stars

Being able to include any file detail as a search criterion is especially useful when you are working with photos, music, and videos because they have special properties for their file types, such as album artists, album, rating, and length.

When searching in a folder window, you can use the Other properties button in the Refine group on the Search Tools Search tab to display a list of properties you can use in a search, such as Authors, Tags, and Title. In each case, when you click a property on the Other properties list, Windows inserts the property name and a colon in the Search box. Using the Other properties button can help you create advanced criteria using the proper shorthand notation. If you know the correct shorthand notation, you can enter it directly in the Search box.

For the updates Howard is planning for the Ithaca Imports website, Howard wants to show French art. Howard inserted the nationality of the artist as a tag for the photos in the Prints and Sculpture folders. You can search the tags of the files in the Ithaca folder to find art photos Howard can use.

To find files by specifying a property in the Search box:

1. Open the Ithaca folder in the Documents folder on your hard disk, if necessary.
2. Click in the **Search Ithaca** box, and then type **tag:french**. As you type, Windows filters the view of the files in the folder window, and then displays three files that contain the text "french" in their Tags property: Print03, Print08, and Sculpture05.
3. Click **Print03** and examine the information in the Details pane. This is a photo of *The Kitchen Table*, a painting by Cezanne, a French painter, created from 1880–1890.
4. Click **Print08** and examine its details. This is a photo of *Woman with a Parasol*, a painting by Monet, also a French painter, created in 1875.
5. Click **Sculpture05** and examine its details. This is a photo of *Young Dancer*, a sculpture by Degas, a French artist, created in 1881.

By searching for text in the Tags property, you found three photos to display on the Ithaca Imports website.

Combining Criteria When Searching File Contents

TIP

When you use two or more words as a search condition, Windows searches as if the condition includes the AND Boolean filter.

To perform a precise search, you can combine criteria in the Search box. For example, suppose you store your financial documents on your computer and need to find a list of charitable donations you made in 2018. You don't recall where you've stored this information, and scanning the filenames in your Financial folder doesn't reveal the file. If you search the contents of the files using *donation* as the search criterion, you'll find lists of donations for many years as well as other documents, including those with text such as "Thanks for your support! Every donation helps." If you search the contents of files using *2018* as the search criterion, you'll find dozens of documents that mention that year. To pinpoint your search, you can combine the criteria to find files that contain the word "donation" and the year "2018." When you search file contents, you can use **Boolean filters**, which are filters that let you search for specific information using the words AND, OR, and NOT to combine search criteria. You can use quotation marks and parentheses to refine the search conditions further. Figure 6-18 describes how to use AND, OR, and NOT along with quotation marks and parentheses when combining search criteria.

Figure 6-18 **Combining search criteria**

Word or Punctuation	Examples	When to Use
AND	donation AND 2018 donation 2018	To narrow the search to files that contain "donation" and "2018" even if the words are not next to each other
OR	donation OR 2018	To broaden the search to files that contain "donation" or "2018"
NOT	donation NOT 2018	To restrict the search to files that contain "donation" but not "2018"
"" (quotation marks)	"donation 2018"	To pinpoint the search to files that contain the exact phrase "donation 2018"
( ) (parentheses)	(donation 2018)	To open the search to files that contain both items next to each other in any order

When you use the words AND, OR, and NOT, you must enter them using all uppercase letters.

One of your ongoing projects for Ithaca Imports is maintaining an archive of quotations, which Howard uses on the shop's website. Howard, employees, and customers provide these quotations in various ways, such as in a word-processing document or an email message. You store the quotations in TXT documents to make sure anyone at the shop can use the documents. However, this means that you cannot add tags or other properties to the files; you can add these details only to Microsoft Office documents.

Along with the photos of French art, Howard wants to include at least one quotation about art collecting. You can use Boolean logic to combine search criteria and search the contents of the Quotations folder to find suitable quotations.

INSIGHT

Preparing to Combine Search Criteria

Before you combine search criteria, select the search text, select the filter you plan to use, if any, and then select the condition. For example, choose **.txt* as the search text to find text files. If you want to find text files modified after a certain date, use the datemodified: filter, and then select the appropriate date, such as >8/31/2018. Next, determine whether you should use AND, OR, or NOT to combine the criteria, and whether you need quotation marks or parentheses to find the files you want. For example, if you want to find files that use "Ithaca" as a tag and have "Howard" as the author, you use the AND filter, whether you insert AND or not. In other words, *tag:Ithaca AND author:Howard* is the same as *tag:Ithaca author:Howard.*

If you want to find either text files or Word documents, you need to insert OR, as in **.txt OR *.doc**. (The search condition **.doc** finds Word documents that have a .doc or a .docx filename extension.) To determine the best criteria, test each method in order, starting with AND. Keep in mind that AND narrows the search results, whereas OR broadens the results. For example, if you search for files that are photos and use "Ithaca" as a tag, you find fewer files than searching for files that are photos or use "Ithaca" as a tag.

Although you want to find quotations about art collecting, using *art* and *collecting* as search criteria won't find quotations that include "collection" or "collector" or even "collect," which might be appropriate quotations. A good rule of thumb when specifying search text is to use the root of the word; for example, use *collect* to find documents containing "collecting," "collection," "collector," and "collect." Using the root of a word is also called **stemming**. For Howard's search, you can use *art* and *collect* as search criteria.

Next, determine the best way to combine the criteria, as shown in the following list:

- *Art collect* (or *art AND collect*) finds documents that include both words.
- *Art OR collect* finds documents that include at least one of the words.
- *Art NOT collect* finds documents that include "art" but not those that include "collect."
- *"Art collect"* finds documents that include the exact phrase "art collect."
- *(Art collect)* finds documents that include the exact words "art" and "collect" consecutively in either order.

Because the phrase *art collect* will produce the results you want, you'll use it as your search criteria to find quotations about art collecting.

To find files using AND criteria:

1. Click the **Close search** button on the Search Tools Search tab to return to the Ithaca folder in the Documents folder.
2. Click in the **Search Ithaca** box, and then type **art collect**. As you type, Windows searches filenames and file contents that meet your criteria and finds one file. See Figure 6-19.

Figure 6-19 Finding files that contain *art* AND *collect*

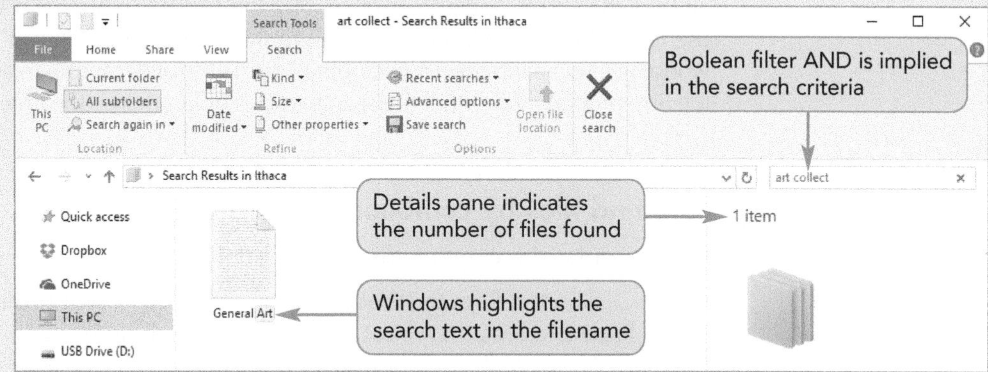

3. To verify this file contains a quotation you can use, double-click **General Art** to open it in a text-editing program such as Notepad.
4. Press the **Ctrl+F** keys to open the Find dialog box, type **collect** in the Find what box, click the **Find Next** button until you find a quotation Howard can use, and then close the Find dialog box and Notepad.

Try your search again, this time using the Boolean filter OR to find files that contain either "art" or "collect."

To find files using OR criteria:

1. Display the contents of the Ithaca folder again.
2. In the search box, modify the criterion to **art OR collect**. Now Windows finds four files that contain the word "art" or "collect." See Figure 6-20.

Figure 6-20 Finding files that contain *art* OR *collect*

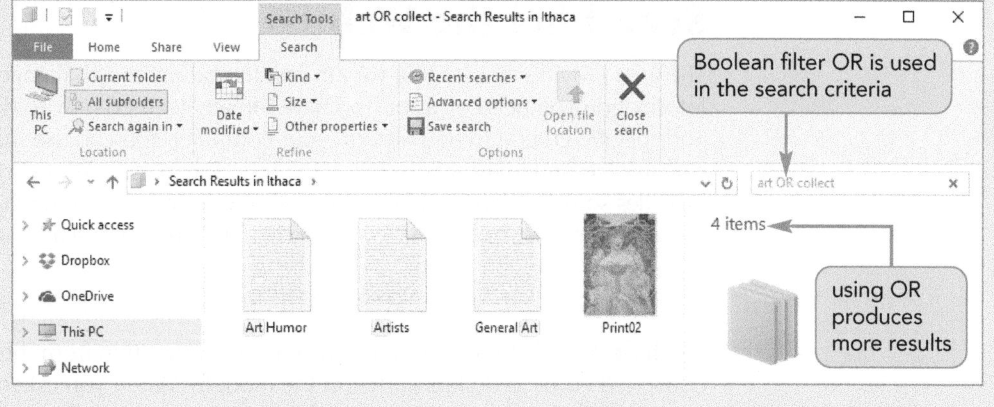

To pinpoint what you want to find and to refine your search criteria, you can combine Boolean filters and file properties.

Combining Boolean Filters and File Properties

When you search files by file property, you can use Boolean filters to combine criteria. For example, suppose Howard is working on the website and requests a photo of Italian art from the 1400s. You can search the tags of the photo files to find those that contain this text. To search efficiently, you can use the Boolean filter AND to combine the criteria and use an asterisk (*) wildcard to search for photos that include the tags "Italian" and "14*." (If you used the Boolean filter OR, you would find photos of Italian art, but not necessarily art from the 1400s, and photos of art from the 1400s that are not necessarily Italian.) If you use *tag: Italian 14**, Windows searches for files that include "Italian" as a tag and a number whose first two digits are 14 (including 140, 1499, and 14,500) in any property, including the Size property. To restrict the search to tags only, enclose the criteria in parentheses.

To find files by combining file property criteria:

1. Display the contents of the Ithaca folder.
2. Click in the **Search Ithaca** box, and then type **tag: (Italian 14*)**. Windows finds two files that meet your criteria. See Figure 6-21.

Figure 6-21 **Combining Boolean filters with file properties**

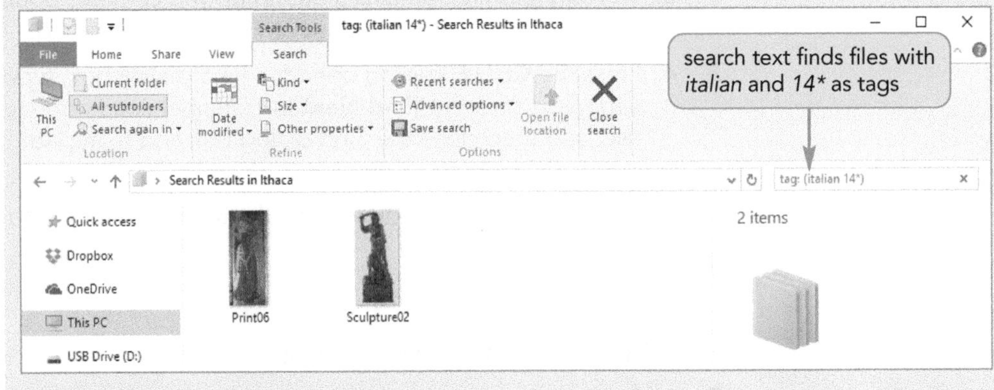

3. Close File Explorer.

You now know many expert techniques to search for files, so you can turn your attention to searching for information on the web.

Searching the Web

The web provides access to a wealth of information; the challenge is to find the information you need or want. You have already learned how to develop search strategies and specific criteria to find files on your computer. You can use many of the same search strategies to find information on the Internet. The first place to start is Cortana, which provides some information from the web. If Cortana can't find what you're seeking, you can click the Web button in Cortana to conduct the same search using Microsoft Edge.

Searching for Web Information with Cortana

You have already used Cortana to search for information from the web when you converted euros to dollars earlier in the module. When you asked Cortana to tell you how many euros equal one dollar, Cortana found the current rate for the currency conversion on the web to use in the calculation. In fact, all of the instant results Cortana provides for calculations, conversions, definitions, flight information, stocks, sports scores, weather, and restaurant information involve gathering information from the web.

INSIGHT

Cortana Voice Search

Instead of typing search text in the Ask me anything box, you can set up Cortana to respond to your voice and use spoken words as search text. You need a microphone attached to or built into your computer to use voice search. To set up Cortana, you click the microphone icon in the Ask me anything box and then complete a wizard (a series of dialog boxes) so that Cortana can detect a microphone and learn to recognize your voice and how you speak. (Cortana is available only in certain regions and recognizes certain languages, including English, Chinese, French, Italian, German, and Spanish.) After you set up Cortana, you can click the microphone icon in the Ask me anything box and then start speaking. Cortana recognizes your speech and uses it as search text. To skip clicking the microphone icon altogether, set up Cortana to respond when you say "Hey, Cortana." Click the Ask me anything box, click the Notebook icon, and then click Settings. Click the slider button to turn the Hey Cortana setting from Off to On to activate it.

Howard is traveling to New York City in a few days to attend a conference for small businesses in the import/export field. He wants to know what kind of weather to expect in New York. For a presentation he will make at the conference, he also needs to find a few facts. For example, he needs to know the population of New York City. You'll show him how to use Cortana to find this information. Unlike searching for files using the Search box in a folder window, with Cortana, you can provide search text using more natural language.

To find weather and flight information with Cortana:

1. Click in the **Ask me anything** box on the taskbar. Cortana opens in a pane on the desktop.
2. Type **What's the weather forecast for New York** to display the results in Cortana. See Figure 6-22. Your results might differ.

Figure 6-22 Finding weather information with Cortana

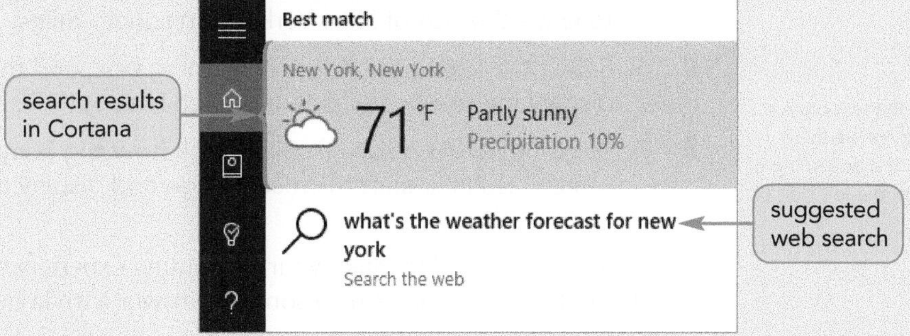

The search results show the current conditions in New York. Cortana can also display the forecast for the next few days.

3. In the search results, click **what's the weather forecast for new york** to display a more detailed forecast for the week in Bing, the Microsoft search engine. See Figure 6-23. Your results might differ.

   Trouble? If Cortana displays the forecast instead of opening Edge, click the See more results in Bing.com link.

Figure 6-23 Weather search results in Bing

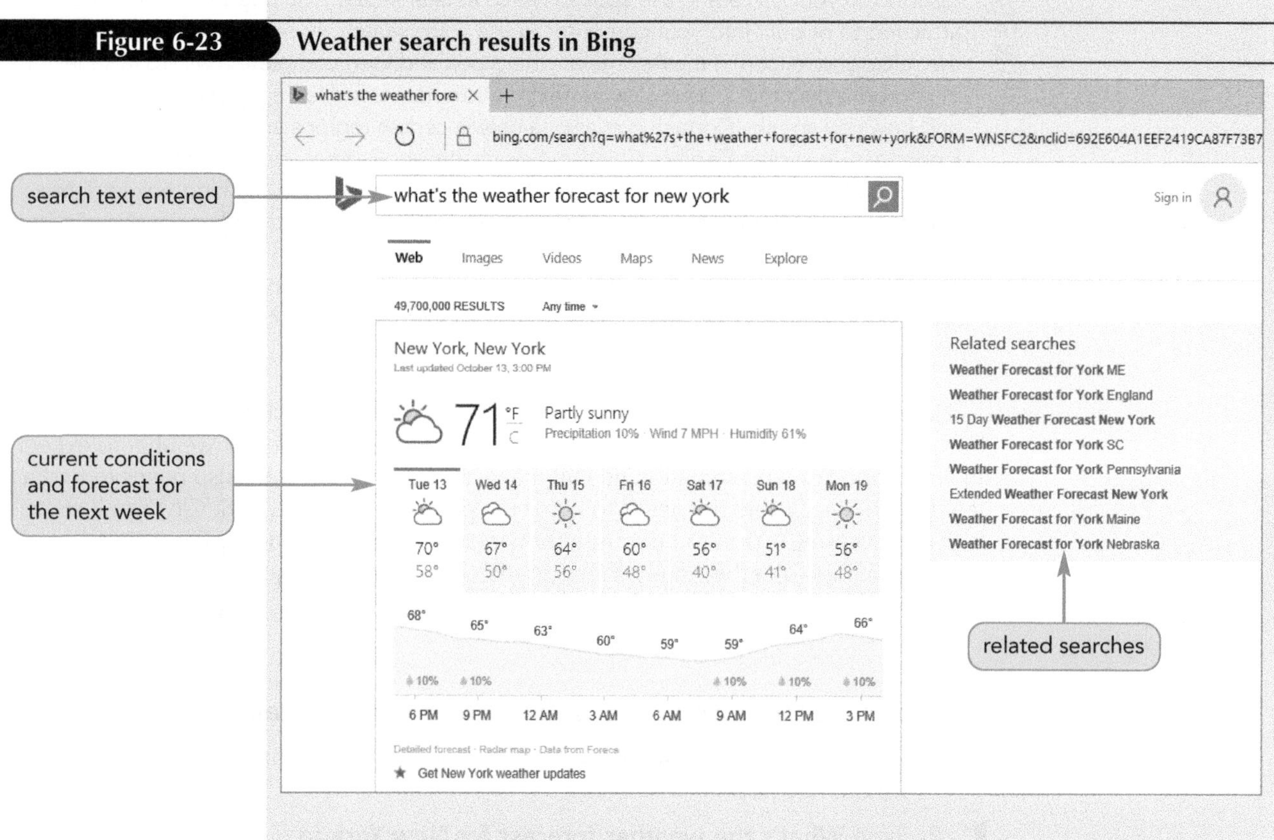

4. Close Microsoft Edge. Next, you can ask Cortana about the population of New York City.
5. Click in the **Ask me anything** box, and then type **population nyc** to display the results in Cortana, which is about 8.5 million people. Howard also wants to know the size of New York city in square miles.
6. Select the text in the Ask me anything box, and then type **how big is nyc** to display the results in Cortana, which is about 470 square miles.
7. To compare the results to Bing, click **how big is nyc** in the Web section of the search results to start Microsoft Edge and display the same results in Bing.

TIP

To select the text quickly in the Ask me anything box, click the beginning of the text on the left side of the box.

Cortana is designed to make your computing experience enjoyable, so you can ask Cortana to tell you a joke, sing a song, or answer a trivia question.

Searching the Web with Microsoft Edge

Instead of using Cortana to search the web, you can use the more full-featured search tools provided in Microsoft Edge, including the Address bar and a search engine.

The terminology that you use when searching the web with a browser is slightly different from the terminology you use to search for files or settings on your computer. As shown in the Session 6.2 Visual Overview, the word or phrase you use to search the web is typically called a search expression. Each word in the search expression is called a **keyword**. After you enter a search expression in the Microsoft Edge Address bar or the search engine's Search box, Microsoft Edge displays the results, which are links to webpages that meet your criteria. You can click these links, or hits, to access webpages that contain the keywords in your search expression.

When you enter a search expression in the Address bar of Microsoft Edge, it uses a search engine such as Bing or Google. Because searching all of the webpages on the Internet to find those that contain your search expression would take a prohibitive amount of time, search engines typically search a database of indexed webpages. These databases are updated periodically, though not often enough to keep all of the indexed webpages up to date. This is why a page of search results might include inactive or broken links.

Website designers and owners can make their webpages easier for search engines to find by **optimizing** the site. In its webpage headings, an optimized site lists keywords and phrases that you and other web users are likely to use to find the information on the webpages. Conversely, you are more likely to find the webpages you want if you are aware of the types of keywords web designers often use.

PROSKILLS

Problem Solving: Searching the Web Effectively

Because the web provides access to a vast amount of information, finding the information you need can be a problem. Conducting a search that finds millions of results is inefficient, even if search engines list the webpages most relevant to your search first. To work effectively, you need to use search techniques that provide a few high-quality results. Keep the following guidelines in mind to search the Internet efficiently:

- Be specific. If you search for general categories, you'll find an overwhelming number of pages. Searching for specific terms or details is more likely to provide results you can use. For example, instead of searching for "desserts," search for "pear cake recipe."
- Form a question. Think of your search expression as a question you want answered, such as "Which restaurants in the Denver area serve vegetarian food?" Eliminate the articles and common words to form a workable search expression, such as "restaurants Denver vegetarian."
- Modify the search expression. Add keywords to a search expression to reduce the number of pages to review. For example, suppose you search for "pear cake recipe" and find many thousands of results. If you want a recipe similar to the one your Swedish grandmother made, you can add "Swedish" to your search expression.

Now that you've found some general information Howard can use during his trip to New York, he wants to find more specific information. He wants to expand into vintage posters and prints that include travel and movie posters, and he plans to visit a few shops in New York that carry these types of pieces. You offer to search the web to find shops that specialize in vintage art. You'll start the search by using *New York City vintage art shop* as the search expression to find webpages describing shops that specialize in vintage art in New York City.

Because webpages and search indexes change frequently, the search results you find when you perform the steps in this section will differ from those shown in the figures. The following steps use Bing as the search engine. If you are using a different search engine, your results will differ.

To search using a search expression:

1. In Microsoft Edge, select the text in the Address bar, type **New York City vintage art shop**, and then press the **Enter** key. Bing looks for webpages containing the search expression you entered, and then displays the results. See Figure 6-24.

Figure 6-24 **Search results for the search expression *New York City vintage art shop***

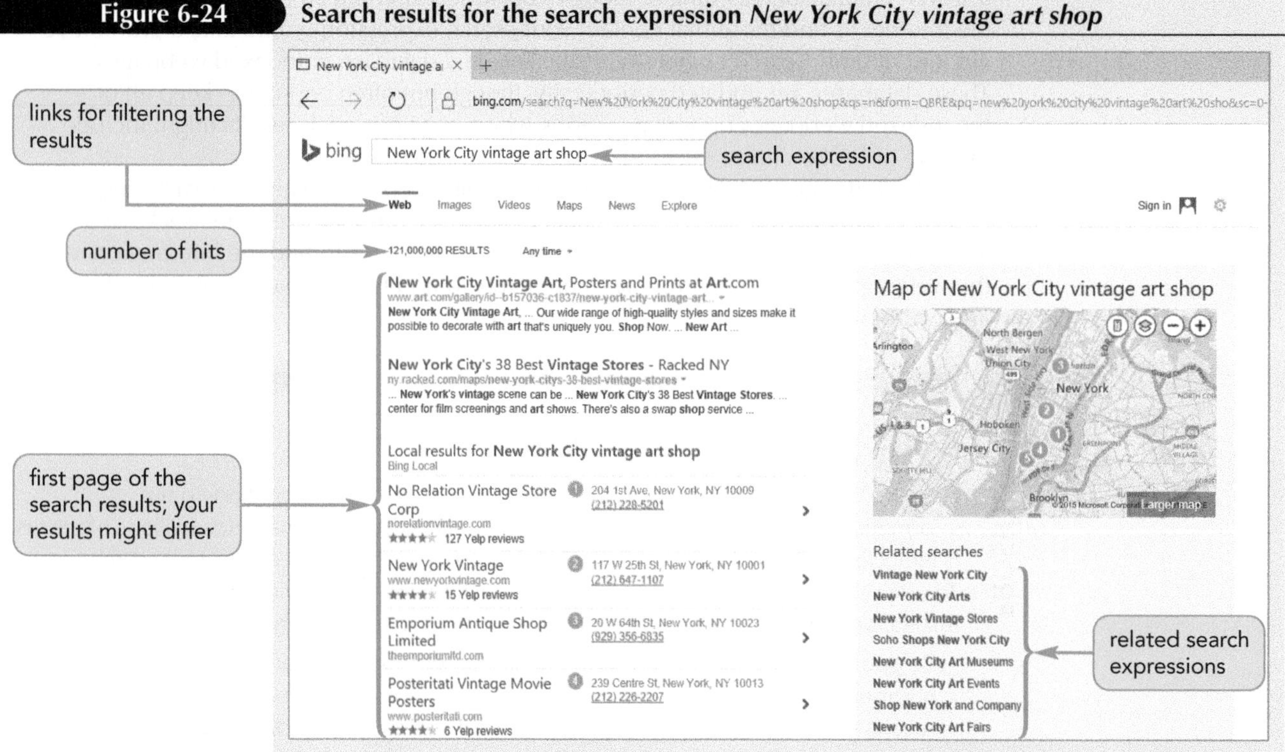

Using "New York City vintage art shop" as the search expression produced about 121 million results, which is not unusual and can change daily. You need to narrow your search to find more useful webpages.

Narrowing Your Search

You can narrow your web search by modifying your search expression or by limiting the kinds of webpages you want in your results. One way to modify your search expression in most search engines is to use quotation marks to search for specific phrases. If you enclose a phrase in quotation marks, you restrict the results to webpages that contain that exact phrase. For example, using a search expression such as *vintage art shop* finds webpages that include those three words anywhere on the page. If you enclose a search expression in quotation marks, as in "vintage art shop," you find only webpages that include the exact text in the specified order.

Another way to modify your search expression is to use the advanced search features that search engines typically offer. Figure 6-25 shows the Advanced Search page from Google, a popular search engine.

Figure 6-25 **Google Advanced Search page**

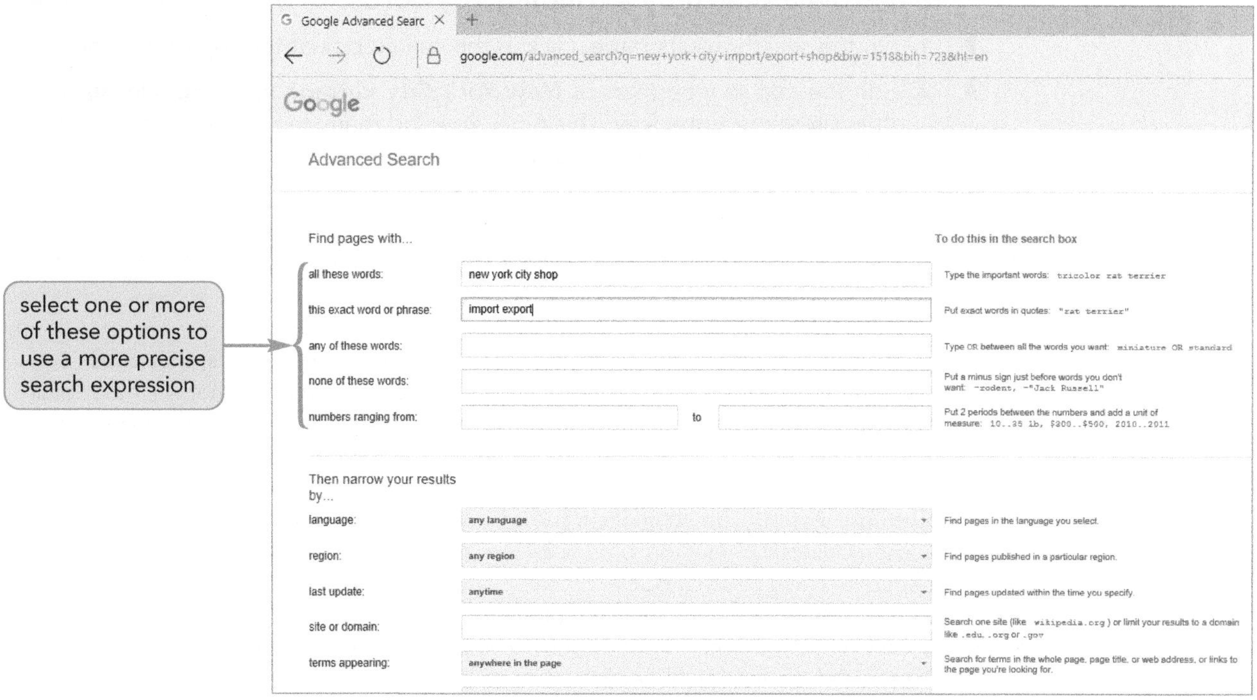

Google Advanced Searc
google.com/advanced_search?q=new+york+city+import/export+shop&biw=1518&bih=723&hl=en
Google
Advanced Search

Find pages with...		To do this in the search box
all these words:	new york city shop	Type the important words: tricolor rat terrier
this exact word or phrase:	import export	Put exact words in quotes: "rat terrier"
any of these words:		Type OR between all the words you want: miniature OR standard
none of these words:		Put a minus sign just before words you don't want: -rodent, -"Jack Russell"
numbers ranging from:	to	Put 2 periods between the numbers and add a unit of measure: 10..35 lb, $300..$500, 2010..2011

Then narrow your results by...		
language:	any language	Find pages in the language you select.
region:	any region	Find pages published in a particular region.
last update:	anytime	Find pages updated within the time you specify.
site or domain:		Search one site (like wikipedia.org) or limit your results to a domain like .edu, .org or .gov
terms appearing:	anywhere in the page	Search for terms in the whole page, page title, or web address, or links to the page you're looking for.

select one or more of these options to use a more precise search expression

Source: Google

Although Bing does not have an Advanced Search page, you can use the same advanced search tools that let you specify and combine search conditions. Most advanced search tools provide the following types of options:

- Find pages that include all of the words. This is the default for most search engines.
- Limit the results to pages that match the exact phrase. This is the same as using quotation marks to enclose an expression.
- Find pages that include at least one of the words in the search expression. This is the same as using OR between each search term.
- Specify keywords that you do not want included on the webpage. This is the same as inserting NOT or a hyphen before the keyword to exclude.

Search engines often provide extensive help information. For example, enter a search term in Google, click the Options button, and then click Search help to display the Search Help webpage, which provides links to basic search information and more advanced tips for searching. In Bing, click the Help link at the bottom of the Bing home page to display the Bing Help page.

Besides providing an advanced search page for narrowing your search expression, most search engines include tabs or links that specify the kind of results you want. For example, the Bing results page shown earlier includes a navigation bar near the top of the page with links such as Web, Images, Videos, and Maps. By default, Bing displays webpages in the results. If you are searching for images, such as photos and drawings, you can click the Images link before or after you enter a search expression to restrict the results to pages including images that meet your criteria.

When you search for *New York City vintage art shop*, many of the results are for vintage clothing shops in New York. Because Howard has time to visit only a couple of shops, he wants to refine the search to exclude vintage clothing stores. To specify this kind of search condition, you can insert a hyphen, or minus sign, before the keyword you want to exclude from the search results. Using NOT before a keyword has the same effect. For Howard, you want to search for vintage art shops in New York City, but not those that sell clothing.

To narrow a search by excluding keywords:

1. On the search results page, click in the search box at the top of the page.
2. Edit the text so it appears as **New York City vintage art shop -clothing** and then press the **Enter** key. This time, you find many fewer results, some of which are promising for Howard.

INSIGHT

Evaluating Webpages in the Search Results

Although a webpage might be listed at the top of the search results, that doesn't guarantee the page provides reliable and up-to-date information that will meet your needs. On a search engine's webpage, the search results are usually organized into sections. At the top or in another prominent location on the page are sponsored links; companies pay to have these links appear when certain keywords are used in a search expression. The companies pay an additional fee when you click one of their sponsored links. Using sponsored links helps search engines offer their services free to the public. However, that doesn't mean a sponsored link will lead to the information you want. Before using a webpage or citing it as a source, review the content with a critical eye. At the bottom of the webpage, look for the author's name and evidence of the author's credentials. Look for links to the original source of quoted information, which tends to validate the information on a webpage. Also look for signs of bias, such as unsubstantiated claims or extreme points of view.

Howard wonders if you can quickly show examples of vintage art available in New York. To fulfill his request, you can use the Images link on the navigation bar. Google and other search engines include a similar tool. First, however, you should edit the search expression. If you click the Images link now, the results would show images of art shops, not art itself.

To display images of vintage art:

1. On the search results page, click in the search box at the top of the page.
2. Edit the text so it appears as **New York City vintage art** and then press the **Enter** key. The results include a section that previews images of vintage art, most of them using New York City as the subject. This isn't exactly what Howard was looking for, but the results might help him find the kind of vintage travel art he is seeking.
3. In the navigation bar, click the **Images** link. At the top of the search results, Bing displays suggested keywords for narrowing the search and a toolbar of buttons for filtering the results by image size or color, for example. In the main part of the page, Bing displays many images that meet the search criteria, whereas, at the bottom, it displays images that other users search for after searching for "New York City vintage art." See Figure 6-26. Your results might differ.

Figure 6-26 Displaying images in the search results

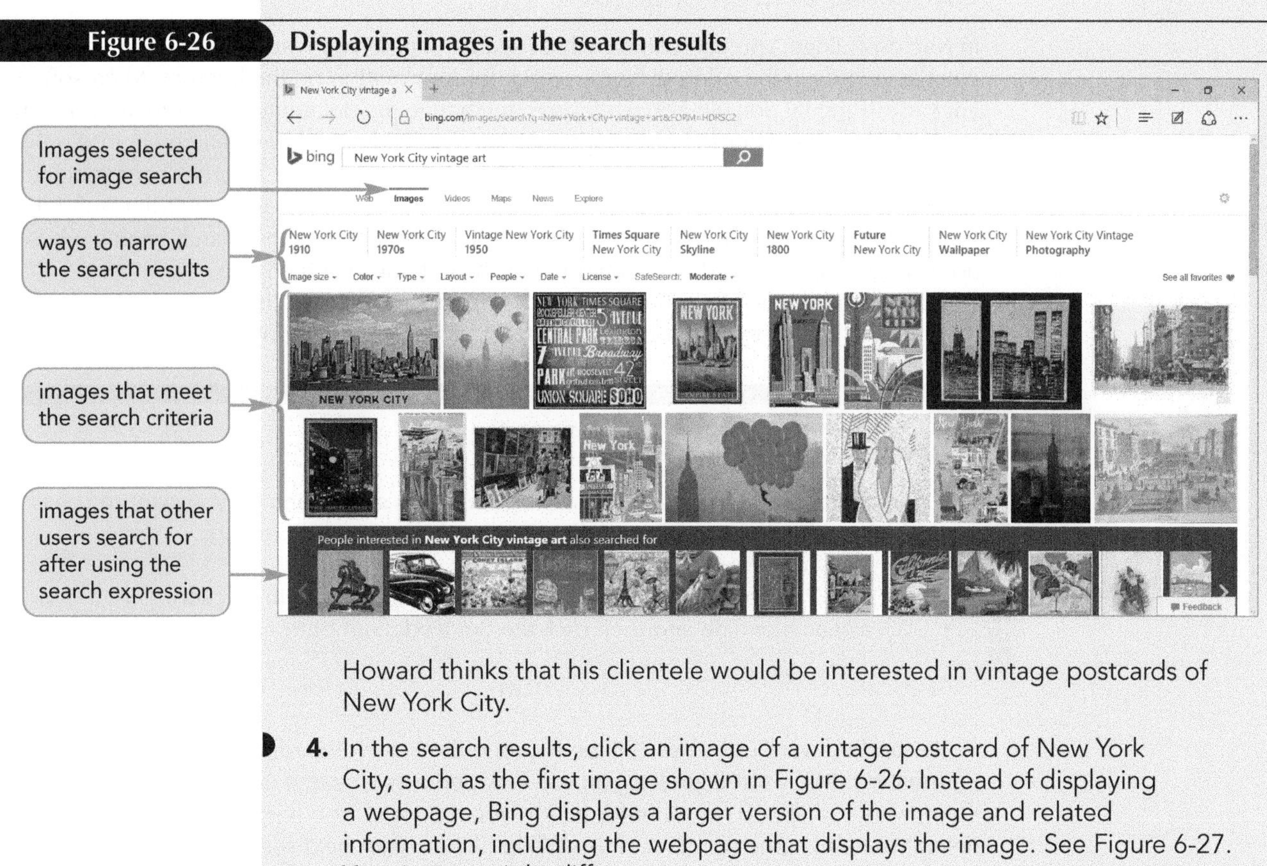

Howard thinks that his clientele would be interested in vintage postcards of New York City.

4. In the search results, click an image of a vintage postcard of New York City, such as the first image shown in Figure 6-26. Instead of displaying a webpage, Bing displays a larger version of the image and related information, including the webpage that displays the image. See Figure 6-27. Your image might differ.

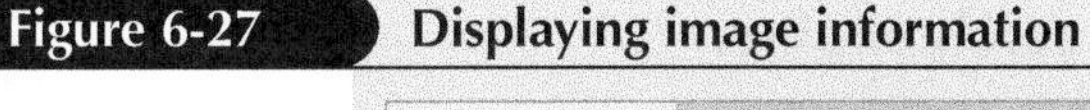

Figure 6-27 Displaying image information

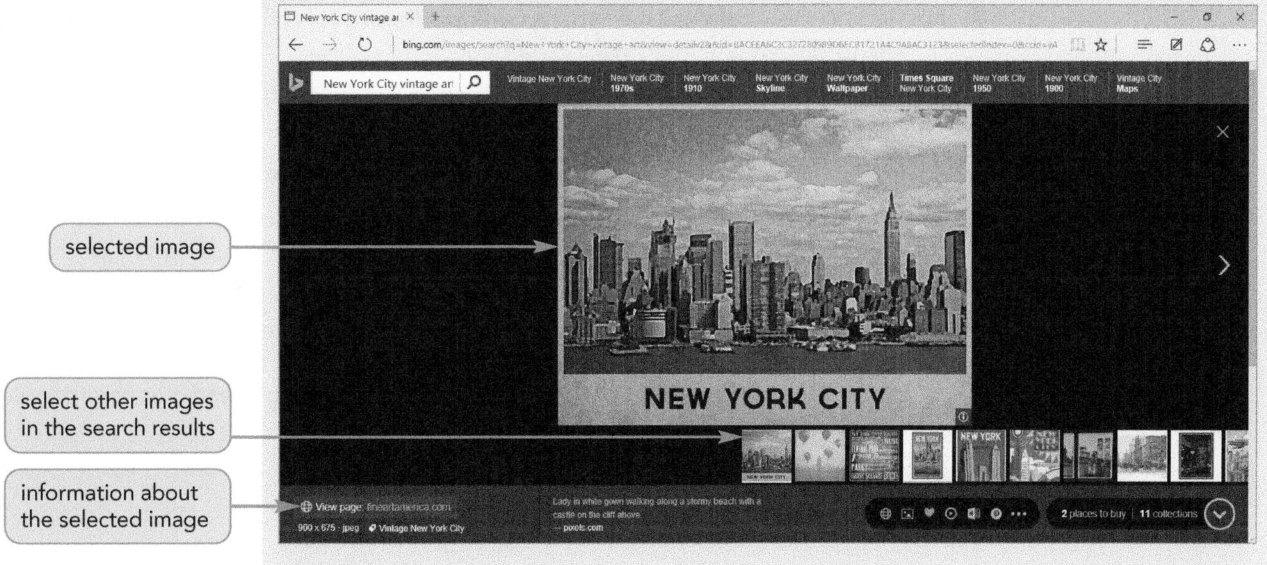

From here, Howard can explore other vintage New York City postcards, view and possibly purchase the postcard at a commercial website, or search for other types of vintage New York City images.

Choosing Search Engines

In Microsoft Edge, you can choose which search engine you want to use when you enter keywords in the Address bar to search for information on the Internet. Microsoft Edge uses Bing by default; however, you can change the default to use a different search engine to increase your searching options. Microsoft Edge includes search engines only if they use Open Search technology, so it might not support your favorite search engine. Open the home page of the search engine's website and then change the Microsoft Edge settings to select a default search engine. If Microsoft Edge lists the search engine whose home page you displayed, you can use it as the default search engine.

Keep in mind that you can use a search engine's website, such as google.com, to perform a search even if it is not selected as your search engine.

REFERENCE

Adding a Search Engine

- In Microsoft Edge, navigate to the website of the search engine you want to use.
- Click the More button in the navigation bar, and then click Settings.
- Click the View advanced settings button.
- Click the Change button in the Search in the address bar with section.
- Click a search engine and then click the Set as default button.

You and Howard often use Wikipedia, an online encyclopedia, to search for information. Microsoft Edge lets you use Wikipedia as a search engine, which is handy if you want to look up factual information about a topic. You'll set Wikipedia as the default search engine so you can use Wikipedia for your next search.

To change the default search engine:

1. Click in the **Address bar**, type **en.wikipedia.org**, and then press the **Enter** key to display the main Wikipedia page.
2. Click the **More** button [...] in the navigation bar, and then click **Settings** to display the Settings pane.
3. Scroll the Settings pane and then click the **View advanced settings** button.
4. Scroll the Advanced settings list, click the **Change** button in the Search in the address bar with section to display search engines, including Wikipedia. See Figure 6-28.

   Trouble? If Wikipedia is not listed, close Microsoft Edge, and then repeat Steps 1–4 to allow Microsoft Edge to detect Wikipedia. If it still does not detect Wikipedia, click the webpage to close the Change search engine pane.

Figure 6-28 **Setting the default search engine**

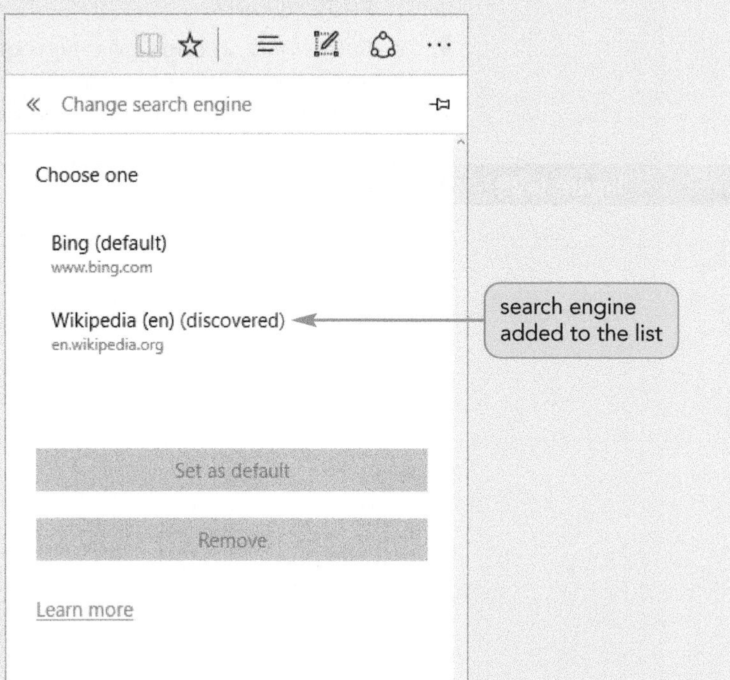

5. Click **Wikipedia (en) (discovered)** and then click the **Set as default** button to make Wikipedia the default search engine.

   Trouble? If you selected Wikipedia as a search engine before performing these steps, the Change search engine pane lists the search engine as Wikipedia (en).

6. Close Microsoft Edge.

One of Ithaca Imports' most popular prints is *Woman with a Parasol* by Claude Monet. Customers often ask about Monet's biography, especially his period in Giverny, where he created *Woman with a Parasol* and his famous water lily paintings. Howard would like you to write a short biography of Monet to post on the Ithaca Imports website. You can use Wikipedia as the search engine to find a summary of Monet's life and works. When you are displaying a webpage, you can use the Find toolbar in Microsoft Edge to find specific information on the page. After you find suitable biographical information about Claude Monet, you'll show Howard how to search for information about Monet's life in Giverny using the Find toolbar in Microsoft Edge.

To use Wikipedia as the search engine:

1. Start Microsoft Edge, click in the **Address bar**, type **claude monet**, and then press the **Enter** key. Microsoft Edge uses Wikipedia as the search engine and finds a Wikipedia entry for Claude Monet.

   Trouble? If you could not select Wikipedia as the search engine in the preceding set of steps, click in the Address bar to select the text, type "en .wikipedia.org," and then press the Enter key. Click in the Search box on the Wikipedia page, type "claude monet," and then press the Enter key.

2. Press the **Ctrl+F** keys to display the Find toolbar at the top of the Microsoft Edge window.
3. In the Find on page box, type **giverny**. Microsoft Edge highlights all instances of "giverny" and displays the number of matches on the page. Your number might differ. See Figure 6-29.

Figure 6-29 Using the Find toolbar

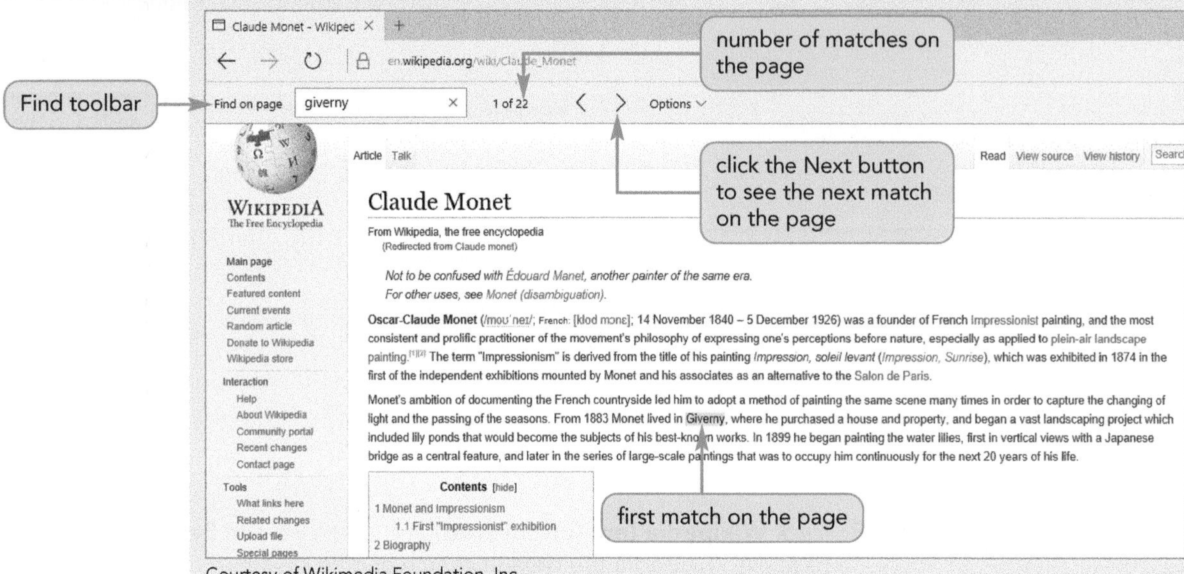

Courtesy of Wikimedia Foundation, Inc.

4. Click the **Next** button [>] as many times as necessary to display the section titled "Giverny" with the subtitle "Monet's house and garden," which describes Monet's life and works at Giverny.
5. Click the **Close** button [X] to close the Find toolbar.
6. Close Microsoft Edge.

Howard plans to provide biographies on other artists, so you can use Wikipedia as a search engine to find information about their lives and works.

Restoring Your Settings

If you are working in a computer lab or on a computer other than your own, complete the steps in this section to restore the original settings on the computer.

To restore your settings:

1. Open File Explorer, navigate to the **Users > user name** folder (where *user name* is your user name), and then open the **Searches** folder.
2. Move the **JPG Sept** saved search to the Ithaca folder in the Documents folder.
3. Click in the **Search Ithaca** box to display the Search Tools Search tab, click the **Advanced options** button in the Options group, and then click **File contents** under the In non-indexed locations section to remove the checkmark.

4. Move the **Ithaca** folder to the Module6 > Module folder provided with your Data Files.
5. Close the Details pane in the folder windows, and then close File Explorer.
6. Start Microsoft Edge, click the **More** button [...] in the navigation bar, and then click **Settings** to display the Settings pane. Click the **View advanced settings** button, click the **Change** button in the Search in the address bar with section, click **Bing (www.bing.com)**, and then click the **Set as default** button. Close Microsoft Edge.
7. Click the **Start** button, type **clock**, click **Add clocks for different time zones**, click the first **Show this clock** check box to remove the checkmark, and then click the **OK** button to close the Date and Time dialog box.
8. Close any open windows.

REVIEW

Session 6.2 Quick Check

1. What shorthand notation would you use to find files that include the word "artist" in the Title property?
2. If you use tag: French OR 1900 as search criteria, what files would you find?
3. Explain how you can quickly find weather conditions in Los Angeles.
4. The word or phrase you use to search the web is typically called a(n) _______________.
5. If you enclose a phrase in quotation marks in a search expression, how does that affect the results?
6. After using a search expression to search the web, how can you specify that you want to display only news stories in the results?
7. Explain what happens if you use Wikipedia as the search engine in Microsoft Edge and use Michelangelo as the search expression.

PRACTICE

Review Assignments

Data Files needed for the Review Assignments: Japan01.jpg–Japan10.jpg, Japanese Prints.mp4

Ithaca Imports purchased a collection of Japanese prints, and you are now working with Howard on developing and showcasing the collection. You have taken photographs of the Japanese prints and created a video featuring a few of the prints. Howard wants you to help him search for apps that can play video and find Japanese prints for the shop's website. Just for fun, he also wants to include a joke on the home page. Complete the following steps:

1. In the Documents folder on your hard disk, create a folder named **Prints**. Move all of the files in the Module6 > Review folder provided with your Data Files to the Prints folder.
2. Use Cortana to search for a file that contains the word "Japanese" in its filename. Select a media file and then play the file.
3. Press the Print Screen key to capture an image of the screen, and then paste the image in a new Paint or WordPad file. Save the file as **Video App** in the Module6 > Review folder provided with your Data Files. Minimize Paint or WordPad, and then close the Movies & TV app.
4. Search for an app you can use to play media files, and then start the app. (*Hint*: If a dialog box opens where you can select initial settings, click the Recommended settings option button, and then click the Finish button.) Click Videos in the left pane of the app window, drag the Japanese Prints video stored in the Prints folder to the app's window, and then click the Play button to play the video.
5. Press the Print Screen key to capture an image of the screen, and then paste the image in a new Paint or WordPad file. Save the file as **Media App** in the Module6 > Review folder provided with your Data Files. Close the media app. Minimize Paint or WordPad.
6. Search for a setting on your computer related to AutoPlay settings for media files, and then display the setting for using AutoPlay for all media and devices. Press the Print Screen key to capture an image of the window, and then paste the image in a new Paint or WordPad file. Save the file as **AutoPlay** in the Module6 > Review folder provided with your Data Files. Close the window with the AutoPlay settings. Minimize the Paint or WordPad window.
7. Search for all of the JPG files in the Prints folder.
8. Add the following tags to Japan03: **Mt. Fuji; landscape; Japan**. Change the filename to **Mountain Landscape**.
9. Add the following tags to Japan04: **woodblock; traditional; Japan**. Change the filename to **Kimono**.
10. In the Prints folder, search for JPG photos that have *woodblock* as a tag. Save the search as **JPG woodblock**. Move the JPG woodblock file to the Prints folder.
11. Move the files you found to a new subfolder named **Woodblocks** in the Prints folder.
12. In the Prints folder, find a photo that has *watercolor* and *zen* as tags. Change the name of this file to **Zen**. Close File Explorer. Minimize the Paint or WordPad window, and then close all other open windows.
13. Ask Cortana to tell you a joke. Press the Print Screen key to capture an image of the search results, and then paste the image in a new Paint or WordPad file. Save the file as **Joke** in the Module6 > Review folder provided with your Data Files.
14. Start Microsoft Edge and use Bing to find webpages providing information about traditional Japanese prints. Narrow the search to find images of traditional Japanese woodblock prints. (*Hint*: Click the Images link on the navigation bar.) Press the Print Screen key to capture an image of the first screen of search results, and then paste the image in a new Paint or WordPad file. Save the file as **Traditional** in the Module6 > Review folder provided with your Data Files.
15. Use a search engine other than Bing to search for Hiroshige woodblock prints. (Hiroshige is a Japanese artist.) Press the Print Screen key to capture an image of the search results, and then paste the image in a new Paint or WordPad file. Save the file as **Hiroshige** in the Module6 > Review folder provided with your Data Files.

16. Restore your computer by restoring Bing as the default search engine in Microsoft Edge. Move the Prints folder from the Documents folder on your hard disk to the Module6 > Review folder provided with your Data Files. Close the Details pane in the folder window, and then close all open windows.

APPLY

Case Problem 1

Data Files needed for this Case Problem: Flag01.jpg–Flag10.jpg

Sister Cities Association Richard and Debra Cowen run the Sister Cities Association in York, Pennsylvania. The organization is devoted to promoting international goodwill and educating Americans about other countries by forming sister city relationships between their city and a city in another country. You work as an all-around assistant to Richard and Debra. Currently, they want you to help them find graphics for their webpages using flags of the world. They also want to back up their files online, and ask you to find information about apps they can use to do so. Complete the following steps:

1. Search for an app you can use to read news stories. Start the app, maximize the window, and then click a link to display technology news.
2. Press the Print Screen key to capture an image of the app, and then paste the image in a new Paint or WordPad file. Save the file as **News App** in the Module6 > Case1 folder provided with your Data Files. Close the app.
3. Search for a setting on your computer related to backups. Display the setting or tool for backing up using File History.
4. Press the Print Screen key to capture an image of the tool, and then paste the image in a new Paint or WordPad file. Save the file as **Backups** in the Module6 > Case1 folder provided with your Data Files. Close the window.
5. Use Cortana to find the current time in Arles, France, which is the sister city to York, Pennsylvania. Press the Print Screen key to capture an image of the result, and then paste the image in a new Paint or WordPad file. Save the file as **Time** in the Module6 > Case1 folder provided with your Data Files.
6. Open File Explorer and then review the tags and other properties already assigned to the files in the Module6 > Case1 folder. Add a tag to the Flag04 and the Flag09 files based on information in the other properties.
7. Using the Details pane, add **Liz Kerr** as the author of the following images: Flag06, Flag07, and Flag10.
8. Use the Search box to find a photo that includes the tag *2018* and has C Maki as the author. Rename the file **2018**.
9. Start Microsoft Edge and use Bing to find webpages providing information on Arles, France. Narrow the search to find images of the city. Press the Print Screen key to capture an image of the screen, and then paste the image in a new Paint or WordPad file. Save the file as **Arles** in the Module6 > Case1 folder provided with your Data Files.

Explore 10. If necessary, set Google as the default search engine in Microsoft Edge, and then use Google to search for information about Arles, France. Display a map of the city. (*Hint*: Click the Maps button near the top of the webpage.) Press the Print Screen key to capture an image of the screen, and then paste the image in a new Paint or WordPad file. Save the file as **Arles Map** in the Module6 > Case1 folder provided with your Data Files.

11. Restore your computer by restoring the original default search engine in Microsoft Edge. Close all open windows.

CHALLENGE

Case Problem 2

Data Files needed for this Case Problem: Music01.png–Music10.png

Sonoma Chamber Orchestra Isabel Williams is the marketing director of the Sonoma Chamber Orchestra in Sonoma, California. She is developing new print brochures to make available at ticket windows and throughout the orchestra hall during concerts. As an intern at the Sonoma Chamber Orchestra, you help Isabel prepare promotional materials. She asks you to help her find and organize images that will fit within the design of the new brochure and to research general information about composers and orchestral music. Isabel is also interested in information about music-playing apps that she can use to listen to music. Complete the following steps:

Explore 1. Search for an app you can use to play music. Start the app, maximize the window, and then click a link to get music in the Store.

Explore 2. In the Store window, scroll to the bottom of the page, and then select Classical as the genre. Press the Print Screen key to capture an image of the music app and the Store, and then paste the image in a new Paint or WordPad file. Save the file as **Music Store** in the Module6 > Case2 folder provided with your Data Files. Close the Store window and the music app.

3. Search for a setting that lets you adjust the system volume. Open the setting window, and then press the Print Screen key to capture an image of the window. Paste the image in a new Paint or WordPad file. Save the file as **System Volume** in the Module6 > Case2 folder provided with your Data Files. Close the volume setting window.

4. Using the Details pane, add a Date taken of **11/14/18** to the following files in the Module6 > Case2 folder: Music01, Music06, and Music09.

Explore 5. Using the Details tab in the Properties dialog box, add a Date taken of **10/24/18** to the following files: Music02, Music04, and Music05. (*Hint*: Right-click the file and then click Properties on the shortcut menu to open the Properties dialog box for the file.)

Explore 6. Using **dimensions** as the property name in the Search box, find files in the Module6 > Case2 folder that have 600 pixels as one of their dimensions. Move the file(s) to a new folder named **Dim 600** in the Module6 > Case2 folder provided with your Data Files.

Explore 7. Using **size** as the property name in the Search box, find files In the Module6 > Case2 folder that are larger than 100 KB in size. (*Hint*: Add KB to the search text.) Move the files to a new folder named **Large** in the Module6 > Case2 folder provided with your Data Files.

Explore 8. Start Microsoft Edge and use Bing to find webpages providing information on classical music styles. Select a link listed in the "Related searches for classical music styles" list. Press the Print Screen key to capture an image of the screen, and then paste the image in a new Paint or WordPad file. Save the file as **Classical Music** in the Module6 > Case2 folder provided with your Data Files.

9. Explore at least one of the links in the results and then select a classical music genre.

10. Use any other search engine to conduct a search for information on the classical music genre you selected. Open a page displaying information about this topic. Use the Find toolbar to find information on the page about a composer. Press the Print Screen key to capture an image of the screen showing the Find toolbar, and then paste the image in a new Paint or WordPad file. Save the file as **Composer** in the Module6 > Case2 folder provided with your Data Files. Close all open windows.

11. Restore the original default search engine, and then close all open windows.

CREATE

Case Problem 3

Data Files needed for this Case Problem: House01.jpg–House10.jpg

Great House Walking Tour Dwight Payton is an America architect living in London, England. Wanting to combine his two major enthusiasms—British great houses and walking for fitness—Dwight started a small travel business that conducts walking tours to great houses throughout Great Britain. Dwight publishes an online newsletter to attract travelers to his tours. He has a collection of images of the great houses he tours and needs to organize them. He also wants to find a new app he can use for his online newsletter. He's heard about Flipboard and wants to know if that app would be suitable. As his editorial assistant, you offer to help him find this information and organize the images for the newsletter. Complete the following steps:

1. Search for Flipboard and then start the app. Press the Print Screen key to capture an image of the app. Paste the image in a new Paint or WordPad file. Save the file as **Flipboard** in the Module6 > Case3 folder provided with your Data Files.
2. Use the app to select Travel as a category of content to include. Press the Print Screen key to capture an image of the opening window showing your selection. Paste the image in a new Paint or WordPad file. Save the file as **Travel** in the Module6 > Case3 folder provided with your Data Files. Close Flipboard.
3. Working in the Module6 > Case3 folder, add **Yorkshire** as a tag to the House01 and House03 files. Add the tag **Wales** to the House02 file and the tag **Scotland** to the House05 file.
4. Conduct a search in the Case3 folder to find files with the word "palace" in any of the properties. Move the files you found into a new folder named **Palaces** in the Module6 > Case3 folder.
5. Conduct a search in the Case3 folder to find files with "park" in any of the properties. Move the files you found into a new folder named **Parks** in the Module6 > Case3 folder.
6. Conduct another search in the Case3 folder to find files with "Yorkshire" as a tag. Copy the files you found into a new folder named **Yorkshire** in the Module6 > Case3 folder. (*Hint*: Be sure to copy rather than move the files.)
7. Start Microsoft Edge and conduct a search to produce results similar to those shown in Figure 6-30.

Figure 6-30 Google search results

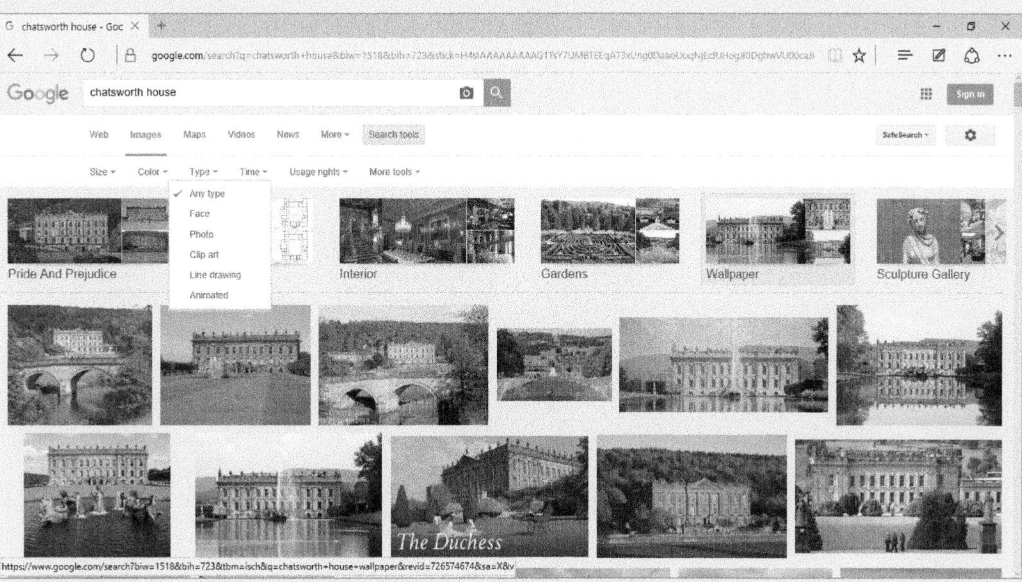

8. Press the Print Screen key to capture an image of the first screen of search results, and then paste the image in a new Paint or WordPad file. Save the file as **Chatsworth** in the Module6 > Case3 folder provided with your Data Files.
9. Close all open windows.

RESEARCH

Case Problem 4

There are no Data Files needed for this Case Problem.

Sabota Reference Tanya and Gary Sabota are starting a company called Sabota Reference. They plan to provide research services for businesses and others, especially those who need demographic information for marketing research. They hired you as an assistant and want you to investigate the types of information available on the web, including tools that search engines provide. Complete the following steps:

1. Start Microsoft Edge and use any search engine to research the following terms:
   Web 2.0
   Web 3.0
   Keyword search engines
   Blog search engines (provide examples)
2. Use WordPad or another word-processing program to create a document that lists these terms and provides a definition for each one. Save the document as **Research** in the Module6 > Case4 folder.
3. Search engines such as Google and Bing offer tools for marketing research. For example, Bing has a collection of tools called Bing solutions that help businesses reach more customers. Google has the AdWords, AdSense, and Analytics tools for business. Research one of these tools to learn its purpose and how it works.
4. In the Research document, describe the Bing or Google business tool you researched and then explain how Sabota Reference or another business might use it. Save the document.

INDEX

D

E

V

W

Y

Z